HANS WILHELM HERTZBERG

I & II SAMUEL

HANS WILHELM HERTZBERG

I & II SAMUEL

A Commentary

SCM PRESS LTD
BLOOMSBURY STREET LONDON

Translated by J. S. Bowden from the German
Die Samuelbücher
(Das Alte Testament Deutsch 10)
second revised edition, 1960
published by Vandenhoeck & Ruprecht, Göttingen

FIRST PUBLISHED IN ENGLISH 1964
© SCM PRESS LTD 1964
PRINTED IN GREAT BRITAIN BY
W. & J. MACKAY & CO LTD, CHATHAM, KENT

Dedicated to Dr Otto Dibelius
in admiration and gratitude

CONTENTS

PREFACE TO THE FIRST GERMAN EDITION

LIKE MY COMMENTARY on the Books of Joshua, Judges, and Ruth, which appeared three years ago, the present treatment of the Books of Samuel is concerned to examine and expound the material not only with regard to its individual details, but also with regard to its place within the whole book, and, where possible, with regard to its place within Holy Scripture. This seems to me to be a standpoint which, at a time of predominantly literary-critical work on the Old Testament, has been too much neglected, understandable though this neglect may be, and one which should now come into its own, particularly in a series like the *Altes Testament Deutsch*. The method also makes it more possible to stress theological threads running through the book, another necessary concern of the series.

This does not, however, mean that a careful examination of individual details is to be dispensed with. In the Preface to his commentary on Jeremiah, Weiser has rightly indicated that his book is concerned to make such a detailed examination and has thus laid upon contributors to the series the obligation of giving a clearer place to matters of scholarship. The present commentary does just this, but in order to keep it readable, textual, topographical and other such explanations have been relegated to the notes unless exegesis of the text demands their inclusion within the body of the commentary. The principle may therefore be established that a proper concern with the details of the text does, in fact, facilitate that insight into its essential meaning and its total significance which were mentioned above.

The book is dedicated to the man who, as I shall never forget, awakened in me years ago in Lauenburg in Pomerania, a love of the Old Testament and its language, and to whom I am even now gratefully indebted.

Kiel, 23 January 1956

PREFACE TO THE ENGLISH EDITION

IT IS WITH great satisfaction that I greet the appearance of the
English translation of the Commentary on the Books of Samuel in
the German *Altes Testament Deutsch* series. The only commentary
on these books which has appeared since those of Karl Budde (1902)
and Hugo Gressmann (1910) has been the very learned and difficult
one of Wilhelm Caspari (1925), so the ATD one was virtually the first
for a generation, and was received accordingly. It is my earnest wish
that the one in the Old Testament Library series may be equally
warmly welcomed.

If this happens the merit will belong in the first place to the trans-
lator, who has succeeded in rendering not only the words but the
spirit of his text. His translation is a masterpiece. I must also thank
Dr Hans Harald Mallau, *Assistent* in the Theological Seminary in
the University of Kiel, who with his wife gave valuable help in reading
the proofs of the English edition.

The Introduction and Commentary on I and II Samuel by
William McKane in the Torch Bible Commentary series appeared
after this translation was completed. I hope that they will make a
useful pair.

Kiel   H. W. HERTZBERG
25 May 1964

TRANSLATOR'S PREFACE

For the German editions of this commentary, the author made his own translation from the Hebrew, making full use of the Septuagint where this seemed to offer a better text. Because of the many variants and corruptions which are a notorious feature of the text of I and II Samuel, the resultant version differs widely in substance from the Revised Standard Version. To avoid adding to the already numerous textual notes, it has proved the simplest course to print an English equivalent of the author's German text, checked against the Hebrew and Greek, based on RSV but deviating from it wherever this is necessary for a faithful reproduction of the author's work. It has not been practicable to indicate these deviations in print, but a comparison of the commentary with RSV will reveal them and the reasons why they have been made.

Miss Jean Cunningham, of the SCM Press, has, as always, been tireless in hunting down elusive references and detecting errors and inconsistencies. I am most grateful to her.

Nottingham,
4 April 1964

BIBLIOGRAPHY

COMMENTARIES:

O. Thenius, 2nd ed., 1864; Hummelauer, 1866; K. F. Keil, 1875; A. Klostermann, 1887; M. Löhr (3rd ed. of Thenius), 1898; H. P. Smith (International Critical Commentary), 1899; K. Budde, 1902; W. Nowack, 1902; N. Schlögl, 1904; P. Dhorme, 1910; H. Gressmann, 1910, 2nd ed. 1921; A. Schulz, 1919–20; R. Kittel (4th ed. of Kautsch), 1922; W. Caspari, 1925; de Groot, 1934–5; K. A. Leimbach, 1936; H. Asmussen, 1938; P. Ketter, 1940; C. J. Goslinga, 1948; M. Rehm, 1949; S. Goldman (Soncino Press), 1951; R. de Vaux, 1953; K. Gutbrod (I), 1956; (II), 1958.

Other literature (in chronological order):

J. Wellhausen, *Der Text der Bücher Samuelis*, 1871

S. R. Driver, *Notes on the Hebrew Text of the Books of Samuel*, 1890, 1913[2]

O. Procksch, 'Der Schauplatz der Geschichte Davids', *PJB* 5, 1909, pp. 58–80

A. B. Ehrlich, *Randglossen zur hebr. Bibel*, Band 3, 1910

O. Procksch, 'Die letzten Worte Davids', *Kittel-Festschrift*, 1913, pp. 113–25

C. Steuernagel, 'Die Weissagung über die Eliden', *ibid.*, pp. 204–21

H. Tiktin, *Kritische Untersuchungen zu den Büchern Samuelis*, 1922

A. Bruno, *Gibeon*, 1923

A. Alt, 'Jerusalems Aufstieg', *ZDMG* 79, 1925, pp. 1–19 (*Kleine Schriften* III, 1959, pp. 243–57)

L. Rost, *Die Überlieferung von der Thronnachfolge Davids*, 1926

S. Mowinckel, 'Die letzten Worte Davids', *ZAW* 45, 1927, pp. 30–58

H. W. Hertzberg, 'Mizpa', *ZAW* 47, 1929, pp. 161–96

H. M. Wiener, *The composition of Judges II 11 to I Kings II 46*, 1929

A. Alt, 'Die Staatenbildung der Israeliten in Palästina', Reformationsprogramm, 1930 (*Kleine Schriften* II, 1953, pp. 1–65)

O. Eissfeldt, *Die Komposition der Samuelisbücher*, 1931

K. Budde, 'Besprechung zu Eissfeldt, *Komposition* . . .' *OLZ* 34, 1931, pp. 1056–62

I. Hylander, *Der literarische Samuel-Saulkomplex (1 Sam. 1–15)*, 1932

A. Bruno, *Das hebräische Epos, eine rhythmische und textkritische Untersuchung der Bücher Samuelis und Könige*, 1935

K. Elliger, 'Die 30 Helden Davids', *PJB* 31, 1935, pp. 29–74

A. Weiser, 'I Sam. 15', *ZAW* 54, 1936, pp. 1–28

A. Alt, 'Zu 2 Sam. 8.1', *ZAW* 54, 1936, pp. 149–52

R. Press, 'Der Prophet Samuel', *ZAW* 56, 1938, pp. 177–225

W. Vischer, *Das Christuszeugnis des Alten Testaments*, Zweiter Teil, 1942

M. Noth, *Überlieferungsgeschichtliche Studien* I, 1943

O. Eissfeldt, *Geschichtsschreibung im AT*, 1948

D. M. C. Englert, *The Peshitto of Second Samuel*, 1949

L. Kreyssig, *Gerechtigkeit für David*, 1949

A. Alt, 'Das Grossreich Davids', *TLZ* 75, 1950, cols. 213–20 (*Kl. Schriften* II, pp. 66–75)

N. Glueck, *Explorations in Eastern Palestine*, IV, 1951

O. Eissfeldt, 'Ein gescheiterter Versuch der Wiedervereinigung Israels', *La nouvelle Clio* 3, 1951, pp. 110–27 and 4, 1952, pp. 55–59

G. von Rad, *Der Heilige Krieg im alten Israel*, 1952²

F. M. Cross, 'A new Qumran biblical fragment to the original Hebrew underlying the Septuagint', *BASOR* 132, December 1953, pp. 15–25

H. J. Stoebe, 'Anmerkungen zu I Sam. 8.16 and 16.20', *VT* 4, 1954, pp. 177–84

A. S. Kapelrud, 'King and Fertility, a discussion of II Sam. 21.1–14', *Interpretationes ad Vetus Testamentum, pertinentes Sigmendo Mowinckel*, 1955, pp.113–22

A. S. Kapelrud, 'König David und die Söhne des Saul', *ZAW* 67, 1955, pp. 198–205

M. Buber, 'Die Erzählung von Sauls Königswahl', *VT* 6, 1956, pp. 113–73

H. J. Stoebe, 'Die Goliathperikope I Sam. 17.1–18.5 und die Textform der Septuaginta', *VT* 6, 1956, pp. 397–413

P. A. H. de Boer, 'Texte et traduction des paroles attribuées à David en 2 Samuel XXIII 1–7', *SVT* IV, 1956, pp. 47–56

L. M. v. Pákozdy, 'Elchanan, der frühere Name Davids?' *ZAW* 68, 1956, pp. 257–9

F. Maass, 'Zu den Qumran-Varianten der Bücher Samuel', *TLZ* 81, 1956, cols. 337–40

M. Bíč, 'Saul sucht die Eselinnen', *VT* 7, 1957, pp. 92–97

H. J. Stoebe, 'Noch einmal die Eselinnen des Kisch', *VT* 7, 1957, pp. 362–70

H. J. Stoebe, 'Die Einnahme Jerusalems und der Ṣinnôr', *ZDPV* 73, 1957, pp. 73–99

H. Wildberger, 'Samuel und die Entstehung des israelitischen Königtums', *TZ* 13, 1957, pp. 442–69

M. Noth, 'David und Israel in II Sam. 7', *Mélarges Bibleques, rediges en l'Lonneur de André Robert*, 1957, pp. 122–30

H. Cazelles, 'La titulature du roi David', *ibid.*, pp. 131–6

H. J. Stoebe, 'David und Mikal, Überlegungen zur Jugendgeschichte Davids', *Von Ugarit nach Qumran* (Eissfeldt-Festschrift, BZAW 77) 1958, pp. 224–43

G. A. Wainwright, 'Some early Philistine history', *VT* 9, 1959, pp. 73–84

ABBREVIATIONS

ANET	J. B. Pritchard, *Ancient Near Eastern Texts*, 2nd ed., 1955
AOT (B)	H. Gressmann, *Altorientalische Texte (Bilder) zum Alten Testament*
ATD	Das Alte Testament Deutsch
BASOR	*Bulletin of the American Schools of Oriental Research*
BH	*Biblia Hebraica*, ed. Rudolf Kittel, 3rd ed., A. Alt and O. Eissfeldt, 1952
BRL	Galling, *Biblisches Reallexicon*
BZAW	Beihefte zur *Zeitschrift für die alttestamentliche Wissenschaft*
ET	English translation
GB	Gesenius-Buhl, *Hebr. und aram. Handwörterbuch über das AT*
GK	Gesenius-Kautzsch, *Hebrew Grammar*, 2nd English edition, rev. by A. E. Cowley, 1910
JBL	*Journal of Biblical Literature*
JPOS	*Journal of the Palestine Oriental Society*
LXX	Greek translation of the Old Testament (Septuagint)
MSS	Manuscripts
MT	Massoretic text
OLZ	*Orientalische Literaturzeitung*
PJB	*Palästinajahrbuch*
PG	Migne, *Patrologia Graeca*
RB	*Revue Biblique*
RHPR	*Revue d'Histoire et de Philosophie Religieuses*
RSV	The Revised Standard Version of the Bible
SVT	Supplement to Vetus Testamentum
Syr.	Syriac translation of the Old Testament (Peshitta)
Targ.	Targum
TLZ	*Theologische Literaturzeitung*
TZ	*Theologische Zeitschrift*
Vulg.	Latin translation of the Bible by Jerome (Vulgate)
VT	*Vetus Testamentum*
ZAW	*Zeitschrift für die alttestamentliche Wissenschaft*
ZDMG	*Zeitschrift der Deutschen Morgenländischen Gesellschaft*
ZDPV	*Zeitschrift des Deutschen Palästinavereins*

The First and Second Books of Samuel are usually described with the Roman numerals I and II.

INTRODUCTION

THE BOOKS OF SAMUEL contain that part of the history of Israel which describes the foundation of the State, running from the close of the period of the Judges to the establishment of the united kingdom. It may be wondered why the first two chapters of I Kings have not been added to the Books of Samuel to conclude the comprehensive picture of David's life, given in forty chapters and one and a half books of the Bible, with an account of his death. There is all the more reason for such a question since these two chapters belong to the great source which describes the succession to the throne and now occupies the centre of II Samuel. The point is clearly brought out by L. Rost (*Die Überlieferung von der Thronnachfolge Davids*, 1926). It is evident that whoever made the present division thought it more appropriate to attach the two chapters to the complex describing the reign of Solomon (on this see the note appended to section VII). The final compiler was, however, quite aware of the connection between II Samuel and the beginning of I Kings, as is already clear from the present position of the account of the purchase of a site for the temple in II. 24 (on this see the Commentary on II. 24).

The division in the material after II. 24 is old, and goes back to the time of the formation of the Old Testament Canon. But the strength of the feeling that the Books of Samuel and of the Kings belong together can be seen from the way in which the ancient Greek translation, the Septuagint, has combined them under the common title 'Books of the Kingdoms'. The division of the work into four books, instead of two as previously, was made at the same time. The purpose of this division, so familiar to us now, was surely to prevent the books from becoming too large; it was only applied to the Hebrew Bible from the time when this began to be printed, in the fifteenth century. The fact that the two Books of Samuel originally existed as a single book also explains why we should speak of the 'Second Book of Samuel', when Samuel makes no appearance in it; as kingmaker, he could legitimately lend his name to the combined book. It is manifestly impossible to regard him as the author of the work, a view occasionally put forward in late Jewish literature, as there is a report of his death as early as I. 25. Roman Catholic scholars for the most part retain the Septuagint title and speak of four books of Kings (Rehm's commentary in the Echter-Bibel series differs in this respect).

A considerable number of the events described in the Books of Samuel are not far removed in time from the composition of the work, so that in some passages in Part III (Samuel and Saul) and in the David stories we feel that we are listening to the words of contemporaries. This gives the Books of Samuel an importance over and above all the other prose books of the Old Testament. It is not for this reason, however, that large portions of the text of these books have been very badly transmitted, but because of chance accidents to the text; in this respect, too, the Books of Samuel unfortunately stand out among the prose literature of the Old Testament. The relationship between the Massoretic text and that of the LXX is a special problem; the commentary will refer to it as far as is possible within the limits of a series of this nature.[a]

In the present commentary the material in the Books of Samuel has been divided into seven parts, some of which are determined by their content and others by their literary prehistory (Parts II, VI, VII). Here, as in other 'historical books' of the Old Testament, we are not dealing with a completely unified presentation. True, from time to time, especially in Parts II and VI, it is possible to trace a continuous thread, but in other parts it is quite obvious that the narratives are of varied origin and have only later been arranged in accordance with certain definite points of view.

It is becoming more and more uncommon in discussions about the formation of these books for scholars to assert that they contain some sort of continuation of the Pentateuchal sources. There seemed to be some justification for this assumption in the material contained in Part III (Samuel and Saul), but closer examination is proving that the literary-critical method is unable to do justice to such diverse matter. This question and the whole matter of the formation of the books will be discussed both in the commentary and in the sections on the formation and structure of the material which follow each of the seven parts into which the work is divided, so that it is unnecessary to go into detail here.

[a]The importance of the LXX text of Samuel or its underlying Hebrew has been strongly emphasized by the finding of fragments of Samuel at Qumran (cf. Cross in *BASOR* 132, December 1953). The Qumran texts evidently represent the same tradition as a Hebrew text underlying the LXX. This is particularly important because the MT, as has been said above, has been badly transmitted in places and the text-form underlying the LXX offers us valuable assistance in elucidating the sense. Maass comments well on the significance of this in *TLZ* 81, 1956, cols. 337–40.

The material contained in the books offers a variegated picture. Some narratives quite clearly originated in a particular neighbourhood, other sections seem to be taken from archives; there are poetic passages which originally existed independently, and larger entities which already had their own literary history in the time before the formation of the Books of Samuel. As the above-mentioned work by L. Rost on the 'Succession History' has shown in detail, there were documents which presented as continuous narratives certain parts of the history with which we are here concerned: 'The History of the Ark' (I. 4-6, II. 6) and the 'Succession History' (II. 9-20; I Kings 1-2), into which an account of the Ammonite war has been inserted (in II. 10-12). A continuous account of David's rise to power has been recognized, but with nothing like the same degree of certainty. The juxtaposition of different traditions comes out most clearly in the stories strictly concerned with Saul in Part III. Here, as in many other passages, we can see the careful, conservative treatment of the traditional material by the final compiler. At the same time, we can see his intention, realized with skill, of arranging this material in a particular manner, in accordance with clear theological principles. As in the Books of Joshua and Judges, and, of course, also in the Books of Kings, this compiler[a] belongs to deuteronomistic circles. As he deals differently with Samuel, Saul and David in turn, we can detect both in his attitude to the traditional material and his basic approach: Samuel is the man of God, chosen for his task from his mother's womb, who, like Moses, combines the divinely ordained leadership of the people with priestly and prophetic traits and so is completely equipped for his position. The tradition fluctuates in its picture of Saul, the king appointed by Yahweh and anointed and instituted by Samuel. Wonder, even reverence, gives way to fear and terror. He is the chosen one, and at the same time he is rejected. Doubtless he was of greater historical significance than has sometimes been allowed; even the tradition about David—and this the final compiler has in no way suppressed—is conscious that throughout his life David had to compete with the shadow of Saul; moreover, the creation of the united kingdom would have been quite unthinkable without the preliminary work done by Saul. This is quite clear from the content and arrangement of the material, even though the personal feelings and theological attitude of the final compiler are in closer sympathy

[a] Or perhaps 'these compilers', cf. my commentary on Joshua, ATD 9, p. 8.

with that part of the Saul tradition which regarded the development
from Samuel to Saul as a mistaken one, even if it was permitted by
Yahweh. One of the most attractive features of these texts is the way
we can see how the friendly disposition towards the first king has
not been eliminated, but has been overlaid by this different approach.

David, on the other hand, is to the final compiler and the tradition
which he uses the man 'with whom' Yahweh is, fore-ordained and
specially chosen, the man whom II. 7, which marks a high point in
the whole narrative, sees arrayed in messianic splendour. He is not
just the great soldier or adroit politician, but the instrument of
Yahweh, who is to bring the conquest to its completion. He is thus the
appointed successor of Joshua and the Judges, and at the same time
the king who begins to make Jerusalem the holy city, the place of
worship and revelation. Everything, however, is described and
arranged in such a way that here we have no kind of hero-worship,
as can be seen above all from the chapters describing the struggle
for the throne, which occupy the centre of the second book. The
theological basis of the Books of Samuel is not so obvious as that of
the other historical books; it is there unobtrusively, and is more often
to be read between the lines than in explicit statements. Sometimes
a point is made chiefly by the way in which the material is arranged,
but it is always sufficiently recognizable, and the reader will again
and again be particularly struck by the way in which the basic
theological pattern is continued throughout the material, told as it
is for the most part in so masterful a way.

The Books of Samuel provide a mass of excellent material to illustrate the historical situation of about 1000 BC. It is not the purpose
of a commentary of this character to examine their contents with this
chiefly in mind, but the exegesis of the text will of itself produce a
picture of the conditions of the period. At the same time we are
above all led to realize that the early history of the kingdoms of
Israel and Judah depicted here forms an essential part of the history
of the kingdom of God. Samuel and David, who make a frame round
the dark, problematical figure of King Saul, are figures of striking
significance in this history of the kingdom, and much of the message
of the Bible is embodied in their lives and in their struggles; and all
three, each in his own way, are forerunners and heralds of the real
King.

I

ELI AND SAMUEL
I. 1–3

1. THE CHILD ASKED OF GOD: 1.1–20

1 ¹There was a certain man of Ramathaim,[a] of (the) Zuphites,[b] of the hill country of Ephraim, whose name was Elkanah the son of Jeroham, son of Elihu, son of Tohu, son of Zuph, an Ephrathite. ²He had two wives; the name of the one was Hannah, and the name of the other Peninnah. And Peninnah had children, but Hannah had no children.

3 Now this man used[c] to go up year by year from his city to worship and to sacrifice to the LORD of hosts at Shiloh, where the two sons of Eli, Hophni and Phinehas, were priests of the LORD. ⁴Now there was a day when Elkanah sacrificed.[d] And he used to give portions to Peninnah his wife and to all her sons and daughters, ⁵but he would give Hannah one portion, (the portion) of the face,[e] for he loved Hannah, although the LORD had closed her womb. ⁶And her rival used to provoke her sorely, to humiliate her,[f] because the LORD had closed her womb. ⁷So it went on[g] year by year; as often as she went up to the house of the LORD, she used to provoke her. Therefore Hannah wept and would not eat. ⁸And Elkanah, her husband, said to her, 'Hannah,[h] why do you weep? And why do you not eat? And why is your heart sad? Am I not more to you than ten sons?'

[a]The reading should probably be Ramah or Ramatha, cf. v. 19.

[b]The text fluctuates between *ṣōpī* and *miṣṣūpīm*, the first consonant of which would be borrowed from *hārāmātayim*.

[c]GK 112 dd.

[d]The continuation of this sentence follows in v. 7b. What stands in between describes things which used to happen year by year.

[e]The phrase is dubious, see Commentary.

[f]Uncertain hiphil, the above translation follows the Arabic *raghama*, 'be contemptuous'.

[g]See Kittel, *Biblia Hebraica*³ (henceforward cited as BH); MT reads 'So he did'.

[h]The LXX has a longer text at this point: 'Hannah!' She answered him, 'Here am I, Lord.' And he said to her, 'Why . . .' This will be the original text, see Budde.

9 But Hannah rose, after they had eaten the boiled meat[a] and had drunk, and went before the LORD.[b] Now Eli the priest was sitting on his seat beside the doorpost of the temple of the LORD. [10]She was deeply distressed and prayed to the LORD, and wept bitterly. [11]And she vowed a vow and said, 'O LORD of hosts, if thou wilt indeed look on the affliction of thy maidservant, and remember me, and not forget thy maidservant, but wilt give to thy maidservant a son, then I will give him to the LORD all the days of his life, and no razor shall touch his head.'

12 As she continued praying before the LORD, Eli observed her mouth. [13]Hannah was speaking in her heart; only her lips moved, and her voice was not heard; therefore Eli took her to be a drunken woman. [14]And Eli said to her, 'How long will you be drunken? Put away your wine from you.' [15]But Hannah answered, 'No my lord, I am only[c] a woman sorely troubled;[d] I have drunk neither wine nor strong drink, but I have been pouring out my soul before the LORD. [16]Do not regard[e] your maidservant as a base woman, for all along I have been speaking out of my great anxiety and vexation.' [17]Then Eli answered, 'Go in peace, and the God of Israel grant your petition which you have made to him.' [18]And she said, 'Let your maidservant find favour in your eyes.' Then the woman went her way and ate with her husband and drank,[f] and her countenance was no longer sad.

19 They rose early in the morning and worshipped before the LORD; then they went back to their house at Ramah. And Elkanah knew Hannah his wife, and the LORD remembered her; [20]and Hannah conceived, and in due time bore a son,[g] and she called his name Samuel, for she said, 'I have asked him of the LORD.'

[1] The history of the beginnings of the time of the kings opens with a narrative which bears all the external characteristics of an idyll. It does not, however, resemble the folk tale, with anonymous figures, as we are told the names of everyone involved, including the second wife, who is not essential to the story. In this way the beginnings of the time of Samuel (and hence of the kings) are fixed quite definitely in certain people at a certain place. Elkanah, whose genealogy is given as far back as his great-great-grandfather—the sign of a noble and well-known family—is described as an Ephra-

---

[a]Reading *'aḥᵃrē 'ᵉkōl habbᵉšēlā.*

[b]So LXX, which wrongly omits here the words 'and had drunk', cf. v. 14.

[c]This is perhaps the best translation for the emphatic 'I' of the MT.

[d]MT reads 'hard in respect of the spirit', which should perhaps be emended with LXX to *qᵉšat yōm,* 'one who has had a hard time', cf. Job 30.25.

[e]This represents a reading *lᵉpāneka* with the Syriac; the MT preserves in the hard *b* of *bat* a reminiscence that *lipnē* does not belong with *bat.*

[f]So LXX.

[g]Word order following LXX.

thite. Here the word is meant to indicate the Ephraimite descent of the family and not, as in Ruth 1.2 (cf. Micah 5.2), to describe a clan of Bethlehem. In I Chron. 6.1ff., Samuel is given a Levitical ancestry, a change understandable in the light of later ideas. Otherwise the names of the ancestors in I Chron. 6.11f. are similar to those mentioned in I Sam. 1. Zuph, the last named of these ancestors, not only stands behind the word 'Zuphite', but evidently also gave his name to a definite area, the 'land of Zuph', I Sam. 9.5.[a] Here the family are said to live at Ramathaim; elsewhere Haramah (Ramah) is taken to be Samuel's home and native place (1.19, etc.). In English it means 'the height', an understandable name in Palestine and one which occurs frequently. The mention of the 'twofold Ramah' here and later—in the LXX, also I Macc. 11.34 and Matt. 27.57—shows that the tradition distinguished the place from Ramah of Benjamin (Judg; 4.5; 19.13, etc.). Evidently two places (at least) of the same or a similar name were claimed as the home of Samuel. The bulk of the tradition associates Samuel with the well-known Ramah of Benjamin (now er-ram). According to Judg. 4.5, this was counted as part of the 'hill country of Ephraim', near the boundaries of the tribes of Joseph and Benjamin (I Sam. 10.2; Jer. 31.15). At a later time, however, the present rentis, a long way north-west of er-ram, was regarded as the biblical 'Arimathea' and so as the abode of Samuel.[b]

[2–3] Elkanah has two wives; polygamy is thus unquestionably practised. The close association of wives is particularly likely to lead to discord if one of the two is childless, the most bitter misfortune possible for an Eastern woman.[c] The hostility between the wives comes clearly to light on the pilgrimage which Elkanah used to make each year with all his family, and which shows that he was 'not only a pious man, but, as we should now say, a churchman' (Ketter). The place of pilgrimage is Shiloh, the present selun, lying between Bethel and Shechem. Danish excavations have established the site beyond question.[d] The sanctuary there was of considerable importance as the resting-place of the ark. Men went up 'to

---

[a]The Arabs call the great estate of the Syrian Orphanage near Lydda not Bir Salem, the name given to it, but arḍ-ešpon, the land of Spohn, who was for a long time its director.

[b]Cf. A. Alt, PJB 24, 1928, p. 70; see further on ch. 9. Alt's observation (loc. cit.) that we should ask 'whether any narrative as graphic as this is meant to be read as a topographical document' is strongly to be endorsed.

[c]Gen. 30.1; hence Budde's remark that Elkanah shares 'Jacob's fate'.

[d]Hans Kjaer, The Excavation of Shilo, the place of Eli and Samuel, Jerusalem, 1930.

Shiloh, to Yahweh, the Lord of hosts'.[a] This is the technical term for a pilgrimage (cf. Luke 18.31, etc.). Why Elkanah went up to Shiloh in particular, and not to other equally famous sanctuaries which perhaps lay nearer to his home, such as Bethel, Mizpah or Shechem, is not explained. The fact that he goes to the shrine of the ark is meant on the one hand to show that Elkanah means to serve the true God at the legitimate place and on the other hand to provide an 'historical' confirmation of Samuel's association with Shiloh, which is well known elsewhere. Hophni and Phinehas, the sons of Eli, function as priests—according to the LXX the father still continues in his priestly office; a son of Eleazar is also known under the name of Phinehas, and 'Gibeah of Phinehas', with the grave of Eleazar, lies in the hill country of Ephraim (Josh. 24.33), in all probability not a great way from Shiloh, so that the same figure was evidently included at different points in the tradition.

[4–7a] The climax of the pilgrimage is a sacrificial meal at which the pilgrims rejoice before Yahweh with eating and drinking. The portions, of the sacrifice, of course, are divided by the head of the household, and it is emphatically stressed that even the women and children receive appropriate portions from him. This is a particularly kind gesture, as the women and children usually remained in the background during a feast and waited until the mealtime proper was over. Hannah, Elkanah's favourite wife, is evidently singled out for special attention. The text, however, is obscure: 'He used to give her one (the word is stressed) portion, (the) face (?) . . . for he loved Hannah . . .' The word 'appāyim, properly 'nose' (and sometimes 'wrath'), frequently means 'face', especially in the context of bowing down before God or before men in high positions. Perhaps 'portion of the face' signifies a particularly large piece, a portion of honour: earlier exegetes suggested a portion for two people (cf. Gen. 43.34, where Benjamin receives portions five times as large as those of his brothers). In any case, Hannah must have been treated by her husband in some special way to explain the taunts which Peninnah used to fling on such an occasion.

[7b–18] The description of the present visit begins again in v. 7b. Hannah, who cannot eat for grief, is addressed by her husband with exceptionally loving words of consolation. Nevertheless, she leaves

---

[a] Mizpah had similar importance as the place of the tent sanctuary, cf. *ZAW* 47, 1929, pp. 161ff.; men likewise went up 'to Yahweh at Mizpah', Judg. 20.1, 21.5.

THE CHILD ASKED OF GOD: I.I—20

the family meal—the text here is again obscure—as soon as possible[a] to 'pour out her heart' before the Lord, i.e. at the entrance to the temple. Her prayer is wholly concerned with her own distress, and, like that of Jacob in Gen. 28.20f., is bound up with a vow. It is completely in accordance with Eastern custom that Hannah asks not for a child, or children, but for a son. All the stories in the Bible which describe the events leading up to the birth of a child are concerned with boy children. Her pledge to consecrate the longed-for boy to the service of the sanctuary is meant to make the Lord willing to fulfil her request; there is no later mention that the boy, like Samson, was placed under Nazirite vows. This feature may possibly have been taken over from the Samson story, to which the narrative bears a certain similarity in other respects as well. During her long prayer Hannah has been watched by the old priest Eli, whose seat is outside at the temple gate. The silent prayer, in which only her lips move, seems to him so unusual that he takes her to be drunk; it is clear from this that drinking was quite customary at sacrificial meals (cf. vv. 9 and 18). Hannah's modest reply so obviously bears the stamp of truth that Eli believes her completely and not only makes the salutation of peace—still regularly used in the Arabian East to those departing on a journey—but also consoles her, wishing or promising (both are grammatically possible) the fulfilment of her request. Hannah's thanks are expressed in a formula which is again meant to show her humble bearing, and she goes away comforted.

[19—20] The sequel to the story is as we would imagine and expect. Hannah has not appealed in vain to the Lord of hosts at Shiloh. God blesses her womb, as the Fathers would put it; the phrase 'and she conceived', which has by mistake found its way into the wrong place, is not to be deleted (as Budde, etc.). The mere fact that a wife is pregnant raises her status considerably (see Gen. 16.4). Then the hoped-for son is born. He is named Samuel. The word $\check{s}^e m\bar{u}'\bar{e}l$ is apparently made up of $\check{s}\bar{e}m$ (name) and $'\bar{e}l$ (God); 'he over whom the name of God has been said' (Budde) is an appropriate designation of the great man of God.

Now it has been noticed for some time that the story itself has, in fact, another point. Twice in Eli's promise and most particularly

[a] Perhaps the 'eating of the boiled meat' was the part of the meal at which she had to be present.

in the naming of the child, the root *šā'al*, ask, is used in a kind of word-play. True, this is not far removed from the word *šᵉmū'ēl*, but it is without doubt more reminiscent of *šā'ūl*, 'he who is asked for'. In view of this, scholars, especially Hylander,[a] have sought to establish that the story originally described the birth of Saul, who, like Samson, was regarded as a deliverer from the Philistine oppression. Now without doubt[b] the mere fact that someone brings about 'deliverance' from the hand of the classical enemy is an understandable reason for narrating how the Lord made a personal intervention right from his mother's womb. Nevertheless, it is impossible[c] to establish that the original literary form of this passage was a narrative connected with the birth of Saul. It is, however, quite conceivable that such a narrative about the longed-for Saul, the future deliverer from the Philistines, was current in the pre-literary period; more than this we cannot say. If this material then attached itself to the figure of Samuel, the reason was surely not just a similarity in the names (though this made the process easier), but the fact that Samuel, to a greater degree than Saul, became and continued to be the formative figure, in other words the man sent of God. This may well be already an appearance of a thought which overshadows the first half of I Samuel. The real deliverer is not the first king, but the last judge. The sudden intervention of God has called him into being, and this fact makes it clear that we are now to hear not a history of monarchs, but the story of the continuing guidance of God.

2. SAMUEL COMES TO ELI: 1.21–2.11a

1 [21]And the man Elkanah and all his house went up (again) to offer to the LORD the yearly sacrifice, and to pay his vow. [22]But Hannah did not go up, for she said to her husband, '(I will remain here) until the child is weaned; then I will bring him to see[d] the face of the LORD, and abide there for ever.' [23]Elkanah her husband said to her, 'Do what seems best to you, wait until you have weaned him; only, may the LORD establish his word.' So the woman remained and nursed her son, until she weaned him. [24]And when she had weaned him, she took him up with her, along with a three-year-old bull,[d] an ephah of flour, and a skin of wine; and she brought him to the house of the

---

[a]pp. 13f.; earlier representatives of this view are also mentioned there.
[b]On this point see what is said in my commentary on Judg. 13.
[c]Cf. Press in *ZAW* 56, 1938, pp. 189f.
[d]See BH.

LORD at Shiloh, although the child was still young.[a] [25]Then they slew the bull, and they brought the child to Eli. [26]And she said, 'O my lord! As you live, my lord, I am the woman who was standing here in your presence, praying to the LORD. [27]For this child I prayed; and the LORD has granted me my petition which I made to him. [28]Therefore I have lent him to the LORD; as long as he lives,[b] he is lent to the LORD.'[c]

And they worshipped[d] the LORD there.

2 [1]Hannah also prayed and said,
   'My heart exults in the LORD,
      my horn is exalted in my God[b]
   My mouth derides my enemies,
      because I rejoice in thy salvation.

[2]'There is none holy like the LORD, for there is none besides thee;[e]
      there is no rock like our God.
[3]Talk no more so very proudly,[f]
      let not arrogance come from your mouth;
   for the LORD is a God of knowledge,
      and by him[b] actions are weighed.
[4]The bows of the mighty are broken,
      but the feeble gird on strength.
[5]Those who were full have hired themselves out for bread,
      but those who were hungry have ceased (to hunger) for ever.[g]
   The barren has borne seven,
      but she who has many children is forlorn.
[6]The LORD kills and brings to life;
      he brings down to Sheol and raises up.

[7]The LORD makes poor and makes rich;
      he brings low, he also exalts.
[8]He raises up the poor from the dust;
      he lifts the needy from the ash heap,
   to make them sit with princes
      and inherit a seat of honour.
   For the pillars of the earth are the LORD's,
      and on them he has set the world.

[a]we*hanna*'ar na*'ar*, already misinterpreted by LXX, is to be explained on the lines of Judg. 8.20, where the two words similarly stand close together.

[b]See BH.

[c]Hebrew uses the same root for 'to ask' and 'to borrow, lend'. There is therefore a word-play here which it is impossible to render in English.

[d]MT speaks only of 'he', but a 'w' has probably fallen out.

[e]The second clause is uncertain, see LXX and the Commentary.

[f]In the original text, the line is unusually long for the metre, but this may be intentional.

[g]Against the accentuation; read *lā'ad*; the unusual dagesh in the *l* of *ḥādēllū* may well have preserved a recollection of an omitted *l*. (But cf. D. W. Thomas, *SVT* 4, 1957, pp. 8–16. Tr.)

9'He will guard the feet of his faithful ones;
but the wicked shall be cut off in darkness;
for not by (his) might shall a man prevail.
10The adversaries of the LORD shall be broken in pieces.
The highest one in heaven will shatter thema
The LORD will judge the ends of the earth;
he will give strength to his king,
and exalt the power of his anointed.'
11AAnd they left him there before the LORD and went home to
Ramah.b

[21-23] The story moves on swiftly to the point towards which the narrative of the previous section was directed: the arrival of the promised child at the sanctuary in Shiloh. At the same time we are told why the vow is not performed immediately; it is postponed for as long as the child is being suckled. But the fact that the married couple are in earnest is emphasized by the note that Elkanah pays 'his vow' at the first opportunity which presents itself, the pilgrimage of the next year. We have not heard previously of a vow made by Elkanah; the writer assumes that the husband has accepted what his wife has determined as a matter of course. This is in accordance with the regulations for vows in Num. 30.1ff., especially v. 14, according to which a husband can confirm or invalidate any vow made by his wife. Elkanah even went beyond a confirmation of this nature by his personal participation in the vow; this may be what the writer is suggesting. In any case, Elkanah appears as the man responsible before God, who has to see that his wife also discharges her vow correctly, and at the right time. On the other hand, it is understandable that the woman draws out the time until she must give up her child as long as possible: the fact that children in the East are often suckled by their mothers for several years (three years, in II Macc. 7.27) would make her action seem quite reasonable.

[24-28] After the boy has been weaned, almost certainly a festive occasion, as in Gen. 21.8, and as still today in the East, he is taken along to Shiloh. A rich sacrifice is offered: a full-grown, and therefore particularly valuable, bull, wine, and about a bushel of flour. The child is then presented to the priest and the wife seeks to recall the earlier events to Eli's mind. Here, too, we have the word-play with *šā'al*, but in a new form (v. 28): 'he who is asked' now becomes

---

aThe corrupt 'against him' in the MT may well have given rise to the present pointing 'will thunder'; the early conjecture *'elyōn* and *y'rō'ēm* may well be right.
bSo LXX; MT speaks only of Elkanah and 'his' home. See Commentary.

'he who is lent', the Hebrew *šā'ūl* represents both. The presentation
of Samuel to the sanctuary is once again (cf. 1.11) expressly stated
to be for life. **[2.11a]** The personal touches which would accompany
the parting of mother and child are, as usual in the Bible, left unmentioned. MT records that Elkanah[a] (only?) returned to his home,
which is here said to be Ramah; it is not impossible that there was
a variant tradition according to which the mother remained for a
time with so small a child and perhaps temporarily took over some
duty at the sanctuary (as 2.22b). The LXX, however, whose reading
is certainly to be preferred, mentions the return of both parents.

[2.1–10] Before this last verse, the 'Hymn of Hannah' has been
inserted. The very way in which 2.11 joins on to 1.28 without any
lacuna shows it to be an insertion; it is further abundantly clear
that the content of the psalm is only loosely connected with the
story of Hannah. We thus have a parallel instance to the psalm in
the Book of Jonah. In either case an already existing psalm, which
seemed appropriate to the compiler, has been inserted. We should
take this in the same way as the addition of a suitable hymn to a
Bible reading.

So we have to ask two questions of the psalm, 'What does it mean
in itself?' and 'What does it mean in its present context?' Originally
it was a hymn. **[1–3]** The very beginning, which describes the joy of
the singer, makes this clear. An opening of this kind expresses the
complete and confident certainty of the person who speaks. The
word 'in' is most important; the man 'in God' is quite unassailable
because he is under the protection of the mighty God. One can see
from this alone that a hymn of this kind belongs to the sanctuary.
This is also noticeable from the way in which the second person is
sometimes used by the worshipper (v. 1b)[b] although Yahweh is
usually spoken of in the third. The confidence of the singer 'in' God
gives him steadfastness in the face of his 'enemies', and the strength
with which he is endowed is particularly emphasized in the image
of the 'horn'. Here 'my' enemies are, in fact, God's enemies, as the
works of God, and not personal experiences, are the object of the
praise and the content of the psalm. This is immediately recognizable
because directly after the introduction the uniqueness of the Lord is
acknowledged; v. 2, in fact, contains a confession which has a framework similar to that underlying the Israelite *sh'ma'*, 'Yahweh our

[a]MT of 1.28 also speaks of Elkanah only.
[b]Cf. Gunkel, *Einleitung in die Psalmen*, 1928, p. 47.

God is one Yahweh' (Deut. 6.4) and the first half of the Islamic creed, 'There is no God but God'. We find this word for word in v. 2b. This particular clause, however, appears to be a later expansion, as in it Yahweh is celebrated as the one who alone exists, an advance over the rest of the verse which praises his supremacy over all men and all things ('there is none like . . .'). Because the Lord is so strong, no one can go against him; the Psalmist therefore turns to the 'enemies' and in vivid language warns them against persisting in their presumptuous attitude, as the eyes of God penetrate all things and he is a righteous God. Here the sin of *hybris*, the primal sin of Gen. 3, constantly recognized, by Isaiah and others, as the root sin, is denounced; it is a revolt against God, a questioning of his primacy.

[4-9] The earlier verses described God's power, his holiness and his omniscience; the antitheses in the central section glorify his ability to intervene in a material way in the events of the world by virtue of these attributes. First, the perfect is used; this signifies that these claims have been experienced and proved. Then from v. 6 to v. 8 we have the participle; with it attention is transferred from the acts of God to the God who is of this nature. For *he himself* is the real theme of the psalm; in this respect it corresponds to the way of worship, which always assigns the pre-eminence to God. Consequently it is of no use for men to be mighty, satisfied, prolific, alive, prosperous, exalted, nobly born; God can put in their place the feeble, the hungry, the barren, the dead, the poor and the lowly, thereby using the weak to put the strong to shame (I Cor. 1). The LXX has inserted Jer. 9.22 at this point—quite pertinently, as it has the same theological viewpoint. The whole is not meant as praise for the righteousness of the God who makes all equal, but as praise of his lordly might which is exercised in a mercy which condescends to the needy. Among the remarks made here about God, particular attention should be paid to that which ascribes to the Lord power to bring men down to the kingdom of the dead—Sheol, imagined as being in the bowels of the earth—and to raise them up again. A specific faith in the resurrection from the dead lies more on the periphery and at the conclusion of the OT, but its theological starting-point is without doubt the consciousness of the unconditioned might of Yahweh. The remark that the 'pillars of the world' belong to him is surely put intentionally at this point. As creator of the world, he is the Almighty; is his power to be limited by what is under the earth?

[9–10] All this is not, however, to be regarded as a dogmatic expression with the status of a doctrine. Here the Lord is praised simply as the unique and wonderful one, the holy one, who will therefore also preserve his own, the 'faithful ones', as they stand against the 'wicked' (properly 'guilty'). It is important that the psalm once again stresses that no one can do this through his own strength. Here the psalm (as early as the middle of v. 8) changes from the perfect and the participle to the imperfect. Now, at the conclusion, it considers what is of permanent and final validity. The concern of the individual and his hopes therefore merge once again into general expectations: Yahweh, the creator of all the world, is also judge of all the world and at the same time the bringer of salvation. It is uncertain whether the reference at the end is to the earthly king depicted in messianic colours or to the king of salvation of the last times;[a] presumably the boundaries here are blurred.

This powerful, virile psalm, which nevertheless derives the strength to which it witnesses wholly and entirely from the power of God, is now put in the mouth of Hannah, chiefly, of course, because of the mention of the barren woman who is compared with the one 'who has many children'. But the basic theological standpoint also fits her situation in other respects: the Lord can make something out of nothing, a victor from the oppressed, and can thus testify to his abundance in the life of one poor human being. It is precisely this remedying of chronic childlessness which is frequently said to be the working of God's power (Gen. 18.14; Luke 1.36f.; Rom. 4.19–21; Heb. 11.11). The final compiler of the whole work wished to stress that here too. In so doing he has at the same time given a theological interpretation to the beginning of Samuel's life. What we have here is not a charming, idyllic narrative with a happy ending and piety rewarded. The psalm puts the birth, and hence the life, of Samuel in the context of the all-powerful saving acts of God. These stories are intended to be history, the history of God's dealings with the chosen people.

Hannah's song of praise has had a further sequel of a special nature. It is extremely like the Magnificat (Luke 1.46–58), which, while being, in fact, simply a catena of Old Testament quotations,[b] bears the closest resemblance to I Sam. 2 (and 1.11). Hannah's song

---

[a]Cf. W. Stärk, *Lyrik*[2], 1920, pp. 71f.
[b]Even v. 48b, not printed by Nestle in bold type, is to be understood in the light of Gen. 30.13.

of praise has been understood as the thanksgiving of a woman on whom God has bestowed the blessing of a child after a long period of waiting, and this in turn means that the reading of 'Elisabeth' for 'Mary' in Luke 1.46—with ancient testimony—is deserving of notice. On the other hand, we can easily understand how the powerful theological expressions running through the psalm of Hannah would have led to its New Testament successor being considered significant enough to be placed in the mouth of the 'blessed among women'.[a]

3. SAMUEL AT THE TEMPLE AND THE SINS OF THE SONS OF ELI: 2.11b–36

2 [11B]And the boy ministered to the LORD, in the presence of Eli the priest.

12 Now the sons of Eli were worthless men; they had no regard for the LORD, [13]nor for what was due to the priest from the people.[b] When any man offered sacrifice, the priest's servant would come, while the meat was boiling, with a three-pronged fork in his hand, [14]and he would thrust it into the pan, or kettle, or cauldron, or pot; all that the fork brought up the priest would take for himself. So they did to all the Israelites who came to sacrifice to the name of the LORD in Shiloh.[c] [15]Moreover, before the fat was burned, the priest's servant would come and say to the man who was sacrificing, 'Give meat for the priest to roast; for he will not accept boiled meat from you, but raw.' [16]And if the man said to him, 'Let them burn the fat first, and then take as much as you wish,' he would say, 'No, you must give it now, and if not, I will take it by force.' [17]Thus the sin of the young men was very great in the sight[d] of the LORD; for the men treated the offering of the LORD with contempt.

18 Samuel was ministering before the LORD,[e] a boy girded with a linen ephod. [19]And his mother used to make for him a little robe and take it to him each year, when she went up with her husband to offer the yearly sacrifice. [20]Then Eli would bless Elkanah and his wife, and say, 'The LORD give you children by this woman in place of the demand which the LORD has made';[f] so then they would return to

[a]Cf. Hertzberg on Luke 1.46–58 in the North German appendix to *Für Arbeit und Besinnung* 4, 1951, pp. 886–8.

[b]See BH. Another way of translating would be: 'And the custom of the priests with the people was this' (RSV: cf. ZAW 40, 1922, pp. 265f.).

[c]Pointing the penultimate Hebrew word *šēm* and expanding the evidently mutilated verse after LXX.

[d]The same expression as in v. 11b; literally 'before the presence'.

[e]The words *mᵉšārēt 'et-pᵉnē yahweh* can mean either 'he served (without object) under the eyes (as v. 11b, there associated with Eli) of Yahweh' or, 'he served the countenance of Yahweh', i.e. Yahweh himself.

[f]*lᵉyahweh* is formed on the pattern of 1.28, where it occurs twice; *yahweh* is grammatically correct.

his[a] home. [21]And[b] the LORD visited Hannah, and she conceived and bore three sons and two daughters. And the boy Samuel grew in the presence of the LORD.

22 Now Eli was very old, and he heard all that his sons were doing to all Israel, and how they lay with the women who served at the entrance to the tent of meeting. [23]And he said to them, 'Why do you do such things? For I hear from all the people of your evil dealings.[c] [24]No, my sons; it is no good report that I hear the people of the LORD spreading abroad. [25]If a man sins against a man, God will mediate for him; but if a man sins against the LORD, who can intercede for him?' But they would not listen to the voice of their father; for it was the will of the LORD to slay them.

26 Now the boy Samuel continued to grow both in stature and in favour with the LORD and with men.

27 And there came a man of God to Eli and said to him, 'Thus the LORD has said,[d] "I revealed myself to the house of your father when they were in Egypt (subject)[e] to the house of Pharaoh. [28]And I chose him out of all the tribes of Israel to be my priest, to go up to my altar, to burn incense, to wear an ephod before me; and I gave to the house of your father all my offerings by fire from the people of Israel. [29]Why then kick at my sacrifices and my offerings which I commanded for my dwelling, and honour your sons above me by fattening yourselves upon the choicest parts of every offering of Israel?"[f] [30]Therefore the LORD the God of Israel declares: "I promised that your house and the house of your father should go in and out before me for ever"; but now the LORD declares: "Far be it from me; for those (alone) who honour me I will honour, and those who despise me shall be lightly esteemed. [31]Behold, the days are coming, when I will cut off your strength and the strength of your father's house, so that there will not be an old man in your house. [32] . . . [g]In all the prosperity which (the LORD) shall bestow upon Israel; and there shall not be an old man in your house

[a]So MT and the majority of the ancient witnesses. The 'their', suggested even at an early date, is a simplification.

[b]Presumably a *way^ehī* has fallen out (Thenius); LXX abbreviates to *wayyipqōd*.

[c]The words *'et-dibrēkem rā^īm* belong with *'ēlle*, at the end of the verse.

[d]See BH.

[e]Inserted by LXX.

[f]The puzzling *mā^ōn*, 'dwelling' (as II Chron. 36.15, etc.) appears to be the remains of an original *lim^ōnī:* the incomprehensible *l^ammī*, at the end of the verse, seems to be a marginal correction of *mā^ōn*, having very similar consonants, which then found its way into the text at a wrong place. LXX connects *mā^ōn* with *^ayin*, 'eye', and thus obtains a different meaning, which is accepted by many recent exegetes. The chief difficulty is the fact that *mā^ōn* recurs at v. 32, see *ad loc.*

[g]The three words *w^ehibbaṭṭā ṣar mā^ōn* 'and you will look upon the enemy of (my) dwelling' (?) may possibly refer to the destruction of Shiloh mentioned in Jer. 7.12, though Eli himself did not live to see it. On the other hand, it is more probable that the words represent a doublet to the beginning of v. 29: *tib^ṭ^ū . . . ṣiwwītī mā^ōn.*

S.—B

for ever. ³³Not that I intend to cut off any man of you from my altar (and thus) cause your eyes to weep and your heart to grieve; but all the increase of your house shall die in (the prime of) manhood. ³⁴And this which shall befall your two sons, Hophni and Phinehas, shall be the sign to you: both of them shall die on the same day. ³⁵And I will raise up for myself a faithful priest, who shall do according to what is in my heart and in my mind; and I will build him a sure house, and he shall go in and out before my anointed for ever. ³⁶And every one who is left in your house shall come to implore him for a piece of silver or a loaf of bread, and shall say, 'Put me, I pray you, in one of the priest's places, that I may eat a morsel of bread.' " '

The content of this section is exactly what the title shows: two activities which take place alongside one another. One continues the line of the previous narrative and describes how Samuel grows up and becomes accustomed to his destined office. The other describes the sins of the house of Eli and adds a forecast of its punishment. But these two strands do not stand side by side as distinct entities; they are purposely worked together by the compiler. One curve sinks, the other rises, as is recorded in II Sam. 3.1 of the house of Saul and David and in John 3.30 of John the Baptist and Jesus. This contrast and juxtaposition is not just the work of the final compiler; it appears to be old. The story of Samuel's youth has certainly never been just an account which narrated the rise of Samuel as it were with no fixed purpose. The child asked of Yahweh and then lent to him again is chosen and equipped by him for the leading part he is to play. Hitherto this has been suggested only in hints. Now it becomes clearly recognizable.

[11b] From his earliest days onwards, it is stressed, Samuel serves at the sanctuary; *leitourgōn* is the word with which the LXX translates this sacral 'service'. He is instructed by the bearer of the tradition, Eli, of the house of Aaron; he serves 'in his presence'. [12-14] It is noticeable how, as early as this, the sons of Eli are said to present a contrast. They are 'worthless' and 'do not know' (the Hebrew word whose sense RSV correctly renders as 'have no regard for') the Lord. In other words, they are concerned for their own profit and not for the correct performance of the will of God. Their present preoccupation is with the maintenance of their privilege; that is the meaning of the sentence, whether we render the first Hebrew word of v. 13 'custom' or 'claim'. The procedure described here is contrary to what was enjoined and allowed. Custom and ordinance (cf. Lev. 7.31ff., Deut. 18.3) had strict regulations about the portions of the sacrifice

available to the priest, even if they might have differed at individual
sanctuaries. The sons of Eli put arbitrariness in place of law, human
selfishness in place of the will of God. The fact that they acted 'while
the meat was still boiling' is meant to show the greed which governed
all their actions. [15–17] The second example mentioned here points
in the same direction; in their desire to obtain raw meat instead of
the permissible boiled meat they put themselves in first place, before
the Lord. The laity, who want first to give Yahweh the fat which is
his due, are better protectors of the holy law than the priests
appointed for that very purpose. All this shows that here we have
something more serious than a few lapses. Sacral law is being
perverted and the holy office disgraced. And to crown all, this is
being brought about through a rule of terror. The final clause of the
paragraph is therefore no exaggeration. Here is sin being committed
in the immediate presence of the holy God.[a]

[18–21] The contrast between this gloomy scene and the bright,
serene picture of the boy Samuel serving at the sanctuary is surely
intentional. Perhaps the form of the text (see note *ad loc.*) is meant to
stress that he was the personal servant of the Lord; similarly 3.3 shows
his sleeping-place to have been immediately beside the ark. He
already wears the priestly garment. 'Linen ephod' is its official
description, and whoever 'wears' it is characterized as a priest. As is
well known, the word ephod is sometimes used in the OT to describe
a fixed object which can be made out of precious metal (cf. Judg.
8.27 and 17.1ff.) and sometimes to describe the priestly garment.
The fact that both have something to do with oracles may explain
why the same word is used in either case.[b] Be this as it may, 'Samuel is
thus depicted virtually as a little priest' (Budde *ad loc.*). The little
robe which the mother makes for her son year by year and brings
with her when she comes on pilgrimage is an indication of her
motherly care—the boy would grow out of the previous year's robe
—and pride; such a garment is a sign of distinction (cf. the mantle in
Isa. 3.6). This visit does more, however, than bring about the mutual
joy of an occasional reunion; the couple derive from it a new, special
blessing from Yahweh. The 'loan' (again the root *šā'al* is involved)

---

[a]The expression 'young men' should in no way be taken as a plea for 'extenuat-
ing circumstances' (Caspari).

[b]'Perhaps it was thought of as a garment of the deity which gave the priest
magic power when he wore it' (O. Procksch, *Theologie des AT*, 1950, p. 109.
Further literature there).

which they have made to the Lord by surrendering the child yields high interest; presumably the sentence means that the blessing continued to bring good fortune and that the couple were endowed with five more children. This charming feature is surely related to show once again how important Samuel's service at the sanctuary was in the eyes of the Lord, to merit such a blessing.

[22–25] The years go by. The boy grows up, but at the same time the guilt of the sons of Eli becomes greater. This is evidently implied by the note that they pollute the sanctuary by excesses in yet another direction. The sentence—lacking in Codex Vaticanus—could have been added later from another tradition; it has been formed along the lines of Ex. 38.8. In fact, a proper building to house the ark had been standing in Shiloh for some time. The women mentioned here (and in Ex. 38.8) have the task of keeping the entrance clean; this was particularly important[a] for what took place in the sanctuary. The fact that the women are counted among the sacral personnel by virtue of their task is meant to make the sins of the priests seem all the more culpable. The remonstrances of their father, whose age is mentioned at the beginning of the section apparently to excuse him, are, on the other hand, not so weak as they are often represented to be. He begins, quite correctly, with popular rumour, knowing full well that this alone is a disastrous thing for the priestly office, whose holders live in houses with glass walls. Eli's second argument is still more telling: in a sin between men God can act as arbitrator and exercise his mercy, but in any matter between man and God, God can no longer act as an impartial moderator (Job 16.21 differs). The root *pālal* used here means 'determine' ('act as an attorney') without any specific connotations, but in this passage the tone is favourable. This has been noticed by LXX (and RSV) who render it in the sense of *hitpallēl*, intercede. Eli argues that God himself has been challenged in such a way by the sins of the priests that his goodwill can no longer be invoked. Here the old man gives an impressive warning. The complete disregard for it shown by his sons is ominous for later developments. There is, however, no mention of any lack of concrete repentance which we might suppose could have stayed the disaster. Even the guilt of the sons of Eli is taken up into the omnipotence of God. This is the theological situation which is elsewhere characterized by the biblical phrase 'having the heart hardened'.

[a]Hertzberg in *ZAW* 47, 1929, pp. 169, 175.

[26] Immediately afterwards, our attention is once again drawn to the young Samuel. The purpose of this arrangement is quite clear: first decline, then increase; evil repute, then favour with men; the judgment of God, then his mercy. To remove the sentence from its present context is to misunderstand the whole point of the passage. The phrase is not applied to Jesus purely by chance in Luke 2.52; we will return to this at the end of the next chapter.

[27a] A speech by a man of God forms the conclusion to the section. Passages of this kind often occur in texts edited by the deuteronomistic school, and are particularly important. They represent the theological explanation of the events which have been described (cf. Judg. 6.8–10, also Judg. 9.7–20 and my commentary *ad loc.*). History here is never a mere sequence of events, but what happens under the guidance and explanation of God. Men go their way in guilt or good favour, but the Lord is constantly at their side. Such prophetic insertions, moreover, frequently offer a cross-section of history. They give an event its place in the context of the divine plans extending throughout all time.

[27b–28] This passage presents some difficulty not only in the text, which is in part badly preserved, but also, to a greater extent, in the meaning of the subject-matter. It is indubitably concerned with the overthrow of the house of Eli; on the other hand, there is no indication of who is to emerge in their place. In the general context we would, of course, think of Samuel, but the conclusion of the passage seems to point towards the later priestly dynasty of the Zadokites.[a] First we hear of the call of the tribe of Levi (and of the sons of Aaron in particular) to be bearers of the priestly office, during the time in Egypt; the expression 'house of your father' might mean either the tribe of Levi or the sons of Aaron. The duties of the priestly office mentioned here are serving in the forecourt, in which the altar stood, serving in the inner sanctuary, where the altar of incense was situated, and the giving of oracles: in other words, the cultus in its entirety. The revenues were regulated accordingly. [29] Here, too, the sins in the priestly sphere are regarded much more seriously. The change in the form of address (second person singular instead of second person plural, a change which cannot be reproduced in modern English idiom) where Eli is being personally charged with honouring his sons more than the Lord, is intended to lay special

---

[a]Cf. II 15.24ff. and on II 6.3 and II. 8.17. On this see Budde in *ZAW* 52, 1934, pp. 42–50 and O. Procksch, *Theologie*, p. 124.

stress on his share of the responsibility. **[30-34]** A formal threat is now uttered (and that means here a threat in prophetic form) with the twofold use of the word *n^e'um* (word of God, whisper). As the earlier part of the speech recalled the former promise that the house of Eli (or the tribe of Levi) should be the permanent holders of the priestly office, the following passage must mean that this promise has now been revoked. That is the meaning of the clause 'Far be it from me.' Only those (note the plural) who honour Yahweh can in turn be honoured by him, i.e. be entrusted with high dignity. Now a sentence ought to follow reading, approximately, 'Therefore I deprive you of your office and put . . . in your place.' But strangely enough this is not what happens. Instead, we have a second declaration, that in the future there will no longer be an 'old man' in the house of Eli: the male persons of the family are all to die in the prime of life. The 'shame' announced here seems to consist in the future absence of those persons, the old, who by nature are owed the reverence of the community. There is, however, no mention of a complete dispossession from the priestly office; on the contrary, v. 33a rather seems to discount this most fearful and overwhelming punishment, even if the wording suggests that the family's enjoyment of high office is to be restricted. It is possible, but not certain, that this remark may contain an allusion to Abiathar, who, at a later date, was the only one to escape the blood bath which Saul brought about among the sons of Eli. In addition, the death of the two chief culprits is announced as a sign that the death of men in their prime will very soon be a grim reality.

[35-36] Only now does there follow what might originally have been expected, and was interrupted by the train of thought in vv. 31-34, the replacement of the rejected priestly dynasty by a new one. At first sight, these remarks seem to imply that Samuel is the 'faithful priest'. He can be described thus; he is a man after God's heart, and the remark that he shall go out and in before 'Yahweh's anointed' reminds us that Samuel had a special relationship to the first two kings. On the other hand, what is said in the third place does not fully accord with the relationship in which Samuel stood to Saul and David. It seems much more to be concerned with a priestly family lasting from generation to generation. Finally, the mention that the sons of Eli will become a common order who have to entreat the new master for the position of a subordinate priest may be a hint at the circumstances in which the house of Eli found itself after the

banishment of Abiathar to Anathoth (I Kings 2.26) and more particularly later, after the dismissal of the priests of the land by the Deuteronomic reform. Here, in fact, our attention is drawn to the house of
Zadok, the *homo novus* who became the ancestor of the priestly family.

We have here, then, generally speaking, a speech constructed by
the deuteronomistic compiler which describes the downfall of the
sons of Eli to the advantage of the Zadokite priesthood. It is not,
however, just a work composed at a late period, but makes use of
older material. Of this older material, the most prominent is the
threat 'there will not be an old man in your house'. We may have
traces here of material which belonged to the tradition of the death of
the sons of Eli and the history of the ark, and was introduced into the
description of Samuel's youth for the obvious reason that the latter
narrative also told of the sins of the sons of Eli. Most of the speech,
however, treats of the deposition of the sons of Eli. It is no longer
possible to see at all clearly whether in the primary form of the
tradition the speech of the man of God prophesied that Samuel was
to take the place of Eli and his sons; viewed at a distance, the main
concern seems to be the removal of the tribe of Levi, and that could
mean the office being taken over by a member of the tribe of Ephraim,
in other words Samuel (cf. Budde on 2.27). Were this the case, the
material would have been elaborated further in reflection upon the
historical events themselves. This had two consequences: the downfall of the priestly tribe became an obscure matter (indeed, even the
house of Zadok set great store by its legitimate descent—from
Aaron!); and not just a reliable priest—that would, as has been said,
have applied equally well to Samuel—but a faithful priestly family
(which Samuel could not boast, cf. 8.3) took the place of the now
unworthy clan. The providence of the Lord thus goes beyond
Samuel and guarantees into the future the holy office whose present
bearer is Eli and whose next bearer will be Samuel. It is of this that
the next section speaks.

4. THE LORD CALLS TO SAMUEL: 3.1–4.1a

3 [1]Now the boy Samuel was ministering to the LORD under Eli.
And the word of the LORD was rare in those days; there was no frequent vision.

2 At that time Eli, whose eyesight had begun to grow dim, so that
he could not see, was lying down in his own place; [3]the lamp of God
had not yet gone out and Samuel was (still) lying down,[a] within the

[a]Here the MT has a caesura, which emphasizes what follows.

temple of the LORD, where the ark of God was. ⁴Then the LORD called Samuel and he said, 'Here I am!' ⁵and ran to Eli, and said, 'Here I am, for you called me.' But he said, 'I did not call; lie down again.' So he went and lay down. ⁶And the LORD called again, 'Samuel!' And Samuel arose and went to Eli, and said, 'Here I am, for you called me.' But he said, 'I did not call, my son; lie down again.' ⁷Now Samuel did not yet know the LORD, and the word of the LORD had not yet been revealed to him. ⁸And the LORD called Samuel again the third time. And he arose and went to Eli, and said, 'Here I am, for you called me.' Then Eli perceived that the LORD was calling the boy. ⁹Therefore Eli said to Samuel, 'Go, lie down; and if he calls you, you shall say, "Speak, LORD, for thy servant hears." ' So Samuel went and lay down in his place.

10 And the LORD came and stood forth, calling as at other times, 'Samuel, Samuel!' And Samuel said, 'Speak, for thy servant hears.' ¹¹Then the LORD said to Samuel, 'Behold, I am about to do a thing in Israel, at which the two ears of every one that hears it will tingle. ¹²On that day I will fulfil against Eli all that I have spoken concerning his house, from beginning to end, ¹³and (what) I have told him,ᵃ that I am about to punish his house for ever, for the iniquity which he knew because his sons were setting God at noughtᵇ and he did not restrain them. ¹⁴Therefore I swear to the house of Eli that the iniquity of Eli's house shall not be expiated by sacrifice or offering for ever.'

15 Samuel lay until morning; then he opened the doors of the house of the LORD. And Samuel was afraid to tell the vision to Eli. ¹⁶But Eli called Samuel and said, 'Samuel, my son.' And he said, 'Here I am.' ¹⁷And Eli said, 'What was it that he told you? Do not hide it from me. May God do so to you and more also, if you hide anything from me of all that he told you.' ¹⁸So Samuel told him everything and hid nothing from him. And he said, 'It is the LORD; let him do what seems good to him.'

19 And Samuel grew, and the LORD was with him and let none of his words fall to the ground. ²⁰And all Israel from Dan to Beersheba knew that Samuel was established as a prophet of the LORD. ²¹And the LORD appeared again at Shiloh, for the LORD revealed himself to Samuel at Shiloh. 4 ¹ᴬThus the word of Samuel was as the word of the LORDᶜ to all Israel. Now Eli was very old, and his sons continued in their way and their way was evil in the eyes of the LORD.ᵈ

ᵃThis is apparently the meaning of wᵉhiggadtī, without consecutive stress; this is better than the proposal to emend the text to wᵉhiggadtā 'and you shall tell him'; in the context of the text he has already been told!

ᵇThe transmission of the text here is defective. An original yaʿan before ʾᵃšer (see BH) was displaced by the baʿᵃwōn, which for its part originally belonged with bānāw. mᵉqalᵉlīm stands for mᵉqallīm, lāhem is what is left of ʾᵉlōhīm, cf. Budde ad loc.

ᶜSee BH.

ᵈThis sentence stands after v. 21 in LXX.

The main part of this chapter is taken up with an excellent piece of narrative, both simply and dramatically told. It has a twofold purpose. In the foreground we have (yet again) an announcement of the punishment of the house of Eli which refers back to what has already been said in ch. 2. But over and above this, the chapter depicts as it were the call of Samuel. This emerges from two features. First, we hear of a theophany similar to those associated with other men of God (Moses, Gideon, some of the prophets, and Samson). We further learn what sort of a person Samuel was from his boyhood up, namely one who was capable of receiving 'the word'. He has this capability, however, not of himself, but as a man who has received a special qualification. We hear several times in the chapter just what is 'special' about it in comparison with what has gone before.

[1–3] At the beginning, the narrative takes up the note 2.11b (cf. 2.18). Samuel grows used to his service in the sanctuary; it is important for the writer to stress this. The ordination to his later office, however, is not a consequence of this service, but of a special calling. The first four verses form a single sentence, which can be reproduced in translation only by a paraphrase. First of all the general situation is described (by the use of the participle and then of the perfect). It is expressly stated that the word of the Lord had become 'rare' and there was no 'frequent vision'. Thus nothing came from the hand of God, and in the world of men the waters flowed only sluggishly. The chief reason for this is certainly assumed to be the conduct of the house of Eli; God had hidden his face. Eli himself is described as infirm, as is Isaac in Gen. 27.1. His infirmity of vision may have been mentioned to show why Samuel and not he himself was sleeping at the sanctuary. Why this was the priestly duty, we are not told. One might connect it with the tending of the lamp,[a] but it may have been simply a watch by the ark, originally in order to receive the divine instructions (incubation). This watch, as we are emphatically told, had for a long time been unsuccessful. [4–9] The scene now depicted takes place towards morning; we are told that the lamp of God has not yet gone out. The call of the Lord, which consists in the mention of the person who is called, once or twice, happens three times without Samuel and Eli, who is mistakenly taken for the person who is calling, knowing what is happening. Only on the fourth occasion does Samuel give the answer suggested to him by Eli; the word 'hears', a participle in Hebrew, means 'is ready to hear'. Such

[a] Caspari, p. 50, n. 3.

readiness to receive the divine manifestation is evidently regarded as a necessity. [10–14] Only now does the Lord 'come' to make an appearance. The OT is generally very restrained in this connection (cf. Isa. 6 and Ex. 33); here, too, there is more in hints than in explicit statements. Still, what is said is sufficient to show the young man, and especially the hearers of the story, that something is now to take place for which the earlier call was just a signal. Samuel is now to hear a real threat, such as we later find frequently in the prophetic writings, a threat in which guilt and punishment are closely bound together as cause and effect. The material here runs parallel to the earlier threat (2.27ff.), so the two scenes have almost certainly been transmitted independently of one another. Following one another as they do now, they serve as a confirmation of what the future is to bring for the house of Eli; this second divulging of the divine will appears as an explicit underlining and strengthening of the first. Thus the sins of the house of Eli are represented as inexpiable still more clearly than in ch. 2.

[15–18] Samuel receives the divine revelation, apparently more asleep than awake (vv. 9 and 15), and remembers it well because of its impressive content. At first, however, he keeps silent. Only at the direct command of the priest, whose words reveal both insight (he speaks only of 'him') and tension, does he pass it on literally and without regard for the consequences. In form and content Eli's reply accords with Eastern attitudes, but also reveals a man who knows that he stands under God. Much is packed into the short sentence.

[19–21] The previous sentences already assume that some years have passed since his mother brought the boy Samuel to Shiloh. The closing verses describe his growth to manhood. The phrase 'the Lord was with him' can itself be used to describe any successful man, but here it means one who is especially blessed by God, the man of God. And Samuel is indeed depicted as one who is himself capable of receiving the word of the Lord. 'His' words are those which the Lord allows to come to Samuel and which 'he', the Lord, authenticates by bringing them to pass. This is the way in which the word of a prophet is shown to be true in the Deuteronomic law, too (Deut. 18.22). Here, then, Samuel is already assumed to have prophetic gifts going far beyond that first occasion when he was entrusted with the word of God. Samuel's repute, which reaches from the northernmost sanctuary of classical Palestine to the most southerly, is fully in accord with this. Shiloh now becomes a great place for the revelation

of God. This, however, is not because of the ark of God, but by virtue
of the person who is considered worthy of so great a gift of the word.
[4.1a] The more the reputation of Samuel rises, the more Shiloh
loses credit as a place of worship through the conduct of the sons of
Eli, as we are told in the sentence which occurs in the LXX. This
sentence shows rise and decline together and so prepares for the
following chapter.

In these three chapters Samuel appears as a man who has been
associated with the sanctuary from his youth, who has grown up and
gained his experience in the priestly service, and who is destined to
become in reality the true priest in Israel. He succeeds to this office,
however, only through the revelation of the word accorded to him.
In this way he unites the priestly office with the prophetic vocation.
He becomes the spiritual leader of his people, and that means that he
receives a public, indeed a political status. This will be discussed
later. By now, however, it is already clear that there has not been a
man like him since the days of Moses. Samuel should be regarded in
this light. Joshua was Moses' successor, the 'servant of God'. But he is
never called prophet, nor is he a priest. Here is more than a Joshua.
Here, too, we have something more than the prophets of later times,
who stood in the midst of the people as the spokesmen of God, but in
other respects were still on their periphery. Samuel unites in his
person the three offices of the Christ who is to come, prophet, priest
and king. It is no wonder that the shadow of this particular figure
falls over the 'Books of Samuel' which bear his name. Nor is it by
chance that in the passage which describes the growth of the boy
Jesus (Luke 2.42) we find the same words which describe the growth
of the young Samuel and that, as has been remarked above, the
thanksgiving of the mother of Jesus also makes use of words of the
thanksgiving of the mother of Samuel. The Bible regards him as being
to a special degree one of the forerunners of Christ, and does so with
justification.

NOTE ON FORMATION AND STRUCTURE: I

The meaning of the story of Samuel's youth is, in its present form,
quite clear. It is meant to show how Samuel is the first to come
forward to take the place of the line of Eli. The opening narrative
matches this pattern. Samuel is asked of the Lord and 'borrowed' by
him, and this we find confirmed by the prophetic saying which
accompanies the story (in ch. 2), and above all by the call, which

contains a threat of punishment against the sons of Eli and at the conclusion emphasizes Samuel's position. These observations are in no way altered by the fact that 2.35ff. looks beyond Samuel to the priestly dynasty of the sons of Zadok. And if the story of his childhood in its original form really referred to Saul, the first king, its present application to Samuel confirms with sufficient certainty the high position which the figure of the man now occupies (see the remarks at the end of the previous section).

The hand of the final compiler is to be seen at the conclusion of the account in ch. 2. He knew the later history of Samuel's family, i.e. the fact that Samuel's descendants did not succeed to the place of Eli's descendants. He knew, moreover, that the priests who did service before the 'anointed', the king of Judah of his time, were of the family of Zadok. But it was, of course, also clear to him that Samuel was the effective successor of Eli, the last of the judges, and also the king-maker. So Samuel is for him the truly great figure who possessed not only priestly, but also prophetic and political powers of leadership. The story of his youth was welcome, indeed absolutely necessary material for him to bring this out.

We may also be indebted to the final compiler for the insertion of the psalm of Hannah. Its character has been described in the commentary *ad loc.*, and in its present position it is intended as a theological interpretation of the beginning of Samuel's life. Yahweh's way of making something come out of nothing is here displayed with great clarity and confirms that the story of Samuel does not depict the rise of a man to fame; it is God who calls this man into existence, sets him to his service, is 'with him', calls him, helps him and blesses him.

The accounts of the fall of the sons of Eli and rise of Samuel need not necessarily have been linked together from the first. In chs. 4–6 we hear only of the former, and not of the latter. But the final compiler received the material already worked together as it is now. It may have been handed down at one of the sanctuaries mentioned in 7.16, which perhaps continued to keep a remembrance of Samuel. It is impossible to say more on the point. The story of his youth is of extreme importance for a theological appreciation of the rise of Samuel and of the period of the kings, which was to be inaugurated by him, and is in any case something more than a pleasant introduction which might as well be omitted as retained.

II

THE HISTORY OF THE ARK
I. 4–6

1. THE ARK IS TAKEN: 4.1b–22

4 ¹ᴮNow in those days the Philistines gathered together to fight against Israelᵃ and Israel went out to battle against the Philistines; they encamped at Ebenezer, and the Philistines encamped at Aphek. ²The Philistines drew up in line against Israel, and when the battle spread,ᵇ Israel was defeated by the Philistines, who slew about four thousand men on the field of battle. ³And when the troops came to the camp, the elders of Israel said, 'Why has the Lord put us to rout today before the Philistines? Let us bring the ark of the covenant of the LORD here from Shiloh, that he may come among us and save us from the power of our enemies.' ⁴So the people sent to Shiloh, and brought from there the ark of the covenant of the LORD of hosts, who is enthroned on the cherubim; and the two sons of Eli, Hophni and Phinehas, were (there)ᶜ with the ark of the covenant of God.

5 When the ark of the covenant of the LORD came into the camp, all Israel gave a mighty shout, so that the earth resounded. ⁶And when the Philistines heard the noise of the shouting, they said, 'What does this great shouting in the camp of the Hebrews mean?' And when they learned that the ark of the LORD had come to the camp, ⁷the Philistines were afraid; for they said, 'Their God has come into the camp to them!'ᵈ And they said, 'Woe to us! For nothing like this has happened before. ⁸Woe to us! Who can deliver us from the power of this mighty God? This is the God who smote the Egyptians with every sort of plague in the wilderness. ⁹Take courage, and acquit yourselves like men, O Philistines, lest you become slaves to the Hebrews as they have been to you; acquit yourselves like men and fight.'

ᵃThis sentence stands in LXX in place of v. 1a, which has been incorporated in the previous section.
ᵇHere the qal is used instead of the usual niphal. The LXX *eklinen* perhaps means 'was drawing to an end', so Klostermann, but this is improbable, as in that case something would have to have been said earlier about the course of the battle.
ᶜThis word is in the MT, but not in LXX, and is probably a scribal error.
ᵈSee BH.

45

10 So the Philistines fought, and Israel was defeated, and they fled, every man to his own home; and there was a very great slaughter, for there fell of Israel thirty thousand foot soldiers. [11]And the ark of God was captured; and the two sons of Eli, Hophni and Phinehas, were slain.

12 A man of Benjamin[a] ran from the battle line, and came to Shiloh the same day, with his clothes rent and with earth upon his head. [13]When he arrived, Eli was sitting upon his seat by the gate, watching towards the road,[b] for his heart trembled for the ark of God. And when the man came into the city and told the news, all the city cried out. [14]When Eli heard the sound of the outcry, he said, 'What is this uproar?' Then the man hastened and came and told Eli. [15]Now Eli was ninety-eight years old and his eyes were set, so that he could not see. [16]And the man said to Eli, 'I am he who has come from the battle; I fled from the battle today.' And he said, 'How did it go, my son?' [17]He who brought the tidings answered and said, 'Israel has fled before the Philistines, and there has also been a great slaughter among the people; your two sons also, Hophni and Phinehas, are dead, and the ark of God has been captured.' [18]When he mentioned the ark of God, Eli fell over backward from his seat by the side of the gate;[c] and his neck was broken and he died, for he was an old man, and heavy. He had judged Israel forty years.

19 Now his daughter-in-law, the wife of Phinehas, was with child, about to give birth.[d] And when she heard the tidings that the ark of God was captured, and that her father-in-law and her husband were dead, she bowed and gave birth; for her pains came upon her. [20]And about the time of her death the women attending her said to her, 'Fear not, for you have borne a son.' But she did not answer or give heed. [21]And she named the child Ichabod, saying, 'The glory has departed from Israel!' because the ark of God had been captured and because of her father-in-law and her husband. [22]And she said, 'The glory has departed from Israel, for the ark of God has been captured.'

The second main section of the Books of Samuel has no direct connection with the first. A concrete link is, in fact, only provided by the place Shiloh, with the ark and priesthood there. But not a word is said of the offence of the sons of Levi, nor is Samuel men-

[a]The MT can only be translated 'the men of Benjamin'. We must, along with LXX, add either an *m* before or a *y* after *binyāmīn*.

[b]So LXX, probably correctly. The textually easier reading 'by the road to Mizpah' does not fit in well with the helplessness of Eli described later, nor does it suit the situation; in that case the messenger would have to pass Eli. MT 'by the road looking', impossible as it stands, represents a combination of two readings; *derek* would at least require the article.

[c]*be'ad yad*, properly, 'through the side of the door'. *be'ad* is presumably a conflation of *be* and *'ad*, leaving the choice between *beyad* and *'ad-yad*.

[d]See BH.

tioned. Conversely, nothing in the first main section suggests the urgent political situation, and Eli appears only as priest, not as judge. Both sections do, however, mention Eli's extreme old age. From these features it has rightly been concluded that the second main section originally had an independent existence. It is a history of the ark. The subject is strictly maintained. The narrator is only concerned with political and military events so far as they involve the ark. The destruction of the temple at Shiloh is not mentioned once—it is almost as though without the ark it were an empty shell, of no further interest. 'Only from Jer. 7.12, 14; 26.6 (Ps. 78.60), from the change of abode of Eli's descendants (21.2ff.; 22.9ff.), and from the absence of the name Shiloh in passages like Amos 5.5 and I Kings 12.29, could we conclude that the sanctuary of Shiloh was at that time not only robbed of the ark, but also destroyed and non-existent' (Budde, p. 30). We see from this that the history of the ark represents not a Shiloh tradition but an ark tradition, part of the *hieros logos* for the sanctuary of the ark.[a] We may assume from the presence of an account of the fortunes of the house of Eli that the formation of the report belongs to the time when the house of Eli was still in the service of the ark, i.e. the time of David. This could explain the positive attitude to the sons of Eli, which differs from that in chs. 2 and 3. The compiler, who put the history of the ark between chs. 3 and 7, was able to use it, as it was, as a welcome expansion and continuation of the earlier material. At the same time, we are introduced here to a particular concern of the Books of Samuel: for the books as a whole the ark of Yahweh is of considerable importance. Alongside the figures whom Yahweh calls and makes the bearers of his will—Samuel, Saul, David—there stands the great sanctuary, which right from the early days in the wilderness accompanies the history of the people as a special sign of the divine revelation.

[1b] In addition, another important factor in the Books of Samuel as a whole comes to light here: the Philistines make an appearance. They have already been mentioned several times during the period of the judges (Shamgar and Samson, cf. also Judg. 10.7), and in the Samson stories they are regarded as the real lords of the land. Counteractions from the Israelite side, such as the deeds of Samson, are limited to individual occasions and do nothing to alter the general situation. Even this text has the same presuppositions (v. 9).

[a] Cf. Rost, *Die Überlieferung von der Thronnachfolge Davids*, pp. 4–47.

We gain the impression that we now for the first time have a serious hostile encounter between the two claimants to the rule of Palestine. The scene of the battle, Aphek, the present *ras el-ʿen*, lies immediately north of the Philistine territory in the narrower sense, which is bounded by the five towns of Gaza, Ashkelon, Ashdod, Ekron and Gath. It is impossible to determine the location of Ebenezer, the place mentioned as the Israelite camp, but it must have been situated within earshot of Aphek (v. 6). The name ('stone of help')[a] sounds like a bad joke in the light of subsequent events (but cf. on 7.12).

[2] The events of the war take place in two episodes, the first of which ends disastrously for Israel. Nevertheless, although they have sustained heavy losses, they are still not completely defeated. [3–11] The 'elders of Israel' promise themselves effective and victorious redress as soon as the morale of their troops has been strengthened. To this intent, the holy ark, around which Israel used to assemble in its twelve-tribe confederation, is brought from Shiloh. The ark is given its most ceremonious title, 'Yahweh, the God of hosts, who is enthroned on (between? above?) the cherubim', a description which suggests the exterior form of the ark. It is, as its name *ʾarōn* implies, primarily a chest, and thus a container; at the same time it serves as a throne for the Lord most High. The figures of cherubim attached to the ark belong in the context of this second idea. In this way Yahweh is immediately characterized as 'God of hosts'. Again, as it is he who disposes the heavenly hosts, he is the Lord of war (Josh. 5.13ff.). Hence here, in the context of a war, we have his full name mentioned. The priests, Eli's sons, accompany the ark, as they are accustomed to service at the shrine. This is a dangerous occupation, as is evident from several later incidents. Here, too, the people's cry of joy and the terror of the Philistines themselves point in the same direction. It is not surprising that the latter should have had tidings of the events in Egypt; the Old Testament several times relates that the God of Israel is taken quite seriously by other peoples (Josh. 2.9; 5.1; I Kings 20.23; II Kings 5.15, etc.).[b] The Philistine

---

[a]Literally, 'the stone, (namely) the help', but read 'the stone of help', as in 5.1, with BH.

[b]The text in v. 8 should not be emended. The replacement of *bammidbār* (in the wilderness) with *baddeber* (by the pestilence) is unfortunate, as the pestilence was not the only blow to fall on the Egyptians. On the other hand, Egypt was not, strictly speaking, smitten 'in the wilderness'. The Philistines, however, need not be expected to know the individual details; the keywords 'Egypt' and 'wilderness' themselves suggest the whole story. LXX skilfully inserts an 'and' before 'in the wilderness'.

reaction is not, however, anxiety or even flight, but a resolution to exert all their strength lest they, too, become 'slaves'. So the result of the battle is a victory for the Philistines. In addition to great losses on the battlefield we hear of complete rout; the host is scattered, and worst of all, the ark falls into the hands of the enemy and Hophni and Phinehas are killed. The way in which these events are narrated is completely dispassionate. We hear only the facts, but that is quite sufficient.

[12–18a] The scene shifts from the battlefield to Shiloh. An anonymous Benjaminite brings the ill tidings to Shiloh. The terrible shock of events leads him to cover the long distance (over eighteen miles as the crow flies) on the same day. He comes in mourning and is received with cries of grief. The narration of the section is particularly impressive. The aged Eli is the focus of interest. Now very old, and smitten with the blindness of old age, he sits in his seat at the entrance to the temple. The description of his 'watching' should not be regarded as inconsistent with the detail of his blindness (and hence as an indication of another source). The verb ṣāpā can be used to mean 'wait', 'expect'. The blind man, who can still hear well, is concentrating on the street leading to the temple and anxiously awaits the messenger. The temple apparently lay in that part of the place furthest from where the messenger arrives, for he meets the people of the town and gives them the news first. The report to Eli is once again quite factual. But one blow follows another, just as in the message brought to Job; here, as there, the most dreadful news occupies the fourth and last place. It is the news that the ark has been captured, and not that his sons have been killed, that is the direct cause of the old man's death.

[18b] The brief note about his forty years as judge is surprising, as we have heard nothing of it previously; elsewhere Eli appears merely as a priest. On the other hand, there is no evident reason why he, the priest of the most eminent sanctuary, should not also have held the office of judge. It is not an improbable assumption that Eli's name originally occurred in the list of 'Minor Judges', parts of which are still preserved in Judg. 10 and 12.[a] The years of his office as judge make up a round number and a usual one for the East. The LXX has the number 20 instead. The note about Eli's office as judge is meant in this context to show the extent of the damage done to the Israelite structure by the loss of the ark; it was a

[a]Cf. Hertzberg, 'Die Kleinen Richter' *TLZ* 79, 1954, cols. 285–90.

catastrophe like that of 587, for both the central sanctuary and its leading personnel perished at the same time.

[19–22] The episode of the birth of Ichabod gives us a picture of the grave seriousness of the situation from another side. As a narrative, it is no less compelling than the earlier one. The bad news so terrifies the pregnant wife of Phinehas that the birth takes place prematurely;[a] the word *hāpak*, used to describe the onset of the birth-pains, is the same as that used for the destruction of Sodom and Gomorrah and means 'to turn over and over'. The depth of her grief can be seen from the way in which she pays no attention to the news that she has given birth to a son—the most wonderful tidings a woman can have. Her sole concern in her last hours is the loss of the holy ark. Her last words express this clearly, and the naming of the boy is an allusion to it.[b] The formulation of the phrase that the 'glory' (*kābōd*) has vanished from Israel along with the ark is intentional; it is at the sanctuary of the ark that the 'glory' of Yahweh manifests itself. This saying of the dying woman is therefore quoted twice on purpose;[c] it is not only possible, but probable, that when the story was recited at the sanctuary, special emphasis was laid on this saying, which reaches to the heart of the matter; it may have been repeated by the community. Psalm 78, which alludes to these events towards the end, says in v. 61: 'He delivered his power into captivity, his glory into the hand of the foe.' The expression 'the ark is taken' occurs five times in the chapter (cf. 5.1) and is its essential content. With it we reach a point in Israelite history lower than any since the captivity in Egypt. The author resists the temptation to depict the horror of the situation in any deeper colours. Hearer and reader nevertheless hold their breath and ask how God can find a way out of such distress again.

Here we should notice two further things. This chapter should be read in conjunction with the preceding chapter. True, as was said, there is no mention here of the sins of the sons of Eli. But the compiler of the whole work surely felt nevertheless that Israel no

[a]The word 'bowed' describes the usual position which a woman takes up, even today, in the East, when giving birth; the same term occurs in Job 39.3.

[b]The first syllable *'i* is felt as a negation. Etymologically, however, this is quite uncertain. Gressmann (p. 16) suggested 'man' or 'father of renown'.

[c]To explain the repetition of the sentence at the end as the working together of two sources is to misunderstand the matter. Would both sources have been formulated in the same way, and would the redactor have added a second sentence saying exactly the same thing?

longer appeared worthy of the personal presence of the Lord (cf. Ps. 78.56ff., where this train of thought is carried through in detail). There is also, however, another thought. On entering camp the ark is greeted by both friend and foe as though it exerted some sort of magic influence. In contrast to this, the text teaches that 'the ark is not a supernatural means of guaranteeing victory' (Caspari, p. 60). Yahweh is not bound to the ark; he shapes history independently of the symbol of his constant presence. Israel must recognize that the Lord is present even when the place of his self-revelation has vanished. This is an extraordinarily far-reaching insight, the last consequences of which are drawn by Jesus in his conversation with the woman of Samaria (John 4.19–24).

2. THE ARK IN THE LAND OF THE HEATHEN: 5.1–12

5 [1]When the Philistines captured the ark of God, they carried it from Ebenezer to Ashdod; [2]then the Philistines took the ark of God and brought it into the house of Dagon and set it up beside Dagon. [3]And when the people of Ashdod rose early the next day and went into the temple of Dagon they saw that[a] Dagon had fallen face downward[b] on the ground before the ark of the LORD. So they took Dagon, and raised him up,[c] and put him back in his place. [4]But when they rose early on the next morning, behold, Dagon had (again) fallen face downward[b] on the ground before the ark of the LORD, and the head of Dagon and both his hands were lying cut off upon the threshold; only the trunk[d] of Dagon was left to him.[e] [5]This is why the priests of Dagon and all who enter the house of Dagon do not tread on the threshold of Dagon in Ashdod to this day.

6 The hand of the LORD was heavy upon the people of Ashdod, and he wrought havoc with them. He afflicted them with tumours,[f] both Ashdod and its territory, and mice appeared in the midst of their land and there was a fearful, deadly confusion in the city.[g] [7]And when the men of Ashdod saw how things were, they said,[h] 'The ark of God must not remain with us; for his hand is heavy upon us and upon

[a]This phrase is lacking in MT, but is preserved by LXX.
[b]MT means 'before his face', i.e. before the face of Yahweh, but the interpretation of LXX, Syr, Targ, which render the text as if it were *'al-pānāw*, is correct.
[c]So LXX.
[d]Lacking in MT, but preserved in the ancient translations.
[e]*'al* is here used as is *b*[e] sometimes.
[f]The text fluctuates between 'boils' (literally 'hills'; on Thenius' conjecture 'he smote them in the hinder parts' see Commentary) and 'sores on the anus'.
[g]So LXX, Vulg.
[h]Here, as often in Sam., there is a perfect with a copulative *waw* instead of the usual *waw* consecutive; perhaps this a peculiarity of dialect.

Dagon our God.' [8]So they sent and gathered together all the lords of the Philistines and said, 'What shall we do with the ark of the God of Israel?' And (those of) Gath answered, 'Let the ark of the God of Israel be brought around to Gath.'[a] So they brought the ark of the God of Israel to Gath.[b] [9]But after they had brought it around, the hand of the LORD was against the city, causing a very great panic, and he afflicted the men of the city, both young and old, so that tumours broke out upon them. [10]So they sent the ark of God to Ekron. But when the ark of God came to Ekron, the people of Ekron cried out, 'They have brought around to us the ark of the God of Israel to slay us and our people.' [11]They sent therefore and gathered together all the lords of the Philistines, and said, 'Send away the ark of the God of Israel, and let it return to its own place, that it may not slay us and our people.' For there was a deathly panic throughout the whole city. The hand of God was very heavy there; [12]the men who did not die were stricken with tumours, and the cry of the city went up to heaven.

Despite the observations made at the end of the last section, it does not now transpire that the Lord abandons the ark. He has surrendered it to the enemy and by so doing has shown that the disappearance of the ark is as little to be equated with his own disappearance as the end of the temple in 587 is to be regarded as the end of the Old Testament religion of revelation. But the ark has not become simply a piece of wood, it remains the possession of Yahweh; he is not confined to the ark, but it remains his property. Thus his relationship to the ark remains the same as his relationship to the land and the people of Israel.

The Philistines now come to experience the truth of this last sentence. Throughout the story they appear not so much as political opponents, but as heathen. The Philistines, the ancient enemy of Israel, are, in fact, the former *par excellence*. Setting out to conquer Canaan at approximately the same time as the Israelites, they attempted to take possession of the land from the coastal side, while Israel used the approach from the desert. In the long run, Israel proved themselves the stronger, but it is no mere chance that the Philistines gave the name 'Palestine' to the land, a name which it bore until 1948. The first kings of Israel had to defend themselves against the Philistines in a life and death struggle; indeed, it was only as a result of these battles that the Israelite state was formed. Here,

[a]'Gath' has been omitted in one place because of a neighbouring 'Gath' or 'Gittites'; cf. LXX *pros hemas*.
[b]Expanded by LXX, but the text makes sense without.

then, we have a real historic conflict. Nevertheless, Israel always regarded her differences with the Philistines, the 'uncircumcised', as being in the realm of sacral theology rather than of politics. Although none of her neighbours held Israel subject so severely and for so long a period as the Philistines, Israel for her part did not pursue the battle with that embittered hate which was to become a characteristic attitude of the Jews of later times towards their opponents (Babylon, Edom, Moab, the foreign powers in the Books of Esther and Daniel), and *vice versa*. The heathen on the coastal plain were regarded with that superiority with which the believers in the one God could look upon polytheists. We can look at the matter in another way. It is striking, particularly in the Samson stories, how despite the gravity of the situation the stories are told not without a touch of humour (see my commentary *ad loc.*). There is a similar instance in this chapter. The audience would have been overcome with laughter on hearing how the God of Ashdod fell down on his nose before the ark of Yahweh or on listening to the consummate way in which the God of the stolen ark dealt with those who had taken it. The Lord in no way allows the 'uncircumcised' to dictate the way in which events are to proceed. He is manifestly supreme.

[1] The Philistines bring the captured ark, the most important piece of their plunder, to the city of Ashdod, which lies in the centre of their territory. We do not hear at this point whether they pursue their victory any further. The original narrator of the history of the ark and the final compiler are governed not by political and military, but by theological interests. We are thus given the impression, quite erroneous from a purely historical point of view, that the capture of the ark was the real objective of the war; what was, in fact, at stake was shown clearly enough in 4.9. On the other hand, it is the basic theme of the 'historical books' of the Old Testament to show that Yahweh is the Lord of history, of the history of his people and of the world. To that extent the historical point is still preserved.

[2–4] The Philistines put the ark in their temple, where, in their view, it belongs as a cult emblem. Their overriding purpose, however, is to let the victory over Israel manifest itself on a higher level—god against god. The Philistine god is called Dagon, cf. the Hebrew *dāgān*, corn; the connection with *dāg*, fish, sometimes put forward earlier, should be abandoned. It is remarkable how the God, or at least his name, thus has associations with the language of Palestine; it shows that the Philistines, unlike Israel, did what was usual in religious matters and adapted themselves to the circumstances of the country. The statue of Dagon is found the next morning lying on its face, in the attitude of a slave before his master, a vassal before his king, or a worshipper before his god. The next day, moreover, both his head and his hands are cut off and he is left completely powerless. The Philistine plan thus fails completely and the superiority of the God of Israel is brilliantly demonstrated. [5] This is the occasion for indicating a custom for which ch. 5 provides the aetiological text; no one treads on the threshold, because it has been as it were infected by the amputated members of the god. Such was the explanation given in Israel, again quite humorously, for this custom. Religious ideas concerning the thresholds both of temples and of houses occur throughout the history of religion in a number of contexts.[a] In the Old Testament, cf. in addition to this passage I Kings 16.34, Zeph. 1.9; all three passages show the negative attitude of the Old Testament to this thought-world.

[6] But this god is not the only one to discover the supremacy of the Lord of the ark. His people learn it, too. Wherever the ark comes, devastating, fatal consequences ensue. The ark of Yahweh may not be taken round the land of the heathen with impunity. It is not wholly clear in what way the hand of the Lord lies heavy upon the Philistines. There is a fluctuation even in MT in the details of the sickness with which the Lord smites his enemies, between boils (literally 'hills') and sores on the anus, the second word probably being intended as an interpretation of the first. The translation 'tumours' is perhaps the most convenient rendering of an awkward Hebrew text. We are evidently to imagine something like a plague of boils, an epidemic which brings added shame to the Philistines because of the part of the body which is affected. We cannot leave on one side the reference, or rather the allusion, to which Thenius draws attention (when commenting on the Vulgate): 'he smote them in the hinder parts;' such a tone suits the tenor of this passage, and is moreover suggested by Ps. 78.66, 'he smote his enemies backward'.[b] The present form of the text, however, gives the impression that the other interpretation has been preferred (on grounds of decency). Moreover, LXX and Vulgate are certainly right here in preserving a verse which additionally records a plague of mice; this makes it easier to understand why the expiatory gifts described in ch. 6 should

[a]Material in Gressmann, pp. 19f.
[b]This is the rendering of RV; RSV does not illustrate the point. Tr.

have included golden mice. **[7–12]** Under these circumstances it is twice as easy to see why the people of Ashdod should have wished once again to be rid of the dangerous ark, because of which their persons and their fields had suffered so much damage. In this passage we have renewed indications of the purpose of the section; it is to demonstrate the superiority of Yahweh to Dagon and his people. The description of the summoning of the council of the five lords of the Philistines is meant to show the important position the matter occupies in state politics. If the LXX and Vulgate are also right here, Gath[a] spontaneously offers to take care of the ark. It would appear from this that the Philistines are still sitting on their high horse. But this soon comes to an end, and the ark is as quickly as possible passed on to Ekron, the city state which lies nearest of the five to Israel. Here, however, a loud and vehement protest is made as soon as the ark enters the city, so that the magnificently narrated chapter[b] can end 'and the cry of that city went up to heaven'. Thus the God whom the Philistines think they have defeated is not defeated. He is the real victor, who can give his people into the hand of the enemy and yet remain the Lord throughout.

3. THE ARK RETURNS: 6.1–7.1

6 [1]The ark of the LORD was in the country of the Philistines seven months.[c] And the Philistines called for the priests and the diviners and said, 'What shall we do with the ark of the LORD? Tell us with what we shall send it to its place.' [3]They said, 'If you send away the ark of the God of Israel, do not send it empty, but by all means return him a guilt offering. Then you will be healed, and it will be known to you why his hand does not turn away from you.' [4]And they said, 'What is the guilt offering that we shall return to him?' They answered, 'Five golden tumours[d] and five golden mice, according to the number of the lords of the Philistines; for the same plague was upon all of you[e] and upon your lords. [5]So you must make images of your tumours and images of your mice that ravage the land, and give glory to the God of Israel; perhaps he will lighten his hand from off you and your gods and your land. [6]Why should you harden your hearts as the Egyptians and Pharaoh hardened their hearts? After he had made sport of them,

---

[a]Gath, the location of which is disputed, has recently been identified with *a'raq el-menšiye*, about 15 miles WSW of Ashkelon.

[b]To divide this chapter into sources is wrong in every respect; cf. the objections made as early as Budde, p. 38.

[c]LXX inserts here 'and their land teemed with mice'.

[d]See on 5.6.

[e]See BH.

did not they let the people go, and they departed? [7]Now then, prepare a new cart and take[a] two milch cows upon which there has never come a yoke, and yoke the cows to the cart, but take their calves home, away from them. [8]And take the ark of the LORD and place it on the cart, and put in a box at its side the figures of gold, which you are returning to him as a guilt offering. Then send it off, and let it go its way. [9]And watch; if it goes up on the way to its own land, to Bethshemesh, then it is he who has done us this great harm; but if not, then we shall know that it is not his hand that struck us, it happened to us by chance.'

10 The men did so, and took two milch cows and yoked them to the cart, and shut up their calves at home. [11]And they put the ark of the LORD on the cart, and the box with the golden mice and the images of their tumours. [12]And the cows went straight[b] in the direction of Bethshemesh along one highway, lowing as they went; they turned neither to the right nor to the left, and the lords of the Philistines went after them as far as the border of Bethshemesh. [13]Now the people of Bethshemesh were reaping their wheat harvest in the valley; and when they lifted up their eyes and saw the ark, they ran to meet it, full of joy.[c] [14]The cart came into the field of Joshua of Bethshemesh, and stopped there. A great stone was there; and they split up the wood of the cart and offered the cows as a burnt-offering to the LORD. [15]And the Levites took down the ark of the LORD and the box that was beside it, in which were the golden figures, and set them upon the great stone; and the men of Bethshemesh offered burnt-offerings and sacrificed sacrifices on that day to the LORD.[d] And when the five lords of the Philistines saw it, they returned that day to Ekron.

17 These are the golden tumours, which the Philistines returned as a guilt offering for the LORD: one for Ashdod, one for Gaza, one for Ashkelon, one for Gath, one for Ekron; [18]also the golden mice, according to the number of all the cities of the Philistines belonging to the five lords, both fortified cities and unwalled villages. The great stone,[e] beside which they set down the ark of the LORD, is a witness to this day in the field of Joshua of Bethshemesh.

19 But the sons of Jeconiah did not share in the joy of the men of Bethshemesh when they looked upon the ark of the LORD,[f] so he slew

---

[a]The text has 'take and prepare'.

[b]The anomalous (despite GK § 47k) *wayyišarnā* is a conflation of *weyiššerū* and *watteyaššarnā* (see Budde *ad loc.*).

[c]See BH.

[d]The verse is an expansion, occasioned by later reflection on the original events. See Commentary.

[e]Instead of *weʿad ʾābēl* ('and as far as Abel'?), *weʿēd hā-ʾeben* should be read (with some MSS and versions). *ʿōd* ('still') would also be possible.

[f]*welō ḥādū benē yekonyā* should be supplied at the beginning of the verse, after LXX. The MT 'and he slew some of the men . . .' only hints at this; in fact, the present text gives the impression that the looking upon the ark was the reason for their death, cf. Num. 4.15, 20. Following this latter trend, Bewer—developing

THE ARK RETURNS: 6.1–7.1

of the people seventy men—fifty thousand men. And the people mourned because the LORD had made a great slaughter among the people. ²⁰Then the men of Bethshemesh said, 'Who is able to stand before the LORD, this holy God? And to whom shall he go up away from us?' So they sent messengers to the inhabitants of Kiriath-jearim, saying, 'The Philistines have returned the ark of the LORD. Come down and take it up to you.' **7** ¹And the men of Kiriath-jearim came and took up the ark of the LORD, and brought it to the house of Abinadab on the hill; and they consecrated his son, Eleazar, to have charge of the ark of the LORD.

[1] The note that the 'panic' caused by the ark lasted for seven months is meant to shed a special light on the events described in ch. 5. The writer's view is that the vigorous protest of the people of Ekron was calculated to put an end to a situation which was becoming unbearable. The long period of trouble and unrest has created for the Philistines a situation from which they want release at any price. Yet even here there is the danger of making another false step and incurring further punishment. [2] The advice of the theologians is therefore sought. 'Diviners' are mentioned as well as priests; the LXX names yet a third group. The *qōsemîm* are people versed in the extra-sensory realm. The term derives from the heathen world. The question put to these specialists, 'What shall we do with the ark?' is that considered by the lords in 5.8; here, however, it serves more to introduce the question, 'How is the ark to be taken back?' It is striking that once again, as in 5.11, the possibility of restoring the ark 'to its place' (*māqōm*) is mentioned as something quite obvious. Was it not known that this place no longer existed? And why is this possibility of taking the ark to 'its' place given no consideration at all later? As we may not assume that the proposal is tacitly rejected in the theologians' reply—were that the case it would have had to be stressed—we must understand the expression to have quite general significance, 'go back where it belongs'. This is an important consideration; for the restitution of the ark is, in fact, the recognition of an incapacity, indeed of a defeat, and it is therefore already essential that the Philistines withdraw themselves from the affair in a way which, while not being too damaging to their

---

a suggestion originally made by S. J. Feigin—attempts to repair the faulty text as follows: 'But Yahweh took no delight in the men of Bethshemesh because they had looked into the ark, and he slew seventy men of them (LXX)' (*JBL* 57, 1938, pp. 89–91).

political prestige, at the same time obviates the danger of their being similarly afflicted again. We will return to this point at the end.

[3–5] The answer given by the specialists recommends the payment of a 'guilt offering' ('āšām); this will bring about 'healing'. Here the answer displays a recognition of the cause of the present lack of wholeness: it is because, as we must add by way of expansion, the Lord has hitherto not been given his due honour.[a] The sin offering is now described in two aspects, golden tumours and golden mice. According to the present text, both of these are involved throughout, so that the LXX is right in placing the plague of mice alongside the sickness affecting the people as early as ch. 5 (cf. 5.6 and on 6.1); otherwise the means of propitiation is incomprehensible. The procedure follows the well-known 'homeopathic maxim': *similia similibus*, and is also resorted to elsewhere in the Old Testament in the story of the fiery serpents (Num. 21). Recently (since F. Hitzig), the almost universal explanation has been that the mouse was regarded as a bearer of pestilence (material in Gressmann, p. 17); the failure of the MT to mention the mice in ch. 5 could be an argument for this. On the other hand, quite apart from the LXX, vv. 17–18a of the MT surely regard the plague of mice as additional to the sickness, and the phrase in v. 5 'that ravage the land' can only refer to a real plague of mice. The word 'figures', used later, which covers both categories, also points in the same direction. The most important point of all, however, is that the former explanation of the sickness would point more to a natural cause than to the Lord, and thus would run contrary to the purpose of the whole text. The theological sense of the present text requires that two plagues be mentioned, each of which represents a direct punishment from the Lord, the one affecting the people and the other the land. This does not exclude the possibility that at an earlier stage in the history of the text there could have been a circumstantial connection between the mice and the pestilence, but it is inadmissible to alter the present form of the text to produce this sense. The number of figures set out for the guilt offering represents a further obscurity. It is quite understandable that they should be limited to five, the number of the lords of the Philistines, and this is expressly confirmed by

[a]The emendation suggested by LXX and Targ., changing *wᵉnōdaᶜ* to *wᵉyitkappēr*, would be easier. The end of the verse would then run, 'Then you will be healed and your sins will be expiated; why should his hand (then) not turn from you?'

the additional note of v. 17. In the case of the mice, however, the tradition fluctuates between five, as in the former instance, and the information in v. 18, namely that a golden mouse was offered for each of the places afflicted. In itself, this is a consistent idea, but precisely by virtue of this consistency it betrays itself as a theoretical development, quite apart from its being a barely conceivable exaggeration.

[6] The renewed introduction of Egypt as a precedent is as little surprising here as it is in 4.8. The comparison is both pertinent and impressive. Men must honour this God, instead of 'hardening' their hearts; perhaps it is no coincidence that a word is used here which comes from the same root as *kābōd*, honour, glory.

This recognition of the need to give to the mighty God the glory which is his due is a counsel of wisdom and is in any case to be implemented. [7–9] At the same time, however, it is possible to ascertain whether the situation is really what appearances suggest. It is therefore thought advisable to make a test similar to those which occur sometimes elsewhere in the Old Testament (Moses, Gideon). The test is well devised. If milch cows, who have never before been yoked and thus are still young beasts, are hitched to a cart, it is most improbable that everything will go off smoothly. If in addition their calves are left behind, they will normally follow the urge to give suck and return to the stall, all the more so if they are left to their own devices. If despite these difficulties the cows and the cart which bears the ark and the sin offerings take the road to the nearest Israelite dwelling-place, this may be regarded as proof that God himself is here at work. Should it, however, be impossible for the difficulties to be overcome, there are no theological undertones to the situation. Such is the reasoning of the Philistine men of religion.

[10–15] All is carried out according to plan. But things do not turn out as expected. As though under compulsion—the lowing is here to be understood as an expression of the reluctance of the animals[a]—the cows go straight down the road to Bethshemesh and there stop in the field of a man called Joshua, who is not mentioned elsewhere. The great stone which lies there seems to be their goal. Here is the first place on Israelite soil suitable for a sacrifice and here the inhabitants of Bethshemesh, delighted at the reappearance of the ark, offer the 'burnt-offering', using what the Lord himself

[a]The Hebrew infinitive absolute *gāʿō* vividly suggests the beasts' lowing.

has provided for them, the wood of the cart and the yoke animals. The golden figures of the Philistines were the tribute due from the heathen to a superior Lord; the burnt-offering is the homage of the Lord's own people. Therefore posterity is enjoined to continue to carry out this sacrifice in a way which corresponds with the will of the Lord laid down in the law. This is the explanation of the supplementary v. 15. Not laymen, but qualified Levites, offer the sacrifice; not any stone, but only the altar provided can be used for the purpose. This verse is meant to be understood as implying that the sacrifice took place elsewhere, on the legitimate altar; in reality, it is said, the great stone was only the resting-place of the ark and the offerings. From Deuteronomy onwards it was felt that this was the only way things might have happened; before v. 15 we must imagine a clause, 'The details were as follows . . .' It is useless to ask 'Where did the Levites come from?' or 'Could the lords of the Philistines have waited long enough for the complicated burnt-offering and sacrifice—in which those who sacrificed took part in a meal—to be completed?' 'Where did the beasts for the sacrifice come from, once the whole burnt-offering had been made?' No, v. 15 is simply intended to give a *correct* description of events, that is all. The 'historical' element, for which the modern reader searches, is completely secondary.

[16–18] We are expressly told that the Philistines waited. Their actions confirm that the decision sought from the priests and the diviners was correct. Now, for them—and for the later hearers of the story—it has finally been demonstrated that the Lord has been at work. In Philistine eyes also, the sacrifice offered in his honour is the seal of this. But the great stone is the manifest proof for all time. Here we have once again one of those aetiological motifs in which the Old Testament is so rich. Not only are people shown this stone 'to this day', to wonder and to have brought before them the various features of the narrative, but we may assume that there was a sacrificial feast of which this story formed the sacred legend. Not only v. 15 but also vv. 17–18a are an indication of how the individual details and the customs described have been transformed in a living process of growth and thus show us how later generations meditated on events which were so important to them.

[19] The continuation of the account also points in the same direction. The LXX has certainly once again preserved the original text for us here. We are told that those who did not share in the joy

over the return of the ark incur the punishment which overtakes
people who do not show due respect to the high God, be they
Philistines or Israelites. The number seventy preserved in the text
is the number of those that perish. From the MT at the beginning
of v. 19 it seems that merely looking at the ark[a]—as in Num. 4.15–20
—was the cause of the divine retribution. Even here, then, we again
find the tendency to describe the events in accordance with the word
and purpose of God as found elsewhere. Whether the number
50,000, which has been written alongside the number 70, is similarly
meant to underline the great seriousness of the situation, must remain
uncertain. The ancient versions have exercised a great deal of thought
on the question without reaching a satisfactory result. In any case,
this 'great slaughter' strikes as great terror into the people of Bethshemesh as had earlier fallen upon the Philistines. [20] Under such
circumstances no one can 'stand' before God; the word here has a
double meaning, to 'serve before' or to 'exist'. The most important
word here is 'holy'. That is the point of the whole narrative; the
Holy One expects man to keep himself holy. It is fatal to meddle
with him, and any mistake can bring down death and destruction.
Here one of the strongest theological concepts of the Old Testament
is expressed, that of the holiness of God which sets him completely
apart from man. 'God is in heaven and you upon earth', as the late
Book of Ecclesiastes still recognizes (5.2).

[6.21; 7.1] So the ark journeys farther, to the town of Kiriath-
jearim, and there on the 'hill', i.e. in the most ancient holy place of
the town, it finds a temporary resting-place until years later new
provisions are made for it by David. Here we find ourselves faced with
a riddle. Why is the ark not brought to one of the well-known sanctuaries? Shiloh, though this is not mentioned, may have been
destroyed, but there were other holy places, for example Mizpah,
not far from Kiriath-jearim, where the traditions of the holy tent
from the wilderness were kept.[b] Above all, where were the members
of the house of Eli? The end of ch. 4 showed the closeness of their
connection with the ark; where were they now? Nor is Samuel
mentioned here, though in ch. 7 he is said to have been active at a
number of different sanctuaries. Was it not possible for the ark to go
to one of these? Was the reason for the apparent 'cold-storage' of
the ark the fact that it had been 'taken'? This cannot possibly have

[a]Or looking *into* the ark? See textual note on v. 19.
[b]On this cf. Hertzberg, *ZAW* 47, 1929, pp. 161ff.

been the case, for ch. 5 glorifies it in such a way that no dishonour falls either upon the ark or upon its God. There remains only the thought that the Philistines, the lords of the land, must have attached importance to the ark staying in Israelite territory because of its dangerousness, but did not want it too far away from the centre of their realm. They could keep a close watch upon both Bethshemesh and Kiriath-jearim. It might perhaps be noted that David's decisive defeat of the Philistines took place to the east of these places, in the plain of Rephaim; the land lying to the west, including Kiriath-jearim, was therefore in the narrowest sense 'Philistine-occupied' territory. None of this is mentioned here, because, as has been said, no secular historical account is intended.

The narrative is not concerned further with the ark until the point at which David intervenes and is able once again to establish the ark in a place worthy of it. From an historical point of view this is surely quite correct. Until that point it remains in the house of Abinadab; his son Eleazar is 'consecrated'—how, by whom, or with what authority we are not told—to 'have charge' of the ark, i.e. to do the necessary holy service with it and before it.

NOTE ON FORMATION AND STRUCTURE: II

Little need be added to what has been said here (and is said later at II. 6). The purpose of the chapters stands out quite clearly: they describe the fortunes of the holy ark. The political events are only an object of interest in so far as they concern the ark. The clearest indication of this is the way in which we hear of the fate of Eli and of his daughter-in-law, but not of the fall of Shiloh. This is therefore a history not of the sanctuary at Shiloh and of the house of Eli, but of the ark, that migrating sanctuary, which was at one time kept there. The three, or rather four, chapters represent its *hieros logos*. It was suggested that the composition of the history of the ark belongs to a time before the family of the sons of Eli were expelled from court and from their office by Solomon (I Kings 2.26f.). As the account of Eli and his family has no overtones and in particular does not seek to defend a family which was regarded with suspicion at court after the death of David, it seems more probable that the account was written in the time of David than in the early days of Solomon's reign.

Generally speaking, the account is a unity in form and content.

This has been worked out in detail, particularly by L. Rost.[a] In his view, the chief expansion, apart from smaller additions such as have been assumed in the present commentary, is to be seen in 6.5–9. Something of this kind is, of course, inherently probable. The very character of a *hieros logos* invites sermon-like additions to the sacred narrative. Such additions hardly alter the events described, but can clarify the content, underline the chief concern and strengthen the kerygmatic element. Such reflection on the meaning of past events is familiar from many passages of the Old Testament. On the other hand, the grounds advanced by Rost on pp. 13f. do not seem conclusive enough to compel the literary verdict that in the original text v. 10 followed immediately upon v. 4. The purpose of the narrative, chiefly the display of the power of Yahweh, is without doubt expressed more clearly if vv. 10–12, 14 are prepared for, as they are in vv. 5–9. Here, as generally in the three chapters, the strictness of the way in which the subject is maintained, without digressions to one side or the other, is amazing. If we go on to consider the connection between I. 4–6 and II. 6—which Rost has, in fact, convincingly demonstrated—and the reasons why the final compiler has attached II. 7 to II. 6 and later makes the whole book finish at II. 24 (cf. the remarks on the passages in question), we shall see the fundamental importance of the contents of these chapters for the Books of Samuel as a whole. The events described here are far more than an episode. Here the intervention of the hand of God in the history of Israel, and the background to this history, become extremely clear. In the description of how the God who is honoured in the 'ark of the Lord' shows himself to be supreme and takes up his dwelling in Jerusalem after his apparent wanderings, the message of the Books of Samuel as a whole begins to emerge: after long journeyings, God sets up his throne in the city of David, there to be honoured and to continue his work of shaping the further destinies of his people and of the world.

[a]*Die Überlieferung von der Thronnachfolge Davids*, pp. 4–47.

III

SAMUEL AND SAUL
I. 7-15

1. SAMUEL THE JUDGE: 7.2-17

7 ²From the day that the ark was lodged at Kiriath-jearim, a long time passed, some twenty years, and all the house of Israel lamented after the LORD.ᵃ

3 Then Samuel said to all the house of Israel, 'If you are returning to the LORD with all your heart, then put away the foreign gods and the Ashtaroth from among you, and direct your heart to the LORD, and serve him only, and he will deliver you out of the hand of the Philistines.' ⁴So Israel put away the Baals and the Ashtaroth, and they served the LORD only.

5 Then Samuel said, 'Gather all Israel at Mizpah, and I will pray to the LORD for you.' ⁶So they gathered at Mizpah, and drew water and poured it out before the LORD, and fasted on that day, and said there, 'We have sinned against the LORD.' And Samuel judged the people of Israel at Mizpah. ⁷Now when the Philistines heard that the people of Israel had gathered at Mizpah, the lords of the Philistines went up against Israel. And when the people of Israel heard of it they were afraid of the Philistines. ⁸And the people of Israel said to Samuel, 'Do not cease to cry to the LORD our God for us, that he may save us from the hand of the Philistines.' ⁹So Samuel took a sucking lamb and offered it as a whole burnt-offering to the LORD; and Samuel cried to the LORD for Israel, and the LORD answered him. ¹⁰As Samuel was offering up the burnt-offering, the Philistines drew near to attack Israel; but the LORD thundered with a mighty voice that day against the Philistines and threw them into confusion; and they were routed

---

ᵃSo the literal text. It is, however, not inconceivable that instead of the doubtful (see the versions) *wayyinnāhū* there stood the word *wayyizne*, the consonants of which are very similar. When this word was no longer recognizable, a *mē* fell out before *'aḥᵃrē*, so that the original text would have run, 'And all Israel departed from Yahweh to serve idols.' The beginning of Samuel's speech in v. 3 does, however, presuppose some positive act on the part of the house of Israel; cf. Commentary.

before Israel. ¹¹And the men of Israel went out of Mizpah and pursued the Philistines, and smote them, as far as below Beth-car.

12 Then Samuel took a stone and set it up between Mizpah and Jeshanah,ᵃ and called its name Ebenezer; for he said, 'Hitherto the LORD has helped us.' ¹³So the Philistines were subdued and did not again enter the territory of Israel. And the hand of the LORD was against the Philistines all the days of Samuel. ¹⁴The cities which the Philistines had taken from Israel were restored to Israel, from Ekron to Gath; and Israel rescued their territory from the hand of the Philistines. There was peace also between Israel and the Amorites.

15 Samuel judged Israel all the days of his life. ¹⁶And he went on a circuit year by year to Bethel, Gilgal, and Mizpah; and he judged Israel in all these places. ¹⁷Then he would come back to Ramah, for his home was there, and there also he administered justice to Israel. And he built there an altar to the LORD.

With ch. 7 we begin a new complex of the Books of Samuel, which, while not having the relative compactness of such sections as I. 1–3 and 4–6, nevertheless shows a certain unity of subject. It describes the rise of the first king and his achievements, and particularly the struggle against the Philistines. It is again significant, though at the same time not unexpected, that these are no 'historical' reports; the 'historical situation' may only be read out of the texts with some difficulty. From the very beginning, the monarchy is given a distinctly theological evaluation. This is principally evident from the way in which Samuel, the man of God, appears as the figure who stands behind, alongside, even above the king. In the view of the text it was he who played the decisive part in the formation of the monarchy. In this way the guiding hand of Yahweh himself, whose instrument Samuel is, is shown with great clarity to be the determining power. Like the birth of the nation, the conquest, the destruction and the rebuilding of Israel, the formation of the state is shown in a special sense to be the work of God.

On this the accounts are agreed. In other respects, however, both in their attitudes and in individual details, they diverge. The greatest difference is between the deuteronomistic final compiler and that part of the accounts which sketches a completely positive picture of the development of the monarchy and of Israel's first king. It is fascinating to see how not only political, but also theological, attitudes of different times and different places are reflected in the arrangement and presentation of events. This will be noted

ᵃSee BH.

S.—C

in detail. It is, however, impossible to regard those passages which criticize Saul and his office as unhistorical and the others as historical; we can neither disregard the one in an attempt to construe the course of events nor use the other uncritically for the same purpose.

Ch. 7 should be regarded as a factual, and above all as a theological introduction to the whole section. Its concern with Samuel and way of dealing with him is meant to demonstrate that God is here at work through the man he has chosen. Thus Samuel appears as judge; indeed, as we learn from the general outline of the Books of Samuel, as the last judge,[a] in whom all the characteristics of the leading personalities of the period of the judges appear once again to a heightened degree. This does not, however, mean that his judge's robe makes him a schematized, colourless figure. His personality is clearly distinguishable even in this first chapter, which at first sight might seem farthest removed from the 'historical' situation.[b]

[2] The chapter begins with a note intended to link its narrative with the previous section. The number 20 thus represents one of those details which go to make up the deuteronomistic outline of chronology.[c] The 20 years are apparently meant to represent half of Samuel's period of office (the first), the second half of which is filled with the activity retailed at the end of the chapter. It looks as though the figure is a note added later. Unfortunately the sense of the second half of the verse is obscure. The unemended text evidently envisages mourning rites as mentioned in Judg. 20.23, 26; 21.2; Jer. 3.21, and connects them with the adverse political (and cultic) situation resulting from the defeat at Aphek.[d] [3–4] Samuel's attitude resembles that of Joel 2.13, 'Rend your hearts and not your garments', and thus represents the prophetic voice in time of necessity. This conversion will be made more evident by a renunciation of strange gods, among whom special mention is made of the Ashtaroth, female figures whose widespread occurrence has time and again been confirmed by excavations, and later of the Baals, the deities of the land. This is an attitude in accord not only with Deuteronomy (12.29ff.) but also with the prophetic movement. The

[a]Samuel's office as judge has recently been investigated by Wildberger, 'Samuel und die Entstehung des israelitischen Königtums', *TZ* 13, 1957, pp. 442–69.
[b]Cf. the remarks made by Noth in *Überlieferungsgeschichtliche Studien* I, p. 55 and *The History of Israel*, ET², 1960, p. 172, n. 2.
[c]Cf. ATD 9, pp. 141f. Also Noth, *Überlieferungsgeschichtliche Studien* I, pp. 18 ff.
[d]But see the textual note.

end of ch. 3 and 15.22f. should be remembered as an indication of
this prophetic side to Samuel.

[5–6] When Israel has duly repented, Samuel summons the people
to the sanctuary of Mizpah, which lay in the Benjaminite part of the
central hill country of Palestine and was of considerable importance
right down to a late period (Jer. 40; I Macc. 3).[a] The custom
mentioned here of drawing water and pouring it out before the
Lord is not known elsewhere, but it certainly has some connection
with fasting and the confession of sins—both are mentioned. There
is a similar connection between water and sin in the 'baptism of
repentance for the forgiveness of sins' in Mark 1.4, even if the
situation there is different (Schulz, p. 116). On the other hand, Lam.
2.19 says that the Israelites are to 'pour out your heart like water'.
In any case, the action is to make evident the change of heart
previously demanded of the people by Samuel. As the action takes
place at the sanctuary where Samuel at the same time acts as inter-
cessor, he also appears to hold the priestly office, as is said in Jer.
15.1 (remarkably enough alongside Moses, cf. Ex. 17.10ff.). He is
also described here and three times later in the chapter as judge.
We therefore gain the impression that Samuel holds the title 'judge'
not because of his act of deliverance, nor because of the Deuteronomic 'conception' that 'all persons living between the conquest and
the time of the kings who were of significance for all Israel were called
"judges" '. His functions as judge are expressions of a permanent
office such as we find in the case of the 'minor' judges (Judg. 10.1ff.;
12.6ff.). We cannot pass any judgment on the phrase 'judged
Israel' in v. 6 without taking into consideration the later details in
v. 16.[b] Samuel appears as judge because the 'old tradition' 'will have
known of Samuel's work in a judicial capacity'.[c]

[7–11] What is done by Samuel and Israel is not to be regarded
as a preparation for hostile action against the Philistines, though the
sanctuaries were frequently enough used as starting-points for such
undertakings. So while the Philistine reaction now described may
be regarded as unjustified, it is at the same time understandable.
The 'lords' of the Philistines are so called in chs. 5 and 6, but they

[a]Cf. ATD 9[2], pp. 249f. *en-nebi samwil*, the site generally accepted earlier for
Mizpah, preserves its connection with the figure of Samuel in 'Samuel's grave'.

[b]Against Noth, *Überlieferungsgeschichtliche Studien* I, p. 55, esp. n. 3; Buber (*VT*
6, 1956, p. 119) says that Samuel is not intended to appear here as one of the
great judges, in the sense of a 'heroic saviour'.

[c]Noth nevertheless allows this as a possibility, *loc. cit.*

are not, of course, imagined as 'going up' without a host as they do in 6.12, 16. They therefore consider the Israelite assembly to be directed immediately against themselves. Hence we may infer the correct historical situation, that the overlordship of the Philistines was complete, at least in the territories lying on the borders of Philistia proper. The only weapon available to an unarmed (cf. 13.19ff.) Israel against the oncoming enemy is prayer. Samuel, as we are expressly told, becomes the 'saviour' through his prayer; the same word is used here as for the saving action of the 'great' judges, *yāša'*.[a] His offering at the same time of a clearly defined, evidently extraordinary, sacrifice[b] likewise stresses that his proper concern is that of the priest; he makes intercession—the expression 'cry' chosen to describe the prayer is meant to indicate the urgency of the intercession—and offers sacrifice. In like manner, the help accorded by the Lord is described as an 'answer', which is manifested as an intervention from heaven, as in the case of the walls of Jericho (Josh. 6), the miracle of the sun in the valley of Aijalon (Josh. 10.13) or the stars at the brook Kishon, which fought against Sisera (Judg. 5.20). So, too, here the decisive action comes from the Lord. It is he who deals with the enemy; the human share in the action is prayer and faith. Pursuit alone is left to Israel, to go after those whom Yahweh has smitten. We are meant to learn from all this that this humbling of the Philistines takes place on another plane from that on which victories are usually won. Samuel's battle with the Philistines is not of a military, but of a theological nature. For this reason it does not have historical, but programmatic significance. Israel's real victories are won in the manner described here; they are not the victories of Israel, but of Yahweh. This is the prophetic way of regarding history, as can be seen, for example, from Hosea or Isaiah. Here, then, is the prelude to the history of the kings which now begins. This is the special way in which things will have been regarded and handed down at the sanctuary of Mizpah,[c] and the deuteronomistic compilers have made this viewpoint completely their own. In this sense the chapter has all the marks of *kerygma*.

[12] This may be underlined by yet another special feature, the

---

[a]Judg. 2.16, 18; 3.9, 15, 31; 6.14f.; 10.13f.; 13.5; I Sam. 9.16, cf. Judg. 9.17; 10.15; I Sam. 12.10f. (*nāṣal*).

[b]The synonyms *'ōlā* (whole offering) and *kālīl* (also a complete sacrifice) stand juxtaposed. Perhaps the whole young animal is also meant to signify something special.

[c]Caspari even speaks of a special 'Mizpah source'.

erection of the 'stone of help' (*'eben hā'ēzer*). It is hardly fortuitous that the same geographical designation also appears in the account of Israel's defeat (4.1; 5.1). In that case it was the false Ebenezer; this time it is the real one. Whether we have, or are meant to have (so Budde and Schulz), the same locality here, cannot be ascertained, despite what has just been said, because of the intimate geographical details in either case; it will be a place near Mizpah. Here, too, however, the theological element is more important than the historical.

[13–14] Samuel appears throughout as the man who carries on the work of 'deliverance' from the Philistine oppression 'begun' by Samson (Judg. 13.5), in which Shamgar had already played a part (Judg. 3.31). The compiler knows that this work was carried on by Saul and only completed by David. For this reason, while describing the victory as fundamentally great and real, on the grounds mentioned above, he nevertheless adds that the success was limited, both geographically and temporally. The extent to which the fairly precise details correspond with historically concrete events is questionable. We cannot exclude the possibility that the Philistines found the great man of God as uncanny as the holy ark and that an attempt to capture him was as unsuccessful as the corresponding undertaking on an earlier occasion. Thus the phrase 'all the days of Samuel' could have a pregnant significance not only in the light of the deuteronomistic scheme, but also in accordance with historical fact. The details of the towns restored to Israel could be understood in a similar way: the Israelites of the border territories once again came under the jurisdiction of the 'judge', who thenceforward performed his office unhindered. The note that relations with the original inhabitants were good does not imply that this was the consequence of a victory (Budde, Schulz, etc.). It is intended rather to give a further indication of the influence of the powerful personality of Samuel, who was everywhere respected.

[15–17] The chapter closes with the brief account of Samuel's activity as judge at the three great sanctuaries in the southern part of the hill-country of Ephraim. This activity is said to be pursued before the presence of the Lord. His erection of an altar in his own dwelling-place also points in the same direction. Such an altar would naturally have existed in Ramah and would have been pointed out by posterity as Samuel's altar; perhaps the story went that it had been built after the destruction of Shiloh. Strangely enough, there is no mention of the ark except at the beginning, though the manner of the victory described here would suggest that it might have been at least possible to take it from Kiriath-jearim perhaps to Mizpah. Were there differences between Mizpah, the sanctuary with the tradition of the holy tent, and the ark? Unfortunately we can discover no more.

In the centre of the chapter stands Samuel, the last judge, who, like the first judge Othniel, appears as a man who combines the charismatic work of deliverance of the 'great' judges with the institutional office of the 'minor' judges. In this way the chapter shows that Israel is cared for. There is no need to take thought either for the present or for the future. The Lord provides all necessary guarantees for peace within and to counter threats from without.

2. NOT JUDGE, BUT KING: 8.1–22

8 ¹When Samuel became old, he made his sons judges over Israel. ²The name of his first-born son was Joel, and the name of his second, Abijah; they were judges in Beersheba. ³Yet his sons did not walk in his ways, but turned aside after gain; they took bribes and perverted justice.

4 Then all the elders of Israel gathered together and came to Samuel at Ramah, ⁵and said to him, 'Behold, you are old and your sons do not walk in your ways; now appoint for us a king to govern us like all the nations.' ⁶But the thing displeased Samuel when they said, 'Give us a king to govern us.' And Samuel prayed to the LORD. ⁷And the LORD said to Samuel, 'Hearken to the voice of the people in all that they say to you; for they have not rejected you, but they have rejected me from being king over them. ⁸According to all the deeds which they have done, from the day I brought them up out of Egypt even to this day, forsaking me and serving other gods, so they are also doing to you. ⁹Now then, hearken to their voice; only, you shall solemnly warn them, and show them the ways of the king who shall reign over them.'

10 So Samuel told all the words of the LORD to the people who were asking a king from him. ¹¹He said, 'These will be the ways of the king who will reign over you: he will take your sons and appoint them to his chariots and to be his horsemen, and to run before his chariots; ¹²and he will appoint for himself commanders of thousands and commanders of fifties, and some to plough his ground and to reap his harvest, and to make his implements of war and the equipment of his chariots. ¹³He will take your daughters to be perfumers and cooks and bakers. ¹⁴He will take the best of your fields and vineyards and olive orchards and give them to his servants. ¹⁵He will take the tenth of

your grain and of your vineyards and give it to his officers[a] and to his servants. [16]He will take your menservants and maidservants, and the best of your cattle,[b] and your asses, and put them to his work. [17]He will take the tenth of your flocks, and you shall be his slaves. [18]And in that day you will cry out because of your king, whom you have chosen for yourselves; but the LORD will not answer you in that day.'

19 But the people refused to listen to the voice of Samuel; and they said, 'No! but we will have a king over us, [20]that we also may be like all the nations, and that our king may govern us and go out before us and fight our battles.' [21]And when Samuel had heard all the words of the people, he repeated them in the ears of the LORD. [22]And the LORD said to Samuel, 'Hearken to their voice, and make them a king.' Samuel then said to the men of Israel, 'Go every man to his city.'

The present chapter is of great significance among the historical books of the Old Testament. Here the basic transition from the time of the judges to the time of the kings takes place, and it is described in a way that shows its significance. A continuation of the period of the judges was not, in fact, impossible. Why could the Lord not have raised up new judges once again? But the biblical writer knows that historically this was not the case. With Samuel, the period of the judges was at an end, a new page of the history of God's dealings with Israel was opened, and this chapter shows that it had to be opened. It was the will of the two protagonists, the people of the time and the Lord himself; and the judge Samuel, who—at first— does not understand and thereby expresses the critical voice of a certain section of opinion, must also be enlightened. Indeed, he is compelled, once again by the people and by the Lord, to give up his old office and institute the new one. Samuel, the last judge, becomes the kingmaker. His historical position is thus fully recognized; he is one of those men who stand at the junction of two ages.

[1–3] The story begins, like that of Eli, with the failure of Samuel's sons, who have been appointed assistant judges by their father in Beersheba, the southernmost of the great sanctuaries. This is the third example, after Gideon and Eli, where the attempt to advance from the institution of the judgeship to a new competence, or, more accurately, the attempt to replace the individual call to office by a hereditary succession, is to be regarded as a failure. Each time it is

[a]Literally 'eunuchs'.
[b]So LXX; MT reads 'young men'. Stoebe (*VT* 4, 1954, pp. 177ff.) retains MT and thinks of the king's encroachments on the best Israelites in using them for forced labour. But the juxtaposition of young men and asses remains strange, especially as sons have already been mentioned in vv. 11f.

wrecked by the attitude of the persons concerned, who, be they
Abimelech, the house of Eli, or now others, each in a different way
try to assert their own personality. In this third instance, the selfishness of the younger generation appears in the sphere most closely
connected with the office of judge, that of the law. To help on the
slow or unfavourable course of the law with a bribe is a sin censured
most severely by the prophets and all too well known in the East,
right up to the present day.

[4–5] This, then, is the occasion for the 'elders', who, as in earlier
times (Moses, Joshua), appear as the representatives of the people
(v. 10), to seek for the replacement of the office of judge by that of
king. The use of the word 'judge' shows that this is the content of the
passage. The whole chapter speaks of 'judging' and of 'judgment'.[a]
The king is to be 'judge', indeed he is to be a just, incorruptible
judge, as the contrast with the sons of Samuel is meant to show.
The narrator will have taken this feature in the wish of the people
in a positive way. But he regards it as a negative factor that the desire
of the elders for a king is a consequence of what they have seen in
all the other 'nations' (cf. Deut. 17.14). The word *gōyim* is used here,
stressing the non-Israelite, heathen element. With this concern,
then, Israel departs from her special position to sink to the level of
the others. [6–9a] As a result, Yahweh, to whom Samuel turns with
this 'evil thing', interprets the people's request to mean that they
wish to forsake him, the real king, just as they did at the time of the
Exodus. Here one of the basic features of world history emerges:
the struggle of man against God—already beginning in Gen. 3—a
struggle which, according to the general outline presented in the
Bible, has its roots in the special position given to man in Gen. 1.
Samuel experiences what Moses, the prophets, and even Jesus experience: 'We do not want this man to reign over us' (Luke 19.14).

Nevertheless, the Lord accedes to the will of the people. Twice
Samuel is told to 'hearken to the voice of the people'. These instructions could, in the author's view, be the result of a careful consideration of the pros and cons of the situation, but they have as their
principal and essential basis the historical fact that the institution of
the monarchy took place at that time, and so could not have taken

---

[a]The necessary use of different words ('govern', 'justice', 'the ways of') in the
English version to render Hebrew words all of which come from the root *šāpat*
unfortunately obscures the frequency with which this root occurs. A glance at the
Hebrew text will make Hertzberg's point clear. Tr.

place without the wish of the Lord of history. Behind this chapter
there also stands the consciousness—which will later be revealed
quite clearly—that the king is not simply the representative of an
ill-willed people, but is the chosen one of God. The time was ripe for
the king, i.e. for the development of a state, even though the manifold dangers which could now cause theological chaos were seen all
too well. God sanctions the king, indeed the king is an expression of
his will; but the people must know that his appearance opens a new
way to apostasy from the first commandment (v. 8).

[9b–17] Samuel must therefore now proclaim to the people 'the
ways of'[a] the king. The Hebrew word does not mean 'the rights of
the king', i.e. the limits to be set to the powers of the king to put a
check to the danger of *anomia* (I John 3.4). The word here almost
means 'conduct', i.e. the conduct of the king towards Israel. It is,
however, foreseen that this conduct on the part of the king will
be 'of right', because of his elevation to the throne. The Hebrew
word *hēʿīd* ('witness') therefore has the sense of 'warn', as the RSV
correctly indicates, particularly in the general context. The outline
of a king's claims now put forward accords with the picture of a
sultanate, familiar in the East. The king, who intervenes in the private affairs of his subjects and 'has the right' to dispose of fields,
cattle, servants, even sons and daughters, really is a ruler 'such as
all the (heathen) nations have'.[b]

This, then, is the comprehensive description of the king for whom
the elders, on behalf of the people, have asked. It must be said,
however, that by and large, apart from some isolated instances, the
monarchy in Israel does not give this impression of being an abso-
lutist régime; care is taken, indeed by God himself, that the trees
do not grow right up to heaven. Not the least important factor here
is the emergence of the prophets. But the office of king, in which son
follows father and is followed in turn by his son (Judg. 8.22f.), by
virtue of its nature offers different possibilities of danger from those
of the office of judge, which, as the three above-mentioned instances
show, are much more easily obviated. It is hardly fortuitous that the
form and content of the description of the extent of the king's jurisdiction recalls the tenth commandment in its deuteronomistic form

[a]Hebrew *mišpāt*, see previous note. Tr.

[b]The similarity of the actions described here with the conditions of the 'semi-
feudal Canaanite society' revealed in the texts of Alalakh and Ugarit is stressed
by J. Mendelssohn in *BASOR* 143, 1956, pp. 17 22. The writer uses this similarity
to draw conclusions about the age of the description in I. 8.

(Deut. 5.18). **[18]** At the close of the speech it is stressed that there will be no divine deliverance from this difficult situation into which Israel can or will be led by the king; thus the Israelite king is rather different from Midianite or Ammonite, against whose oppressions the 'cry' of the people can summon the mercy and help of the Lord. The king is now the representative of God, even when he is not one of the 'kind and gentle' masters (I Peter 2.18).

[19–22] The people must therefore know, now, and for all time to come, that they themselves have wished for this master and have taken the burden upon themselves. They nevertheless abide by their choice, and their answer shows the advantages of the monarchy, as they conceive them. Regulated government, leadership in war—a 'trained soldier' instead of the temporary charismatic leader—and above all the responsibility for 'our' war, are all rated high by the people, and their view is correct. Even here, then, it is clear that the king is in no way caricatured and held up to be a bad thing. So the people stand firm, and the Lord gives his express sanction to the step now to be taken.

The literary form of the end of the chapter is such as to provide a place for the rest of the material pertinent to the origins of the monarchy. Here we recognize the guiding hand of the final compiler. It is a debatable question whether ch. 8 in its present form belongs to a 'source', perhaps the 'Mizpah source' (cf. on ch. 7), close to the 'Elohistic' position, or whether here the deuteronomistic compiler has himself by and large shaped the material.[a] Even in this case, we would, of course, assume that he worked with traditional material which already maintained an attitude critical not only of the first king, but of the monarchy in general, an attitude based above all, as has been said, on theological presuppositions. For the Lord is the real king (v. 7). Thus the literary-critical question raised here is hard to answer, but, in view of the similarity of the basic position of the final compiler and the material with which he was working, it is at the same time not over-important. What is without doubt the most important thing is that this chapter is a theological guide for all that is to follow, and though it is primarily a hint at the history of King Saul, it is not a hint at this alone. The reader leaves ch. 8 in great tension, wondering how, in view of the evident matter for conflict between God, the king and the people, and of course Samuel, the divine history will work itself out.

[a]So most energetically Noth, *Überlieferungsgeschichtliche Studien* I, p. 57.

3. THE ANOINTING OF SAUL: 9.1–10.16

9 [1]There was a man of Gibeah[a] of Benjamin whose name was Kish, the son of Abiel, son of Zeror, son of Becorath, son of Aphiah, a[b] Benjaminite,[c] a man of wealth; [2]and he had a son whose name was Saul, a handsome young man. There was not a man among the people of Israel more handsome than he; from his shoulders upward he was taller than any of the people.

3 Now the[d] asses of Kish, Saul's father, were lost. So Kish said to Saul his son, 'Take one of the servants with you, and arise, go and look for the asses.' [4]And he passed through the hill country of Ephraim and passed through the land of Shalisha, without finding them. And they passed through the land of Shaalim, but they were not there. Then they passed[e] through the land of Benjamin, but did not find them.

5 When they came to the land of Zuph,[f] Saul said to his servant who was with him, 'Come, let us go back, lest my father cease to care about the asses and become anxious about us.' [6]But he said to him, 'Behold, there is a man of God in this city, and he is a man that is held in honour; all that he says comes true. Let us go there; perhaps he can tell us about the journey on which we have set out.' [7]Then Saul said to his servant, 'But if we go, what can we bring the man? For the bread in our sacks is gone, and there is nothing left[g] to bring to the man of God. What have we?' [8]The servant answered Saul again, 'Here, I have with me the fourth part of a shekel of silver, and I will give it to the man of God, to tell us our way.' ([9]Formerly in Israel, when a man went to inquire of God, he said, 'Come let us go to the seer'; for he who is now called a prophet was formerly called a seer.)[h] [10]And Saul said to his servant, 'Well said; come, let us go.' So they went to the city where the man of God was.

11 As they went up the hill to the city, they met young maidens coming out to draw water, and said to them, 'Is the seer here?' [12]They answered, 'He is; behold he is just ahead of you. Make haste;[i] he has come just now to the city, because the people have a sacrifice today on the high place. [13]As soon as you enter the city, you will find him,

---

[a]So Wellhausen's conjecture, see BH.

[b]*ben-'īš y°mīnī* could be a conflate reading of *ben y°mīnī* and *'īš y°mīnī*. It is better to transpose *'īš* and *y°mīnī*. *'īš gibbōr ḥayil* also occurs at Ruth 2.1.

[c]This is explicitly emphasized, as it was not a matter of course, see Judg. 19.16.

[d]MT 'the', i.e. all that he had. Deletion of the article is unjustified, see Stoebe, *VT* 7, 1957, pp. 362f.

[e]See BH.

[f]See above on 1.1.

[g]Doubtful word; Caspari will be right in assuming a connection with the root *šā'ar*, 'remain over'.

[h]This note belongs after v. 11, where the word 'seer' occurs for the first time.

[i]The simpler text of LXX (see BH) is unnecessary. The change in MT to the second person singular [Not discernible in English. Tr.] corresponds to the observation of the maidens, who immediately notice the more distinguished (and more attractive) man.

before he goes up to the high place to eat; for the people will not eat till he comes, since he must bless the sacrifice; afterward those eat who are invited. Now go up, for you will meet him immediately'.[a] [14]So they went up to the city. As they were entering the gate,[b] they saw Samuel coming out toward them on his way up to the high place.

15 Now the day before Saul came, the LORD had revealed to Samuel: [16]"Tomorrow about this time I will send to you a man from the land of Benjamin, and you shall anoint him to be prince over my people Israel. He shall save my people from the hand of the Philistines, for I have seen the affliction of[b] my people, because their cry has come to me.' [17]When Samuel saw Saul, the LORD told him, 'Here is the man of whom I spoke to you! He it is who shall rule over my people.' [18]Then Saul approached Samuel in the gate, and said, 'Tell me where is the house of the seer?' [19]Samuel answered Saul, 'I am the seer; go up before[c] me to the high place, for today you shall eat with me, and in the morning I will let you go and will tell you all that is on your mind. [20]As for your asses that were lost three days ago, do not set your mind on them, for they have been found. And for whom is all that is desirable in Israel? Is it not for you and for all your father's house?' [21]Saul answered, 'Am I not a Benjaminite, from the[b] least of the tribes of Israel? And is not my family the humblest of all the families of the[b] tribe of Benjamin? Why then have you spoken to me in this way?'

22 Then Samuel took Saul and his servant and brought them into the hall and gave them a place at the head of those who had been invited, who were about thirty persons. [23]And Samuel said to the cook, 'Bring the portion I gave you, of which I said to you, "Put it aside".' [24]So the cook took up the leg and the fat tail[d] and set them before Saul; and he[e] said, 'See, what was kept is set before you. Eat; because it was kept for you until this time.'[f] So Saul ate with Samuel and with the guests[g] that day. [25]And when they came down from the high place into the city, a bed was spread for Saul[h] upon the roof and he

---

[a]So BH; the emphasis on 'him' given in the MT, but missing in LXX, is hardly correct.

[b]See BH.

[c]A mark of especial courtesy.

[d]So Targ. The fat tail of the sheep is still a special delicacy today.

[e]'He' is certainly the cook. LXX differs; but Samuel is mentioned only at the end of the verse.

[f]Literally 'the appointed time'.

[g]The phrase lēmōr hā'ām qārātī 'for he said, "I have invited the people"' which stands before 'So' in MT, makes no sense. Perhaps the two last words stood at the end of the verse in the form we'im haqqerū'īm (cf. Budde ad loc.); where the lēmōr comes from is obscure. Buber (VT 6, 1956, p. 131) renders mō'ēd 'assembly' in accordance with his exegesis which identifies this assembly with that described in ch. 8, and translates the closing words: '. . . that you may be right in saying, "I have invited the people."' Apart from everything else, this breaks down on the interpretation of lēmōr. We can do no more than recognize textual corruption here; so, too, Stoebe, VT 7, 1957, p. 366.

[h]So almost certainly correctly, according to LXX.

lay down to sleep.[a] Then at the break of dawn Samuel called to Saul upon the roof, 'Up, that I may send you on your way.' So Saul arose, and both he and Samuel went out into the street.

27 As they were going down to the outskirts of the city, Samuel said to Saul, 'Tell the servant to pass on before us'—and he passed on[b]—'and stop here yourself for a while, that I may make known to you the word of God.'

10 ¹Then Samuel took a vial of oil and poured it on his head, and kissed him and said, 'Has not the LORD anointed you to be prince over his people Israel? And you shall reign over the people of the LORD and you will save them from the hand of their enemies round about. And this shall be the sign to you[c] that the LORD has anointed you to be prince over his heritage. ²When you depart from me today you will meet two men by Rachel's tomb in the territory of Benjamin in the shade of a rock,[d] and they will say to you, "The asses which you went to seek are found, and now your father has ceased to care about the asses and is anxious about you, saying, 'What shall I do about my son?' " ³Then you shall go on from there further and come to the oak of Tabor;[e] three men going up to God at Bethel will meet you there, one carrying three kids, another carrying three loaves of bread, and another carrying a skin of wine. ⁴And they will greet you and give you two loaves of bread, which you shall accept from their hand. ⁵After that you shall come to the hill of God, where the prefect[f] of the Philistines is; and there, as you come to the city, you will meet a band of prophets coming down from the high place with harp, tambourine, flute, and lyre before them, prophesying in ecstasy. ⁶Then the spirit of the LORD will come mightily upon you, and you shall prophesy in ecstasy with them and be turned into another man. ⁷Now when these signs meet you, do (only) whatever your hand finds to do, for God is with you. ⁸And you shall go down before me to Gilgal; and behold, I am coming to you to offer burnt offerings and to sacrifice peace offerings. Seven days you shall wait, until I come to you and show you what you shall do.'

9 When he turned his back to leave Samuel[g] . . . all these signs came

---

[a]So likewise according to LXX.

[b]Marginal note.

[c]This clause was omitted in MT through a scribal error, but has been preserved in LXX, Vulg.

[d]MT has beṣelṣaḥ, usually explained as a proper name. It would be better to read beṣēl ṣeḥiᵃḥ. The second word, perhaps written in abbreviated form (ṣḥ) would have been misunderstood at an early date. Some of the ancient versions were already in doubt whether ṣelṣaḥ was a proper name.

[e]It is hardly possible to make a distinction between the palm of Deborah (Judg. 4.5), the oak (also of Deborah) in Gen. 35.8, and the oak of Tabor. The word Tabor might even be a textual error for debōrā. But the name may also have been altered following Judg. 4.6.

[f]See BII.

[g]The clause which follows here belongs at the end of v. 10.

to pass that day[a] . . . [10]When he had come thence[b] to the hill, behold, a band of prophets met him; and the spirit of God came mightily upon him, and he prophesied among them, and God gave him another heart.[c] [11]And when all who knew him before saw how he prophesied in ecstasy with the prophets, the people said to one another, 'What has come over the son of Kish? Is Saul also among the prophets?' [12]And a man of the place answered, 'And who is their father?' Therefore it became a proverb, 'Is Saul also among the prophets?' [13]When he had finished prophesying, he came to Gibeah.[d]

14 Saul's uncle said to him and to his servant, 'Where did you go?' And he said, 'To seek the asses; and when we saw they were not to be found, we went to Samuel.' [15]And Saul's uncle said, 'Pray, tell me what Samuel said to you.' [16]And Saul said to his uncle, 'He told us plainly that the asses had been found.' But about the matter of the kingdom, of which Samuel had spoken, he did not tell him anything.

The story of the young peasant who went out to look for lost asses and found a king's throne has always given especial delight to both hearers and readers. It is told in a vivid way, which reflects the pleasure with which the narrator regarded both the subject and the persons involved. Everyone, right down to the servant and the maidens drawing water, seems to stand out quite clearly, and the way in which Samuel and Saul are described is suffused with a warmth right from the heart. True history is surely reflected here: despite his critical attitude towards the institution of the monarchy and the first king, Samuel was deeply attached to Saul.

The narrative flows on in an attractive way, but this does not prevent an occasional amplification—the conversation with the maidens, the sacrificial meal—which, as it were, marks time. This is not characteristic of the biblical narrative style, which usually rushes on to the climax in great strides. The unity of the narrative, which even extends to its style, should not, however, prevent us from noticing one or two discrepancies. The search for the asses takes the two travellers a considerable distance from their town, and we are given the impression that the abode of the man of God is about the furthest point of their journey. On the other hand, according to the information given in ch. 10, Samuel's place appears to lie quite near

---

[a]There is perhaps a gap here where the happening of the other things mentioned earlier was recorded.

[b]According to LXX: *wayyābō' miššām.*

[c]The clause is taken earlier in MT as being the most important point.

[d]The word, which here means the proper name Gibeah (of Saul) (so LXX), has been interpreted as 'high place' = 'hill' in MT.

to Saul's home, as Saul is immediately known on the 'hill of God', and all the events which followed the anointing manifestly took place on the same day. Another thing is even more striking. At the beginning, the man of God is given no name. He is as little known to Saul as Saul is known to him. Only the pressing recommendation of the servant encourages Saul to seek the advice of the man of God. Moreover, the way in which the man of God is first described as a professional diviner does not at all fit the picture of Samuel which we have been given hitherto, the man who rose from the position of assistant to Eli to become his successor, and who then emerged as chief among the people. At the end of the text, on the other hand, Samuel is the man known to all, whose word is worth a great deal (10.14f.). There may be a third discrepancy in the fact that according to the account of the maidens, 'the seer' went into the city shortly before Saul, and did so expressly because of the sacrifice, whereas in the general course of the chapter we are given the impression that the place was his usual abode. These differences can only be explained by assuming that the present narrative had two primary forms, native to different places. The details of these cannot, of course, be distinguished clearly, indeed they cannot be distinguished at all by literary critical methods. One will have told how Saul, searching for the asses, far from his home, enlisted the help of the—unknown— 'seer', who, as sometimes happens in folk tales, promised him the future crown. The other account may have described a visit of Saul to Samuel, who would be living in the neighbourhood of Gibeah, the astonishing invitation, the sign with the exact details of the place concerned, and, above all, the anointing. Both accounts were originally attached to different localities, the former perhaps to the 'land of Zuph'; the different places given as Samuel's abode, Ramathaim-sophim and Ramah (cf. on 1.1), seem to meet us even here. The second account would then have been native to Ramah (er-ram). The former account predominates at the beginning, the latter at the end of the narrative; it seems that the latter has merely been expanded and enlarged by the other. The union of the two 'primary stories' and the formation of them into the present text was then achieved in the attractive and delightful way which we see before us. Perhaps it took place in Bethel, a sanctuary often mentioned here alongside Ramah, and which is, in fact, also explicitly associated with Samuel (7.16). It is further remarkable that a point of contact is frequently made with both earlier and later matter.

The story of the anointing is thus by no means intended as an episode as it were enclosed in brackets; it plays its full part in the onward flow of the whole.

Events are so far advanced that Samuel, convinced by the Lord himself that the request of the Israelites must be granted and that a king must be nominated, finds himself at the end of the preceding chapter in a kind of expectant obedience. **[9.1–2]** The compiler makes a new beginning at this point by first introducing the prospective king. The extensive list of his ancestors is intended, as was Samuel's family tree earlier, as an indication of a good and respected family. The town of Gibeah (= hill), according to Wellhausen's attractive conjecture already mentioned at this point, later called 'Gibeah of Saul', is the present *tell el-ful*, lying barely an hour's journey north of Jerusalem at the meeting of two roads. It is the same town which acquired a bad name from the events described in Judg. 19–21 (the 'disgrace of Gibeah', cf. Hos. 10.9), but was later restored to favour. There, too, the Benjaminites, and particularly the men of Gibeah, are described as bold daredevils. Saul, the son of Kish, and evidently still young, is portrayed with unconcealed delight as imposing and handsome, a man who makes an impression on everyone. It is not the only occasion on which Saul is thus depicted. In this way, like David at a later date (16.12, 18), he is designated as one chosen beforehand and destined for a special career.

[9.3–8] The loss of 'the' asses is reason enough for Saul's travels, on which he is accompanied by one of his father's servants.[a] The text, in which the verb forms fluctuate between singular and plural here

---

[a]Some would-be exponents of the 'symbolic character of the loss of the asses' (Stoebe, *VT* 7, 1957, p. 362) have recently appeared. The protagonist of this view has been Bič in his article 'Saul sucht die Eselinnen' (*VT* 7, 1957, pp. 92–97). He sees in the search for the asses part of a forgotten cult which would have included the visiting of the four 'lands' (9.4f.). The consequent connection of Zuph with the honeycomb, making it a paradisal place (!), of Shalisha with the number three, a reference to the resurrection on the third day (Hos. 6.2), and Shaalim with the jackal's head of Anubis makes the whole thing imaginative enough, but not plausible. And if at the back of it all there is really the cultic custom that a 'young man, sitting on an ass,' was brought 'in triumphal procession into the sanctuary' (p. 94), then should not Saul in the narrative at least have ridden into Gibeah (of God) on an ass's back? The symbolic background is much less marked in Stoebe (*loc. cit.*). He refrains from any effort to find something definite behind the names Shalisha and Shaalim, which are perhaps in themselves incidental. But he, too, thinks that Saul is confirmed 'as *gibbōr ḥayil*, as warrior and deliverer'(p. 370), by the events of 10.2–8 (see below). He argues that the

and also at times elsewhere, shows by this very fluctuation that 'he' is the chief person. Unfortunately it is impossible to locate the places mentioned; the occurrence of Ephraim and Benjamin does, however, indicate the extent of the journey. The land of Zuph, which presumably has something to do with the word mentioned twice in 1.1, is, as has been said, the point at which Saul thinks of turning back and giving up the search, for understandable reasons. The way in which the hitherto negative results are transformed into something positive just at this point will seem to every reader to be a conclusive proof of the mysterious workings of fate. For now comes the advice of the servant that they should go to the famous man of God living in the neighbourhood, who, as the servant is aware, knows everything. The offering of a present, the need for which Saul is quick to point out, is the usual payment. This very feature, however, shows the figure of the man of God in a different light from other passages, even from the way in which Samuel appears at the end of the narrative.

[9.9] At this point we have the important note about the identification of 'seer' and 'prophet'. It must be later than the surrounding words and is primarily meant to underline the identity of the 'man of God', viz. seer, with the 'prophet'. In the present context this means the identity of the unnamed diviner with the figure of Samuel, who has earlier been called a prophet. This note thus confirms what was said earlier, that we have here an amalgamation of two earlier stories, and it may derive from the man who constructed the present account of the anointing from these two stories. This is not, however, the only reason for the importance of this verse to us; there is also the more far-reaching reason that here we learn something of the early history of prophecy. The early period knew two groups of such men of God. Seers were those who, as their name implies, could 'see' something imperceptible to others, not only, say, lost asses, but even events in the future. This special gift was profitable to them, as it was to the owners of the slave girl endowed with powers of divination in Acts 16.16. Prophets (Hebrew *nābī'*), on the other hand, are men on whom God has laid his hand, men who have been

---

gifts presented to Saul have symbolic significance because of their connection with motifs from David's anointing and call. This is in itself correct, cf. below on 16.1ff., but 16.20, which is for him the most important feature, has a different meaning (see below *ad loc.*). And after all, it is not Saul, but his father, who is the *gibbōr ḥayil* (9.1); the phrase is an expression of his position as a citizen (and as a warrior)—as also in the case of Boaz, Ruth 2.1.

fully accepted by him, as indeed we go on to learn in this story. In the early period these groups were completely distinct. Gradually, however, the texts 'allow characteristic features to pass from one to the other, the more so as time goes on'.[a] The later classical prophets took over definite characteristics of both groups, so that the statement advanced here is correct and important not only historically, but also theologically.

[9.10–13] The question to the maidens, who have come down from the elevated position of the city to draw water—a scene which can be noticed again and again in the East—is answered by a speech 'which is lively and ceremonious in a feminine way—female speech is almost always clearly distinguished in the Old Testament—' (Budde on 9.12f.). As a result, the travellers are now informed and try to meet the seer before he goes up to the 'high place' (bāmā), which lies even higher than the city. [9.14–16] In fact, they meet Samuel, who is here named for the first time, 'in the gate'. We are now brought up to date with what, of course, had happened earlier. Samuel received a 'revelation', a revelation perceptible to the ear, as the literal rendering of the Hebrew shows. 'A man' of Benjamin will come to Samuel; he is to be the awaited king. The word 'king' (melek) is not, in fact, used here; twice we have nāgīd, prince, properly the 'one who has been announced'.[b] Thus the king is entitled 'the one designated of Yahweh' until political honour is added to theological recognition by the 'acclamation of the people'[c] (11.15). Then he is called 'king'. The word 'king' is also used in ch. 8, where the will of the people is expressed. By putting the narrative 9.1ff., which is of a completely different nature and comes from a completely different context, in its present position, the compiler demonstrates that designation by the Lord must come first. Without his will and his calling, the new office is impossible. The hierarchy disrupted by the wish of the people for a king is once again made good by the fact that chs. 9 and 10 recount the 'revelation' and the anointing—and 10.17ff. the election by lot.

[a]Hertzberg, *Prophet und Gott*, 1923, p. 13, with details on the whole problem of prophecy.

[b]There is a preparation for and introduction to the word *nāgīd* in the use of the verb *nāgad* in vv. 6, 8, 18, 19; 10.15f.; on this see the impressive explanation by Buber in *VT* 6, 1956, pp. 126, 142, who adds: 'Anyone who insists on maintaining that this is a coincidence throws away the key to the inmost heart of the Hebrew Bible.' See also Gutbrod, p. 70.

[c]Alt, *Die Staatenbildung der Israeliten in Palästina*, 1930, p. 29; *Kleine Schriften* II, p. 23.

[9.17] The extent to which the direction of the Lord underlies all this is made clear by the second message to Samuel, which is given at the moment of meeting. It is quite obvious that this section of the narrative again presupposes that the two are not yet acquainted. It is said to be the task of the *nāgid*, as in the case of Shamgar and Samson (Judg. 3.31; 13.5) to 'save' Israel from the hand of the Philistines and then to 'rule over' the people. The Hebrew word *'aṣār*—used only here and in 10.1—has the meaning 'keep in check'. These are mighty acts which can only be done by one 'with whom the Lord is'.

[9.18–21] In answer to Saul's question, Samuel reveals himself as the seer, issues the invitation to the sacrifice, so important in the general context, and without being asked expressly, gives the desired information. 'Samuel, by knowing in advance what Saul had to ask, here solves the task which king Nebuchadnezzar vainly put to his interpreters in Dan. 2 until Daniel proved their superior' (Budde, *ad loc.*). The servant was right; this seer knows his business; he knows that the asses have been found. But this is now only a matter of secondary importance; to underline the fact, events are put in a wider context. Saul and his family can lose neither asses nor anything else in Israel, for from now on all the precious things which belong to the people are his.[a] Saul, like Gideon (Judg. 6.14), brushes off the obscure allusion by referring to the small resources of his own tribe and family. Here, as in the case of Gideon, the reader will see a confirmation of the divine law according to which God chooses the weak in the world and gives grace to the lowly.

[9.22–24] Saul's amazement must be growing continually. He is welcomed, along with the servant—a remarkable but not unique example of the status of servants in Israel (cf. Gen. 24; Job 31. 13–15), into the special group of thirty guests gathered in the 'hall'. The existence of such a 'hall', intended to offer protection against sun and rain, shows that the sanctuary is not an insignificant one. Saul is the awaited guest of honour, for whom the best portion has been saved; the size of the portion given to him indicates the special extent of the honour due to him (cf. Gen. 43.34). The description of the huge portion as a 'little remnant'[b] accords with a courtly style

[a] As pointed, MT really means 'all that is desirable' (cf. Targ., so RSV); the *optima* of the Vulgate is, however, without doubt better.

[b] Stoebe (*VT* 7, 1957, p. 366) differs. He envisages a confusion of two readings which may at one time have been associated under the influence of the incomprehensible *lēmōr*—see p. 76 n.[g] above.

native to the East ('your servant', or II Kings 8.13) and not unknown even in the West where food is concerned (e.g. 'will you have a bite', etc.). Thus the foresight of Samuel, or rather in the last resort that of Yahweh, is operative right down to these individual details. The reactions of the 'guests' to the strange situation are no more mentioned than its effect upon Saul, the chief person concerned. As so often in biblical history, it is the theological and not the psychological side of the matter that is important.

[9.25–27] Nor is any further comment made on the invitation to Saul to sleep—during the Eastern summer the flat roof is a favourite place for spending the night; this is simply taken for granted, as is the ceremonial escort provided by Samuel in the morning. Samuel stops at the boundary of the city territory. To have come this far would have been a usual mark of courtesy; the place may later have been shown as the place of the anointing, as everything that follows betrays an extremely detailed knowledge of the area. Both the early hour of the morning and the despatch of the servant indicate Samuel's desire that the sacred action which he intends should take place without witnesses; the political situation of Israel at the time could also be a contributory factor.

[10.1] Anointing is a sacramental act by which a man destined for a special office—like that of priest, and particularly that of king— is demonstrably consecrated by God. In no Old Testament figure more than Saul is it clearer that this action stamps on the person concerned a special character, which never disappears. Even his later rejection does not alter the fact that he is 'the anointed of Yahweh'. The sacred character of the anointing does not derive from the material used, the oil, as there is also Old Testament evidence of anointings with no sacramental significance. It derives from the person who does it. In the last resort, in fact, it derives from the Lord himself. Samuel acts as representative and instrument of the most high God and, moreover, stresses that it is really the Lord who does the anointing. Now Saul is *nāgîd*, prince 'by the grace of God'. Even here, the duties of the future ruler are stressed once again; the decisive words are preserved in LXX. The report that Samuel kisses Saul after the anointing is over is perhaps a record of part of the solemn act, but is surely also an indication of Samuel's affection for Saul, which never ceased, even at a later time.

Again there is no word from Saul. But as though to counter certain questions and objections, Samuel now indicates the signs by which Saul is to recognize the reality of what has happened. [10.2] The first is to confirm from a neutral mouth what Samuel has previously asserted; two men will say to Saul that the asses have been found and will describe how things now are at his home. The place of this meeting is to be Rachel's tomb, which was originally on the border between Benjamin and Joseph—so, too, in Jer. 31.15, where it is mentioned alongside Ramah.[a] The oak of Tabor is to be located not far away (see above). [10.3–4] The three men mentioned here are on their way 'to God', to Bethel—the palm of Deborah is also located 'between Ramah and Bethel' in Judg. 4.5—and have with them abundant sacrificial offerings. They will give to the travellers two of their three loaves of bread; this is meant to refer back to 9.7 and is to be regarded as an act of providence from the Lord. This is the best interpretation of the end of v. 4. [10.5-7] Gibeath-elohim, 'the hill of God', is also not far away, and would be a well-known sanctuary; this would seem the most obvious reason for stationing a Philistine 'prefect'[b] there. The identification of the place with Mizpah, 'the watch', is highly probable.[c] The reason for this third and most important sign is Saul's foretold encounter with the prophets. These are a group of n[e]bī'îm, such as are often to be found at a sanctuary, who, inspired by music, are sent into a prophetic ecstasy. Saul is to be seized by this ecstasy, through the working of the spirit of the Lord, so that he is 'turned'[d] into another man. This sign is therefore to be perceptible in Saul himself and is to make it clear that he is called to be an instrument of God, open at any time to the onset of his power. From now on he will be able to seize the opportunities placed before him by God, confident that God is 'with' him. But at the same time he will have to seize them. [10.8] The conclusion of Samuel's speech directs Saul to Gilgal near Jericho (twice he says 'go down'), to a sacrifice and to await Samuel's further instructions. It should be noticed that Saul appears here as altogether the man called by God, who is ready for his instructions. In this

[a]Here we have the most definite evidence that for the narrator Ramah was *er-ram*. The tomb of Rachel was later located in Bethlehem, as in the gloss on Gen. 35.19 and in Matt. 2.17f., and is so today.

[b]Renderings of the word *nāṣīb* vary between 'prefect', 'garrison' and 'pillar'. Even in the last instance, such a pillar must have stood in an often-frequented place (against Buber, *VT* 6, 1956, p. 134).

[c]On the pros and cons see *ZAW* 47, 1929, pp. 179f. Other possibilities are listed there.

[d]The word used here is the same as that used in the Old Testament for the 'overthrow' of Sodom and Gomorrah.

position he is reminiscent of judges like Barak, Gideon, Jephthah and Samson.

[10.9–12] The present text records only the realization of the last sign,[a] in such a way that the change of 'heart' is stressed as the most important factor. Despite this formula, which deviates somewhat from v. 6, we should not, however, think of a conversion in the spiritual sense, but merely of a readiness in Saul for the intervention of the Lord, in a way yet unknown. While Saul was a stranger at Samuel's home, he has been known at the sanctuary for a long time, so his prophetic ecstasy arouses general wonderment. The writer takes this as the explanation of the origin of the proverb 'Is Saul also among the prophets?' Another explanation is given in 19.18ff. The proverb means, 'How does a reasonable man, well placed in civic life, come to be in this eccentric company?' Among people who, as a contemptuous aside puts it, 'have no father', i.e. come from anywhere! This assessment of the situation is to be compared with that made in Acts 2.13, where it is said of those seized by the spirit of God that they are full of new wine. In any event, the writer gives as positive a judgment on the seizing of Saul by the spirit of Yahweh as does Luke in the case of the apostles in Acts 2.

[10.13–16] Saul then comes home, but on being questioned by a relative who is, of course, interested in Saul's meeting with Samuel— here obviously well known to all (see above)—he does not give away his secret. From the passing mention of the 'kingdom', we see that we are already being led on towards the sequel. The hearer waits in burning expectation as to what the Lord will do next.

4. THE CHOOSING OF THE KING: 10.17–27

10 [17]Now Samuel called the people together to the Lord at Mizpah; [18]and he said to the people of Israel, 'Thus says the Lord, the God of Israel, "I brought up Israel out of Egypt, and I delivered you from the hand of the Egyptians and from the hand of all the kingdoms that were oppressing you." [19]But you have this day rejected your God, who saved you from all your calamities and your distresses; and you have said, "No![b] but set a king over us." Now therefore present yourselves before the Lord by your tribes and by your thousands.'

20 Then Samuel brought all the tribes of Israel near, and the tribe of Benjamin was taken by lot. [21]He brought the tribe of Benjamin near by its families, and the family of the Matrites was taken by lot; finally

[a]Something, however, has fallen out, see above.
[b]See BH.

he brought the family of the Matrites near man by man,[a] and Saul the son of Kish was taken by lot. But when they sought him, he could not be found. [22]So they inquired again of the LORD, 'Did the man come hither?'[b] and the LORD said, 'Behold, he has hidden himself among the baggage.' [23]Then they ran and fetched him from there; and when he stood among the people, he was taller than any of the people from his shoulders upwards. [24]And Samuel said to all the people, 'Do you see him whom the LORD has chosen? There is none like him among all the people.' And all the people shouted, 'Long live the king!'

25 Then Samuel told the people the rights and duties of the kingship; and he wrote them in a book and laid it up before the LORD. Then Samuel sent all the people away, each one to his home. [26]Saul also went to his home at Gibeah, and with him went those of the[c] host whose hearts God had touched. [27]But some useless fellows said, 'How can this man save us?' And they despised him, and brought him no present. But he acted as though he did not notice it.[d]

Whereas the previous section described the anointing of Saul as *nāgīd*, we hear now of his election as king. This is told as though in complete ignorance of the passage 9.1–10.16, and forms an immediate sequel to 8.22a. Saul's rise to the throne was evidently narrated in different places in different ways; here we have the Mizpah tradition. All accounts, however, agree in one thing—it is always the Lord who plays the leading role, and he uses Samuel as his instrument.

[**17–19**] First comes the assembly 'of the people'—later they are called 'all the people'—at the sanctuary of Mizpah. This is not the elders alone, as in 8.4.[e] The phrase describes the full citizens, who formed the host (cf. *haḥayil*, v. 26). Proceedings begin with some remarks of Samuel, similar in tone to those made in ch. 8; he refers to Yahweh's gracious acts in the Exodus and at the time of the judges and compares with them the ungratefulness of the people towards their 'saviour' which finds expression in their desire for a king. As in ch. 8, the theological pattern is thus once again clearly marked. Here, as at the close of the section, we are listening to the

[a]To be expanded thus according to LXX.

[b]MT reads: 'Is there yet a man to come hither?' LXX will, however, have been right in reading *hā'īš* and presumably also *'ad* (instead of *'ōd*).

[c]LXX simplifies with *benē* before 'host'.

[d]Literally: 'And he acted as though dumb.' Buber (*VT* 6, 1956, p. 146) '. . . like a deaf-mute . . . he returned the insulting remark by acting as though it had made no impression upon him'. LXX renders the words as though the consonants were similar (and the pointing different): 'And it happened about a month later.' Cf. on 11.13f.

[e]'The people', in fact, also appears at 8.10; at the end (8.22b) we have the neutral phrase 'the men of Israel'.

view of the final compiler, who is, however, without doubt bringing out a theme already present in his material.[a]

[20–21] In spite of this critical outlook, it is once again possible to discern the Lord's will to fall in with the wishes of the people, here in the way that the sacred lot is used. The procedure is as in Josh. 7.16–18.[b] There is a process of elimination, from the larger entity to the smaller entity and finally to the individual 'man'. This leads to the discovery of Saul, who is not, as in the previous section, the son of his father, but a full citizen. In the general context, the choice by lot seems to be a miraculous confirmation of the revelation given to Samuel in ch. 9 and of the secret anointing which followed it. The juxtaposition of the different accounts thus appears not as addition, but as multiplication.

Strangely enough, the chosen man is now nowhere to be found. This is a clear contradiction of what was said earlier, as we must assume that the 'men' of the family of the Matrites were 'brought near' *in figura*. And why should Saul have hidden himself just when matters were concerning him? If we examine the general context, this feature, like Saul's remark in 9.21, might seem to be intended as a sign of his modesty. But for reasons mentioned earlier, this explanation is insufficient. Moreover Samuel, who is at first completely opposed to the choice, is later very much in favour of it. [22–24] There is therefore much to be said for Eissfeldt's conjecture that here we have a different account of the election of the king, in which the divine reply at the sanctuary marked out as future king the man who stood head and shoulders above the rest of the people. In that case, MT has preserved the original form of the text in v. 22; after no one has appeared to fulfil the necessary requirement, they ask 'Is there yet a man to come hither?' Then would come the reference to the baggage. This would be the best introduction to vv. 23, 24.[c] Eissfeldt now uses this observation to support his division of the material into three sources and finds here a combination of his continuous sources III and I (corresponding to E and L). This,

[a]'This day' in v. 19 is surprising. It makes it seem as though this assembly took place on the same day as that of ch. 8. Perhaps this was, in fact, the original way in which events were described in the 'Mizpah source'. Buber describes vv. 18f. as 'an insertion of kerygmatic character' (*VT* 6, 1956, p. 145).

[b]Details there are more accurate; as an intermediate stage 'houses' also appears. MT is still shorter than LXX in I Sam. 10.

[c]O. Eissfeldt, *Die Komposition der Samuelbücher*, p. 7. K. Budde, *OLZ* 34, 1931, pp. 1059f., strongly disagrees.

however, is improbable, as despite the argument advanced by Eissfeldt, the 'rights and duties of the kingship' in v. 25 are not to be distinguished from the 'ways of the king' in 8.11 (see *ad loc.*), so that there can be no literary-critical grounds for separating 10.21b*b*–27a from ch. 8 and 10.17ff. Here too, the Mizpah tradition will generally be in evidence, its theology now and then being made more clear by the hand of the deuteronomistic compiler, who had a similar viewpoint. First, it must be stressed that the account 10.17–27 came to the final compiler when already in its present arrangement; the chief support for this is the phrase 'rights and duties of the kingship' in v. 25. More will be said on this point. At the same time, however, we must concede that, as in 9.1ff., two different traditions of the choice of the king in Mizpah preceded this text; one described the choice of the candidates as taking place by lot, the other is concerned with the imposing stature of the aspirant. To this latter belongs the business of the 'baggage'. The amalgamation of the two narratives then expresses something characteristic of the tone of the general account, as described earlier: the institution of the monarchy is of itself an expression of a lack of confidence in the Lord and his capacity, constantly put to the test, always to send the right man at the right time. On the other hand, he is now prepared to allow the people a king, and Samuel, in whose person the basic objections were most clearly concentrated, is personally well disposed to the figure of the first king.

It has already been said that it is the men of the host from whose midst the king is chosen. The word 'baggage' (*kēlîm*, utensils, baggage or weapons) also points in the same direction. In this particular context, the choice of the most imposing man, who 'does not have his like' among the people, is quite understandable. The similarity of the formulas here and in 9.1 is not to be attributed to editorial assimilation. As 10.11f. shows, King Saul is a man to whom proverbial phrases attached themselves—an indication of his popularity. The 'acclamation of the people' (A. Alt) follows, with the joyful cry 'Long live the king'. The chosen of the Lord thus becomes the people's king.

[25] The proclamation of the 'rights and duties of the kingship' and their preservation in writing represents the final act of the important drama which, as is explicitly stressed, takes place 'before the Lord' and resumes the matter mentioned in 8.11.[a] In the view

[a]Cf. M. Noth, *Überlieferungsgeschichtliche Studien* I, p. 58.

of the text, however, the written law was not intended to contain just the complicating factors mentioned as a warning to the people in ch. 8. We have an example of such a 'law for the king' in Deut. 17.14ff.

[26–27] The people are then dismissed, and Saul too returns to Gibeah. He is accompanied by men 'whose hearts God had touched', men who are ready not only to recognize him, but also to make his cause their own. It is assumed that they bring him gifts of homage. The account speaks with abhorrence of those of a different opinion who even refrain from offering gifts. Such an attitude is tantamount to doubting the decision of God, which has now been made.

5. THE AMMONITE WAR AND THE ELEVATION TO THE THRONE: 11.1-15

11 ¹Then Nahash the Ammonite went up and besieged Jabesh-gilead; and all the men of Jabesh said to Nahash, 'Make a treaty with us, and we will serve you.' ²But Nahash the Ammonite said to them, 'On this condition I will make a treaty with you, that I gouge out all your right eyes, and thus put disgrace upon all Israel.' ³The elders of Jabesh said to him, 'Give us seven days respite that we may send messengers through all the territory of Israel. Then, if there is no one to save us, we will give ourselves up to you.' ⁴When the messengers came to Gibeah of Saul, they reported the matter in the ears of the people; and all the people wept aloud.

5 Now Saul was coming from the field behind the oxen; and Saul said, 'What ails the people, that they are weeping?' So they told him the tidings of the men of Jabesh. ⁶And the Spirit of God came mightily upon Saul when he heard these words, and his anger was greatly kindled. ⁷He took a yoke of oxen, and cut them in pieces, and sent them throughout all the territory of Israel by the hand of the[a] messengers, saying, 'Whoever does not come out after Saul—and Samuel[b]—so shall it be done to his oxen!' Then the dread of the LORD fell upon the people, and they came out as one man. ⁸When he mustered them at Bezek, the men of Israel were three hundred thousand, and the men of Judah thirty thousand. ⁹And he said[c] to the messengers who had come, 'Thus shall you say to the men of Jabesh-gilead: "Tomorrow, by the time the sun is hot, you shall have

[a]So MT. It is thus the messengers from Jabesh who take round the pieces. But the reading 'of messengers' also has ancient testimony.

[b]'And after Samuel' is frequently regarded as a later addition. But this source, too, like the whole tradition, knows that Saul's beginnings have something to do with Samuel.

[c]MT 'they said'.

deliverance." ' When the messengers came and told the men of Jabesh, they were glad. ¹⁰Therefore the men of Jabesh said, 'Tomorrow we will come out to you, and you may do to us whatever seems good to you.' ¹¹And on the morrow Saul put the people in three companies; and they came into the midst of the camp in the morning watch, and cut down the Ammonites until the heat of the day; and those who survived were scattered, so that no two of them were left together.

12 Then the people said to Samuel, 'Who is it that said, "Shall Saul reign over us?"ᵃ Bring the men, that we may put them to death.' ¹³But Saul said, 'Not a man shall be put to death this day, for today the LORD has wrought deliverance in Israel.' ¹⁴Then Samuel said to the people, 'Come, let us go to Gilgal and there renew the kingdom.' ¹⁵So all the people went to Gilgal, and there they made Saul king before the LORD in Gilgal. There they sacrificed peace offerings before the LORD, and there Saul and all the men of Israel rejoiced greatly.

The present narrative is the third we have which describes the beginning of Saul's kingship. The reason for so many forms of tradition, as was remarked briefly in the previous section, can hardly be the presence of a number of continuous sets of narratives. It will simply be that the individual sanctuaries possessed established traditions of Saul's rise to the throne. As a Benjaminite sanctuary, Mizpah would be the first concerned; what was known there about the beginnings of Saul's kingship has been collected, as we saw, in 10.17–27. In 9.1 to 10.16 there are traditions which will have been current at Samuel's dwelling-place, or rather at the two places which claimed this honour. The details of the eleventh chapter may have been transmitted at Gilgal, near Jericho. Of course, some things may have been handed down in similar or identical fashion at different places.

[1] The account starts again with the Ammonite invasion. We find a hostile encounter with them as early as the judgeship of Jephthah. Even then, as here, the Ammonites picked the quarrel. A real or supposed weakness on the Israelite side is used to bring about the invasion. Nahash,ᵇ described as 'the Ammonite', is, of course, the king. Jabesh-gilead is a town east of the Jordan, mentioned frequently in the Old Testament; its name has been preserved until today in

ᵃLXX simplifies by making the sentence a statement and adding *lō*: 'Saul shall not be king over us.'
ᵇ'Snake', 'but we may not conclude the existence of snake-worship from this' (Schulz *ad loc.*).

the *wadi yabis*.[a] Its destruction is mentioned in Judg. 21.[b] The deduction to be made from that passage that there were evidently special relationships between the tribe of Benjamin and this city is important; this is also the background to I Sam. 11, even if it is not mentioned explicitly.

The situation of Jabesh is desperate, demonstrating with historical accuracy the powerlessness of Israel as a whole. Evidently the defeat at Aphek had serious consequences. At this point the significant word *b*erit* ('treaty', but also of course 'covenant') makes an appearance, in the Israelite offer. The *b*erit* is a solemn (cf. Gen. 15) agreement between two partners, but it is not in the first place made by parties of equal standing; it is a matter of the terms of a settlement being dictated by the stronger party. The Israelite offer is an indication of this. In their view, servitude and the making of a covenant quite naturally belong together. A second element is, however, also important. The stronger party puts himself under an obligation as well, thereby providing the weaker party with a sacred sphere of rights. A *b*erit* is therefore by no means an unconditional surrender. The obligations which go with it are important for the Israelites. [2–3] Nahash replies with bitter scorn; in the *b*erit* which he proposes, the whole meaning of the act is completely changed—law becomes arbitrariness. His words reveal his consciousness of the inferiority of Israel, indeed he even allows the men of Jabesh seven days to look for help among their kinsmen. This is the lowest ebb of pre-exilic Israelite history. Such is the intended meaning. But the reader knows that the deliverer is already at hand.

[4] The narrative speeds to its climax in great strides. We learn nothing of a journey by the messengers through the hill-country of Israel and of vain attempts to get help. It seems rather as though they rush directly to Gibeah of Saul. LXX even says that they went 'to Gibeah, to Saul' (instead of 'to Gibeah of Saul'), in other words that they went to what was now the proper place. This is not sur-

[a]For its location see N. Glueck, *Explorations in Eastern Palestine* IV, 1951, pp. 261–75. He advocates *tell abu kharaz* (along with *tell el-meqbereh*), lying near the Jordan, not only with good archaeological justification, but also in view of the consideration that a place lying further inland would make Saul's action incomprehensible, taking into account the distances involved. In the present account, the expression 'he went up', if anything, might sound suspicious, as the Ammonites would have had to 'go down'. But an approach from the south through the Jordan valley might be envisaged. Moreover, *'ālā* often has just the sense of going up to war. Noth produces other considerations in *ZDPV* 69, 1953, pp. 28–41.

[b]On this, see ATD 9², p. 254.

prising, as LXX regarded these accounts as a whole even more than MT; Saul has been anointed and chosen, therefore he is the person to go to. It is, however, easy to see that this was originally an independent story. In the original form, the messengers would have come quite by chance—i.e. as a result, of course, of higher guidance— to Gibeah. There they deliver their sorrowful message. The people are deeply moved, but at the same time quite helpless. [5–6] Saul comes from the fields—again 'by chance', in the same sense—sees and hears, and in the same moment the spirit of God 'leaps' (this is the literal meaning) upon him. As in the case of Samson (Judg. 14.19), being possessed by the spirit of the Lord is not comparable with being inflamed with human anger, but is clearly differentiated from it. Here we have a new description of the Lord's nomination which reminds us of the way in which such acts of deliverance were introduced in the time of the judges. Once again God has brought his help in a time of deep need, as he did before. [7] Saul's action under the influence of the spirit of God is similar to that of the Levite in Judg. 19.[a] Strangely enough the concubine, too, is killed in Gibeah. It is in the course of this same story that the connection of Benjamin with Jabesh, mentioned earlier, is related. The agreement can hardly be coincidental.

Saul's appeal to Israel, made so vividly and so seriously, is not without effect. The fear of the Lord falls upon the people. God's hour has come. [8–11] Of course the numbers given, as in Judg. 20, are a fantasy,[b] in LXX even more so than in MT. The muster takes place in Bezek, the modern *khirbet ibziq*, from which the march to Gilgal could easily be managed. The inhabitants of Jabesh are informed, and they in their turn give the Ammonites tidings intended to make them confident. The hidden double meaning of the phrase 'tomorrow we will come out to you' is thus an especially subtle touch, which the ancient audience would have applauded loudly. Saul's attack takes place in the early hours of the morning and ends with the defeat and rout of the Ammonites and the deliverance[c] of Jabesh.

[a]G. Wallis produces 'a parallel . . . from the letters in the Mari Archives' in *ZAW* 64, 1952, pp. 57–61.
[b]One feels that the number 1,000 has simply been added. Three hundred is the number of men with which Gideon defeated the Midianites. The distinction between 'Israel' and 'Judah' is remarkable.
[c]Phrases incorporating the word 'deliver' (*yašuʿ*) occur three times in the chapter; Saul is meant to appear and be celebrated as a 'deliverer' here.

[14] All this is merely a prelude to the real climax intended by the narrator: the choice of Saul as king in Gilgal.[a] Here Samuel once again makes an appearance;[b] in view of the other indications of his connection with Gilgal, this is hardly surprising. Nevertheless, here, too, the earlier use of the material is evident. First of all it will have shown how Saul was seized by the spirit of Yahweh, fear of whom fell on all the people about. These events would emphasize that a calling had taken place here like that which took place in chs. 9 and 10 through the 'anointing' (and Saul's subsequent prophetic ecstasy).[c] Here too, then (see above), the 'designation by Yahweh' is followed by the 'acclamation of the people'. The parallelism of events is made even clearer by LXX, which, unlike MT, also mentions an anointing of Saul at this point. On the other hand, the final compiler sees this account as a continuation of the earlier ones. This may explain the word 'renew'; originally it will have been no 'renewal', but an institution of the kingship. We are also able to see in the sequel that here an editorial hand has tried to represent things as a succession rather than a juxtaposition of accounts.

[12-13] Verses 12 and 13 make an awkward break between the events of Jabesh and those of Gilgal. Originally they will have belonged to the conclusion of the Mizpah narrative, that is, to the end of ch. 10. The compiler has not unskilfully placed the episode of Jabesh between 10.27 and 11.12, thus impressively demonstrating that the Lord is with Saul and the doubters are wrong. Saul's generosity now appears as a particularly gracious act on the part of the victor. So once again we have an impressive description of a rise from the gloomiest depths to great heights. It is truly a day of 'deliverance'. [15] At the conclusion, all are assembled at the sanctuary at Gilgal for a feast to celebrate the victory and Saul's kingship. The LXX emphasis that Samuel was present in the happy throng is meant to indicate something alluded to before: Samuel is associated with the beginning of Saul's kingship not only by virtue of his office, but also because he has a personal relationship with the king.

One more observation on the whole complex of narratives may be added. In gathering together all the material he could find to

[a]For the site of Gilgal see ATD 9², p. 26. Remarkably enough Muilenburg (*BASOR* 140, 1955, pp. 11-27) once again advocates *khirbet el-mefjir*; cf. also Noth, *ZDPV* 71, 1955, p. 47.
[b]On the other hand, there is no reason for the mention of Samuel as early as v. 7; cf. *ad loc.*
[c]On this cf. A. Alt, *Staatenbildung*, p. 23; *Kleine Schriften*, p. 18.

describe the beginning of the monarchy, the final compiler must have been steeped in the consciousness that a decisive event had taken place here. In this he was right, not only from an historical point of view—the incoming people now formed themselves into a state—but also in respect of the course of sacred history. A new leaf of this history has now been turned.

6. SAMUEL'S FAREWELL: 12.1–25

12 ¹And Samuel said to all Israel, 'Behold, I have hearkened to your voice in all that you have said to me, and have made a king over you. ²And now, behold, the king walks before you; and I am old and grey, and behold, my sons are with you; and I have walked before you from my youth until this day. ³Here I am; testify against me before the LORD and before his anointed. Whose ox have I taken? Or whose ass have I taken? Or whom have I defrauded? Whom have I oppressed? Or from whose hand have I taken a bribe to blind my eyes with it? (Or a pair of shoes? Testify against me!)ᵃ I will restore it to you.' ⁴They said, 'You have not defrauded us or oppressed us or taken anything from any man's hand.' ⁵And he said to them, 'The LORD is witness against you, and his anointed is witness this day, that you have not found anything in my hand.' And they said, 'He is witness.'

6 And Samuel said to the people, 'It was the LORD who appointed Moses and Aaron and brought your fathers up out of the land of Egypt. ⁷Now therefore stand still, that I may plead with you before the LORD (and tell you)ᵇ all the saving deeds of the LORD which he performed for you and for your fathers. ⁸When Jacob went into Egypt and your fathers cried to the LORD, the LORD sent Moses and Aaron, who brought forth your fathers out of Egypt, and made them dwell in this place. ᶜ ⁹But they forgot the LORD their God; and he sold them into the hand of Sisera, commander of the army of (Jabin king of) Hazor, and into the hand of the Philistines, and into the hand of the king of Moab; and they fought against them. ¹⁰And they cried to the LORD, and said, "We have sinned, because we have forsaken the LORD, and have served the Baals and the Ashtaroth; but now deliver us out of the hand of our enemies, and we will serve thee." ¹¹And the LORD sent Jerubbaal and Barak,ᵈ and Jepthah, and Samuel, and delivered

ᵃThe words in brackets take the place of the preceding infinitival clause in LXX. Written in Hebrew, they are very like MT and are held to be the original text by most exegetes. This cannot, however, be determined with certainty.

ᵇThe words in brackets are in LXX; so, too, in v. 9 (but not in vv. 14, 21).

ᶜThe versions read: 'he (i.e. Yahweh) made them dwell'; but this will be a later simplification.

ᵈMT *bᵉdān*, so Vulg. The versions offer different alternatives. The word *ʿaḥdān*, the letters of which bear most resemblance to *bᵉdān*, is improbable; 'Deborah' or 'Gideon' would be possible. LXX Barak.

you out of the hand of your enemies on every side; and you dwelt in safety. [12]And when you saw that Nahash the king of the Ammonites came against you, you said to me, "No, but a king shall reign over us", when the LORD your God was your king. [13]And now behold the king whom you have chosen, for whom you have asked; behold, the LORD has set a king over you. [14]If you will fear the LORD and serve him and hearken to his voice and not rebel against the commandment of the LORD, and if both you and the king who reigns over you will follow the LORD your God (it will be well); [15]but if you will not hearken to the voice of the LORD, but rebel against the commandment of the LORD, then the hand of the LORD will be against you and against your king, to destroy you, like[a] your fathers. [16]Now therefore stand still and see this great thing, which the LORD will do before your eyes. [17]Is it not wheat harvest today? I will call upon the LORD, that he may send thunder and rain; and you shall know and see that your wickedness is great, which you have done in the sight of the LORD, in asking for yourselves a king.' [18]So Samuel called upon the LORD, and the LORD sent thunder and rain that day; and all the people greatly feared the LORD and Samuel.

19 And all the people said to Samuel, 'Pray for your servants to the LORD your God, that we may not die; for we have added to all our sins this evil, to ask for ourselves a king.' [20]And Samuel said to the people, 'Fear not; you have done all this evil, yet do not turn aside from following the LORD, but serve the LORD with all your heart; [21]and do not turn aside after vain (gods) which cannot profit or save, for they are vain. [22]For the LORD will not cast away his people, for his great name's sake, because it has pleased the LORD to make you a people for himself. [23]Moreover as for me, far be it from me that I should sin against the LORD by ceasing to pray for you; and I will instruct you in the[b] good and the right way. [24]Only fear the LORD, and serve him faithfully with all your heart; for consider what great things he has done for you. [25]But if you still do wickedly, you shall be swept away, both you and your king.'

This chapter is usually regarded as a direct continuation of the source which appeared in chs. 7 and 8 and also in 10.17–27, displaying, in contrast to 9.1–10.16 and ch. 11, an anti-monarchical tendency. We saw that matters are not quite so simple. There were, however, Mizpah traditions whose attitude was decidedly critical of the institution of the monarchy, from a theocentric position. At the same time, it should be noted that the deuteronomistic final compiler could continue immediately from this point. His procedure

[a]To some extent in accordance with LXX, part of the text which has been omitted through a scribal error has here been replaced to read: *bākem ub^emalk^ekem l^eha'^abīd^ekem ka'^abōtēkem.*
[b]See BH.

was either to reproduce the traditional matter as it stood (so, to some extent, in ch. 10) or to use it as material for an account which was largely his own. Thus the text is sometimes virtually his work. This is the case with ch. 12.

Chapter 12 is a sermon. At least as far as the form is concerned this is strictly true only of vv. 6–15 and 20–25. But this part is the nucleus, and all else is additional. The preacher is Samuel, the audience the people of his time. The real auditors, however, are the Israelites of a much later period, the period in which the compiler was living, the sixth century; we will come back to this later. It is important to notice that the account of the period of the judges begins and ends with a sermon. Judg. 2.6–3.6 is preached history, even if it is not put in direct speech.[a] It is the same with I Sam. 12. It is significant that statements of this nature are made before the work of the first judge and after the work of the last. This is the theological light in which the period of the judges should be seen. Nor should we fail to notice that the former account looks back to Joshua, while the latter gives a preparatory glance at the time of the kings.

[1] The place where Samuel deals with the people is not mentioned. According to the context it is the sanctuary at Gilgal. The serious disputation is, however, incompatible with the joy over the king which occupies the conclusion of ch. 11. The tradition of Samuel's farewell, which is to be included in the complex of Mizpah traditions, was added at this point because it in fact belongs at the end of the events which precede the beginning of the first king's reign. For this reason, the opening section of 8.7 is repeated word for word right at the beginning. Samuel has complied with the voice of the people; that this was done at the Lord's command is not said here, but is made quite clear in a later remark (v. 13). Here, far more stress is laid on the opposition of the people's will to that of the Lord. The attitude of the deuteronomistic theology of history is thus quite clear. From a theological point of view the whole period of the kings was fundamentally a mistake. This will later be demonstrated in still more detail.

[2] First of all, however, we look back to the time of the last judge, who used to have to 'go before' the people, as the king must from now on. The reference fits Samuel particularly well, as he has been in a place of public eminence 'from his youth' right until his old age. His sons are not mentioned with reproach, as in 8.3, but

[a] Cf. ATD 9, p. 162.

S.–D

quite neutrally, to show how long he, their father, has been in office. Samuel is more concerned with the probity of his term of office than with its length. **[3–5]** He is asking for his discharge before the high court of the Lord and of his anointed. The question is raised whether he, as judge, has used force and unjust dealing, a charge levelled, according to 8.3, at his sons. The incorruptibility of the judge, who has exercised his office before God without subterfuge and without favouring private interests, is confirmed in solemn form by the people at Samuel's request. All this is relevant to Samuel and *his* office. In the wider context, however, it is of greater significance. During the period of history now coming to an end, God has chosen honourable men to be his instruments; there may at times have been an unsuitable person among them, like Abimelech, but the prophetic voice is soon heard (Jotham) to show him up, and even more than this, there is the correcting hand of the Lord, who does not let the trees grow right up to heaven. Thus, as the people have expressly testified, care has been taken that in the case of men like Samuel everything has been done in order. This description of the time of the judges differs from that in Judg. 17.6; 19.1; 21.25,[a] according to which every man did what seemed right to him, a state of affairs to which only the time of the kings offered a remedy. The two approaches go along side by side.[b] The former view predominates where the emphasis is more upon God, who intervenes as helper in time of need, calls the judges to be his instruments, and accords them his protection and blessing; the latter is more widespread where we see how men seek to depart from the Lord, to rebel and fall away.

[6–8] Here, then, the former view predominates, particularly now, in what is Samuel's sermon proper. Here, too, the form of a lawsuit is chosen, but now, more clearly than before, Yahweh is the protagonist, whereas earlier Samuel confronted the people. We have a short survey of history, which appears as a history of continuing guidance. This is clear right from the start; it begins with the word 'Yahweh'. He 'made' (the literal Hebrew) Moses and Aaron, who here (as in Josh. 24.5) are mentioned together; in other words, he called them to life and to their office. The Exodus from Egypt, the decisive act of the early history, is expressly mentioned twice. These are real saving works, literally 'manifestations of righteousness' (so

[a]Cf. ATD 9², p. 255.
[b]Ibid., p. 144.

already Judg. 5.11), which can be evidenced from the past. [9–11] From the Exodus, Samuel moves on to the entry into the Promised Land and thus to the time of the judges. The description is couched in terms which often recall the Book of Judges: they 'forget' the Lord, are 'sold' into the hands of foreigners, 'cry' to the Lord, confess their sins and their apostasy to the 'Baals and the Ashtaroth' and are 'delivered'. Some of the oppressors, particularly the enemies of Judg. 3 and 4, are mentioned by name, but in reverse order, as are some, the most important, of the judges. The occurrence of Samuel's name among them is not to be regarded as a slip of the pen (for 'Samson', for example). It reveals rather that the sermon is meant as more than the statement of a certain historical situation. The whole period of the judges *including* the time of Samuel is under review here, under the two aspects mentioned above: the mercy of God, who 'sends' the judge and allows the people to 'dwell in safety', and the ever-recrudescent will of the people to sever themselves from the Lord and follow other gods, in other words to go their own way.

[12] The people's desire for a king is put in this context; it is a new form of the constantly renewed apostasy. The name Saul does not occur in the chapter, but the frequent (vv. 13, 17, 19) occurrence of the word *šā'al*, 'ask for', is surely meant to be an allusion to *šā'ūl*, the 'one who is asked for'. The new sin exceeds all previous sins in so far as the aspiration for a king puts in question the desire and capability of the Lord to bring about deliverance. This is particularly evident in the fact that when a new adversary, Nahash, appears, there follows not the usual, well tested 'cry to Yahweh', but the demand for a king, coupled with a disregard of the true king, Yahweh. Surprisingly, the expedition against Nahash in this context appears to be the occasion for the people's wish for a king; this cannot be read out of either ch. 8 or ch. 11. We may therefore ask whether the deuteronomistic compiler has made a free compilation from the general picture here,[a] or whether an original feature of an older tradition does not underlie the passage. In any case, the demand for a king is meant to demonstrate the attitude of a discontented people, ready for apostasy. It is nevertheless significant that here, in agreement with what has been said earlier, the Lord has 'given' the king to the people at their request. From the mere presence of this note, it is again evident that we do not have simply

[a]Cf. Noth, *Überlieferungsgeschichtliche Studien* I, p. 60.

a consistent reproduction of source-material, but the drawing of a conclusion.

[13–15] Attached to this is a survey of the period of the kings which is now beginning. In spite of the conduct of the people, the Lord has not changed from his steadfastness—as even the note in v. 13 indicates! It is his grace in which people and king will share if he wills to direct his further steps in accordance with what is done on man's side. In themselves, then, things are easy; men need only follow the 'voice' of the Lord, i.e. the commandment, which throughout the whole chapter (see v. 10) is primarily taken as the first commandment. The history of the people of God has to follow the direction of the first commandment. If it does this, all is in order. It is worth remembering how the history of the kings is described from a similar point of view. Except for Hezekiah and Josiah, the kings responsible for reform, all fell short. Had they not done so, and made their conduct conform more closely to the first commandment, the events of 587 would not have taken place. The standpoint of the preacher and his audience accordingly lies in the time after 587. Samuel's sermon reaches a long way over the ages.

[16–19] For in all this it is not forgotten that Samuel is the speaker. The episode of the thunderstorm at the time of the wheat harvest—about our Whitsuntide—may again be part of the material which lay to hand in the Mizpah tradition, along with the report of the account rendered by Samuel. In the normal course of events there is no more 'thunder and rain' after the end of May. Its occurrence is to be regarded as an extraordinary manifestation of Yahweh, especially as it happens as a direct result of Samuel's prayer. The event is reminiscent of 7.10ff. The direct intervention of the Lord drives the people to fear and repentance. [20–25] Otherwise the close of Samuel's sermon brings the admonition, as previously, to follow the Lord 'with all your heart' and not to follow useless gods who are unable to save. God's faithfulness is emphasized, and, as a new element, Samuel's readiness for further intercession and teaching. So things go on. Bad as the matter of the king must seem—in the context of Israel's history as a whole—the possibility of 'deliverance' is still present in it. Samuel will counsel the people as before in the path they are to follow; and after Samuel, we must add, there will be others, prophets and teachers of the law. The Lord, for his part, has made provision. It is now up to the people and the king whether they keep to it.

7. THE BEGINNING OF THE PHILISTINE WAR: 13.1–23

13 [1]Saul was . . . years[a] old when he began to reign; and he reigned two (?)[a] years over Israel. [2]Saul chose three thousand men of Israel; two thousand were with Saul in Michmash and the hill country of Bethel, and a thousand were with Jonathan in Geba[b] of Benjamin; the rest of the people he sent home, every man to his tent. [3]Jonathan defeated the prefect of the Philistines stationed on the hill[c] of God; and the Philistines heard of it and[d] proclaimed, 'The Hebrews[e] have risen!'[f] [4]And Saul blew the trumpet throughout all the land, and all Israel heard it and said, 'Saul has defeated the prefect of the Philistines. Israel also has become odious to the Philistines.' And the people were called out to join Saul at Gilgal.

5 And the Philistines mustered to fight with Israel, three thousand chariots,[g] and six thousand horsemen, and troops like the sand on the sea-shore in multitude; they came up and encamped in Michmash, to the east of Bethaven. [6]When the men of Israel saw that they were in straits,[h] the people hid themselves in caves and in holes[i] and in rocks and in tunnels[j] and in cisterns, [7]and great crowds[k] crossed the Jordan to the land of Gad and Gilead. Saul was still at Gilgal, and all the people followed him trembling.

8 He waited seven days, the time appointed by Samuel;[f] but Samuel did not come to Gilgal, and the people were scattering from him. [9]So Saul said, 'Bring the burnt-offering here to me, and the peace offerings.' And he offered the burnt-offering. [10]As soon as he had finished offering the burnt-offering, behold, Samuel came; and Saul went out to meet him and salute him. [11]Samuel said, 'What have you done?' And Saul said, 'When I saw that the people were scattering from me, and that you did not come within the days appointed, and

[a]See Commentary.

[b]In MT 'Gibeah', as in v. 15. The details of place in vv. 2 and 3 were evidently transposed.

[c]The place is called this according to 10.5, 10, and not Geba as in MT.

[d]The last three words of the verse fit better after *pelištīm* and thus in the mouth of the Philistines. According to MT, Saul would have spread the message round 'Let the Hebrews hear' (or 'let them rise'), but this is not feasible because of the word 'Hebrews'. Saul would have had to say 'Israel'.

[e]LXX reads *'abādīm*, slaves, which is written similarly.

[f]See BH.

[g]So versions; MT 'thirty thousand'.

[h]The words which now follow, '(for the people were hard pressed)', represent a variant reading to the previous 'that'-clause, which has perhaps been formed along the lines of 14.24.

[i]MT 'thorn bushes'; hardly suitable as a permanent hiding-place.

[j]Judg. 9.46, 49. Underground passages and vaults are meant, perhaps even in abandoned settlements.

[k]Read *'am rab*, instead of the surprising 'and Hebrews', which is also not confirmed by LXX.

that the Philistines had mustered in Michmash, [12]I said, "Now the Philistines will come down upon me at Gilgal, and I have not entreated the favour of the LORD"; so I forced myself, and offered the burnt-offering.' [13]And Samuel said to Saul, 'You have done foolishly; you have not kept the commandment of the LORD your God, which he commanded you; for now the LORD would have established your kingdom over Israel for ever. [14]But now your kingdom shall not continue; the LORD has sought out a man after his own heart; and the LORD has appointed him to be prince over his people, because you have not kept what the LORD commanded you.'

15 And Samuel arose, and went up from Gilgal and went his way. And those of the people that remained went up (to the hills) behind Saul, to meet the warriors. And they came from Gilgal[a] to Geba[b] of Benjamin. And when Saul numbered the people who were present with him, there were about six hundred men. [16]And Saul, and Jonathan his son, and the people who were present with them, stayed in Geba of Benjamin; but the Philistines encamped in Michmash. [17]And raiders came out of the camp of the Philistines in three companies; one company turned toward Ophrah, to the land of Shual, [18]another company turned toward Beth-horon, and another company turned toward the height[c] that looks down upon the valley of the hyenas toward the wilderness.

19 Now there was no smith to be found throughout all the land of Israel; for the Philistines said, 'Lest the Hebrews make themselves swords or spears'; [20]but every one of the Israelites went down to the Philistines to sharpen his ploughshare, his share,[d] his axe or his sickle;[e] [21]and the charge was two thirds[f] for the ploughshares and the shares, and a third of a shekel for sharpening[g] the axes and for setting the goads. [22]So on the day of the battle there was neither sword nor spear found in the hand of any of the people with Saul and Jonathan; but Saul and Jonathan his son had them. [23]And the garrison of the Philistines went out to the pass of Michmash.

Saul's real task, and at the same time his fate, was the war against

---

[a]A long section here, which has fallen out of MT by scribal error, is preserved in LXX and Lat.

[b]'Gibeah' is improbable here, as in v. 2, although best attested. In view of v. 16 it is better to read 'Geba'.

[c]MT 'place', LXX 'Geba'. A high-lying locality must be meant.

[d]It is impossible to distinguish between the expressions. Cf. Dalman, *Arbeit und Sitte in Palästina* II, 1932, p. 76.

[e]Doubtful, see BH.

[f]On the meaning of the word see Bewer in *JBL* 61, 1942, pp. 45f. The solution adopted here is better than all previous ones; but the repetition of the introductory *weḥāyetā* is not unsuspicious.

[g]Here, too, the text is to be read according to Bewer: *ušelīš šeqel lāšōn*. The obscure word *qilleśōn* contains the three radicals of the word *šeqel*. LXX points in the same direction.

the Philistines. It was in face of this that he was chosen, here that the triumphs of his life occurred, and here that he finally met his end. If we look deeper, however, it was not his country's enemy which exercised him and was the nucleus of his most pressing dangers, but the mysterious quarter in which the God of Israel dwelt and from which Samuel, as the representative of the Lord, intervened in the fate of people and king. Chapter 13, difficult as individual details may be, makes both these points clear.

[1] At the beginning, we find a note such as is customary in the Books of Kings (I Kings 14.21, etc., and earlier II Sam. 2.10 and 5.4); it stems from the hand of the deuteronomistic compiler. In using the customary formula, this compiler includes Saul in the sequence of kings which now continues without interruption until the destruction of Jerusalem (587). At the same time, however, the numbers given in the sentence deviate from the pattern which is normal later. There is no figure at all in the note of Saul's age. For this there is no evident reason. Presumably the fact that Saul appears first as the (young) son of his father (9.1ff.), then as a leader (11.1ff.) capable of bearing rule (10.17ff.), and even as the father of a son of military age (13.2ff.), led to some uncertainty about his age which resulted in the note being left open. The number 30, given by the Greek minuscules, is a conjecture, but may well be approximately correct. A number 'two' is given as the length of his reign, but in so unusual a form—in Hebrew 'two years' is usually *š^enātayim*—that it cannot be original. The number is given because it was the later view that Saul was actually 'king' for only quite a short time (cf. also on 15.1). In fact, the number 40, which is given both in Josephus[a] and in Acts 13.21 as the length of Saul's reign, may originally have stood here;[b] as has been said, it would have been replaced by the figure two on dogmatic-historical grounds.

[2] The note about the military side of Saul's monarchy at the beginning of the account proper of his reign is a correct recognition that this formed the basis of his rule. His was a definite military kingship,[c] which arose in view of the Philistine situation.[d] The force

[a]*Antiquitates* 6.14.9 divides the reign into 18 years before and 22 years after the death of Samuel; in *Ant.* 10.8.4, however, the number 20 occurs.

[b]The plural *šānīm* need not tell against this (so Noth, *Überlieferungsgeschichtliche Studien* I, p. 25). Cf. GK § 134e.

[c]A. Alt, *Staatenbildung*, p. 37, *Kleine Schriften* II, p. 30.

[d]*Staatenbildung*, p. 34; *Kl. Schr.*, p. 27; G. von Rad, *Der Heilige Krieg im alten Israel*, 1952, p. 34.

numbering 3,000 men was chosen on grounds of suitability (cf. 14.52); the implication is that the recruitment took place in connection with the Ammonite war. This was an organic development, as the levy was an old institution (cf. v. 2b)—an important psychological factor for Israel. We have here, then, the beginning of a standing army. The neighbourhood in which Saul exercised his troops was the territory north of Gibeah of Benjamin, right up to Bethel. A part was stationed south, but the majority north of the deep *wadi eṣ-ṣwenit*. For the first time Saul's brave and noble son Jonathan appears, though he is introduced not specially as being Saul's son,[a] but first as the leader of the smaller of the two detachments, [3] and principally as the initiator of the Philistine War: he defeats the prefect of the Philistines[b] on the hill of God. Hitherto the Philistines had evidently not troubled themselves over the new events in Israel. Perhaps the disarming of the Israelites—described later—may have seemed sufficient protection, perhaps the dispute between Israel and Ammon may have appeared even desirable as a means of weakening both sides, but only now does the word go out that the 'Hebrews' are in revolt. The LXX reading 'slaves' here rightly stresses that the new events seem no more than a slave revolt to the Philistines. [4] The Philistine verdict on Israel's military capability is vividly attested by the echo aroused by Jonathan's deed, which, significantly described as Saul's deed, goes round like wildfire, and by Saul's call to the people to join the host. We hardly gain the impression that this is seen as a torch for freedom; the disruption of the existing situation is rather viewed with displeasure. This is, in fact, always the case, as in the time of the fleshpots of Egypt (Ex. 16.3) and the searchings of heart at the brooks of Reuben (Judg. 5.16 RV).[c] The chapter is hardly a paean to the warlike spirit of the people of Israel.

[5–7a] Still, that is understandable, as the military supremacy of the Philistines is evident. First, mention is made of the terrible chariots, in the face of which Israel had for long been completely powerless; the number of 'horsemen' works out at two men to each chariot. For hill-fighting, however, the infantry—said to be extremely

[a]Perhaps the word *bᵉnō*, 'his son', has fallen out; it occurs in v. 16 and v. 22. On 'Geba' instead of 'Gibeah' as in the MT, see above.

[b]Cf. the note on 10.5.

[c]The 'also' in the Israelite saying could refer to a second hostile event, perhaps the formation of Saul's guard.

numerous—is of far greater importance. Here the Philistine strategy is more one of terror. It is tacitly assumed that Saul has now given up the territory north of the *wadi eṣ-ṣwenit*, so that Michmash (the modern *mukhmas*, directly north of the *wadi*) is now in the hands of the Philistines and is the centre of their operations.[a] The Philistine tactics bear their expected fruit. There is a mass flight of the Israelite population which makes full use of the countless possibilities afforded both by the east slopes of the hills, little inhabited and rich in caves, and by the nearby territory to the east of the Jordan.

[**7b**] In this context the episode at Gilgal begins;[b] it is described by Gressmann as 'thoroughly improbable'. It is, in fact, curious, and represents the chief difficulty of the chapter. Its content, sometimes described as 'the rejection of Saul', is not presupposed in the later course of events; all would, in fact, be simpler were there no account of a stay of Saul in Gilgal. Accordingly the section is often deleted as an insertion. This does not, however, make matters any easier.

There would be no objection to Saul's journey to Gilgal in itself, in the context of the other events. In v. 4b the summoning of the host is expressly said to take place at Gilgal, and this is quite understandable. In the conditions then prevailing, Mizpah and Bethel were completely out of the question as meeting places. Moreover, even in 10.8—presuming the verse in fact belongs in that context— Gilgal is named as the starting-point for the acts imposed on Saul. The idea is evidently that Jonathan should remain in position at Geba with his men, while Saul gathers reinforcements in the Jordan plain.

[**8–15a**] But the real difficulty lies in the events centred on Samuel. Saul waits for seven days, as he was bidden, and then himself offers the 'burnt-offering'; the 'peace offerings' are not mentioned after v. 9. Samuel comes when all is finished, accuses Saul of disobedience, declares that Saul's kingdom will not continue and that the Lord has sought out someone else—clearly David— and departs. Saul, on the other hand, justifies his conduct in a modest and at all points irrefutable way. From the description of the affair we seem to have a vindication of Saul rather than a charge against him. Saul has done what was permissible for him to do according to Samuel's express instructions, indeed what he had to

[a]The note 'to the east of Beth-Aven' is meant to describe the site of the camp. The writer, acquainted with the locality, knew the exact place.

[b]On its location, see Commentary on 11.14.

do as commander-in-chief, especially in view of the dwindling of his manpower. If anyone is in the wrong here it is Samuel, and not Saul. But if we look at the history of Saul as a whole, the contrary is intended. The compiler of the work means to convey here what is elsewhere expressed in connection with sentences like v. 1: the king 'did what was evil in the sight of the Lord'. It is his purpose to show that Saul's kingship was perverted right from the beginning; the first king trod a path with which the Lord was not pleased. This theological verdict is made on the strength of the Gilgal episode, and is put before the period of Saul's reign like a clef on a music stave. This is fully in accord with what we felt able to detect earlier in v. 1. Saul's trespass, always in relationship with the general picture of him, could then consist in the fact that he did not act in obedience to the letter, had no patience, i.e. no faith, and allowed the disturbing situation to be the most important factor in his decision. Thus we have here a manifest contradiction between the proper content of the material used and the purpose for which the compiler wanted to use it. The account itself could originally derive even from a group standing close to Saul and well disposed towards him.

In making an historical assessment, it should first be noted that there is a similar scene later, in ch. 15. That is, the dispute between Samuel and Saul at the Gilgal sanctuary has been transmitted twice, but one tradition connects it with the Philistine war and the other with the expedition against the Amalekites. The sanctuary is the same; it was there that the event was narrated, and doubtless too people pointed to the place at which it had happened. But Saul's 'rejection' really only comes about in the second episode. The argument in ch. 13 is not as sharp as that in ch. 15; indeed in this chapter we do not really have the rejection of Saul, but a declaration that his kingdom is not established and will not continue. He still therefore remains king, even though the eyes of the Lord are already looking farther afield, to his successor. Nevertheless, we are concerned with the same event, which is meant to describe the separation of Samuel and Saul. Historically, it happened that the king had differences with the man of God—who was, moreover, the last judge—differences which stemmed from the fact 'that the relationship between the king's sacral and secular functions was ill-defined, and the secular requirements of the monarchy conflicted with the ancient sacral traditions'.[a] The most important thing is, of course, this: from all

---

[a]Noth, *The History of Israel*, ET², pp. 175–6.

we learn of him, Saul is a man in whom the element of faith plays a predominant, even terrifying part. He crossed Yahweh, his will, and even his representatives. The king anointed by the Lord and chosen by lot is shattered—on the Lord. It seems as though the compiler of the work saw something of this. The insertion of the Gilgal episode into this chapter corresponds with this historical reality. From this point onwards, the reader sees the dark destiny over the head of the first king.

[15b–16] Saul's unexpectedly long stay in Gilgal has doubtless damaged the Israelite cause in other respects. The number of men willing to fight, in any case greatly lessened through fear of the Philistines, is further diminished, so that when Saul goes up into the hills he has only 600 men left with him. This is thought to include the troops of 'warriors' (v. 15), doubtless the force stationed at Geba under Jonathan (cf. 14.2). Thus the military situation is that the *wadi eṣ-ṣwenit* represents the boundary between the opposing sides; Geba and Michmash are the places immediately adjacent, to the north and to the south. The deep valley offers such good protection to both sides that Saul can venture his expedition to Gilgal just as the Philistines send out raiders into the countryside. [17-18] These plundering actions extend to the north, west and east (the south, being occupied by the Israelites, is excluded), and are meant, it is said, to increase the general fear and thus indirectly to damage the Israelite cause.

[19–22] At this point we are given, very appropriately, a picture of the general situation, and learn that the Philistines have disarmed the Israelites of all weapons, to such an extent that not even their iron agricultural implements can be repaired and put in order by their own smiths. Similar actions are also known elsewhere in history. 'This general rule was, of course, never in force over a long period.'[a] King and crown prince are expressly excluded from the general lack of weapons.

[23] The chapter ends with the report of a Philistine measure which is probably connected with their plundering forays. To guard the camp, greatly weakened in this way, an outpost is sent right to the bank of the wadi. We are thus well prepared for the next chapter. In general, the accounts in ch. 13 stand close in time to the events which they describe and are well acquainted with the locality. These accounts derive from someone who was close to the events in every respect, even to the king and his action, and are thus of special value.

[a]Gressmann, p. 52.

No less important, however, is the way in which these events are put in the light of the guidance of God, who always has a hand in what happens to the people of God.

8. THE PHILISTINES ARE DEFEATED: 14.1–46

14 [1]One day Jonathan the son of Saul said to the young man who bore his armour, 'Come, let us go over to the Philistine garrison on yonder side.' But he did not tell his father. [2]Saul was staying in the outskirts of Geba[a] under the pomegranate tree which is at Migron; the people who were with him were about six hundred men, [3]and Ahijah the son of Ahitub, Ichabod's brother, son of Phinehas, son of Eli, the priest of the LORD in Shiloh, wore the ephod.[b] And the people did not know that Jonathan had gone. [4]Between the passes by which Jonathan sought to go over to the Philistine garrison, there was a rocky crag on the one side and a rocky crag on the other side; the name of the one was Bozez, and the name of the other Seneh.[c] [5]The one crag rose on the north in front of Michmash, and the other on the south in front of Geba.

6 And Jonathan said to the young man who bore his armour, 'Come, let us go over to the garrison of these uncircumcised; it may be that the LORD will work for us; for nothing can hinder the LORD from saving by many or by few.' [7]And his armour-bearer said to him, 'Do all that is in your mind and make the expedition.[d] I am with you; as is your mind so is mine.'[e] [8]Then said Jonathan, 'Behold, when we cross over to the men,[f] we will show ourselves to them. [9]If they say to us, "Wait until we come to you," then we will stand still in our place and we will not go up to them. [10]But if they say, "Come up to us," then we will go up; for the LORD has given them into our hand. And this shall be the sign to us.' [11]So both of them showed themselves to the garrison of the Philistines; and the Philistines said, 'Look, Hebrews are coming out of the holes where they have hid themselves.' [12]And the men of the garrison hailed Jonathan and his armour-bearer, and said, 'Come up to us, and we will show you a thing.' And Jonathan said to his armour-bearer, 'Come up after me, for the LORD has given them into the hand of Israel.' [13]Then Jonathan climbed up on his hands and feet and his armour-bearer after him. And they fell before

---

[a]This is surely to be read in place of Gibeah. See Alt in *PJB* 23, 1927, pp. 18–20; his proposed identification of Migron with the present *tell miryam* is certainly to be adopted.

[b]Ichabod (as indeed the whole genealogy) is mentioned to show the link with 4.19ff.

[c]On the locality cf. Dalman, *PJB* 7, 1911, pp. 11f. Abel, *Géographie de la Palestine* II, 1938, p. 328, differs.

[d]The construction of this largely misunderstood saying is as at II Sam. 2.21.

[e]Preserved in LXX.

[f]This is expressed by a participle in the Hebrew.

Jonathan,^a and his armour-bearer killed them after him; ¹⁴and that first slaughter, which Jonathan and his armour-bearer made, was of about twenty men within as it were half a furrow's length in a yoke of land.^b ¹⁵And there was a panic in the camp and among all the people in the field;^c the garrison and even the raiders trembled; the earth quaked; and it became a very great panic.

16 And the watchmen of Saul in Geba^d of Benjamin looked; and behold, the multitude was surging hither and thither. ¹⁷Then Saul said to the people who were with him, 'Number and see who has gone from us.' And when they had numbered, behold, Jonathan and his armour-bearer were not there. ¹⁸And Saul said to Ahijah, 'Bring hither the ark of God.' For the ark of God was on that day with^d the people of Israel.^e ¹⁹And while Saul was still^f talking to the priest, the tumult in the camp of the Philistines increased more and more; and Saul said to the priest, 'Withdraw your hand.' ²⁰Then Saul and all the people who were with him uttered a cry^g and went into the battle; and behold, every man's sword was against his fellow, and there was very great confusion. ²¹Now the Hebrews who had been with the Philistines before that time and who had gone up with them into the camp, even they also turned^d to be with the Israelites who were with Saul and Jonathan. ²²Likewise, when the men of Israel who had hid themselves in the hill country of Ephraim heard that the Philistines were fleeing, they, too, followed hard after them in the battle. ²³So the Lord delivered Israel that day; and the battle passed beyond Beth-aven.^h

24 And the men of Israel were distressed that day;ⁱ for Saul laid an oath^d upon the people, saying, 'Cursed be the man who eats anything^j until it is evening and I am avenged on my enemies.' So none of the people tasted anything. ²⁵Now the whole land had an abundance of^k

---

^aLXX perhaps: 'hardly had they seen Jonathan than he struck them.'

^bThe text, largely incomprehensible in both ancient and modern versions, is meant to show the extent of the area within which the 'slaughter' took place. See Dalman, *Arbeit und Sitte* II, 1932, pp. 49f., 171.

^cThe words *ūbᵉkol-hā-ʿām* and the preceding *bassāde* are better transposed.

^dSee BH.

^eLXX reads: 'Bring the ephod here! For he wore the ephod on that day before Israel.' See Commentary.

^fRead *ʿōd mᵉdabbēr*.

^gTo be pointed as qal.

^hThe reading 'Beth-horon' (more than nine miles from Michmash) attested by ancient MSS in place of the (nearer) Beth-aven takes in the whole of the battlefield; the nearer place is, however, more appropriate, as Saul's oath fits better at the point when the pursuit begins.

ⁱThe *niggaš* of BH³ is a misprint for *niggas*. Instead of this sentence, LXX has a longer text, which contains the useful point that the battle 'stretched out over all the hill country of Ephraim', but is otherwise unskilful.

^jThe text has 'bread'; it is used quite generally to mean 'food'.

^kMT 'come in' (*bāʾū ba*); the evidently corrupt word, not even understood in LXX (*erista*, 'breakfasted'), could have read *mālᵉʾū*, better *zābū* or *zūbū*, 'flowing in', which is frequently associated with *dᵉbaš* 'honey'.

honeycombs, so that there was honey in the open field.ᵃ ²⁶And when
the people came to the honeycombs, where the honey was there to
see,ᵇ no man put his handᶜ to his mouth; for the people feared the
oath. ²⁷But Jonathan had not heard his father charge the people with
the oath; so he put forth the tip of the staff that was in his hand, and
dipped it in the honeycomb, and put his hand to his mouth; and his
eyes became bright. ²⁸Then one of the people said, 'Your father
strictly charged the people with a holyᵈ oath, saying, "Cursed be the man
who eats anythingᵉ this day." And so the people are faint.' ²⁹Then
Jonathan said, 'My father has troubled the land; see how my eyes
have become bright, because I tasted a little of this honey. ³⁰How much
better if the people had eaten freely today of the spoil of their enemies
which they found; for now the slaughter among the Philistines has not
been great.'

31 They struck down the Philistines that day from Michmash to
Aijalon. And the people were very faint. ³²So the people flew upon the
spoil, and took sheep and oxen and calves, and slew them on the
ground; and the people ate on the blood.ᶠ ³³Then they told Saul,
'Behold, the people are sinning against the LORD, by eating on the
blood.' And he said, 'You have dealt treacherously; roll a great stone
to me here.' ³⁴And Saul said, 'Disperse yourselves among the people,
and say to them, "Let every man bring his ox or his sheep, and slay
them here, and eat; and do not sin against the LORD by eating on the
blood." ' So every one of the people brought with him that night what
he hadᶜ and they slew them there. ³⁵And Saul built an altar to the
LORD; it was the first altar that he built to the LORD.

36 Then Saul said, 'Let us go down after the Philistines this nightᶜ
and plunder among themᵍ until the morning light; let us not leave a
man of them.' And they said, 'Do whatever seems good to you.' Then
he said to the priest,ʰ 'Let us draw near hither to God.' ³⁷And Saul
inquired of God, 'Shall I go down after the Philistines? Wilt thou give
them into the hand of Israel?' But he did not answer him that day.
³⁸And Saul said, 'Come hither, all headsⁱ of the people; and know and
see how this sin has arisen today. ³⁹For as the LORD lives who saves
Israel, though it be in Jonathan my son, he shall surely die.' But there
was not a man among all the people that answered him. ⁴⁰Then he
said to all Israel, 'You shall be on one side, and I and Jonathan my
son will be on the other side.' And the people said to Saul, 'Do what

ᵃ'On the surface of the field.'
ᵇLit.: 'And behold, a flowing of honey'; ḥēlek is to be interpreted like hālak
in Josh. 4.18.
ᶜSee BH.
ᵈMT: infin. absol.
ᵉSee note ʲ, p. 109.
ᶠOn the place where the blood had run on to the earth. Cf. Commentary.
ᵍThe expression is surprising, but well attested.
ʰSee BH and Commentary.
ⁱLit. 'pinnacles' as Judg. 20.2.

seems good to you.' [41]Therefore Saul said to the LORD: 'God of Israel,[a] give a right judgment.' And Jonathan and Saul were taken, but the people escaped. [42]Then Saul said, 'Cast the lot between me and my son Jonathan.' And Jonathan was taken.

43 Then Saul said to Jonathan, 'Tell me what you have done.' And Jonathan told him, 'I tasted a little honey with the tip of the staff that was in my hand; here I am, I will die.' [44]And Saul said, 'God do so to me[b] and more also; you shall surely die, Jonathan.' [45]Then the people said to Saul, 'Shall Jonathan die, who has wrought this great victory in Israel? Far from it! As the LORD lives, there shall not one hair of his head fall to the ground; for he has wrought with God this day.' So the people ransomed Jonathan, that he did not die. [46]Then Saul went up from pursuing the Philistines; and the Philistines went to their own place.

In spite of a difficult text, this chapter makes complete sense and is written in an uncommonly vivid way. Everywhere it is again evident that the original writer knew the locality well and stands near to the time when the events took place.[c] The account represents an important part of the Saul tradition, which is not extensive and sometimes stands in an unfavourable light.

[1–3] We have already mentioned the *wadi es-swenit*, on whose two high-lying banks the opposing sides had encamped. The Philistines in particular felt themselves quite secure because of their forward outpost, though Saul held a good key position in Migron, which is in the territory of Geba. From there it was quite easy to go along the road to Michmash, as they found out later. On the other hand, Jonathan could not have put his bold plan, certainly not sanctioned by his father, into operation here, as this route was, of course, under constant surveillance from both sides; we are given the general impression that this is not a well-considered plan of Jonathan's, but a sudden idea. Saul is sitting in the shade of a pomegranate tree, certainly an identifiable tree later pointed out by those who knew the place as Saul's tree. Pomegranate trees (Arabic *rumman*, Hebrew *rimmōn*) are often found in Palestine even today. They are imposing, and dominate the landscape. The mention of the priest prepares

[a]In the LXX there is the following extended version, which was earlier generally preferred: 'Why hast thou not answered thy servant this day? If this guilt is in me or in Jonathan my son, O LORD, God of Israel, give Urim; but if this guilt is in thy people Israel, give Thummim.' (See RSV. Tr.)

[b]See BH.

[c]Those who handed the text down were not informed to the same extent. Otherwise the confusion between Gibeah and Geba (v. 2) could not have occurred.

for the role which the holy lot is later to play in the narrative; anyone who 'bears the ephod' is *ipso facto* characterized as a priest (see 2.18). The mention of the priest's ancestry is meant to stress the fact that Ahijah (who is identical with Ahimelech, I. 22) belongs to the priestly family of Eli; the unusual mention of his brother Ichabod is meant to provide some connection with 4.19.

[4–6] Jonathan's surprise attack, as is stressed twice, is undertaken at his own responsibility; it is the purpose of this element, as of the whole chapter, to show that the victory of Saul (and of Israel) is properly the victory of Jonathan, whose impulsive attack was as early as 13.3 given as the occasion for the beginning of the Philistine war. At the same time, however, we are left in no doubt that the Lord himself is standing in the background and shaping events. First, we have a description of the impassable landscape with its high rock-formations, two particularly striking features of which are known by name (the 'slippery one' and the 'thorny one'). As far as the approach and the attack are concerned, the whole undertaking is either madness or faith. Who could cross country like this? And even if that were successfully accomplished, who could carry out an attack with two men on an enemy ten or a hundred times superior? The answer to such questions is the saying that the Lord finds no difficulty in helping with many or with few. Thus, too, it is stressed that Jonathan appears as instrument in an event which is really accomplished by God himself. The usual description of the Philistines as the uncircumcised is at the same time meant as an indication that this war is not an expedition like any other, but 'a crusade, a holy war' (T. Körner).

[7] In contrast, the armour-bearer—intentionally?—lacks any 'sacral' characteristics; he is a faithful servant to his master, with every inclination to 'show off', but brave and ready, a true picture of the good oriental servant. [8–15] It again accords with Jonathan's —and the narrator's—manner that what now follows is represented not as a foolhardy risk, but as obedience to a declared judgment of God. The Philistines' shout that the two may come up to them is to serve as a sign from the Lord. And so events turn out; the Philistines, sure of their superiority, make mock of the 'Hebrews' who have crept out of their 'holes'. Their invitation to climb up is sarcastic, as they take such an attempt to be impossible, especially in view of the terrain. But by them the Lord has proclaimed his will. The two climb down into the wadi, thus disappearing from the view of the

enemy watchmen, and, still unseen, climb up again on the other
side. The precipitousness of the terrain, described most vividly, while
making the enterprise more difficult, in fact makes it possible. The
surprise is complete. It is not clear whether the men in the outpost
fall to the ground in fear or are wounded; in any case, the armour-
bearer gives them the *coup de grâce*. The number of dead is given as
twenty, and the scene of the battle is accurately described; a definite
field, known for its size, would certainly have been called 'the
field of Jonathan' or something similar at a later date. We are not
told whether the event becomes more widely known through indivi-
duals who escape or through the noise of battle which penetrates
throughout the Philistine camp. The news goes round like the wind.
Even detachments outside the camp hear it; the 'panic' fear grips
them all: it really is the 'fear of God'. The Lord himself intervenes, as
in the slaughter brought about by Deborah, the battle in the valley of
Aijalon, and as earlier at the Red Sea.

[16–18] There is a striking and vivid description of how the
Israelite battle-force, too, is now drawn into Jonathan's surprise
attack. The site of the enemy camp can be seen from the neighbourhood of Geba, and the noise which comes from it is clearly audible.
Thereupon Saul, who partly guesses what is up, investigates who is
missing, and, in view of the new situation and the decisions which
must necessarily be taken, begins to inquire of the holy oracle. MT
reports that the ark was at that time with Saul's troops and that
Saul ordered it to be brought. LXX, on the other hand, mentions
the 'ephod', as Ahijah wore the ephod. This could mean something
different from v. 3, which apparently refers only to a priestly
garment, while in LXX, v. 18, the ephod should have something to
do with the oracle. The difference between MT and LXX is usually
(Wellhausen, Schulz, etc.) understood as follows: the tradition did
not favour the ephod as a means of obtaining an oracle—perhaps
because of Judg. 8.26f. and 17.1ff.—and so the legitimate ark was
mentioned instead; thus LXX has preserved the original text,
especially as the ark was in distant Kiriath-jearim, and is not mentioned between I. 6 and II. 6. But the matter can be seen from the
opposite point of view. As it was generally known that the ark was
restored to favour only by David, the LXX could have altered the
text or preferred a tradition which spoke, not of the ark, but of the
ephod. We may do no more here than assume that there were two
traditions current. The most difficult reading in the general context

is that of the MT; it is quite remarkable that it has been preserved at all, and this fact should at least tell against its being discarded too hastily.

[19–23] Saul does not, however, get as far as finding out God's will, as the increasing uproar on the other side of the valley demands immediate intervention. The sacred action had, in fact, already begun; the priest had stretched out his hand to take the lot, but he is next told to withdraw it. Saul's next move is not expressly reported, but he will now have crossed the wadi, shallower at this point and thus more easily fordable, at a rapid march. He finds the Philistines in complete confusion, especially as their Israelite partisans now strengthen their compatriots' attack, and even the men who had hidden reappear. The confusion among the Philistines is, of course, a consequence of the 'fear of God'. Express mention of the help of the Lord is made intentionally. The word *yāša'* used here is the usual expression for the classic act of deliverance; it is applied, for example, to the acts of the judges and makes the present action appear as a saving work.

[24] The seriousness with which Saul in particular regarded the battle now emerges from the oath which he had laid upon his people, probably right at the beginning of the battle (see the remarks above on v. 23). K. Budde will be right in associating this step with the enforced omission of the inquiry of the oracle. It becomes more and more clear how earnestly Saul takes his relations with God. By reading 'And Saul did a great folly on that day', LXX, while appropriating Jonathan's later verdict, misunderstands Saul's concern. Perhaps the reading arose because the text was unclear at just this place. According to MT, it seems that the occasion for Saul's oath lay in the fact that the Israelites—in the ensuing pursuit or because of growing resistance on the part of the enemy—ran into difficulties, a feature which is so surprising that it can hardly have been invented. Saul therefore lays upon himself and his warriors a fast until sundown,[a] so rendering Israel in an emphatic way the war troop of Yahweh. The reference to his, Saul's, 'vengeance' is not, of course, meant to make the battle seem a private concern of the king's. It is tragic that the king's decision, meant in all seriousness, has the opposite effect; tactically it was a mistake. Not only the LXX reading mentioned above, but also the MT, regards Saul's

[a]This is still present practice in the Mohammedan fast month of Ramadan.

conduct as hasty, even foolish. For people who may neither eat nor drink are, of course, hampered in their capacity for action.

[25-26] Here there occurs an episode which is important for the further course of events. The background to it is the richness of the country in wild bees' honey, a fact also attested elsewhere. It was such that the incoming Israelites said that it 'overflowed with milk and honey'.[a] There was evidently a particularly rich supply of honey just in the region of this battle. The text (in v. 26) is put in such a way that we are meant to see how the men's mouths water as they notice the gleam of the honey. But the oath which has been laid on them is stronger than their physical desire. [27-30] Jonathan, who knows nothing of the oath, takes advantage of the inviting nourishment as he passes by, and it is twice emphasized what an immediate effect this has. It is only a man from the troop who points out to him that all are under an oath and shows him the adverse consequences it has had for them.[b] This is expressly confirmed by Jonathan. He is right. Saul's oath has 'troubled the land', for it is now impossible to make such full use of the victory as would otherwise have been possible. The original writer may have been conscious that it was a tragedy that Saul and his measures were viewed thus. The final compiler thought otherwise, as his verdict on Saul was completely negative.

[31-32] Nevertheless, Saul had already gained a far-reaching victory. The distance to Aijalon as the crow flies is over fifteen miles. Aijalon lies at a point where the hills give way to plain, so that the hill country may be considered to have been cleared of the Philistines. In the meanwhile, we must suppose, evening has fallen; the terminus of the oath has thus been reached, and now everyone falls on the plundered beasts which are supposed to have been brought from the Philistine camp.[c] In so doing, the hungry people neglect the cultic regulations, so that Jonathan's earlier remark is proved justified in yet another sense. Their conduct is not as serious as exegetes usually suppose. It is not that the men had eaten the flesh

[a]Perhaps the word *zūb*, overflow, similarly stood here originally (see on v. 25).

[b]Verse 28b is usually not taken as part of the soldier's remarks, but like v. 31b is regarded as a general expression. This, however, would 'pointlessly anticipate' (Budde) the latter verse, so that it is usually either deleted or amended. It is simpler to understand it as above; the soldier feels just as Jonathan does.

[c]Hence Gressmann concludes that the battlefield was much smaller than the text suggests. On the other hand, this day had cleared the hill country of Philistine rule, so the details will be right. Cf. also the words 'go down' and 'went up' in vv. 36 and 46.

'with' its blood—that would have to be b^e and not '*al*, cf. Gen. 9.4—but that they prepared the meal 'on' the blood. The blood did not go, as we are to see later, to the place that belonged to Yahweh, and thus the spatial and, as a result, the actual separation between God's due and man's due was lacking.[a] **[33–35]** Saul's seriousness in all his dealings with the Lord is again clear from the way in which, when he learns what is happening, he intervenes, and, as in 6.14, appoints a stone for sacral slaughtering. The 'first altar', which he then erects, presumably by incorporating the stone into some structure, was almost certainly pointed out for a long time at the place where it stood (in Aijalon) as 'Saul's altar'.

[36] After the probably lengthy stay and the strengthening of the people, Saul means to go 'down' from the place, which is to be imagined as in the hill country, and pursue the Philistines. The mention of 'spoil' might be meant as incitement for the men. They are in agreement, but first the priest, according to the words of the MT, requires the divine authorization. This is an extraordinary piece of interference, 'and in no one's case does it seem more superfluous that he should be prompted in his devotion to Yahweh than in Saul's' (Budde *ad loc.*). The initiative must rather have stemmed from Saul, and not from the priest.[b] But in that case, what now transpires seems fraught with unusual tragedy. Had he not been detained by the events which now follow, Saul could have recovered much more. His honest, yet anxious, concern to be on a right footing with the Lord is a practical hindrance to his exploiting the victory to the full. The present form of the text, according to which the priest, apparently against Saul's will, insists on an inquiry being made of Yahweh, of course makes it appear that the Lord's verdict is already fixed, in agreement with ch. 13. The original writer had a different, more equitable attitude to the figure of Saul than the final compiler.

[37–44] Saul's question to the Lord, i.e. to the oracle served by

---

[a]Cf. also Budde and Schulz *ad loc.* The method of slaughter here adopted by the people is itself a profane slaughtering, as is expressly allowed in the Deuteronomic law (Deut. 12.15ff.). So the Deuteronomists need not have disapproved of it. Presumably they already misunderstood the passage in the same way as later exegetes. There is a similar commandment in Lev. 19.26.

[b]In addition, if Saul is speaking, the word 'hither', hardly comprehensible in the mouth of the priest, is immediately understandable; the priest is, of course, thought of as being present at sacrifices. As far as the text is concerned, it is quite sufficient to assume that originally *lakkōhēn* stood in place of *hakkōhēn*.

Ahijah, remains unanswered. God is silent.[a] The only possible interpretation of this is that someone has provoked the wrath of God.
The deep seriousness with which Saul is inspired emerges very clearly
from his inclusion of his own person in the procedure of the sacral
investigation. The question to the oracle is again in the form of an
alternative: the people or the king's house? The answer is, 'Not the
people'; their precipitous and ritually objectionable conduct in
slaying the animals has thus been put right in Yahweh's eyes. And
now: Saul or Jonathan? The lot falls on Jonathan, who now, through
the information given him by the soldiers, knows that the trouble
is his tasting of the honey, which is a transgression against the oath.
The way in which he acknowledges his guilt shows that he does not
consider his conduct to have been so serious. The people, too, who
first of all (v. 39) had not answered Saul a word and later (v. 40)
had replied very briefly,[b] view the matter completely differently
from the king, whose deadly seriousness in the situation has something even piteous about it. He is ready and prepared to give up
both himself and his son to the will of God. The action is described
with the utmost brevity. Only the absolute essentials are given, so
that there is an uncanny tension about the nocturnal proceedings.
In v. 42 LXX has expanded the narrative and records the people's
objection, carefully announced before the lot is finally given. The
people mean to lose neither Saul nor Jonathan. But Saul, so this
insertion says, has his own way. Not that he can have his own way
when the lot has declared Jonathan liable to death. **[45–46]** Here
the *vox populi* stands over against the *vox Dei*, but in such a way that
the victory, which is really Jonathan's victory, is regarded as
confirmation that God does not wish the death of the king's son.
The very word $y^e \check{s} \hat{u}^c \hat{a}$ = saving deed, used here by the people, again
testifies that the success of the day is one of God's saving acts. 'With
God', Jonathan has won his victory over the uncircumcised. How
could it be God's will for him to die? Here, then, there is more than
sympathy for the beloved young warrior. One manifestation of the
will of God stands over against another. So it comes about that
Jonathan is ransomed. It must be regarded as improbable that a
special procedure lies behind the brief description, a procedure

[a]Technically speaking, it seems that neither the 'no' lot nor the 'yes' lot appeared.
[b]The answer 'Do what seems good to you' is truly oriental. The Arab today
would say his *ṭaiyib* (good) in just the same way when he thought otherwise. A
biblical instance of this is Hezekiah's answer in Isa. 39.8a.

whereby another man is accepted as ransom for Jonathan and is put to death, as has been inferred from the use of the word *pādā* (= redeem), from Ewald onwards. For in that case expiation would have been made, and the action against the Philistines could have gone on. The actual state of affairs is shown by the way in which Saul breaks off the battle, goes 'up' once more and allows the Philistines to return home without pursuit. On the one hand the king cannot completely disregard the arguments of the people; he, too, must concede that the Lord was 'with' Jonathan. But in Saul's eyes this does not bring a solution to the question of the Lord's reply. So the day ends with a success which is no victory, and in Saul's case with the uncertainty about whether the Lord is satisfied or not. Saul could have dealt with the Philistines; he has not been able to deal with the Lord—and so he cannot deal with the Philistines either.

Difficult questions thus stand behind this many-sided chapter. The gloomy man, who constantly strives after God's will, is overshadowed by the constant worry whether he is now really king by the grace of God. God chose him, the people gave their approval, God gave his help. Saul is not a king like Abimelech, in whom all this was lacking and who therefore came to ruin; Saul is a pious man. *But is he the man after God's heart?* The history of Saul is overshadowed by this dark question. Knowing how events turn out, the final compiler says, 'He is not.' The ancient report was of a different opinion. But Saul stands right between the two, and as we now have the text, this bitter uncertainty appears disturbingly clearly.

9. REMARKS ON SAUL'S KINGSHIP: 14.47–52

14 [47]When Saul had taken the kingship over Israel, he fought against all his enemies on every side, against Moab, against the Ammonites, against Edom, against the kings of Zobah, and against the Philistines; wherever he turned he did saving acts.[a] [48]And he did valiantly, and smote the Amalekites,[b] and delivered Israel out of the hands of those who plundered them.[c]

49 Now the sons of Saul were Jonathan, Ishyo[d] and Malchishua;

[a]With Schulz, read *yōšiʿa* for *yaršiʿa*. Cf. Commentary.

[b]The phrase 'and smote the Amalekites' is perhaps an addition, because of ch. 15.

[c]*šōsēhū* really means 'his plunderer', but will be a defective form of *šōsēyhū* (plural).

[d]See Commentary.

and the names of his two daughters were these: the name of the first-born was Merab, and the name of the younger Michal; [50]and the name of Saul's wife was Ahinoam the daughter of Ahimaaz. And the name of the commander of his army was Abiner the son of Ner, Saul's uncle; [51]Kish, the father of Saul, and Ner the father of Abner were sons[a] of Abiel.

52 There was hard fighting against the Philistines all the days of Saul, and when Saul saw any strong man, or any valiant man, he attached him to himself.

[47–48] These notes are of considerable significance for our knowledge of Saul's ability and personality, though whether this verdict applies to the first remarks is sometimes disputed. Here Saul is described as a man who was constantly engaged in wars with neighbouring peoples. As three of these peoples, Ammon, the Philistines, and Amalek, are also known to the other, more detailed, material as opponents of Saul, the observations made here are not in themselves striking. Edom is attached in the south to Moab; the 'kings of Zobah' belong in Aramaean territory. True, we hear nothing elsewhere of these particular opponents, but it can easily be imagined that the co-ordination of Israelite strength under one king and the formation of a standing guard excited uneasiness and hostility not merely among the Philistines, but also among the other neighbouring peoples. Now these people are approximately those mentioned in II. 8 and 10 as David's opponents, but the order here is different and the Aramaeans are not mentioned by name. The addition *bet rehōb* in LXX, on the basis of II. 10, makes it clear that the similarity was noted of old. We may not therefore exclude the possibility that perhaps the mention of the Edomites was added later to complete the list. In itself, the list made here, which is no slavish imitation of II. 8 and 10, is not surprising.[b] We are completely free to assume that for a long time all that we know of Saul did not find a place in the Bible.

The biblical writer is most interested in the material which describes the history of God's dealings with Saul. This is clear from a characteristic phrase. MT runs 'Wherever he turned he acted wickedly' (*yaršī^ca*). Whoever wrote this regarded Saul's warlike actions as constantly rooted in sinful conduct. The LXX, on the other hand, has *esōzeto*, 'he was saved', instead, representing

[a]See BH.
[b]Gressmann's remark that 'in unhistorical fashion the victories of David are ascribed to him' (p. 52) is in any case too summary and therefore incorrect.

wayyiwwāšēᶜᵃ. The correct reading of the original text will lie between the two: *yōšīᶜᵃ*, 'he did saving acts'. We have here what is virtually a scale of valuations: from saving deeds to being saved and finally to folly. Originally the account will have been well disposed towards Saul, as we can also see, particularly in v. 48. Saul appears in the series of 'saviour' figures, an interpretation which would not, of course, have been acceptable to other tendencies hostile to Saul.

[52] The closing remark also gives an objective report; indeed, it is sympathetic towards Saul. The sentence is important to us, as it shows how the king was concerned to develop military strength. He did what he could.

[49–51] In between there are details of his family relationships. Among the sons it is striking that Abinadab (31.2) is missing and that Ishbaal is written as Ishyo—the text has the similar word Ishvi; the objectionable word 'Baal', which was later frequently changed to *bōšet* (God of Shame) is thus here replaced by *yō* = *yahweh*. Perhaps this was his real name, and it was only later writers, ill disposed towards the king, who also wished to slander him as having given Baalistic names to his sons. It is possible that only the textual alteration to Ishvi prevented a similar change from being made here. Abner, frequently mentioned later, is here (and only here) given the name Abiner; his appearance as Saul's cousin is surely authentic.

The section is very significant for us, because here we have a factual account of some details in the life of the first king, whose historical portrait otherwise fluctuates, distorted more by partisan hate than by sympathy.

10. THE AMALEKITE WAR AND THE REJECTION OF SAUL: 15.1–35

15 ¹And Samuel said to Saul, 'The LORD sent me to anoint you king over his people Israel; now therefore hearken to the voiceᵃ of the LORD. ²Thus says the LORD of hosts, "I have seen wellᵇ what Amalek did to Israel in opposing them on the way, when they came up out of Egypt. ³Now go and smite Amalek, and utterly destroy him andᶜ all that he has; do not spare, but kill both man and woman, infant and suckling, ox and sheep, camel and ass." '

4 So Saul summoned the people, and numbered them in Telaim,

ᵃAlternative reading, 'the words'.
ᵇSo the perfect should be translated. The usual rendering, 'I will take vengeance' is incorrect, despite GK § 106m.
ᶜSee BH.

two hundred thousand men on foot and ten thousand men, namely the men of Judah.[a] [5]And Saul came to the city of Amalek, and lay in wait[b] in the valley. [6]And Saul said to the Kenites, 'Go, depart, go down from Amalek,[c] lest I make you to vanish along with him;[d] for you showed kindness to all the people of Israel when they came up out of Egypt.' So the Kenites[e] departed out of Amalek. [7]And Saul smote Amalek from Havilah as far as Shur, which is east of Egypt. [8]And he took Agag the king of Amalek alive, and utterly destroyed all the people with the edge of the sword. [9]But Saul and the people spared Agag, and the best of the sheep and of the oxen—the fatlings[f] and the lambs—and all that was good, and would not utterly destroy them; all that was despised[g] and worthless[h] they utterly destroyed.

10 The word of the LORD came to Samuel: [11]'I repent that I have made Saul king; for he has turned back from following me and has not performed my commandments.' And Samuel was angry; and he cried to the LORD all night. [12]And Samuel rose early to meet Saul in the morning; and it was told Samuel, 'Saul came to Carmel, and behold, he set up a monument for himself and turned, and passed on, and went down to Gilgal.'[h] [13]And Samuel came to Saul,[i] and Saul said to him, 'Blessed be you to the LORD; I have performed the commandment of the LORD.' [14]And Samuel said, 'What then is this bleating of the sheep in my ears and the lowing of the oxen which I hear?' [15]Saul said, 'They have brought them from Amalek;[j] for the

[a]This is the literal translation of the text. Perhaps instead of *raglī* (foot soldier), or after it, there occurred the similar *miyyisrāēl*, as 'foot soldier' is a striking word to use in contrast with 'men of Judah'. At that time there were still no horsemen in Judah.

[b]See BH.

[c]See BH; here and in v. 15 there are variant readings of *ᶜamālēq* and *hāᶜamālēqī*.

[d]Virtually 'take in'; Lagarde and most later writers have conjectured *'espᵉkā*, 'blot out' (from *sāpā*), but MT is more vivid here.

[e]Here, too, as in the case pointed out in n.[c] above, the text fluctuates between *qayin* and *haqqēnī*.

[f]See BH, MT: those of the second birth (?), which will have been regarded as particularly good (?). The words in parentheses are probably a later addition.

[g]The text offers a choice between *nibzā* and *mubzā* (see Schulz *ad loc.*). The *h* of the article was lost after the previous word.

[h]This translation follows LXX, which reads *hiṣṣīb* instead of the *maṣṣīb* of MT. In this way it is Saul who has 'turned' and gone to Gilgal after setting up the monument. According to the MT, as Samuel approaches, Saul is *in the process* (participle) of setting up a monument; thereupon *Samuel* turns and goes to Gilgal. But then v. 13 causes difficulties; it gives the impression that Saul is already at Gilgal on Samuel's arrival, and we are compelled to ask how Saul managed to reach Gilgal before Samuel. The word *maṣṣīb* must therefore be regarded as an early corrupt text.

[i]LXX continues here (or at the end of v. 12), 'who was in the process of offering a sacrifice to the Lord of the best of the plunder which he had brought from Amalek' The sentence is derived from vv. 15 and 21.

[j]See n. [c] above.

people spared the best of the sheep and of the oxen, to sacrifice to the LORD your God; and the rest we have utterly destroyed.' ¹⁶Then Samuel said to Saul, 'Stop! I will tell you what the LORD said to me this night.' And he said to him, 'Say on.'

17 And Samuel said, 'Though you are little in your own eyes, are you not the head of the tribes of Israel? The LORD anointed you king over Israel. ¹⁸And the LORD sent you on a mission, and said, "Go, utterly destroy the sinners, Amalek, and fight against him, until you have consumed them."ᵃ ¹⁹Why then did you not obey the voice of the LORD? Why did you swoop upon the spoil, and do what was evil in the sight of the LORD?' ²⁰And Saul said to Samuel, 'I have obeyed the voice of the LORD, I have gone on the mission on which the LORD sent me, I have brought Agag the king of Amalek, and I have utterly destroyed Amalek. ²¹But the people took of the spoil, sheep and oxen, the best of the things devoted to destruction, to sacrifice to the LORD your God in Gilgal.' ²²And Samuel said,

> 'Has the LORD as great delight in burnt-offerings and sacrifices
>   as in obeying the voice of the LORD?
> Behold, to obey is better than sacrifice,
>   and to hearken than the fat of rams.
> ²³For rebellion is as the sin of divination,
>   and stubbornness is like the iniquity of idolatry.ᵇ
> Because you have rejected the word of the LORD,
>   he has also rejected you from being king.'

24 And Saul said to Samuel, 'I have sinned; for I have transgressed the commandment of the LORD and your words, because I feared the people and obeyed their voice. ²⁵Now therefore, I pray, pardon my sin and return with me, that I may worship the LORD.' ²⁶And Samuel said to Saul, 'I will not return with you; for you have rejected the word of the LORD, and the LORD has rejected you from being king over Israel.' ²⁷As Samuel turned to go away, Saul laid hold upon the skirt of his robe,ᶜ and it tore. ²⁸And Samuel said to him, 'The LORD has torn the kingdom of Israel from you this day, and has given it to a neighbour of yours, who is better than you. ²⁹And also the Glory of Israelᵈ will not lie or repent; for he is not a man, that he should repent.' ³⁰Then he said, 'I have sinned; yet honour me now before the elders of my people and before Israel, and return with me, that I may worship the LORD your God.' ³¹So Samuel turned back after Saul; and Saul worshipped the LORD.

ᵃ'Them' stands twice in MT; these will again be variant readings.

ᵇDelete the *waw* with LXX. The usual emendation of *'āwen* to *ʿawōn* is unnecessary.

ᶜ*meʿīl* is the upper garment, virtually a man's coat, somewhat like the *kumbas* of the Arab and the *kaftan* of the Jew.

ᵈAn obscure title of God, which includes the elements both of brightness and of unchangeableness.

32 Then Samuel said, 'Bring here to me Agag the king of Amalek.' And Agag came to him with tottering step.ᵃ Agag said, 'Surely the bitterness of death is past.' ³³And Samuel said,

> 'As your sword has made women childless,
>   so shall your mother be childless among women.'ᵇ

And Samuel hewed Agag in pieces before the LORD in Gilgal.

34 Then Samuel went to Ramah; and Saul went up to his house in Gibeah of Saul. ³⁵And Samuel did not see Saul again until the day of his death, but Samuel grieved over Saul. And the LORD repented that he had made Saul king over Israel.

Is Saul the man after God's heart? That is, as we have said, the theme of Saul stories hitherto. Here we have the last of them. The answer runs: sadly, no. The deuteronomistic final compiler may have stressed the 'no' more strongly, but the material which lay before him and which he used indicated the 'sadly' so clearly that it could not be suppressed.

It is not clear where ch. 15 originally belonged in the Saul tradition. Budde, Eissfeldt and other proponents of the source-theory thought of putting it with ch. 12. This makes difficulties because of the by no means merely negative attitude towards Saul adopted by ch. 15.ᶜ Moreover, the beginning joins directly on to the anointing of Saul in 10.1, and v. 17 may well recall 9.21. Nevertheless, ch. 15 has no direct connection with, for example, 10.16, simply because there Saul's anointing is associated with the Philistine war (9.16), whereas here there is no mention of the Philistines. In addition, Saul in ch. 15 is no longer an unknown quantity, but is imagined as the leader of a considerable force. At best, therefore, we might imagine a connection between ch. 15 and ch. 11, because in ch. 11 Samuel is with Saul and, for that matter, in Gilgal, and because ch. 11, like ch. 15, makes no mention of the Philistines. We might also point out that, like 15.1, at least LXX at the end of ch. 11 speaks of Saul's anointing. The numbering in v. 4 is reminiscent of

---

ᵃFrom *māʿad*? No satisfactory rendering of the word has yet been found. One would expect something like 'full of contempt for death'. But the connection with the root *ʿādan* ('Eden', delight, loveliness) does not suggest that. The often used 'cheerfully' (as RSV) is impossible.
ᵇThe original is in verse form, with a rhyme.
ᶜSee Weiser, *ZAW* 54, 1936, pp. 2f.

11.8. Chapters 11 and 15 may therefore once have been connected[a] by virtue of the fact that both were traditions native to the Gilgal sanctuary.[b] It was only the compiler of the whole work who broke the connection, which still, however, as was said, remains recognizable despite the insertion of chs. 12–14. The presence of another account of the dispute between Samuel and Saul belonging to the Philistine traditions, in ch. 13, shows that the sanctuary at Gilgal is the scene of the former dispute and also that the event belongs at the beginning of Saul's reign, but has been associated with different campaigns. For the compiler of the whole work, the details of ch. 13, which has no express mention of the rejection, represent the lightning, while the storm breaks in ch. 15. Therefore the narrative of David's anointing, to which 15.28 expressly refers, follows immediately on this account.

[1–3] Neither Saul's plans nor a particular historical situation led to the expedition against Amalek; it was the will of the Lord and his servant Samuel—to Saul it comes as something quite unexpected. Hence the strong stress at the beginning on Samuel's 'I'; the mention of the anointing points in the same direction. As the Lord's anointed, Saul is to wage the holy war; for such it is. The opponent makes that clear. Amalek is a Bedouin tribe from the steppes of the deep south, and was Israel's chief enemy during the time in the desert, as the saying in Ex. 17.16 shows: 'The LORD will have war with Amalek from generation to generation.' Amalek, then, is the adversary of the Lord. This people is regarded by the tradition as *the* opponent, which first and most obviously sought to deny Israel entry into the Promised Land. Therefore the victory over Amalek is expressly a victory of prayer (Ex. 17.8ff.) and thus of the Lord; and the answer to anyone who puts himself in opposition to God 'with

---

[a]As far as I can see, no one has yet considered the possibility of an earlier connection between chs. 11 and 15. Perhaps the reason for this lies in 13.2b, a verse which apparently points back to ch. 11, but which could as well stem from the editorial hand of the final compiler. On the other hand, it must, of course, be conceded that the beginning of the Philistine war also assumes an official acceptance of the kingship by Saul, as in ch. 11. It should merely be pointed out that chs. 11 and 15 belong in the same tradition and seem to have come into the hand of the final compiler still connected in this way. In view of what was said above, this would be more enlightening than Weiser's thesis of the 'relatively old individual narrative' (*ZAW* 54, 1936, p. 3); cf. Noth, *Überlieferungsgeschichtliche Studien* I, p. 62, n. 1. He describes I Sam. 15 as a 'later addition' to the old Saul tradition.

[b]Perhaps the strange figure 2 for Saul's reign in 13.1 is based on this.

a high hand' can only be the ban. So, too, when in the monarchy Israel has achieved a previously unsurpassed consolidation of her forces, the adversaries of the Lord must be put under the ban. Here, then, the king in no way appears as a kind of theological competitor to Yahweh, as he does in ch. 12 and also in ch. 8, but on the contrary appears as one who is primarily chosen to get the Lord his due. In this particular context, the reference to the anointing is extremely important.

[4–9] Saul readily obeys, and holds a mustering, the wording of which recalls 11.8, though the numbers are not the same. The name of the place has been handed down as Telaim or Telam, and will be identical with the Telem of Josh. 15.24, a place lying deep in the south of Judah. LXX has 'in Gilgal' here, thus—rightly—regarding Gilgal as the place of Samuel's instructions to Saul. But the other place, occurring seldom and not far from Amalek, is the more suitable location for the mustering. The 'city' of the Amalekites, next mentioned, is unknown to us;[a] there can be no question of the Bedouin people having had a city in our sense of the word. The ambush represents an evidently favourite means of strategy in earlier days (Josh. 8; Judg. 20, also Judg. 9.32ff.). The most frequent arrangement was to lay a trap for the (besieged) enemy, to be put into operation as soon as he made a sally against the main body of attackers. Here we have quite simply a concentration of the attackers in a wadi situated near to the 'city'. It is in accordance with courtesy, and also with the character of this war, that the Kenites, who occupy territory bordering on the Amalekites, but are, unlike the latter, old friends of Israel from the sojourn in the wilderness, are invited to depart. Judg. 1.16 already speaks of their transition to a settled life; our passage seems to refer to their last Bedouin remnants. Saul's victory is reported only briefly; other factors are more important to the writer than strategy and geography. The same details are given in describing the field of operations as for the country of the Ishmaelites in Gen. 25.18. With the capture of the Amalekite king the war is virtually at an end. The naming of the personification of anti-Semitism, Haman, in Esther 3.1 as Agagite shows clearly that Agag became almost the type of the enemy of Yahweh and his people. Saul's subsequent action must therefore have been regarded all the more seriously at a later time. Quite apart from the sparing of Agag,

---

[a]The suggested emendation of 'city' to 'cities' does not help. Caspari proposed *har* (hill) *ʿamlēq*, but then finds difficulties with the 'lying in wait'.

the ban is only partially carried out. Only the worthless cattle are killed. The best of them remain in Saul's hand and—as is mentioned purposely—in the hands of his people. Later generations apparently took particular interest in this passage, and supplied it with additions. This is understandable enough, as here we have the place where it was determined whether Saul was the man 'after God's heart'. It was his sin that he waged this war after the fashion of other wars; that was regarded as a profanation of the realm of the holy. There will be more to say about this.

[10–11] The Lord's verdict follows immediately. The reasons given for the decision to reject Saul follow a line which has already been drawn. Here we have the theologically important concept of the repentance of God: God is not slavishly bound by his own decisions, but is almighty to such an extent that he is Lord even of them. Just as he takes the action of men into consideration in his decisions, so that omnipotence never means that man is deprived of his responsibility, so, too, the election of the king is not irrevocable. God can at any time lay aside the instrument which he is using if it appears to him to be neither tried nor suitable. Here it is remarkable that Samuel is painfully distressed and evidently does not agree. Samuel's 'crying' all night to the Lord can only mean that he is attempting to make him change his mind. 'Samuel pleads for the sinner as does Abraham for Sodom' (Budde)[a], but he must—though this is not expressly stated—fall in with the will of the Lord and agree with him. [12] Accordingly he goes straight to meet Saul the next morning. He supposes him still to be in the south, but then hears that he has erected a 'hand', a pillar, in Carmel in Southern Judah as a mark of his victory, and has gone on to Gilgal. This will certainly still have been pointed out for a long time as Saul's pillar, and its existence will have been the reason for its being mentioned. Only if we follow MT and not LXX (see critical notes) does this note have a distinctive, critical accent, suggesting that Saul ascribed the glory of the victory to himself, as there it appears that Samuel wished to have nothing to do with it, but returned immediately.

[13–21] The greeting with which Saul meets Samuel in Gilgal and the news that he has fulfilled his task are not signs of a guilty conscience (so Schulz); rather Saul—and at the same time the

[a]It is quite wrong to transpose the names Saul and Samuel on the support of LXX MSS in v. 12 and also v. 10, as Caspari proposes. Cf. further Schulz on v. 12.

reader—is only convinced that he has done wrong during the course of his conversation with Samuel. First of all, of course, Saul has not only a plausible but also a pious answer ready for Samuel's question about the significance of the cattle round about. Is it not the same thing for him to set aside the cattle for sacrifice and to offer them now at this holy place as to put them to the 'ban' in the place where they were taken? But sacrifice and the 'ban' are not the same thing; the 'ban' is complete destruction, the surrender of the whole, whereas sacrifice (*zābaḥ*) usually presupposes a portion for men as well. Above all, however, Saul, by bringing the plunder undestroyed from the place of the 'ban', has thereby introduced it into the profane sphere of life, where it is exposed to the usual contamination. Thus in Samuel's ears, Saul's answer must seem hollow talk, and Samuel therefore begins his message immediately. First, he touches on something in Saul's words which seems like self-justification, namely the fact that it was the 'people' who were responsible for the measures that were taken. In reference to this, Samuel points to Saul's special position which is his by virtue of the anointing; did he have to fall in with the will of the people?[a] As the anointed *of the Lord*, did he not have sufficient authority behind him? No, Saul himself is guilty, and his answer cannot alter that fact, especially as it brings nothing new, except perhaps the mention of Agag, whose presence Samuel discovers in this way, though at first he does nothing about it. Behind this conversation[b] lies the question whether the 'ban' and sacrifice are equivalent, as Saul at first assumes. The discussion of this is particularly important, because it recalls the criticism of sacrificial worship in classical prophecy.[c]

[22–23] This becomes clearest in the saying, whose rhythmic form alone shows it to be the central point of the chapter. Sacrifice, and even the burnt-offering (*'ōlā*), in which the whole animal goes up in smoke and in which the sacrificer has no share, is contrasted with obedience (literally 'hearing') in a way which shows that here there are two different realms. The difference may lie in an opposition of institution to direct action, then perhaps of priestly order to pro-phetic command. But this would be too external. Basically, the fact

[a]The phrase 'although a little man in your own eyes' could, as was said, refer back to 9.21 and 10.22 (see *ad loc.*). Evidently the tradition in its different parts is aware of the personal modesty of the first king.

[b]Cf. Weiser, *ZAW* 54, 1936, p. 10.

[c]*Inter alia*, Amos 5, Isa. 1, Jer. 7, Zech. 7, and on this, Hertzberg, 'Die pro phetische Kritik am Kult', *TLZ* 75, 1950, cols. 209–26.

is that the offering of a sacrifice, though it may be originally an action
enjoined by the Lord, becomes in the practical course of events an
occasion which is incumbent upon man and is performed by him,
whereas in the ban, man is the instrument of a higher hand and thus
lives completely in 'obedience'. Obedience is therefore, even from a
theological point of view, more than the best fat of rams. 'Hence
Samuel rejects Saul's view that it did not matter how God came into
possession of the plunder.'[a] As a consequence of this, disobedience
is identified with the sin of divination—which Saul himself practised
(28.9)—and with 'iniquity of idolatry', which in this context is
thought to come to the same thing (cf. also Judg. 17.4f.). Disobedience itself is mentioned by Ezekiel among others; he uses the term
bēt merī, 'rebellious house', for Israel. 'Stubbornness' is also meant
in a similar way;[b] it is imagined as a sort of passive resistance which
is to be seen in Saul, who is by no means a rebel against the Lord.
What was required was clear, active obedience, not a hidden non-
co-operation. The instrument which the Lord uses must be completely adapted to his hand, and quite dependable. This is the basis of
the theological, in other words, the proper and authoritative criticism
of King Saul. For this reason, we find here in solemn form the rejection of the man who has rejected the word of the Lord.

The description continues in such a way as to show us that Saul
has evidently not understood the seriousness of the situation. [24–31]
In his eyes, what has happened seems to be a 'transgression' (*ʿābar*),
as v. 24b clearly shows, in other words a failing which is expiable in
the usual way; hence the form of his request to Samuel. Samuel's
refusal is consistent with the insights of v. 23. His speedy departure
then leads to the dramatic act of the tearing of the robe, which
Samuel, on the spur of the moment, interprets as the tearing away
of the kingdom.[c] Here, too, as in 13.14, there is a reference to the
better king who is to come, a reference which must necessarily be
incomprehensible to the protagonists in their present situation. At
the same time, the compiler takes the opportunity to give a theological safeguard to the earlier remark about the repentance of the
Lord, along the lines of Num. 23.19 ('God is not man that he should

[a]Weiser, p. 11.

[b]The hiphil form *hapṣar* need hardly (with Weiser, p. 12) be emended to
niphal.

[c]Cf. the anecdote, used in Uhland's ballad *Taillefer*, in which William the
Conqueror, on landing on the coast of England, falls on his hand and immediately
reinterprets this unpropitious event, 'I seize and grasp thee, England!'

lie, or a son of man that he should repent'), in case of any possible misinterpretation. God's repentance is in no way comparable with the untruthfulness or occasional shortcomings of men. Even in his treatment of Saul, the Lord remains true to himself and is far removed from any fickleness. The external and internal connections with that sentence from the sayings of Balaam are thus manifest.

We might ask whether the original narrative was later extended, perhaps from v. 25 onwards.[a] On the other hand, the matter of the tearing of the robe is completely original. If there has been an expansion here, it derives from another, old tradition. In any event, these verses are meant to attest and explain the rift—which was wanted neither by Saul, the man faithful to Yahweh, nor by Samuel —between the king and his God in its historical and particularly its theological significance. The excursus about the repentance of Yahweh is an integral part of this section. Samuel's subsequent 'turning back' to Saul and his presence at Saul's 'worship', after his earlier refusal, can now no longer be regarded as an attempt at camouflage. The tradition knew that Samuel was there, too; perhaps a place was pointed out in Gilgal as the place where the two worshipped and where Agag was later killed. There was therefore a tradition of the breach between the two men, externally symbolized in the story of the torn robe, and another, according to which they stood together 'before Yahweh' (v. 33) in Gilgal. The preceding section would accordingly represent the bridge between the two traditions. We are not told the form of Saul's worship; presumably it was the sacrifice of the plunder that he intended to make, as we are told in v. 15. This is certainly the view of LXX, which makes an addition to v. 12 (see above).

[32–33] The killing of Agag forms a conclusion. Samuel's performance of it does, of course, express criticism of Saul, who had spared him. It is hard to find in the text the idea that in so doing Samuel declares himself against the king, but for the kingdom (Weiser). It is better put in different terms: the fact that Agag is hewed in pieces 'before the Lord' takes the event from the sphere of sacrifice into that of the ban. Samuel, who gave the orders for the Amalekite war, and not Saul, who has separated himself from the sphere of the ban, performs the judgment of God; and with his action—and with the rejection of Saul—the infringed law of the ban

[a]Cf. Weiser, pp. 4f.; Jepsen, *Nabi*, 1934, pp. 105f.

is restored, as in the punishment of Achan (Josh. 7). The section is vividly narrated, and speaks for itself, even if all the details are not clear (cf. on v. 32). In particular, one would like to know whether Agag's remark, 'Surely the bitterness of death is past', represents the liberating certainty of a sure death or the hope that with the appearance of the old man actions will be governed by mercy; Samuel's completely different conduct then proclaims that here no human rule but the clear harshness of the holy ban holds sway. The remark with which Samuel begins his task is formulated so as to correspond both inwardly and outwardly (chiasmus) with Gen. 9.6.

[34–35] Then the ways of Samuel and Saul separate for ever, surely not to the grief of Samuel alone, as is expressly said here. But the old servant of God, even against his feelings, is keeping to the ruling of the Lord, who has 'repented' that he gave Saul the kingdom.

NOTE ON FORMATION AND STRUCTURE: III

It is immediately obvious that the history of the beginnings of the Israelite monarchy is marked with strongly different accents. As ch. 7 speaks of the last judge, so chs. 8 and 12 have a negative attitude to the monarchy, and particularly towards this king, whereas in ch. 15, which records his rejection, this is by no means generally the case; the monarchy is not criticized at all, and even the king is depicted not without sympathy. This fact alone precludes the combining of the three chapters into a 'source', as was usual earlier. The account of the rejection in ch. 13 judges the king if possible still more favourably. The narration of the choice of the king in Mizpah (10.17ff.) does, it is true, stand in the shadow of ch. 8, with which it is organically connected, but still leaves room for another tradition, more positive towards Saul. That is still more the case with the report of the anointing of the young Saul in 9.1ff. Here the monarchy stands completely under the mark of the divine grace, and the man chosen to be ruler is shown to be endowed with the spirit of God. This, too, is the case in the account of the Ammonite war and the enthronement in Gilgal, and surely also in the descriptions of chs. 13 and 14, standing as they do so close to the historical events and also to people directly associated with Saul.

These differences and nuances explain why the earlier thesis, that the Saul stories could be divided into two or three sources, detectable by literary criticism, and each with a continuation both backwards and forwards, has now been increasingly discarded. We must, however, ask whether there are not connections within the different reports which could then give us some explanation of the growth of this complex. The principal question which arises is that of the *locale* of these traditions. It is clear that the Mizpah sanctuary possessed and maintained a tradition critical not only of the king, but also of the monarchy in general. Nevertheless, even here, a tradition attesting a more positive attitude of Samuel to Saul (10.17ff.) seems to have been preserved. It was not unknown, even in these circles, despite all theological objections, that the hour of the kingdom had come and was willed by God.

The traditions apparently associated with the Gilgal sanctuary are of a different nature. To them belongs first the history of the Ammonite war and the subsequent enthronement (and, according to LXX, the anointing) in Gilgal (ch. 11), and the account of the rejection in ch. 15. The commission given by Samuel to Saul, to undertake the holy war against the Amalekites, which it reports at the beginning, could be directly connected with ch. 11. As has been said, the narrative of the rejection is not unfavourably disposed towards Saul and gives extensive and plausible reasons for it, having compassion, while at the same time regarding it as a theological necessity. Here the distinction between sacrifice and the ban, admirably worked out—it was, of course, in Gilgal (see the texts in the first half of Joshua) that this theme was well-known—and the discussion of the repentance of God are particularly significant. It is striking that neither narrative says anything about the Philistines. It could be that the Philistines were in every respect most remote from the Jordan valley. The theme of the rejection in Gilgal occurs in ch. 13 in yet another context. There it is used in such a way that Saul appears to be vindicated. In this way the rejection is interwoven into the Philistine battles as well. One reason for this is that the Gilgal sanctuary was traditionally a mustering place for troops during the Philistine war; another reason is, of course, that the account of the rejection was firmly rooted at Gilgal. It is easy to see how the two complexes exercised mutual attraction and helped to shape the account of Saul's battles with the Philistines.

This account itself occupies a special place among the material collected here in that it stands nearest to the events which it describes. Its author is well informed about details of people, places and events. Only these two chapters talk of Jonathan, and do so 'after the fashion of the hero-narratives of the Book of Judges.'[a] They see more clearly than do the other narratives the real tragedy in Saul's life. Thus it has rightly been assumed that the man writing here comes from the period and entourage of Saul himself. Here, perhaps, we have the beginnings of court history writing. This would be particularly true of the notes in 14.47–52; but the description of the Philistine war could also be based on court documents. It is recognizable that the report gives a true-to-life description of the king, but at the same time seeks to understand him and vindicate him. Perhaps this was done to combat other voices which were already raised against Saul during his lifetime. In any case, we can reckon with the possibility that it was localized in Gibeah itself.

Independent of this, and quite separate from it, was the charming narrative which, in folk-tale style, tells of the young Saul and his anointing. More accurately, as was said in the exposition, it is made up of two stories, of which one takes place far from Gibeah and brings Saul face to face with an unnamed seer, whereas the other, well acquainted with the neighbourhood of Gibeah, describes the meeting of Saul and Samuel (in Ramah). The two closely related stories are woven together to such an extent that it is no longer possible to separate them into 'sources'. Perhaps the story as a whole was handed down at Bethel; but this is not important. Like 10.23f., it praises Saul's exceptional stature and is also in other respects as devoted to him as is Samuel, from all that we hear both here and elsewhere. Here, as in 15.17, his modesty is stressed. We are also told here, as in ch. 11—though somewhat differently—that Saul comes under the influence of the spirit of God.

Now these different materials have not just been worked together by the deuteronomistic compiler; they have also been seen as a whole. It is clear that his theology and basic standpoint are closest to the Mizpah traditions, so that in these we occasionally have the impression that the deuteronomistic final compiler is himself speaking (especially in ch. 12). Chapters 7 and 8, which open the sequence, give a tone to the whole which is maintained throughout: Saul, wrongly asked for by the people, but graciously given by the Lord, is not the man after the Lord's heart.[b] In this respect, the Deuterono-

[a] L. Rost, *Einleitung*, 8th edition. p. 91,
[b] 'The kingdom granted by YHWH is . . . affirmed, but in the view of the anti-Saul group Saul is merely an unsuccessful prototype and hence not the legitimate founder of a dynasty' (Buber, *VT* 6, 1956, p. 167).

mist has left the material generally untouched. Still, occasionally, as in the Gibeah report, the discrepancy between material and final compiler is evident, and here and there his ordering and connecting hand is visible. This is particularly clear in the general structure. Chapter 8 showed that Yahweh had granted the king. Then there follows the story of the choice and anointing of the chosen ruler, which at once makes clear that Samuel, despite his basic objection in ch. 8, is now preparing the way for the coming king, not simply in obedience, but with affection and sympathy. The Mizpah account of the choice of the king and the acclamation of the people has an organic connection with this. The affair of the Ammonites is the occasion of his first appearance, and the enthronement in Gilgal, described by the final compiler as the 'renewal of the kingdom', is then the consequence of the first victory. The Philistine narrative starts here, first with the usual, though recognizably altered, formula with which the deuteronomistic compiler tends to mark the beginning of a reign in the Book of Kings. The tragic conflict in which Saul, the pious man who is nevertheless unsure in his zeal towards God, is engaged, is already visible in several places, but particularly in the insertion of the rejection at Gilgal. The rejection itself does not yet appear here explicitly as such, partly because the pertinent material occurs in greater detail and in a more appropriate context in ch. 15, in the Gilgal story. The expedition against the Amalekites and the command to use the ban was indeed the best occasion to make it theologically clear that Saul was not the king 'after God's heart'. Nevertheless Saul is not, even in the eyes of the Deuteronomist, a man like Abimelech. He is the anointed; he is loved by many, even by his opponent Samuel, he is pious in the extreme, brave yet modest, without doubt a man of the stuff of which kings are made. But despite his zeal for Yahweh, he appears, in fact, more as the king which other nations have than as the instrument of Yahweh, which the king over the people of God must be. This is the view of ch. 15, and it is the view which the final compiler appropriated and made his own. Here he saw the outcome correctly. Saul is the inaugurator of the kingdom. But the king set over the people of God must be a man of God's grace, called by him and a real instrument in his hand. This Saul is not. To this extent, the history of the beginning of the kingdom at the same time also provides the theological evaluation of the kingdom in Israel.[a] Only the man 'on whom the

[a]Buber, purposely avoiding the word 'theology', stresses 'that for the narrator',

spirit of the Lord shall rest' (Isa. 11.2) can really be the king in Israel. The first king is like a sign pointing towards the true kingly office, but at the same time also a sign showing that the man who holds this office can come to grief in it. Only he who allows God to be wholly king, and who is therefore himself completely obedient, can be king over the people of God. The first king is measured strictly by this standard and cannot come up to it. But he remains the anointed one nevertheless, and continues to bear the insignia of the kingship which have been handed to him; even as rejected king he remains king, the first of the line at the end of which stands the One who alone was completely obedient.

—whom he sees as the same person throughout, apart from some additions— 'here, at the very beginning, lies the mystery of the kingdom, the problem of the encounter of God and man within it, the feeling of historical tragedy, and even at this stage the nucleus of a promise which will overcome the tragedy' (*VT* 6, 1956, p. 116).

IV

SAUL AND DAVID
I. 16–II. 1

1. THE ANOINTING OF DAVID: 16.1–13

16 ¹The LORD said to Samuel, 'How long will you grieveᵃ over Saul, seeing that I have rejected him from being king over Israel? Fill your horn with oil, and go; I will send you to Jesse the Bethlehemite, for I have provided for myself a king among his sons.' ²And Samuel said, 'How can I go? If Saul hears it, he will kill me.' And the LORD said, 'Take a heifer with you, and say, "I have come to sacrifice to the LORD." ³And invite Jesse to the sacrifice, and I will show you what you shall do; and you shall anoint for me him whom I name to you.' ⁴Samuel did what the LORD commanded, and came to Bethlehem. The elders of the city came to meet him trembling, and said, 'Does your coming meanᵇ peace?' ⁵And he said, 'Peace; I have come to sacrifice to the LORD; consecrate yourselves, that you may come with me to the sacrifice.'ᶜ And he (himself) consecrated Jesse and his sons, and invited them to the sacrifice.

6 When they came, he looked on Eliab and thought, 'Surely the LORD's anointed is before him.' ⁷But the LORD said to Samuel, 'Do not look on his appearance or on the height of his stature, because I have rejected him; for the LORD sees not as man sees; man looks on the outward appearance, but the LORD looks on the heart.' ⁸Then Jesse called Abinadab, and made him pass before Samuel. And he said, 'Neither has the LORD chosen this one.' ⁹Then Jesse made Shammah pass by. And he said, 'Neither has the LORD chosen this one.' ¹⁰And Jesse made seven of his sons pass before Samuel. And Samuel said to Jesse, 'The LORD has not chosen these.' ¹¹And Samuel said to Jesse, 'Are all your sons here?' And he said, 'There remains yet the youngest, but behold, he is keeping the sheep.' And Samuel said to Jesse, 'Send and fetch him; for we will not close the circle till he

ᵃHithpael participle.
ᵇSee BH.
ᶜFor the 'that' clause LXX has, 'and rejoice today with me.' This is presumably meant to avoid the difficulty that later evidently only the family take part in the sacrifice. See Commentary.

comes here.' [12]And he sent, and brought him in. Now he was ruddy, and had moreover[a] beautiful eyes, and was handsome. . . .[b] And the LORD said, 'Arise, anoint him; for this is he.' [13]Then Samuel took the horn of oil, and anointed him from the midst[c] among his brothers; and the Spirit of the LORD came mightily upon David from that day forward. And Samuel rose up, and went to Ramah.

The account of the anointing of David occupies the same position in the traditions about the rise of David as the episode of the asses does in the Saul tradition. Peculiar to both is not only the secret anointing, undertaken at the express command of the Lord, but also the fact that the person concerned is a young man, who is as yet no more than the son of his father. Nevertheless, we may not simply assume that the narrative came into being for the sake of these parallels and even describe it as a late midrash. Even Budde, who comes to this conclusion, has to concede that 'our section hardly displays the linguistic characteristics of very late origin'. Here, rather, we have a tradition which narrated how Yahweh directed his attention to David at an early stage and which holds it extremely important to demonstrate the connection between judge and king in this second instance, too. As the account is clearly connected with ch. 15, we must assume that it, like the former, belongs to the Gilgal tradition. Originally the material will have been native to Bethlehem[d] and will have been narrated in detail there. It is remarkable how compressed everything is in the present narrative; the gap in v. 12 could well mark the place of an omission. In the present form of the material only the bare essentials are mentioned. We will return to this point shortly.

[1] We begin with the situation described in ch. 15. Samuel receives the order to anoint a new king. The Lord is thus concerned not to let the kingdom fall with the 'rejected' king, but, on the contrary, to take care that it is preserved. The fact that this is to be

[a]The ʿim must be rendered in this way. The usual emendation to nāʿīm does not commend itself, as the ʿim is also transmitted at 17.42 and in addition the general descriptive word 'charming' would not fit very well between 'ruddy' and 'beautiful in respect of the eyes'.

[b]There is a gap here in the text. It might be supposed (Schulz) that a sentence has fallen out which perhaps described the sacrificial meal. LXX here has the word kyriō; see Commentary.

[c]This must be the rendering of the 'in the midst'; see Commentary.

[d]Budde (ZAW 12, 1892, pp. 46ff., cf. p. 114 of his commentary) assumes a connection between the sources of this narrative and those of the Book of Ruth. This is quite possible, at least as far as the history of the tradition is concerned.

effected by an anointing is a sign that a call from the Lord is the decisive factor for taking up the office. Both Saul and David are wholly elected by divine grace. There is a variation to this only at II Sam. 7. A man no more 'becomes' king through human initiative than he 'becomes' prophet by such means.

The divine choice has fallen on a son of Jesse of Bethlehem, not defined more closely at this point. **[2–3]** Samuel's fear that his journey to Bethlehem would arouse Saul's mistrust is connected with the geographical situation. If Samuel goes from Ramah to Bethlehem he must pass through Gibeah of Saul. There is also, of course, the fact that Samuel feels himself exposed to the constant surveillance of the king. So Samuel is ordered to offer sacrifice in Bethlehem,[a] one of his obligations at other times, too (cf. on ch. 9). He is to take the sacrificial beast as authentication in case the king notices anything.

[4] The reception given to him by the elders, who seem more terrified than honoured, may be a result of their knowledge of the discord between Samuel and Saul and their fear of involving themselves in trouble, as did later the inhabitants of the priestly city of Nob. This is more comprehensible than the assumption that Samuel's coming was as alarming to the Bethlehemites as is the sick visiting of the parson to many members of a congregation. Samuel gives the reassuring news that his visit is of a 'pastoral' nature. The text leaves us in doubt as to whether the elders really take part in the planned sacrifice. The divergent reading of LXX has arisen because they make no further appearance, playing a part similar to the thirty guests in 9.22; the abbreviation, already mentioned, may account for this lack of a further appearance. In any case, the anointing is not to be regarded as a public affair. The account of David's second anointing (II. 5.3) expressly mentions the presence of the 'elders' at the act.

[5] How Samuel carried out the 'consecration' of the male members of Jesse's family, we are not told. Whatever happened, they were drawn into the holy sphere by a special act of consecration performed by Samuel himself—the elders are to consecrate themselves! Thus the real purpose of Samuel's visit remains hidden from the elders, and even from the sons of Jesse. Jesse must be regarded as knowing something, but the decisive word 'king' is mentioned neither to him, nor later to David, almost certainly on purpose.

[a]Not as a subterfuge. Some commentators argue unnecessarily over this 'white lie'.

[6] Samuel uses the word 'anointed' only in his verdict on Eliab.
But we are hardly to suppose that it was said out loud. It is, like the
Lord's 'word' to Samuel, something which takes place between the
Lord and Samuel, without other witnesses. In this way it accords
generally with the rest of this section; the other people are really
only supernumeraries, mentioned as far as is necessary for the circumstances, the divine action of the choosing and anointing of the
king. Even David appears only in order to be anointed. The whole
narrative is completely theocentric; it does not therefore ask how
the details are to be understood, whether historically or psychologically.

Eliab, Jesse's oldest son, is shown as an imposing young man,
like Saul (9.2; 10.23), and Samuel's verdict on him is like that in
10.24. [7–10] But he is turned down; here we have the same word
'rejected' as appears in 15.23 and 16.1. The reason given is the fine
statement that the Lord does not look upon what is external and
visible, but upon what a man is like within. The other sons also
pass before Samuel, but with none of them does the Lord give a
sign. [11] The one upon whom the Lord has cast his eyes—a long
time ago according to the general context (13.14; 15.28)—is not
numbered among them. Here again we have the divine law of I Cor.
1.27: God has chosen what is weak in the world. The men, particularly the father, Jesse, have not considered David at all, seeing that
he is the youngest and probably not yet qualified to take part in the
cult (Caspari, p. 189); the feeling that the flock could not have been
left unattended (Caspari, *ibid.*, cf. also 17.28) plays no part here.
But as a son of Jesse, David, however young he may be, belongs
within the bounds laid down in Yahweh's instructions (v. 1), and
this is confirmed by Samuel's final sentence. 'Closing the circle'
(*sābab*) presupposes the company assembled for the sacrifice. Elsewhere, in accordance with the intent of the whole section, the sacrifice is not mentioned. [12] As in the case of Saul, so here the writer
speaks particularly lovingly of the figure of the coming king. The
word translated 'ruddy' is normally used to describe someone of
fair hair and colouring; his whole attitude, as later developments
show, displays something fair and winning. Nevertheless, the
establishment of David's suitability is not, as with Eliab, a result of
his appearance and of Samuel's judgment, but is based on the
command of the Lord immediately given to Samuel. LXX has even
inserted the words '(pleasing) to the Lord', presumably to smooth

over the supposed contradiction with vv. 6f. [13] Thereupon the anointing takes place; we might conclude from the word *b*ᵉ*qereb* ('in the midst') that David was anointed in the presence of the whole company at the sacrifice, perhaps even of the elders. In that case, Samuel's previous (v. 2) precautions are completely left aside, for now there would be no more guarantee of secrecy, especially as such a guarantee is not even demanded. Surely, however, as in the case of Saul (9.27; 10.16), the action is thought to be performed in secret; *b*ᵉ*qereb* is therefore to be rendered 'from the midst' (cf. Schulz *ad loc.*). With the anointing, David is chosen as the instrument of God, and as with Saul and many of the judges, the spirit of the Lord comes upon him now and henceforth. At the same time, the line running towards the king of the final age (Isa. 11.2) is extended, seeing that at the baptism of Jesus, which, in fact, corresponds to the anointing, the Spirit of God (Mark 1.10; Matt. 3.16; Luke 3.22, cf. John 1.32) descends upon him. Thus the story reaches its goal; Samuel can leave Bethlehem. All other questions, the completion of the sacrifice, the feeling of the brothers, the elders, the father, David himself, are left unanswered as being inessential.

Precisely because of this, however, the meaning of the narrative becomes very clear; here we have the keynote to the whole history of David. David is the long foreseen, pre-elected, forethoughtfully anointed one. So we are told here. For the further course of this history the anointing remains, of course, without importance (but cf. on II. 12.7). For the reader of the whole work, however, the rise of David, the man 'with' whom the Lord is (v. 18), which now begins, has its theological foundation in the anointing which has just taken place.[a]

---

[a]The question of the name 'David' has recently been raised again as a result of the Mari texts. The word *dawidum* occurring in them was interpreted to mean 'commander'. This made possible the assumption that 'David's' title of office had suppressed his real name. Thus, *inter alia*, Jirku, *Forschungen und Fortschritte* 27, 1953, p. 28; Noth, *History of Israel*, ET², p. 179, note 2 (with reference to W. v. Soden). v. Pákodzy (*ZAW* 68, 1956, pp. 257–9) points to modern parallels—Duce, Tito; from the biblical period we could think of Pharaoh, as well as apostles' names (v. Pákodzy, *ibid.*). The original name of 'David' is presumed to be Elhanan, who in II. 21.19 is taken to be the victor over Goliath; cf. also *ad loc.* But this whole thesis, attractive in itself, cannot be maintained, as was demonstrated most recently by J. J. Stamm in his paper given at the Old Testament Congress held in Oxford in 1959 (now published in *SVT* 7, 1960, pp. 165–83), which he kindly put at my disposal. The expression *dawidum daku* (or *maḥaṣu*, *šakanu*) simply means 'to inflict a defeat', so that all the hypotheses based on the supposed equation *dawdidum* = commander are shown to be untenable. The word David has rather originally something to do with 'father's brother'.

2. DAVID COMES TO THE COURT OF SAUL: 16.14–23

16 [14]Now the Spirit of the Lord departed from Saul, and an evil spirit from the Lord continually[a] tormented him. [15]And Saul's servants said to him, 'Behold now, an evil spirit from God is tormenting you. Let our lord now command your servants, who are before you, to seek out a man who is skilful in playing the lyre;[b] and when the evil spirit from God is upon you, he will play it, and you will be well.' [17]So Saul said to his servants, 'Provide for me a man who can play well, and bring him to me.' [18]One of the young men answered, 'Behold I have seen a son of Jesse the Bethlehemite, who is skilful in playing, a man of valour, a man of war, prudent in speech, and a man of good presence; and the Lord is with him.' [19]Therefore Saul sent messengers to Jesse and said, 'Send me David your son, who is with the sheep.'[c] [20]And Jesse took an ass, and loaded it with bread,[d] and a skin of wine and a kid, and sent them by David his son to Saul. [21]And David came to Saul, and entered his service. And Saul loved him greatly, and he became his armour-bearer. [22]And Saul sent to Jesse, saying, 'Let David remain in my service, for he has found favour in my sight.' [23]And whenever the evil spirit from God was upon Saul, David took the lyre and played it with his hand; so Saul was refreshed, and was well, and the evil spirit departed from him.

[14] In both the Old and the New Testaments the stories of the men of God are largely narrated as a history of the Spirit of God with them. It is made quite clear that this is not a human history. This is true of the time of the judges, and Saul, whose fortunes bring to the end the period of the judges, is no exception. With his anointing, the Spirit of God is with him, and only on his being rejected does it depart from him. True, he is still king for a number of years, but king without that divine legitimation which is a necessity among the people of God.

Not only, however, is he no longer ruled by the Spirit of God, but an 'evil spirit' continually visits him in its place. This evil spirit is not permanent, but he is inflicted with it over and over again. The fact, at first surprising, that even the evil spirit comes 'from Yahweh', expresses how all things in the end are caused by the one

[a]This is the sense of the consecutive perfect here.
[b]The text allows of a choice between *yōdēʿa naggēn* and *mᵉnaggēn*.
[c]Neither David nor the herd were mentioned in v. 18. On the other hand, Saul's messengers would have had to have details, to find the right son of Jesse.
[d]The words *wayyissā' ʿālāw*—cf. BH—are probably to be supplied, after LXX. Stoebe (*VT* 4, 1954, p. 183) seeks to keep MT (. . . an ass 'and' bread, a . . .); Jesse sent the riding animal and the first victuals for the young warrior. But in that case, he should have been mentioned first!

God. Whence else should it come? The Old Testament speaks of Satan only three times, all in later passages, and one of them, Job 1f., expressly describes the 'accuser' as subordinate to the Lord. So, too, it is with the evil spirit. Saul's suffering is described theologically, not psychopathetically or psychologically. And rightly so, for in an obscure way the hand of God invades the life of this man who, as can be seen often, exerts himself so much for Yahweh.

[15–16] It says a great deal for the esteem in which Saul was held at his court that his 'servants'—footmen, officials, soldiers—should think about a remedy and thus hit upon music, a means customary elsewhere in such situations. The instrument named is not the harp, but the smaller lyre (*kinnōr*).[a] [17–18] When the opportunity arises, one of the younger attendants recalls having met David; the words which he uses to describe him are again, as in v. 12, put in such a way that David appears particularly attractive, both in character and appearance. This side of David has evidently left a general stamp on the tradition. The further mention of his valour and skill at arms is not a later adjustment to other traditions, but is quite pertinent, seeing that Saul was still on the look-out for good soldiers (14.52). Saul is thus said to have had the most favourable picture possible, from the start, of this young man of whom it is said that 'Yahweh is with him'. [19–20] Saul then immediately sends messengers to have David brought; the fact that he is able to have this done from Judah shows how his kingdom extends without question beyond his own tribe. Saul is not thought to know that David has been anointed shortly beforehand, nor do we have the impression that Jesse and David are afraid that Saul's request is connected with this anointing. The presents which Jesse sends to the king by David are not signs of anxiety in this direction, but an understandable act of homage to the king (cf. 10.25).[b]

[a]Cf. Eino Kolari, *Musikinstrumente und ihre Verwendung im AT*, Helsinki, 1947, pp. 64–72.

[b]Stoebe rejects this interpretation: 'for the gifts would really be too trivial for this' (*VT* 7, 1957, p. 369). He would prefer to see them as equipment for the young warrior. That, however, is not apposite here, as David is being called because of his musical capabilities. That Saul's servants would wish to recommend the young man to the king for other qualities as well (v. 18) does not in any way alter the fact that David *here* comes to court as a musician, and *only then* (vv. 21f.) enters Saul's 'service' as a soldier. Had Jesse sent him to Saul equipped as a soldier from the first, he would have paid no attention to David's real task with Saul, indeed, he would have anticipated Saul's later request for his permission. Moreover, the gifts are not so trivial for a mere Judaean farmer!

[21–23] So David comes to the court. And in accord with his character as described earlier, he quickly wins the heart of the king, as he later wins the hearts of the king's son and the king's daughter. At the same time he also enters the king's service in a military capacity; but his chief task is the use of his skill at music, to help the king when he is possessed. In this respect, too, then, the Lord is 'with' David. So the purpose of Saul's servants is fully accomplished. But in the general context this episode means far more, and is really the continuation of the account of the anointing in a deeper sense. The Lord, who allows the anointing to be done by the last of the judges, so joins the threads that the man who is rejected, but is still bearer of the kingly office, takes the newly chosen one, of whose election neither are conscious, into his court, to allow him, all unknowing and unexpectant, to make the first steps towards the throne which will be his according to the will of the Lord.

3. DAVID AND GOLIATH: 17.1–18.5

17 [1]Now the Philistines gathered their armies for battle; and they were gathered at Socoh, which belongs to Judah, and encamped between Socoh and Azekah, in Ephes-dammim. [2]And Saul and the men of Israel were gathered, and encamped in the valley of the terebinths, and drew up in line of battle against the Philistines. [3]And the Philistines stood on the mountain on the one side, and Israel stood on the mountain on the other side, with a valley between them. [4]And there came out from the battle line[a] of the Philistines a champion[b] named Goliath, of Gath, whose height was six cubits and a span. [5]He had a helmet of bronze on his head, and he was armed with a coat of mail, and the weight of the coat was five thousand shekels of bronze. [6]And he had greaves[a] of bronze on his legs, and a javelin of bronze on his shoulder.[c] [7]And the shaft[a] of his spear was (as strong) as a weaver's beam[d] and his spear's head weighed six hundred shekels and was of iron; and his shield-bearer went before him. [8]He stood and shouted to the ranks of Israel, 'Why have you come out to draw up for battle? Am I not a Philistine, and are you not servants of Saul? So determine[e] a man for yourselves, and let him come down to me. [9]If he is able to

[a]See BH.

[b]See Commentary.

[c]Literally, 'between the shoulder blades'; he thus carried it lightly—not drawn right back to throw, but with half-stretched-out arm, so that the tip of the head pointed over the neck to the other side.

[d]This means the 'weaving- or cloth-beam of the standing loom'; Dalman, *Arbeit und Sitte* V, 1937, p. 113.

[e]The word *b^{e}rū*, which only occurs here, has been replaced in LXX by *baḥ^{a}rū*, 'choose'.

fight with me and kill me, then we will be your servants; but if I prevail against him and kill him, then you shall be our servants and serve us.' [10]And the Philistine said, 'I have this day defied the ranks of Israel (in saying), "Give me a man, that we may fight together." ' [11]When Saul and all Israel heard these words of the Philistine, they were dismayed and greatly afraid.

12 Now David was the son of an Ephrathite—already mentioned[a]—of Bethlehem in Judah, named Jesse, who had eight sons. In the days of Saul the man was already too old to go among the men (of war).[b] [13]The three eldest sons of Jesse had followed Saul to the battle; and the names of his three sons who went to the battle were Eliab the first-born, and next to him Abinadab, and the third Shammah. [14]David was the youngest; the three eldest followed Saul, [15]but David went back and forth from Saul to feed his father's sheep at Bethlehem. [16]For forty days the Philistine came forward and took his stand, morning and evening.

17 And Jesse said to David his son, 'Take for your brothers an ephah of this parched grain, and ten of these loaves,[c] and carry them quickly to the camp to your brothers; [18]also take these ten cheeses to the commander of their thousand. See how your brothers fare, and bring some token from them. [19]Saul and they and all the men of Israel are in the valley of the terebinths, fighting with the Philistines.'

20 And David rose early in the morning, and left the sheep with a keeper, and took the provisions, and went, as Jesse had commanded him; and he came to the encampment[d] as the host was going forth to the battle line, shouting the war cry aloud.[e] [21]And Israel and the Philistines drew up for battle, army against army. [22]And David left the things in charge of the keeper of the baggage, and ran to the ranks, and went and greeted his brothers. [23]As he talked with them, behold, the champion, the Philistine of Gath, Goliath by name, came up out of the ranks[c] of the Philistines, and spoke the same words as before. And David heard him.

24 All the men of Israel, when they saw the man, fled from him, and were much afraid. [25]And the men of Israel[f] said, 'Have you seen

[a]*hazze*; the pronoun represents the transition to ch. 16.

[b]Reading *mibbō' bā'ᵃnāšīm* and following Klostermann's brilliant conjecture. It would also be possible to take the *m* at the end as an abbreviation for *milḥāmā* and then to read *bᵉ'anšē milḥāmā*. 'To go among the men of war' means 'to become a soldier'.

[c]See BH.

[d]The text has 'wagon-barricade', an expression from a later time, when the Israelites had wagons of their own.

[e]The text may have run *wᵉhārēᶜa hērīᶜū* instead of the unusual Hebrew *wᵉhērēᶜū*.

[f]Linguistic usage as Josh. 9.6f., cf. Judg. 7.23; 8.22 = the Israelites. The usual translation 'an Israelite' is wrong; that would have to be *'īš mibbᵉnē yisrāēl*, as I Sam. 9.2; Num. 25.6. The phrase *'īš yisrāēl* in Num. 25.8 and 14 means 'the Israelite'. 'A servant of Saul' is similarly in 21.8 not *ᶜebed šā'ūl*, but *'īš mēᶜabdē šā'ūl*.

this man who has come up? Surely he has come up to defy Israel; and the man who kills him, the king will enrich with great riches, and will give him his daughter, and make his father's house free in Israel.' [26]And David said to the men who stood by him, 'What shall be done for the man who kills the Philistine, and takes away the reproach from Israel? For who is this uncircumcised Philistine, that he should defy the armies of the living God?' [27]And the people answered him in the same way, 'So shall it be done to the man who kills him.'

28 Now Eliab his eldest brother heard what he spoke to the men; and Eliab's anger was kindled against David, and he said, 'Why have you come down? And with whom have you left those few sheep in the wilderness? I know your presumption, and the evil of your heart; for you have come down to see the battle.' [29]And David said, 'What have I done now? Was it not but a word?' [30]And he turned away from him toward another, and spoke in the same way; and the people answered him again as before.

31 When the words which David spoke were heard, they repeated them before Saul; and he sent for him. . . . [32]And David said to Saul, 'Let no man's[a] heart fail because of him; your servant will go and fight with this Philistine.' [33]And Saul said to David, 'You are not able to go against this Philistine to fight with him; for you are but a youth, and he has been a man of war from his youth.' [34]But David said to Saul, 'Your servant used to keep sheep for his father; and when there came a lion, or a bear,[b] and took a lamb from the flock, [35]I went after him and smote him and delivered it out of his mouth; and if he arose against me, I caught him by his beard,[c] and smote and killed him. [36]Your servant has killed both lions and bears; and this uncircumcised Philistine shall be one of them, seeing he has defied the armies of the living God.' [37]And David said, 'The LORD who delivered me from the power of the lion and the power of the bear, will deliver me from the hand of this Philistine.' And Saul said to David, 'Go, and the LORD be with you!' [38]Then Saul clothed David with his armour; he put a helmet of bronze on his head, and clothed him with a coat of mail,[d] [39]and he also girded a sword on David's armour.[e] And he tried in vain to go, for he was not used to them. Then David said to

[a]LXX reads *'adōnī* instead of *'ādām*, and this is mostly preferred. It would, however, be most disrespectful for the young David to talk to the king about his lack of courage.

[b]The words *we'et-haddōb* in v. 34 and *gam-haddōb* in v. 36 have exchanged places by mistake and are to be transposed (see LXX).

[c]LXX reads 'at the throat', presumably because only the lion has a beard, and not the bear.

[d]The last words are missing in LXX MSS, from the correct reflection that the 'armour' includes a coat of mail. On the other hand, *maddīm* in Hebrew is normally the lower garment (cf. Dalman, *Arbeit und Sitte* V, 1937, p. 208).

[e]So LXX MSS. MT says 'And David girded his sword . . .' which makes it seem as if David himself had a sword. Of course, the reading could have arisen in order to avoid this misunderstanding.

Saul, 'I cannot go with these; for I am not used to them.' And David put them off. [40]Then he took his staff in his hand, and chose five smooth stones from the brook and put them in his shepherd's bag, which served him as a wallet;[a] his sling was in his hand, and he drew near to the Philistine.

41 And the Philistine came on and drew near to David, with his shield-bearer in front of him. [42]And when the Philistine looked, and saw David, he disdained him; for he was but a youth, ruddy, and moreover[b] comely in appearance. [43]And the Philistine said to David, 'Am I a dog, that you come to me with sticks?' And the Philistine cursed David by his gods. [44]The Philistine said to David, 'Come to me and I will give your flesh to the birds of the air and to the beasts of the field.' [45]Then David said to the Philistine, 'You come to me with a sword and with a spear and with a javelin; but I come to you in the name of the LORD of hosts, the God of the armies of Israel, whom you have defied. [46]This day the LORD will deliver you into my hand, and I will strike you down, and cut off your head; and I will give your dead body and[c] the dead bodies of the host of the Philistines this day to the birds of the air and to the wild beasts of the earth; that all the earth may know that there is a God in Israel, [47]and that all this assembly may know that the LORD saves not with sword and spear; for the battle is the LORD's and he will give you into our hand.'

48 Now[c] when the Philistine arose and came and drew near to meet David, David ran quickly from[c] the battle line to meet the Philistine.[d] [49]And David put his hand into his bag and took out a stone, and slung it, and struck the Philistine on his forehead; the stone[e] sank into his forehead, and he fell on his face to the ground.

50 So David prevailed over the Philistine with a sling and with a stone, and struck the Philistine, and killed him; there was no sword in the hand of David. [51]Then David ran and stood over the Philistine, and took his sword and drew it out of its sheath, and killed him, and cut off his head with it. When the Philistines saw that their champion was dead, they fled. [52]And the men of Israel and Judah arose with a shout and pursued the Philistines as far as Gath[f] and the gates of Ekron, so that the wounded Philistines fell on the way from[c] Sha-araim as far as Gath and Ekron. [53]And the Israelites came back from chasing the Philistines, and they plundered their camp. [54]And David took the head of the Philistine and brought it to Jerusalem; but he put his armour in the tent of the LORD.[g]

[a]Perhaps a marginal note by someone who knew that the word *yalqūt* (only occurring here), is the pertinent technical term.

[b]See on 16.12.

[c]See BH.

[d]The second half of the verse is missing in the Vaticanus of LXX. See Commentary.

[e]The LXX addition 'through the helmet' at this point may have arisen later because of the consideration that the Philistine was wearing a helmet.

[f]So LXX. MT reads *gay'* (= valley).   [g]See Commentary.

55 When Saul saw David go forth against the Philistine, he said to Abner, the commander of the army, 'Abner, whose son is this youth?' And Abner said, 'As your soul lives, O king, I cannot tell.' [56]And the king said, 'Inquire whose son the stripling is.' [57]And as David returned from the slaughter of the Philistine, Abner took him, and brought him before Saul with the head of the Philistine in his hand. [58]And Saul said to him, 'Whose son are you, young man?' And David answered, 'I am the son of your servant Jesse the Bethlehemite.'

18 [1]When he had finished speaking to Saul, the soul of Jonathan was knit to the soul of David, and Jonathan loved him as his own soul. [2]And Saul took him that day, and would not let him return to his father's house. [3]Then Jonathan made a covenant with David, because he loved him as his own soul. [4]And Jonathan stripped himself of the robe that was upon him, and gave it to David, and his armour, and even his sword and his bow and his girdle. [5]And David went out and was successful wherever Saul sent him; so that Saul set him over the men of war. And that[a] was good in the sight of all the people and also in the sight of Saul's servants.

Although the story of David and Goliath is well and attractively told, and the text is in a very good state of preservation, its exposition offers considerable difficulties. These lie in two directions. First, in II. 21.19, Elhanan, one of David's men, is named as the victor over Goliath the Gittite. This difficulty is usually stressed to such a degree that Elhanan's deed is held to be the actual event, and it is assumed that it was later transferred to David. On the other hand, the tradition according to which David came to Saul's court and made a covenant of friendship with Jonathan (later marrying the king's daughter) because of his special skill at arms is itself credible, especially as David also appears as the slayer of Goliath in I. 21.5; 22.5. It could therefore be that in the course of the tradition the well-known name Goliath became used to describe an unknown or anonymous man.

A second feature is more difficult. The Goliath narrative completely contradicts ch. 16, in both parts. Neither David's anointing nor his arrival at the court of Saul are presupposed; Saul, as we are expressly told in v. 55, does not yet know David. Now those passages in which ignorance of ch. 16 is most conspicuous (17.12–31; 17.55–18.5) are missing in the Vaticanus MS of the LXX. The remaining part of the narrative can at a pinch be harmonized with the account

[a]Only this rendering fits the Hebrew use of *wayyîṭab*. It is usually translated 'he', i.e. that David is loved. In fact, the sentence is concerned with public reactions to David's unusual promotion.

of David's arrival at the court of Saul in ch. 16, though even in this part David appears as a shepherd, and his musical capabilities and duties remain unmentioned. Here Saul appears throughout as an amiable man who is 'completely normal'. How are we to overcome this difficulty? We must certainly dismiss the view, put forward by Wellhausen and others, that the text was later abbreviated for the sake of a good balance. We must dismiss it because the omitted passages fit well into their context[a] and are not, as it were, clippings. Nor, on the other hand, do they look like subsequent enlargements. David's arrival at Saul's court may have been recorded in different ways at different places. We have such a story in 16.14–23; in the passages omitted by LXX we have another of a different kind; it is meant to tell us quite explicitly how David made the personal acquaintance of Saul and his family. We may say that its interest is to show that the rise of David was legitimate. God so disposed matters that David, the lowly man, should come upon the way by which he became a great man: esteemed by the king and set in office by him, solemnly chosen by the crown prince as friend and brother, designated consort for the princess because of his bravery, David here looks the future king. This form of the narrative will certainly have been widespread where it was thought important that David should appear not as an upstart but as the rightful successor according to God's will and ordinance.

The part of the narrative common to LXX and MT differs. It is possible, though by no means completely certain, that Saul's acquaintance with David is presupposed here. The setting of these passages becomes quite clear once we notice how often the weapons are mentioned in them. Not only is the equipment of the Philistine noted in detail; the 'armour' which Saul handed over to David is mentioned piece by piece and this same subject is the essential content of the remarks exchanged between the two contenders. At the conclusion, the weapons of the vanquished are said to have been deposited at a definite place. We cannot therefore exclude the possibility that this place was that at which the account was preserved. We will return to this point at v. 54.

It was then the task of the compiler of the whole work to collect all these similar narratives and to adjust the details to fit in with other material. It was his chief concern to accommodate them to the demands of the narrative first mentioned. So we now have here an

[a]This is disputed, hardly correctly, by Stoebe (*VT* 6, 1956, p. 405).

account of the rise of David, willed by God and disposed by him.
But it is evident from the form of the LXX text how clearly it was
remembered that originally two points of view were expressed here.

[**17.1–3**] This story, an episode from the battles between Israel
and the Philistines, takes us into the hill country of western Judah,
a border territory. The location of some, but not all, of the places
mentioned can be established. 'The valley of the terebinths' in
particular is to be identified with the present *wadi es-sant* (valley of
the acacias), about twelve miles west of Bethlehem. The valley itself,
which is to be imagined, of course, as being waterless, especially in
the summer, which is the only possible season for waging war,
marks the boundary between the opposing troops which day by day
occupy the declivities and form a 'battle line' about half-way up
the sides of the valley, returning to their camps at night. We must,
of course, imagine the camps then to have been guarded by patrols
in case of possible surprise attacks (cf. Judg. 7). At first there is no
mention of hostilities in the proper sense; in the morning the troops
take up position with the indispensable war cries, but for the moment
that is all. [**17.4–7**] The situation changes when the 'champion' appears; the Hebrew wording *'iš-habbēnayim* is unusual, and should
perhaps be translated 'man who fights between the battle lines'.[a]
Anyone who comes forward from the front line becomes a 'man
between the battle lines' and is thus a sort of 'challenger' or 'champion'. The custom of beginning with single combat is not unknown
to the Old Testament (II. 2.14ff.),[b] but appears to accord more
with Greek practice. It is indeed the Philistine—coming from non-
Semitic territory—who acts in this way. The name Goliath
(Alyattes?)[c] is of course foreign, and his armour is no less so; 'the
equipment of the Philistine was, as we know from Egyptian representations also, characteristically different from that of the Israelite'.[d]
The weapons are of bronze; the armour weighing more than a
hundredweight, in the form of a coat of mail, is particularly striking.
With the helmet, it must have made the man's figure look particu-

[a]This interpretation has now also been taken up by de Vaux, *RB* 65, 1958,
p. 125; cf. also *Ancient Israel*, p. 218. Gutbrod translates similarly, 'the dueller',
p. 144.
[b]But de Vaux, *loc. cit.*, and Wainwright (*VT* 9, 1959, p. 79) rightly refer to
Sinuhe's fight, the action of which is remarkably similar (cf. *AOT*, pp. 57f.).
[c]Cf. Caspari, p. 200, Hempel, *PJB* 1927, p. 65.
[d]Gressmann, p. 71. Earlier literature on the 'Homerically armed hero' in
Hempel, *loc. cit.*, now, too, in Wainwright, *loc. cit.*, and Yadin, *Pal. Exp. Q* 86,
1955, pp. 58–69.

larly terrifying. The bronze greaves on his legs complete the martial picture. The shield, large enough to cover even so tall a man, is carried by a special shield-bearer. All this is mentioned to show that the Philistine was protected as well as possible, so that the assailant would have no possible opening. In addition, there are his offensive weapons, among which the sword is nowhere mentioned;[a] the smaller javelin which he carries loosely on his shoulder, ready to use at any time (see above on v. 6), and the spear proper, perhaps carried by attendants, whose strength is made clear by the comparison with the weaver's beam and the mention of the iron head weighing upwards of a stone.[b] [17.8–11] In this frightening array he challenges the Israelites to a duel, to decide who is to serve whom. His 'ridiculing' consists in the fact that in all seriousness he does not imagine that there is one Israelite who will dare to engage in a contest with him. The consequent insult, not only to Saul, and with him the Israelite monarchy (v. 8), but also to the God of Israel, only emerges as the narrative proceeds, when David makes an appearance.

[17.12–15] Here the narrative, as it were, makes a new start by giving a brief biography of David. It seems to be speaking of David for the first time. This was, of course, intended in the original form of the narrative. Whoever gave the story its present form or brought it together marked the connection of the whole with the word *hazze* (see above) and also with the mention of the eight sons.[c] In fact, the continuation of the narrative gives us the impression that originally only four sons were mentioned, of whom three went to war and one stayed behind. This is the only way in which the reproaches later made by Eliab to David are comprehensible. Verse 15 is the clearest attempt to balance the material; whoever wrote it imagined that David went to the court at Gibeah only occasionally, when Saul's sickness necessitated it, and otherwise remained, now as before, the son of his father, with the duties which that involved. The sentence is valuable, because it is a significant interpretation of the way in which the later compiler undertook to present the whole material not only as a theological unity, which would have been quite legitimate, but also as an historical unity.

[a]Perhaps this is because it is not immediately visible; the picture of the 'giant Goliath' is not considered in the mind, but visualized.

[b]The text is particularly interested that the head is made of iron; we are in the transition period between the 'bronze age' and the 'iron age'.

[c]Cf. 16.10. In I Chron. 2.15, David is the seventh.

Like the family into which Ruth was married (Ruth 1.2), and from which, according to Micah 5.1, the Messiah is to come, Jesse is connected with Ephrath, the name of a district in or around Bethlehem. He appears as an older man, past the age of military service, but still fully the head of his family. **[17.16–19]** His task for David reveals both consideration and sagacity. David is to take bread to his three brothers; as the war is not one of movement, in which there is spoil for the taking, but a long-drawn-out (v. 16) and sedentary war, and the soldiers are evidently responsible for supplying themselves with their own provisions, Jesse's measures are understandable and necessary. 'Parched corn' was a delicacy (cf. Ruth 2.14). The special offering to the commander is a gesture as realistic as it is friendly. The 'token' which is required of David is to confirm the safe delivery of the gifts and also that his brothers are still alive; this custom of the 'arbun (Arabic, from the Greek arrabōn) has survived in the East until now. There is certainly no idea of taking their pay back to their father (so Schulz). **[17.20–22a]** We are then given a charming description of how David, who evidently set off very early, reached the Israelite camp at the very moment when the troops were going out to take up position. The military procedure so grips David that for the moment he forgets his commission—which he cannot as yet carry out, as those whom he has come to see are occupied—and goes forward with the troops. This really human touch serves the end of a higher guidance: David comes into contact with the Philistines. We hear no more of his carrying out of his father's orders, but the reader can assume from the depositing of the—not inconsiderable—baggage with the baggage guard that all will eventually reach its destination. All this is left on one side as being irrelevant to the course of events; only up to this point was Jesse's commission important; it was the way by which David reached his God-willed goal.

[17.22b–25] Hardly has he found and greeted his brothers[a] than he catches sight of the Philistine. The reaction of the men of Israel is described as before; in this way the narrator shapes the background to David's subsequent venture. It should, however, be remembered that 'fear' in the biblical sense is not simply to be equated with anxiety or even cowardice. It is frequently just the

---

[a]Asking how a person is in the East is considered most important and takes up a great deal of time; the kif ḥalak, 'How goes it?' occurs often in such conversations.

human reaction to unusual and terrifying circumstances (compare the attitude of the shepherds in the Christmas story) and often the mention of men's fear is simply meant to make it clear that God, and not man, is at work (e.g. Judg. 7). At the same time, the opportunity arises of mentioning something that we do not yet know, that the king has promised to give the man who conquers the Philistine great riches, and even the hand of the princess. This is a theme familiar from folk tales; here it is used because it fits with the historical course of events. **[17.26–31]** The narrative goes on to show that David has apparently not caught the words of the previous speakers; in this way he can express his indignation and readiness to fight, not to receive any reward, but quite simply because he finds it scandalous that an uncircumcised man, a worshipper of dead gods (cf. ch. 5) should insult the people of God and therefore the living God himself. This is very important for our assessment of the whole story. Even the interlude with the brothers is more than a skilful naturalistic touch on the part of the narrator; it is meant to show that David is involved in this episode neither through arrogance nor through zeal for adventure. As with Joseph's dreams,[a] there is a mysterious, divine plan behind the young man's words. The reader of the whole book will here recall the anointing, of which this story knows nothing. Eliab's criticism of David's words and conduct is rather to send David elsewhere with his remarks and thus—though this was not, of course, the intention—brings it about that they circulate among the troops and reach the ear of the king.[b]

[17.32–37] Saul's conversation with David goes straight to the point with a speed quite unexpected after what has gone before. David now quite unmistakably offers to fight with the giant. He bases his offer primarily on the experience which he has gained as a shepherd with lions and bears who preyed upon his flock. The bravery of Palestinian herdsmen is part of their professional pride,[c] but also has other grounds: the shepherd is responsible to his master for every member of the flock. Unless he can prove, say by showing the remains of a savaged animal (cf. Amos 3.12; Ex. 22.12), that a wild beast was really responsible for the loss, he must himself replace

---

[a]Stoebe, *VT* 6, 1956, pp. 402ff., recalls other 'traditional elements from the Joseph narratives'.

[b]Perhaps there was an inquiry from Saul about the bold speaker immediately after v. 31, which ends very abruptly. LXX adds at least 'and they brought him to Saul'. The omission could have been caused by vv. 55ff.

[c]This is important, e.g. in the exegesis of Ps. 23.3, 'for his name's sake'.

the plundered animal. More than anything, however, David here
expresses the fact that the Lord himself has been called forth by
Goliath's invitation. Thus Goliath is a representative of the ungodly
powers and David appears not merely as a simple and bold believer
who entrusts himself in all situations to the Lord, but at the same
time as an instrument under the divine guidance.

Saul, who is at first extremely dubious about the undertaking,
accordingly gives his consent, probably recognizing that here there
is more than a young man's boldness. [17.38–40] In placing his,
the royal, weapons, at David's disposal, he shows how strongly he
feels the impending battle as an official event. David in Saul's armour
—the reader may have seen here more than an attempt on the part
of the king to give all possible help to the 'brave young man'. But
David is not yet ready; the armour is too large for him. And the
Lord means to overcome the heavily armed giant not by an armed
man, but by an unarmed man. David takes the stones he needs
for his sling from the watercourse and goes to meet the Philistine in
shepherd's clothing. [17.41–47] The description of David is drawn
here with particular affection, and the wording is reminiscent of
16.12; this was evidently the classic description of the young David.
Goliath, of course, observes only his small stature and his beardless
face. In his 'scorn' he points out that it is no well-equipped warrior
who comes out to meet him; his opponent does not even have the
right weapons. The conversation between the two is remotely reminiscent of the speeches made by the Homeric heroes before battle,
though it is precisely here that David's words allow the theological
purpose of the chapter to come through particularly clearly. The
whole account is intended to demonstrate that the uncircumcised
Philistines, indeed 'all the world', are to see that Israel has a God
whose name alone is sufficient to strike the strongest man to the
ground. David's remark that this God needs neither sword nor
spear to aid him, and that he uses what is weak to put the strong to
shame reveals a basic law of the kingdom of God.[a] It is remarkable
that at the end the qāhāl, the (cultic) assembly, and not the people,
is mentioned. This text, too, has its basic setting among the hearing
community.

[17.48–51a] The description of the actual battle is not entirely

[a]This is completely misunderstood by E. Hirsch, who thinks that the Goliath
story should be expounded in the light of the Book of Judith (Das Alte Testament
und die Predigt des Evangeliums, 1936, pp. 33–49).

clear. The MT, but not the Vaticanus of LXX, reports that not only does David run towards Goliath, but also the Philistine approaches David (vv. 40f.). In v. 48, this is put the other way round. Moreover, MT suggests that David ran 'towards the battle line', which is hardly right (see above). If the clause 48b, superfluous in itself, is to make sense at all, it must mean that David goes forward from the Israelite battle line towards Goliath to the point at which he can best put his sling to use. There then follows, with unerring certainty, the shot which lays the Philistine out on the ground. We are probably to understand that Goliath falls down stunned and is only slain by the blow from David's sword. The interposed v. 50, referring to v. 47, underlines the fact that the victory was not won with ordinary weapons. Here we have the climax of the theological standpoint which has been adopted here. We need therefore see no contradiction to the surrounding sentences in the statement of v. 50 that the Philistine was 'killed' by the stone and only afterwards had his head cut off. What is stressed here, and was certainly taken up and celebrated by the community which heard this story and handed it down, was that God had done his saving work without there having been a sword in the hand of his chosen instrument.

[17.51b–54] We hear only briefly of the Israelite advance, the flight of the Philistines and the taking of the spoil. The whole action is only an episode in the historical course of the Philistine war and by no means what Goliath had promised in his confidence of victory, a decision as to who was to exercise the mastery. The narrative does not return to this point again; instead it continues to the point where we hear what happens to the head and weapons of the decapitated giant. The verse in which this happens is striking, because it ends the narrative, which is nevertheless (vv. 55ff.) not really at an end. It is still stranger that David should have taken the head to Jerusalem, which was at that time still in the hands of the Jebusites. Here we are only helped by the reflection that the 'relic'[a] will, in fact, have been brought to Jerusalem and displayed there later.[b]

---

[a]So Uhland in the ballad 'Roland Schildtrager', which is similarly concerned with the head of a giant (and his amputated hand).

[b]Cf. *ZAW* 47, 1929, p. 178, note 2. We may not exclude the possibility that there was a rock formation called 'Goliath's skull' in Jerusalem. There has still been no explanation of the origin of the name Golgotha ('skull') (cf. J. Jeremias, *Golgotha*, 1926, pp. 1f.). There is perhaps a connection here, later forgotten in favour of the tradition of the 'skull' of Adam, who was also imagined as being of gigantic size.

The weapons of Goliath are, however, treated differently. David is said to have put them 'in his tent'. This is an incomprehensible remark; as David had hitherto been merely the son of his father, he had no tent. b^e'$oh^ol\bar{o}$ will rather be a miswriting of b^e'$oh^ol\bar{\imath}$, with the final letter being an abbreviation for *yahweh*. The reference will then be to the tent-sanctuary of Yahweh, from which David later, in ch. 21, takes the sword of Goliath back again.[a] The hypothesis has already been advanced above that the location of the tent-sanctuary, i.e. Mizpah, was the place at which this part of the history of David, which is particularly interested in the weapons, was handed down.

[**17.55–58**] Somewhat lamely, if we view the narrative as a whole, the continuation and conclusion of the account next brings Saul's inquiry about David's descent. Here he is unknown both to Saul and to his commander, Abner. It has already been intimated that this extremely vividly narrated part of the tradition will have had its *Sitz im Leben* at a place where David was represented as the legitimate successor to the throne of Saul. Where that was, we cannot of course discover. We can, however, say this much: in view of the way in which the accents are placed it could only have come from someone who was privy to David's intentions; this is the way in which David himself might have wished to interpret his entering into the succession, sparing the first wearer of the crown and his family as much as possible.

[**18.1–4**] For that reason, the most beautiful description of a friendship which the Bible offers us—that between Jonathan and David—belongs here. On Jonathan's side it is completely disinterested; whether the same was true of David, we are not told, at least here, but there will have been a corresponding echo on his side (cf. especially II. 1). David is evidently a man with particularly attractive features, as we are shown here and often elsewhere; he takes hearts by storm, and everyone falls for him. He is indeed someone 'with whom' the Lord is (16.18; 17.37).[b] Here Jonathan goes beyond the personal feelings of a friendly disposition and makes a solemn 'covenant' which was certainly concluded under

---

[a]On this cf. Hertzberg, 'Mizpa', *ZAW* 47, 1929, pp. 161ff., esp. p. 178. In n. 5 of that page it is recalled that in I. 31.10 the Philistines, too, bring the weapons of their most prominent enemy into their temple.

[b]'It could be a particularly subtle feature of this narrative that Saul himself has to acknowledge it' (Stoebe, *VT* 6, 1956, p. 407).

Yahweh's eyes and in a fixed (cultic) form.[a] Jonathan's gift of his clothing and weapons to David is more than the generous action of a prince to a shepherd boy who has neither clothing for the court nor equipment for battle. It is a recognition of the *alter ego* in the covenant of friendship, and clothing especially is so much a part of the person who wears it that the giving of it to another person is equivalent to giving away one's own self. Twice here we also have the expression *k enapšō*—'as his own soul', like himself.[b] The covenant was kept by both until Jonathan's death, by David even afterwards. They were truly 'brothers' (II. 1.26).

[**18.5**] But the father,[c] too, is trusting and affectionate towards David. David now remains at the court and is given military commissions which he carries out successfully. The high status which he thus acquires is ungrudgingly recognized not only by the 'people', here particularly the troops, but also by the court—by no means a matter of course! As yet, however, there is still no mention of the victor's prize, the king's daughter. This is the subject of a later section.

4. SAUL'S JEALOUSY TOWARDS DAVID: 18.6–16

18 [6]As they were coming home, when David returned from slaying the Philistine, the women came out of all the cities of Israel, singing and dancing,[d] to meet King Saul, with timbrels, with songs of joy, and with instruments of music. [7]And the women sang to one another as they made merry, 'Saul has slain his thousands, and David his ten thousands.' And Saul was very angry,[e] and this saying displeased him; he said, 'They have ascribed to David ten thousands, and to me they have ascribed thousands; and what more can he have but the kingdom?' [9]And Saul eyed David from that day on.

10 And on the morrow an evil spirit from God rushed upon Saul, and he raved within his house, while David was playing the lyre, as he did day by day. Saul had his spear in his hand; [11]and Saul prepared to throw[f] the spear, for he thought, 'I will pin David to the wall.' But David evaded him twice.

[a]Cf. Budde at 18.9. He takes up Klostermann's conjecture that the *basileus* of LXX (i.e. Hebrew *melek*) should be read as *melaḥ*, thereby suggesting a 'covenant in salt'.

[b]Cf. Gressmann, p. 75.

[c]Eissfeldt (*Komposition*, p. 12) has put forward the conjecture that the subject in v. 2 was originally not Saul, but Jonathan, who, in fact, according to 'the source' which occurs here, became David's 'liege lord'. On the other hand, the tradition knows that even Saul's relationship with David was originally completely positive; cf. also on 18.20ff., etc.

[d]MT literally, 'To sing and the dances.'

[e]Words missing in LXX, see Commentary.

[f]See BH.

12 Saul was afraid of David, because the LORD was with him but had departed from Saul. ¹³So Saul removed him from his presence, and made him a commander of a thousand; and he went in and came out before the people. ¹⁴And David had success in all his undertakings; for the LORD was with him. ¹⁵And when Saul saw that he had great success, he stood in awe of him. ¹⁶But all Israel and Judah loved David; for he went out and came in before them.

The tragedy in Saul's life is manifest. Hardly has the Lord called him to be king than he incurs guilt in his sight. And hardly has he found an aide so fitting in every respect than rising mistrust poisons the relationship which began so hopefully. The picture sketched out here is not only remarkably vivid, but also extremely gripping. Saul's misfortune makes itself increasingly felt as David's star rises. This passage is narrated in such a way that only shadows fall upon Saul. In a way none too frequent in the Bible the course of events is given what amounts to a psychological basis.

[6] This is underlined by the structure which we have before us. The section is made up of three parts, each of which appears originally to have had a separate existence. This is particularly clear in the second passage. First we hear of the return from the war. The verses round off the Goliath narrative and properly belong to it. In the LXX, v. 6 runs: 'And the dancing girls came out to meet David from all the cities of Israel with timbrels, with (shouts of) joy and with cymbals.' The introductory sentence is lacking; on the other hand, it appears twice in MT! Evidently the tradition was not sure whom the women went out to meet. According to one account, attested in the second introductory clause of MT ('when David . . . returned') and in LXX, the women came out to meet David; according to the other, Saul; 'As they were coming home' would fit as an introduction to the latter. The mere fact of the duplicate introduction well reflects the uncertainty of the tradition. The first of the traditions is the more comprehensible; it is inconceivable that the women could have dared sing to Saul a verse which puts him in second place, whereas this would be quite understandable were David alone. On the other hand, the present form of MT makes it much easier to understand how Saul could have developed such jealousy of David. Anyone who knows how events are to turn out, of course, also knows the deeper justification of his mistrust: David is really destined to be Saul's successor.

The dance with which the women extend their greeting accords with modern Eastern custom. It is a *fantasia*, such as can often be seen, for example, at weddings. The women (and similarly, of course, the men) go in long lines, stepping backwards and forwards, often repeating certain verses. That is also the case here. The drumming on the hand drums and the playing on the (three-stringed) instrument is interspersed by the shout of joy, a high trilling produced by a speedy forward and backward movement of the tongue which can still be heard from women's lips on any joyful occasion. **[7–8]** The verse, which is rhymed in the original text, is certainly not meant to disparage Saul, but it must have had that effect on him. In the description of this effect it also looks as if the first clause— missing in LXX—belongs to the tradition which reported that the women came out to meet *Saul*. Saul's reaction is felt to be exaggerated because of his sickness, but is nevertheless—within the context of all the Saul-David material—regarded as justified: David really has everything but the kingdom. From a psychological point of view, Saul is seeing ghosts. But within the general framework of the material, his perception was correct.

[9–11] At this point an episode has been inserted which properly belongs to a later stage of developments and which, unlike the other parts, describes David not as a young warrior but as a lyre player; moreover, it recurs, though in a different, independent form, in 19.9f. The fact that vv. 10f. are lacking in the Vaticanus shows that there were circles who were conscious of the disparate nature of the material. On the other hand, the appearance of the theme at this early stage is by no means unskilful. If Saul maintained an attitude of jealous mistrust towards David from the return onwards, the attempt to remove him from the scene with a spear-throw,[a] a consequence of this attitude, is understandable, particularly if the reading *wayyiṭṭōl* ('and he raised'), and not MT *wayyāṭel* ('and he cast') is correct. We may further assume that David often had similar experiences. In the general context, it looks as if Saul's inward disturbance over the women's song, in fact, brought on the new attack. It is remarkable and by no means by chance that the words used here correspond to those in 10.6 and more particularly in 10.10, where the 'spirit' 'comes mightily' upon Saul 'in the midst' of the prophets, so that he goes into 'prophetic ecstasy'. It is the same

[a]Here for the first time the figure of Saul appears, as often later, connected with the spear (see esp. Gressmann, pp. 78f.). This may have been the way he was handed down to posterity.

thing, except that in ch. 18 an 'evil' spirit from God brings about this seizure. Saul is by nature extremely susceptible to such attacks in one way or another. The whole tragedy of his life is linked up with this. We should not fail to notice that we have here an attempt to understand Saul's nature and to forgive him much because of it. The whole passage is suffused with an understanding sympathy.

[12–16] Of course, this does not prevent the writer from showing how David rises higher and higher, despite the king's mistrust. Saul now sends David, whose presence he finds uncomfortable, to the front. It is not said here that this is to put him in danger, but it may be read between the lines. This, too, however, from Saul's point of view, is again a tragic move: David increases, rather than decreases, by the move. He develops his special abilities as a soldier and a leader and his way of winning the hearts of all those with whom he comes in contact. There he stands in his glory, loved by all, not only by his own tribe of Judah but also by Israel, as we are expressly told, whereas the king remains behind in his gloomy solitude, seized with dread that his measures have gone so contrary to the way which he had hoped for and planned. So they are contrasted, one the man 'with whom' the Lord is, and the other the man from whom the Lord has removed himself. And that is the meaning of the whole section. It is no expression of human capabilities and aims, but shows how God directs the destinies of two men and with them—the point with which we are concerned here—the history of the people of God.

5. DAVID BECOMES THE KING'S SON-IN-LAW:
18.17–30

18 17Then Saul said to David, 'Here is my elder daughter Merab; I will give her to you for a wife; only be valiant for me and fight the LORD's battles.' For Saul thought, 'Let not my hand be upon him, but let the hand of the Philistines be upon him.' 18And David said to Saul, 'Who am I, and who is my family*—the clan of my father*—in Israel, that I should be son-in-law to the king?' 21BAnd Saul said to David, 'In two years* you can become my son-in-law.' 19But at the time when Merab, Saul's daughter, should have been given to David, she was given to Adriel the Meholathite for a wife.

20 Now Saul's daughter Michal loved David; and they told Saul, and the thing pleased him. 21ASaul thought, 'Let me give her to him,

---

aSee BH.
bThis remark is meant to confirm the unusual meaning of *ḥay* = family.
cSee BH and the next note.

that she may be a snare for him, and that the hand of the Philistines may be against him.'ᵃ ²²And Saul commanded his servants, 'Speak to David in private and say, "Behold, the king has delight in you, and all his servants love you; now then become the king's son-in-law." ' ²³And Saul's servants spoke those words in the ears of David. And David said, 'Does it seem to you a little thing to become the king's son-in-law, seeing that I am a poor man and of no repute?' ²⁴And the servants of Saul told him, 'Thus and so did David speak.' ²⁵Then Saul said, 'Thus shall you say to David,"The king desires no marriage present except a hundred Philistine foreskins, that he may be avenged of the king's enemies." ' Now Saul thought to make David fall by the hand of the Philistines. ²⁶And when his servants told David these words, it pleased David well to be the king's son-in-law (in this way). Before the time had expired, ²⁷David arose and went, along with his men, and killed two hundred of the Philistines; and David brought their foreskins, and they laidᵇ them in full number before the king, that he might become the king's son-in-law. And Saul gave him his daughter Michal for a wife. ²⁸But when Saul saw and had to recognizeᶜ that the LORD was with David and that Michal, Saul's daughter, loved him, ²⁹Saul was still more afraid of David. So Saul was David's enemy continually. ³⁰Then the princes of the Philistines came out to battle, and as often as they came out David had more success than all the servants of Saul; so that his name was highly esteemed.

The narrative of how David becomes the son-in-law of Saul describes a new and particularly important stage in David's rise. The legitimacy of his claim to the succession becomes very clear. Of course, the material in its present form is meant to illustrate a different point: the breach between Saul and David becomes deeper. If, however, we look closely at the text, we will see that the material does not immediately provide a smooth continuity. **[17b, 21a, 25b]** It is remarkable that Saul, if he means to do away with David, uses so high a stake as his daughter. Could he not have set David the task of bringing back the Philistines' foreskins without the inducement of the princess's hand? The references to Saul's ulterior motives run parallel to the rest of the material without really being integrated in it. We can make a test and read the section without vv. 17b,

---

ᵃIn 21b, the *bištayim* of MT is a corruption of *bišnātayīm*; this corruption could be the reason why the half-verse has been moved from what is presumably its original position after v. 18 to after v. 21a. It is completely inapposite in this latter position, as the negotiations over Michal are indirectly anticipated. Whoever put the half-verse here thought that Saul had now 'twice' promised a daughter to David.

ᵇMSS 'And he laid'; but this is presumably a simplification.

ᶜ'Recognize' is omitted in LXX Vat. and may really not be part of the text. MT wishes to portray the sequel as a product of observation and inference.

21a, 25b. The result is a completely self-contained narrative, in which Saul views David not only without mistrust, but even with a degree of goodwill (v. 22). Moreover, the three half-verses mentioned are so similar that one involuntarily recognizes the same interpretative voice in each. Verses 28f. belong to the same point of view, while v. 30 adopts yet another standpoint.

If these observations are correct, we can see that the material has undergone a development, and if we establish this development we can see the historical situation. We must further consider the possibility that the Merab episode is a sort of parallel to the story of Michal; the latter in no way presupposes the former. We could say that the Merab affair is connected with 17.25. In the case of Michal, however, the situation is different; here the starting-point is not an earlier promise, but the young girl's love. Nevertheless the compiler has woven a picture with extremely vivid colours out of the two stories. To understand the section rightly, we must look at the individual elements from which it developed as well as its final form.

[17] As has been said, the beginning gives the impression of being an intentional allusion to the king's promise of 17.25. Here Budde ('the mere word order shows that Saul's promise stems from an obligation he has undertaken') is to be upheld against Gressmann ('no syllable of the present text refers back to the reward for victory offered in the Goliath story'). At least, this will be the intention of the compiler of the whole work; otherwise this particular feature of ch. 17 would have completely disappeared. The Merab episode is missing in Codex Vaticanus, as is that part of ch. 17 which contains the relevant promise; this speaks indirectly for their association. According to it David is a youth just grown out of boyhood, who is really not yet of an age to marry. Saul is therefore quite justified in telling him that he must first prove himself for a time as a *ben ḥayil* in the 'wars of Yahweh'; in ch. 17, David's success might in the end be just a piece of luck, and the king will have wanted to give his daughter to a tried warrior rather than to a reckless shepherd boy.

[18] This understandable attitude of Saul is expounded *in malam partem* in v. 17b, but, as has been said before, this need not have originally been the case. David's answer accords with oriental courtesy, both ancient (Judg. 6.15; I. 9.21, II. 7.18) and modern; it is not a refusal, but shows that David knows his duty. Within the sentence, the words 'in Israel' should not remain unnoticed; David, in fact, comes from Judah, and so has nothing by virtue of which he

can lay claim to such honour 'in Israel'. [21b] If the conjecture about v. 21b is right, then Saul put the space of time for David to prove himself at two years. [19] Why the king does not then keep his word, we are not told.[a] In the Lucianic recension there is an addition, that Merab 'feared' David; in the East, however, the emotional agitation of a young girl is usually no argument for a father to call off a wedding. Be this as it may, Saul's arbitrary conduct is the point which prompted the later inclusion of these events among the measures stemming from the king's mistrust. This need not originally have been the case, but we now have an action similar to that of Laban (Gen. 29).

[20] In the general context, Saul's action in the case of Michal then looks very much like that of a man who has afterwards been smitten with conscience. But this impression is given only by the juxtaposition of the two episodes. The text itself has nothing to say, and thus shows that the Michal account once led an independent existence and originally had nothing to do with the Goliath narrative. It is rather that all, one after the other, are captivated by David's irresistible appearance—the father and the son, the court and the army. How can the king's daughter be an exception? [22–24] The father's approval of his daughter's wishes will originally have come from a desire to join David to his house. Saul's use of his middle-men corresponds with Eastern custom current even today.[b] The unusual fact that the initiative is on the side of the woman can be explained from the special circumstances. David is not, of course, in a position to offer the usual presents to the bride, presents which are determined by the status and wealth of her family, and which in the case of the king would have been virtually unattainable. It is evident here, too, that David has no prior right to his bride, as, say, in connection with 17.25.

[25–27] Saul's request for a hundred Philistine foreskins instead of the bride-price is meant to give David the opportunity of winning

---

[a]Stoebe (*Eissfeldt-Festschrift*, 1958) thinks that the Jacob tradition has exercised some influence here (pp. 241f.). He holds it possible (p. 243) that there was an original (written) form of an account of a marriage between David and two daughters of Saul, as in the case of Jacob. But it is more probable 'that David was cheated of them both by Saul' (cf. I. 25.44). Stoebe is himself fully conscious of the problems attached to this line of thought. These problems are also augmented by the fact that the David material was committed to writing very soon after the events themselves would have taken place.

[b]L. Bauer, *Volksleben im Lande der Bibel*, 1903[2], p. 97.

S.–F

his bride in a way which befits a warrior (see Judg. 1.12). Here we
have a parallel with the offer of 17.25. The king's demand not for
amputated noses or ears, but for foreskins as evidence, i.e. that
part of the body in which the cultic-religious contrast of the 'uncircumcised' is manifest, is again (cf. v. 17) connected with the fact
that the war being waged here is not just any war, but the war of
Yahweh. We have already commented on the remark that Saul
devised this as a way of doing away with David. Agreement is
evidently reached on a definite time by which David is to have
accomplished his task, which seems so barbaric to us. Despite the
evidence of LXX and II. 3.14, it is hardly a scribal error that we
read of *two* hundred foreskins being given to the king before the
time is up; this is meant as a 'bold over-trumping' of the prescribed
task (Budde).

[28–30] So Michal becomes David's wife, and we read that this,
too, serves to elevate David's status and to deepen the gulf between
Saul and David. The episode is once again fitted into the general
pattern. But the closing remark could belong to the original tradition, for here we have no more than the fact that David's ever-
increasing fame at arms is mentioned with wonderment. This note
alone confirms that events did not take place in the concentrated
brevity with which they are here described. Quite a long time passed
before the young David became an experienced leader and rose to
be a member of the royal family. The mistrust of the king, plagued
by an 'evil spirit', must soon have been aroused, however, even if
not from the earliest days. The present account sees the relationship
and the consequences of things which happened at very different
times. Viewed from this lofty perspective, Saul would have had reason
for regarding David as an enemy from the very beginning. Just as
the 'possessed' of the New Testament see the divine reality (Mark
1.24; 5.7; Acts 16.17), so Saul, in the grips of an evil spirit, sees
what God has in store and attempts to go against it. Hence we are
given a very clear picture both of the deep tragedy in which the
history of Saul is submerged and of the mysterious background to it,
shaped by the will of God.

6. JONATHAN AS MEDIATOR: 19.1–7

19 ¹And Saul told Jonathan his son and all his servants that he
wanted to kill David. But Jonathan, Saul's son, delighted much in
David. ²And Jonathan told David, 'Saul my father seeks to kill you;

therefore take heed to yourself in the morning, stay in a secret place and hide yourself; ³and I will go out and stand beside my father in the field where you are, and I will speak to my father about you; and if I learn anything, I will tell you.' ⁴And Jonathan spoke well of David to Saul his father, and said to him, 'Let not the king sin against his servant David; because he has not sinned against you, and because his deeds have been of good service to you; ⁵for he took his life in his hand and he slew the Philistine, and the LORD (through his hand)ᵃ wrought a great victory for all Israel. You saw it and rejoiced; why then will you sin against innocent blood by killing David without cause?' ⁶And Saul hearkened to the voice of Jonathan; Saul swore, 'As the LORD lives, he shall not be put to death.' ⁷And Jonathan called David, and Jonathan showed him all these things. And Jonathan brought David to Saul, and he was in his presence as before.

Relations between Saul and David come to a crisis. Saul—if we look at the whole narrative context—has not reached his goal by indirect methods. For the first time, he says quite deliberately and in the presence of others that he means to do away with David. [1] This sentence thus marks an important step forward in the direction of a split between Saul and David. And at just this point, with consummate skill, the compiler has inserted the attempted reconciliation by the crown prince, to slow up the pace of the tragedy. This attempt is at the same time a real test of the friendship between David and Jonathan, and no easy test at that. [2–3] It has been noticed that Jonathan does not immediately express his feelings about his father's intention, but first advises David to go away and waits for a suitable opportunity. There are, of course, difficulties here for the exegete. It is absolutely impossible to harmonize Jonathan's advice to David to stay in a secret place with his decision to hold the decisive conversation with Saul at the place 'in the field' where David will be. Does Jonathan then already know where Saul means to go, and does he think of a definite hiding-place, with room enough for his purpose? Nothing, however, is said about this. Caspari thought that Jonathan envisaged a particular piece of agricultural work in which Jonathan would stand 'at the side' (literally) of his father. But then the clause 'where you are', in turn becomes incomprehensible, and has to be emended or deleted. Or was this relative clause misunderstood at an early date? Did it originally mean that Jonathan would occupy David's position (as a substitute) (e.g. perhaps, 'there where you—usually are'),

ᵃSee BH.

intending to advance his interests on that occasion? The most we can assume is that two different traditions have been juxtaposed here, one of which contained the beginning of v. 3 'where you are', and the other its conclusion. The second is the one which originally belonged to the entire report. According to it, Jonathan wanted to advise David to hide and then merely promised to speak to his father about him. The first tradition, like ch. 20, knew of a scene 'in the field'ᵃ which took place in such a way that David himself could overhear the conversation. Then, of course, it was no longer necessary for Jonathan to bring the news. But this tradition is still preserved only by the half-verse, which should properly be put in parenthesis.

[4–7] Jonathan's argument is clear and simple, especially in its reference to the Philistines. It is so simple that it must convince anyone, even the king, who does not, in fact, always appear as a man blinded with fury, but also as someone accessible to reasonable argument. So he guarantees David's life with an oath, and the reconciliation takes place without any special action. David simply reappears, and, as the literal translation runs, 'was in his presence', i.e. did him service. In the general context this is, of course, as has been said before, no more than a brief postponement of the inevitable consequence of David's increasing successes, Saul's mistrust, and over and above these the Lord's direction of history.

7. DAVID IS SAVED FROM SAUL'S AMBUSH: 19.8–24

19 ⁸And there was war again; and David went out and fought with the Philistines, and made a great slaughter among them, so that they fled before him.

9 Then an evil spirit from the LORD came upon Saul, as he sat in his house with his spear in his hand; and David was playing the lyre. ¹⁰And Saul sought to pin David to the wall with his spear; but he eluded Saul, so that he struck the spear into the wall. And David fled, and escaped.

That same nightᵇ ¹¹Saul sent messengers to David's house to watch him, that he might kill him in the morning. But Michal, David's wife, told him, 'If you do not save your life tonight, tomorrow you will be killed.' ¹²So Michal let David down through the window; and he fled away and escaped. ¹³Michal took the teraphim and laid it on the

---

ᵃPresumably again a definite place was pointed out as the scene of the event.
ᵇSee BH. The two words ballayᵉlā hahū have been drawn into v. 10 in MT.

bed and put a pillow of goats' hair at its head, and put a covering over it. [14]And when Saul sent messengers to take David, she said, 'He is sick.' [15]Then Saul sent the messengers to see David, saying, 'Bring him up to me in the bed, that I may kill him.' [16]And when the messengers came in, behold, the teraphim was in the bed, with the pillow of goats' hair at its head. [17]Saul said to Michal, 'Why have you deceived me thus, and let my enemy go, so that he has escaped?' And Michal answered Saul, 'He said to me, "Let me go; why should I kill you?"'

18 Now David fled and escaped, and he came to Samuel at Ramah, and told him all that Saul had done to him. And he and Samuel went and dwelt at Naioth. [19]And it was told Saul, 'Behold, David is at Naioth in Ramah.' [20]Then Saul sent messengers to take David; and when they[a] saw the company[b] of prophets prophesying, and Samuel standing as head over them, the Spirit of God came upon the messengers of Saul, and they also prophesied. [21]When it was told Saul, he sent other messengers, and they also prophesied. And Saul sent messengers again the third time, and they also prophesied. [22c]Then he himself went to Ramah, and came to the great well that is in Secu; and he asked. 'Where are Samuel and David?' And one said, 'Behold, they are at Naioth in Ramah.' [23]And he went from there[a] to Naioth in Ramah; and the Spirit of God came upon him also, and as he went he prophesied, until he came to Naioth in Ramah. [24]And he too stripped off his clothes, and he too prophesied before Samuel, and lay naked all that day and all that night. Hence it is said, 'Is Saul also among the prophets?'

While this section has a single thread running through it, it is, in fact, composed of four different parts. **[8]** First we have a note about the increasing skill at arms of the young David, who is making a great slaughter in the incessant Philistine war (14.52). The form of expression is the same as that in Judg. 15.8. But the note is not inserted at this point merely for the greater glory of David; it explains why the settled relations between David and Saul brought about by Jonathan did not last long. And it is the reason why immediately afterwards we are told of Saul's (second) attempt to murder David with his spear. **[9–10]** The episode is again vividly narrated; we have a clear picture of Saul with his spear and David with his lyre. The danger of David's position is thus strongly emphasized; the account knows, however, how sick an act Saul's is. But as the Lord is 'with' David, he is able to avoid the spear and escape.

[a]See BH.

[b]The root *qhl* has here been transmitted in reverse order; *q[e]hillat* is meant.

[c]LXX attractively begins the sentence: 'Then Saul was seized with burning anger.' But there seems to be no reason why that should have been omitted.

From time to time in Old Testament poetry, and in prose,[a] certain terms are given special emphasis by being repeated several times. This is the case throughout ch. 19 with the hiphil of *mūt*, which appears four times in vv. 1–7 and a further four times afterwards, and with *mālaṭ* in the piel, which occurs five times. These are, in fact, the key words: Saul means to 'do away with' David, David 'escapes'.

Now, this material is used three times, though the key words themselves are not used in the third. The first time, David escapes through his own dexterity; the second time with the help of Michal, and the third time with the help of Samuel. In all three cases, however, the narrator would claim that the Lord was the real deliverer. For in the background there stands the fact that Saul is in no position to thwart the divine plan in which David is destined for great tasks. Saul therefore appears in the three narratives as someone vainly running his head against a brick wall. Neither his spear nor his various messengers can succeed against anyone 'with' whom the Lord is.

[11–12] The Michal story is told with particular charm; despite the seriousness of the account there is considerable humour woven into it. Whether it is connected with what goes beforehand is questionable. Nevertheless, in its present context it is meant to show that David regarded the spear-throw as an impulsive act brought on by the evil spirit, and went home. It is his watchful wife who sees the continuing danger. She arranges his escape, which, as in the case of Joshua's spies (Josh. 2.15) and of the Apostle Paul (II Cor. 11.33), is made through the window of the house. We are to imagine the house, as in the other two cases, as being in or on the town wall— otherwise David would have fallen into the watchers' hands.

[13–17] Michal's ruse with the teraphim is meant to gain time for David's flight. As the king's daughter, she has little to fear for herself, but she protects herself against any eventuality by lying. The way in which the figure of the sleeping man is made up of the household god, the goats' hair pillow and the covering is magnificent. We do not, however, hear the story aright if we regard it merely as a commendation of the cunning wife who comes to the aid of her husband. Surely the listener felt her conduct—we hear something similar at a later stage (II. 5)—to be that of Saul's daughter, and thought less of the two lies, which would not have been held against

[a]Cf., e.g., Josh. 3f., Judg. 1, and my commentary *ad loc.*

her. The presence of a *teraphim*,[a] which were regarded as taboo, at least by the later tradition, in David's house is quite astonishing, and would only have been accepted because 'the person concerned was the daughter of the rejected Saul' (Budde on v. 13). Her deception of the messengers with the help of the teraphim and the readiness of the messengers, indeed of Saul himself, to be deceived, is narrated with furious joy and put to the discredit of the first king. With all the greater thankfulness is the description of the 'escape' taken up and impressed upon hearers and readers.

[18–24] The narrative of David's stay with Samuel is now attached to the preceding account by a brief transitional sentence. It is, however, an independent legend which may have been transmitted at Ramah. It is a parallel to the story told in 10.10–12 to explain the origin of the saying 'Is Saul also among the prophets?' which is quoted in both places. It is reminiscent of II Kings 1, where the king similarly tries three times to seize someone under the protection of God by means of his messengers. It suggests that the episode of David's anointing by Samuel was also known in the circles in which this form of the narrative was current, though there is no direct preference. The name of the place to which Samuel goes with David cannot be explained, though some reference to *nāwe* (meadow, dwelling-place) has much to commend it. In any case, it describes the place where the prophets would live (Schulz: monastery). They were, in fact, accustomed to assemble at sanctuaries. Perhaps Naioth is the description of a settlement of prophets, just as Nob, which we meet later, is that of a settlement of priests. The place Secu, with the great well, is also unknown to us. The word may describe some pasturage. LXX has interpreted the name as 'the well of the threshing-floor on the bare hill', but this is hardly right. In any case, the narrative displays a good knowledge of the topography throughout.

Samuel's journey with David to Naioth, begun as soon as he learns of David's position, surely suggests that he hopes to find safety for his protégé in the sanctuary there. This is immediately confirmed. No one can escape the influence of the Spirit of God which is at work there. Samuel appears as the 'principal of a theological college' (Cornill, cf. Budde on v. 20) without giving the impression that he

[a]There is no evidence of a singular form of this word. But in our passage the plural form is used as a singular, as the form lying on the bed is meant to simulate a man. (But cf. P. R. Ackroyd, *Expository Times* 62, 1950/51, pp. 378f. Tr.)

himself is seized by the prophetic spirit. We do not hear whether David was similarly affected. The narrative is much more concerned to bring Saul into contact with the prophetic ecstasy and thus to give the basis for the proverb. Saul is evidently drawn more strongly into the workings of the spirit than are his messengers, as he tears the clothes from off his body and lies on the ground in this state like a paralytic. Indeed, he is first gripped by the mere approach of the prophetic fury. We can see elsewhere that Saul is particularly affected by all that is holy. The description here, however, is not written in praise of the king. This is so both in the case of the account itself and of the position it occupies in the narrative sequence. For in the general context this event is, of course, meant to show that here the Lord is finding yet another way of procuring David's 'escape' from danger.

8. DAVID'S PARTING FROM JONATHAN:
20.1–42 (Heb. 20.1–21.1)

20 [1]Then David fled from Naioth to Ramah, and came and said before Jonathan, 'What have I done? What is my guilt? And what is my sin before your father, that he seeks my life?' [2]And he said to him, 'Far from it! You shall not die. Behold, my father does nothing either great or small without disclosing it to me;[a] and why should my father hide this from me? It is not so.' [3]But David replied,[b] 'Your father knows well that I have found favour in your eyes; and he thinks, "Let not Jonathan know this, lest he be grieved." But truly, as the LORD lives and as your soul lives, there is but a step between me and death.' [4]Then said Jonathan to David, 'Whatever you say, I will do for you.' [5]David said to Jonathan, 'Behold, tomorrow is the new moon, and I should not fail to sit at table with the king; but let me go, that I may hide myself in the field until the evening (and) to the third (evening).[c] [6]If your father misses me at all, then say, "David earnestly asked leave of me to run to Bethlehem his city; for there is a yearly sacrifice there for all the family." [7]If he says, "Good!" it will be well with your servant; but if he is angry, then know that evil is determined by him. [8]Therefore deal kindly with your servant, for you have brought your servant into a covenant of the LORD with you. But if there is guilt in me, slay me yourself; for why should you bring me to your father?' [9]And Jonathan said, 'Far be it from you! If I

---

[a]Literally: Uncovering my ear.

[b]The ʿayin at the end of wayyišābaʿ is a dittograph; the wayyāšeb of LXX will be right. David's 'swearing' seemed understandable because of v. 3b.

[c]The word 'third' is missing in LXX B L. It has been supplied in MT in view of the continuation of the story (v. 19), because the events, in fact, take place two days after this conversation.

knew that it was determined by my father that evil should come upon you, would I not tell you?' [10]Then said David to Jonathan, 'Who will tell me if perhaps[a] your father answers you roughly?' [11]And Jonathan said to David, 'Come, let us go out into the field.' So they both went out into the field.

12 And Jonathan said to David, 'By the LORD[b] the God of Israel, if about this time tomorrow[c] I have sounded my father and he is well disposed toward David, then[d] I will send no one to disclose it to you. [13]But should it please my father to do you harm, the LORD do so to Jonathan, and more also, if I do not disclose it to you, and send you away, that you may go in safety. May the LORD be with you, as he has been with my father. [14]And do you,[e] if I am still alive, do you[e] show me the loyal love of the LORD, that I may not die; [15]and do not cut off your loyalty from my house for ever. But when the LORD cuts off every one of the enemies of David from the face of the earth, then [16]Jonathan's name shall not be cut off[e] from the house of David, but the LORD will avenge himself on David's enemies.' [17]And Jonathan made David swear again[f] by his love for him; for he loved him as he loved his own soul.

18 Then Jonathan said to him, 'Tomorrow is the new moon; and you will be missed if your seat is empty.[g] [19]And on the third day you will be greatly missed;[h] then go to the place where you hid yourself on the day of the deed,[i] and remain beside yonder[j] stone heap. [20]And I will shoot three arrows to the side of it,[k] as though I were shooting them at a mark.[l] [21]Then watch! I will send the boy, saying, "Go, find the arrows." If I say to the lad, "Look, the arrow[e] is on this side of you, take it",[e] then you are to come, for, as the LORD lives, it is safe for you and there is no danger. [22]But if I say to the youth, "Look, the arrow[e] is beyond you", then go; for the LORD has sent you away. [23]And as for the matter of which you and I have spoken, behold the

[a]Ewald translates the difficult 'ō ma thus; it is the best conjecture hitherto, if one maintains the integrity of the text (LXX *ean*). Schulz supposes a variant reading: 'ō ('whether', GK § 150i) *ya'ankā 'ābīkā qāšā* or *ma ya'ankā 'ābīkā*. It could also be that the text was soon corrupted from *ma ya'ankā 'ābīkā ṭōbā 'ō qāšā* (what your father answers you good or bad); the loss of the *ṭōbā* would then have caused the confusion.

[b]Perhaps a *ḥay* has fallen out before *yahweh*.

[c]'The third day' is a later addition, see on v. 5.

[d]*āz* and *lō* must be transposed. The MT 'shall I not then . . .' tries to square the thought with vv. 18ff. See Commentary.

[e]See BH.

[f]This is the way *wayyōsep* should probably be translated.

[g]Here, too, the same word *pāqad*—'miss, look round for'.

[h]So the versions; but the misreading of *tērēd* as *tippāqēd* is striking. Perhaps the sentence *we'šillaštā tippāqēd me'ōd* was followed by something like *we'attā tērēd*?

[i]See Commentary.

[j]Read *hallāz*.

[k]Read *ṣiddāh*; the suffix refers to the 'stone'.

[l]An alteration of the prefix from *le* to *ke* is unnecessary.

LORD is between you and me for ever.' ²⁴So David hid himself in the field.

And when the new moon came, the king sat down to eat food. ²⁵The king sat upon his seat, as at other times, upon the seat by the wall; and over against him was Jonathan's seat,ᵃ and Abner sat by Saul's side, but David's place was empty.

26 Yet Saul did not say anything that day; for he thought, 'Something has befallen him; he is not clean.'ᵇ ²⁷But on the second day, the morrow after the new moon, David's place was empty. And Saul said to Jonathan his son, 'Why has not the son of Jesse come to the meal, either yesterday or today?' ²⁸Jonathan answered Saul, 'David earnestly asked leave of me to go to Bethlehem; ²⁹he said, "Let me go; for our family holds a sacrifice in the city, and my brother has commanded me to be there. So now, if I have found favour in your eyes, let me get away and see my brothers." For this reason he has not come to the king's table.'

30 Then Saul's anger was kindled against Jonathan, and he said to him, 'You son of a degenerate, rebelliousᶜ woman, do I not know that you have chosen the son of Jesse to your shame, and to the shame of your mother's nakedness? ³¹For as long as the son of Jesse lives upon the earth, neither you nor your kingdom shall be established. Therefore send and fetch him to me, for he shall surely die.' ³²Then Jonathan answered Saul his father, 'Why should he be put to death? What has he done?' ³³But Saul brandishedᵈ his spear to smite him; so Jonathan knew that his father was determined to put David to death. ³⁴And Jonathan rose from the table in fierce anger and ate no food the second day of the month, for he was grieved—because of Davidᵉ—because his father had disgraced him.

35 In the morning Jonathan went out into the field to the appointment with David, and with him a little lad. ³⁶And he said to his lad, 'Run and find the arrows which I shoot.' As the lad ran, he shot an arrow beyond him. ³⁷And when the lad came to the place of the arrow which Jonathan had shot, Jonathan called after the lad and said, 'Is not the arrow beyond you?' ³⁸And Jonathan called after the lad, 'Hurry, make haste, stay not.' So Jonathan's lad gathered up the arrow, and came to his master. ³⁹But the lad knew nothing; only Jonathan and David knew the matter. ⁴⁰And Jonathan gave his weapons to his

---

ᵃMT incomprehensible: 'And Jonathan stood up'. The *wayᵉqaddēm* suggested by LXX is no better; for this passage the translation is just 'and J. sat opposite'. Perhaps the original text ran *ūlᵉpānāu mᵉqōm*; this may have become illegible early on, with only the four consonants *wyqm* remaining.

ᵇThe added clause, 'for he is not clean' could have arisen from an intention to interpret the previous, linguistically strange, sentence by a more usual one (Caspari).

ᶜ'Degenerate through rebellion'; other examples, GK § 128x.

ᵈSee BH.

ᵉA marginal note, almost certainly incorrect. It is not David, but Jonathan himself who has been disgraced.

lad, and said to him, 'Go and carry them to the city.' [41]And as soon as
the lad had gone, David rose from beside the stone[a] and fell on his face
to the ground, and bowed three times; and they kissed one another and
wept with one another to excess.[b] [42]Then Jonathan said to David, 'Go
in peace, forasmuch as we have sworn both of us in the name of the
LORD, saying, "The LORD shall be between me and you, and between
my descendants and your descendants, for ever".' (Heb. 21.1.) And
David[c] rose and departed, and Jonathan went into the city.

David's departure from the royal court, like his arrival there, was of
particular concern both to his contemporaries and to later generations. This interest is to be explained not just as an interest in
David's person, but also as an interest in the monarchy. We have
already pointed out how important it seems to have been to the
tradition to show that David's path in succeeding to the throne was
a legitimate one. David's disappearance from the court could have
given the impression that this path, which the compiler prefaced
with the anointing, ended before it had begun. Such a view could
have commended itself all the more because David now seemed to
sink back again into his nothingness—indeed, his desertion to the
land of the Philistines and to a fugitive's life in the wilderness seemed
to have put him completely out of the running. It is therefore important that one after another Saul's daughter Michal, the prophetic
leader Samuel, and now, too, the crown prince and heir to the
throne, should all have helped David's flight.

In the present chapter this can be seen above all by the way in
which the actual narrative has been developed by later writing so
as to reveal the concern of the final compiler. The chapter in its
present form is directed towards David's future position as king.

[1] The narrative begins with a sentence intended to link the
material with the Samuel episode. Both accounts originally led an
independent existence and have here, like the story of Michal, been
combined to serve the dominant theme. Nevertheless, we might ask
how the compiler envisages the transition from ch. 19 to ch. 20. 'If
the chapter stands in its original context and does not introduce

[a]*hannegeb* ('the south') is certainly wrong. LXX has here, as in v. 19, a word
'*ergab*, left untranslated from the Hebrew. It is usually rendered 'heap of stones'.
The word, which does not occur elsewhere, was also unknown to the Massoretes,
because on v. 19 it is paraphrased '*eben* (stone) and here *negeb*.

[b]This is what the LXX must have read, with its *heōs synteleiās megalēs* ('*ad
taklīt gᵉdōlā*?). MT: 'to David; he has done great' is incomprehensible.

[c]So LXX. Perhaps the word found its way into the margin and thence wrongly
into the text at v. 41? See the previous note.

events from the time before David's flight, then David used the hours
of Saul's ecstasy with hasty resoluteness to rush to Gibeah and speak
with his faithful friend' (D. Ketter). As an attempt to reconstruct the
course of events, such a sentence is mistaken, for the events related
in ch. 19 are so described that further investigation of Saul's intentions would have been unnecessary. If we are looking for an earlier
event with which to connect the present story, we must attach it
directly to the story of the spear (19.9ff.), where the question
whether Saul's attack on David rested on the deliberate intention
of the king to do away with David could still arise. Here there would
be room for an investigation of the king's intentions. In attaching
ch. 20 directly to the Naioth narrative, the compiler seems to have
imagined that Saul's conduct appeared so impossible and so un-
believable to David that David felt he should make one more close
investigation. In the view of the compiler of the whole work, Saul
is thus, as it were, given one more chance to rehabilitate himself.
But at the same time David comes to look like the innocent exile, and
his right to the later succession to the throne is made all the more
secure.

The story begins very vividly. David's excitement is impressively
stressed by the threefold question. He is conscious of no guilt in
himself, but after what has happened he must fear that Saul is
seeking his life. [2–3] Even Jonathan's words of consolation cannot
make him waver in his view. Unlike Jonathan, who imagines himself
to be in full possession of his father's confidence, he supposes that
the mere fact of Jonathan's relations with him, David, on this
occasion prevents the king from being open with his son. David thus
shows himself to be the better psychologist; Jonathan is the *anima
candida*. In the figure of Jonathan, the Old Testament has a real
nobleman of high sensibility.

In their relationship as friends, Jonathan has the higher position
and excels in affectionate, unselfish friendship, whereas David is
more resolute and is superior in intellect. [4–8] In any case, the plan
for discovering Saul's attitude comes from him, and Jonathan
follows his advice almost literally. The verses here give the impression
that David is more Jonathan's than Saul's subordinate, that Jonathan is David's 'liege lord'.[a] It is, however, sufficient to assume that
Jonathan here acts as representative and proxy of his father. David's

[a]Eissfeldt uses this fact for distinguishing the sources, *Komposition der Samuelisbücher*, pp. 12, 15.

plan rests on the fact that in the normal course of events he would be invited to the royal table with Abner and Jonathan for the two-day new-moon feast; whether because of his status or his kinship with the royal house, we are not told. His plan is well devised. In the event, an innocent interpretation of his absence on the part of Saul would show the groundlessness of his fears, while an outbreak of anger on the part of the king would show that he was set against David. David does not, of course, want to fall into Saul's hands. In view of the previous incident—and this becomes all the more serious if we think not only of the spear-throw but of everything reported in ch. 19—David no longer dares to go into the king's presence, and would if need be rather be killed at the hand of his friend. Here, too, Jonathan seeks to dispel David's fears and promises him news if the king is set on his downfall.

[9–10] If the text in v. 10 is correct, we then have the details of how an *unfavourable* message is to be brought to David. We cannot, however, exclude the possibility that in the original form of the text David asked for news to be brought to him in any event (cf. the note on v. 10). The present form of the text could be explained from the fact that both before and after we are only told that bad news reached David's ears. We will return to this point shortly. [11–13] Jonathan now makes a suggestion, and in order to make it takes David out of his, Jonathan's, house, into the open. Here two different ideas of Jonathan's are expressed. The second, the business with the arrows, is logically connected with going out into the field. On the other hand, Jonathan could have made the earlier remarks as well in his house as anywhere else. To suggest that 'in the open . . . they are safe from eavesdroppers'a is not convincing; it would only make sense if they were both hard of hearing and had to shout their secrets to one another! Quite clearly we have here two different accounts of the matter discussed. The first is the one which is, in fact, continued and developed later, and is theologically the more important. It is there-fore introduced with a solemn oath, to increase the tension in the reader's expectation. Here there are no details of how the news is to be brought, except that Jonathan will only warn David should it be bad. Otherwise he will not send a messenger. The present form of the text of v. 12 does not, however, give us to understand this clearly; it gives the impression of having been harmonized with v. 10, where David is to be given news in any event. But not only

aSchulz, p. 306.

v. 12, but also v. 13, indicates that Jonathan feels it necessary to send news only in the second event. In that case he would let his friend depart 'in safety'.[a] No word is said about how the news is to be brought, in answer to David's request of v. 10. Jonathan's remarks are leading in a different direction. The end of v. 13 already puts David and Saul together, and this can only be understood as an allusion by Jonathan to David's future kingdom. **[14–17]** Then comes the request that David, in his later glory, will not treat him, Jonathan, and his descendants in the way in which the ruler from another house so often treated the supporters of the old king (even David to some degree acts like this, cf. II. 21.1ff.). Jonathan asks David for this evidence of 'Yahweh's grace'. An assurance by David that he will play his part belongs at the end of this request. Usually it is imagined that Jonathan offered an oath to David or 'swore' to him.[b] The passage only makes sense, however, if Jonathan made David swear. This could also be inferred from II. 21.7. The oath is a consequence of Jonathan's love for David, who is for Jonathan completely safe, indeed sacred. David kept the oath and proved true to his friend (II. 9). More important still is the open reference to David's future. David is on the brink of flight, he is now dependent, and will soon be an outlaw; in the foreseeable future he will have to make decisions such as those now made by Saul and Jonathan, royal decisions. The Lord's plans are firmly and clearly contrasted to the present moment. The man shortly to be exiled will nevertheless become a king.

[18–24a] The curtain has been raised on the distant future, but the narrative now returns to the matter in hand. Jonathan, as has already been said, takes up David's suggestion about the new-moon feast, and recommends him to hide outside at a certain place. 19.2f. mentions such a hiding-place, and it will be the same spot. It is marked by a stone or heap of stones (*'ergab* LXX?); the stone will certainly have been pointed out later, and the event will have been located there. We do not know what is meant by the 'day of the deed'. Commentators differ between 'work-day' and 'day of the attack' (with the spear); neither is particularly apt, but the second is much better than the first. Jonathan will then inform his friend

[a]Cf. also v. 42a and the farewell greeting *ma' salame*, still given in the Arabian East by the person remaining to the one going away.

[b]Already by LXX, so too exegetes; Schulz, p. 308, has the right idea, but does not go on to draw the necessary conclusions.

in his hiding-place about the situation by means of the play with the arrows, which is to be done near the stone, i.e. in fact by the words which he shouts out to his boy. An arrow shot beyond the boy is to represent bad news; an arrow which falls between Jonathan and the boy, good news. Then David will have his answer. Should the worst happen, there is a further reference to the inviolability of the agreement that has been concluded. It is very beautifully said that the Lord stands 'between' the friends, probably a relic of old ideas about the covenant. In Gen. 15.17 the flame—representing the deity —goes to and fro 'between' the sacrificial offerings.

[24b–26] The scene in the king's house is depicted with the utmost vividness. Only four men are expected to the festal meal; women, as still today in the East, have no part in it. Saul occupies the place by the wall, the best (and safest) place. Even here, as we hear later, he has the spear beside him. Jonathan may have regarded it as a hopeful sign that Saul does not mention David at all on the first day. We are told, however, that the reason for Saul's silence is his assumption that David has become involved in temporary uncleanness—we are to think of a pollution—which according to ancient custom excluded participation in a cultic meal until the evening (Lev. 15.16; 7.20f.); a new-moon feast would certainly come under these conditions. [27–31] Matters are different on the second day, when the earlier reason no longer obtains. Saul's mistrust is clear simply from the way in which he speaks of the 'son of Jesse'; in contrast, Jonathan gives him his proper name. Jonathan now tells the story of the family sacrifice which David put into his mouth; the personal invitation by the brother, as being particularly pressing, would have had to have been accepted. The excuse does not sound bad, but it does not dispel the king's mistrust, and in a burst of foul-mouthed anger, he curses his son and his son's mother.[a] These are not, of course, reproaches against the mother herself. Saul is rather saying that Jonathan is utterly 'degenerate', the opposite of Samson, whose Nasirate is already prepared for by the conduct of his mother, and—a more appropriate example—of Christ, whose holiness already begins in his mother's womb. Saul also accuses his son of rebellious conduct,[b] of making common cause with the rebels. Indeed, the revolt is in the last resort against Jonathan himself,

[a]The usual way of giving vent to one's feelings today in the Arabian East is to curse one's father (yil‘an or yin‘al ’abuk).

[b]Mardūt, to be derived from mārad.

seeing that as hereditary successor he is the person most affected. This is a skilful and legitimate argument on the part of the king, and it would have made some impression on anyone else. **[32–34]** It says a great deal for the depth of his friendship with David that Jonathan does not yield. Jonathan takes David's side to the point of putting himself in danger, and then leaves the table in fierce anger, without having eaten a bite (MT 'bread' without article). The present form of the text, according to which Jonathan leaves the king's house because of David, can be explained from the strength of feeling about Jonathan's plea for David. In any case, he now knows where he stands.

[35–40] The agreed shooting of the arrows now takes place outside. Evidently only one arrow is shot. The textual tradition does not agree over this, as can be seen particularly at vv. 20–22, where 'arrows' and 'arrow' are juxtaposed. It could be that in the description of the affair only the most important part, the shooting of the decisive arrow, was mentioned. Jonathan makes it as clear as possible, so that his friend can have no doubt. The repeated call to the boy not to wait is to prevent him from looking round or from looking in the wrong direction and possibly discovering David; Jonathan's concern for David is evident right to the last.

[41–42] With this the story is really at an end, and in its original form it would, in fact, have ended here. David has been informed, and now he must leave his hiding-place and flee from Saul. Subsequent happenings do not fit with what has gone before. True, we need not be surprised that Jonathan sent the boy home with the arrows; the oriental servant is not taken aback by sudden whims of his master, even if they are the opposite of what he would have expected; he puts up with them quite naturally.[a] The business of the arrows would, however, be quite superfluous if the friends had been able to take their leave in the way depicted at the end. There will be another tradition here which described the farewells of the two—probably at the well-known stone. The deep feeling of the parting, which is not impaired even by David's gestures of thanks and honour, once again shows the inwardness of their friendship. For this reason the compiler will have felt it important not to suppress the scene, even if he damaged the logic of the narrative by its inclusion. Moreover, it once again brings out the theological pattern

[a]The classical example of this is the Babylonian conversation between the master and the servant. Text in *AOT*², pp. 284–7, Pritchard, *ANET*, pp. 437f.

of the material, like v. 23. The Lord will stand 'between' Jonathan and David, as a holy bridge, for all time, even if they must now part.

The chapter forms the introduction to the most uncertain period of David's life, which leads him farthest away from the goal marked out for him at the anointing. It is therefore important that here we are not simply told of mere events, but that the Lord's unchangeable plan for David is brought into the foreground.

9. DAVID IN NOB: 21.1-9 (Heb. 21.2-10)

21 ¹Then came David to Nob to Ahimelech the priest; and Ahimelech came to meet David trembling, and said to him, 'Why are you alone, and no one with you?' ²And David said to Ahimelech the priest, 'The king has charged me with a matter, and said to me, "Let no one know anything of the matter about which I send you, and with which I have charged you." I have made[a] an appointment with the young men for such and such a place. ³Now then, whatever you have at hand—five loaves—give me, or whatever (else) is here.' ⁴And the priest answered David, 'I have no common bread at hand, but there is holy bread; if only the young men have kept themselves from women.' ⁵And David answered the priest, 'Of a truth women have been kept from us yesterday and the day before. When I went out, the bodies[b] of the young men were (under) holy (law), and that was a common journey. How much more will they[c] be holy today?' ⁶So the priest gave him the holy bread; for there was no bread there but the bread of the Presence, which is removed from before the LORD, to be replaced by hot bread on the day it is taken away.

7 Now a certain man of the servants of Saul was there that day, detained before the LORD; his name was Doeg the Edomite, the chief of Saul's herdsmen.

8 And David said to Ahimelech, 'And have you not here[d] a spear or a sword to hand? For I have brought neither my sword nor my weapons with me, because the king's business required haste.' ⁹And the priest said, 'The sword of Goliath the Philistine, whom you killed in the valley of the terebinths, behold, it is here wrapped in a cloth behind the ephod; if you will take that, take it, for there is none but that here.' And David said, 'There is none like that; give it to me. . . .'[e]

---

[a]MT *yōdaᶜtī* would have to be a poᶜal form (not attested elsewhere) of *yādaᶜ* ('shown'). Better qal or hiphil (*yāᶜadtī* or *hōᶜadtī*) of *yāᶜad*.

[b]MT 'vessels', here euphemism for the male organ, because of vv. 5, 6a (against Stoebe, *Baumgärtelfestschrift*, 1959, pp. 182f.). A similar Greek use of *skeuos* is often attested.

[c]See BH.

[d]MT *weᵓīn yeš* is obscure. It is a conflated reading: *weᵓim yeš* (*ᵓim* as interrogative particle) or *weᵓēn yeš* (as Ps. 135.17).

[e]See Commentary.

The narrative of Ahimelech and David shows the latter in flight, a flight begun so hastily and so suddenly that it seems most plausible to assume that the situation immediately preceding was that of 19.11–17 (the story of Michal). It is, however, relatively useless to posit associations here. There was one tradition according to which David sought refuge with the prophets and another according to which he fled to the priests. David's relations of this kind—in character unlike those which Saul evidently had with both groups—are certainly historical, and have something to do with his rise to power. It is important that in the picture which they give they represent what is also expressed by David's anointing and the statement that the Lord is 'with him'; even in the worst period of his humiliation, indeed in just that period, he receives symbolic deliverance and help, first from the prophets and now from the priests; in other words, from those who are specially engaged in the service of God.

The account is again written as briefly as possible. In particular, we miss what is later given prominence by Doeg: the fact that David asks for and receives an oracle, or instructions, from the priest. We are not to assume that Doeg is therefore to be accounted a liar, especially as even Ahimelech himself returns to the point (22.15). Nothing is more likely than that a man like David should wish to assure himself in such a situation of the blessing and the approval of God (cf. Judg. 18.5f.). It is hard to understand why this is not also recorded in ch. 21. The usual solution offered (by Budde and others) is that we have a different source in ch. 22, especially as 22.10 speaks of 'provisions' and not of 'the bread of the Presence'. The explanation of the discrepancy may, however, be that the only important point for the king to know was that David had been given sustenance by the priest. As far as the other discrepancy is concerned, it can, in fact, hardly be explained, except perhaps by pointing out that the narrative does not really have a conclusion, but ends before David receives or takes the sword. Might a missing part have contained David's request to the priest to inquire of the Lord for him—while they were standing right in front of the ephod!—and the granting of the request? And at this point v. 7 would also make sense; its present position is not happy. We will come back to this point shortly.

[1] Nob is said to be where the action occurs. Its peculiarity is that the place, which is later described as a 'city of priests' (22.19), is

associated with a significant sanctuary, which, as 17.54 in all probability leads us to suppose, is called the 'tent of Yahweh' and possesses
the 'tent tradition' from the time of the wilderness;[a] it would
therefore be Mizpah (or the 'great height' of Gibeon). In that case,
this city of priests cannot have been situated where Nob is later to be
located according to Isa. 10.32 and Neh. 11.32, i.e. in the neighbourhood of Anathoth and thus very close to Jerusalem (cf. Alt in *PJB* 21,
1925, pp. 12f.). Evidently the settlement of priests, destroyed according to 22.19, was later rebuilt elsewhere; the fact that this rebuilding
took place in the neighbourhood of Anathoth fits in with what
Abiathar, the only surviving member of the priesthood of Nob, is
commanded in I Kings 2.26. Ahimelech, the son of Ahitub (22.19),
is the grandson of Eli, and will be identical with Ahijah, the son of
Ahitub (14.3). In any case, these are descendants of the priests of
Shiloh, and therefore what is referred to here is no small village
sanctuary, but a well-known central shrine.

[2] David is, of course, no stranger to the priest. The surprised
question why he comes without any troops is not a sign of mistrust
but of astonishment. The reason given by David is evidently regarded
by Ahimelech as satisfactory. How is the priest to know how such
secret political or military missions are carried out in practice? The
account follows without further comment. There is no perceptible
sympathy for the priest, who is thus innocently drawn into a dubious
enterprise, and there is no rebuke for David, who is the responsible
party, because of his tissue of lies. On the other hand, neither is
'David's agility and presence of mind extolled' (so Gressmann). We
have a simple report, no more; only later does David condemn his
own conduct as culpable (22.22), and even then it is less because he
gave the priest false information than because he was not sufficiently
careful. Moral categories have no part here. We are rather given
primarily a glimpse into the bitter need of a flight which has such
consequences as these.

[3-6] But light falls on the proceedings from another angle. It
should certainly be noted that David concerns himself not with
'common' (profane) bread—in view of the famous oriental hospitality
(cf. 10.4) and David's well-known figure, would it really have been
hard for him to get bread?—but with 'holy bread', the 'bread of
the Presence' (AV 'shewbread'), the bread that was put in the house

[a] For the details of this tradition see Hertzberg, 'Mizpa', *ZAW* 47, 1929,
pp. 161-96; on Nob, esp. pp. 177-9.

of God as a cereal offering and then fell to the Aaronite priests
(Lev. 24.9). The priest's hesitation in giving it to David stems from
the fact that it is holy bread. He therefore hands it over only when
David has assured him that both he himself and his men have
definitely placed themselves in the sphere of the 'holy', both for their
previous undertakings, even though they were of a profane nature,[a]
and in the present event. If David's present statement, at least as
far as the presence of his men is concerned, does not apparently
correspond with the facts[b] it may still be significant that he begins
his flight by taking bread and also the sword from the sanctuary.
[8–9] Even when deprived of all expectations, a fugitive and in need,
we might almost add, compelled to be a perfect liar, he remains
in the sphere of the holy.[c] Such patterns of thought have already
been mentioned in the first paragraph. We might also think of the
blessing of Jacob; here, too, events start from a manifest act of
deception. But despite it all, Jacob remains the possessor of the
blessing.

[7] Between the giving of the bread and the conversation about
the sword, there is the sentence about Doeg, very important for the
compiler, because it represents the bridge to the events of ch. 22.
The sentence can in no way be regarded as a later insertion; it is
necessary to the course of events and is, moreover, completely
original. It only remains to ask whether the present position of the
verse is original, or whether v. 7 did not rather, as has been said,
form the end of the pericope. In that case, as the verse at the end
of the section, it might have become unreadable or have otherwise
been lost, and then perhaps have been put after v. 6 because in v. 6,
as in v. 7, the phrase 'before the Lord' appears. Doeg the Edomite
(LXX Aramaean) is here introduced as a new character, as a kind
of antagonist. The fact that he is an Edomite fits with the general
attitude of the Old Testament, according to which there were hostile
exchanges between Edom and Israel before, as well as after, the
exile. They began, in fact, with Esau, Edom (Gen. 25.25, 30),
obtained during the wanderings in the desert (Num. 20.14ff.), at
the time of the judges (cf. on Judg. 3.7–11 and ATD 9², pp. 163ff.),
of Saul (I. 14. 17), David (II. 8. 13ff.) and Solomon (I Kings

[a]*hū'* refers to the previous undertakings.
[b]Mark 2.25f. par. differs.
[c]According to the synoptic tradition Jesus deduces another idea from this
scene (Mark 2.25f.; Matt. 12.3f.; Luke 6.3f.). But even there it is connected with
the holy bread.

11.14ff.), and developed until after 587 they broke out in fearful bursts of hatred which at a later time still characterize the relationship between the Jewish people and the Idumaean Herod. The brief mention of the Edomite at this point would certainly have made the listener prick up his ears and think, 'This means no good.' The priest, of course, appears unsuspecting in this respect, too. It is later said by David, however, that he immediately had misgivings (22.22). Doeg is introduced as the 'chief' (literally 'strong man', '*abbīr*) among Saul's herdsmen. This will hardly mean that he had the office of an overseer; it is rather meant to indicate that he was robust in every way, as we are to see later. His 'detention' in the house of God ('before the Lord') may have been connected with an act of penance, the performance of which was perhaps the cause of Doeg's later visible animosity against the priests.

This short section, then, is of considerable importance within the framework of the David stories, far above the level of a mere episode in his flight, as it is vitally connected with earlier and later events, and therefore has a part in the theological view of the reports of David's rise to the throne.

10. DAVID WITH ACHISH AT GATH:
21.10–15 (Heb. 21.11–16)

21 ¹⁰And David rose and fled that day from Saul, and went to Achish the king of Gath. ¹¹And the servants of Achish said to him, 'Is not this David the king of the land?ᵃ Did they not sing to one another of him in dances, "Saul has slain his thousands, And David his ten thousands"?' ¹²And David took these words to heart, and was much afraid of Achish, the king of Gath. ¹³So he dissembledᵇ before them, and feigned himself mad in their hands, and drummedᶜ on the doors of the gate, and let his spittle run down his beard. ¹⁴Then said Achish to his servants, 'Lo, you see the man is mad; why then have you brought

---

ᵃThis, and not 'king of the earth', is the only legitimate translation. In his article 'La folie de David' (*RHPR* 37, 1957, pp. 156–62), Bič, starting from the impermissible translation, attempts to give a theological interpretation of David's feigned madness, claiming that David appears as the representative of the true God in the land of the Philistines; he makes special use of David's writing on the wall (v. 13) in his argument. But even Bič concedes that the present text no longer understood the position.

ᵇLiterally: 'He altered (it? The *waw* perhaps the third radical?) his behaviour.' (This is the probable rendering of *ṭaʿam*, 'taste', here; LXX and Vulg. think of 'countenance'.)

ᶜSo according to LXX; MT has 'and he scribbled (figures)', here also thought of as a sign of madness.

him to me? [15]Do I lack madmen, that you have brought this fellow to
play the madman in my presence? Shall this fellow come into my
house?'

Not only the beginning of this strange story, but also its content,
show that it was not originally connected with the narrative about
Nob. It is not devoid of humour (Gressmann). Had David planned
to desert to the Philistines, he would hardly have asked to be given
the Philistine sword, of all weapons. The beginning of the account
could originally have been attached to one of the flight narratives,
perhaps that to Samuel (19.18ff.); indeed, it could have had a
point of its own, that after Saul had fallen into prophetic ecstasy
there, David, too, must at least simulate madness. But we cannot
get beyond conjectures. The episode also remains strange because
David later formally went over to the Philistines, and indeed to the
same Achish[a], who was evidently well disposed towards him. Here
we have a local tradition which may have been preserved in Gath
itself, like the tradition of the house and hill of Samson (cf. on Judg.
16.1–4). Indeed, it may even have been attached to a definite place.
In the general context, the story is meant to show three things.
First, David's capacity for coping with a difficult situation. The
Israelites learnt with pleasure how David outwitted the Philistines.
But this does not disguise—and here is the second point—the
desperate situation in which David finds himself. What a contrast:
the radiant hero whose praise was passed from mouth to mouth,
even among the enemy, and the apparent madman, whose spittle
ran down his beard! These are real depths, more serious than prison
was for Joseph. But despite everything, the guiding and protecting
hand of God is still with him, even if this is not explicitly stressed.
We will hear more almost immediately.

[10] In letting David flee abroad, the narrative shows that Saul's
power is considered greater than is often felt by the historian. There
is evidence for this elsewhere: Saul's search in Bethlehem specially
for David is another indication, as are his further dealings with
David. Perhaps the idea behind David's move is that he will enlist
as an unknown soldier in the service of Achish. Whatever it may have
been, the attempt misfires. David cannot rebuild his life with and
among the Philistines. [11] Here once again we find an aspect which
goes beyond the framework of the episode; inappropriate human

[a]Achish is the equivalent of Anchises. On this see most recently Wainwright,
VT 9, 1959, pp. 77f.

thoughts are cut short by the rule from above. In this case, it happens that the soldiers in Gath know David, whom they describe as 'king of the land', as a consequence of the saying at 18.7. The title, chosen by non-Israelites and enemies, is once again meant to underline the fact that the divine plan is inviolably bound up with David. This element, however, stands only in the background; in the foreground matters are very different. Here we have the sudden revelation of the danger in which David now finds himself. It is particularly acute, because the soldiers have seized him and brought him to Achish; this is to be concluded from the expressions, 'in their hands', 'brought'. **[12–15]** With great presence of mind, David seizes upon the expedient of behaving as though he were raving mad. He is thus certain of protecting himself; in both ancient and more recent times the insane man has stood under the special care of the deity. He also succeeds in making his identity as assumed by the servants seem incredible to Achish. David can therefore—though this is not expressly recorded—leave the court again without danger, without ending up in a Philistine troop or in the prison of Achish. The way God has prepared for him remains sure and opens up further.

11. DAVID IN ADULLAM AND MIZPEH: 22.1–5

22 ¹David departed from there and escaped to the cave of Adullam; and when his brothers and all his father's house heard it, they went down there to him. ²And every one who was in distress, and every one who was in debt, and every one who was discontented, gathered to him; and he became captain over them. And there were with him about four hundred men.

3 And David went from there to Mizpeh of Moab; and he said to the king of Moab, 'Pray let my father and my mother come out (and stay) with you, till I know what God will do for me.' ⁴And he led them before the king of Moab, and they stayed with him all the time that David was in the stronghold. ⁵Then the prophet Gad said to David, 'Do not remain in the stronghold; depart, and go into the land of Judah.' So David departed and went to Yaar Hereth.

[1] The place to which David betakes himself 'from there', i.e. in this case from Gath, is Adullam, the name of which has been preserved up to the present in *khirbet 'id el-ma*, lying about six and a half miles east of *bet jibrin*. The place conjectured for Adullam itself is the height directly south of this, which bears the sanctuary of *šeḥ madkur* and is characterized by a large number of caves. It is therefore understandable that both the 'cave'—of course, a definite cave which would later have been pointed out by tradition—and the 'stronghold' are mentioned here. The David tradition was connected with both alike. But the original text will have read *m*^e*ṣūdat* (stronghold) instead of *m*^e*ārat* (cave, very similar in the Hebrew).[a] The height, riddled with caves, offers a suitable resting-place for the fugitive. So it is quite understandable that he receives reinforcements, first from members of his family who seem to be dangerously near to Saul in Bethlehem—how necessary this was is shown by the subsequent story—and further, [2] from all kinds of discontented and reckless elements who had some reason for escaping from the situation in their homeland and who, under a leader like David, could form a dangerous band. We hear the same sort of thing about Abimelech (Judg. 9.4) and Jephthah (Judg. 11.3). We learn something of the difficulty of maintaining such troops in ch. 25.

[3–4] The note about David's concern for his parents is, of course, connected with v. 1. They could hardly be expected to live an outlaw's life permanently. David's gaze turns towards Moab, because he has family associations with it, as the Book of Ruth shows (4.17). The beginning of the Book of Ruth also mentions Moab as a place for fugitives from Bethlehem. The fact that David, unlike the former Bethlehemites, goes straight to the king with his request may be a consequence of his previously high status. David's harsh treatment of the Moabites later is surprising (II. 8.2)—David evidently brought his parents along with him and left them there. How long their exile lasted, we are not told. The time given here, 'all the time that David was in the stronghold', is hardly meant to signify just the length of his stay at Adullam; it probably means all the time until his unsettled life came to an end. The reading of the Syriac, occasionally preferred by commentators, which here and in v. 5 has the word 'Mizpeh' instead of 'stronghold', is connected with v. 5, and would, in fact, make the question of the length of David's parents' stay still more difficult to answer.

[5] The prophet Gad now appears, evidently after David's return to Adullam; he has not been mentioned hitherto, but comes again in II. 24. He advises David to go into the land of Judah. This, in fact, sounds as though David were being called back to his home-

<hr />

[a]Both are also in juxtaposition in II. 23.13f. and I Chron. 11.15f.

land from abroad, and it is the reason for the discrepancy in the Syriac version mentioned above, which knew that Adullam was territory belonging to the tribe of Judah (Josh. 15.35; cf. Neh. 11.30). On the other hand, Adullam is an old Canaanite royal city (Josh. 12.15), and lies so near to Philistine land—an important consideration here—that it can be regarded as being a part of it. Wherever this note may have originated, in its present position it must mean that David is to return from the borderlands of the territory of Judah into Judah proper. Thus prophetic utterance confirms what was recognizably the ultimate meaning of the previous section: despite the danger which this step brings, and in contrast to what would be practical and expedient in human judgment, David is to remain where he is 'under the wings of Yahweh, the God of Israel' (Ruth 2.12).[a] Such a reference to the supreme divine guidance must be noted; here the background of the David narratives shows through. The sentence ends with the news that David obeys. Unfortunately, the location of the new spot which he chooses, shown by both its names to be wooded, is unknown. There is, however, much to be said for Ewald's assumption (cf. Wellhausen and Budde) that the word *ḥeret* is a dialect form of *ḥōreš* (cf. 23.15–19). In that case, the 'forest of Horesh' would lie in the Judaean wilderness of Siph, south of Hebron.

12. SAUL'S VENGEANCE ON THE PRIESTS OF NOB: 22.6–23

22 [6]Now when Saul heard that David and some[b] men whom he had with him were discovered—Saul was sitting at Gibeah, under the tamarisk tree on the height,[c] with his spear in his hand, and all his servants were standing about him—[7]Saul said to his servants who stood about him, 'Hear now, you Benjaminites; will the son of Jesse give every one of you fields and vineyards and[d] will he make you all commanders of thousands and commanders of hundreds? [8]You have all conspired against me and no one discloses to me when my son makes a league with the son of Jesse, none of you has supported[e] me or has disclosed to me that my son has stirred up my servant against me, to

---

[a]Quite remarkably, David speaks to the heathen king not of Yahweh, but in general terms, of God, v. 3.

[b]Note the absence of the article.

[c]Instead of *rāmā*, LXX reads the similar *bāmā*, high place, at least a right interpretation.

[d]See BH.

[e]Read *hōmēl*, after LXX; MT 'has fretted himself sick over me' is too strong.

lie in wait, as at this day.' ⁹Then answered Doeg the Edomite, who stood by the servants of Saul, 'I saw the son of Jesse coming to Nob, to Ahimelech the son of Ahitub, ¹⁰and he inquired of the LORD for him, and gave him provisions and gave him the sword of Goliath the Philistine.'

11 Then the king sent to summon Ahimelech the priest, the son of Ahitub, and all his father's house, the priests who were at Nob; and all of them came to the king. ¹²And Saul said, 'Hear now, son of Ahitub.' And he answered, 'Here I am, my lord.' And Saul said to him, 'Why have you conspired against me, you and the son of Jesse, in that you have given him bread and a sword, and have inquired of God for him, so that he has risen against me, to lie in wait, as at this day?' ¹⁴Then Ahimelech answered the king, 'And who among all your servants is so faithful as David, who is the king's son-in-law, and captainᵃ over your bodyguard,ᵇ and honoured in your house? ¹⁵Is today the first time that I have inquired of God for him? No! Let not the king impute anything to his servant or to all the house of my father;ᵃ for your servant has known nothing of all this, much or little.' ¹⁶And the king said, 'You shall surely die, Ahimelech, you and all your father's house.' ¹⁷And the king said to the guard who stood about him, 'Turn and kill the priests of the LORD; because their hand also is with David, and they knew that he fled, and did not disclose it to me.' But the servants of the king would not put forth their hand to fall upon the priests of the LORD. ¹⁸Then the king said to Doeg, 'You turn and fall upon the priests.' And Doeg the Edomite turned and fell upon the priests, and he killed on that day eighty-five persons who wore the linen ephod. ¹⁹And Nob, the city of the priests, he put to the sword; both men and women, children and sucklings, oxen, asses and sheep, he put to the sword.

20 But one of the sons of Ahimelech, the son of Ahitub, named Abiathar, escaped and fled after David. ²¹And Abiathar told David that Saul had killed the priests of the LORD. ²²And David said to Abiathar, 'I knew on that day, when Doeg the Edomite was there, that he would surely tell Saul. I have the death of all the persons of your father's house on my conscience.ᶜ ²³Stay with me, fear not; for he that seeks my life seeks your life;ᵈ with me you shall be in safekeeping.'

[6–8] This episode, dramatically told and very important for the course of events, begins with an assembly evidently summoned because of David's decision to stage an armed revolt in his own land, thereby raising the standard of rebellion. His conduct is described

---

ᵃSee BH.

ᵇLiterally, 'your men-in-waiting'.

ᶜLXX with its *aitios* presumably thinks of *ḥabtī*, but this is an unusual word. MT read *sābab*, occurring in vv. 17f.: 'I have endangered the life = I am the occasion of.' The meaning, then, is the same.

ᵈThe subject is Saul. It is unnecessary to interchange 'my' and 'your' (BH, etc.).

with the word *'ōrēb*, to set an ambush, to stab in the back. Had David vanished abroad, Saul would presumably have arranged things differently. We notice how important the prophetic saying of v. 5 is for the whole proceedings. The assembly takes place at Gibeah, by the holy tree of the place, a tamarisk. Tamarisks, like palms, are rarely found in the hill country, and so with the latter (Judg. 4.5) are particularly striking, and appropriate as holy trees. Like Deborah in Judg. 4.5, Saul 'sits' under the tree, with the spear once more in his hand, as a sign of his rank. To sit is the right of the chieftain; his subordinates 'stand' before him, so that 'to stand before him' is in the Old Testament virtually a technical term for 'serving' (I Kings 17.1, etc.). The form of address with which Saul opens the proceedings leads us to expect no good. We learn incidentally that Saul's court is formed of members of his tribe; but this need not imply that his kingdom was in fact a tribal kingdom (against Budde).[a]

Saul's brief speech chiefly contains accusations against Jonathan, who has 'set David on his feet' (*hēqīm*) and smoothed the way towards his treacherous action. We are to assume that Jonathan took no part in the assembly of the 'servants of Saul'. On the other hand, Saul's accusations seem to have had no consequences for him. We are perhaps to understand that the king is put on another scent by Doeg and so now thinks that he has discovered the guilty party (Schulz, *ad loc.*). The mistrustful king wavers between exaggeration and injustice. The mere fact of his having been told nothing is, in his eyes, already betrayal. He accuses his servants of siding with the coming man even now, all of them—we should note the frequent repetition.

[9–16] The Edomite Doeg, who does not himself belong to the 'Benjaminites' and is perhaps present only by chance, uses this opportunity to tell Saul what he has observed in Nob and to denounce Ahimelech. The priest is summoned, along with 'all his father's house'. The very form of address, 'son of Ahitub', shows the seriousness of the situation. After Saul has told him to his face of his alleged guilt, Ahimelech defends himself in a way which must convince everyone, particularly the reader. The enumeration of David's high positions, the reference to earlier inquiries at the oracle—an important piece of information for our assessment of David—and his complete lack of suspicion are, in fact, compelling

[a] Shortly before his death, King Ibn Saud formed a government which was composed only of members of his family.

arguments. But to no avail; the king pronounces the death sentence, which, according to the principle of tribal membership, applies to all who belong to the tribe. This incident will not, however, be the sole ground for Saul's action, even if it is the only one of which we hear. It has already been said in comments on ch. 21 that David had prophets and priests on his side. Saul has both groups against him. This may be because of the attitude of Samuel, who was, in fact, closely connected with the house of Eli: anyway, it was the case. It is yet another indication of the tragedy in Saul's life that he who was at first so intent on the will of God appears more and more as a man 'forsaken by God'. [17] We should therefore take particular note that Saul tells his 'runners' to kill the priests of Yahweh. This is open war against the servants of the Lord, and therefore against the Lord himself, and the refusal of the servants, who are by no means sensitive men, to lay a hand on the Lord's anointed is intended as a deliberate contrast. [18–19] Only Doeg is prepared to act as executioner, and he is no man of Israel, but an Edomite. The number of those killed is astonishingly large, especially as it represents only the males. Perhaps there was a place near the tamarisk of Gibeah with which the number 85 was especially associated. To heighten Saul's guilt, it is expressly said that all the slain were priests in office. The destruction of the city of the priests and the slaughter of its inhabitants and their animals completes the gruesome work. It is done after the manner of the ban, and this leaves a particularly horrifying impression; the ban is the way in which the worshippers of Yahweh act against the heathen, and here it is used against the servants of the Lord! The subject of v. 19 remains obscure; originally it will have been Saul himself, and it is possible, and often supposed, that here we have the remnant of a special tradition according to which the real punishment was not the massacre at Gibeah, but the sacking and destruction of Nob, and that Saul set out to carry out the punishment immediately after Doeg's betrayal, without first summoning Ahimelech. In its present combination, however, the whole complex makes a particularly horrifying impact.

[20–23] Whereas Saul is in this way alienating the priests, David gains possession of one, a 'real' priest, of the house of Eli. We must regard this as the focal point of the chapter. Both prophet and priest appear before the fugitive. Saul, in possession of all the sanctuaries, a neighbour to the city of Samuel, brusquely and roughly severs the connections between himself and them. David, pursued by all, receives a prophetic message and now has with him a consecrated bearer of the ephod.

We are not told how Abiathar managed to escape the blood bath. Perhaps he was keeping watch at the temple; it is, however, sufficient to regard the incident in the same way as Judg. 9.1ff. There, too, moreover, the escaped person represents the *vox dei* (cf. my commentary *ad loc.*). David's heart is smitten because he sees the unfortunate chain of events in which he is culpably involved. He can only seek to make things good in the person of the sole survivor. The friendship between him and Abiathar lasted until David's death. It has often been supposed that Abiathar had a special position as a historiographer at David's court, and later.

13. DAVID AT KEILAH: 23.1–13

23 [1]Now they told David, 'Behold, the Philistines are fighting against Keilah, and are robbing the threshing-floors.' [2]Therefore David inquired of the LORD, 'Shall I go and attack these Philistines?' And the LORD said to David, 'Go and attack the Philistines and save Keilah.' [3]But David's men said to him, 'Behold, we are afraid here in Judah; how much more then if we go to Keilah against the armies of the Philistines?' [4]Then David inquired of the LORD again. And the LORD answered him, 'Arise, go down to Keilah; for I will give the Philistines into your hand.' [5]And David and his men went to Keilah, and fought with the Philistines, and brought away their cattle, and made a great slaughter among them. So David delivered the inhabitants of Keilah.

[6] Now when Abiathar, the son of Ahimelech, fled to David he brought the ephod with him, and he came down to Keilah with David.[a] [7]And it was told Saul that David had come to Keilah. And Saul said, 'God has sold[b] him into my hand; for he has shut himself in by entering a town that has gates and bars.' [8]And Saul summoned all the people to war, to go down to Keilah, to besiege David and his men. [9]David knew that Saul was plotting evil against him; and he said to Abiathar the priest, 'Bring the ephod here.' [10]Then said David, 'O LORD, the God of Israel, thy servant has surely heard that Saul seeks to come to Keilah, to destroy the city on my account. [11]Will the men of Keilah surrender me into his hand? Will Saul come down, as thy servant has heard? O LORD, the God of Israel, I beseech thee, tell thy servant.' And the LORD said, 'He will come down.' [12]Then said David, 'Will the men of Keilah surrender me and my men into the hand of Saul?' And

---

[a]MT (as RSV) '. . . fled to David to Keilah; the ephod was brought down in his hand.' LXX: '. . . he went down with David to Keilah and he had taken the ephod with him' (lit. 'he had the ephod in his hand'). From this we may conjecture an original Hebrew text. *weha'ephod beyado wehu yarad 'im-dawid qe'ila.*

[b]See BH.

the LORD said, 'They will surrender you.'[13] Then David and his men,
who were about six hundred, arose and departed from Keilah, and
they went wherever they could go. When Saul was told that David had
escaped from Keilah, he gave up the expedition.

[1] The fortified town of Keilah (Hebrew $q^e{}^c\bar{\imath}l\bar{a}$) is to be identified
not with *khirbet qila* (in the neighbourhood of the Jaffa-Jerusalem
road, about three miles south of *latrun*), but with the ruins of the
same name, about six miles east of *bet jibrin*, south of Adullam.[a]
Keilah, like Adullam, is exposed to the attack of the Philistines, the
real masters in the hill country. The inhabitants are men of Judah.
Threshing-floors are the obvious thing for the enemy to plunder, as
the whole harvest is laid down, threshed and winnowed on them,
and the process takes some time. Such plundering of the harvest is,
of course, a fearful blow for the peasant inhabitants. [2] David's care
for the people of Keilah is determined not only by the wish to help
men of his own tribe, but also by something which is only hinted at
in the contemptuous sounding words 'these Philistines'. We are
reminded of the story of Goliath; the (uncircumcised) Philistines are
the real enemies of the people of God. Battles against them are the
wars of the Lord. David appears here as the man who takes up the
task of the king of Israel although he does not occupy his throne.
For this reason, the word $y\bar{a}\check{s}a^c$ = 'save' is used twice, a word which
in the Book of Judges often characterizes the action of the judge.
David's action here is clearly opposed to that of Saul.

[3–4] The special character of David's undertaking is further
underlined by a twofold inquiry made of the Lord. This seems to
have consisted in the putting of alternative questions to the ephod,
the holy oracle by lot (cf. ch. 14). Here, too, as in ch. 14, the *vox
populi* makes itself felt. But in this case it does not coincide with the
vox Dei; it is merely an expression of fearfulness. The Lord and his
'servant', as he is called later, argue on a higher level.

[5] So David sets out and attacks the Philistines. It is strange that
he begins by driving away the Philistine cattle; they could not have
taken cattle with them on their plundering foray, as that would only
have hindered them. We would also expect that the victory would
have been mentioned before the plunder. Caspari's assumption that
it was the Philistines who had driven away 'their' cattle, i.e. the cattle
of the people of Keilah, is certainly worth noticing, but it necessitates
greater alterations in the text than that of *wayyinhag* to *wayyinh^{a}gū*.

[a]Cf. *PJB* 21, 1925, pp. 21f., and 22, 1926, pp. 72f.

The animals would be better taken as beasts of burden which the Philistines would need to transport the grain. Strategically, the attack on the baggage was a skilful beginning. The scant mention of David's victory once again shows which events concern the writer and which do not. The military side of the affair is narrated as briefly as possible. It is, however, expressly said that this is an act of deliverance. **[6]** We should pay particular attention to v. 6, the text of which can be established with the help of LXX. In contrast to MT, it certainly does not mean that Abiathar only now fled to David, but that Abiathar had accompanied him into action. This prepares the way for the third inquiry, about Keilah. At the same time, the Lord's will is clearly brought into the centre of the picture. Against the rules of wisdom, David goes to Keilah, and, equally surprisingly, he leaves it again very quickly. Nevertheless both his actions are not only what the lot commanded, but also correct, the first for the reasons advanced earlier, the second for the sake of David's safety. The Lord, who has the greater power, is clearly in charge.

[7–13] Saul's plan, too, is well conceived, but, despite the mention of God, it is a 'human' plan of war. Saul has deprived himself of the ephod and its bearers and hence of the means of ascertaining what is necessary for his undertakings. So he can 'plot' evil, but no more. Nevertheless, it again becomes clear what power Saul has at his disposal. His ability to destroy the priests was a sign of it. We notice here that, given the chance, the inhabitants would immediately take the side of Saul and not that of their deliverer. We must also keep this distinct difference of power in mind in assessing the meaning of the episode. But as so often in the Bible (cf., e.g., on Judg. 7.1ff.), God is not on the side of the big battalions.

David appears here in a particularly attractive light. It is purposely said that he is ready to go to the aid of the city and that he is equally ready to depart, not because of his own uncertain position, but also because Keilah could incur new misfortunes on his account. Not once does he reprove the citizens for their attitude, of which he is informed by means of the oracle. And if the Lord is the chief actor, guiding everything towards the realization of his plans, then David appears as the instrument which the Lord can use.

14. DAVID AND SAUL IN THE WILDERNESS: 23.14–28

23 **14**And David remained in the strongholds in the wilderness, in the hill country of the Wilderness of Ziph. And Saul sought him every

day, but God did not give him into his hand. 15Now David saw that Saul had come out to seek his life.

While David was in the Wilderness of Ziph at Horesh, 16Jonathan, Saul's son, rose, and went to David at Horesh, and strengthened his hand in God. 17And he said to him, 'Fear not; for the hand of Saul my father shall not find you; you shall be king over Israel, and I shall be next to you; Saul my father also knows this.' 18And the two of them made a covenant before the LORD; David remained at Horesh, and Jonathan went home.

19 Then the Ziphites went up to Saul at Gibeah, saying, 'Does not David hide among us in the strongholds—at Horesh—in Gibeath Hachilah, which is south of Jeshimon?ª 20Now come down, O king, according to all your heart's desire to come down; and our part shall be to surrender him into the king's hand.' 21And Saul said, 'May you be blessed by the LORD; for you have had compassion on me. 22Go, make yet more sure; know and see the place where his fleetingᵇ foot stays; for it is told me that he is very cunning. 23Take note of all the lurking places where he hides, and come back to me to a certain (place).ᶜ Then I will go with you; and if he is in the land, I will search him out among all the thousands of Judah.'24 And (when they returned,)ᵈ they arose and went to Ziph ahead of Saul, while David and his men were in the wilderness of Maon, in the foothillsᵉ to the south of Jeshimon. 25And Saul and his men went to seek him. And David was told; therefore he went down to the rock which isᵇ in the wilderness of Maon. And when Saul heard that, he pursued after David in the wilderness of Maon. 26Saul went on one side of the mountain, and David and his men on the other side of the mountain; and David was making haste to get away from Saul, as Saul and his men were closing in upon David and his men to capture them, 27when a messenger came to Saul, saying, 'Make haste and come; for the Philistines have made a raid upon the land.' 28So Saul returned from pursuing after David, and went against the Philistines; therefore that place was called the 'Rock of Parting'.

[14–15] We now find David in the region south and south-east of Hebron, more accurately in the 'wilderness' directly east of the great watershed. The Hebrew word *midbār* need not be wilderness in the strict sense; it primarily means pasture land as opposed to

---

ªThe geographical references are to be taken as marginal notes which arose in respect of 23.15 and 26.1.

ᵇSee BH.

ᶜThe rendering of *'el-nākōn* is uncertain. It could mean 'definitely' or 'with definite news'. But in view of 26.4, some reference to a place is preferable. Saul will have agreed a definite meeting-place with the Ziphites to which they were to 'return'.

ᵈA *wayyāšūbū* seems to have fallen out here.

ᵉThe 'Arabah' is here synonymous with the eastern declivity of the hill. Maon itself is still in the 'hill country'.

cultivated land. The whole description represents the 'desolate' eastern declivities of the hills falling down to the Dead Sea. Ziph lies on the watershed (the present *tell ez-zif*; cf. *PJB* 22, 1926, p. 77), likewise, south of it, Maon (the present *tell ma'in*). The pasture-land is thus east of these places, on the lower slopes of the hills, which are here for once described by the word *'arābā* (lowland; v. 24). Hill country (*har*) is the Judaean highland proper. This is the reason why in v. 14 we first have a mention of the wilderness in general and then of the wilderness of Ziph 'in the hill country'. Horesh, the name of a place or of some pasture-land, must similarly be sought near the watershed, as 'in the wilderness of Ziph' is expressly inserted.[a]

The different localities, the repeated occurrence of the wilderness, the mention of hill country and lowland, then again of a mountain and a rock, show from the start how hunted and hemmed in was the life of David and his men once they had given up as too dangerous the attempt to secure a fortified place by a treaty of friendship. David now sees himself exposed to a real chase. He knows that Saul is constantly on his tracks. Hence the remark at the beginning, that God did not give David into Saul's hand, is an important one. It gives a title to the whole section. Saul may pursue and David may be pursued, but it is firmly fixed in the divine plan that David will remain safe. No man can alter anything in this long-arranged course of events.

[16 18] Jonathan's visit makes it even more clear that thoughts of this kind govern the whole narrative. The account of it is not meant to describe a new act of friendship which, in fact, in point of danger exceeds everything that Jonathan has previously done for David. But in the omission of all the details we would so much like to know—how Jonathan made the journey, how his visit escaped the notice of Saul, what attitude David's men took up towards the son of their enemy—the reason for the introduction of the scene at this point becomes all the clearer. David (and the reader!) are to be assured that David is to be the future 'king over Israel'. So Jonathan strengthens David 'in God'. He himself fades into the background, like the 'friend of the bridegroom' when the hour comes. We shall learn later, in still more detail, that as Jonathan says, Saul is indeed clear about this divinely ordained course of events. The covenant,

---

[a]Alt's conjecture that it should be identified with *ḥarās* (*PJB* 24, 1928, pp. 25f.) in the western hill country cannot therefore be accepted. Buhl, *Geographie des alten Palästina*, p. 97, mentions a ruin Huresa, south of *tell ez-zif*.

renewed afresh, seals the friendship and shows how seriously Jonathan means what he has said.

[19–24] The episode with the Ziphites is governed by this twofold preface. It is most vividly described, both in respect of the conversation with Saul and of the pursuit. Between the two a brief section, at least one word (see above), has fallen out. Meanwhile, David, guessing perhaps what is to come, has gone farther south into the wilderness of Maon, and, as the danger becomes more acute, he keeps moving east, into the wilderness proper, his best place of refuge. **[25–28]** A definite rock, the name of which recalls the 'parting', later preserved the memory of these events. David's enemies are separated from him only by a spur of the hills, and his end seems certain. But the news of an attack by the Philistines, who have taken advantage of Saul's absence to go on a plundering expedition, compels him to break off the pursuit. This must be understood in the light of what is said in v. 14. The rock of parting has become a memorial of David's preservation.

15. THE MEETING IN THE CAVE OF ENGEDI:
23.29–24.22 (Heb. 24.1–23)

23 ²⁹And David went up from there, and dwelt in the strongholds of Engedi. **24** ¹When Saul returned from following the Philistines, he was told, 'Behold, David is in the wilderness of Engedi.' ²Then Saul took three thousand chosen men out of all Israel, and went to seek David and his men in front of the Wild-goats' Rocks. ³And he came to the sheepfolds by the way, where there was a cave; and Saul went in to relieve himself. Now David and his men were sitting in the innermost parts of the cave. ⁴And the men of David said to him, 'Here is the day of which the LORD said to you, "Behold I will give your enemy^a into your hand, and you shall do to him as it shall seem good to you." ' Then David arose and stealthily cut off the skirt of Saul's robe. ⁵And afterward David's heart smote him, because he had cut off Saul's skirt. ⁶He said to his men, 'The LORD forbid that I should do this thing to my lord, the LORD's anointed, to put forth my hand against him, seeing he is the LORD's anointed.' ⁷So David persuaded his men with these words, and did not permit them to attack Saul. And Saul rose up and left the cave, and went upon his way.

8 Afterward David also arose, and went out of the cave, and called after Saul, 'My lord the king!' And when Saul looked behind him, David bowed with his face to the earth, and did obeisance. ⁹And

---

^a'Your enemies' is also possible. Then this would be a quotation of an earlier saying of God, couched in general terms.

David said to Saul, 'Why do you listen to the words of men who say,
"Behold, David seeks your hurt?" [10]Lo, this day your eyes have seen
how the LORD gave you today into my hand in the cave, and some[a]
bade me kill you, but I[b] spared you. I said, "I will not put forth my
hand against my lord; for he is the LORD's anointed." [11]See, my father,
see the skirt of your robe in my hand; for by the fact that I cut off the
skirt of your robe, and did not kill you, you may know and see that
there is no wrong or treason in my hands. I have not sinned against
you, though you hunt my life to take it. [12]May the LORD judge between
me and you, may the LORD avenge me upon you; but my hand shall
not be against you. [13]As the proverb of the ancients says, "Out of the
wicked comes forth wickedness"; but my hand shall not be against you.
[14]After whom has the king of Israel come out? After whom do you
pursue? After a dead dog! After a flea! [15]May the LORD therefore be
judge, and give sentence between me and you, and see to it, and plead
my cause, and deliver me from your hand.'

16 When David had finished speaking these words to Saul, Saul said,
'Is this your voice, my son David?' And Saul lifted up his voice and
wept. [17]He said to David, 'You are in the right, more than I; for you
have repaid me good, whereas I have repaid you evil. [18]And you have
declared this day how you have dealt well with me, in that you did not
kill me when the LORD put me into your hands. [19]For if a man finds his
enemy, will he let him go away safe? So may the LORD reward you
with good for what you have done to me this day. [20]And now, behold,
I know that you shall surely be king, and that the kingdom of Israel
shall be established in your hand. [21]Swear to me therefore by the LORD
that you will not cut off my descendants after me, and that you will not
destroy my name out of my father's house.' [22]And David swore this to
Saul. Then Saul went home; but David and his men went up to the
stronghold.

[23.29–24.2] This beautiful, vivid story is directly connected with
the previous one. Saul has again found a breathing space after
repelling the Philistines and can therefore continue his action against
David without delay. David has meanwhile moved to the hilly
wilderness of Engedi, perhaps in the middle of the eastern slopes
towards the Dead Sea; the name has been preserved until now in the
oasis *'en jidi*. As is especially stressed, the danger for David lies in
the fivefold superiority and the special quality of Saul's men. The
place where they meet is again characterized by a peculiar rock-
formation which certainly kept alive the memory of the events

[a]Vulg. seems to have read *wā'ōmar* instead of the grammatically difficult
we'āmar, i.e. 'and I said to myself'.
[b]*wattāḥos* needs an *'ēnī*, which Vulg. has preserved. Other versions read
wā'āḥus.

narrated here for a long time. There is no lack of caves in the wilderness of Judah; among them are some which run back, as it were, in sections: the immediate entrance gives way to further caves, often connected by half-blocked passages. **[3–7a]** The text suggests that the front part of the cave was occasionally used for sheltering herds of cattle, perhaps in storms, cold weather, etc. Saul goes in here, as the euphemistic expression has it, 'to cover his feet'. He does not guess that at this very moment Yahweh has given him 'into David's hand', as David's men put it, quite appropriately and in a way which corresponds with the theological insights of the Old Testament. In this case the phraseology may be influenced by a divine saying spoken earlier. For these men it is quite settled that David will now kill his enemy to save himself and his people from a position which is becoming more and more difficult. Indeed, it seems to them to be the will of the Lord, who has graciously brought about this situation: 'a unique application of the maxim *vox diei vox Dei*' (Schulz, p. 348). David's refusal to follow their advice, which is not, as has been said, simply the advice of rough and thoughtless warriors, follows from his clear recognition that the sanctity of the king's person, effected by his anointing, is stronger than anything else. Thus the title 'David's generosity', so often given to this section, does not reach right to the roots of the matter. True, David is meant to appear as a chivalrous opponent.[a] But it is more important that he complies with the will of God where it is unmistakably clear. What appears to the others as the will of God seems to him to be a temptation from which God will 'preserve' him. It is not clear from the wording whether or not an inner struggle took place at this point. The fact that David 'arose' after the men had spoken at first sight suggests that he was going to follow their advice. And why is it his heart that smites him? Did the text here originally suggest that his conscience—as we would say—struck him just as he reached out to strike the death blow? If we were to accept these considerations it would in any case mean deep inroads into the text; not only would v. 5b have to be deleted, but a clause would have to be inserted in v. 4 after 'and David arose', perhaps saying, 'and David took the sword to kill Saul'. And then it would have to go on 'then David's heart smote him and he cut . . .' It is not impossible that the first form of the

---

[a]'Now no women receive him in the round dance to sing his praises, but the choir of angels lauds him from the heights, full of wonderment at his wisdom and meekness' (Chrysostom *Hom.* 2.2 *on David and Saul* [PG 54. 688–9]).

narrative went in this way. As things are now, David's 'fine feelings' (Budde) are expressed in his present action towards Saul. This point is further made by his injunction to the men that they are to do nothing on their own account. There is no suggestion, as many commentators suppose, that Saul's position is meant to be degrading. What Saul does is natural, not comic and ridiculous. It is simply said that Saul is here clearly given into David's hand.

[7b–15] The story does not end with David sparing Saul. Its second part is, as it were, an evaluation of the earlier events. Saul leaves the cave, David likewise. David calls to the king, causing him to turn round, and pays him his due homage. Then he gives a true description of what happened in the cave, in such a way that the theological position becomes clear. He has the skirt of the robe in his hand as evidence that he took as the highest standard the will of God confirmed in Saul's anointing. This is further developed, to the effect that he did not take the execution of the 'vengeance' upon himself, but feels that it belongs only to the Lord. This is appropriately underlined by the saying which David quotes. All this is very important for the history of David; what we have here is not meant to be just an individual event. David knows and says that in comparison with Saul he is in the right, and Saul, too, sees it in this way. But the decisive factor is that David does not stand upon his rights, but leaves their realization to the Lord.

[16–21] To this Saul says two things. First, he concedes with deep emotion that David is right, and secondly, he confirms what Jonathan said of him in 23.17: he knows that David will be his successor and that only with him will the kingdom be established. Thus Saul's battle against David and the hunt organized by him in the rocky wilderness[a] are shown to be pointless and senseless. Saul is really possessed by an evil spirit; he acts, indeed he rages, against his better judgment and therefore against the will of God, which he knows full well. He seeks to secure a kingdom which does not remain his own. Once again this narrator, and indeed the compiler who puts the events in order, is conscious of the tragedy under which Saul lives and fights. It is, however, more important in events like this for him to make clear the divine line which, despite all appearances, runs towards David's elevation.

David's action, too, is ordered along this line. It is not the generous and the humble man who is the real person acting here. The Lord

[a] W. Vischer, *Christuszeugnis* II, p. 223.

gives Saul into his hand, but protects him from following up a false interpretation of the situation and confirms anew his, David's, present and future rights, even through the mouth of God's anointed. For the moment, that means deliverance from a highly dangerous situation, and for the future, a promise of the goal planned by God.

[22] In contrast, David's oath, which assures the king that his descendants will be honoured, is of little significance, and is merely meant to underline what has been said: even as king, David is not to execute 'vengeance', but is to remain true to the previous line, the line ordained of God.

Quite remarkably, the event has no immediate sequel. A novelist would have had David return to Saul's court to take up his old position again. Instead of this, Saul goes to Gibeah, and David to his mountain stronghold. The temporary respite is a relatively insignificant occurrence for David. But we see the compiler's concern: it is to set the points rightly, so that we know which way the train is to run. David has openly given a correct picture of his situation in v. 14; this has in no way been altered. But the direction in which God means to work, despite everything, is now evident with a new clarity to all the participants and to the audience.

16. THE DEATH OF SAMUEL: 25.1a

25 ¹ᴬNow Samuel died; and all Israel assembled and mourned for him, and they buried him in his house at Ramah.

[1a] The note about the death of Samuel, to which reference is made in the same words in 28.3, could belong here simply because it in fact belongs to the time during which David was in Engedi (so Thenius). Nevertheless, we should ask whether there is not also a 'causal nexus' here (*ibid.*). 'This one man could have prevented fights between brothers for their enemies to see, as in I Kings 12.23f.' (Caspari, p. 304). It could be that the death of Samuel, a man well disposed towards David, appeared to the compiler to be a setback which had its effect on what might have been a good result of the encounter between Saul and David. In any case, a root which David had in Israelite soil was plucked up.

Be this as it may, Samuel's death once again directs all eyes not only to the 'grand old man' but also to the phenomenon of 'all Israel', which is in process of being consumed by skirmishings and factions, and which is losing consciousness of its unity. Not only are there Saul and David; there were also Samuel and with him 'all Israel'. But now he is dead, and there is an imminent danger that there might be no more Israel.[a]

There is both literary and archaeological evidence elsewhere that a person could be buried 'in his house'. The place of Samuel's grave was certainly as well known in ancient days as is the case with the *nebi samwil* in Palestine today.[b] The lamentation is appropriate to the status of the dead man (see Gen. 50.1–14).

17. DAVID AND ABIGAIL: 25.1b–44

25 [1B]Then David rose and went down to the wilderness of Maon.[c] [2]And there was a man in Maon, whose business was in Carmel. The man was very rich; he had three thousand sheep and a thousand goats. He was shearing his sheep in Carmel. [3]Now the name of the man was Nabal, and the name of his wife Abigail. The woman was of good understanding and beautiful, but the man was churlish and ill-behaved —a real Calebbite dog.[d] [4]David heard in the wilderness that Nabal was shearing his sheep. [5]So David sent ten young men; and David said to the young men, 'Go up to Carmel and go to Nabal, and greet him in my name. [6]And thus you shall salute my brother:[e] "Peace be to you, and peace be to your house, and peace be to all that you have. [7]I hear that you have shearers; now your shepherds have been with us, and we did them no harm, and they missed nothing, all the time they were in Carmel. [8]Ask your young men, and they will tell you. Therefore let my young men find favour in your eyes; for we come on a feast day. Pray, give whatever you have at hand to your servants and to your son David." '

9 When David's young men came, they said all this to Nabal in the name of David; and then they waited. [10]And Nabal answered David's servants, 'Who is David? Who is the son of Jesse? There are many servants nowadays who are breaking away from their masters. [11]Shall I take my bread and my water and my meat that I have killed for my shearers, and give it to men who come from I do not know where?' [12]So David's young men turned away, and came back and told him all this. [13]And David said to his men, 'Every man gird on his sword!' And

---

[a]Similarly, Budde and Nowack, *ad loc.* They therefore—in accordance with their views on the sources—regard the verse as an editorial insertion.

[b]On this see *PJB* 22, 1926, pp. 103f., 105; *ZAW* 47, 1929, pp. 190f.

[c]So according to LXX. The place name 'wilderness of Paran' mentioned in MT belongs in the north-east part of the Sinai peninsula. The mistake may be the result of an orthographic error; the word *māʿōn* was perhaps written with an *'aleph* and not an *ʿayin*. From there the miswriting of *māʿōn* as *pā'rān* is a small step.

[d]The word *kālibbī* or *kᵉlibbō* (*kethibh*) can be explained in three ways; 'Calebbite', 'like his heart' (i.e. his nature accorded with his evil deeds) or 'like a dog'.

[e]See BH.

every man of them girded on his sword; David also girded on his sword;[a] and about four hundred men went up after David, while two hundred remained with the baggage.

14 But one of the young men told Abigail, Nabal's wife, 'Behold, David sent messengers out of the wilderness to salute our master; and he railed at them. [15]Yet the men were very good to us, and we suffered no harm, and we did not miss anything when we were in the fields, as long as we went with them; [16]they were a wall to us both by night and by day, all the while we were with them keeping the sheep. [17]Now therefore know this and consider what you should do; for evil is determined against our master and against all his house, and he is so ill-natured that one cannot speak to him.'

18 Then Abigail made haste, and took two hundred loaves, and two skins of wine, and five sheep ready dressed, and five measures[b] of parched grain, and a hundred clusters of raisins, and two hundred cakes of figs, and laid them on asses. [19]And she said to her young men, 'Go on before me; behold, I come after you.' But she did not tell her husband Nabal. [20]Now[c] as she rode on the ass, and came down under cover of the mountain, behold, David and his men came down towards her; and she met them. [21]Now David had said, 'Surely in vain have I guarded all that this fellow has in the wilderness, so that nothing was missed of all that belonged to him; and he has returned me evil for good. [22]God do so[c] to David and more also, if by morning I leave so much of all who belong to him as one who pisses against the wall.'

23 When Abigail saw David, she made haste, and alighted from the ass, and fell before David on her face, and bowed to the ground. [24]She fell at his feet and said, 'Upon me alone, my lord, be the guilt; pray let your handmaid speak in your ears, and hear the words of your handmaid. [25]Let not my lord regard this ill-natured fellow, Nabal; for as his name is, so is he; Fool is his name, and folly is with him; but I your handmaid did not see the young men of my lord, whom you sent. [26]Now then, my lord, as the LORD lives, and as your soul lives, seeing the LORD has restrained you from bloodguilt, and from taking vengeance with your own hand, now then let your enemies and those who seek to do evil to my lord be as Nabal. [27]And now let this present which your servant has brought[c] to my lord be given to the young men who follow my lord. [28]Pray forgive the trespass of your handmaid; for the LORD will certainly make my lord a sure house, because my lord is fighting the battles of the LORD; and evil shall not be found in you so long as you live. [29]If[c] men rise up to pursue you and to seek your life, the life of my lord shall be bound in the bundle of the living in the care of the LORD your God; and the lives of your enemies he shall sling out as from the hollow of a sling. [30]And when the LORD has done to my lord according to all the good that he has spoken concerning you, and has appointed you prince over Israel, [31]my lord shall have no cause of

[a]The omission of this clause in LXX B is no reason for deleting it.
[b]'Seah'; five seah = something over a bushel and a half.
[c]See BH.

grief, or pangs of conscience, for having shed blood without cause or for my lord taking vengeance himself. And when the LORD has dealt well with my lord, then remember your handmaid.'

32 And David said to Abigail, 'Blessed be the LORD, the God of Israel, who sent you this day to meet me! [33]Blessed be your discretion,[a] and blessed be you, who have kept me this day from bloodguilt and from avenging myself with my own hand! [34]For as surely as the LORD the God of Israel lives, who has restrained me from hurting you, unless you had made haste and come to meet me, truly by morning there had not been left to Nabal so much as one who pisses against the wall.' [35]Then David received from her hand what she had brought him; and he said to her, 'Go up in peace to your house; see, I have hearkened to your voice, and I have raised your countenance again.'[b]

36 And Abigail came to Nabal; and, lo, he was holding a feast in his house, like the feast of a king. And Nabal's heart was very merry within him, for he was very drunk; so she told him nothing at all until the morning light. [37]And in the morning, when the wine had gone out of Nabal, his wife told him these things, and his heart died within him, and he became as a stone. [38]And about ten days later the LORD smote Nabal; and he died.

39 When David heard that Nabal was dead, he said, 'Blessed be the LORD who has avenged the insult I received at the hand of Nabal, and has kept back his servant from evil; the LORD has returned the evil-doing of Nabal upon his own head.' Then David sent and wooed Abigail, to make her his wife. [40]And when the servants of David came to Abigail at Carmel, they said to her, 'David has sent us to you to take you to him as his wife.' [41]And she rose and bowed with her face to the ground, and said, 'Behold your handmaid is a servant to wash the feet of the servants of my lord.' [42]And Abigail made haste and rose and mounted on an ass, and her five maidens attended her; she went after the messengers of David, and became his wife.

43 David also took Ahinoam of Jezreel; and both of them became his wives. [44]Saul had given Michal his daughter, David's wife, to Palti the son of Laish, who was of Gallim.

[1b] Here we find David once again south of Hebron, where he had been staying earlier (23.14ff.); the place Carmel—also mentioned at 15.12—is to be thought of as being near Maon. Of all the narratives from the time of David's flight, this is the one which shows him least constrained. It is very different from 23.14ff.! The report of Nabal's shepherds about David does not betray any special needs and shows him as the leader of what is virtually a tribe, which

---

[a] *ṭaʿam*, properly: taste. The slang phrase 'have a good nose for' would be the best translation.
[b] In the sense of granting the request and thus comforting her. The usual rendering 'I have hearkened to you' is too weak.

has already been there for a considerable time. The marriages presuppose a certain growth of stability in his circumstances. It could
be the narrator's purpose to show that the fact of Samuel's death has
caused David to move farther into the south, but that his encounter
with Saul first of all resulted in an improvement in his situation.

[2–3] The story is told very vividly and charmingly; the three
main figures stand out clearly. We first make the acquaintance of
Nabal. His name, 'fool', has the connotation 'simpleton', 'silly'. He
is introduced as a very well-to-do owner of herds, though the
number of small cattle in his possession amounts to only half that
attributed to Job (Job 1.3). As a man he appears rough, stubborn
and thoughtless, the Calebbite type which the writer—closely associated with the court—regards with considerable contempt, and
pertinently characterizes with the pun at the end of v. 3. His wise
and charming wife, who more and more becomes the real protagonist of the narrative, is completely different.

[4–8] The occasion of the events described is the sheep-shearing,
which represents the harvest festival of the flock-owner and is
celebrated accordingly (II. 13.23). On such occasions it is usual for
something to be given to needy neighbours. David therefore sends
some of his young men to 'his brother' Nabal. Their number, ten,
may indicate how big the expected gift should have been. David's
request is not groundless. Wandering groups such as his own, and
plundering Bedouin tribesmen, themselves represent a danger not
only to the lonely traveller (Jer. 3.2; Luke 10.30) but also to the
herdsmen and their cattle (Job 1.15). If their attitude is friendly and
they leave the herdsmen unmolested, they expect some sort of tribute
in return, and this is regarded by the herdsmen, as we learn now, as
being completely justifiable. David does not exaggerate in the reasons
which he advances for his request. He has appropriated none of
Nabal's cattle (probably because he did not wish to wrong the people
of the land). Nabal's servants even go so far as to say that David has
been a 'wall' to them, in other words that he has kept off dangers from
other quarters. This is all completely grounded in the relationships
of the open wilderness, [9–13] and Nabal is really a 'fool' if he takes
no notice. He moreover offends David in the coarsest way possible
by judging him and his men from a sight which he often sees, calling
David a runaway slave. When David is given an account of what
happened he maintains an uncanny silence and merely gives the
order to start. What that means, everyone knows.

[14–19] In the meanwhile, Abigail discovers from the servants what has happened and the most probable consequences of her lord's action. She immediately recognizes that only swift action will be of any use. She has the necessary supplies, which are mentioned in detail—no great amount for six hundred men, but perhaps what David with his ten messengers expected to receive—loaded on asses and herself goes out to meet David, sending the gifts before her (see Gen. 32.14–22). It is presumed that the servants know the place where David is encamped. **[20–22]** In the event, Abigail meets David on the way; coming round a hill she suddenly finds herself face to face with him. David's angry monologue is once again meant to show the seriousness of the situation: he will leave no man alive. This time, not as in the occasion with Saul, he is convinced that he is right to take up the sword. **[23–31]** Abigail shows propriety and skill in her attitude and in her reply. Her almost exaggerated courtesy is meant to stand in intentional contrast to the boorishness of her husband. Her address is a masterpiece. Feminine charm and exceptional sagacity stand out vividly. She takes the guilt for everything upon herself, for she—as she says later—did not see the messengers, and tells David that it would not be seemly for him to take notice of the notorious 'fool'. Although not put in so many words, the request that David should put the blame on her is effectively supported by her beauty. Would David really exact vengeance on her for the insult paid to him? By the action which she rightly feels him to have planned would he not have to take bloodguilt on himself by going beyond the admissible limits of self-defence and in so doing would he not be anticipating the Lord? And therefore would he not himself appear as the guilty one? In her words she always sees David's conduct in the light of his promised future; she is an instrument of the Lord to keep the future king's escutcheon clean for David. It is expressly emphasized that David is already acting in accordance with his future by waging Yahweh's war. The appeal to his generosity also belongs to the same theme. How different does David's position appear here from the way in which it was presented in Nabal's words! In this section Abigail represents the prophetic voice. We can see this in detail: the remark of v. 26b which leads the reader to guess at Nabal's early death, and the request that David will later 'remember his handmaiden', by which the reader's attention is focused on what happens at the end of the story, are meant to show that more stands behind her words than she herself knows. The prophetic element in her speech occurs still more clearly in her vision of David as the predestined ruler over 'Israel', which here means all Israel. From this point of view, the wish that David should have a long life and that his enemies should perish is also understandable. Also present is the image of the 'bundle of life' (or of those who live in Yahweh), an obviously ancient idea according to which the 'self' (*nepeš*, better not translated 'soul') of a man is protected and preserved by the Lord himself. We should also take careful note of Abigail's definite assurance that the Lord will make for David a sure (*ne'emān*) house, a promise which exactly recalls II. 7. Abigail cannot, of course, know that she herself will contribute to this (II. 3.3); this is another of the small subtleties which characterize this speech and which will have gained the approval of the audience of the day. As it were in passing, Abigail takes the liberty of giving to David, i.e., wisely, to his men, the present which she has brought with her (Heb. *berākā* = blessing), a 'presumption' for which she asks to be excused. But the psychological subtleties of the speech are not its most important elements. The chief point is something different; it reminds David of the responsibility before the Lord which he is in the process of abrogating, and preserves him from thus forfeiting his place in God's plan. The main concern of the compiler makes itself felt here. Through Abigail, the Lord saves David from a danger different from that in the cave with Saul, but none the less great. It consists, as has been said, in the possibility that David may take matters into his own hand and thus make himself master of his fate, instead of letting it be guided by the Lord.

[32–35] The nature of David's answer makes it clear that this is, in fact, the concern of the chapter. He mentions by name the two offences from which Abigail has preserved him. In so doing, he praises the Lord, whose guiding can be seen quite plainly, and also includes the tactful wife. In this, and still more in the statement that he hearkened to her voice and 'raised her countenance', we have a gentle hint at the conclusion of the chapter.

[36–38] With swift and sharp strokes the narrative is now brought to its end. The details are laid vividly before us. The princely sheep-shearing festival, the heavily drunken man, the dreadful soberness in the morning, the effect of his wife's story, and finally the new and fatal 'blow' of Yahweh after ten days. Nabal is dead and David is right in saying that the Lord has taken vengeance into his own hands after graciously preserving him, David, from effecting it. [39–42]

David's request to Abigail to become his wife is in accord with the plan of the whole story. Nothing is said about the time which elapses between the death of Nabal and David's wooing of Abigail, as in II. 11.27, where we hear only of the lamentation after Bathsheba's widowing. In both places we are given the impression that the inessentials are omitted where possible while the essential elements are delineated all the more lovingly and in detail. Enough, the very brief and almost imperatively abrupt courtship follows and is received by Abigail with the same courteous humility which we have come to recognize in her. She follows the messengers and becomes David's wife. A son of this marriage is mentioned at II. 3.3.

Not a word hints that this association with the widow of a rich sheep-owner represented a material or a moral support for David. This is, however, to be assumed. No doubt the inhabitants of the place now have a different attitude to David from the people of Keilah and Ziph. The fact that he has already previously taken to wife Ahinoam from neighbouring Jezreel (Josh. 15.56)—she becomes the mother of his firstborn Amnon in II. 3.2—points in the same direction. So he has indeed strengthened his position. But this is not said. What is said is directed rather towards the guidance from above which is evident behind events. That is the most important element here.

[44] The note about David's first wife Michal, whom Saul had given to someone else, is opportunely introduced here. It should not be forgotten for a moment that the danger threatening from Saul has not been lifted. Chapter 25 belongs completely to the time of David's extremity.

18. DAVID SPARES SAUL THE SECOND TIME:
26.1–25

26 [1]Then the Ziphites came to Saul at Gibeah, saying, 'Is not David hiding himself in Gibeath Hachilah, which is on the east of Jeshimon?' [2]So Saul arose and went down to the wilderness of Ziph, with three thousand chosen men of Israel, to seek David in the wilderness of Ziph. [3]And Saul encamped in Gibeath Hachilah, which is beside the road on the east of Jeshimon. But David remained in the wilderness; and when David[a] saw that Saul came after him into the wilderness, [4]he—David[b]—sent out spies and learned that Saul had come to a certain (place).[c] [5]Then David rose and came to the place where

[a]So in LXX.   [b]Perhaps an explanatory gloss.
[c]See the note on 23.23.

Saul had encamped; and David saw the place where Saul lay, with Abner the son of Ner, the commander of his army; Saul was lying within the innermost circle of the camp,[a] while the army was encamped around him.

6 Then David said to Ahimelech the Hittite, and to Joab's brother Abishai the son of Zeruiah, 'Who will go down with me into the camp to Saul?' And Abishai said, 'I will go down with you.' [7]So David and Abishai went to the people[b] by night; and there lay Saul sleeping within the innermost circle of the camp, with his spear stuck in the ground at his head; and Abner and the army lay around him. [8]Then said Abishai to David, 'God has given your enemy into your hand this day; now I will pin[c] him to the earth with one stroke of the spear, and I will not strike him twice.' [9]But David said to Abishai, 'Do not destroy him; for who can put forth his hand against the LORD's anointed, and be guiltless?' [10]And David said, 'As the LORD lives, the LORD will smite him; or his day shall come to die; or he shall go down[d] into battle and perish. [11]The LORD forbid that I should put forth my hand against the LORD's anointed; but take now the spear that is at his head, and the jar of water, and let us go.' [12]So David took the spear and the jar of water from Saul's head; and they went away. No man saw it, or knew it, nor did any awake; for they were all asleep, because a deep sleep from the LORD had fallen upon them.

13 Then David went over to the other side, and stood afar off on the top of the mountain, with a great space between them; [14]and David called to the people, and to Abner the son of Ner,[e] saying, 'Will you not answer, Abner?' Then Abner answered, 'Who are you that calls to the king?'[f] [15]And David said to Abner, 'Are you not a man? Who is like you in Israel? Why then have you not kept watch over your lord the king? For one of the people came in to destroy the king your lord. [16]This thing that you have done is not good. As the LORD lives, you deserve to die, because you have not kept watch over your lord, the LORD's anointed. And now see where the king's spear is, and the jar of water that was at his head.'

17 Saul recognized David's voice, and said, 'Is this your voice, my

[a]The translation 'wagon stockade' is misleading, as no wagons could be used in this landscape and Saul in any case did not possess any.

[b]The word is surprising, but *hammaḥᵃne*, 'the camp', often proposed as an emendation, is so different from *hāʿām* that a scribal error would seem to be excluded.

[c]Construction similar to 18.11; 19.10.

[d]Probably thinking of the Philistine wars, in which they 'went down' from the hills.

[e]For *ben-nēr*, LXX has *dibbēr*, 'he spoke', which looks similar: it is an intentional simplification. But even with MT we must suppose that David first—to no effect—called the people, and then—successfully—Abner, by name.

[f]The words 'to the king' are missing in LXX B, a significant (simplificatory) omission. But the lack of a reason for the possible insertion of the words in itself tells against any attempt at deletion.

son David?' And David said, 'It is my voice, my lord, O king.' [18]And he said, 'Why does my lord pursue after his servant? For what have I done? What guilt is on my hands? [19]Now therefore let my lord the king hear the words of his servant. If it is the LORD who has stirred you up against me, may he accept an offering; but if it is men, may they be cursed before the LORD, for they have driven me out this day that I should have no share in the heritage of the LORD, saying, "Go, serve other gods." [20]Now therefore let not my blood fall to the earth away from the presence of the LORD; for the king of Israel has come out to seek my life,[a] like one who hunts a partridge in the mountains.'

21 Then Saul said, 'I have done wrong; return, my son David, for I will no more do you harm, because my life was precious in your eyes this day; behold, I have played the fool and have erred exceedingly.' [22]And David made answer, 'Here is the spear, O king! Let one of the young men come over and fetch it. [23]The LORD rewards every man for his righteousness and his faithfulness; for the LORD gave you into my[b] hand today, and I would not put forth my hand against the LORD's anointed. [24]Behold, as your life was precious this day in my sight, so may my life be precious in the sight of the LORD, and may he deliver me out of all tribulation.' [25]Then Saul said to David, 'Blessed be you, my son David! You will do many things and will succeed in them.' So David went his way, and Saul returned to his place.

It is evident that this narrative and 22.19–24.22 make use of the same material. [1] In each case it is the Ziphites who put Saul on David's track. In each case Saul has three thousand men with him, and an act of generosity on David's part eases the position of the fugitive. On the other hand, there are such remarkable differences in places and events that we can understand the hesitation of the compiler to suppress one of the reports in favour of the other. It is 'not easy', as Budde concedes, to assign each to a different source; this remains unsatisfactory, because it is too schematic. We should rather first of all establish that the material was associated with different localities; the 'rock of parting' in ch. 23, the cave at Engedi in ch. 24, and here in ch. 26 a formation in the wilderness of Ziph where a plateau suitable for a camp was divided by a valley from a hill of some height. The 'place' (Hebrew *māqōm*) bore the name of 'the hill of Hachilah'. The word is probably connected with *ḥaklīl*, reddish, and may have been given because of the colour of the earth. Perhaps the place was also called 'the camp of Saul'.[c]

[a]So LXX. MT has incorporated the marginal note 'a single flea' (from 24.14) into the text.
[b]See BH.
[c]Cf. the 'camp of Dan' (Mahaneh-Dan), Judg. 13.25; 18.12.

The compiler did not simply include the story because he had the material in front of him and did not feel himself entitled to suppress it. Nor is the vivid and ancient (cf. especially Gressmann *ad loc.*) form of the story a sufficient explanation. We must ask at the same time why it should stand here. It has been preceded by the story of Abigail, which shows David's position to be relatively secure. It is followed by David's move to the territory of the Philistines. This intermediate chapter is meant to show that David remains constantly exposed to Saul's pursuit, and therefore in the utmost danger. It will not always be the case that Saul goes into a cave alone or sinks into a deep sleep along with his men. These are rather particular dispensations of the Lord, to save David by a miracle. David cannot rely on his attitude towards Saul making a permanent impression, perhaps leading to a reconciliation. The end of this narrative shows that clearly enough. But the chapter is important in the general framework in yet another respect. As before, David, at a disadvantage militarily and politically, comes out on top by the Lord's guidance. Saul's life is given into his hand. He emerges not only as the moral victor, but also as one to whom the Lord will grant further success, as Saul himself recognizes—but not expressly, as in ch. 24. Thus the basic theme of the whole is again clearly recognizable.

The way the Ziphites bring news to Saul is told much more briefly than in 23.19ff. Their co-operation is really irrelevant in the material adduced here. But they live on in tradition as the notorious betrayers of David, and are therefore mentioned by name, more especially because the adventure takes place in their neighbourhood. [2–4] Precisely at this point it becomes clear that this is the same story as 23.19ff. The insertion of the geographical details of 26.3 at 23.19 suggests that the final compiler was fully conscious of this. It is also strange that the phrase '*el-nākōn* (see note on 23.23) should occur only in these two places in the Old Testament. On close examination it seems that Saul at first had his camp 'on the way', a reference perhaps to the road running from north to south near the watershed, and that he then followed David into the wilderness.

Unlike ch. 24, this meeting does not take place by chance. It is purposely brought about by David. He discovers the site of the camp and goes there by night. [5–6] Perhaps with the help of the moonlight and from the same hilltop which he climbs once he has completed his mission, he is able to see the layout of the camp.

Saul, who has his cousin and field-commander Abner with him (14.50; 20.25), sleeps in the middle of the camp with the men around him, protecting the king with their bodies. It may be remarked in passing that three thousand is far too high a number for this situation. David does not mean to carry out his plan of penetrating the camp right up to Saul by himself, but, like Gideon in Judg. 7.9 and Jonathan in I. 14, takes someone with him. Of the two men asked to go, the Hittite[a] Ahimelech and Abishai, the latter, a real daredevil, offers immediately. He is, moreover, a nephew of David; according to I Chron. 2.16, Zeruiah is David's sister—certainly considerably older. Her sons are always described as sons of Zeruiah, perhaps because their father was long dead (II. 2.32), but more especially because of their mother's relationship to David.

[7–11a] Abishai has no opportunity of assisting David in action. The Lord himself has taken care that no one wakes by means of a stupefying sleep (tardēmā) which he has spread over everyone. Abishai is really only David's tempter; he plays the same role as David's men in ch. 24. The spear standing in the ground at Saul's head, the constantly present sign of his rank, is to be the weapon with which Abishai means to do away with the king. Here, too, he can appeal to the God who has delivered David's enemies into his hand. As in ch. 24, David rejects the proposal by referring to the 'Lord's anointed'. The Lord himself must be left to decide when and how Saul's hour will come. This train of thought is reminiscent of what is said in ch. 25 about 'self-help', and is very important for the general sense. It is not 'men' who make history; history is shaped by a higher hand and it should be clearly understood that not only is David the instrument of the Lord; he is, and means to be, nothing else. All this, however, is said not simply in praise of David's piety and generosity, but above all to clarify the theological position. Here David, as it were, himself represents the 'prophetic voice'.

[11b–12] David then orders Abishai to take Saul's spear with him. The jar of water, similarly taken as evidence, does not appear again as such in v. 22; the word may derive from a special tradition. Probably only the spear originally stood at Saul's head, as emerges from v. 22; if we compare vv. 12 and 16 with this, it seems possible to

---

[a]There were individual Hittites in the country here and there who had, of course, long been accepted by the Israelite tribes. The most well known of them is Uriah, II 11 3ff. In Gen. 23 they are the inhabitants of Hebron and its neighbourhood.

establish that the remark about the water jar is an additional note.[a]
It is also strange that after ordering the things to be taken, David
then goes on to take them himself; in fact, Abishai is no longer
mentioned after v. 12. There was almost certainly a tradition
according to which David carried out the undertaking alone;
Abishai is merely, as has been said, the tempter, through whom the
theological concern of the narrative is well brought out.

[13–16] The second part of the narrative also takes place at night.
Separated from Saul by a valley,[b] David calls from high on the hill
to the men, and particularly, by name, to Abner. Only then is the
deep sleep broken. Abner regards the shout as a disturbance of the
king's rest, without noticing who it is that is calling, a point on
which David does not enlighten him. Instead of this, he sneers at
Abner over his 'good' watch. His words give a vivid picture of the
danger that threatened the king and with the disappearance of the
spear—and the jar—show both his, David's, attitude and Abner's
negligence. [17–20] Saul is the first to recognize David's voice.
David can now use the occasion to make clear to him the sense-
lessness of his pursuit. The issue is not in his, David's, hands. Were
it a spirit of discord sent by Yahweh, as, for example, in Judg. 9.23,
one—and here David could be referring to himself—could make an
offering for a 'sweet-smelling savour';[c] if men were responsible, it
would be possible to make the curse operative against them. David
does not touch on the fourth possibility, that Saul might be at fault.
It is thus recognized and felt all the more clearly by Saul himself.
David makes yet another point. Things will come to the stage—
here the compiler is already turning his eyes towards the next chapter
—when David has to leave the soil of the land belonging to Yahweh,
to flee abroad, and so has to 'serve other gods.' This is an ancient
idea which is soon countered in the Old Testament by the consciousness that as God of the world, the Lord reaches out even beyond the
boundaries of 'his' land. But when Ruth goes from Moab to
Bethlehem of Judah, she puts herself under the wings of the God of
Israel (2.12), and the Aramaean Naaman even takes with him a
load of the holy land so as to be able to show his veneration for
Yahweh correctly in pagan Damascus (II Kings 5.17). If David, in
view of such thoughts, expresses the request that his blood may not

---

[a]Cf. also the surprising *we'et* in v. 16.
[b]This is implied in the word *'ābār*, cross, which is used here.
[c]W. Vischer, *Christuszeugnis* I, p. 118.

fall to the ground away from the presence of the Lord, i.e. the place where he reveals himself and is worshipped, he thus appears not only to appeal to Saul's compassion, but also to remind him of his responsibility as the Lord's anointed.[a] This is more probable than the assumption that he does not wish to 'die in a foreign land . . . in case his innocently shed blood does not come before Yahweh . . . If it comes before him with a cry (Gen. 4.10; Job 16.18), Yahweh will avenge it and so give rest to David's soul.'[b] For if that were David's meaning, it would be an encouragement to Saul to drive him out of the land as quickly as possible, to avoid the consequences!

[21–25] As has been said, Saul, without going into the previous remarks, takes the blame for the conflict on himself, and in so doing expresses the view of both the compiler and the reader. No use is made in the sequel of his promise to spare David and his invitation to David to return, either by David—he 'knows his man' (Schulz)—or by Saul himself. Saul is described throughout the tradition as a man of sanguine temperament. His words are certainly not untrue subjectively; but his temporary emotion does not last. So the narrator cannot make a 'happy ending'. Saul's spear may be fetched back; it has served its purpose. It is more important that the events of the night have once again assured David—and with him the narrator and the reader—that he will be safe under the protection of the Lord, even in the future. We should not fail to notice that David puts this to the Lord as a request. Saul likewise stresses that the way to David's future will lead clearly to the appointed goal. The closing verses, viewed in the general context, serve at the same time as a prelude to the events of the next chapter, where David goes into a foreign land and therefore at first places himself a very long way from his goal.

And so the two men part. They never saw each other again.

19. DAVID AMONG THE PHILISTINES:
27.1–28.2

27 [1]And David said in his heart, 'I shall now perish one day by the hand of Saul; there is nothing better for me than that[c] I should escape to the land of the Philistines; then Saul will despair of seeking me any longer within the borders of Israel, and I shall escape out of his hand.' [2]So David arose and went over, he and the six hundred men who

---

[a]Note the 'therefore' in v. 20.
[b]See Budde on v. 20 and Gressmann, p. 99.
[c]Here *kī* replaces the usual *kī 'im*. The *'im* is probably to be added to the text.

were with him, to Achish the son of Maoch,[a] king of Gath. [3]And
David dwelt with Achish at Gath, he and his men, every man with his
household, and David with his two wives, Ahinoam of Jezreel, and
Abigail of Carmel, Nabal's widow. [4]And when it was told Saul that
David had fled to Gath, he sought for him no more.

5 Then David said to Achish, 'If I have found favour in your eyes,
let a place be given me in one of the country towns, that I may dwell
there; for why should your servant dwell in the royal city with you?'
[6]So that day Achish gave him Ziklag; therefore Ziklag has belonged
to the kings of Judah to this day. [7]And the number of the days that
David dwelt in the country of the Philistines was a year and four
months.

8 Now David and his men went up, and made raids upon the
Geshurites, the Girzites, and the Amalekites; for these were the
inhabitants of the land from Telam[b] as far as Shur, to the land of
Egypt. [9]And David smote the land, and left neither man nor woman
alive, but took away the sheep, the oxen, the asses, the camels and the
garments, and came back to Achish. [10]When Achish asked, 'Where[b]
have you made a raid today?' David would say, 'Against the Negeb
of Judah,' or 'Against the Negeb of the Jerahmeelites,' or, 'Against the
Negeb of the Kenites.' [11]And David saved neither man nor woman
alive, to bring tidings to Gath, thinking, 'Lest they should tell about
us, and say, "So David has done." ' Such was his custom all the while
he dwelt in the country of the Philistines. [12]And Achish trusted David,
thinking, 'He has made himself utterly abhorred by his people Israel;
therefore he shall be my servant always.'

28 [1]In those days the Philistines gathered their forces for war, to
fight against Israel. And Achish said to David, 'Understand that you
and your men are to go out with me in the army.' [2]David said to Achish,
'Very well, you shall know what your servant can do.' And Achish
said to David, 'Very well, I will make you my bodyguard for life.'

[27.1] During the period of his flight David spent a certain time,
fixed to the month, among the Philistines. We have already discussed
the necessity of this step: it was impossible to evade Saul for ever in
the land of Israel. What is said here at the beginning is also completely correct from an historical standpoint.

David's desertion has a twofold significance in the general framework. First, a negative one: David runs the risk of being alienated
from the Israelite cause by his action. The Philistines are the classic
enemies of Israel. In Israelite eyes, anyone who goes over to them
renounces his part in Israel. It is one of the concerns of the last

[a]On the Philistine names Maoch and Achish, see most recently Wainwright
in *VT* 9, 1959, pp. 76-78.
[b]See BH.

chapters of I Samuel to show that although David flees before Saul
to the Philistines, he none the less remains true to the Israelite cause.
Or more accurately: the Lord preserves him from being a partisan
of the Philistines. But that is the positive element which here must
be read between the lines. In this difficult situation, which can jeopardize not only David's life, but also his role in the ordering of
sacred history, matters are so arranged that not only can a loss be
avoided, but David even achieves a gain for the future. Therefore
although this section has no spiritual overtone—quite the opposite,
it is completely unedifying in its account and indeed praise of fraud
and power—it is nevertheless completely involved in the general
theological pattern.

We have already heard of some time spent by David in Gath with
Achish at 21.11–16. This was a local saga which, like ch. 27, is
meant to show how David was saved from a difficult situation in
the land of the Philistines. Accordingly, the two passages look like
parallel accounts, but they have such clear differences that the relation between them is very different from that between chs. 24 and 26.

[27.2–4] The most important difference is that in the earlier narrative David appears as a forsaken fugitive, whereas here he comes as
the head of a powerful, indeed much-feared, band. He is, moreover,
a man who is himself related to families living in the hill countries
of Caleb and Judah, and, of course, has among his troops men in
a similar position. Again, as he represents one of the strongest
figures in Israel, Achish is not just doing a good turn, but is bene-
fiting himself by being able to attract such a man to his side. Their
association is thus to the interest of both parties. We hear nothing of
the conversations and negotiations which may have preceded David's
action. We are merely told that David went with all his men and
their families straight to Achish, i.e. to Gath itself. As Achish also
appears as David's liege lord in the sequel, the stationing of the troops
under the eyes of the Philistine king could have been some sort of
condition or test for David. Looking at things more closely, Achish
may well have wanted to create for himself a foreign legion similar
to that which we find later with David. Be this as it may, it is first
of all established that David has now, in fact, escaped from Saul's
pursuit.

[27.5–7] We are next told that David leaves Gath—presumably
after some time. No reason is given for his request to Achish; the
close of David's speech, however, suggests that his departure from

Gath would give Achish a respite from the necessary provisioning of David's large number of men. We might suppose that religious differences would have made some sort of peaceful isolation desirable, but surprisingly enough there is nothing to hint at this, not even later. Anyway, the king seems immediately ('that day', v. 6) ready to give David Ziklag, a place which after Alt's conjecture[a] has recently been identified with *tell el-khuweilifeh*, about twelve miles north of Beersheba. It should be noted that David's stay at Ziklag had later juridical consequences. Because it belonged to David, Ziklag later became the crown property of the king of Judah, so we may conclude that David felt the place to be in an important position and was perhaps also attached to it, despite the shortness of his stay there. The number given here, precise as it is,[b] is not to be doubted, but it refers to the whole of David's stay among the Philistines. This has sometimes led to vv. 5–7 being moved to the end of the chapter, so that the expeditions described in vv. 8ff. would have been undertaken from Gath. It is, however, simpler to imagine Ziklag as the base of David's operations, and to keep to the traditional verse order.

[27.8–12] David's raiding expeditions stand in well-considered relationship to his hoped-for future position. They are directed towards the tribes deep in the south. Among these, the Amalekites are well known as Israel's most hated enemies (cf. ch. 15). The Geshurites are also mentioned at Josh. 13.2 as a southern group; they are not to be confused with the people of the same name living in the northern territory east of the Jordan (Josh. 13.11, 13, etc.). We do not know who the Girzites were.[c] They are only mentioned here. David's method is both practical and brutal; he destroys all the people he captures, so as to leave no witnesses alive, and takes as plunder only cattle and possessions. The text says nothing about a ban here, precisely because of the treatment of the last-named objects. To the inquiries of Achish,[d] David replies by referring to

---

[a] Cf. *JPOS* 15, 1935, pp. 318f.

[b] LXX gives only four months, which is surely wrong. The omission of 'a year' is perhaps a consequence of the uncommon expression *yāmīm*.

[c] Certainly not inhabitants of Gezer. Perhaps it is another form of the name 'Girgashites', some of the 'original inhabitants' of Palestine.

[d] This is a second reason for the conjecture, mentioned above, that vv. 5–7 should be transferred to the end of the chapter. It is assumed that Achish watched David's actions from near by. He would, however, have exercised some degree of control even as far as Ziklag, and David could hardly have played this risky game from Gath itself.

certain areas belonging to the tribes of South Judah in the 'Negeb'. It is expressly said that he had to bring some plunder to Gath, perhaps because there was a slave market there. Probably these desert dwellers were well disposed to the Philistines, as they were hostile to Israel. In this way, David gives the impression of making enemies for himself among his own people, as Achish triumphantly asserts, whereas in reality he is doing damage to the enemies of his own people. The later audience will have listened to all this with great wonderment at the wise man who played this dangerous game so as not to be untrue to his destiny. David is already beginning the task which he was later to complete: that of conquering the whole of the neighbouring peoples.

[28.1–2] The precariousness of David's position, in spite of everything, becomes clear when the emergency occurs. The Philistines arm for a great attack against Israel. Both Achish's earlier trust and his prominent position compel David to follow the army. The Bible does not usually describe psychological situations, and even here nothing is said of the feelings with which David goes into the field as a Philistine vassal. Presumably here, too, he will have left himself to the divine guidance—and rightly, as we shall see. The king's words are given with some uncertainty; David's reply is manifestly ambiguous. His appointment to be the bodyguard of Achish, i.e. the leader of his guard, could even be a measure directed against David; 'Achish in anticipation promotes him to a highly undesirable fettering to his person' (Budde).

So things are on the razor's edge. How will David—how will the Lord find a way out?

20. SAUL AND THE 'WITCH' OF ENDOR: 28.3–25

28 ³Now Samuel had died, and all Israel had mourned for him and buried him in Ramah,^a his own city. And Saul had put the mediums and the wizards out of the land. ⁴The Philistines assembled, and came and encamped at Shunem; and Saul gathered all Israel, and they encamped at Gilboa. ⁵When Saul saw the army of the Philistines, he was afraid, and his heart trembled greatly. ⁶And when Saul inquired of the Lord, the Lord did not answer him, either by dreams, or by Urim, or by prophets. ⁷Then Saul said to his servants, 'Seek out for me a woman who is a medium, that I may go to her and inquire of her.' And his servants said to him, 'Behold, there is a medium at Endor.'

---

^a'And' occurs in MT, but is understandably omitted by some MSS. It is easier to delete it than to explain its origin.

8 So Saul disguised himself and put on other garments, and went, he and two men with him; and they came to the woman by night. And he said, 'Divine for me by a spirit, and bring up for me whomever I shall name to you.' [9]The woman said to him, 'Surely you know what Saul has done, how he has cut off the mediums and the wizards from the land. Why then are you laying a snare for my life to bring about my death?' [10]But Saul sware to her by the LORD, 'As the LORD lives, no punishment shall come upon you for this thing.' [11]Then the woman said, 'Whom shall I bring up for you?' He said, 'Bring up Samuel for me.' [12]When the woman heard the name Samuel,[a] she cried out with a loud voice; and the woman said to Saul, 'Why have you deceived me? You are Saul.' [13]The king said to her, 'Have no fear, (but say to me) rather[b] what you see.' And the woman said to Saul, 'I see a spirit coming up out of the earth.' [14]He said to her, 'What is his appearance?' And she said, 'An old man is coming up; and he is wrapped in a robe.' And Saul knew that it was Samuel, and he bowed with his face to the ground, and did obeisance.

15 Then Samuel said to Saul, 'Why have you disturbed me by bringing me up?' Saul answered, 'I am in great distress; for the Philistines are warring against me, and God has turned away from me and answers me no more, either by prophets or by dreams; therefore I have summoned you to tell me what I shall do.' [16]And Samuel said, 'Why then do you ask me, since the LORD has turned from you and become your enemy? [[17]The LORD has now[c] done as he spoke by me; for the LORD has torn the kingdom out of your hand, and given it to your neighbour, David. [18]Because you did not obey the voice of the LORD, and did not carry out his fierce wrath against Amalek, therefore the LORD has done this thing to you this day. [19]Moreover the LORD will give Israel also with you into the hand of the Philistines;] and tomorrow you and your sons shall be with me; the LORD will give the army of Israel also into the hand of the Philistines.'

20 Then Saul fell at once full length upon the ground, filled with fear because of the words of Samuel; and there was no strength in him, for he had eaten nothing all day and all night. [21]And the woman came to Saul, and when she saw that he was terrified, she said to him, 'Behold, your handmaid has hearkened to you; I have taken my life in my hand, and have hearkened to what you have said to me. [22]Now therefore, you also hearken to your handmaid; let me set a morsel of bread before you; and eat, that you may have strength when you go on your way.' [23]He refused, and said, 'I will not eat.' But his servants, together with the woman, urged him; and he hearkened to their words. So he arose from the earth, and sat upon the bed. [24]Now the woman had a fatted calf in the house, and she quickly killed it,

[a]See Commentary.
[b]This is the meaning of $k\bar{i}$ (see Budde).
[c]$l\bar{o}$ is the so-called *dativus commodi*; for examples see GK § 119s. The $l^ek\bar{a}$ of some MSS is an intentional simplification.

and she took flour, and kneaded it and baked unleavened bread of it, [25]and she put it before Saul and his servants; and they ate. Then they rose and went away that night.

In this thrilling story we can see clearly that the compiler of the whole work has taken up some independent material and placed it in its present context. This is evident both from individual details and from the whole. As far as the whole is concerned, we might first of all feel that the text would be in a better position before ch. 31, especially as ch. 29 would then join directly to ch. 27, of which it is the continuation. The reason why this did not happen may be as follows. In ch. 27, David finds himself at a point of depression, far removed from his intended goal. Chapter 28 shows that it is not he but Saul who has come to the end of the road, and that the promise still remains in force for David. The fact that it is Samuel, the very man who published Saul's rejection and performed David's anointing, who appears, adds special weight to the section. In addition there are two individual details. At the beginning we have two clauses which look like stage directions. They have been placed here, one from 25.1, the other from the text itself, to make the narrative which follows intelligible. We will similarly have to notice a subsequent expansion of the original narrative in vv. 17–19aa. Now it is just this section in which the main point is made, so that it, too, provides confirmation of what has been said above. The very ancient narrative will itself derive from a local tradition; the house of the woman will later have been pointed out as 'Saul's house' in the place Endor.[a]

[3] Samuel's death and burial were mentioned at 25.1. The remark at 3b is put in abrupt juxtaposition. With it we descend into the mysterious world of a belief about spirits and the dead, similar to that which can be found everywhere under the veneer of the higher religions, and even that of modern secularism (spiritism, etc.). It is a feature of the matter that there is little open mention of it in literature—except perhaps in polemic. For this reason we can gain no clear picture of it from the Old Testament. The word '$\bar{o}b$ is usually translated 'ghost'. But this does not do for this particular story. The apparition of Samuel is called not '$\bar{o}b$, but '$^e l\bar{o}h\bar{\imath}m$ (see below), and his appearance is brought about $b\bar{a}$'$\bar{o}b$, i.e. 'in the' or 'with the help of' '$\bar{o}b$. In his article "'$\bar{o}b$'[b] Hans Schmidt has drawn

[a] $^c\bar{e}n$ $d\bar{o}r$, the present $endur$, lies south of Tabor. Cf. Alt in PJB 23, 1927, p. 41.
[b] $Marti$ $Festschrift$, 1925, pp. 253–61.

attention to this fact and refers to the 'bull-roarer' of the Australians. We may not regard all the details of his conclusions as convincing, but we must take his point when he asserts that this word describes not the ghost itself but the mechanism or means whereby the conjuring of the ghost is brought about. The formulation both of this verse and of v. 9 is the principal evidence for this.[a] Otherwise we can form a clear picture neither of oracles from the dead nor of spirit-oracles.[b] That Saul took some action against this religion of the underworld once again shows his manifest desire for scrupulous piety both in himself and in his people. This feature is highly important for an assessment of Saul.

[4–8a] The narrative proper begins with a report of the Philistine advance; the name of their camp survives in the place *solem*.[c] The Israelite camp is south of this, on or near the hill spur of Gilboa, where the high land of Samaria goes down into the plain of Jezreel.[d] The superiority of the Philistines is so great that Saul, seized with terror, seeks ways of discovering the will of God. He is unsuccessful. By annihilating the priests of Nob he has deprived himself of the holy oracle by lot; God sends him neither dreams nor prophets. In pressing need not to be left all alone, he resorts to means which otherwise he had put far from him, the conjuring up of the dead. His followers are immediately[e] able to name a woman who lives outside the territory occupied by the enemy and is accessible from the hills. Clothed in a style which is not altogether clear, but which conceals all his royal insignia, Saul goes on his nocturnal journey with just two servants, presumably so as not to arouse suspicion.

[8b–14] The story now mounts to its climax. Saul, who at first really remains unrecognized, expresses his wish, and in reply the woman voices her hesitations, prompted by the king's prohibition. These are, however, overcome by Saul's oath, and only then does she learn that it is Samuel whom she is to 'bring up'. There now follows in MT the sentence: 'When the woman saw Samuel, she cried . . .' This, however, is very strange. Samuel's coming up is

---

[a]Here the verb used means 'expel', in v. 8 'extirpate'. The basic meaning is 'cut off', 'cut down'.

[b]*yidde'ōnī*, properly 'the one who knows'; perhaps here it means a sort of medium.

[c]South-west of Tabor, west of the *nabi daḥi*; cf. *PJB* 23, 1927, pp. 47f.

[d]On the site see *PJB* 23, 1927, p. 38.

[e]Their ability to name someone straight away shows how these matters, though forbidden, were an open secret which reached right into court circles.

only reported in v. 13b. Moreover, no one has yet been able to explain why the woman recognizes Saul at the very moment when Samuel becomes visible. It has therefore seriously been conjectured that 'Saul' should be read for 'Samuel' and 'see' should be understood to mean 'take a close look at'; but this would have to be expressed otherwise, and at the least more clearly. So another way must be put forward. We would expect: 'Now when the woman heard the name of Samuel'. Now the word *šēm* (name) could easily have fallen out in front of *šᵉmū'ēl*, as it contains the two initial consonants of the word. This omission could have been the occasion of the alteration 'and she heard' into 'and she saw', as a sentence which began 'Now when the woman heard Samuel' would be incomprehensible. The reading *wattiqrā* (and she spoke) instead of *wattēre* (and she saw) would also be possible, as only one consonant would have to be added. However, 'Now when the woman spoke the name of Samuel' would not be as plausible an opening to the verse as that provided by the former conjecture.

The woman, then, concludes from the request for so prominent a man as Samuel to be 'brought up' that the person who made the request must likewise be prominent, and now recognizes the king, even through his disguise. Saul quietens her rising fears, and on closer questioning learns from her that she sees *'ᵉlōhīm* coming up. The word can mean 'God', but also means 'godlike being' and is therefore most appropriately rendered 'spirit'. Its form is that of an old man wrapped in a robe. Samuel is immediately recognizable from this description (cf. 15.27), especially as the robe is itself the sign of a special rank and status (18.4; 24.5, 12. cf. Job 1.20; 2.12, etc.). Saul himself sees nothing but the woman. At the apparition, however, he reverently throws himself to the ground.

[15–19] Samuel now speaks. It is evidently felt that the conversation between him and Saul takes place without intermediary. On being asked why he has disturbed the rest of the dead, Saul describes his straitened position and in particular points out that the Lord has turned from him. The omission here of any mention of the possibility of a decision by the holy lot ('Urim and Thummim'), mentioned earlier, may be intentional, so as to make it unnecessary to mention to Samuel the circumstances under which Saul lost possession of the oracle. The information asked for is refused for two reasons. The Lord has let him fall, and moreover the fate of Saul and his men is sealed. In other words, it does not matter now what he does or intends to do. In between there is a section which with particular reference to 15.28 recollects to Saul the events of the war against the Amalekites. Verses 17–19aa, put in parentheses above, are a real piece of later interpretation and are meant to associate the events depicted here with those earlier ones, in the proclamation which Samuel is now made to give. The original message of the spirit from the dead was surely limited to v. 16 and the close of v. 19. Here a line is drawn under the whole of Saul's life; the words which stand in between suggest that it was merely the unforgiven guilt of that occasion which was the ground of his destiny as it is now being realized.

[20–25] The effect upon Saul is fearful. Weakened in any case by having taken no 'bread' for twenty-four hours, he falls to the ground like a hewn oak-tree. Everything, including the closing description of the hospitality offered by the woman, is related not without sympathy for him. The way in which she and then the two companions trouble themselves over the hard-hit man who lies there on the floor is most moving. Only after being strengthened do the men walk out into the night, to meet their fate the following day.

Without doubt, this chapter as a whole is directed against Saul, and it sees in his fate a well-deserved punishment. It is equally certain that his recourse to the 'witch of Endor' is regarded as new proof of the fact of his rejection and thus as justification for his rejection. So the narrative is meant to be taken as the penultimate act of a man who is involved in guilt and who now meets his deserts. After the events described in ch. 15, Saul's kingship appears in such a light that the unavoidable end is felt only to be postponed. From that point onwards Saul was ripe for his downfall. We have said that the present position of this chapter is motivated by similar patterns of thought. But the narrative proper has a different point of view. It spoke with sympathy of the events of this night. If the account is to be taken to have been originally associated with its particular location, we may say that in those villages in the north Saul was not assessed in the same way as in the theological view of the Deuteronomist. They saw the tragic element in Saul, and surely his contemporaries, without discounting his errors, were of a similar opinion.

Both points of view have one thing in common; they take the event narrated here extremely seriously. There is no indication that anyone either earlier or later regarded the apparition of Samuel as a fraudulent fiction perpetrated by the woman. Both the earlier account and the deuteronomistic compiler are convinced that Samuel was really present. Although we know that Saul himself regarded this form of spiritist session as hostile to Yahweh, although the Deuteronomist, as we have said, certainly took an unfavourable view of Saul's acting in this way, no one doubted the capability of the woman to bring about something of this kind. They believed as much in this 'witch' as the Middle Ages believed in its witches. We must certainly assume that the narrative was uncanny for the compiler, because here we have a report of something which is 'improper' (v. 15a), namely a glimpse into the inaccessible land of the dead. Nevertheless, the local saga has been incorporated into the train of events surrounding Saul and David because here once again the will of God could be proclaimed from the mouth of Samuel, namely that Saul's time was past and that David's time was coming.

21. DAVID IN THE PHILISTINE HOST: 29.1–11

29 ¹Now the Philistines gathered all their forces at Aphek; and the Israelites were encamped by the fountain which is in Jezreel. ²As the lords of the Philistines were passing on by hundreds and by thousands, and David and his men were passing on in the rear with Achish, ³the commanders of the Philistines said, 'What are these Hebrews doing here?' And Achish said to the commanders of the Philistines, 'Is not this David, the servant of Saul, king of Israel, who has been with me now for days and years, and since he deserted to me I have found no fault in him to this day.' ⁴But the commanders of the Philistines were angry with him; and the commanders of the Philistines said to him, 'Send the man back, that he may return to the place to which you have assigned him; he shall not go down with us to battle, lest in the battle he become an adversary to us. For how could this fellow reconcile himself to his lord? Would it not be with the heads of the men here? ⁵Is not this David, of whom they sing to one another in dances, "Saul has slain his thousands, and David his ten thousands?" '

6 Then Achish called David and said to him, 'As the LORD lives, you have been honest, and to me it seems right that you should march out and in with me in the campaign; for I have found nothing wrong in you from the day of your coming to me to this day. Nevertheless the lords do not approve of you. ⁷So go back now; and go peaceably, that you may not displease the lords of the Philistines.' ⁸And David said to Achish, 'But what am I meant to have done?ᵃ What have you found in your servant from the day I entered your service until now,

---

ᵃThis translation follows from the introductory kī which gives the reason for the remarks of Achish and supports them from David's point of view.

that I may not go and fight against the enemies of my lord the king?' [9]And Achish made answer to David, 'I know[a] that you are as blameless in my sight as an angel of God; nevertheless the commanders of the Philistines have said, "He shall not go up[b] with us to the battle." [10]Now then rise early in the morning with the servants of your lord who came with you and go to the place to which I have assigned you. And think no evil of me, for you are in the right with me.[c] Start early in the morning, and depart as soon as you have light.' [11]So David set out with his men early in the morning, to return to the land of the Philistines. But the Philistines went up to Jezreel.

In view of its content, this brief but vividly narrated account belongs before ch. 28, as has been said. In its present position it is an interpolation. Apart from the reasons for this arrangement given earlier, it should also be noted that it is closely connected with the events of ch. 30, which in turn is contemporaneous with ch. 31 (cf. II. 1.1). So it is in every respect right that ch. 29 should have been given its present position.

[1–2] According to this account, the Philistines are still at Aphek, the place on the coastal plain mentioned in ch. 4, in the neighbourhood of which they achieved the victory over Israel described in that chapter. Saul's army is encamped, perhaps awaiting the enemy, by the fountain in Jezreel,[d] near the mountain spur of Gilboa mentioned at 28.4. The narrative confines itself to the events in the Philistine camp. Some sort of parade is taking place; the lords (*s^erānīm*), including Achish—who is the only one to be called 'king'— evidently take part personally in the march past. The commanders (*sārīm*), who are also mentioned, should properly, according to their title, be subordinate to the 'lords'; here they appear to be the commanding officers of the host, before whom the parade is being held.[e] [3–5] David and his men appear right at the rear, in the company of Achish. The Hebrews are recognizable at once both by their distinctive weapons and their marked racial characteristics; as the

[a]The conjecture 'you know', sometimes put forward, would be better, but there is no evidence for it.

[b]In v. 4 we have 'go down', as though that verse were written so to speak from the point of view of the 'field-marshal's hill'. V. 9 represents the geographical situation.

[c]These words are supplied from LXX (and the Latin versions).

[d]Cf. *PJB* 23, 1927, p. 48.

[e]In fact, the distinction is made clear neither by LXX nor by MT. MT speaks of the 'lords' in v. 6 instead of the 'commanders' as in v. 9—perhaps one or other of the 'lords' belonged among the 'commanders'.

war is against Israel, they are, of course, regarded with mistrust. Achish pleads for David, the turncoat, with skill and determination. We learn once again that he has not seen through David's double game, and still has complete trust in him. The commanders, however, are justifiably suspicious of having the Hebrews in their camp, especially as one of them is the renowned David. He could become a secret 'satan' (adversary—perhaps the word also means a disturber of the peace, *enfant terrible*, like the common Arabic *šiṭan*). The logic of the Philistines is irrefutable, and they judge David, as the reader well knows, better than they themselves guess. The fact that the verse from 18.7 is quoted again here, as at 21.12, where it is also the Philistines who know the saying, shows how far his fame has spread. The Philistines, moreover, seem to have been generous enough to acknowledge foreign fame in war, even in an adversary (cf. Judg. 16.24). We are given the general impression that the Philistines were not only familiar with Hebrew, but regularly made use of the language.

[6–10] Achish naturally feels that the decision of the commanders is embarrassing, indeed a slur on himself. But he must hold to it and send for David. He clothes the news, which he thinks will be bitter for David as well, in words of praise and personal trust, at the same time using, almost certainly on purpose, words of assurance which include the name of Yahweh. The wish for another to depart 'in peace' corresponds with an Arabic greeting still used today. David finds it easy to play the injured and angry soldier. The beginning of his answer (see the note on v. 8) seems to suggest that he is already prepared for the situation brought about by the attitude of the commanders, and says basically the same thing as Achish has said earlier. Achish, who understands David's words as an expression of regret that he is not to be allowed to go into the field, once again confirms his view of David in words of exaggerated kindness[a] and goes on to arrange David's now unavoidable march back to Ziklag. This takes place. [11] The chapter ends with a note on the Philistine advance to the plain of Jezreel, and thus connects it with the situation depicted at the beginning of the previous section.

Despite the vigour with which it moves, the account is both factual and dispassionate. The most important information it provides is not given explicitly, but is to be read between the lines; the development of events has now proved extremely favourable to David.

[a]The comparison with 'an angel of God' is also applied to David in II. 14.17–20; 19.28.

Imagine the fateful dilemma in which he would have found himself had he really had to provide further support for Achish, on the battlefield, too. At this point everything was at stake. We may, moreover, reflect that his return was also a matter of pressing need for other reasons (cf. ch. 30). Although the actual words do not say as much, we have here a section which is concerned with God's dealings with David. This chapter occupies a prominent place among the many indications of the way in which the Lord protected and guided the future king during his greatest time of need. Even the mistrust of the Philistines is worked into the plans of the God of Israel. 'David's deliverance here is remarkable. He is protected from himself and from unfaithfulness to his calling by the enemies of the Lord.'[a]

22. DAVID'S EXPEDITION AGAINST THE AMALEKITES: 30.1-31

30 [1]Now when David and his men came to Ziklag on the third day, the Amalekites had made a raid upon the Negeb and upon Ziklag. They had overcome Ziklag, and burned it with fire, [2]and taken captive the women and[b] what was in it, both small and great; they killed no one, but carried them off, and went their way. [3]And when David and his men came to the city, they found it burned with fire, and their wives and sons and daughters taken captive. [4]Then David and the people who were with him raised their voices and wept, until they had no more strength to weep. [5]David's two wives also had been taken captive, Ahinoam of Jezreel, and Abigail the widow of Nabal of Carmel. [6]And David was greatly distressed; for the people spoke of stoning him, because all the people were bitter in soul, each for his sons and daughters. But David strengthened himself in the LORD his God.

7 And David said to Abiathar the priest, the son of Ahimelech, 'Bring me the ephod.' So Abiathar brought the ephod to David. [8]And David inquired of the LORD, 'Shall I pursue after this band? Shall I overtake them?' He answered him, 'Pursue; for you shall surely overtake and shall surely rescue.' [9A]So David set out, and the six hundred men who were with him, and they came to the brook Besor. [10B]Two hundred men stayed behind, who were too exhausted to cross the brook Besor. [10A]But David went on with the pursuit, he and four hundred men, [9B]while the others stayed behind.[c]

11 They found a man, an Egyptian,[d] in the open country, and

---

[a]H. Asmussen, *Das erste Samuelisbuch*, 1938, p. 169.
[b]A *waw* seems to have fallen out.
[c]The transposition of v. 10a and v. 10b was made as early as Wellhausen. 9b need not be a gloss (against Wellhausen, etc.), but can be transposed with 10b.
[d]Presumably a (correct) gloss.

brought him to David; and they gave him bread and he ate, they gave him water to drink, [12]and they gave him a piece of a cake of figs and two clusters of raisins. And when he had eaten, his spirit revived; for he had not eaten bread or drunk water for three days and three nights. [13]And David said to him, 'To whom do you belong? And where are you from?' He said, 'I am a young man of Egypt, servant to an Amalekite; and my master left me behind because I fell sick three days ago. [14]We had made a raid upon the Negeb of the Cherethites and upon that which belongs to Judah and upon the Negeb of Caleb; and we burned Ziklag with fire.' [15]And David said to him, 'Will you take me down to this band?' And he said, 'Swear to me by God, that you will not kill me, or deliver me into the hands of my master, and I will take you down to this band.'

16 And when he had taken him down they had them[a] (before them), spread abroad over all the land, eating and drinking and dancing, because of all the great spoil they had taken from the land of the Philistines and from the land of Judah. [17]And David smote them from dawn until the evening of the next day;[b] and not a man of them escaped, except four hundred young men, who mounted camels and fled. [18]David recovered all that the Amalekites had taken; and David rescued his two wives. [19]Nothing was missing, whether small or great, sons or daughters, spoil or anything that had been taken; David brought back all. [20]And they took[c] all the flocks and herds and[d] drove these cattle before David,[e] and said, 'This is David's spoil.'

21 Then David came to the two hundred men, who had been too exhausted to follow David, and who had been left at the brook Besor; and they went out to meet David and to meet the people who were with him; and when David drew near to the people he saluted them.[f] [22]Then all the wicked and base fellows among the men who had gone with David said, 'Because they did not go with us,[g] we will not give them any of the spoil which we have recovered, except that each man may lead away his wife and children, and depart.' [23]But David said, 'You shall not do so, my brothers, with what the LORD has given us he has;[h] preserved us and given into our hand the band that came against us. [24]Who would listen to you in this matter? For as his share is who goes down into the battle, so shall his share be who

---

[a]So LXX.

[b]MT: the day following 'them'. For further details see Commentary.

[c]Read *wayyiqeḥū*; perhaps the form had been written defectively, so that the word *dāwīd*, which belongs after v. 20b, could have found its way into the text from there.

[d]See BH.

[e]The word *dāwīd* originally belonged after *lipnē*; it must have found its way into the margin by mistake. Perhaps an *'et* before *hammiqne* gave rise to its omission.

[f]See Commentary.

[g]MT vividly 'with me'.

[h]LXX reads *'aḥarē* instead of *'eḥay 'et*; but the resulting 'after' clause then has no object, so MT is preferable.

S.–H

stays by the baggage; they shall share alike.' ²⁵And from that day forward he made it a statute and an ordinance for Israel to this day.

26 When David came to Ziklag, he sent part of the spoil to the elders of Judah, according to their cities,ᵃ saying, 'Here is a present for you from the spoil of the enemies of the LORD'; ²⁷it was for those in Bethul,ᵇ in Ramoth Negeb,ᶜ in Jattir, ²⁸in Arara,ᵈ in Siphmoth, in Eshtemoa, ²⁹in Carmel,ᵉ in the cities of the Jerahmeelites, in the cities of the Kenites, ³⁰in Hormah, in Borashan, in Athach, ³¹in Hebron, for all the places where David and his men had roamed.

This episodic story is more than just an episode. First of all, it describes the last of David's perils during the time of his flight. With the destruction of the settlement, the abduction of its inhabitants, including David's wives, and the crisis in confidence among his men which accompanied this disaster, all is once again put in the melting-pot, even David's life. It is this which gives the chapter its tense drama, especially in the context in which it has been placed. The narrative looks both forward and backward in yet another respect. It deals with a warlike encounter with the Amalekites, and thus makes a peculiar contrast to Saul's undertaking in ch. 15. The former expedition resulted in the rejection of the king, whereas the latter prepares the way for his elevation. So the Amalekites have almost fateful significance for the beginning of the history of the kings. David's undertaking, despite the use of the oracle, does not, however, come into the category of the holy war, so it would be inappropriate to introduce the word *wayyaḥᵃrīmēm* (cf. BH), 'he put them under the ban', as a conjectural emendation of *lᵉmoḥᵒrātām*, especially as David's conduct is not that of the ban. The connection with later events is also important, as has been said; by the portions of spoil which he sends to different places in Judah, David opens up and establishes relationships which are certainly of use to him on his way towards becoming king of Judah, and this was doubtless his purpose.

[1–8] When David returns from Aphek to Ziklag, a journey of

ᵃThis is probably to be read instead of the '(and) to his friends' of MT.

ᵇMT *bēt-'ēl*; the place mentioned in Josh. 19.4 is meant. There is *bᵉtū'ēl* in I Chron. 4.30.

ᶜThe place *rāmat negeb* in Josh. 19.8 is the same.

ᵈThis is the usual emendation from the *ᶜᵃrōᶜēr* of MT, which lies in the land east of the Jordan. In Josh. 15.22 there is the word *ᶜadᶜādā*, which has similar consonants. Alt has pointed to an identification with *khirbet ᶜarᶜara*, about thirteen miles east-south-east of Beersheba, *JPOS* 12, 1932, p. 133.

ᵉSo LXX. MT *rākāl*.

some sixty miles, he finds a plundered city, razed to the ground. From the Amalekite point of view it has been purely a raiding expedition; it is expressly reported that no one has been killed, so we must assume that no battle took place. It is, of course, the Amalekite aim to use or to sell the captives as slaves. The burning of Ziklag—apparently the only city—to the ground (v. 14) looks like an act of vengeance, as David's actions against the Amalekites will certainly have been spoken of, despite his practice described at 27.8ff. As he stands with his men before the ruins of his life, David's position is unenviable. The loud lament and the rebellion of the warriors, occasioned by the fact that their city was left without a garrison, illustrates this very well; and David cannot, of course, know who the plunderers are and where they have gone. In these circumstances, David would have been completely desolate, had he not been strengthened 'in God'. David lives on in tradition as a man under God, and this is surely also a correct historical description of him. The phrase certainly does not mean that his trust is merely in an inquiry of the holy oracle. The same expression is used at 23.16, where Jonathan 'strengthens' David's hand 'in God'. Now confident and assured, he inquires of the oracle whether pursuit is advisable and promising. The answer—in the positive—is of such significant brevity that we are given an indication of how such oracles may have been obtained.

[9–10] Further events centre partly on a wadi named $b^e s\bar{o}r$, which is indeed the real focal point. As it always occurs with the article, it was probably understood as the 'valley of good news'; this would be confirmed by the further course of the narrative. We first learn that a third of the troop has been unable to keep up with the evidently fierce pace of the pursuit; the crossing of the wadi appears to be the critical point. David therefore continues with four hundred men. [11–15] The episode with the Egyptian is meant to show without an explicit statement how the undertaking is still under favourable auspices, although its chances are less promising with the diminishing of the troop. 'The text is evidently meant to demonstrate how by this means David's path is smoothed without his having to move a finger.'[a] The slave, who is found completely exhausted in the open country, has simply been left to lie there by his master, an indication of the Amalekites' desire to get away as far as possible from the

[a]Asmussen, *op. cit.*, p. 171.

enemy as soon as possible, without stopping. It also shows their attitude towards their slaves. The prisoner, revived by bread, water, and a few delicacies, declares himself ready to show the men the way. Further light is shed on the position of a slave by his prior demand for a guarantee that David will neither hand him back to his former master (for punishment) nor have him killed as a now superfluous traitor once the expedition has been completed. We learn incidentally how extensive the Amalekite raid has been. The Negeb (south) of the Cherethites (Cretans) refers to southern Philistia —the Old Testament knows connections between the Philistines and Crete elsewhere—the Negeb of the Calebbites lies east of this, south of Hebron (Josh. 14.13f.). The spoil taken corresponds with the size of the area ravaged, which also includes places in Judah.

[16–20] The picture confronting David and his men when the Egyptian has led them to the Amalekite camp accords with this. It is not clear whether it was the shape of the land or the time of day (arrival in darkness?) which made this survey possible. In any case, the expression 'from twilight until the evening' does not mean, as is often assumed, that the time is the evening twilight and that David gains a lightning victory. Quite apart from the fact that the word for 'twilight', *nešep*, usually means 'morning light', *'ereb*, 'evening', primarily means the time at which the sun goes down and hence the hours from the middle of the day until it becomes dark, as it still does to the Arab peasants; the word *layᵉlā*, 'night' is normally used for darkness itself. 'The evening *nešep* of the Old Testament may never be put too early after sundown.'[a] Were *nešep* to mean the evening twilight, the text would have to run 'from evening until twilight'! David, then, fell on the Amalekites, exhausted after the festivities of the previous day, in the early morning; the battle and pursuit in that case last into the afternoon. The victory is complete—only four hundred camel riders are able to escape. As camels are not mentioned among the spoil, the fugitives will have comprised the whole 'cavalry'. So David is able not only to gain back everything that he has lost, but also to take a great quantity of booty corresponding to the extent of the territory visited by the Amalekites (v. 14). The bringing of the plundered cattle by David's men—referred to by the 'they' in v. 20—to their leader and their assignment of it to him is not only an important mark of their trust after the surmounting of the crisis,

[a]Dalman, *Arbeit und Sitte* I, p. 630. Unfortunately, Dalman has not noticed our passage.

but also establishes ownership in accordance with the law of war; the original owners now have no more claim to it. David's act in sending parts of the spoil into the territory of Judah despite this is no act of justice, but one of favour—and of policy.

[21–25] In another respect, however, this event did have legal consequences. When David comes back to the Besor valley, the two hundred, who, of course, will have heard the noise of the cattle and the men, and may have seen the horde from afar, emerge from their position. David gives them the greeting of peace still customary today; the emendation attempted by LXX and Syriac (see BH), according to which it is they who greet him, corresponds neither to Eastern custom nor to the intentions of the passage: whereas David's men, not completely illegally, take the lawful standpoint that those who are left behind should receive no more share of the plunder than their own relatives, David judges otherwise, not from generosity or for other motives, but because he is conscious that he has received everything, victory, life, and plunder, from the hand of Yahweh. This feature is an important one in the understanding of the narrative and equally so in assessing David. A regulation is now derived from his decision which determines the share of plunder to accrue to those who remain behind with the baggage. This decision of the Besor valley—as it might later have been called—from now on acquires the character of law,[a] but it was not forgotten that it was a result of the *pietas* of David. This certainly contributed towards the preservation of the account and the affection with which it was regarded. Both the victory proclaimed to those who remained behind and David's philanthropic decision may have contributed to the naming of the Besor valley (see above).

[26–31] As has already been said, the end of the chapter reports that David sent shares of the spoil to a number of places in southern Palestine. In so doing he probably meant to provide some sort of recompense for those whose land had been plundered, but also, more especially, to take up, or rather take up again, the associations which were broken off when he went over to the Philistines. Thus David once again stands at the entrance to his people and his land, and it is carefully arranged that the history of the people of God, though put in grave danger by the imminent catastrophe of Saul, nevertheless advances further.

[a]On this cf. *ZAW* 40, 1922, p. 271.

23. THE FATE OF SAUL AND JONATHAN: 31.1–13

31 [1]Meanwhile, the Philistines were fighting[a] against Israel; and the men of Israel had to flee before the Philistines, and (many)[b] fell slain on Mount Gilboa. [2]And the Philistines overtook Saul and his sons; and the Philistines slew Jonathan and Abinadab and Malchishua, the sons of Saul. [3]The battle pressed hard upon Saul, and the archers[c] found[d] him; and he was badly wounded[e] by the archers. [f] [4]Then Saul said to his armour-bearer, 'Draw your sword, and thrust me through with it, lest these uncircumcised come[g] and make sport of me.' But his armour-bearer would not; for he feared greatly. Therefore Saul took his own sword, and fell upon it. [5]And when his armour-bearer saw that Saul was dead, he also fell upon his sword, and died with him. [6]Thus Saul died, and his three sons, and his armour-bearer, and all his men, on the same day together.[h] [7]And when the men of Israel who were on the other side of the valley and those beyond the Jordan saw that the men of Israel had fled and that Saul and his sons were dead, they forsook their cities and fled; and the Philistines came and dwelt in them.

8 On the morrow, when the Philistines came to strip the slain, they found Saul and his three sons fallen on Mount Gilboa. [9]And they cut off his head, and stripped off his armour, and sent them throughout the land of the Philistines, to carry the good news to the houses of their idols[i] and to the people. [10]They put his armour in the temple of Ashtaroth; and they fastened his body to the wall of Bethshan.[j] [11]But when the inhabitants of Jabesh-gilead heard of him,[k] what the Philis-

[a]This is the meaning of the niphal participle. LXX and I Chron. 10.1 read the perfect, which would have to be translated as our pluperfect.

[b]Budde inserts a *rabbīm*.

[c]The text 'the archers, men' arose from two variant readings: *hammōrīm* or *'anāšīm mōrīm*.

[d]This is certainly the meaning of *māṣā'*. 'Discover' (GB) comes to grief with the mention of the 'bow'. Caspari translates well 'they placed him', but unnecessarily deletes *baqqāšet*.

[e]The pointing, in view of the *etraumatisthē* of the LXX MSS, should probably be *wayyaḥal* (cf. II Kings 1.2—MT *wayyāḥel* 'and he trembled'?).

[f]For the *mēhammōrīm* of MT, LXX mentions the part of the body where he was wounded, 'in the abdomen' (*eis ta hypochondria*), perhaps *mēhammotnayim*. Similarly Dhorme, Schulz.

[g]MT adds 'and thrust me through', but this is probably to be omitted, with I Chron. 10.4.

[h]The words 'and all his men' are omitted in LXX, presumably because nothing has been said about this hitherto. There seems to be no clear reason why it should have been added if it was not there originally.

[i]So MT (literally 'their . . . temple'). Usually *bēt* is altered to *'et*, along with LXX and I Chron., but this is subsequent assimilation. The proclamation of the victory in the 'temples of their idols' in any case makes more sense than if the Philistines notified it 'to their idols'.

[j]The usual way of writing this is 'Beth Shean'; Arabic *beisan*.

[k]The *'ēlāw* is ugly, but is incomprehensible as a gloss.

tines had done to Saul, ¹²all the valiant men arose, and went all night, and took the body of Saul and the bodies of his sons from the wall of Bethshan; and they brought^a them to Jabesh and anointed them there. ¹³And they took their bones and buried them under the tamarisk tree in Jabesh, and fasted seven days.

The account of Saul's end is presented in a way worthy of the first king. There is no hint that his death is deserved, as a punishment from God and as the result of his own disobedience. Whereas in his parallel report (I Chron. 10) the Chronicler makes an express reference to Saul's guilt (vv. 13f.), even including his inquiry of the 'ghost', there is nothing of this kind here. All is described with great solemnity, even reverence. The narrator knows of the tragedy surrounding the end of the first king, and the compiler of the whole work has not taken upon himself the right to alter anything in an implicit *De mortuis nil nisi bonum*.

[1–2] The events follow directly upon the night at Endor. The construction, however (with the use of participles), shows that the writer is conscious of the interpolation of other events. Indeed, the close of ch. 30 already reaches beyond ch. 31. We are brought in at the moment when the Israelite front wavers and a bloody pursuit begins. Why Saul and his sons do not take to flight, we are not told. Anyway, the narrator does not think that Saul sought death because of the defeat, like a captain going down with his ship. It seems that he could no longer escape. First he had to witness the death of his three sons—Ishbaal is not mentioned—among them the outstanding figure of Jonathan, whom only the LXX names alongside Saul in describing the burial at v. 12;^b [3–6] then the battle goes on around him alone. We are given the impression that the Philistines did not dare to approach the mighty man; at any rate, they attack him from a distance with bow and arrow and, according to the most probable reading, wound him severely. This, then, is evidently the reason why Saul gives his armour-bearer orders to kill him. He wants neither the shame nor the torture which are the consequence of falling into the hands of the 'uncircumcised', like

---

^aSee BH.

^bCompare the incident with the ballad 'Die Sendlinger Bauernschlacht', by Hans Hopfen, with the verse about the 'smith of Kochel, the strongest man in the land':

> 'When earthwards looked the sun again,
> There seven sons were lying slain
> About the flag and broken mast,
> And there the father, slain the last.'

Samson. His faithful armour-bearer, whose name has unfortunately not been handed down to us, no more dares to touch the Lord's anointed than did David. So Saul kills himself, and his escort follows his example. Further resistance seems to have been offered from Saul's position. Both the note 'with all his men' (wrongly doubted), and the fact that Saul's death did not prove the signal for an immediate Philistine onslaught would support such a view. In fact, the battle seems to have continued until dusk, as Saul's body is only found the next morning.

[7] The most far-reaching consequence of Saul's death is that first mentioned, its political consequence. Saul was the strongest bulwark against the Philistines, and prevented them from exercising their rule over Israel. His political and military influence reached further than is sometimes thought. Not only does it reach far into the south of Judah, as is clear from earlier chapters; we now hear indirectly that both the north and the east of Israelite territory were noticeably affected by the existence of a central Palestine kingdom. In any case, only now do the Philistines bring parts of the land lying to the north and east of the battlefield under their dominion. 'On the other side of the valley' will mean the northern part of the plain of Jezreel, whose Israelite inhabitants had always had a hard fight against the original occupants; it may even refer to the southern border of the Galilean hill country. 'Beyond the Jordan' is unmistakable; we must not, however, imagine too great an extension of the sphere of Philistine influence east of the Jordan, as Jabesh-gilead was certainly not affected. Perhaps the Philistine advance was essentially limited to certain fords over the Jordan. It is also significant that the central Palestinian hill country is not mentioned here. We hear later that Saul's son Ishbaal, and more particularly his commander-in-chief Abner, are masters of the situation there afterwards, as before, so the Philistine success is not to be overestimated.[a]

[8–10] The end of the chapter is taken up with the immediate consequences of the battle. The fallen are, as usual, plundered. Only now is Saul's body found, stripped, and disfigured. As also happens elsewhere with a defeated enemy,[b] his head is cut off. It is not clear whether the Philistines displayed this trophy, too, in their temples and elsewhere, or whether they limited themselves to Saul's armour

[a]So, e.g., Noth, *The History of Israel*, ET², p. 183.
[b]Goliath, I. 17; cf. the saga of the giant in the forest of the Ardennes used by Uhland in the ballad 'Roland Schildträger'.

and weapons. According to I Chron. 10.10, Saul's head was eventually fastened in the temple of Dagon, and his weapons in the Astarteion (so LXX at 31.10), a temple evidently dedicated to the Ashtaroth (so MT). It is understandable that this view should have developed, as in the case of the Philistine champion the weapons (and the head) were also brought into the victors' temple (see above at 17.54). As the text in I Sam. mentions only the depositing of the weapons in the Philistine sanctuary, it is more probable that Saul's head was fastened to the wall of Bethshan with the rest of his body and the corpses of his sons. Factual as it is, the report is permeated with disapproval and a vivid feeling of the shame to which Saul is subjected. The Chronicler, on the other hand, cannot suppress a certain satisfaction over this fate in his description, even if much of the wording is similar. The town of Bethshan (Beisan) is still the most important place between the plain of Jezreel and the Jordan valley today, and was still more important in ancient times,[a] so that the Philistines as far as they could achieved their purpose of making the dishonour as public as possible.

[11–13] A friendly light dawns over the horrible picture at the end. The inhabitants of Jabesh-gilead[b] have not forgotten Saul's act which saved them (11.1ff.). Hardly has the news been rushed to them than the men make a night march to Bethshan and bring the bodies back to Jabesh. Their 'burning'—this is the usual translation—of the bodies is, of course, surprising in view of the generally hostile Old Testament attitude to cremation. On the other hand, it would be understandable if that means were adopted here. The bodies will have been considerably damaged by the process of decomposition, which sets in quickly during the heat of the day, and by the ravages of carrion birds; and it was important to remedy the disfigurement of the bodies and rescue the bones for burial.[c] In that case, the burning would have had to have been arranged so that the bones were left intact, i.e. not as we read in Amos (2.1), where the bones of the king were burnt to lime, an act held up as a grievous sin. It is, however, simpler to assume another meaning for the root *śārap*, 'anoint' (with resinous spices) here.[d] Saul's bones were then later laid in the family grave (II 21.12 ff.).

[a]A good guide to the early history in Galling, *BRL*, pp. 101–3.
[b]On its situation see Commentary on 11.1ff.
[c]On this see K. Bornhäuser, *Die Gebeine der Toten*, 1921, pp. 8ff.
[d]So Driver, *ZAW* 66, 1954, pp. 314f.; now also L. Koehler, *Supplementum ad Lexicon in VT libros*, 1958, p. 175.

So Saul's life ends not in dishonour, but in honour, as befits the Lord's anointed. The curtain falls where his reign began. In between, there lies a life full of tragic greatness, of which the ancient narrators were fully aware; and, as has been said before, even the compiler of the whole work did not overlook the connection between this last end and the relationship in which Saul stood to the Lord and the Lord to Saul.

24. THE NEWS IS TAKEN TO DAVID: II. 1.1–27

II. 1 [1]After the death of Saul, when David had returned from the slaughter of the Amalekites, David remained two days in Ziklag; [2]and on the third day, behold, a man came from Saul's camp, with his clothes rent and earth upon his head. And when he came to David, he fell to the ground and did obeisance. [3]David said to him, 'Where do you come from?' And he said to him, 'I have escaped from the camp of Israel.' [4]And David said to him, 'How did it go? Tell me.' And he answered, 'The people have fled from the battle, and many of the people also have fallen and are dead; and Saul and his son Jonathan are also dead.' [5]Then David said to the young man who told him, 'How do you know that Saul and his son Jonathan are dead?' [6]And the young man who told him said, 'By chance I happened to be on Mount Gilboa; and there was Saul leaning upon his spear; and lo, the chariots and the horsemen were close upon him. [7]And when he looked behind him, he saw me, and called to me. And I answered, "Here I am." [8]And he said to me, "Who are you?" I answered him, "I am an Amalekite." [9]And he said to me, "Stand beside me and slay[a] me; for anguish has seized me, and yet I am still fully conscious".[b] [10]So I stood beside him, to slay him,[c] because I was sure that he could not live after he was fallen; and I took the crown which was on his head and the armlet which was on his arm, and I have brought them here to my lord.'

11 Then David took hold of his[d] clothes, and rent them; and so did all the men who were with him; and they mourned and wept and fasted until evening for Saul and for Jonathan his son and for the people of the LORD and for the house of Israel, because they had fallen by the sword. [13]And David said to the young man who told him, 'Where do you come from?' And he answered, 'I am the son of a sojourner,

---

[a]The word *ūmōt^etēnī*, 'and slay me', is deleted by Caspari. According to him, originally Saul had asked the Amalekite to save him, as there was still life in him. This made the young man's action still worse.

[b]Presumably—cf. LXX, Syr., and Budde *ad loc.*—a conflation of readings, 'all my life is in me' and 'my life is still in me'.

[c]According to Jewish explanations, the *waw* is to be taken as a *waw* consecutive; it is therefore usually translated, 'and I slew him . . .'

[d]See BH.

an Amalekite.' ¹⁴David said to him, 'How is it you were not afraid to put forth your hand to destroy the LORD's anointed?' ¹⁵Then David called one of the young men and said, 'Go, fall upon him.' And he smote him so that he died. ¹⁶And David said to him, 'Your blood be upon your head; for your own mouth has testified against you, saying, "I have slain the LORD's anointed." '

17 And David lamented with this lamentation over Saul and Jonathan his son, ¹⁸and said—it should be taught to the sons of Judah (as the song of the) 'bow'; behold it is written in the book of the Upright[a]—

¹⁹'Thy glory, O Israel, is slain upon thy high places!
    How are the mighty fallen!
²⁰Tell it not in Gath, publish it not in the streets of Ashkelon;
    lest the daughters of the Philistines rejoice, lest the daughters of the
    uncircumcised exult.
²¹Ye mountains of Gilboa,
    let no dew or rain fall on you,[b]
you false fields![c]
For there the shield of the mighty was defiled:
    the shield of Saul, no (longer) anointed with oil.[d]
²²The bow of Jonathan turned not back,
    and the sword of Saul returned not empty,
from the blood of the slain,
    from the fat of the mighty.[e]
²³Saul and Jonathan, beloved and noble to each other![f]
    In life and in death they were not divided;[g]
they were swifter than eagles, they were stronger than lions.

[a]See Commentary.

[b]Only the *waw* of *yipp*ᵉ*lū*, or whatever it was, now remains, and now stands in front of *s*ᵉ*dē*.

[c]*t*ᵉ*rūmōt* (= sheaves of firstfruits) is better emended to *tarmīt*.

[d](?) Or is a consonant to be altered, and *k*ᵉ*lī* to be read instead of *b*ᵉ*lī*? 'The "weapon" of the one anointed with oil.'(?)

[e]V. 22a*a* is here put at the end of the verse. This is better than connecting it with the closing line of v. 21, as is done by Leimbach: 'The shield of Saul was not anointed with oil, but with the blood of the slain.' For it is not the shield, but the sword, that is the weapon fouled with blood, cf. Deut. 32.42. If both lines are left at the beginning of the verse, they would have to refer both to the bow of Jonathan and to the sword of Saul (Kittel, etc.); the former is most inappropriate, as it is the arrow and not the bow which makes the blood of the enemy flow.

[f]The niphal is here to be translated reciprocally, cf. Gressmann, Caspari and GK § 51d.

[g]LXX reads, 'Saul and Jonathan, beloved and undivided in the prime (of life), lovely in their lives, were not divided even in death.' The possibility of this representing the original text is not to be excluded; the middle of the text would then have run *w*ᵉ*hann*ᵉ*ʿimīm lō*ʾ *niphrādīm nā*ʾ*wīm*, and the eye of the copier would then have been distracted in the MT from the *w*ᵉ*hann*ᵉ*ʿimīm* to the similar *nā*ʾ*wīm*.

²⁴Ye daughters of Israel, weep over Saul,
     who clothed you[a] in purple and finery,[b]
     who put ornaments of gold upon your apparel.
²⁵How are the mighty fallen in the midst of the battle!
     Jonathan on the high places, amongst the slain![c]
²⁶I am very distressed for you, my brother Jonathan;
     very pleasant have you been to me;
     your love to me was more wonderful than the love of women.[d]
²⁷How are the mighty fallen, and the weapons of war perished!'

Because of the division of the Books of Samuel, this chapter has
been taken up into the large section which describes the reign of
David and occupies the whole of II Samuel. This may have been
done to make a similarity between Josh. 1.1, Judg. 1.1 and II. 1.1:
[1] 'After the death of Moses', 'After the death of Joshua', 'After
the death of Saul'.[e] But we do better to take the chapter as the end
of the Saul-David complex; although in its way it is a prelude to
David's elevation to the throne, it still more brings the reign of Saul
to a close, particularly with the eulogy.

[2] The messenger appears with the news of the unsuccessful
battle in a mixture of grief and calculating hope. Externally, the
young man has the usual signs of the mourner, clothes rent and
earth upon his head, but his purpose is, in fact, to bring to Saul's
enemy a message which promises a reward. [3–10] Perhaps the
gesture of obeisance is already meant to be an act of homage to the
future king, to whom indeed he brings the royal insignia. The reader
can recognize the man's concern simply from the way in which his
account does not tally with that of ch. 31. The main facts are, of
course, given correctly: the crushing defeat and the deaths of Saul
and Jonathan. In reply to David's request for details, however, the
messenger seeks to underline his part in the matter, thus unsuspectingly taking himself into an extremely dangerous realm. His description of himself as an Amalekite, twice repeated, must have made

[a]The grammatically dubious text is better read as *hammalbîš 'etkem.*

[b]The Massoretic 'with delight' (*'im ʿădānîm*) is not as good as the *ʿădāyim*
suggested by LXX. The recurrence of the word in the same verse is, in this song
(cf. 20b; 21b), no reason for suspicion.

[c]The conclusion is uncertain, cf. Targ. The corruption may have arisen from
the omission of an *m* at the end. Read *ʿal-bāmot bᵉtōk ḥᵃlālîm.*

[d]The non-existent form *niphlᵉ'atā* is a conflated reading of *niphlā'ōt* and
niphlᵉ'ā. Presumably both forms were originally used side by side in the text.

[e]This assimilation may have been the reason for the circumstantial formulation
of vv. 1 and 2; it is, of course, no reason for distinguishing separate sources.

his action seem all the more horrible in the eyes of David and his
men, newly returned from battle against Amalek. Amalekites remain
Amalekites, even if they are sojourning in Israel; these born robbers
do not even shrink from the Lord's anointed! Doubtless this is the
way the narrative was understood and judged. [13–16] Moreover,
the man betrays himself as an obvious liar, out for what he can get.
True, it is not expressly said that David sees through him and
therefore holds him responsible. But the narrator seems to think
that his death is a just punishment. Of course, the chief ground
remains, that he has laid hands on the Lord's anointed. In reality
he has done nothing of the sort, as the reader knows from ch. 31,
but merely wishes to put his statement to David in a favourable
light. It is therefore the truth when at the end David says of him that
his own mouth testified against him. He is also credited with the
realization that the anointed of Yahweh is fundamentally an unassailable person; he claims that Saul himself asked to be given the
coup de grâce, and adds, again in agreement with the facts, that the
king could not have survived his fall. But all this only makes his
case worse. He receives the due reward of the plunderer of the
battlefield.

[11–12] The expectation that David would receive the news of
Saul's death with satisfaction is shown to be unjustified in other ways,
too. When the Amalekite has finished his report, the narrative purposely stresses how David and his men give themselves over to
lamentation, once the insignia shown to them make Saul's defeat
and death a certain fact. The narrator is concerned to show us that
this is real grief; he has made it clear in two ways: by the place
assigned to vv. 11f., and by the insertion of the lament. As far as the
former is concerned, we find a twofold reaction to the news from
David—on one hand what is described in vv. 11f., and on the other
the events of vv. 13–15. Both happen as a direct result of the news.
The answer to this twofold reaction has been given on literary-critical
grounds; there were two accounts, the one containing vv. (1–)4, 11,
12 and the other vv. 5–10, 13–15 (Budde, Dhorme, Gressmann,
Eissfeldt, etc.). This solution is manifestly too schematic; there must
surely have been something about the punishment of the messenger
and David's grief in any possible account, and it seems hardly likely
that one account should preserve only one element, and the second
account the other. Kittel therefore states at the beginning, 'The
account is a unity.' If the narrator wanted to record both reactions,

how else could he have done it? One of the two must have happened slightly later; if the punishment of the Amalekite came first, the note about David's grief would look, if anything, still more strange. The possibility of there having been several accounts of the event is nothing to do with this.[a]

The second part of the chapter introduces the famous lament on the death of Saul and Jonathan. There is no reason for doubting David's authorship. According to tradition he was a particularly skilled musician, and that certainly means that he was able not only to play, but also to sing.[b] We need add no praise to what has been called the most beautiful heroic lament of all time.

[17–18] The lament has a title which can hardly be interpreted. It consists of a normal introduction in v. 17 and the beginning of v. 18, to which the lament must have been directly attached, and a further note destroying this connection. The conclusion gives details of a source which recurs in Josh. 10.13 and I Kings 8.53 LXX. We do not know what the name 'Book of the Upright' signifies, but in the light of the three biblical examples we can regard it as certainly representing a collection of documents in poetic form. The preceding clause, 'be taught to the sons of Judah, bow' seems to have a twofold purpose. First there is a regulation for the practical use of the song. The ordinance that the people of Judah are to learn the song must come from a time when David was ruler only of Judah. It was thus the wish of higher circles that the song should be known and spread abroad. The people are to know of the king's feelings expressed in the song, as in the similar case of Abner's death (4.33f.). It remains unknown whether this was the command of David himself or of a 'Minister of Information'. 'Bow' may have been added to the title as a characteristic word featuring in the poem,[c] just as, for example, the second *Sura* of the Koran has been called 'the

[a]Supported by II. 4.10, Budde and Schulz posit an original form of the text according to which David, like an oriental despot, struck down the messenger—originally an Israelite—out of hand; it was only gradually that the present narrative arose, and the Israelite became an Amalekite. These things are not demonstrable here, but we can see from the juxtaposition of I. 31, II. 1 and II. 4.10 that the material was of great concern to later generations. This stems from the importance attached to the transition from Saul to David.

[b]Cf. 16.18, where he is celebrated not only for his musical ability but also for his powers of expression.

[c]Eissfeldt (*VT* 5, 1955, pp. 232–5) has a different and more ingenious suggestion. Following earlier scholars, he would understand 'teach the sons of Judah (the) bow' as 'make fit for war'.

cow'. The whole note may at first have stood at the end of the song, or in the margin (see Budde on v. 18). This explanation makes superfluous all attempts to make v. 18 by textual emendation into the supposedly corrupt beginning of the song.

Although the song is expressly described as a *qīnā*—lament for the dead—it is not written in the verse form of this type; the measure is predominantly 2 : 2—a three-stress line occurs only rarely. It is not, however, the beautiful, artistic form which characterizes the song, but the tone of real mourning which is, of course, particularly evident where Jonathan is mentioned.

[19] The lament begins with thoughts of the flower of Israel, the young men fallen in war, and in so doing takes up a note which is bitterly familiar to all peoples and times. In the Old Testament we may recall particularly Jeremiah's dirge of Death the Reaper (9.20f.), of which C. H. Cornill (commentary *ad loc.*) has said, 'It is one of the most masterly poems that has ever been written.' Israel is addressed first—here for once imagined as a man. [20—21] The subsequent focus on the victor's towns, in which the joyful cries of the women ring out as they hear the glad news (the word *bāsar*, used in v. 20, is the same as the Greek *euangelizein*) is reminiscent of I. 18.7, where we see the same custom in Israel. David's wish that it may not come to that in this particular event is a vain one. The deep emotion of the singer expresses itself in the curse on the ill-fated place, that it may be condemned to everlasting barrenness; here one thinks of Job's lament in Job 3. The conclusion of the verse could mean— the text is unsure—that the good shields, even Saul's shield, which was known to be particularly large, now lie about there without receiving the customary care. Only at this point does the lament turn to Saul and Jonathan, who are praised with a proud sadness, as befits mighty warriors. [22—23] The picture of the ravenous sword is common in the Old Testament. I. 20 confirms that the bow was Jonathan's weapon, as the spear was that of Saul. In stressing that they were not divided either in life or in death, David has said something which is also important historically: close as was the relationship between him and Jonathan, this friendship never led to the real breaking of the bonds between father and son. [24] The appeal to the women of Israel recalls how often Saul gave them spoil after successes in war, no wonder in the case of a king who had to wage war all his life (I. 14.52). In Sisera's war, too, the women wait, of course in vain, for the rich spoil (Judg. 5.30). [25—27] The lament

has a special depth at the point where David thinks of his friendship with Jonathan. The root *pālā* (be wonderful), which perhaps occurred twice in the original text, is particularly beautiful here. With a repetition of the third line of the first strophe we come to the end of this masterly song in which David has raised a memorial not only for Saul[a] and Jonathan but also for himself.

There is one more thing which is not directly mentioned in the text. Later, David actually (4.10) described the message brought to him as 'good news'. This was what the messenger thought, and it was, in fact, the case. For what would have been David's position had Saul been victorious? As has been said already, it is a particularly fine feature of this chapter that here only sorrow is expressed, sorrow, as it were, uninterested in the consequences for David himself. But this feature, which does credit both to the narrator and to David, cannot prevent us from seeing how the course of events shows and is meant to show in a remarkable way what was openly said at the beginning of the history of David: the Lord is 'with' David. The hearers certainly recognized with reverence the miraculous way in which David's fortunes were disposed; for Saul's fall—and Jonathan's death—leave the way open for David, a way which *inter alia* leads to the overthrow of Philistine domination. And thus a new leaf is begun in the history of the people of God.

NOTE ON FORMATION AND STRUCTURE: IV

In the exposition just ended it has been considered important to show what considerations guided the hand of the compiler in his presentation of the material. It is immediately obvious that he looked with reverence at the divine guidance and with personal interest at the rise of David—and thus the decline of Saul. Much as he respects Saul as the Lord's anointed, even despite his rejection, much as he stresses David's often expressed thoughts on the matter, right at the beginning of this great section he still intentionally places the account of the anointing of David. If he does not return to it again (but see on II. 12.7), presumably hindered by the fact that it was

[a]Strangely enough, there has never been an adequate dramatic presentation of the figure of Saul. Apart from Handel's oratorio, there is in German only the tragedy 'Saul' written in 1841 by Carl Beck, a Hungarian Jewish poet. This works out the tragic conflict well and also to some extent recognizes that its basis lies in the theological aspect.

not mentioned in the texts, the whole section none the less establishes in all its parts that David is the fore-ordained successor. This is the general theme, so that we might almost give this part the title 'David must increase, Saul must decrease'. We were able to see how this view was made clear in entirely different places (chapters 18, 20, 24, 26, II. 1, etc.). All, even Saul, almost from the beginning (cf. on I. 18.8) onwards, and of course the true and unselfish Jonathan, know in their hearts that David is the coming king.

We may point to two things here. First, to the reports of David's arrival at the court. We should notice that the event they describe is no chance one—it is divinely determined. This lies behind even the description in ch. 16. In ch. 17, the passages omitted by the LXX (17.12–31, 55–18.5) are primary in showing how evident is the interest in demonstrating that David's rise to power is legitimate. This concealed king, with whom Yahweh is, does not usurp the throne or deceitfully snatch it for himself. Step by step, systematically, it is brought to him. And even in the remaining sections of ch. 17, in the sentence where Saul is willing to put his armour at David's disposal, there is at least a hint at David's future rank—even if the armour did not then fit!

The sections which represent David as deposed and pursued are of quite a different order. Here David seems to be far distant from his appointed goal, indeed from time to time he seems to be on the razor's edge. All the more noticeable in this context are the remarks which nevertheless look towards his future status (the words of Abigail, Jonathan, even Saul himself). We can even say that by the mere token of having to escape to the wilderness and to hostile Philistines, David is shown not to be in a position to shape his own fortune. He is completely dependent on the Lord. Only from this aspect does the essential element emerge rightly and the whole pattern become excitingly dramatic.

Nevertheless, the history of David was not simply given its final form and presentation by the compiler; even the theological approach we have outlined is older than the final compiler. The material came to him already in such a fixed form that he thought it neither warranted nor necessary to interfere with it to any great extent; we will return to this point shortly. The arrangement of the material is, however, to a considerable degree his own work.

As to the earlier history of the material, in a number of cases we can recognize a tradition connected with a particular place. This will be true of the very first section, 16.1–13. Originally the material was native to Bethlehem, but it is clear from the present connection with ch. 15 that the narrative found its way to the rest of the material by way of the Gilgal traditions. The question of how David came to the court is answered in different ways. To the report of 16.14–23 in which David's musical capabilities are the reason given, is opposed ch. 17, which states quite clearly that David's skill at arms was the reason for his being summoned. Moreover, within ch. 17 two reports have been woven together, each of which will have led an independent existence, not only in oral tradition but also in a written form. The one, also used by the LXX, can be distinguished by the keyword 'weapon'; perhaps it belongs to the material transmitted at Mizpah, as it ends with the depositing of Goliath's sword in the 'tent of Yahweh'. We have already spoken of the other report, which is intended to show David not as a usurper but as a rightful successor. It is certainly not to be described as a later accretion; we have here a well narrated and well considered account[a] which, we may reasonably assume, has lent its accents to the whole. With respect to ch. 17, we have already pointed out that this attitude must be that of those circles which were most closely associated with David's own view. It is hard to understand why the Vatican MS of the LXX omitted it, i.e. why it found a form of the Hebrew text which did not contain this part of the narrative. It is, however, sufficiently clear that the dissimilarity of the subsidiary narrative (Caspari) was still recognized at a later date. The union of the two reports must at the latest be a result of the deuteronomistic editing, as the latter has many references to the victory over Goliath.

We have here a juxtaposition of different traditions; in 18.17–30, too,—David becomes the son-in-law of Saul—we may recognize something further of the kind: the Merab story presupposes the 'subsidiary narrative' mentioned above, the Michal story does not. From this it becomes more clear how the original material, which maintained a neutral attitude towards Saul, was eclipsed by a view which was full of the deepest mistrust towards him. Here we meet the view of the final compiler; of course, he had enough raw material for it in the traditional accounts. The narrative about the spear, which occurs at both 18.11 and 19.9f., should first be mentioned in this connection. We might even call it the historical starting-point for this theme of mistrust. The Jonathan pericopes (19.1–7; 20.1ff.)

[a]For a characterization of it see Budde, p. 121 (middle).

also bear similar testimony. In them, too, the amalgamation of different traditions is evident, as well as traces of an original local setting for the material.

Just as there were different traditions of David's arrival at the court of Saul, so, too, there were different traditions of his flight. These were familiar to both priestly and prophetic circles, and, as was known, there were friendly relations between David and both groups, whereas in the case of Saul things were very different. The tradition also knows that both Saul's son and his daughter helped David to flee. Similarly, we are twice told that his course led towards the Philistines, once at the beginning of his exile, and once at the end. The details of the accounts are very different; there could be a connection between the first and the Naioth story (ch. 19). Again and again it is made evident that the material was at first native to certain places from which it then spread farther afield. This is very clear in the narratives describing David's flight; an eye-catching stone, a certain rock formation, a valley, once even the definition of a right of war (30.24), preserve the memory 'until this day'. On the other hand, the connection of the material with definite conditions (*Sitz im Leben*) colours it very deeply, with the result that similar reports, e.g. the accounts of David's generosity in chs. 24 and 26, have been preserved side by side. In Endor, too, there was certainly something like a 'Saul's house' in sight of which the events of the night before the battle of Gilboa may long have been recalled. At this very point we can again see clearly how there was a difference between the original form connected with a certain place and the present shape of the material, i.e. in its assessment of Saul.

This statement may be supported most clearly from the material: the picture which results from the original form of the accounts and the final form as it corresponds with the deuteronomistic view of history. It is therefore not true that we 'do not have a single trace of any working over of the Saul narratives . . . by the Deuteronomist'.[a] It is, however, correct to say that the picture of Saul held by the earlier period—perhaps particularly in the northern regions (cf. on ch. 28), but elsewhere, too—was not erased by the Deuteronomist, but merely overlaid. Both aspects are important, the one more for historical investigation, the other for determining the theology of history, but the former is not merely a part of profane history and the latter is not unhistorical.

[a]Noth, *Überlieferungsgeschichtliche Studien* I, p. 63.

It is difficult to discover whether the final compiler already possessed consecutive series of narratives from which he conceived his own work. Without doubt the pericopes are not simply juxtaposed; there are connections. On the other hand we can recognize, as for example in ch. 28, a direct development from the early shape of the narrative, native to a particular locality, to its present form. The attempt to see fixed 'sources', made often, and most recently by Eissfeldt, takes too literary a view of the matter and goes beyond the actual evidence. If, on the other hand, we assume an author 'at the court amongst David's intimates'[a]—the name of the priest Abiathar has been mentioned as being likely[b]—to whose work 'all kinds of secondary accretions'[c] have been added as 'accretions from oral tradition',[d] then such suppositions would seem more hypothetical than proven. We may not, however, exclude the fact that even in early days the local traditions were narrated at definite places and were moulded to a fixed form, and we can often see here an astonishing proximity to the events described. More than this, however, it is hard to say.

Native to the old material and also preserved by the hand of the deuteronomistic compiler was the consciousness of the constant influence of the Lord. The rise of David is represented not as having been a piece of chance good fortune or a wise piece of policy, but as a miraculous event disposed by a higher hand. In this way the material is brought into the larger context of all Scripture and becomes an episode in the history of God's guidance.

[a]A. Weiser, *Introduction to the Old Testament*, ET 1961, p. 164.
[b]E.g. Rost, *Einleitung*[8], p. 91; *Thronnachfolge*, p. 128.
[c]Noth, *op. cit.*, p. 62.
[d]Weiser, *loc. cit.*

KING DAVID
II. 2–8

1. THE DOUBLE KINGDOM: 2.1–3.1

2 [1]After this David inquired of the LORD, 'Shall I go up into any of the cities of Judah?' And the LORD said to him, 'Go up.' David said, 'To which shall I go up?' And he said, 'To Hebron.' [2]So David went up there, and his two wives also, Ahinoam of Jezreel and Abigail the widow of Nabal of Carmel. [3]And David brought up his men who were with him, every one with his household; and they dwelt in the towns of Hebron. [4]And the men of Judah came, and there they anointed David king over the house of Judah.

When they told David that the men of Jabesh-gilead had[a] buried Saul, [5]David sent messengers to the men of Jabesh-gilead, and said to them, 'May you be blessed by the LORD, because you showed this loyalty to Saul your lord, and buried him! [6]Now may the LORD show steadfast love and faithfulness to you! And I will do like[b] good to you because you have done this thing. [7]Now therefore let your hands be strong, and be valiant; for Saul your lord is dead, and the house of Judah has anointed me king over them.'

8 Now Abner the son of Ner, commander of Saul's army, had taken Ishbaal[c] the son of Saul, and brought him over to Mahanaim; [9]and he made him king for[d] Gilead and for the Asherites[e] and for Jezreel and over Ephraim and over Benjamin and (thus) over all Israel. [10]Ishbaal, Saul's son, was forty years old when he began to reign over Israel, and he reigned two (?) years. [f] But the house of Judah followed David. [11]And the time that David was king in Hebron—over the house of Judah—was seven years and six months.

[a]See BH.
[b]This is a possible paraphrase of *hazzōt*.
[c]See Commentary.
[d]The thrice repeated *'el* (= for) stands alongside a thrice repeated *'al* (over), a sign of the interchangeability of these prepositions. It is not worth emending the text.
[e]So Targ.
[f]See Commentary.

12 Abner the son of Ner, and the servants of Ishbaal[a] the son of Saul, went out from Mahanaim to Gibeon. [13]And Joab the son of Zeruiah, and the servants of David, went out from Hebron[b] and met them at the pool of Gibeon; and they sat down, the one on the one side of the pool, and the other on the other side of the pool.[c] [14]And Abner said to Joab, 'Let the young men arise and play before us.' And Joab said, 'Let them arise.' [15]Then they arose and passed over by number, twelve for Benjamin and Ishbaal[a] the son of Saul, and twelve of the servants of David. [16]And each caught his opponent with one hand by the head,[d] and (thrust) his sword in his opponent's side; so they fell down together. Therefore that place was called the 'Field of Sides',[e] which is at Gibeon. [17]And the battle was very fierce that day; and Abner and the men of Israel were beaten before the servants of David.

18 And the three sons of Zeruiah were there, Joab, Abishai, and Asahel. Now Asahel was as swift of foot as a wild gazelle; [19]and Asahel pursued Abner, and as he went he turned neither to the right hand nor to the left from following Abner. [20]Then Abner looked behind him and said, 'Is it you, Asahel?' And he answered, 'It is I.' [21]Abner said to him, 'Turn aside to your right hand or to your left, and seize one of the young men, and take his spoil.' But Asahel would not turn aside from following him. [22]And Abner said again to Asahel, 'Turn aside from following me; why should I smite you to the ground? How then could I lift up my face to your brother Joab?' [23]But he refused to turn aside; therefore Abner smote him in the belly with the butt of his spear, so that the spear came out at his back; and he fell there, and died where he was. And all who came to the place where Asahel had fallen and died, stood still.

24 But Joab and Abishai pursued Abner; and as the sun was going down they came to the hill of Ammah, [f] which lies before Giah on the way to the wilderness of Geba.[g] [25]And the Benjaminites gathered themselves together behind Abner, and became one band, and took their stand on the top of the hill of Ammah.[h] [26]Then Abner called to Joab, 'Shall the sword devour for ever? Do you not know that the end will be bitter? How long will it be before you bid your people turn

[a]See BH.

[b]So LXX.

[c]On the situation of the 'pool' and the topographical problems connected with it, cf. Alt, *PJB* 22, 1926, pp. 19f., and Hertzberg, *ZAW* 47, 1929, p. 185.

[d]So LXX.

[e]MT 'of the rocks'; but this is certainly a miswriting (see LXX).

[f]The name 'hill of the ells', may perhaps have been given because of the shape of the landscape (ell = forearm).

[g]See BH; *midbār* is country only fit for grazing, 'wilderness'. It is improbable that Gibeon had such land, so 'Geba' should be read instead. In I. 13.2f., Geba and Gibeah are also interchanged. On the location, see Dalman in *PJB* 8, 1912, pp. 14f.

[h]MT 'one hill'. Occasionally the 'hill of ells' in v. 24 is also emended accordingly, but that would be hardly possible as a name for the hill which would then occur a second time.

from the pursuit of their brethren?' [27]And Joab said, 'As God lives, if you had not spoken, surely the men would (only) have given up the pursuit of their brethren in the morning.'[a] [28]So Joab blew the trumpet; and all the men stopped so that[b] they pursued Israel no more, nor did they fight any more.

29 And Abner and his men went all that night through the (Jordan) plain; they crossed the Jordan, and marching along the ravine[c] they came to Mahanaim. [30]Joab returned from the pursuit of Abner; and when he had gathered all the people together, there were missing of David's servants nineteen men besides Asahel. [31]But the servants of David had slain of Benjamin three hundred and sixty of Abner's men; (they) were dead.[d] [32]And they took up Asahel, and buried him in the tomb of his father, which was at Bethlehem. And Joab and his men marched all night, and the day broke upon them at Hebron.

3 [1]There was a long war between the house of Saul and the house of David; and David grew stronger and stronger, while the house of Saul became weaker and weaker.

The account of the beginning of the Davidic monarchy, here combined in one chapter, contains three dissimilar parts: a report about David's enthronement in Hebron, a description of his message to the citizens of Jabesh-gilead, and the report of an event in the first battles between David and Ishbaal. This last, told vividly and in detail, is particularly conspicuous.

[2.1–3] It is a pity that the first part has not been handed down with the same loving attention to detail, for just at this point many important questions arise. We would dearly like to know how the Philistines acted after their victory. The first sentences—indeed, the whole chapter—give the impression that the Philistines were nowhere to be seen, at least that they let the course of events take its way after Saul's death without their interference. At all events, from the omission of any mention of them we may conclude that they were not at first dissatisfied with David's transference of his dwelling to Judah; indeed, he may, particularly in the eyes of Achish, have been regarded as a loyal vassal whose resettlement in Judah could be explained as an extension of the Philistine sphere of influence into a

[a]Or, if we read *lū* for *lūlē*: 'If only you had spoken (earlier)! Then the men would (already) have given up . . .'

[b]Consecutive clause, cf. GK § 166a.

[c]The obscure word *bitrōn* occurs only here. A recent conjecture is 'the whole forenoon', as RSV.

[d]The meaning of the word *mētū* is obscure. Perhaps it arose from the word *mē'ōt*, written similarly. There was then perhaps at one time a variant reading *šēš mē'ōt* (600) alongside *šelōš mē'ōt* (300).

distant and hitherto inaccessible area. To the compiler, however, this is irrelevant; he is concerned solely with the question of how the Lord views the step taken by David. His removal to Judah is in express accordance with the will of Yahweh. This alone is reported; we are not even told that David had wisely taken precautions to obtain for himself the goodwill of the men of Judah (I. 30). The two wives are mentioned not to demonstrate David's personal connections with the tribes of Judah, but to show that he left the land of the Philistines for ever a completely new beginning is being made in Judah. David's men likewise have to take their families with them. The Lord wills that a new page in the history of David should begin. This is what we are told here.

We can understand why Hebron rather than a less well-known place was chosen by the oracle[a] as their destination. Not only was Hebron the most important place in Judah, set above the rest by reason of being a sanctuary founded by Abraham, but it was at the same time—and perhaps for that very reason—a place of assembly for other tribes associated with Judah (Caleb, Othniel, Jerahmeel etc.). [4a] Saul's influence certainly reached right into the south of Judah, but after his death David, to whom by no means the whole of Judah was well disposed during the lifetime of Saul (note the case of the Ziphites; I. 23.19; 26.1), was much closer to his fellow tribesmen than anyone else. So his anointing follows: as is laconically reported, he is anointed king in Judah. Nothing is said of either his recognition or his non-recognition by the Philistines, nor do we learn whether David's kingdom extends claims to territory north of Judah. Perhaps, as has been said, the anointing to be king in Judah has a constitutional significance, even in the eyes of the Philistines. When later he becomes king of Israel (5.17) it immediately proves a *casus belli* for them.

[4b-7] David certainly regarded any such limitation as being purely temporary. Such is the significance of the message to the people of Jabesh in this context. The purpose lying behind it is unmistakable. His conduct here is similar to that adopted towards the men of Judah and their southern neighbours (I. 30.26) when he was in the service of the Philistines: he is already carefully envisaging the next step. The reader will have regarded this not only as political

[a]The technique of making this inquiry remains obscure. Where an alternative question is put, as at I. 14 and 23 (and here in v. 1a), we might imagine that one of the two lots appeared (cf. LXX on I. 14.41). Presumably the report here has been abbreviated, and David in fact obtained the answer 'Hebron' in a way similar to that described in the case of Samuel in I. 10 and Saul in I. 14.

wisdom but also as a knowledge of Yahweh's plans for the future. The attempt to make capital of the conduct of the citizens of Jabesh at the death of Saul may appear to us to be remarkably clumsy. However, the fact that we hear of no responding echo need not indicate that the citizens of Jabesh rebuffed him (so Budde); in I. 30.26ff., for example, we hear of no answer from the men of Judah. Jabesh is further mentioned at II. 21.12, but it is not made clear whether David's action in transferring the bones of Saul, reported at that point, is meant for or against Jabesh. If the episode in ch. 2 was felt to be worth reporting, David's action will not have been regarded as a failure. It shows his far-reaching vision under all circumstances.

[8–9] Of course, David's goal is still far distant. Abner, presumably soon after Saul's death, took the initiative and 'made' a son of Saul's 'king'. The way in which this is reported and the later course of events shows that after Saul's death the real leading figure in the kingdom of Israel was always Abner himself. The name of the king appears here in the distorted form Ishbosheth. From I Chron. 8.33; 9.39, however, we learn the name Ishbaal. A twofold intent is thus discernible, not only to express the infamous word Baal as *bōšet* (*bosheth* = shame) but also to calumniate Saul. The real name may be inferred from I. 14.49 and will have been Ishyo (man of Yahweh) (see *ad loc.*). The enthronement of Ishbaal, as we may best name him, at Mahanaim, i.e. in the land east of the Jordan (lying on or near the Jabbok),[a] is to be understood as a consequence of the Philistine victory. At this point they were far out of range. We are given details of the territory ruled over by Ishbaal. It comprised Gilead, in other words the hill country between the Jarmuk and the Jabbok and also the Israelite places east of the Jordan, Ephraim, which refers to the hill country of central Palestine almost certainly including the territory of the tribe of Manasseh, and the lands of the tribe of Benjamin which adjoin it to the south, i.e. Saul's immediate homeland. The Philistine victory was therefore not as complete as the account at first led us to suppose; both central Palestine and the land east of the Jordan were preserved intact, presumably thanks to the energy of Abner. 'The Assyrian and Jezreel' are also mentioned. The latter means the plains; in that case 'the Assyrian' could only include the Galilaean districts, and the remarkable nomenclature would have to derive from the time when the northern part of Israel

[a]Noth suggested *tell hejjaj*, *PJB* 37, 1941, p. 86; *ZDPV* 71, 1955, p. 19.

had already become Assyrian (734). Originally, however, the word *'ašērī* 'the Asherite' would have stood here; the unusual detail in this text, which gives the names of territories or tribes ('Asherite' instead of 'Asher'), may have prompted the alteration to 'Assyrian'. It remains remarkable that it should in particular be Asher, the most westerly of the Galilaean tribes, which is mentioned alongside Jezreel. Did the Philistines, to whom the plains of Jezreel and North Galilee must have fallen after the defeat of Saul, have their administrative centres in 'Asher' and 'Jezreel' (just as at a later date Dor and Megiddo became capitals of provinces after the Assyrian conquest)? At the least, these two districts, if not the whole, may have been ceded by the Philistines to Ishbaal to hold. At any rate, the Philistines will have welcomed the fact that two, as they must have imagined, weak and dependent states, each of which kept the other in check, had arisen in the place of Saul's former kingdom. The names Judah and Israel are here expressly used for the two states.

[10–11] With the round number forty the age of the king is set too high. David is certainly younger than Jonathan, who is perhaps to be imagined as being approximately the same age. David's age at his enthronement is given as thirty (5.4). Ishbaal's youth or his infirmity—in I Chron. 8.33; 9.39, he is the youngest, in I Sam. 14.49, however, he follows Jonathan in age—will have been the reason for his evident absence from the battle. Nor are the years of his reign numbered correctly. David's reign of seven and a half years in Hebron must roughly correspond with the reign of Ishbaal, who was certainly called to be king soon after Saul's death, and the crown will have been offered to David not very long after the death of Ishbaal. Unless there is a textual error here (originally *šebaʿ*, seven, instead of *šetayim*, two), the only possible explanation is that the clause 'and he reigned two years' was originally the introduction to v. 12: 'When Abner . . . went out' (cf. Thenius *ad loc.*). The words 'over the house of Judah . . . six months' represent a parenthesis which perhaps was added later. This may have been the reason for the misunderstanding of the note about the two years and its being interpreted in accordance with I. 13.1, where the length of Saul's reign is also—erroneously, cf. *ad loc.*—put at two years. We therefore have here a juxtaposition of two understandings of the text; the proper, older one is concealed by the present one, which was suggested by the usual deuteronomistic information given when a king of Israel and Judah entered upon his reign.

[12–13] If this is correct, the event which now follows takes place two years after the beginning of the Israelite monarchy, which will in the meanwhile have consolidated itself to some degree. Abner makes a raid on the Benjaminite town of Gibeon with some of the servants of Ishbaal. It is not clear whether the troop consisted of Benjaminites as well as these men—so it would appear from v. 15 and v. 31—or whether the guard is called Benjaminite because it is the guard of the son of Saul who himself belongs to the tribe of Benjamin. The text appears to support the former alternative; in that case we would have to suppose that men of Benjamin had attached themselves to Abner's troop immediately after his entry into Benjamin. Gibeon is a fortified town, lying well to the south of the kingdom of Israel, so that Abner's expedition is understandable. On the other hand, it is also understandable that Joab should have gone there from Hebron. Gibeon was always held in high esteem. Originally the head of a tetrapolis (Josh. 9.17; cf. my commentary on Josh. 9.3), according to the Book of Joshua the city allied itself with Israel and in the days of Solomon still had a special political significance associated with the sanctuary of the 'great high place of Gibeon' (I Kings 3.4).[a] The fact that the meeting of the two troops did not immediately lead to hostilities and more particularly that Abner did not immediately regard Joab's men as enemies who had invaded foreign territory shows how fluid things still were. We are rather given the impression that complications only developed when the harmless military exercises became deadly serious. In other words, neither side trusted the other completely from the beginning. One group sits down at one side of the 'pool', and the other opposite them.
[14–16] The details of how the disastrous blood-bath came about are not clear. The twelve young men from either side were not, of course, set one against the other for each to seize his opponent (with the left hand) by his hair—the text has 'head'—and (with the right hand) drive his sword into his body. That would amount to Hara-kiri, and there is nothing of that here. It appears rather to have been some form of 'mock duel' with definite rules; the swords would not have been used as in a duel, as is implied by the expression *sāḥaq*, 'play',

---

[a] Cf. *ZAW* 47, 1929, pp. 166–77. The topographical identification of the place with *ed jib*, north-east of Jerusalem, is no longer disputed today; cf. ATD 9², p. 66. For recent work see the publication of the excavations by J. B. Pritchard, *Gibeon*, 1962, *Hebrew Inscriptions and Stamps from Gibeon*, Philadelphia, 1959 (and his communication given at the Old Testament Congress at Oxford in 1959, *SVT* 7, 1960, pp. 1–12).

in v. 14.[a] The point at which the combatants seized each other by the head and dealt fatal wounds in the fury of the moment must have been the last phase, which broke through the whole nature of the battle game; it alone is reported here. Quite remarkably, the place is named after the fact that the young men thrust their swords into the 'side'. If the text is in order the injury inflicted reciprocally by both parties must have been regarded as so unusual in a battle fought with swords that it gave the name to the place. It was then, of course, long retained as the name of some pasture-land.

[17–23] The bloody outcome of the mock fight has the result of bringing in those who had hitherto been non-combatants, and Abner's people are compelled to flee after a 'fierce' fight. We learn incidentally that Joab's two brothers, Abishai (I. 26.6ff.) and Asahel, are involved as well as Joab himself; they are, as usual, called sons of Zeruiah, David's sister (I Chron. 2.16). Her husband (v. 32) has already been dead some time. Asahel, who, although a young warrior, did not take part in the mock fight with the other young men, is famed as a runner, and this is his downfall. He determines to overtake Abner himself and to kill him. Joab and Abner have evidently known each other a long while; perhaps Abner also wishes to spare Asahel because the killing of Joab's brother will have personal (because of blood-vengeance) and political consequences. But as Asahel will not abandon his pursuit, Abner, presumably by stopping suddenly, lets him run on to the shaft of his long spear. We are to assume that this was not to kill him but to make him unfit to fight. Unfortunately the spear touches the soft part of the abdomen. Asahel has been running so fast that the shaft goes right through his body and he dies on the spot. The note that all stood still at the place where Asahel had fallen is not a reference to a halt made by the pursuing warriors but to a custom which was in force for later generations. Once again we see how the narrative rests on good local traditions.

---

[a]Eissfeldt (*La nouvelle Clio* 3, 1951, pp. 110–27) understands this expression to mean 'fight a representative battle' to determine the question 'Saul' or David. (In that case it would be similar to I. 17.8f., cf. also de Vaux, *RB* 65, 1958, p. 125). This 'attempt at a reunification of Israel' failed because all the men fell, so that the only consequence was the stronger opposition of the parties. In support of this approach Eissfeldt refers to an article by Y. Sukenik (later = Yadin) in *JPOS* 21, 1948, pp. 110–16, who came to a similar conclusion. In itself this is quite clear; the only question is whether the verb *sāḥaq*, which elsewhere has an element of playfulness and frolic in it, could be the right word here.

[24–32] The brothers continue the pursuit now with redoubled zeal, but are unable to prevent Abner and his men from making a stand on what is evidently a suitable hill, the name and location of which are again well known to the writer. Now Abner raises his voice and warns Joab of the consequences of continuing the battle. Joab's answer is to blame Abner for allowing events to develop as far as they have done. He is thus wise enough to postpone his blood-vengeance to a later time. Both groups make a night-march home. The losses on Abner's side are considerably greater than those suffered by the men of Judah. The number, however, is uncertain— the text varies between 300 and 600, and is anyhow set too high. The number 19, on the other hand, is to be regarded as good tradition. The burial of Asahel with his father in Bethlehem is in accordance with usual custom. The graves of the three brothers were still known in Bethlehem centuries later.[a] Here, too, we find confirmation that the compiler had good local traditions at his disposal. [3.1] The report closes with the important remark that the events described were the start of a civil war, which at the same time led to a gradual shift of the balance of power in David's favour. The end of the chapter, like the beginning, makes it clear that the design of God directed towards David's future reign has now been brought considerably nearer to its fruition.

2. DAVID'S SONS (FIRST LIST): 3.2–5

3 [2]And sons were born to David at Hebron; his first born was Amnon, of Ahinoam of Jezreel; [3]and his second, Chileab, of Abigail the widow of Nabal of Carmel; and the third, Absalom the son of Maacah the daughter of Talmai king of Geshur; [4]and the fourth, Adonijah the son of Haggith; and the fifth, Shephatiah the son of Abital; [5]and the sixth, Ithream, of Eglah, David's wife. These were born to David in Hebron.

The list of David's sons will come from a state archive and belong with that of 5.13–16; the two halves are united in I Chron. 3.1–9. [2] The first part is placed here because the sons named in it were born before David went to Jerusalem. The wording need not lead us to suppose that he had no sons before he settled in Hebron. Nor are we to suppose that each mother bore only one son. Evidently it is

[a] Later distorted into the more familiar biblical names Job, Asaph and Ezekiel. Cf. Hertzberg in *PJB* 22, 1926, p. 95.

always only the first born that is mentioned. We hear nothing of any daughters.

Only the first two of David's wives were associated with him before he went to Hebron. Ahinoam, David's first wife, also produces the crown prince, whose death is reported in ch. 13. **[3–4]** The name of Abigail's son has been uncertainly transmitted. In I Chron. 3.1 the name Daniel surprisingly takes the place of Chileab; the old translations offer further deviations (Daluyah? Dodiyah?). Presumably the name in MT has something to do with the Calebbite descent of the mother (Caspari, for instance, assumes that the original name was Caleb). The boy seems to have died before Amnon, as he is mentioned neither as a claimant to the throne nor in any other respect. The attempt by H. Winckler to make Dodiyah into Jedidiah and to identify Abigail's son with Solomon is not feasible, though the name 'beloved of Yahweh' could have been transferred to Solomon from David's dead son by Nathan, who brought him up. Michal, Saul's daughter, is not mentioned in this list.

As daughter of a king—albeit hardly a powerful one—Absalom's mother has a certain status which seems later to leave its mark on Absalom's character. **[5]** It is striking that Eglah, named last, should be called 'David's wife', as they were, in fact, all his wives. Conjectures that in an earlier form of the text she was David's half-sister or 'wife' of an unknown man cannot be substantiated. It might be assumed that she occupied a special status, if not that of 'first lady', at least that of David's favourite wife.

The section is not meant to detail David's family relationships, but to show that in this sphere, too, David constantly increased, and slowly but surely prepared for himself the dynasty that God willed.

3. ABNER'S TREACHERY AND DEATH: 3.6–39

3 ⁶While there was war between the house of Saul and the house of David, Abner was the strongest man in the house of Saul.ᵃ ⁷Now Saul had a concubine, whose name was Rizpah, the daughter of Aiah, whom Abner had taken to himself.ᵇ And Ishbaalᵇ said to Abner, 'Why have you gone in to my father's concubine?' ⁸Then Abner was very angry over the words of Ishbaal and said, 'Am I a dog's head of

ᵃThe rendering 'had grown strong at the expense of the house of Saul' (Nowack, etc.), while not impossible grammatically, does not make as much sense as the one adopted, which prepares for Abner's subsequent conduct.

ᵇSee BH.

Judah?ᵃ This day I keep showing loyalty to the house of Saul your
father, to his brothers, and to his friends, and have not given you into
the hand of David; and yet you charge me today with a fault concerning a woman. ⁹God do so to Abner, and more also, if I do not accomplish for David what the LORD has sworn to him, ¹⁰to transfer the
kingdom from the house of Saul, and set up the throne of David over
Israel and over Judah, from Dan to Beersheba.' ¹¹And Ishbaal could
not answer Abner another word, because he feared him.

12 And Abner sent messengers to David, saying, 'To whom does the
land belong? Is it not subject to me?ᵇ Make your covenant with me,
and behold, my hand shall be with you to bring over all Israel to you.'
¹³And he said, 'Good; I will make a covenant with you; but one thing
I require of you; that is, you shall not see my face, unless you bring
Michal, Saul's daughter,ᶜ when you come to see my face.' ¹⁴Then
David sent messengers to Ishbaal, Saul's son, saying, 'Give me my
wife Michal, whom I betrothed at the price of a hundred Philistine
foreskins.' ¹⁵And Ishbaal sent, and took her from herᵈ husband—
Paltiel the son of Laish. ¹⁶But her husband went with her, weeping
after her all the way to Bahurim. Then Abner said to him, 'Go,
return'; and he returned.

17 And Abner conferred with the elders of Israel, saying, 'For
some time past you have been seeking David as king over you. ¹⁸Now
then bring it about; for the LORD has promised David, saying, "By
the hand of my servant I willᵉ save my people Israel from the hand
of the Philistines and from the hand of all their enemies." ' ¹⁹And he—
Abner—also spoke to Benjamin; and then he—Abnerᶠ—went to tell
David at Hebron all that Israel and the whole house of Benjamin
thought good to do.

20 When Abner came with twenty men to David at Hebron, David
made a feast for Abner and theᵈ men who were with him. ²¹And
Abner said to David, 'I will arise and go, and will gather all Israel to

ᵃ'Of Judah' is omitted in LXX MSS and is left out by most exegetes.

ᵇThe text is corrupt. LXX tried to find here the place to which Abner sent
the message (Hebron, Telam). But this is only a guess. Emendation must start
from the question 'To whom does the land belong?' This requires the answer 'To
me', i.e. Abner. This, however, is expressed in the word *taḥtāw* (*qᵉrē*)—moved to
the wrong place—which is to be read as *taḥtay*. The second *lēmōr* could have
contained a (*hᵃ*)*lō'* in its first part, while *mōr* would be a dittograph of what
follows. *taḥtay* would then have to be put in its place.

ᶜHere the text allows of a choice between *kī 'im hēbētā* and *lipnē hᵃbī'ᵃkā*. The
former is to be preferred because of the ending of the verse.

ᵈSee BH.

ᵉThere are parallel texts here, one of which reads *bᵉyad*, the other *dāwīd* (so
Caspari *ad loc.*). The two words are very similar in Hebrew. One should read
either *bᵉyad 'abdī 'ōšī'ᵃ* (so MSS) or *dāwīd 'abdī hōšī'ᵃ* (has saved—is destined
to save). In either case the *'el* must be rendered 'in respect of', as Gen. 20.2;
cf. GB on *'el*, 7b.

ᶠThe word 'Abner' is both times an explanatory gloss (see Budde), which on
each occasion separates the *gam* from the word to which it refers.

my lord the king, that they may make a covenant with you, and that you may reign over all that your heart desires.' So David sent Abner away; and he went in peace.

22 Just then the servants of David arrived with Joab from a raid, bringing much spoil with them. But Abner was not with David at Hebron, for he had sent him away, and he had gone in peace. ²³When Joab and all the army that was with him came, it was told Joab, 'Abner the son of Ner came to the king, and he has let him go, and he has gone in peace.' ²⁴Then Joab went to the king and said, 'What have you done? Behold, Abner came to you; why is it that you have sent him away, so that he is gone? ²⁵You know that Abner the son of Ner came to deceive you, and to know your going out and your coming in, and to know all that you are doing.'

26 When Joab came out from David's presence, he sent messengers after Abner, and they brought him back from the cistern of Sirah; but David did not know about it. ²⁷And when Abner returned to Hebron, Joab took him aside into the midst of the gate to speak with him privately, and there he smote him in the belly, so that he died, for the blood of Asahel his brother. ²⁸Afterward, when David heard of it, he said, 'I and my kingdom are for ever guiltless before the LORD for the blood of Abner the son of Ner. ²⁹May it fall upon the head of Joab, and upon all his father's house; and may the house of Joab never be without one who has a discharge, or who is leprous, or who goes upon crutches,ᵃ or who is slain by the sword, or who lacks bread!' ³⁰But Joab and Abishai his brother had marked out Abner,ᵇ because he had killed their brother Asahel in the battle at Gibeon.

31 Then David said to Joab and to all the people who were with him, 'Rend your clothes, and gird on sackcloth, and mourn before Abner.' And King David followed the bier. ³²They buried Abner at Hebron; and the king lifted up his voice and wept at the grave of Abner; and all the people wept. ³³And the king lamented for Abner, saying,

'Should Abner die as a fool dies?
³⁴Your hands were not bound,
    your feet were not fettered;
(and yet) you have fallen, as one falls before the wicked.'

And all the people wept again over him. ³⁵Then all the people came to persuade David to eat bread while it was yet day; but David swore, saying, 'God do so to me and more also, if Iᶜ taste bread or anything

ᵃTranslation uncertain. The phrase is often rendered 'who holds a spindle' (as RSV), = 'effeminate stay-at-home' (Nowack). LXX gives the above, surely more suitable, rendering.

ᵇHere, too, the at least unusual *hāreḡū leʾabnēr* seems to conceal a variant reading, either *hāreḡū ʾabnēr* (= they killed Abner) or *ʾārebū leʾabnēr* (= they lay in wait for Abner, so LXX). The latter is more probable, as Joab alone murdered Abner.

ᶜMT 'If I do not'.

else till the sun goes down!' ³⁶And all the people took notice of it, and
it pleased them; as everything that the king did pleased all the people.
³⁷So all the people and all Israel understood that day that it had not
been the king's will to slay Abner the son of Ner. ³⁸And the king said
to his servants, 'Do you not know that a prince and great man has
fallen this day in Israel? ³⁹I am this day too weak and too helpless[a]
for a king: these men the sons of Zeruiah are too hard for me. The
LORD requite the evildoer according to his wickedness!'

[6–7] Nothing is retailed of individual events in the fratricidal war,
as they are considered irrelevant to the progress of the God-guided
history. The beginning was important, because of the death of
Asahel, and so is this incident with Abner, who played the role not
only of founder but also of gravedigger of Ishbaal's kingdom. The
first sentence is probably meant to show that he is the predominant
figure in the oppressed state, but the interpretation of the verse is
somewhat doubtful (see above). He demonstrates his status by using
Saul's estate as he pleases. He has relations with one of Saul's concubines, Rizpah, who is to present us with such a moving picture in
ch. 21. It is probable that such an action had some legal significance.
In 16.22 Absalom intentionally appropriates David's concubines to
demonstrate that he is his father's successor, and Adonijah's request
to Solomon to be given David's last consort Abishag to wife is interpreted as a desire for the throne which costs him his life (I Kings
2.13ff.). Abner, however, who, as a relative of Saul, could in fact
have taken over the throne immediately, does not seem to have
consorted with Rizpah from political motives, so that Ishbaal's
accusation, though understandable, may still have been quite unjustified. Between the lines we may detect much court gossip and
slander, and Ishbaal was certainly not a strong enough personality
to be able to repudiate such suspicions. Abner, on the other hand,
appears as a strong figure. His answer to Ishbaal is outspoken and
fearless. He knows that it is solely through him that the descendants
of Saul still have their position and status after the catastrophe at
Gilboa. From the logic of the matter, he dismisses his conduct with
Rizpah as a trivial affair which should not be held against a man of

---

[a]The *m* of *māšū*ᵃ*ḥ* can be put before *melek* so as to read *šaḥ mimmelek*. The
text remains obscure. In LXX there is the conjecture that this is a further remark
about Abner, who is 'related' to the king (LXX perhaps reads *rē*ᵃᶜ, 'friend' of
the king, instead of *raq*) and 'anointed by the king' (or 'has anointed the king'?—
then *māšōᵃ*ᵃ*ḥ* would have to be read). But David should here be describing himself,
and not Abner.

S.–I

his stature. His remark about his future intentions is also very open. Here, as again in v. 18, recollection is made of what was probably a widely repeated promise, which assured David of the succession to the throne. [8–10] The story of David is permeated from the beginning with such references and in the general context they should be assessed in the same way as the frequent promises of blessing in the patriarchal narratives. In passages such as this, the reader is meant to perceive the line which runs through all the material; the persons involved are pieces on God's chessboard and events are directed towards their goal by a higher hand. K. Budde has raised the question when, in fact, such a promise was given, and recalls the oracle in I. 22.13. This is impossible to settle. We must be content with the fact that Samuel, Abigail, Jonathan and Saul know of it. The implications of the account of the anointing in I. 16, not mentioned elsewhere, run through events as a secret yet generally recognized piece of knowledge which determines the actions of those concerned, even of David himself. Even Abner's impulsive words and deeds play their part in this programme. They describe David's future kingdom as one which will stretch over Israel and Judah, with the two sanctuaries of Dan in the north and Beersheba in the south as its boundaries (I. 3.20).

[11–12] Abner's blustering remarks are like a blow on the jaw to Ishbaal. The narrator is not concerned whether we are to imagine the king to have taken Abner's remarks as an outburst of wrath. The only important thing is that Abner now seeks a real association with David. If the incomprehensible words in the text have been interpreted rightly, Abner represents himself to David as the *de facto* lord of the land. To make a covenant with him is to gain lordship over 'all Israel'. Abner's unexpected death prevented any possibility of putting his words to the test. The immediate steps of his which are reported, however, show the authority he had. Nevertheless, it was not Abner's downfall but the death of Ishbaal which enabled the goal to be reached.

[13–16] David's reply once again shows his skill as a statesman. He is not happy with Abner's tactically favourable but illegitimate step; in particular, the reserved, almost negative tone of David's reply should be noticed. The author was concerned to repudiate any idea that David became lord over all Israel by an act of treachery. David requires as a preliminary condition for any further action the return of Michal, Saul's daughter, whom Saul had given to someone else after David's flight (I. 25.44). That David's request may also have been motivated by personal considerations (I. 18.20, 19.11f.) is of no interest to the narrator. Surely David takes this step to vindicate the regularity of his claim to Saul's estate. By passing on his decision to Abner, after the latter has offered him as it were 'his' kingdom, David gives a clear answer; Abner can best give help to something which has long been David's. This is underlined by the fact that David makes the return of Michal the subject of an official message to Ishbaal. We may be astonished at David's action, which runs the risk of an insulting refusal,[a] and still more at the compliance of Ishbaal, as the significance of the matter cannot have escaped him. Did he perhaps think, with the daydreams of an inferior man, that he could play off David against Abner, and did David, with sure knowledge of the situation, count on this? At any rate, David's wish is granted. Despite the protests and the lament of the dispossessed husband, whose name is given in a form different from that in I. 25.44, Abner takes Michal to David. David has thus achieved two things: the possibility of being officially regarded as a regular claimant to the throne and an unconcealed opportunity to open negotiations with Abner, who by this means comes to David's court. How Michal feels about all this we are not told. It is not even said that she comes to Hebron. She is merely a pawn in the political game, important as she is in another respect, as the one who provides the way for David to the throne of all Israel.

[17–18] Abner has meanwhile not been inactive, but has taken up negotiations with the elders of Israel. These men, originally, it is to be supposed, in fact the 'oldest' of both tribe and family, experienced and renowned (Job 29), apparently became an aristocratic group which by the pressure of events represented a sort of senate in town or tribe. The 'elders of Israel' mentioned here (and at 5.3; 17.4, 15; I Kings 8.1) may be a nucleus drawn from the elders of the tribes. It is, of course, no longer possible to determine the way in which they were organized.

Our passage requires the assumption that the college of elders did not have its seat at the court of Ishbaal, but elsewhere: just as the 'judge' may have had his seat of office in the territory of the Joseph

---

[a]Noth, *The History of Israel*, ET[2], p. 184, n. 1, regards both this step and David's marriage to Michal at an earlier date as unhistorical. This, however, presupposes such inroads in the traditional material that it would be impossible to explain how the present text came into being.

tribes,[a] so, too, the 'elders of Israel' may have assembled at the declared centre of the land and the place of the covenant, namely the sanctuary of Shechem.[b] The existence of such an organization alongside the monarchy—here we may recall the 'people of the land' during the later period—is of some importance in understanding the people of the Old Testament.

In that case, we might imagine that after the quarrel with Ishbaal Abner stayed in central Palestine and carried out the negotiations there. In so doing he could recollect a favourable attitude shown towards David by the elders at an earlier date. Evidently, immediately after the defeat at Gilboa, the latter named David as their only saviour in time of need, just as in Judg. 11.5 the 'elders of Gilead' call Jephthah, whose position as an outlaw resembles that of David, to be 'head and leader' (Judg. 11.11), with express emphasis on the further duration of the office. Only Abner's strong personality would have hindered their purpose and he acted, as v. 8 in its own way confirms, in order to keep Saul's family (and thereby his own) in power. Now he goes back on his earlier decision. The renewed reminiscence of the promise to David is once again confirmation that neither Abner nor the elders are shaping events. The word 'save' (*hōšiaʿ*) which occurs here is that used to describe Yahweh's acts at the time of the judges.

[19–21] Once Abner has further guaranteed for himself the agreement of his own tribe of Benjamin, he can continue the game at Hebron with good cards in his hand. Nothing is said of a promise made to Abner by David, similar to that made later to Amasa (19.14), namely that he will be commander of the army, in Joab's place or alongside him. We must, however, assume that Abner was destined for the command of the Israelite army, and some envy on this account may have been a contributory factor in Joab's rash decision. Be this as it may, once Abner has proposed the covenant between Israel and David he is allowed to go 'in peace'. This has more significance here than a familiar Eastern greeting to one taking his departure, as the way in which the words are taken up afterwards by Joab and his informers shows.

[22–27] Joab, returning from a successful raid—surely not against Ishbaal—immediately learns what has transpired. His fearless approach is clearly evident; the reader can only be amazed at the

[a] Cf. *TLZ* 79, 1954, col. 290.
[b] Cf. Josh. 24 and on this ATD 9, p. 133.

general way in which the commanders talk to their kings. Whether Joab really suspects in Abner, traitor to his lord, treachery towards David, too, or whether this is merely inserted to explain his subsequent action, remains open, especially as no reply from David is recorded. The reason for this will not be a desire to abbreviate the description; David will not, in fact, have replied (cf. v. 39), so that Joab knows the initiative to be his own. Abner, who is already some miles north of Hebron (the present *sirat el bella'*), is summoned back, unsuspectingly complies, goes with Joab 'into the midst of the gate' and there, though he does not guess that Asahel's death in battle could be an occasion for blood-vengeance, is stabbed by Joab. Blood-vengeance is emphatically given as the reason for Joab's action. This is said twice. This and indeed the whole account is meant to show that David could not possibly be suspected of any guilt in the matter. We should nevertheless ask, as men may have asked even at that time (cf. v. 37), whether Joab did not from the beginning have a secret understanding with David or at least whether Abner did not 'die very opportunely' for David (like Mortimer for the Earl of Leicester). The abruptness which characterizes all David's dealings with Abner could lend support to such a view, as could the king's silence at Joab's remonstrances. Moreover, the presence of Abner as a high-ranking officer in David's army, possibly alongside Joab, would certainly have given rise to many complications. Nevertheless, it must be said after sober consideration that the death of Abner was a very disconcerting incident for David, which in the circumstances could have deeply endangered the hoped-for union with Israel. We also know that David was tormented by Joab's murder of Abner right until the hour of his death (I Kings 2.5, 32). [28–39] So the conduct of David after the death of Abner as reported here will really be in accord with the situation. His first reaction is a curse on Joab's 'house'; this fits the fact that Joab acted because of the attack made on his family. Here we learn that Abishai played a part in the ambush and according to one part of the text—almost certainly incorrect—even shared in the murder of Abner. David thereupon gives the order for a fitting funeral, to which Joab is expressly summoned. David himself plays an active part in it. He sings the customary lament, and adds a song which he has composed, expressing his grief in a moving, and a genuine, way. The verse, skilfully constructed and subtly expressed, laments that this noble man was done to death like a fettered law-breaker, attacked by robbers: 'but the malefactor was not he—it was rather those who stabbed him in the back' (Gressmann). The king's abstinence from food until the evening—like that of the Mohammedans in the fast month of Ramadan—emphasizes his attitude towards the grave event before all the people. It is emphatically stressed that the effect of the king's conduct reached as far as Israel. Moreover, by remarks which must come from David's entourage, we are shown how he felt about Abner and his murder, quite apart from any external demonstrations of grief. Here, for the first time, internal difficulties at the court are brought to light, difficulties over which the king does not have complete mastery. Even features of this kind—which are not without influence on the picture of David—are reported without restraint. Even he is not the hero who carries all before him. Despite this, however, and despite the difficult obstacle which Abner's murder puts in David's way, God's promised plan goes forward.

4. THE DEATH OF ISHBAAL: 4.1–12

4 [1]When Saul's son heard that Abner had died at Hebron, his courage failed, and all Israel was dismayed. [2]Now Saul's son had[a] two men who were captains of raiding bands; the name of the one was Baanah, and the name of the other Rechab, sons of Rimmon, a man of Benjamin from Beeroth (for Beeroth also is reckoned to Benjamin; [3]the Beerothites fled to Gittaim, and have been sojourners there to this day). [4]Jonathan, the son of Saul, had a son who was crippled in his feet. He was five years old when the news about Saul and Jonathan came from Jezreel; and his nurse took him up, and fled; and, as she fled in her haste, he fell, and became lame. And his name was Meribbaal.[a]

5 Now the sons of Rimmon the Beerothite, Rechab and Baanah, set out, and about the heat of the day they came to the house of Ishbaal,[a] as he was taking his noonday rest. [6]And they had already[b] come into the midst of the house (as though) fetching wheat, when they found a woman cleaning wheat. And they smote her in the belly;[c] and thus Rechab and Baanah his brother escaped [7]and came into the house, as he lay on his bed in his bedchamber, and they smote him, and slew him, and beheaded him. They took his head, and went by the way of the (Jordan) valley all night, [8]and brought the head of Ishbaal to David at Hebron. And they said to the king, 'Here is the head of Ishbaal, the son of Saul, your enemy, who sought your life; the LORD has avenged my lord the king this day on Saul and on his

[a]See BH.
[b]Read we‛hinnē.
[c]See Commentary.

offspring.' ⁹But David answered Rechab and Baanah his brother, the sons of Rimmon the Beerothite, 'As the LORD lives, who has redeemed my life out of every adversity, ¹⁰when one told me "Behold, Saul is dead," and thought he was bringing good news,ᵃ I seized him and slew him at Ziklag, which was the reward I gave him for his news. ¹¹How much more, when wicked men have slain a righteous man in his own house upon his bed, shall I not now require his blood at your hand, and destroy you from the earth?' ¹²And David commanded his young men, and they killed them, and cut off their hands and feet, and hanged them beside the pool at Hebron. But they took the head of Ishbaal, and buried it in the tomb of Abner at Hebron.

[1–2] The death of the strongest man lets loose general confusion in Israel. It is marked not only by the reactions of Ishbaal, who appears throughout as a poor specimen, most unlike his father and brother, but principally by the murder plotted by the audacious brothers, who feel that their hour has come. Their descent is described accurately and repeatedly; their actions evidently brought unforgettable shame to their family and their city. The place Beeroth is part of the tetrapolis mentioned at Josh. 9.17 (Gibeon, Chephirah, Beeroth and Kiriath-jearim). The situation of Beeroth is disputed, like that of Gibeon. The bronze age sites of *ed jib* and *el biro* are usually taken for Gibeon and Beeroth respectively; the similarity of names, though philologically incorrect, has led to this identification.ᵇ Accordingly, Beeroth would lie outside the proper territory of Benjamin, as *el-bire* is to be put north of the northern boundary of Benjamin, known to us quite accurately. This could, however, fit in well with the following remark that 'Beeroth also is reckoned to Benjamin.' Beeroth thus has 'Benjaminites' as inhabitants, although it does not belong to their tribe. There were also such enclaves elsewhere (see Josh. 17.9). Moreover, Kiriath-jearim, which properly belongs to Judah (Josh. 15.60), is similarly reckoned to Benjamin (Josh. 18.28, cf. ATD 9², p. 111). [3] Beeroth had then, as we learn here, been abandoned by its inhabitants. Why and when, we do not learn. The reason for its being mentioned at all, however, will

---

ᵃLXX reads *bᵉʿēnāy* instead of *bᵉʿēnāu*: 'Who had good news for me.' Both readings make equally good sense.

ᵇA. Alt, *ZDPV* 69, 1953, pp. 1–27, has suggested the opposite, that *ed-jib* is Beeroth and *el-bire* is Gibeon. But cf. also *ZAW* 47, 1929, pp. 189f. It is suggested there, as by Albright, that Beeroth be identified with *tell en-naṣbe*, which is part of the pasturage of *el-bire*. The theory is, however, hardly tenable in this form (see Alt, *op. cit.*). A discussion of the point is impossible here. For Gibeon, see on II 2.13.

lie in the events which are recorded here; the Beerothites 'fled' because they no longer felt safe. Their new home, Gittaim, is to be located in the neighbourhood of Lydda;[a] so the Beerothites would have gone into Philistine territory. The one and a half verses are, in fact, a marginal note of a later period in the history of the text inserted into the narrative, whose course they interrupt.

[4] This is still more true of the note about Meribbaal,[b] whose name, like that of Ishbaal, has been distorted and has become 'Mephibosheth' ('from the mouth of the God of shame'?). The description of how this—evidently the only—son of Jonathan became lame has no connection with this narrative. It would be in place in ch. 9, to which some commentators would transfer it. Perhaps it is meant to say here 'that after the death of Ishbaal there was no suitable claimant to the throne from the house of Saul' (Nötscher). This is, of course, uncertain (cf. ch. 21), but not impossible. The marginal note would have been incorporated into the text with the other gloss. The narrative proper has v. 5 immediately after v. 2.

[5–6] The two companions succeed in getting inside Ishbaal's house at midday, presumably by some trick. LXX narrates that the doorkeeper had 'nodded off' (so literally in the Greek) while cleaning wheat, so that they slipped in unseen. MT is so completely different that corruption or paraphrase is out of the question; in its present form, however, it is incomprehensible. It seems that the murderers sneaked into the house as wheat-carriers, where they then met someone whom they killed by stabbing in the belly. Perhaps this person was originally the woman found cleaning wheat, and whom LXX made into a doorkeeper. The alteration of the originally feminine suffix to the masculine suffix *wayyakkūhū* can easily be explained, because the person stabbed was expected to be Ishbaal, and because in MT a sentence such as *wᵉhinnē 'iššā bōreret ḥiṭṭīm*, 'and behold, there was a woman cleaning corn', fell out after the word *ḥiṭṭīm*. It is in any case improbable that the king's house was watched over only by a woman worker. But if the two had come in appearing to have some business at the house, they could easily have got past the guard, which would, of course, have been there.

---

[a] In Neh. 11.33, Gittaim is mentioned right between the places in Benjaminite territory and those in the neighbourhood of Lydda; cf. also Abel, *Géographie* II, p. 338.

[b] 'Baal strives' or 'opponent of Baal'? Perhaps the original form was Mippibaal, 'from the mouth of Baal', cf. Schulz *ad loc.*

It continues to remain strange that LXX should merely have retained the clause supposed to have fallen out here and should have given it its present form. One reason could be the corruption of *wayyakkūhā*; after that, the whole sentence would have become obscure.

[7–12] The murderers do their gruesome work on the sleeping man, take his head to David at Hebron, and present him with the *corpus delicti*, representing themselves as executors of the just will of God, deserving a reward. David refuses to accept that the Lord has delivered him and goes on to describe the men as worse offenders than the messenger of II. 1. The expressions 'wicked' (*rāšāʿ*) and 'righteous' (*ṣaddīq*), used here, come from the legal sphere, and mean the one who is in the right and the one who has done wrong towards him. At this moment David is the representative of true justice. So the section ends with the account of appropriate action towards the murderers, who are killed, mutilated, and deprived of the benefit of their own graves, while the head of the murdered man is honourably laid in the tomb of his commander-in-chief. The burial place was shown in the Middle Ages and was visited often (by Rabbi Jacob of Paris, 1258, Peter the Deacon, 1137, Felix Fabri, 1482, and many others). It is still known today.

Infamous as the deed is, even in David's eyes, from a loftier standpoint it represents a great step forward towards his goal. This is not actually said, but it is the real reason for the account. What the murderers say to David, blasphemous as it sounds in *their* mouths, is nevertheless apposite. The divine righteousness has used even this evil act by murderers as a vehicle for carrying forward its design.[a]

5. THE KING OF ALL ISRAEL AND HIS CAPITAL: 5.1–12

5 ¹Then all the tribes of Israel came to David at Hebron, and said, 'Behold we are your bone and flesh. ²In times past, when Saul was king over us, it was you that led out and brought in Israel; and the LORD said to you, "You shall be shepherd of my people Israel, and you shall be prince over Israel." ' ³So all the elders of Israel came to the king at Hebron; and King David made a covenant with them at Hebron before the LORD, and they anointed David king over Israel. ⁴David was thirty years old when he began to reign, and he reigned forty years. ⁵At Hebron he reigned over Judah seven years and six months; and at Jerusalem he reigned over all Israel and Judah thirty-three years.

[a]'By betraying Jesus, even Judas helped in the world's salvation, and yet he died at a rope's end.' E. v. Handel-Mazzetti, from the ballad *Deutsches Recht*.

6 And the king and his men went to Jerusalem against the Jebusites, the inhabitants of the land, who said to David, 'You will not come in here, but the blind and the lame will ward you off'[a]—saying, 'David cannot come in here.' Nevertheless David took the stronghold of Zion; that became the city of David. [8]And David said on that day, 'Whoever smites the Jebusites and reaches the shaft—and (smites) the blind and the lame, who are hated by David because they say, "The blind and the lame shall not come into the house"—(he shall become chief!' And Joab the son of Zeruiah went up first, so he became chief.)[b] [9]And David dwelt in the stronghold, and called it the city of David. And David built the city round about from the Millo inward. [10]And David became greater and greater, for the LORD, the God of hosts, was with him.

11 And Hiram king of Tyre sent messengers to David, and cedar trees, also carpenters and masons who built David a house. [12]And David perceived that the LORD had established him king over Israel, and that he had exalted his kingdom for the sake of his people Israel.

This section, though not clear in all respects, is of the greatest importance. For here the promise to David is fulfilled; he becomes king over all the people, and becomes king in Jerusalem. All that is still to come can only be confirmation, assurance and consequence of this one fact.

On closer examination, we find four sub-sections, which will be taken together here as one. We could equally well treat them independently and even add the two or three remaining parts of the chapter. We treat vv. 1–12 together, however, because here, as has been said, the two most significant factors are linked together: the king of the realm and his capital.

[1–3] The first sub-section deals with the transference of the kingship over Israel to David. It follows as a direct consequence of the murder of Ishbaal, not only because the editorial placing of ch. 5 after ch. 4 allows such a judgment, but also as an historical necessity. David's is the only possible candidacy. It is supported by three reasons: his connection with Saul's family by blood, historical right—as leader of the troops David already virtually exercised the office in practice—and, as in 3.9f., 18, the promise of the Lord. It will be no chance thing that the statement is made by 'all the tribes of Israel', whereas the enthronement and the anointing is per-

---

[a]The $h^e s \bar{\imath} r^e k \bar{a}$ perhaps represents a conflate reading of $h^a s \bar{\imath} r^e k \bar{a}$ and $h^e s \bar{\imath} r \bar{u} k \bar{a}$. The former means, 'You would first have to drive away the blind and lame who say . . .' The latter is more likely and has been chosen above.

[b]Bracketed section expanded from I Chron. 11.6.

formed by 'all the elders of Israel'. This will certainly not be the work of 'later redaction', so that the state act does not appear to be completely 'formless' (Budde; Schulz the reverse). We are to imagine the matter as taking place in two parts, the first of which is undertaken by the active and responsible men of the tribes and has more the nature of a preliminary action; of course, everything would be much more clear were the account not so short, and if we had at least an answer given by David. In any case, v. 3 contains a second act with new personnel: the 'elders' are manifestly a higher authority, and an official body. The fact that David concludes the 'covenant' with them and not they with him signifies that David takes pledges of their loyalty; in other words that there is here an act of homage as a consequence of which they recognize him as king. The events recall Saul's enthronement at I. 11 and also the choice of the king in II. 2. Yahweh's promise was directed towards the *nāgīd*, the prince, or, more accurately, the charismatic ruler willed by Yahweh; now comes, as the corresponding action of the people, their entering into the covenant, which shows David for the first time as the manifest king (*melek*). The subsequent anointing by the elders—it is perhaps not by chance that the 'elders' are also at least mentioned in the account of the anointing of David by Samuel in I. 16—clearly summarizes the constitutional and the sacral situation. Of course, the anointing takes place at the sanctuary of Hebron, as is shown by the addition 'before the Lord'. By it David becomes king in the full sense. In his informative work *Die Staatenbildung der Israeliten in Palaestina*, A. Alt has rightly indicated not only the similarity but also the differences in the procedure of the enthronements of David and of Saul, and also the fact that here not a united state but a personal union is achieved. That this is so is evident many times during David's reign and even more so after the death of Solomon.

[4–5] If the statistical note which is attached derives from another context, it has nevertheless been placed here most skilfully. The mention of Jerusalem, which was only captured subsequently, shows that it did not originally belong in its present context. On the other hand, we are not to conclude that the surprise attack on Jerusalem historically preceded the choice of David as king. The details have occasionally been questioned, as forty, a familiar round number, occurs here. But the number seven and a half has hardly been invented, and in other respects forty may well describe the number of years of David's reign. The placing of such a note at this point underlines the recognition of the historical significance of the moment.

[6] Only now is the report of the capture of Jerusalem produced. Regrettably it is extremely brief. It is first of all important that the capture is achieved not by the host of Israel, as Chronicles (I. 11.4) wrongly represents it, but by 'David's men'. The whole business looks like a systematic undertaking, but done privately and incidentally. The form in which it is transmitted is an anecdote, developed from a proverbial expression. Jerusalem was a city at that time at least a thousand years old; it occurs in Egyptian Execration Texts and in the Amarna correspondence, and also in the accounts of the conquest in the Old Testament. Judg. 1.8 narrates an earlier capture; this may, however, merely deal with the possession of the pasturage of Jerusalem by the men of Judah, to whom it belonged according to the scheme of tribal boundaries.[a] The city was regarded as a foreign element in Israel-Judah (Judg. 19.10–12), and that was, in fact, the case. The reason for Jerusalem having preserved its independence for so long a period was first its detachment from the main north-south routes and secondly its natural position as a fortress. Even today, the south and east sides of the old city hill—the southeast hill—show its good strategic position; at an earlier time the 'valley of the city' to the west was also much deeper. Only to the north was there not such a clear demarcation (see below). The favourable situation of the city is expressed in the remark to David about the blind and the lame. In the evidently original 'ward you off' the perfect is used ('to express the doubtless imminent and therefore already accomplished fact in the consciousness of the speaker' GK § 106n.). Now if the city was impregnable to attacks made at that period, the question arises how capture of it was still possible. [7–8] First of all the capture is quite simply reported as such. Then there follows a puzzling remark which is evidently meant to tell us something about the way in which the attack was launched. It certainly looks as though a distinction is made between the 'stronghold of Zion' and the rest of the city ('Jebus'?); this is even clearer in the account in Chronicles. Verse 8 will be meant to give more accurate details than v. 7. The beginning of the sentence seems to imply that David promised a special reward to the first one to scale the fortress. The mention in Chronicles, though without

[a]Cf. ATD 9, p. 150.

any reference to the blind and the lame, of Joab as the first to succeed, and the subsequent promise that he should have the position of commander (of the city?) may thus be historically correct.[a] It would therefore seem advisable to incorporate the statement by Chronicles in the text of II Sam. Two difficulties still then remain. One concerns the 'watershaft' ($sinn\bar{o}r$). The manifold possibilities must be left undiscussed here. The word most probably describes the shaft which the inhabitants of the city repaired to get water from the spring (the only one in Jerusalem), which lies to the east at the foot of the city hill (Gihon, today the spring of Mary). The upper end of the shaft is meant; the 'Jebusites' would then be the watch stationed there.[b] The text, however, makes it more probable that the bold attackers stormed the slope from the outside, overpowered the watch, and so gained possession of the entrance to the shaft (so Simons, *loc. cit.*) than that they climbed up inside the shaft, an almost impossible venture. Tradition evidently regarded the conquest of the shaft as the decisive event in the capture of the city.[c]

In the case of the second difficulty, the matter of the blind and the lame, we have a subsequent addition which is meant to explain the saying in a similar way to the explanations given of the phrase 'Is Saul also among the prophets?' in I. 10 and 19. The saying 'The blind and the lame shall not come into the house' must have been current in Jerusalem and will have been brought into causal connection with David's aversion to the blind and the lame, which in its turn is associated with the boastful saying of the Jebusites. The passage should therefore be put in parentheses.[d]

[a]The 'Fountain of Job', lying south of Old Jerusalem, the En-rogel of the Old Testament, will originally have been a 'Fountain of Joab'; see Hertzberg in *PJB* 22, 1926, p. 95.

[b]For the details see especially J. Simons, *Jerusalem in the Old Testament*, 1952, pp. 165-73.

[c]Cf. also O. Procksch in *PJB* 5, 1909, pp. 67f.

[d]Stoebe (*ZDPV* 73, 1957, pp. 73-99) suggests a completely different approach. First of all he gives an excellent and complete survey of the history of the interpretation of this passage. His interpretation may be summed up in three parts, which we will present together with our criticisms: (1) He takes the blind and the lame in v. 6 to be David's men: 'You will not come in here unless you ward off the blind and the lame', i.e. from your ranks, which are thus represented as blind and lame in face of the strong fortress. But the whole situation with the practically impregnable fortress suggests that the usual interpretation is the only natural one. The report in Chronicles supports this, as it continues along the lines suggested in II Sam. Should an original form of the text, later no longer understood, have had the sense attributed to it by Stoebe, it has been completely suppressed in favour of the present interpretation. (2) Stoebe renders v. 8: 'Whoever smites

[9] Otherwise we are given no details of the capture, not even of what David did with the inhabitants. It is, however, to be assumed that he spared them and allotted them a place to live; so the observation in I Chron. 11.8 could perhaps mean 'and Joab left the rest of the city alive' (see II. 24; Zech. 9.7). This would fit in with David's usual policy towards the Canaanites, whom he did not exterminate, but incorporated into his kingdom.[a] In any case, as 'the city of David', the captured city was not given to one of the tribes, but remained the property of the throne. David, of course, saw to the fortification of the city. The 'Millo' is a 'stopgap', and evidently lay on the long north side of the city hill, which was most open to possible attack because of its ease of access. Whether David himself erected this fort or built it up to a strategically usable part of the general fortifications is made doubtful first by the wording of the text ('from the Millo inward') and then by the fact that it was Solomon who was the first real constructor of the Millo (I Kings 9.15, 24; 11.27). Be this as it may, David was now master of an easily defensible capital which in addition—an exceptionally important point for him—lay right on the border between 'Judah' and 'Israel' and was extra-territorial to the land belonging to the tribes,[b] so that neither of the two partners in the kingdom could feel themselves at a disadvantage.

[10] The whole action shows the political acumen of this man who is rightly once again emphatically declared to be one 'with whom' the Lord is.

[11–12] The insertion of the fourth sub-section, a note about negotiations with Hiram king of Tyre, was certainly caused by the proximate mention of the king's building plan in Jerusalem. The Phoenicians, skilled in building and rulers of widely forested

---

the Jebusites must take the *ṣinnōr*', i.e. the 'mouthpiece of the spring' or something similar. This therefore means: only the one who possesses the *ṣinnōr* can really conquer the Jebusites. But in that case the sentence must originally have run: whoever captures the *ṣinnōr* can defeat the Jebusites (Hebrew: *kol-nōgēʿa baṣṣinnōr yakke* [*'et-hay*] *yᵉbūsī*). The mere occurrence of *kol* before *makkē* is very damaging for Stoebe's point of view. (3) Stoebe interprets the rest of v. 8: David cannot use the blind and the lame (in the sense suggested by him earlier), that is, in his own ranks. But here, too, the observations made against (1) are valid, so that the reference to a later development given in the Commentary above seems to me to be simpler. Even this way does not seem to have led (in my opinion) to a really effective solution.

[a]Stoebe, *loc. cit.*, has repeatedly brought out this point with special emphasis.

[b]On the complex of questions, see A. Alt's article 'Jerusalems Aufstieg' in *ZDMG* 79, 1925, pp. 1–19 (*Kleine Schriften* III, pp. 243–57).

Lebanon, well stocked in building materials, were important helpers in David's plans. At the same time it becomes clear that David now draws foreign attention upon himself. He finds respect and recognition. The first steps have been taken towards a significant state. The closing remark rightly and intentionally includes this growth in his power and status in the divine plans which the Lord has made 'for the sake of his people Israel' and has carried out up to this point.

6. DAVID'S SONS (SECOND LIST): 5.13–16

5 [13]And David took more concubines and wives from Jerusalem,[a] after he came from Hebron; and more sons and daughters were born to David. [14]And these are the names of those who were born to him in Jerusalem: Shammua, Shobab, Nathan, Solomon, [15]Ibhar, Elishua, Nepheg, Japhia, [16]Elishama, Eliada, and Eliphelet.

[13] The list is a direct continuation of the list in 3.2–5. It is striking that in it the concubines are put before the wives; LXX (Vatic.) therefore alters the order, surely intentionally, and Chronicles omits the concubines altogether. The opposite could, in fact, be the case, that originally only the concubines were mentioned (Wellhausen). On the other hand, Bathsheba, whose son Solomon is mentioned among the others, was surely one of the chief wives. We are therefore to assume that the first part of the sentence which records the taking of the concubines looks out beyond the time in Jerusalem; then the expression 'from Jerusalem' would apply only to the clause 'and wives', and the sons mentioned here, as in I Chron. 3.1ff., would all be sons of legitimate wives. The account in Chronicles would therefore be right in going on to refer to further sons born of concubines (3.9). Moreover, 'from Jerusalem' need not, as happens in I Chron. 14.3, be altered to 'in Jerusalem'; 'the marriages were arranged from the capital' (Caspari). [14–16] Daughters are mentioned, but their names are not given. The series of sons will be in order of their birth. So if we add the sons named in ch. 3, Solomon would stand only in tenth place, and we can understand how Adonijah regards himself, and not Solomon, as the prospective successor to David (I Kings 1). The sons named here do not occur after this; the penultimate son, Eliada, will, in fact, have been called Baaliada (I Chron. 14.7), so that David, like Saul, was easily able to give one of his sons a name compounded with Baal.

[a]See Commentary.

The list has been put here by the final compiler because it could be connected with the capture of Jerusalem. Moreover, the enumeration of his descendants once again shows David's blessing. In this respect, too, the king is great and powerful (cf. Ps. 127.5).

7. VICTORIES OVER THE PHILISTINES: 5.17–25

5 ¹⁷When the Philistines heard that David had been anointed king over Israel, all the Philistines went up in search of David; but David heard of it and went down to the stronghold. ¹⁸Now the Philistines had come and spread out in the valley of Rephaim. ¹⁹And David inquired of the LORD, 'Shall I go up against the Philistines? Wilt thou give them into my hand?' And the LORD said to David, 'Go up; for I will certainly give the Philistines into your hand.' ²⁰And David came to Baal-perazim, and David defeated them there; and he said, 'The LORD has broken through my enemies before me, like a bursting flood.' Therefore the name of that place is called Baal-perazim, that is, 'Lord of breaking through'. ²¹And the Philistines left their idols there, and David and his men carried them away.

22 And the Philistines came up yet again, and spread out in the valley of Rephaim. ²³And David inquired of the LORD and said, 'Shall I go up against the Philistines?' And he answered,ᵃ 'You shall not go up (against them);ᵇ go around to their rear, and come upon them opposite the balsam trees. ²⁴And when you hear the sound of marching in the tops of the balsam trees, then bestir yourself; for then the LORD has gone out before you to smite the army of the Philistines.' ²⁵And David did as the LORD commanded him, and smote the Philistines from Gibeonᶜ to Gezer.

In these important reports of a particularly significant military event, one regrets even more than usual the compressed brevity of the description. It is, however, instructive in two respects. We notice once again that the intention is not to retail political history. Even where the Philistines, the real rivals in the struggle for the land, are concerned, only the bare essentials are narrated. Secondly, we are given the impression that two episodes are here placed one after the other which belong together because of their content, but which need not therefore have been immediately consecutive in time. The reason for their position here is given in v. 17, and there will be something more to be said about this later. The victories, in fact, appear originally to have had some connection with the events of

ᵃA sentence seems to have fallen out here, as in v. 19. The eye of the copyist went straight from the first *wayyōmer* (or *lēmōr*) to the second.
ᵇSo the LXX interprets it.
ᶜSee BH.

ch. 8. The account of them may be an extract from the Davidic archives. 8.1 looks like the conclusion of the report of the Philistine war. The interpolation of chs. 6 and 7 would be a result of the formation of the Books of Samuel; more will be said about this later.

[17] The occasion of the Philistine invasion is the anointing of David to be king over all Israel. His anointing as king of Judah evidently did not arouse their suspicions, especially in view of the rival kingdom of Mahanaim and the hitherto friendly relations between the Philistines and David. The uniting of the realm under one supreme head is, however, a *casus belli*, as it was such as to endanger the fruits of previous Philistine policy. It is striking that the capture of Jerusalem, just narrated, is not given as the reason for their attack. The best explanation of this is that the first of the hostile encounters had already taken place; the way in which they are reported only later is a consequence of the original literary connection of the two accounts, which were left side by side by the compiler of the whole work. Perhaps a second reason was that the compiler identified the stronghold mentioned here with the stronghold which David occupies in 5.7 and which then becomes the 'city of David'. This, however, is impossible; one never goes 'down', always 'up', to Jerusalem. From where would David go down to Jerusalem?[a] The reference here will be rather to the mountain stronghold of Adullam, which (I. 22.4f.) had earlier served David as a base from which to operate; it is this in II. 23.13 and I Chron. 11.15f. Here the name Adullam may have been omitted because of the misunderstanding mentioned above. We are not told why David goes there at all; it could, however, be that when he hears of the Philistines' mobilization he first thinks of an enemy attack in the neighbourhood of Hebron, and means to use Adullam as a kind of outer fort. [18] The Philistines, however, go far to the north—even today the best-known approaches to the hills are by that area—and descend to the plain of Rephaim south-west of Jerusalem, evidently to destroy the connection between Israel and Judah as far as possible. The remark that the Philistines wanted to capture David (literally 'sought him') shows that in their eyes he is still the insignificant man from the wilderness of Judah. They are badly wrong!

[19–21] The oracle is to help the king to decide whether to remain on the defensive or to go over to the offensive. The decision clearly favours the latter course. The name Baal Perazim (Lord of the

[a]In v. 19, 'go up' is used in the sense of a hostile advance, cf. GB ʿ*ālā* 1d.

breaches) will certainly first have arisen as a result of the events described here; according to it, David must have 'broken through' the enemy lines. He himself compares the breakthrough to a phenomenon visible in hilly country during heavy rain: the water which pours down sweeps through and carries away any obstacles which may be in its path, banks of earth, hedges, walls, even a house built on the sand.[a] In view of his approach route, David must have come upon the Philistines from the south, and the battle is to be located here, in the neighbourhood of the present monastery of Elijah, between Jerusalem and Bethlehem.[b] The way in which the Philistines abandon their idols (LXX gods) shows the disorder attending their flight, and at the same time the superiority of the true God, who had promised victory beforehand and himself made the 'breakthrough'. According to I Chron. 14.12, David had the 'gods' burnt; in II Samuel they are innocently taken away as spoil.— This event is preceded by the story of the water from Bethlehem, narrated in 23.12–17, an episode which shows that the tradition of David's wars with the Philistines was richer than now appears (cf. 21.15–22).

[22–25] The second account at first sight looks like a repetition of the first, and this is still more evident if, as above, the omitted clause in v. 23 is replaced. The divine instructions, for which David again asks, run completely differently. This time David is to plan not a breakthrough, but a flanking movement. As Gibeon (MT and RSV Geba) is mentioned later, and it lies to the north of Jerusalem,[c] the battle took place to the north. The balsam-trees, from which the attack is made, are mastic terebinths, 'more like bushes than trees',[d] and are even now a characteristic feature of the hilly country. Those in question must have been a particularly prominent group of bushes. The 'steps' of the Lord, the sign for the attack, will have been seen in distinct, waving movements in the tops of the trees; the whole idea corresponds with that of tree oracles. The manoeuvre is successful, and the result is a great victory which David takes right down to the coastal plain.

[a]Luke 6.49. Here clearer than Matt. 7.27. The words 'breaching a dike' are best avoided, as they do not suit the kind of landscape.

[b]Cf. O. Procksch, 'Der Schauplatz der Geschichte Davids', *PJB* 5, 1909, p. 70.

[c]It cannot have been all that far away from the plain of Rephaim, the area of Philistine operations. The usual identification of Gibeon with *ed-jib* fits better than that with *el-bire* proposed by Alt; the latter is too far away.

[d]Dalman, *Arbeit und Sitte* I, pp. 541f.

We must ask whether David's second attack also took place from Adullam, i.e. from the south. This is improbable. After the first victory, which takes place before the gates of Jerusalem, David will have carried out the surprise attack on the town with his men. We can then understand why, as discussed before, the continuous literary passage about the two victories over the Philistines will have been placed at this particular part of the book and not have been brought in at ch. 8. The bringing up of the ark would then be the best sequel, in the historical order, too. And if David has meanwhile become master of Jerusalem, we can easily understand why the Philistines again advance into the plain of Rephaim. From Jerusalem, David could well carry out the flanking movement and pursue the enemy in a northerly direction.

The part played by the Lord in these important events is recounted on purpose. The conquest of the Philistines is described as his work. It represents the completion of a divine act which begins with the crossing of the Jordan—indeed, with the promise to Abraham—and will give the whole land to the people of God.

8. THE ARK COMES TO JERUSALEM: 6.1–23

6 [1]And David again[a] gathered[b] all the chosen men of Israel, thirty thousand, [2]and he arose and went to Baale-judah.[c] Then David went with all the people who were with him from Baale-judah, to bring up from there the ark of God, over which the name of the LORD is named —the name of the LORD of hosts who sits enthroned on the cherubim.[d] [3]And they carried the ark of God upon a new cart, and brought it out of the house of Abinadab which was on the hill; and Uzzah and

[a]The word has probably been inserted here; it is ambiguous, see Commentary.

[b]The form *wayyōsep* does not reveal textual corruption, but an orthographical deviation. Cf. also L. Koehler, *Lexicon in VT libros*, 1953, p. 71.

[c]The omission of the words *wayyēlek baʿalē yehūdā* assumed here—and still hinted at by the *Paseq*—may have been caused by the scribe's eye going on to the second *wayyēlek*.

[d]The twice-repeated *šēm* (name), and the present position of the *ʿālāw*, seem to show that originally only *šēm yahweh* stood here; the full, solemn nomenclature may then perhaps have been introduced later as a result of the special content of the narrative. Galling has pointed out that a special formula is used here—and also attested elsewhere, cf. on II. 12.28—in which 'the calling of the name accompanies the legal act of appropriation' (*TLZ* 81, 1956, col. 69). In that case, Galling says, we must presuppose here the transference of the cult symbol of 'a strange god (that of Shiloh?)' to Yahweh of Zion. But then we are brought to the point, as Galling himself sees, that in a very strange way the formula which derives from private law here evidently has been used only in a purely 'formal' way.

Ahio, the sons of Abinadab, were driving the new cart; [4]Uzzah went[a] alongside the ark of God, and Ahio went before the ark. [5]And David and all the house of Israel went dancing before the LORD with all their might and with much singing,[b] with lyres and harps and tambourines and castanets and cymbals.

6 And when they came to the threshing-floor of Nacon,[c] Uzzah put out his hand[a] to the ark of God and took hold of it, for the oxen stumbled. [7]And the anger of the LORD was kindled against Uzzah; and God smote him there because he put forth his hand to the ark;[d] and he died there beside the ark of God. [8]And David was angry because the LORD had broken forth upon Uzzah; and that place is called Perez-uzzah, that is, 'the breaking forth upon Uzzah', to this day. [9]And David was afraid of the LORD that day; and he said, 'How can the ark of God come to me?' [10]So David was not willing to take the ark of God into the city of David; but David took it aside to the house of Obed-edom the Gittite. [11]And the ark of the LORD remained in the house of Obed-edom the Gittite three months; and the LORD blessed Obed-edom and all his household.

12 And it was told King David, 'The LORD has blessed the household of Obed-edom and all that belongs to him, because of the ark of God.' So David went and brought up the ark of God from the house of Obed-edom to the city of David with rejoicing; [13]and when those who bore the ark of the LORD had gone six paces, he sacrificed an ox and a fatling. [14]And David danced before the LORD with all his might; and David was girded with a linen ephod. [15]So[e] David and all the house of Israel brought up the ark of the LORD with shouting, and with the sound of the horn.

16 As[a] the ark of the LORD came into the city of David, Michal the daughter of Saul looked out of the window, and saw King David leaping and dancing before the LORD; and she despised him in her heart. [17]And they brought in the ark of the LORD, and set it in its place, inside the tent which David had pitched for it; and David offered burnt-offerings and peace offerings before the LORD. [18]And when David had finished offering the burnt-offerings and the peace offerings, he blessed the people in the name of the LORD of hosts, [19]and distributed among all the people, the whole multitude of Israel, both men and women, to each a loaf of bread, a date-cake and a portion of raisins. Then all the people departed, each to his house.

20 And David returned to bless his household. But Michal the

[a]See BH.

[b]Probably 'singing with all his might'; cf. Kelari, *Musikinstrumente und ihre Verwendung im AT*, 1947, p. 84. The text follows I Chron. 13.8, similarly LXX (cf. BH). With its reading 'with cypress wood', the letters of which are extremely similar, MT imagined wooden instruments.

[c]An unknown proper name, which has been handed down in a number of different forms.

[d]So I Chron. 13.10 in place of an inexplicable word in MT.

[e]The participle in the original text.

daughter of Saul came out to meet David, and said, 'How the king of Israel honoured himself today, uncovering himself today before the eyes of his servants' maids, as one of the vulgar fellows always[a] uncovers himself!' [21]And David said to Michal, 'Praised be the LORD, who chose me above your father, and above all his house, to appoint me as prince over Israel, the people of the LORD!

> Before the LORD will I spring
> and I will dance before the LORD[b]
> [22]I will make myself yet more contemptible than this,
> and will be abased before myself[c]—
> and by the maids of whom you have spoken,[d]
> by them I shall be held in honour!'

23 And Michal the daughter of Saul had no child to the day of her death.

Two things must be noted if this passage is to be understood. In the first place, we have here what is unquestionably a continuation of the ark narratives of I. 4–6. In each case the ark is the theme; the lost ark again finds a new resting-place. Secondly, the account of the introduction of the ark to Jerusalem is in every respect closely connected with the theme of the chapters which surround it; it is there to show the establishment of the throne of David and the fact that he is really, by the grace of God, king of Israel. The text belonging to the 'ark source' has thus been taken out of its original context and placed in another. The chapter therefore affords a good way of seeing how the compiler worked. He knew and used literary complexes as sources, but he felt free to rearrange them so as to demonstrate not only the historical sequence of events but also their theological content. In addition, the Michal episode has been incorporated; this did not originally belong to the ark narrative, but perhaps stood at the beginning of the great complex of the succession work.[e]

[a]The infinitive absolute is extremely unusual after the infinitive construct; the sense is as above.

[b]The text is in disorder. LXX B has the words 'I will spring' and 'praised be the LORD', which are lacking in MT and could easily have fallen out by a mistake in copying. Perhaps the clause 'Praised be . . . Israel' was originally the beginning of David's speech, which then changed later into a rhythmic song; the word w^esihaqti ('and will dance'), which could only be translated in the future tense if it were preceded by an imperfect like '^{a}raqqēd, also suggests this.

[c]Literally 'in my eyes'. An emendation to 'in thy (fem.) eyes' (so already LXX, commentaries and RSV) is an impermissible simplification.

[d]$^uš$er was not spoken in the rhythm.

[e]So L. Rost, Überlieferung von der Thronnachfolge Davids.

[1] Right at the beginning we have an indication of the work done on the text and its rearrangement. The little word 'again' shows us that the present account is to be attached to the narratives of the Philistine war as a new undertaking by David and his host. In the context of the ark narratives, such an 'again' is not only unnecessary, but incorrect. For we are simply told there that when all was ready David went with a great procession to bring up the ark from Kiriath-jearim, where, as we supposed, the ark was kept under Philistine supervision. It is not clear whether in the original context the mission was hostile, or whether it was cultic, and therefore peaceable. The final compiler will, however, be right in connecting the bringing up of the ark with ch. 5: only after the victory over the Philistines will the possibility of bringing the ark and making it once again a national shrine have arisen. It could hardly have been done in the days of Saul. He never obtained the freedom from the Philistines that would have enabled him to take such a step. Moreover, his relationship with the old priesthood of the ark was completely destroyed. David, however, had with him Abiathar, survivor of the catastrophe of I. 22, and heir to the ark tradition. Hence there is nothing more understandable than that David should as soon as possible have set about a task which had been neglected for decades.

[2] So David goes out with his chosen men—the number is again, as often, exaggerated—to Kiriath-jearim, a place lying about seven miles west of Jerusalem, where, according to I. 7.1, the ark was placed in the house of Abinadab 'on the hill'—perhaps the holy place. The place has different names, and as well as being called Kiriath-baal and Baalah (I Chron. 13.6), it is here called Baale-judah. Its very name ('Baal'!) thus has a holy character. The form in which the ark is mentioned shows that this text was also used on solemn occasions; we have here the *hieros logos* of the shrine of the ark at Jerusalem.[a]

[3] According to I. 7.1, Eleazar, the son of Abinadab, was the keeper of the ark. Here Uzzah and Ahio appear in his place. The identification of Uzzah and Eleazar is not a linguistic impossibility, but is, in fact, highly improbable, as the events of I. 7.1 take place even before the reign of Saul. In that case, Eleazar/Uzzah would have to be imagined as an exceedingly old man. 'Son of Abinadab' is better understood in the wider sense = 'grandson'. Wellhausen has

[a]Rost, *op. cit.*, p. 38.

conjectured *'āḥīw*, 'his brother', for the rather remarkable name Ahio. Budde[a] takes this up and adds that originally the proper name Zadok stood alongside the word. He was thus the second, surviving guardian of the ark, and came to the court as such. The name was only omitted here because for obvious reasons (II. 8.17) Zadok found his way into the Aaronite genealogy. This conjecture is to be considered carefully, and would explain how this new man came to the fore and gradually pushed Abiathar aside as chief priest.[b]

[4–8] The ark is brought from Kiriath-jearim under the direction of the brothers. The procession, including David, goes before them in cultic dance, with singing and playing.[c] A serious mishap now occurs, the cause of which is obscure; perhaps the oxen stumble on a steep ledge, 'the threshing-floor'. In any case, the cart and the ark threaten to overturn, so Uzzah leaps quickly at them, evidently disregarding the usual precautions taken when serving the ark. This is regarded as the reason why he falls down dead, smitten by the 'blow of Yahweh'. The place, the threshing-floor of a Nacon who is otherwise unknown to us, is given an appropriate name, and would certainly often have been pointed out with tacit horror.

[9–11] The consequence is that David, filled with angry fear, abandons his plans and has the ark left at a neighbouring farm. The owner of the farm, Obed-edom ('servant of Edom') by name, originally the worshipper of a strange god and further described as a Philistine, will hardly have accepted the ark of his own free will. We are not to assume that being a foreigner he will have had an enlightened point of view.

[12–15] His house now happens to be particularly 'blessed'; we are perhaps to imagine fertility in his family, his cattle and his fields as well as other pieces of good fortune. The neighbours, and David, regard this as a sign that the anger of the Lord has changed to favour. The earlier decision of the king is therefore implemented once again. After the first six steps have been taken—the passage does not, of course, mean 'after each sixth step'—a solemn sacrifice is offered and the procession goes forward. The king plays a

---

[a] *ZAW* 52, 1934, pp. 48f.

[b] Cf. also on 8.17, where there is another theory about Zadok's origin.

[c] On the attempt to find in II. 6 a Canaanite New Year ritual which David is here said to have introduced into the Israelite cultus, see J. R. Porter in *JTS* 5, 1954, pp. 161–73. Further details are sought from references to Ps. 132. In view of David's policy of the peaceful assimilation of the Canaanites (and with them the Jebusites), such a possibility is not to be excluded.

particularly active part. For it he wears the priestly garment, the linen ephod, a short article of clothing which probably covered body and loins.[a] David had put aside the long upper garment; in I Chron. 15.27 the opposite is imagined, that he wore the long outer robe. This was surely not the case in the cultic dance, especially as Michal's feelings are only comprehensible if the tradition knew that David really uncovered himself. For the dancing, there is a word here which is connected with *kikkār* (circle), and represents a rotating movement. Later, another two words are used, which represent quick hopping and springing (v. 16 and cf. on v. 21).[b] It is important that David here exercises priestly functions, just as it is also reported that he blesses the people.

[16–19] The note about the queen looking out of the window already prepares for the end of the chapter. First of all, however, the ark narrative is concluded. There is a tent for the ark, certainly pitched for the occasion, and not to be identified with the wilderness sanctuary ('the tabernacle').[c] An altar, too, must already have been prepared. Peace offerings are made in addition to the burnt-offerings; it is doubtful whether the community was thus given any opportunity of personal participation by the distributions of portions of the sacrifice; in any case, we are not to assume that the word *'ešpār*, which occurs only here, has anything to do with flesh. The ark narrative closes with a description of the general festivities. The fact that the ark has now found a resting-place in Jerusalem is extremely significant. Jerusalem, already the focal point of political life, is now also the centre of worship.

[20–23] Woven into the ark history, or directly attached to it, is the Michal episode. Michal makes her criticism of David's conduct clear with her taunting words. She, the king's daughter, evidently has a feeling for what is seemly, and expresses it, not to shame David, but because she is concerned for the royal dignity. Her attitude should

[a]Cf. Dalman, *Arbeit und Sitte* V, pp. 231f. The linen ephod may have been very similar to the high-priestly ephod, which is of better material (Ex. 28.4–12) and serves to clothe the loins and also the chest and shoulders.

[b]I recollect that the cultic dance I once watched in the chief Ashkenazi synagogue in the Old City of Jerusalem on the feast of the Joy of the Law was of this kind, a combination of rotating and skipping movements.

[c]No other exegesis of the text in its present form is possible (against Kraus, *Gottesdienst in Israel*, 1954, pp. 70f.). The tabernacle tradition will only have come to the Jerusalem sanctuary when the temple was there. Hitherto, the relevant traditions were preserved at the great high place of Gibeon; cf. on II. 21.1ff., and I Kings 3.4ff., also *ZAW* 47, 1929, pp. 167–76, esp. p. 168.

certainly not be described as 'Michal's pride' (Schulz, etc.). Still less does she inveigh against David's participation in the cult of Yahweh at all. It is at this point, however, that David begins to refute her. His answer, beginning with a sentence in prose, changes into a rhythmical form (see above). We may not exclude the possibility that the words 'Before the Lord will I spring and I will dance before the Lord' represent a verse of the kind which was usual in such processional dances. David's answer follows the maxim 'whoever humbles himself shall be exalted'. David knows that he has been appointed ruler by the Lord; here the word *nāgīd*, stressing the vocational side of kingship, occurs once again. Therefore the Lord is to be praised, and David purposely serves the Lord, who is the only great one, precisely by making himself contemptible—conduct to which Michal objects. Two things will claim the reader's assent; that David describes himself as having been chosen 'above Saul', a remark which must hit Saul's daughter very hard, and that he says —taking up her own words—that the maids who are thought to be mocking him on the contrary have more feeling of true reverence than Michal herself: they know that reverence is to become lowly before God. All this is said in complete accord with the view of the final compiler, who sees here, too, the family of Saul rejected in favour of David. This, of course, becomes clearest in the closing sentence. It is hardly meant to imply that David avoided her from then on as a punishment. Her childlessness means rather that the Lord himself takes up the gauntlet that she has thrown down. To alter the saying in I. 8.7 slightly, Michal has rejected not David, but Yahweh. So there is none of the blood of the house of Saul on the throne of Israel. That is meant to be demonstrated here.

Now it is just this feature which shows the purpose of the chapter in its present form. The king, ready to serve the Lord without thinking of what others may say, humble, yet powerful, learns and prospers: Jerusalem becomes not just David's city and the political focal point of the united realm, but the Holy City, which will therefore be a true place of encounter between God and man through the centuries, right until the New Covenant.

9. HOUSE OF GOD AND HOUSE OF DAVID: 7.1–29

7 ¹Now when the king dwelt in his house, and the LORD had given him rest from all his enemies round about, ²the king said to Nathan the prophet, 'See now, I dwell in a house of cedar, but the ark of God

dwells in a tent.' ³And Nathan said to the king, 'Go, do all that is in your heart; for the LORD is with you.'

4 But that same night the word of the LORD came to Nathan, ⁵'Go and tell my servant David, "Thus says the LORD: Would you build me a house to dwell in? ⁶I have not dwelt in a house since the day I brought up the people of Israel from Egypt to this day, but I have been moving about in a tent for my dwelling. ⁷In all places where I have moved with all the people of Israel, did I speak a word with any of the judgesª of Israel, whom I commanded to shepherd my people Israel, saying, 'Why have you not built me a house of cedar?' "⁸ Now therefore thus you shall say to my servant David, "Thus says the LORD of hosts, I took you from the pasture, from following the sheep, that you should be prince over my people Israel; ⁹and I have been with you wherever you went, and have cut off all your enemies from before you; and (thus) I am makingᵇ a great name for you, like the name of the great ones of the earth. ¹⁰And I appoint a place for my people Israel, and plant them, that they may dwell in their own place, and be disturbed no more and that violent men afflict them no more. And as formerly, ¹¹that isᶜ from the time that I appointed judges over my people Israel, I give you rest from all your enemies. Moreover the LORD declares to you that the LORD will make you a house. ¹²Nowª when your days are fulfilled and you lie down with your fathers, I will raise up your son after you, who shall come forth from your body, and I will establish his kingdom. ¹³He shall build a house for my name, and I will establish the throne of his kingdom for ever. ¹⁴I will be his father, and he shall be my son. When he commits iniquity, I will chasten him with the rod of men, with the stripes of the sons of men; ¹⁵but my steadfast love will not depart from him, as I made it depart from Saul, whom I made to depart from you.ᵈ ¹⁶And your house and your kingdom shall stand before meᵉ for ever; your throne shall be established for ever." '
¹⁷In accordance with all these words, and in accordance with all this vision, Nathan spoke to David.

18 Then King David went in and sat before the LORD, and said, 'Who am I, O Lord GOD, and what is my house, that thou hast brought me thus far? ¹⁹And yet this was a small thing in thine eyes, O Lord GOD; thou hast spoken also of thy servant's house for a great while to come, and hast let one man see this,ᶠ O Lord GOD! ²⁰And what more

ªSee BH.

ᵇOn the perfects with *waw* see Commentary.

ᶜ This is a possible translation of the *waw*—deleted by LXX and most exegetes; cf. GB s.v. *waw*, d.

ᵈUsually the text is given a more pleasing form, after Chron. (see BH), but MT is perfectly tenable.

ᵉSee BH. Rost, p. 58 would read 'before him' and take the verse with v. 11b.

ᶠText obscure. MT 'and that as law (wise?) for men' hardly makes sense. One conjecture is *hir'ītā 'ādām*, where the *h* before *'ādām* would have to be put at the end of *hir'ītā*. The verb *rā'ā* (see) also occurs at I Chron. 17.17, where, however, the original meaning seems to have been 'Thou has regarded me after the manner of men' (cf. Bewer, *Bertholet-Festschrift*, pp. 74f.); there, too, the text is not intact.

can David say to thee? For thou knowest thy servant, O Lord GOD! [21]Because of thy promise,[a] and according to thy own heart thou hast wrought, to make thy servant know all these great things.[b] [22]Therefore thou art great, O Lord GOD; for there is none like thee, and there is no God besides thee, according to all that we have heard with our ears. [23]And who is like thy people, like Israel, (is there) a single nation on earth, whom God went to redeem to be his people, making him[c] a name, and doing for them[d] great and terrible things? For thou didst drive[e] before thy people whom thou didst redeem for thyself from Egypt, nations and gods.[f] [24]And thou didst establish for thyself thy people Israel to be thy people for ever; and thou, O LORD, didst become their God. [25]And now, O LORD God, confirm for ever the promises which thou hast spoken concerning thy servant and concerning his house, and do as thou hast spoken; [26]and thy name will be magnified for ever, saying, "The LORD of hosts is God over Israel", and the house of thy servant David will be established before thee. [27]For thou, O LORD of hosts, the God of Israel, hast made this revelation to thy servant, saying, "I will build you a house"; therefore thy servant has found courage to pray this prayer to thee. [28]And now, O Lord GOD, thou art God, and thy words are true, and thou hast promised this good thing to thy servant; [29]now therefore may it please thee to bless the house of thy servant, that it may continue for ever before thee; for thou, O Lord GOD, hast spoken, and with thy blessing shall the house of thy servant be blessed for ever.'

L. Rost[g] has discussed this chapter in detail, and M. Noth[h] has agreed with his views. We may take Rost's view as basically correct without following him in every detail. Here the king, who wants to build a house for the Lord, is told that the Lord will 'build' him 'a house'. Both the intent and the promise, and the form in which they are presented, completely fit the historical situation of the period. It is quite understandable that this important material should have occupied later generations, and that this interest should have found literary expression in later rewriting of the chapter.

[a]Chron.: 'servant'; 'servant' is therefore missing in Chron. at the end of the verse.

[b]On word order see BH. In MT ('thou hast done all these great things to make thy servant know') there is no object. In Chron. the word 'great things' occurs twice.

[c]One could also translate 'himself'; there is a 'thee' in Chron. An understandable interpretation!

[d]MT *lākem ha* . . .; the *ha* is a marginal correction for the wrong *k*. See BH.

[e]Chron. read *l^egārēš*, LXX *l^egāreškā*. MT 'for thy land' is a miswriting of the latter.

[f]See BH.

[g]*Thronnachfolge*, pp. 47–74.

[h]*Überlieferungsgeschichtliche Studien* I, pp. 64f.

Chapter 7 has a unique place among the complexes which are the basic sources for the period in question: the history of the ark, the texts about David's reign, and the succession story. In its present form, it has to do with all these. [1] It is introduced by being attached to the entry of the ark, so as to make its position comprehensible. David is presumed to have reached the point in his reign when all his building plans are completed (ch. 5). The further statement, that 'the Lord had given him rest from all his enemies round about', really only makes sense after ch. 8 or ch. 12; Chronicles therefore carefully omits it (I Chron. 17.1). Its presence here is meant to show that the king's plan to build the temple, and above all the promise evoked as a result, is the conclusion and crown of the whole. Chapter 7 is the climax of the whole Davidic tradition. At the same time it introduces the account of the succession, which contains evidence of many sins and failings. The prefixing of this account of the promise of a lasting dynasty implies that despite everything God still means to build up the house of David. The final compiler has thus placed the chapter at a stage when the history of the ark has come to an end, the secular buildings have been completed, the disputes over the throne have not yet begun, and the king has at least been 'given rest' from the Philistines. Chapter 7 has been given its present position on purpose. The phrase 'given rest' is moreover theologically significant; it is the sign for the special intervention of Yahweh and at the same time—as in Gen. 2.1ff.—the goal of still harder work and the conclusion of the way of blessing (cf. on v. 11).

[2–3] The considerations which lead David to think of building a temple are laudable, and worthy of a godly king. A house of cedar is the supreme example of a well-constructed and distinguished building; tents, on the other hand, are a feature of the lodging of nomads, the lowest members in the social structure, a lodging which is easily destructible and can be broken up at any moment. What an insult to the Lord and to his ark, to have to endure this manifest indignity! No wonder that the prophet Nathan immediately agrees. His name is mentioned here for the first time. As prophetic counsellor of the king he is one of the most important figures at court.

[4–7] The king's plan is now thwarted, however, by a new revelation.[a] The Lord has as yet neither had nor shown the desire to be

---

[a]V. 4 looks like a second beginning. Rost's assumption (pp. 68f.) that a report of the revelation of Yahweh to Nathan took the place of an earlier one given directly to David cannot be proved.

lodged with the ark in a fixed house, and wills even now to remain true to the mode of revelation which has been customary hitherto. It seems remarkable here that the Lord claims that not since the Exodus from Egypt, i.e. never, has he dwelt in a house, when there were well-built houses at the least in Shiloh, and even later, to hold the ark. As the compiler, of course, realized this, the only real way of interpreting the sentence is to make a distinction here between *yāšab*, dwell permanently, abide, and *šākan*, make a temporary stay. The tent-dwelling in the wilderness is here (and often) called *miškān*, dwelling in the latter sense, and even the stay at Shiloh appears to be regarded merely as an episode in a series of temporary stopping-places. Here we have an expression of the original and theologically legitimate view that the Lord is not bound to one place, but can make his dwelling anywhere. This, in the basic monotheistic conception, is what befits him. We could find in this passage the background to much of the prophetic polemic against the temple liturgy, just as in the New Testament also the worship of God in temples is regarded as a stage to be superseded (John 4.21; Acts 7.48f.; 17.24). The preservation of this trend of thought, despite the later construction of the temple, speaks for its age. In particular, in true prophetic fashion, the adornment of the future temple by cedar-wood is rejected.

[8–11a] Now we come to the real point, the promise that the Lord will make a house for the king. It is understandably supported by a recollection of the previous guidance given by the Lord to David. His call from the lowliness of a shepherd to the high position of king is brought to mind; the word *nāgīd*, prince, is again used to express his nomination by Yahweh, and, in addition, the statement that the Lord has been 'with David', so important in the history of David, is now given an emphatic position, as in v. 3. In the assertions which now follow, it is grammatically uncertain whether the tenses are past or future. According to normal rules we would have here the consecutive perfect, and the statements would be future. This, however, raises difficulties. Such clauses are usually preceded by an imperfect or an imperative, and that is not the case here. Moreover, the things mentioned here—the making of a great name, a sure dwelling for the people and the sought-after 'rest'—have already been achieved in fact, as we have been told at the beginning of the chapter. The statements will therefore refer to the past.[a] Perhaps they have been intentionally left ambivalent because it is expected

[a] And therefore not as in RSV. See Rost, pp. 59f.

that what the Lord has done hitherto will remain effective afterwards. (Thus the present tense (as above) is possibly the best way of representing these special forms.)

Verse 11 raises two further exegetical problems. The clause at the beginning 'since I appointed judges over my people' is usually taken with the 'as formerly' at the end of v. 10 in such a way that both refer to the time of oppression by the 'violent men', just mentioned. Both are thus supposed to refer to the afflictions during the time of the judges. To characterize this distress, however, it would hardly be necessary to mention the means by which it was overcome, namely the calling of the judges! It is therefore appropriate to refer the close of v. 10 and the beginning of v. 11 to the deliverance, especially as the concept of 'rest'—though expressed by a different term—is similarly used for the time of the judges (3.11, 30; 5.31; 8.28; but cf. Josh. 1.13, 15; 22.4). [11b–12, 14–17] It is further surprising that in the middle there is a passage in which Yahweh is *spoken of* in the third person, whereas he has previously been *speaking* in the first. The small sentence looks like a stereotyped formula which was handed down and has now been left, as it were, in quotation marks as being the most important part, which gives the main contents:[a] the Lord will make a house for David, i.e. will make him the founder of a dynasty. Immediately afterwards this is explained in more detail, so that the verses up to v. 16 look like a commentary on a previous textual passage. Here—apart from v. 13—the mention of successors is quite general. The further promise of personal protection describes the divine grace which will be the peculiar characteristic of the 'eternal' dynasty of David. The sins of the future king will be taken seriously and punished accordingly, but God will always be the father who chastises his son. These are strains which do not as yet point beyond the historical plane. It is quite simply the favoured dynasty which is principally put before the eyes of the reader. In the post-exilic view of the Chronicler, from a time when there was no king, the line is carefully, but still clearly, extended into the Messianic sphere.[b] This interpretation is not arbitrary, but legitimate. It is already suggested in II. 7 by the constant emphasis on the 'for ever'. With reference to this text, A. Alt has rightly spoken of the 'historical root of the expectation of the Messiah, as simple as

[a]Rost, pp. 58f., supposes that the oldest basis of Nathan's prophecy is to be found here and in v. 16.

[b]I Chron. 17, cf. von Rad, *Das Geschichtsbild des chronistischen Werkes*, pp. 123ff.

it was suggestive'.[a] This is true not only in history and literature, but also in theology: instead of man building a house for God, the Lord declares himself ready to make a house in the midst of the people of God, consisting in a definite succession of men to bear his authority.[b] 'Fulfilment' comes when the Word of the Son of David, who is the 'Son of God', makes his dwelling and 'tabernacles' among us (John 1.14).

[13] The intermediate v. 13 is of a different character. It has a plausible connection with v. 12, which could be interpreted as referring to David's immediate successor, but has an originally general character. Now follows the announcement of the building of the temple by David's son and heir, i.e. Solomon. This, however, represents a transformation of the real meaning of the chapter, that the Lord does not wish to have a fixed house, but will himself build a dependable house in another sense, so that it becomes 'it is not David who is to build the house but his son and successor'. A reason for this is given in I Chron. 22.7–10, where II Sam. 7.14 is expressly cited. According to the Chronicler, it is not David, the man of so many wars, who is to build the temple with blood-stained hands, but he in whose name *šelōmō* the word *šālōm*, 'peace', is to be detected. We can see how this question occupied later generations and may recognize v. 13 as a first stage of a later development, visible only here in ch. 7. Even David's prayer does not refer to it.

[18–29] This prayer is truly 'royal, worthy of a David'.[c] It is evidently made in the tent of the ark. There the king sits or lies down on the ground.[d] The content of his prayer is a thankful acceptance of the divine promise. It begins, as does Nathan's promise, with a recollection of the guidance which David has already received from the Lord. Then comes the promise for 'a great while to come'. If the conjecture advanced above is correct, the king is particularly thankful that the Lord has allowed him, a man, to look into the otherwise hidden secrets of the future. This unwonted demonstration of grace is connected, as the prayer explains, with the 'word' of the promise which came to him earlier (e.g. 3.9f., 18), now comes again (vv. 3, 9), and is a sign of God's feelings towards him ('according to thine own heart'). The three verses represent a digression which

[a] *Kleine Schriften* II, pp. 63f.
[b] Cf. Vischer, *Christuszeugnis* II, pp. 258–62.
[c] Root, *op. cit.*, p. 55.
[d] Cf. Heiler, *Das Gebet*[3], p. 100. ET (abridged), 1932, pp. 41f.

speaks of the long-proved relationship between the Lord and Israel. They need not necessarily be an insertion.[a] Personal prayers are enlarged to take in the people and the community in some of the Psalms (22; 130, etc.); the people are also mentioned expressly in Nathan's prophecy. The promise that the house of David will be 'for ever' corresponds to the choice of Israel to be the people of God 'for ever': both together will magnify the holy name of God 'for ever'. The house of David and the people of God are thus bound together eternally by the promise of Nathan. This certainly has aspects which apply to the history of the time, but also once again clearly opens up perspectives which extend far beyond the history of Israel. The prayer appropriately closes with the request that the Lord will make what he has promised true 'for ever'.

With this echo of the great promise the chapter comes to an end. The central significance of the time and also the person of David is made quite clear, and it is further underlined by the contrast between him and Saul. But it is none the less clear where the focal point of the era of David lies. The man 'with whom' God is is king by the grace of God in the full meaning of the phrase.

10. DAVID'S EMPIRE: 8.1–14

8 [1]After this David defeated the Philistines and subdued them, and David took the leading reins[b] out of the hand of the Philistines.

2 And he defeated Moab, and measured them with a line, making them lie down on the ground; two lines he measured to be put to death, and one full line to be spared. So Moab fell to David; (they became his) servants (and) brought tribute.

3 David also defeated Hadadezer the son of Rehob,[c] king of Zobah, as he went to restore his power at the river Euphrates. [4]And David took from him a thousand and seven hundred horsemen, and twenty thousand foot soldiers; and David hamstrung all the chariot horses, but left enough for a hundred chariots. [5]And when Aram-Damascus came to help Hadadezer king of Zobah, David slew twenty-two

[a]So Rost, pp. 49, 53f., who holds that the verse has a deuteronomistic stamp and was composed in the exile. The character of the prayer, however, allows such deviations.

[b]'Reins of the forearm', a picture which is now obscure to us. Does the original significance of *'ammā* = 'forearm', around which the reins were wound, play a part here? In that case *hā'ammā* would have to be interpreted as a subjective genitive. O. Eissfeldt, *ZDPV* 66, 1943, p. 118, considers the 'extraordinary size of the reins' (?). Chron. and LXX no longer understood the text.

[c]The words 'son of Rehob' are missing in I Chron. 18.3, presumably because Rehob occurs as a place name in II. 10.6.

thousand men in Aram. 6Then David put prefects in Aram-Damascus. So Aram fell to David; (they became his) servants (and) brought tribute. And the LORD gave victory to David wherever he went. 7And David took the shields of gold which were carried by the servants of Hadadezer, and brought them to Jerusalem. 8And from Tebaha and from Berothai, cities of Hadadezer, King David took very much bronze.

9 When Toib king of Hamath heard that David had defeated the whole army of Hadadezer, 10Toi sent his son Hadoramc to King David, to greet him, and to congratulate him because he had fought against Hadadezer and defeated him; for Hadadezer had often been at war with Toi. And he brought with him articles of silver, of gold, and of bronze; 11these also King David dedicated to the LORD, together with the silver and gold which he had dedicated from all the nations he subdued, 12from Aram,d Moab, the Ammonites, the Philistines, Amalek, and from the spoil of Hadadezer the son of Rehob, king of Zobah.

13 And David won a name for himself. When he returned, after he had smitten Aram, he smote Edoma in the Valley of Salt—eighteen thousand men. 14And he put prefects in Edom,e so that all the Edomites became David's servants. And the LORD gave victory to David wherever he went.

This chapter is of great value to the historian, as it gives us an impression of the growth and extent of David's kingdom. David's kingdom was not only the first but also the greatest state to arise on the soil of Palestine. And while that was only possible because at the time, in the tenth century, there were no great states of any considerable power either in Asia Minor and Mesopotamia or in Egypt, nevertheless the chief cause lies in the person of King David, who was exceptionally skilful both at politics and in war. Behind what is catalogued here in such a matter-of-fact way lies the supreme achievement of a man of whom it is twice intentionally said 'The Lord helped him'. Evidently his contemporaries and their successors regarded these deeds as a miracle.

The passage possibly belongs to the collection of texts which

aSee BH.
bThis is the name which has been transmitted here. But Tou, attested by MSS and Chron., is more correct.
cProperly Hadadram. MT reads Joram; 'the divine name Hadad was simply paraphrased with an Israelite one' (Budde *ad loc.*).
d'Aram' is usually emended into the similar 'Edom'; see BH. But Edom is only mentioned in what comes later. 'Aram' will rather be a reference to vv. 5f.
eAt this point there follows the sentence, 'throughout all Edom he put prefects', presumably some indication of the content of the passage originally in the margin.

narrate the rise of David, and could even be its conclusion. In any case, it is not to be included in the complex describing the succession to the throne of David, which begins with ch. 9. Noth's suggestion[a] that ch. 8 is to be regarded as a deuteronomistic compilation of David's wars does not commend itself. The fact that events in ch. 8 are reported again in ch. 10 in a different way suggests rather that we have a special ancient source in ch. 8. R. Kittel calls ch. 8 'a purely annalistic arrangement of the acts of David, perhaps a passage from his royal annals'.[b] So Alt's[c] conjecture that the chapter is to be regarded as having originally been connected with 5.17–25 has much to commend it (see also above, pp. 272ff.).

[1] The hand of the final compiler can be detected at the beginning. 'After this' is meant to refer straight back to ch. 7. According to this, David's train of victories should follow directly upon the bringing up of the ark and Nathan's promise: only the David to whom God's aid was promised right into the distant future could build up the kingdom. This introduction therefore has a theological significance. On the other hand, we have already heard in ch. 5 of two victories over the Philistines, and they may have been sufficient to assure the success described in v. 1.[d] The beginning of ch. 8 should therefore properly read, 'David, then, had defeated the Philistines . . .'

David's victory over the Philistines was the first in a series of wars, and led the way to all the others. It is therefore correct that the mention of the overthrow of the Philistines should be followed by a note that the reins were taken out of their hand. The literal meaning of the phrase is not altogether clear (see above), but the general sense is clear enough. Up to this point, the Philistines were in the saddle in Palestine; from now on it is Israel, i.e. David. The situation never changed again in favour of the Philistines.

[2] The Moabites are next mentioned. David himself has friendly relations with them, even connections by marriage (I. 22.3). The treatment of the Moabites described here, however, takes little regard of this. What we have here is not a means of measuring the land (Caspari), but a gruesome exercise of the rights of war, according to which two out of every three men must be put to death. There

---

[a] *Überlieferungsgeschichtliche Studien* I, p. 65.
[b] Kautsch[4], p. 462.
[c] *ZAW* 54, 1936, pp. 149–52.
[d] Cf. Alt, *op. cit.*, p. 150.

will have been a serious occasion for such a course, unknown to us; the king may have been more offended at the misconduct of friends and kinsmen than at that of others. There could be a hint of some extenuation when it is said that one 'full' line is taken of those to be spared. So at least mercy is given more generously than punishment.

[3–8] Zobah, whose king Hadadezer is mentioned several times, is a region north of Damascus, to the east of the Antilebanon.[a] Here, too, the reason for the war is not given; we learn more about it, however, in ch. 10. In ch. 8 it seems that David chose a moment to attack when Hadadezer was occupied in the direction of the Euphrates; this is what is meant by 'river' in the MT, as is clear from the *qere* to v. 3 (cf. also the LXX) and I Chron. 18.3. The Aramaean was not equal to war on two fronts, so that David was able to achieve a considerable victory. Even if this success did not have a lasting influence on the north Aramaean kingdom, David, by conquering this not insignificant enemy, pushed back the boundaries of his sphere of influence to the Euphrates, so that his kingdom reached 'from the Euphrates . . . to the border of Egypt'.[b] The victory over the Aramaeans of Damascus confederate with Hadadezer is connected with this. This kingdom, which lay much closer to Israel, was, like that of Moab, conquered and made subject to tribute. In this way David brought a great complex of states to the north under his jurisdiction. At this very point which describes the greatest extension of the Israelite kingdom yet to have taken place, express remembrance is therefore made of the 'help' of the Lord; the expression is again that used for 'deliverance' in the time of the judges, etc., and therefore has particular theological weight. Nothing is said about David's treatment of the prisoners. Unlike his son and successor, he was unable to make any use of the captured horses. The precious metal and the bronze taken was more important plunder for him and it would certainly have formed a basic supply for the later building of the temple. The exploitation here will have lasted for some time; it was all the more important because Palestine itself had no mineral resources of this kind. We have no knowledge of the towns mentioned here, but they will certainly be in the Coele-Syrian plain. There is no connection between Berothai and Beirut.

[9–12] A direct consequence of the victory is the approach of the

[a]Cf. Noth, *ZDPV* 68, 1949, p. 26.
[b]I Kings 4.21; on the whole matter see A. Alt, *TLZ* 75, 1950, cols. 213–20; *Kleine Schriften* II, pp. 66–75.

king of Hamath (the present Hama, lying about 120 miles to the
north of Damascus). He seeks to win the friendship of David, now
grown so powerful, with tributary gifts. In fact this king (Toi or
Tou, see above) will have wished to anticipate any hostile moves on
the part of David. The compiler makes the acceptance of this
treasure an opportunity of enumerating the peoples from whom
came the spoils which David brought to Jerusalem and dedicated.
In addition to those already mentioned, we find the Ammonites,
who are first mentioned in chs. 10–12, and the Amalekites, the
enemies in the south. David had hostile encounters with them
earlier (I. 27 and 30); no later contacts are recorded. [13–14] The
summary list makes it clear that David has extended his kingdom in
all directions and has made a 'name' for himself.

The verse and a half about Edom look like an addition, but belong
here. The name 'Valley of Salt' is used even today for the land east
of Beersheba; we would, however, expect somewhere lying farther
east, in the Edomite territory proper. Here, too, as in Aram-
Damascus, garrisons are installed. This shows the degree of subjec-
tion. According to I Kings 11.15–17 Edom was treated still more
gruesomely than Moab. No reasons are given here. The possession
of Edom became important at a later date, as it afforded the Davidic
state an approach to the Red Sea.

In this way David set a bulwark of subject peoples round his own
land. It is no wonder that we are once again told at this point that
the Lord stood at the side of the king with 'saving' power.[a]

11. THE LEADING MEN AT THE COURT OF DAVID (FIRST LIST): 8.15–18

8 [15]So David reigned over all Israel, and David administered justice
and equity to all his people. [16]And Joab the son of Zeruiah was over the
army; and Jehoshaphat the son of Ahilud was recorder; [17]and Zadok
and Abiathar the son of Ahimelech son of Ahitub[b] were priests; and
Seraiah was secretary; [18]and Benaiah the son of Jehoiada was over[c]
the Cherethites and the Pelethites; and David's sons were priests.

[15] The list preserved here affords us a small but nevertheless
significant glimpse into the internal organization of the Davidic
state, whose external growth has just been described. It begins by

---

[a]On the chapter as a whole see the conclusion of the next section.
[b]See Commentary.
[c]See BH.

reporting that David reigned over all Israel, an observation which would fit better at the point when the union of the northern and the southern kingdoms had been effected; there is a similar remark in 5.5. It is said of David that he 'administered justice and equity', a testimony which was always of particular importance to the prophets. Moreover—and this is the significance of the sentence in this context—we are thus told that David himself took over the supreme office of judge. Absalom later criticized the alleged neglect of this duty by his father (15.2–4), and this was evidently one of the contributory factors to his rebellion. The office of judge had a long tradition in Israel; its 'existence . . . indicates the absolutely essential significance of the sphere of law in ancient Israel and is certainly connected with the fact that it was the special character of Israel that it was placed under the dominion of a divine law'.[a] It is therefore extremely significant that the king himself here holds the office. [16, 18a] According to this list, the military command is shared between Joab, who leads the all-Israelite host, and Benaiah, the leader of the foreign mercenaries. These last bear the name Cherethites and Pelethites. This obvious word-play is chiefly connected with the Philistines; 'Cherethites' recalls the island of Crete, which plays a part in Philistine origins (cf. on I Sam. 30.14), and 'Pelethites' can only mean Philistines—it will have been assimilated to 'Cherethites'.[b] The Cherethites and Pelethites are therefore a sort of foreign legion, but with special responsibility for the person of the king. The recorder (*mazkīr*) is the most important figure in domestic politics at the court; he is the spokesman who has to keep the king continually informed and to transmit his decisions.[c] [17] The secretary was responsible for the execution of written matters, including diplomatic correspondence. The duties of the priests are harder to define. Zadok, the *homo novus*, and Abiathar, David's companion in adversity and descendant of the Aaronic priesthood at Shiloh, stood, as we know from elsewhere, side by side; apparently the former was responsible for serving the ark. We learn nothing elsewhere about Zadok's origin (cf. on 6.3); this passage could explain the reason why. For here the text calls Zadok the son of

---

[a]M. Noth, 'Das Amt des Richters Israels', *Bertholet Festschrift*, p. 414; cf. also Hertzberg, 'Die Kleinen Richter', *TLZ* 79, 1954, cols. 285–90.

[b]Hebrew *kᵉrētī* and *pᵉlētī*. Tr.

[c]H. Graf Reventlow speaks of an 'amphictyonic office' which was originally responsible for obedience to the ordinances of the law (*TZ* 15, 1959, pp. 161–75).

Ahitub; according to I. 14.3 the latter is, however, grandson of Eli and according to I. 22.9 father of Ahimelech and therefore grandfather of Abiathar. Ahitub thus belongs without question among the ancestors of Abiathar. Now the later tradition wished to incorporate Zadok, too, in the Aaronite genealogy and made him a son of Ahitub (I Chron. 5.33f.; 6.37f.). This is understandable, in so far as Zadok later became the legitimate chief priest after the defection of Abiathar (I Kings 2).[a] The beginning of this false development is to be found here in v. 17, which should accordingly be restored (see above). The introduction of Zadok into the old priestly line may have been caused by the loss of the name of his real father. [18b] The details of the priestly service of the sons of David cause a further difficulty. Here, too, later ages were puzzled, as the princes were laymen, and did not belong to the priestly tribe. The LXX makes the 'priests' high officials and Chronicles makes them 'chief officials in the service of the king' (I Chron. 18.17). The earlier period did not think it amiss that sons of the patron of a sanctuary should exercise priestly functions (Judg. 17.5), although even there it is regarded as better that the office should be filled by a real Levite (17.12f.). Perhaps II Sam. 8 is a similar case. It is not, in fact, said, as in the case of the other officials, that 'David's sons were priests', a phrase in which in Hebrew the predicative noun is placed alongside the subject without a copula. Instead the word *hāyū* (they had been) is inserted, as though it were a matter which came to an end after a certain period. We do not hear elsewhere of any such activity on the part of David's sons.

A list which differs only slightly is to be found in 20.23–26 (see *ad loc.*). There were certainly documents of this sort in the royal archives. The lists of the sons of David (3.2–5; 5.13–15) are to be assessed in a similar way. The reason for the introduction of the list of officials at this point may be that some mention of the inner structure of the state was thought necessary after the description of its external expansion. This is the significance of ch. 8. In its present position, if we remember that it is preceded by ch. 7, it seems to show the first realization of the promises just given; ch. 8 lays the

[a]On the rise of the family of Zadok see H. G. Judge, 'Aaron, Zadok and Abiathar', *JTS*, NS 7, 1956, pp. 70–74. According to this, the descendants of Zadok were recognized to stem from Aaron after the exile. To the writer, Zadok himself is a former priest of *'ēl 'elyōn* who was taken over into the service of David after the capture of Jerusalem, when the sanctuary there became Israelite.

foundation for the promised kingdom. Once again we should recall the two notes about the help given to the king by Yahweh, and also v. 15. The compiler feels that David's kingdom can now go forward firmly into the future.

NOTE ON FORMATION AND STRUCTURE: V

In this section, the ideas which were determinative for the compiler in his arrangement of the material are easily recognizable. The exegesis of the details of the different passages has afforded us some insights into the matter. Two leading thoughts emerge. First, the compiler means to keep to the historical course of events throughout. The individual incidents are stages on the way to a goal: the fugitive and freebooter, hemmed in between the Philistines and Israel, follows a course at the end of which stands an empire, and from which the Lord's promise points on into the distant future. It is an astonishing, almost legendary career, and it is therefore understandable that in a number of ways we are made to realize that the hand of the Lord has disposed it all. And this is the second important thought: what has unfolded up to now is the result neither of chance nor of the personal qualities of the man David. Wherever it could seem clearest that David has been helped on by his own initiative and capabilities, it is emphatically stressed that he had earlier been given the assent of the Lord (2.1; 5.19, 23; cf. 8.6, 14). For this reason, ch. 7, as was indicated in the commentary, is the climax of this part and indeed of the book as a whole. The work of David is crowned by the promise, which points on towards the messianic hope. Where the previous great part describing the struggle between Saul and David was full of dramatic power, both in its features and in its setting, here everything is more compressed. At the same time, however, it is made much clearer, and above all the theological implications may be more readily grasped.

The compiler has achieved this principally by arranging the material at his disposal in a definite way, to suit his purpose. This is often evident. The list of the sons of David in 3.2–5 originally belonged with the second list in 5.13–15. The compiler split it into two parts, because the birth of the sons mentioned in the second list falls during the Jerusalem period and should only be given after the account of the conquest of the city. The list of officials in 8.15–18 similarly derives from the state archives. The reasons for its place at the end of the part have already been given. The account of the

Philistine wars in 5.17–25 was originally connected with the enumeration of the rest of David's foreign successes (8.1–14). It is possible that this account, which is in fact extremely terse, similarly comes from the royal archives. It is frequently assumed today that we have here the conclusion of a larger work describing 'the rise of David'. To this work would belong (apart from 5.17–25; 8.1–14) the greater part of chs. 2–4 and the account of the capture of Jerusalem. The difficulties of this hypothesis have been discussed earlier, but for want of a better it must remain as a working hypothesis. It is more important for an understanding of this part, 'King David', that we realize why the compiler split the account of the wars into two parts: the victory over the Philistines preceded the introduction of the ark into Jerusalem. It is further very probable that historically the surprise attack on Jerusalem fell between the first and the second defeat of the Philistines. In this instance the compiler has not separated the two accounts of the fighting. Here their connection in literary form and subject-matter evidently weighed heavier than historical sequence, and this probably led to the incorrect understanding of the 'hold'.

Chapter 6 is itself a continuation and conclusion of the history of the ark in I. 4–6. To attach it directly at that point would have been senseless, as the events which it describes occur decades afterwards. The only sensible course was to make the account of the bringing up of the ark follow the account of the capture of Jerusalem and the defeat of the Philistines. For both these had to happen before the ark, which had evidently previously been under the jurisdiction of the Philistines, could be brought to Jerusalem. In a way which is historically quite apposite and theologically equally understandable, the episode with Michal is associated with this narrative about the ark. The Michal episode is in its turn[a] connected with the great complex 9.1ff. The compiler was evidently content to leave ch. 9, the Meribbaal narrative, in the context of the other accounts dealing with the succession to the throne. It seemed to him more apposite to introduce the account of the childlessness of Michal, so important for the question of David's successor, in its historical position. Moreover at this point, when the daughter of Saul made critical objections to David's conduct at the sanctuary of Yahweh, it could be made clear that the Lord on whom the members of the family of Saul had called until then now himself willed their decline. It was not the

[a]Cf. L. Rost, *Thronnachfolge Davids*.

will of David. He had expressly taken back the daughter of Saul to underline his legitimate claim to the throne. Nor was he in any way responsible for the death of Ishbaal; all this happened without his interference. If we examine the way in which these accounts have been woven together, we can recognize what work has been done, on the one hand by careful utilization of existing literary material, and on the other by the development of clear and understandable viewpoints. This becomes especially clear in the way that Nathan's promise comes at the very moment when Jerusalem is beginning to become the political and cultic centre of the land. It would have been quite possible to put ch. 7 after ch. 8, and indeed the remark at 7.1 that the Lord had given David rest from all his enemies, taken up again in v. 11, would fit better after the enumeration of his victories over the neighbouring peoples. Nevertheless ch. 7 is made to follow ch. 6 for the reasons given earlier.

If there are still a great many open questions about the earlier history of these texts,[a] it is nevertheless possible to recognize with sufficient clarity that careful and well-considered work has been done here to bring into prominence the essential historical and theological points: the work and the figure of David is set in the context of divine plans which already reach beyond the soil of Palestine and his own time.

[a]Among them is the question whether there is not in chs. 3 and 4 material which formed the beginning of the account of the succession. On this see the commentary on ch. 9.

VI

THE SUCCESSION TO THE THRONE
OF DAVID
II. 9–20

1. JONATHAN'S SON: 9.1–13

9 [1]And David said, 'Is there still any one left of the house of Saul, that I may show him kindness for Jonathan's sake?' [2]Now there was a servant of the house of Saul whose name was Ziba, and they called him to David; and the king said to him, 'Are you Ziba?' And he said, 'Your servant is he.' [3]And the king said, 'Is there not still some one of the house of Saul, that I may show the kindness of God to him?' Ziba said to the king, 'There is still a son of Jonathan; he is crippled in his feet.' [4]The king said to him, 'Where is he?' And Ziba said to the king, 'He is in the house of Machir the son of Ammiel, at Lo-debar.' [5]Then King David sent and brought him from the house of Machir the son of Ammiel, at Lo-debar. [6]And Meribbaal[a] the son of Jonathan, son of Saul, came to David, and fell on his face and did obeisance. And David said, 'Meribbaal!' And he answered, 'Behold, your servant.' [7]And David said to him, 'Do not fear; for I will show you kindness for the sake of your father Jonathan, and I will restore to you all the land of Saul your father; and you shall eat at my table always.' [8]And he did obeisance, and said, 'What is your servant, that you should look upon a dead dog such as I?'

[9] Then the king called Ziba, Saul's servant, and said to him, 'All that belonged to Saul and to all his house I have given to your master's son. [10]And you and your sons and your servants shall till the land for him, and shall bring in the produce, that your master's son may have bread to eat;[b] but Meribbaal your master's son shall always eat at my table.' Now Ziba had fifteen sons and twenty servants. [11]Then Ziba said to the king, 'According to all that my lord the king commands his servant, so will your servant do.' So Meribbaal ate (always)[c]

[a]On the form of the name, see 4.4.

[b]'Bread' is used here in a wider sense, so it does not contradict what follows (against Budde, etc.).

[c]This is the force of the Hebrew participle.

298

at David's[a] table, like one of the king's sons. [12]And Meribbaal had a young son whose name was Mica. And all who dwelt in Ziba's house became Meribbaal's servants. [13]So Meribbaal dwelt in Jerusalem; for he ate always at the king's table. Now he was lame in both his feet.

This marks the beginning of the great continuous section which is concerned with the succession to the throne of David[b] and which deals first with the problem presented to David by the house of Saul. By making Michal once again his lawful consort, David has shown that he has a legitimate connection with the house of the first king. So the story of the succession must have contained something about the childlessness of Michal (6.16, 20ff., cf. Rost, p. 105). Whether the succession history actually began with this (so Rost, p. 120) must remain in doubt. In fact, Michal's coming to the court of David and, indeed, the story of the fate of Ishbaal should properly form a part of it (chs. 3 and 4); we should at any rate observe that the note giving the reason for Meribbaal's lameness is to be found here. Everything, however, is so dovetailed together that it is difficult to make any progress towards a literary solution. It has long been noticed that the episode of the killing of the seven sons of Saul (21.1ff.) appears to be somehow connected with ch. 9, and in such a way as to be a presupposition for it (Klostermann, Budde, Schulz). There will be something to be said about the reason why 21.1–14 does not come before ch. 9, but is only introduced later in an appendix, when we come to the passage.

[1] Be this as it may, ch. 9 begins with the house of Saul having suffered a considerable loss, a loss of which David is well aware. Shimei, a man of Saul's family, even accuses David later of himself having done the bloody work (16.7f.). The matter may be left open here. David's remark that he would show kindness to any survivors of the house of Saul could, however, have sounded like Herod's wish to come and worship the new-born king (Matt. 2.8). It was the purpose of the man who separated 21.1ff. from 9.1ff. to show that David meant it well and not maliciously. He really wanted to show mercy.

[2–5] The servant Ziba, through whom David tries to make contact with any of the house of Saul who are still living, seems to be

---

[a]LXX, Syr; MT has 'at my table'. But this *difficilior lectio* would only be justified here if something like: 'The king said' had fallen out at the beginning.

[b]This has been convincingly demonstrated to be the case by L. Rost in his work *Die Überlieferung von der Thronnachfolge Davids*, 1926.

faithfully attached to the house of Saul. We are also given the impression that by his immediate mention of Meribbaal's lameness he wishes to represent him as harmless. Similarly, his answers to David are extremely terse. Ziba's later attitude towards his master is somewhat different (16.1–4; 19.27–30). The lame Meribbaal is in Lo-debar, in the land east of the Jordan and north of the Jabbok, evidently in the region of Mahanaim.[a] Jonathan's son has thus been hidden in the immediate vicinity of Ishbaal's earlier residence. His host is a certain Machir, whom we meet again in 17.27 as a man who stands by David even in his ill fortune. The way in which David treated his protégé may have converted Machir from being a follower of the house of Saul to being a supporter of David. This could again confirm that David was really well disposed towards Meribbaal and treated him 'as one of the king's sons'.

[6–7] It is nevertheless quite understandable, particularly if the events described in 21.1ff. had just taken place, that Meribbaal regarded his audience with some trepidation. But David tries to show him the lack of danger in the situation by his 'do not fear'. This is explicitly followed, as earlier, by a reference to David's binding covenant of friendship with Jonathan. The word 'kindness' (ḥesed) occurs for the third time, qualified in v. 3 with the addition 'elōhīm: David promises Meribbaal kindness such as can truly be shown only by God (cf. I. 20.14). In practice, this kindness consists in the return of all the property of the family of Saul, which is due to David as their successor, and, in addition, the provision for Meribbaal's personal presence at court. He is given the same privileges as are accorded to Jehoiachin after his restoration to grace at the Babylonian court. The words used are the same as at II Kings 25.29; Jer. 52.33: 'he dined regularly at the king's table'. This need not necessarily mean that he shared in the king's personal table— as did David at the court of Saul (I. 20)—despite the following remark which explicitly puts him on a par with the princes. Nevertheless, David kept the grandson of Saul under careful watch by these means, so that any plan of being restored to the throne was made impossible from the start. The later development of events shows that such suspicion was not far from David's mind (16.1–4; 19.25–31). David's conduct here combines faithful kindness towards

---

[a]The place has not been identified. Noth's conjecture (*Joshua*[2], p. 82) that it should be identified with *tell el-mghanniye* comes to nothing in view of the archaeological evidence, cf. Glueck, *Explorations in Northern Palestine* IV, pp. 73–76.

his dead friend with the requisite statesmanlike wisdom. **[8]** We cannot discover Meribbaal's personal reactions to the second part of the king's demonstration of kindness from his answer, which is couched in courteous terms exaggerated even for the East; he will certainly have noted the king's purpose, but will at the same time have conceded its necessity.

[9–10] The management of the evidently considerable estate is entrusted to Ziba, as both Meribbaal's infirmity and the command which binds him to the court prevent him from being equal to the task. Ziba has the necessary sons and servants and now of course a sufficient provision for himself and his own. He is to appear at Jerusalem from time to time to give account and to bring in produce from the land. He tries to avoid this by his later conduct.

[11–13] We are expressly told once again of the position which has thus been arranged in a kind of appendix—this is why the remark about the king's sons occurs again—and the social standing of the house of Ziba is finally established. No stress is laid on the note about the little son of Meribbaal which follows. It is not there, however, as a result of any kind of statistical interest, but is once again intended to indicate how right it was of David to keep watch on this possible claimant to the throne. Events could have gone the same way as in the later history of the kings (II Kings 11), where a child who grew up in secret caused the downfall of the queen. In this way it is made impossible that a member of the house of Saul should succeed to the throne. Nathan's promise that the king's successor will have sprung from the loins of the king can now await its fulfilment.

2. THE AMMONITE WAR (PART ONE): 10.1–11.1

10 [1]After this, Nahash[a] the king of the Ammonites died, and Hanun his son reigned in his stead. [2]And David said, 'I will deal loyally with Hanun the son of Nahash, as his father dealt loyally with me.' So David sent by his servants to console him concerning his father. And David's servants came into the land of the Ammonites. [3]But the princes of the Ammonites said to Hanun their lord, 'Do you think, because David has sent comforters to you, that he is honouring your father? Has not David sent his servants to you to search the city, and to spy it out, and to overthrow it?' [4]So Hanun took David's servants, and shaved off half the beard of each, and cut off their garments in the middle, at their hips, and sent them away. [5]When it was told

[a]See BH.

David, he sent to meet them, for the men were greatly ashamed. And the king said, 'Remain at Jericho until your beards have grown,[a] and then return.'

6 When the Ammonites saw that they had become odious to David, the Ammonites sent and hired Aram Beth-rehob, and Aram Zobah, twenty thousand foot soldiers, and the king of Maacah with a thousand men, and the men of Tob, twelve thousand men. [7]And when David heard of it, he sent Joab and all the host of the mighty men. [8]And the Ammonites came out and drew up in battle array at the entrance of the gate, and Aram Zobah and Rehob, and the men of Tob and Maacah, were by themselves in the open country.

9 When Joab saw that the battle was set against him both in front and in the rear, he chose some of the picked men of Israel, and arrayed them against Aram; [10]the rest of his men he put in the charge of Abishai[b] his brother, and he arrayed them against the Ammonites. [11]And he said, 'If Aram is too strong for me, then you shall help me; but if the Ammonites are too strong for you, then I will come and help you. [12]Be of good courage, and let us play the man for our people, and for the cities[c] of our God; and may the LORD do what seems good to him.' [13]So Joab and the people who were with him drew near to battle against Aram; and they fled before him. [14]And when the Ammonites saw that Aram had fled, they likewise fled before Abishai, and entered the city. Then Joab returned from fighting against the Ammonites, and came to Jerusalem.

15 But when Aram saw that it had been defeated by Israel, they gathered themselves together. [16]And Hadadezer sent, and brought out those of Aram who were beyond the river; and they came to Helam, with Shobach the commander of the army of Hadadezer at their head. [17]And when it was told David, he gathered all Israel together, and crossed the Jordan, and came to Helam. And Aram was arrayed against David, and fought with him. [18]And Aram fled before Israel; and David slew of Aram the men of seven hundred chariots, and forty thousand men,[d] and wounded Shobach the commander of their army, so that he died there. [19]And when all the kings who were servants of Hadadezer saw that they had been defeated by Israel, they made peace with Israel and became subject to them. So Aram feared to help the Ammonites any more.

---

[a]Imperfect = Future II. See GB under ʿad B.

[b]See BH.

[c](?) Sometimes ʿārē is emended to ʾᵃrōn (ark), but this involves an awkward change of letters. The word would be better completely omitted as a dittograph of the word preceding, cf. Schulz ad loc. 'City' is also possible, Galling, Die Bücher der Chronik, Esra, Nehemiah (ATD 12), p. 56.

[d]MT: 700 chariots (horses) and 40,000 horsemen. For the latter, Chron. has 'foot-soldiers'. Perhaps 'mounted' (pārāšīm) is a gloss on rekeb (chariot, horse), because the verb hārag (kill) sounded unusual for rekeb, and originally ʾīš (man) stood in that place.

11 [1]In the spring of the year, the time when kings go forth to battle, David sent Joab, and his servants with him, and all Israel; and they ravaged the Ammonites, and besieged Rabbah. But David remained at Jerusalem.

The account of the Ammonite war has been incorporated into the story of the succession because of its associations with the Bathsheba episode, which formed such an important part of it. This can be seen clearly from the division of the account of the war into two parts, the shorter of which only begins in 12.26 and follows on directly from 11.1. Despite the many objections advanced, the section 10.1–11.1 is a unity. This is true both of the section 15–19a—long explained as a later addition—(we are certainly to regard this as 'a second phase of the same war', with Rost p. 77,)—and of the introductory vv. 1–6a. Rost's note of stylistic differences (in one place 'comfortable breadth', in another 'forced brevity', p. 78) is not convincing. We also find an elaboration of the situation in vv. 11f.;[a] these verses do not belong to the Bathsheba narrative in any way at all, but form the natural and necessary introduction to the account of the Ammonite war. The text as a whole, including 12.26–31, was certainly written down by someone near to and familiar with the events described; it could be the official document from the royal archives.

[10.1–6a] The event first described will have fallen at the beginning of David's reign; we can only imagine David having been thus snubbed if he were regarded as an insignificant man on whom such a bad joke could be played. The dead king of the Ammonites, whose name, Nahash, is preserved for us in I Chron. 19.1, is Saul's opponent of I. 11. Saul's opponent David will therefore have had friendly relations with him. This makes the message of sympathy understandable. On the other hand, we can equally well understand the suspicion of the young king's counsellors. The unnatural deaths of Abner and Ishbaal will certainly not have gone unnoticed round about. Moreover, David's embassage to the citizens of Jabesh-gilead (2.4–7)—not unknown to the Ammonites (I. 11.1ff.)!—will have been interpreted by them as an attempt by David to extend his influence beyond his own sphere. King Hanun draws his own conclusions and sends back David's messengers in disgrace. The

[a]One might draw attention to the phrase 'show kindness', which occurs in 10.2 as in 9.1–3, 7; 15.20, four times in the story of the succession; on the other hand, the expression is so common as to be of no great weight.

beard is an Oriental's glory, and a man is most utterly insulted by having the lower half of his clothing cut away. We can imagine them running the gauntlet through a mob of jeering men and women. One might ask whether Hanun was clear that his action was tantamount to a declaration of war—he may have felt that David was fully occupied by the Philistine war—or whether it was simply the unconsidered act of a young king prone to making coarse jokes (see I Kings 12.10f.); the latter view is supported by the way in which the Ammonites apparently became utterly terrified when David took the humiliation of his ambassadors so seriously as to send them immediately into quarantine, and now looked round about for help.

[6b–10] The sequel does not involve an alliance in the strict sense of the word, but the hiring of soldiers. They all come from the great Aramaean region whose population was at that time beginning to consolidate itself, north and east of the Ammonite territory. Zobah, mentioned in 8.3, is northernmost. The location of Beth-rehob is uncertain; perhaps *riḥab*, lying about fifteen miles east-north-east of Jerash, has preserved a reminiscence of it.[a] Maacah (Josh. 13.13) lies south of Hermon, and Tob not far away. The Aramaeans of Damascus are not mentioned, as they are in ch. 8. The hostile encounter with the Aramaeans, described in 10.6-13, is not to be identified with that in ch. 8. In 10.6ff. we have, as was said, merely mercenaries enrolled by the Ammonites for a special occasion. The numbers given are too high and are to be explained from the size of the figures given at v. 18. The summoning by Joab of only the 'mighty men'[b] and not the whole Israelite host also suggests a rather more minor occasion. Nevertheless, the allied enemy forces are numerically superior to the Israelite troops, with the result that they are able to surround Joab with a pincer movement. He therefore decides to attack the Aramaeans with the picked men, and to leave the battle with the Ammonites operating from their capital Rabbah[c] to his brother Abishai. [11–14] Joab's words of encouragement throw some light on the magnitude of the danger. He knows that this is no mere skirmish; people and land are at stake; a victory on the part of the Ammonities, and above all of the Aramaeans, the coming people in the Near East—as Joab seems to have realized—would once again jeopardize the newly won freedom

[a]The gloss on Hadadezer in 8.3, 'son of Rehob', uncertain of course, could point to an old association between Zobah and Beth-rehob.

[b]*gibbōrīm*, i.e. professional soldiers (cf. G. v. Rad, *Der Heilige Krieg im alten Israel*[2], 1952, p. 35).

[c]Rabbath Ammon, the present Amman, the capital of Jordan.

of Israel. But Joab's plan succeeds; the Lord 'was pleased' that it should succeed. The enemy seems not to have expected Joab's main attack and takes flight as soon as he approaches. The Ammonities take the same course before Abishai. Joab may have felt himself not strong enough to lay siege to the capital; after his victory he returns to Jerusalem.

[15–19] What is now described is an undertaking of the Aramaeans, who this time do not come to the aid of others, but fight on their own account. The name Hadadezer, known from ch. 8, occurs here. Quite apart from this, it is probable that the same events are described in the two passages. Chapter 8 records a similar action by Hadadezer on the Euphrates—but differently from here—moreover, the numbers given here could represent the same forces as those in 8.4f. There we have 42,000 foot soldiers, here 40,000 'horsemen'; the latter designation, however, is surely incorrect, and Chronicles (I. 19.18) is right in also speaking of 'foot soldiers'. The 700 'chariots' in 10.18 contrast with 1,700 'horsemen' in 8.4. Remarkably, the word 'horsemen' also occurs at 10.18. Here the number 1,000 could have fallen out before 700; 'horsemen' can be regarded as a correct gloss for 'chariots', which would be a reference to the details in ch. 8. The mention of the place of the battle, Helam (the location is unknown), and the name of the commander, show that a special tradition lies alongside that of ch. 8. Here, too, David eventually makes the Aramaeans subject peoples. As a result, there is no longer any possibility of the Ammonites getting any support from that direction. [11.1] The interrupted action against them can therefore be taken up again at the beginning of the dry season, this time with the summoning of David's guard and the whole Israelite host. Joab is in command. He devastates all the open land and begins the siege of the capital; the position of Ammon is like that of Judah in the days of Sennacherib (701), which we find described in Isaiah 1.4–9. The account breaks off with the note that David remained at Jerusalem, for this is the introduction to the story of Bathsheba.

3. URIAH'S WIFE AND THE BIRTH OF SOLOMON:
11.2–12.25

11 ²It happened, late one afternoon, when David arose from his couch and was walking upon the roof of the king's house, that he saw from the roof a woman bathing; and the woman was very beautiful. ³And David sent and inquired about the woman. And one said, 'Is not this Bathsheba, the daughter of Eliam, the wife of Uriah the

Hittite?' [4]So David sent messengers, and took her; and she came to him, and he lay with her. (Now she was purifying herself from her uncleanness.)[a] Then she returned to her house. [5]And the woman conceived; and she sent and told David, 'I am with child.'

6 So David sent word to Joab, 'Send me Uriah the Hittite.' And Joab sent Uriah to David. [7]When Uriah came to him,[b] David asked how Joab was doing, and how the people fared, and how the war prospered. [8]Then David said to Uriah, 'Go down to your house, and wash your feet.' And Uriah went out of the king's house, and there followed him a present from the king. [9]But Uriah slept at the door of the king's house with all the servants of his lord, and did not go down to his house. [10]When they told David, 'Uriah did not go down to his house,' David said to Uriah, 'Have you not come from a journey? Why did you not go down to your house?' [11]Uriah said to David, 'The ark and Israel and Judah dwell in booths; and my lord Joab and the servants of my lord are camping in the open field; shall I then go to my house, to eat and to drink, and to lie with my wife? As I live,[c] and as your soul lives, I will not do this thing.' [12]Then David said to Uriah, 'Remain here today also, and tomorrow I will let you depart.' So Uriah remained in Jerusalem that day, and the next. [13]And David invited him, and he ate in his presence and drank, so that he made him drunk; and in the evening he went out to lie on his couch with the servants of his lord, but he did not go down to his house.

14 In the morning David wrote a letter to Joab, and sent it by the hand of Uriah. [15]In the letter he wrote, 'Set Uriah in the forefront of the hardest fighting, and then draw back from him, that he may be struck down, and die.' [16]And as Joab was besieging the city, he assigned Uriah to the place where he knew there were valiant men. [17]And the men of the city came out and fought with Joab; and some of the servants of David among the people fell. Uriah the Hittite was slain also. [18]Then Joab sent and told David all the news about the fighting; [19]and he instructed the messenger, 'When you have finished telling all the news about the fighting to the king, [20A]then, if the king's anger rises, and if he says to you, "Why did you go so near the city to fight?" [21B]then you shall say, "Your servant Uriah the Hittite is dead also." '

22 So the messenger went, and came and told David all that Joab had sent him to tell. [23]The messenger said to David, 'The men gained

[a]According to Lev. 15.19ff., the time of uncleanness lasts seven days; the action therefore took place when actual menstruation was over (hence the bath), towards the end of this week or immediately after it. Because of the participial construction, it is impossible to connect the 'purification' with the 'uncleanness' just brought about by the adultery. In that case a consecutive imperfect would have to stand here. It would be possible, though improbable, for the sentence to begin 'although she was just . . .' (see GK § 141e).

[b]It is no coincidence that the same expression is used here as is used about his wife in v. 4 (bō 'ēlāw).

[c]Read ḥayyay; the k of MT could be the remains of a pronoun 'ānōkī which was added (GK § 135f.).

an advantage over us, and came out against us in the field; but we drove them back to the entrance of the gate. ²⁴ᴬThen the archers shot at your servants from the wall; some of the king's servants are dead.' Then David was angry at Joab and said to the messenger, 'Why did you go so near the city to fight?ᵃ ²⁰ᴮDid you not know that they would shoot from the wall? ²¹ᴬWho killed Abimelech the son of Jerubbaal?ᵇ Did not a woman cast an upper millstone upon him from the wall, so that he died at Thebez? Why did you go so near the wall?' ²⁴ᴮThen the messenger said to David,ᶜ 'Your servant Uriah the Hittite is dead also.' ²⁵David said to the messenger, 'Thus shall you say to Joab, "Do not let this matter trouble you, for the sword devours now one and now another; strengthen your attack upon the city and overthrow it." And encourage him.'

26 When the wife of Uriah heard that Uriah her husband was dead, she made lamentation for her husband. ²⁷And when the mourning was over, David sent and brought her to his house, and she became his wife, and bore him a son. But the thing that David had done displeased the Lord.

12 ¹And the Lord sent Nathan (the prophet)ᵈ to David. He came to him and said to him, 'There were two men in a certain city, the one rich and the other poor. ²The rich man had very many flocks and herds; ³but the poor man had nothing but one little ewe lamb, which he had bought. And he brought it up, and it grew up with him and with his children; it used to eat of his morsel, and drink from his cup, and lie in his bosom, and it was like a daughter to him. ⁴Now there came a traveller to theᵇ rich man, and he could not bear to take one of his own flock or herd to prepare for the wayfarer who had come to him, but he took the poor man's lamb, and prepared it for the man who had come to him.' ⁵Then David's anger was greatly kindled against the man; and he said to Nathan, 'As the Lord lives, the man who has done this deserves to die; ⁶and he shall restore the lamb fourfold, because he did this thing, and could not bear to touch his own (property).'ᵉ

7 Nathan said to David, 'You are the man. Thus says the Lord, the God of Israel, "I anointed you king over Israel, and I delivered you out of the hand of Saul; ⁸and I gave you your master's house, and your master's wives into your bosom, and gave you the daughtersᵇ of Israel and of Judah; and if this were too little, I would add to you as

---

ᵃThis part is attached to v. 22 in the LXX. The clauses 20b, 21a which now follow are connected with this in the LXX and, as in MT, put between 20a and 21b. But it is improbable that Joab should anticipate every single detail of David's reaction to the messenger. The confusion may have arisen from the twofold occurrence of the sentence 'Why did you go so near . . .?'

ᵇSee BH.

ᶜThis clause was lost when the sentences were changed round.

ᵈAdded in LXX and Syr.

ᵉRead lō instead of lŏ' in MT; MT means 'because he had no pity', and by itself makes sense. But the verb ḥāmal must be translated here as in v. 4.

much more.[9] Why have you despised the LORD,[a] to do what is evil in my sight? You have smitten Uriah the Hittite with the sword, and have taken his wife to be your wife, and have slain him with the sword of the Ammonites. [10]Now therefore the sword shall never depart from your house—because you have despised me, and have taken the wife of Uriah the Hittite to be your wife." [11]Thus says the LORD, "Behold, I will raise up evil against you out of your own house; and I will take your wives before your eyes, and give them to your neighbour,[b] and he shall lie with your wives in the sight of this sun. [12]For you did it secretly; but I will do this thing before all Israel, and before the sun." ' [13]David said to Nathan, 'I have sinned against the LORD.' And Nathan said to David, 'The LORD has put away your sin; you shall not die. [14]Nevertheless, because by this deed you have utterly scorned the enemies of the LORD,[c] the child that is born to you must[d] die.' [15]Then Nathan went to his house.

And the LORD struck the child that Uriah's wife bore to David, and it became sick. [16]David therefore besought God for the child, and David fasted, and whenever[e] he came home he always spent the night in sackcloth,[f] and lay on the ground. [17]And the elders of his house stood beside him, to raise him from the ground; but he would not, nor did he eat food with them. [18]On the seventh day the child died. And the servants of David feared to tell him that the child was dead; for they said, 'Behold, while the child was yet alive, we spoke to him, and he did not listen to us; how then can we say to him the child is dead? He may do himself some harm.' [19]But when David saw that his servants were whispering together, David perceived that the child was dead; and David said to his servants, 'Is the child dead?' They said, 'He is dead.' [20]Then David arose from the earth and washed, and anointed himself, and changed his clothes; and he went into the house of the LORD, and worshipped; he then went to his own house; and when he asked, they set food before him, and he ate. [21]Then his servants said to him, 'What is this thing that you have done? You fasted and wept for the child while it was alive; but when the child died, you arose and ate food.' [22]He said, 'While the child was still alive, I fasted and wept; for I said, "Who knows whether the LORD will be gracious to me, that the child may live?" [23]But now he is dead; why should I fast? Can I bring him back again? I shall go to him, but he will not return to me.'

[a]MT 'the word of Yahweh'; 'Yahweh', the right text, is evidenced in the versions. The expansion may have been caused by the later reinterpretation of the despising of the Lord as the despising of his (fifth and sixth) commandments.
[b]See BH.
[c]See Commentary.
[d]The Hebrew word *gam* ('also') is better left untranslated here. It corresponds to the *gam* of v. 13 before 'Yahweh' (the LORD)—'on the one hand . . . on the other hand'.
[e]This is the probable meaning of the repeated consecutive perf. (GK § 112f.).
[f]*bassaq*, according to LXX; the word might have been overlooked before *weˇsākab*. Cf. also Budde *ad loc.*

24 Then David comforted his wife, Bathsheba, and went in to her, and lay with her; and she bore a son, and he called his name Solomon. And the LORD loved him, [25]and sent a message by Nathan the prophet; so he called his name Jedidiah—because of the Lord.[a]

The story of David and Bathsheba has long aroused both dismay and astonishment; dismay that King David, with his manifest piety, could stoop to such an act, and astonishment that the Bible narrates it with such unrelenting openness, although the person involved is David, the great and celebrated king, the type of the Messiah. It is significant that Chronicles, which follows the text of Samuel chapter by chapter throughout, omits this incident, almost certainly because of the serious blemish which it leaves on David's reputation. On the other hand, its presence not only shows how the ancient texts have no tendency to whitewash, but stresses that God's cause is advanced not through blameless persons, but by God himself, despite the sinfulness of his best people.

[11.2–3] The story, told brilliantly and excitingly, is so neatly dovetailed into the account of the Ammonite war that a join can hardly be seen. David has left the siege of the capital to Joab and remained in Jerusalem. It is summer (cf. v. 1) and he has spent the heat of the day in the house, where, of course—like King Eglon of Moab (Judg. 3.20)—he has an 'upper room', open to the cool afternoon breeze. Towards 'evening', which here as frequently (cf. ATD 9 on Ruth 3.2 and on I. 30.17) means the late afternoon, he comes out on to the flat roof of the palace, thought to be higher than the neighbouring houses and particularly that of Uriah (cf. the frequently used word 'go down'). There are similar possibilities of looking at life in other roofs and courtyards in the present Old City of Jerusalem. We must, however, ask whether Bathsheba did not count on this possibility. 'One cannot but blame her for bathing in a place where she could be seen' (Schulz, p.114); not, of course, that this possible element of feminine flirtation is any excuse for David's conduct.

David does not recognize Bathsheba, though he will certainly have known her as Eliam's daughter (23.34) and Ahithophel's

---

[a]The construction is strange. The *beyad* could be explained by a variant *wayyiqrā beyad nātān hannābī'* alongside the original version *wayyišlah et-nātān hannābī' wayyiqrā*. The present text would be the somewhat unskilful amalgamation of two variant readings, which would arise more easily in view of the *wayyišlah beyad 'ūriyyā* in 11.14.

granddaughter (*ibid.* and on 15.12), perhaps also as the wife of
Uriah, one of his most prominent officers;[a] the form of the answer to
his inquiry suggests that it is felt that David must know her. He has
evidently seen only her figure, but it was enough to arouse his desire.
Things now develop fast. [11.4] Bathsheba is called to the king, and
all goes as he planned. We learn nothing of Bathsheba's feelings; her
consciousness of the danger into which adultery was leading her
(Deut. 22.22) must have been outweighed by her realization of the
honour of having attracted the king. In any case, all this is unimportant for the biblical narrator. The writer—and later David himself—lays the blame squarely on the king's shoulders. All that is said
is that the earlier bathing which had stirred David's desire had been
connected with the practice of 'purification' after monthly uncleanness. Perhaps this is also stressed because even in ancient experience
this time was regarded as especially favourable for conception.

[11.5–13] The sequel vividly depicts the predicament in which the
king finds himself on learning the consequences of his act; the affair
is not without danger even for him (Deut. 22.22), as in Israel even the
king does not stand *extra legem*. He has Uriah summoned from the
army so that he will later appear to be the father of the expected
child. The conversation about the military situation—literally *šālōm*
of the commander, the people and the war—is only a pretext for
David's real purpose, to get Uriah to go down to his house and 'wash
his feet' there. Here this means no more than 'make himself comfortable' (Budde), but we may nevertheless not exclude an allusion to
another meaning of *raglayim* (feet) = the male genitals.[b] The present
of food sent on by the king is meant to put Uriah in a suitable frame
of mind. It is quite possible that Uriah had wind of the affair and is
confirmed in his suspicions by the king's generosity; at any rate,
we are frequently told that a third party (even 'messengers', v. 4)
went to and fro between David and Bathsheba, so there would have
been a ready source of court gossip.[c] Be this as it may, Uriah is
shaken in his resolve neither by the king's repeated encouragement
nor by the court invitation which requires Uriah's presence for a

[a]Cf. 23.39. The name Uriah is pure Hebrew (Yahweh is my light). 'Hittite'
may indicate the derivation of his family. In Matt. 1, the genealogy of Jesus, the
'wife of Uriah' nevertheless appears among the tribal mothers of pagan origin
(Tamar, Rahab, Ruth).
[b]See ATD 9², p. 275, on Ruth 3.4, 7.
[c]This line is worked out quite dramatically, especially by Kreyssig, *Gerechtigkeit für David*, pp. 73ff.

further day, during which he is to be made drunk and thus desirous. In the face of the king's invitations, Uriah falls back on his loyalty to his comrades, and apparently also on the religious obligations which the 'holy war'[a] imposes upon him. If the interpretation offered earlier is correct, this refusal to accede to the wishes of the king represents Uriah's weapon and his revenge, a revenge, however, which costs him his life.

[11.14–17] For David there is now only one way out: Uriah must disappear. As in the story of Cain, the different stages of David's sin are described with shattering truthfulness. We only learn the facts, nothing of the feelings of the four chief persons involved. The wife's agony, the king's needs, the husband's rancour or the commander's attitude to the whole affair, can only be read between the lines. David writes the 'Uriah letter'; whether Uriah takes it with him unsuspecting or suspecting is again left uncertain. The letter gives detailed instructions about what is to be done. Gressmann supposed that David wrote only the first part (up to 'hardest fighting') and left it to Joab to read the right meaning into this not completely clear order, something which Joab was certainly capable of doing. On the other hand, the execution of the orders is not carried out in the way suggested by the letter in its present form, and it was certainly not the concern of later writers to blacken David still further. Joab then acts even more skilfully and safely. Elsewhere, too, he acts fully in accordance with the wishes of his master. He is not even bothered by a murder, as is clear from the death of Abner and later that of Amasa (20.8ff.). 'How cheering to find a troublesome master, who always speaks from obedience to his faith, for once acting as an accomplice' (Kreyssig, p. 79). The death of other 'servants of David' along with Uriah further increases David's stock of guilt.

[11.18–25] The section containing the messengers' report is badly preserved in MT; in particular, vv. 20b and 21a will occur first in David's answer (cf. 24ᵃ above). The messenger reports the course of the war as he was ordered. Here we gather further details of the fateful occasion and of the losses suffered, but at first there is no mention of Uriah. In consequence, David, perhaps disappointed at hearing nothing of Uriah, reacts with an angry outburst which would do honour to the king's consciousness of his responsibility if it did not

---

[a]The note that Israel and Judah, together with the ark, are lying 'in booths' is meant to make clear the difference between them and the fighting troops, 'the servants of David'. Cf. G. v. Rad, *Der Heilige Krieg*, p. 36.

occur in this particular context. As Joab rightly assumed, David chiefly blames him for his careless approach to the wall (the clause 'Why did you go so near the wall?' occurs three times) and refers to the fate of Abimelech (Judg. 9.53). Only then does the messenger give the news of Uriah's death, once again in accordance with his orders. The immediate change in David's attitude is masterfully expressed. Whether the messenger became suspicious at this is once again not said, as being superfluous to the story.

[11.26–27a] David has thus achieved his aim. Bathsheba makes the necessary lamentation[a] and is then—probably very soon, as on an earlier occasion in the case of Abigail (I. 25)—brought by David to his house. The son is born 'to David' in the palace. The name of the child is not given.

[11.27b] Now comes the climax; the judgment and condemnation of the affair by God. It takes up a considerable amount of space, and is indeed the determining factor in the second half. Occasionally (most emphatically by Gressmann, but also by Kittel) the Nathan scene has been regarded as a later addition and the divine criticism of David's action has been thought to be demonstrated only in the death of the child. It is, however, hard to imagine that the original story, after it had exposed David to such an extent in ch. 11 and had registered the divine judgment upon his action, could end without the king being made aware of this judgment and being brought to realize the nature of his act. There is, of course, a second question, whether in the speech of the prophet there are not thoughts which point in a direction which was not originally intended and are thus to be regarded as later expansions.

[12.1–6] The parable is narrated without an introduction, as an illustration, indeed as a 'case' which Nathan, who apparently comes into the king's presence quite suddenly, submits to him; Nathan's conduct in II Kings 1 is just the same. It is not necessary to inquire whether the instance fits the case of David and Uriah in all its details; it is sufficient that a blatant injustice is described here, which so enrages the king that he pronounces the verdict on himself. This effect is principally achieved by making the lamb, which the poor man had to buy for himself with difficulty, appear as the darling of the whole family. The way in which the rich man acts is thus made to appear not only parsimonious, but also rough and crude. The way in which

---

[a]Seven days; cf. P. Heinisch, *Die Totenklage in Alten Testament*, 1931, pp. 12f.

David reacts towards what he is told shows not only his temperament but also his feeling for right dealing, which does not leave him, even when he sees the real point of Nathan's parable. He is thus far from blaming Nathan for his boldness or for the form in which he tells his sins to his face. Quite the opposite. Right until David's death we find Nathan as a trusted adviser to the king. The prophet evidently stood in relation to David in the same place as the confessors at later courts. David has been criticized (Gressmann, Schulz) for demanding fourfold restitution in addition to the death penalty (Ex. 21.37). This, however, is no 'pedantic' (Gressmann) addition by a later scribe; it is rather quite understandable and necessary if the king is concerned that the poor man as well as the rich should have his 'rights'.

[12.7a] Nathan's 'You are the man', one of the 'most apt' sayings in the Bible, takes up the verdict spoken by David without having to state it explicitly: it is a death sentence. This is important if we are to understand what follows. For this sentence is only annulled on David's acknowledgment of his guilt and not before. Until that point it stands, as otherwise it would not be necessary for it to be taken back *expressis verbis*! [12.7b–10] On the other hand, the two other pronouncements of punishment which stand between v. 7a and v. 13 are framed differently; they put the earlier case in a relationship to later history. The first is remarkable because it presupposes David's anointing; it is extremely probable that the anointing of I. 16 and not that of II. 5 is meant, as it is in this context placed before the pursuit made by Saul. Also original is the remark that Yahweh gave David's 'master's wives into his bosom'; thus David had done just what Absalom does with David's concubines on usurping power (16.20ff.); indeed, the fact that Absalom acts in this way may perhaps be connected with the precedent made by his father. We learn nothing of it elsewhere, however; it possibly happened at the time of Abner's betrayal, which brought Michal to David, or after the death of Ishbaal. In any event it is a piece of old tradition. The preceding remark, that David was given the 'house' of Saul,[a] means principally in this context the possession of the female members of the house; the importance of this matter is clear from the conflict between Abner and Ishbaal (II. 3) and the episode of Abishag the Shunammite and Adonijah (I Kings 2). The purport of these remarks is that it was not necessary for David to have procured a wife in so underhand a way.

[a]Klostermann's conjecture that *bat* (daughter) should be read instead of *bēt* (house) is ingenious but unsupported, and is better not adopted.

The sin of which David is here accused is not adultery, but that he murdered a husband and then took the wife for himself. These offences are mentioned twice and both are described as 'despising the word of the Lord'. The punishment for them is that the blood-stained sword will reappear again and again throughout the later history of the house of David. Perhaps it is the unnatural deaths of three of David's sons which first spring to mind (Amnon, Absalom and Adonijah), but it may be, too, that later events in the house of David (Athaliah) are also recalled. [12.11–12] The second threat, which is given a new introduction, expressly mentions David's adultery—without mentioning the murder—and also announces a fitting punishment; there is the same relationship between guilt and punishment with respect to the sixth commandment in Job's confession.[a] Absalom's action at 16.20ff. is regarded as the execution of the punishment.[b] Thus the two threats each single out one aspect of David's sin and relate it to definite events which occur later. God's righteousness is clearly shown forth in the way beloved of the deuteronomistic and the 'Wisdom' literature. The punishment fits the crime. This need not, of course, be a sign of late composition, but the passage will certainly be a later development. The section would very easily lend itself to emphasis on points which were only implicit and to the consequent demonstration that Yahweh's justice is not suspended, even for the mightiest.

[12.13] Originally, the brief saying in v. 7a, which flashes out like lightning, may have been the only one of Nathan's remarks cited in the account. David's brief confession of repentance and acknowledgment of the Lord's justice would then be the corresponding answer. Thereupon follows—in a way reminiscent of II. 7—Nathan's second judgment, which amends the first. As has been said, the first judgment carries the death sentence. This is now annulled with the promise of forgiveness. Here, too, the Lord does not desire the death of the sinner (cf. Ezek. 18.23, 32; 33.11) but rather that he should turn from his wickedness and live.

[12.14] What follows at first sight appears to be a subsequent qualification of an unqualified announcement of pardon. Why is a further punishment imposed, and why does it concern the child? In answering these questions we should note the reasons given for this

---

[a]Job 31.9–12; cf. Hertzberg, *Das Buch Hiob*, pp. 121, 125.
[b]Absalom is here described as 'your neighbour' (*rēʿekā*), just as David is described as 'your neighbour' in relation to Saul in I28.17.

pronouncement: 'Because by this deed you have utterly (infin. abs.) scorned the enemies of the Lord . . .' As in RSV, 'the enemies' is almost universally deleted as a 'gloss on religious grounds'. From the time of A. Geiger[a] this has been maintained almost without dispute in all the commentaries. But why have these selfsame 'religious grounds' not influenced the other twelve Old Testament passages in which the piel of *nā'aṣ* has as an object God or divine things? The fact that *nā'aṣ* in the piel always occurs as 'blaspheme' and never as 'make to blaspheme' need not exclude this possibility; the meaning of the piel given at GK § 52g and often evidenced, 'to drive and cause another to act', could quite easily be pertinent here. In that case the phrase means: David's action is not only a sin against God—which has been forgiven him—but also a sin which has further effects in the world around him. If a man like David, the anointed one, 'with whom the Lord is', allows himself to be guilty of such offences, then the Lord's cause is seriously damaged. In fact, the enemies of God blaspheme over it even to this day. Matters have been put right between the sinner and the Lord through the grace of God, but the death of the child is to show how God feels about the clear transgression of his commandments and to stop the mouths of all those who might think to forge evidence against him from such an instance. There is accordingly no reason to suppress the word 'enemies', especially as the reading is preserved in all the ancient witnesses.[b]

[12.15–23] As expected, the child falls ill and we learn of the measures taken by David—once again the mother is not mentioned— to move the Lord to 'repent': he offers special prayers, submits to a special fast, which presumably lasts for the whole period of the child's illness, puts on sackcloth (cf. Jonah 3), and lies upon the ground at night. He also refrains from washing and anointing himself—a picture of complete self-abasement. His trusted officials in vain seek to dissuade him. Then the child dies and no one dares to tell David, who appears so determined in his efforts to ward off the blow; it looks as though the court suppressed the news because they feared a desperate act on the part of the king, perhaps even suicide. But David himself finds out, and when his servants confirm the news he immediately dispenses with the attitude of a mourner, once again

[a]*Urschrift und Übersetzungen der Bibel*, p. 267; cf. also Budde *ad loc.*
[b]The opposite thought, that Yahweh does something particularly impressive because of the enemy, i.e. to bring them to silence, occurs in Ps. 8.3—there the power of weakness is in question.

goes to the sanctuary, now in his usual clothes, and, to the utter amazement of the court, calls for food. It is as though he had already anticipated the mourning, but as a penitent. Nevertheless his conduct was barely comprehensible, indeed shocking, to his contemporaries and to posterity. He appears here on the one hand as calculating (v. 23a) and on the other hand (v. 23b) as all too realistic; for David's statement that he cannot bring the child back but must in the end go to him is no expression of hope in a future life, but simply of the immutability of death. It should not, however, be forgotten that with the absolution pronounced over David and the death of the child his sins are regarded as expiated; indeed, the death of the child can be regarded as a confirmation that nothing more will happen to the king himself. The child has, as it were, been accepted as a sacrifice. For this reason, the king may have omitted the mourning customs usual at the time. The explanation for his conduct is thus not to be sought in his own personality, whether with approval or with disapproval—Schulz: 'his strength of will in dispensing with unnecessary grief'; Budde: 'the indication of a sound understanding of man and a manly attitude'[a]—but rather in his recognition of its deeper significance; everything has now been put right between him and God. True, David sought to ward off the threatened loss of the child by prayer and self-abasement. But the Lord replied to him in the negative. The expiation was necessary. And now the path is open for further developments. It was important that David's sin, which was sufficient to jeopardize his life and his kingdom, should find its conclusion precisely within the framework of the theme of the succession to the throne of David, in punishment and in forgiveness, a conclusion which made it possible for a new leaf to be turned over before men and their talk and most important of all before God. David emerges from the situation judged and redeemed. Posterity, with a deep sense of what was appropriate, has regarded Psalm 51 as an expression of his experience.

[12.24] The narrative leaves open the way in which David then expressed his sympathy to Bathsheba. The word *nāham* (piel) can simply mean 'comfort'. Usually, however, definite mourning customs, appropriate to the situation, have been envisaged (Budde, Caspari). When a mother has lost her child in the East today she is usually told, 'May God support your husband'; with great realism this refers

---

[a]Caspari's remark that the king 'refrained from the usual signs of mourning because of the state of the hostilities' is completely off the mark.

to the begetting of a new child in place of the one that has been lost. Presumably the basic meaning of the text points in this direction. In any case, David's 'coming' ($b\bar{o}$' = go in to) to her and the birth of another son—LXX goes on to add 'and she conceived'—are mentioned in immediate connection with David's expression of his sympathy. The name Solomon ($\check{s}^el\bar{o}m\bar{o}$) is, of course, connected with $\check{s}\bar{a}l\bar{o}m$, peace; the name is meant to convey the same thought as the additional observation that the Lord 'loved' him. It has often been pointed out, certainly rightly, that the 'love' of Yahweh showed itself in the fact that the child stayed alive, in contrast to the first one. But while this is indisputable, it is at the same time insufficient. The meaning is that the grace of God once again shines out over this child—and so over David, too. This is a confirmation of what was said in the previous paragraph. [12.25] There then follows the express addition that the child is given a (second) name by Yahweh, who commissions the prophet Nathan to act for him. The name, as it were, demonstrates the Lord's disposition. 'With an intentional reminiscence of the name of the child's father, he thus expresses the oneness which has been established between the king and God' (Caspari, p. 536). And there is more: the child is thus described from the start as a child of God's grace, a most important statement in the context of the succession texts. An attempt has occasionally been made by a slight emendation of the text (Wellhausen, Budde, Nowack) to find here the thought that Nathan was appointed guardian of the child by David; according to I Kings 1 there is, in fact, a particularly close connection between Nathan and Solomon. The text, however, makes sense without this expedient. Moreover, the name Jedidiah does not occur outside this passage. It appears to have chiefly theological significance here.[a] Thus the new son of David has entered with good auspices on his career, which had so shameful an introduction, and with him the signs point towards the successor of David who will bear the promised favour of the Lord through the ages.

4. THE AMMONITE WAR (PART TWO): 12.26-31

12 [26]Now Joab fought against Rabbah, the (city) of the Ammonites, and took the royal city.[b] [27]And Joab sent messengers to David, and

[a]Klostermann's theory that Jedidiah is, in fact, the name of the dead child is not as abstruse but equally as impossible as that of Cook, who holds Solomon to be the child conceived in adultery
[b]See Commentary.

said, 'I have fought against Rabbah; moreover I have taken the city of waters. [28]Now, then, gather the rest of the people together, and encamp against the city, and take it; lest I take the city, and it be called by my name.' [29]So David gathered all the people together and went to Rabbah, and fought against it and took it. [30]And he took the crown of their king from his head; the weight of it was a talent of gold, and in it was a precious stone; and it was placed on David's head. And he brought forth the spoil of the city, a very great amount. [31]And he brought forth the people who were in it, and set them to labour with saws and iron picks and iron axes, and made them toil at[a] the brick-kilns; and thus he did to all the cities of the Ammonites. Then David and all the people returned to Jerusalem.

[26–27] The account of the Ammonite war, interrupted at 11.1, is now resumed. We are not, however, to conclude that the closing battles took place only after the birth of Solomon. First the Bath-sheba episode is told right to its conclusion. The closing phase of the war begins with the capture of the city of waters, part of the present river *sel 'amman*, from whose valley the town rises precipitously and powerfully. Of course, according to MT the phrase 'city of waters' occurs only in the second verse, in Joab's despatch to David, and strangely enough not in the first verse which, however, seems to describe the same event. There we have 'the royal city' (*'îr hamm^e-lūkā*). Because of v. 27, this is generally emended to 'city of waters', as it is rightly assumed that the palace and the rest of the city which surrounded it stood on the hillside, on the site of the present citadel of Amman, and that this was taken by David himself. Nevertheless, we must still put a question which has been completely neglected, namely, how all the ancient translations attest the reading 'royal city' instead of 'city of waters'. This question requires an answer, irrespective of what was the original reading. Possibly we have a position similar to that obtaining in Jerusalem, where the 'king's garden' lay right to the south of the south-east hill, where three valleys run together (the Valley of Kidron, the Valley of the City and the Valley of Hinnom; cf. II Kings 25.4; Jer. 52.7; Neh. 3.15); there, near where the Siloam conduit emerged, was the only possible site for a garden. In Rabbath Ammon the river valley was still more suitable for this purpose. Perhaps the part of the city concerned, which really was a 'city of waters', bore another name in the capital itself, but Joab avoided the alternative in his despatch so as not to give a wrong impression.

[a]See BH.

[28–29] Joab's request to David to summon the reserves of the army and then himself come with these fresh troops to storm Rabbath Ammon is framed in such a way that he seems concerned for the prestige of the king; perhaps he was equally concerned to strengthen his troops. The main factor, however, seems to be 'the taking of Rabbath Ammon into the power and possession' of the victor, a measure taken over from private into public law which is effected in a way 'analogous to a peaceful exchange of property'.[a] In any case, David acts accordingly. He captures the city and with it, of course, the palace, and this must be regarded as the downfall of the Ammonite state. We learn nothing of the fate of the king, only that of his crown. **[30]** This is, of course, assuming that the MT reading *malkām* ('their' king) is in order. LXX instead read 'Melchol' as the name of the king, but this is most surprising, as the young king is called Hanun in 10.1 and there is little to commend the suggestion that he died and the above-mentioned Melchol succeeded him. It has therefore often been suggested that here, as in I Kings 11.5, the name of the Ammonite god Milkom should be read in place of *malkām*. The fact that David seized a god's crown and placed it on his own head is seen to be remarkable (by Budde and others), but not an insuperable difficulty. Nevertheless, it is easier to follow MT, as does the corresponding account in I Chron. 20.2, although the suffix 'their' king is awkward. Another reason against supposing the crown to be a royal one is its heavy weight. Even if the figures given in Benzinger's *Hebraische Archaeologie*, which occur in all the commentaries, that 1 *kikkār* amounts to 130 lb, are too high (cf. the calculations in Galling, *BRL*, pp. 185–8), the crown is still heavy enough.[b] Chronicles therefore states that only the precious stones belonging to the crown were placed on David's head (I Chron. 20.2). So even at that time there was considerable thought about how David managed the heavy crown. Of course, the expression may also have been used figuratively. The main point made is that David becomes king of the Ammonites, whose territory he incorporates into his own.[c] It is certainly not unimportant that the host and not the servants of David were the deciding factor.

[a]So quite rightly Galling, 'Die Ausrufung des Namens als Rechtsakt in Israel', *TLZ* 81, 1956, col. 67.
[b]On the other hand, Palestinian peasant women on occasion carry two metal canisters of water (about 88 lb.) on their heads, to say nothing of the almost phenomenal 'headwork' of eastern porters. Cf. also ATD 9[2], p. 277.
[c]'In a personal union' . . .; Alt, *Kleine Schriften* II, pp. 69f.

[31] It is further obscure how the punitive measures taken against the Ammonite men are to be understood. Earlier the predominant view was that David inflicted a gruesome massacre; he showed his enemies the same treatment as they were accustomed to deal out to their prisoners (Amos 1.13; cf. also Amos 1.3). It would be possible to interpret the text in this way if need be, and MT at I Chron. 20.3 could also point in this direction; moreover, in 8.2 we learn of David taking similar measures against the Moabites. It is, however, more probable here that we should envisage forced labour, in breaking stones, baking bricks and so forth (cf. Ex. 1), especially as it is not easy to see why the punishment should have been inflicted with instruments of manual labour and not simply with weapons. David, and more particularly Joab (I Kings 11.16), would assent to atrocities without a second thought; that was fully in accordance with the rules of war in their day. The second interpretation is, however, the more probable and is generally preferred today. The Ammonite men are thus put to works which will advance considerably the economic progress of the Davidic empire.

5. AMNON AND ABSALOM'S SISTER: 13.1–22

13 ¹Now Absalom, David's son, had a beautiful sister, whose name was Tamar; and after a time Amnon, David's son, loved her. ²And Amnon was so tormented that he made himself ill because of his sister Tamar; for she was a virgin, and it seemed impossible to Amnon to do anything to her. ³But Amnon had a friend, whose name was Jonadab, the son of Shimeah, David's brother; and Jonadab was a very crafty man. ⁴And he said to him, 'O son of the king, why are you so haggard morning after morning? Will you not tell me?' Amnon said to him, 'I love Tamar, my brother Absalom's sister.' ⁵Jonadab said to him, 'Lie down on your bed, and pretend to be ill; and when your father comes to see you, say to him, "Let my sister Tamar come and give me bread to eat, and prepare the food in my sight, that I may see it, and eat from her hand."' ⁶So Amnon lay down, and pretended to be ill; and when the king came to see him, Amnon said to the king, 'Pray let my sister Tamar come and make a couple of cakes in my sight, that I may eat from her hand.'

7 Then David sent home to Tamar, saying, 'Go to your brother Amnon's house, and prepare food for him.' ⁸So Tamar went to her brother Amnon's house, where he was lying down. And she took dough, and kneaded it, and made cakes in his sight, and baked the cakes. ⁹And she called the servants[a] and took the pan and emptied it out before him, but he refused to eat. And Amnon said, 'Send out every

---

[a] *wattiqrā' 'et-hammᵉšārēt* has fallen out before the similar words which follow, see BH.

one from me.' So every one went out from him. [10]Then Amnon said to Tamar, 'Bring the food into the chamber, that I may eat from your hand.' And Tamar took the cakes she had made, and brought them into the chamber to Amnon her brother. [11]But when she brought them near him to eat, he took hold of her, and said to her, 'Come,[a] lie with me, my sister.' [12]She answered him, 'No, my brother, do not force me; for such a thing is not done in Israel; do not do this wanton folly. [13]As for me, where could I carry my shame? And as for you, you would be as one of the wanton fools in Israel. Now, therefore, I pray you, speak to the king; for he will not withhold me from you.' [14]But he would not listen to her; and being stronger than she, he forced her, and lay with her.[b]

15 Then Amnon hated her with very great hatred; so that the hatred with which he hated her was greater than the[c] love with which he had loved her. And Amnon said to her, 'Arise, be gone.' [16]But she said to him, 'No, my brother; for my sake do not do this great wrong; for this wrong would be greater than the[d] other which you did to me, if you sent me away.' But he would not listen to her. [17]He called the young man—his servant—and said, 'Put this woman out of my presence, and bolt the door after her.' [18]Now she was wearing a long robe with sleeves, for thus were the garments[e] which the king's daughters wore while they were virgins. So his servant put her out, and bolted the door after her.[f] [19]And Tamar put ashes on her head, and rent the long-sleeved robe which she wore; and she laid her hand on her head, and went away, crying aloud as she went.

20 And her brother Absalom said to her, 'Has Amnon your little brother[g] been with you? Now hold your peace, my sister; he is your brother; do not take this to heart.' So Tamar dwelt in bitterness[h] and

---

[a]*bō'* 'come, go in to' is here, as often, meant in a sexual sense, cf. 11.4, etc.

[b]MT does not read *'ittā* ('lay with her'), as might have been expected, but the accusative *'ōtā*. Perhaps this is meant to be an expression of the violence of his action.

[c]See BH.

[d]The text is mutilated here, as the old translations show. It may originally have run approximately thus: *'al ('āhī 'el) 'ōdōt(ay 'al ta'as 'et-)hārā'ā hagg'dōlā hazzōt (kī g'dōlā hārā'ā hazzōt) mē(hā)'ªhērōt.* The mistaken tradition may have first come about because the three words *hārā'ā hagg'dōlā hazzōt* occurred twice and were in one place overlooked by the copyist. Such a mistake would, of course, have been easy at the beginning of a verse. The conjecture put forward here tries above all to take note of the *'al-'ōdōt*, which is left out of consideration in other attempts at improvement.

[e]The word *m'îlîm*, which, of course, has a clumsy effect, must nevertheless be left; Wellhausen's emendation to *mē'ōlām*, from time immemorial is quite inappropriate, as a fashion for king's daughters in Israel cannot have been all that old!

[f]The form *w'nā'al* (instead of *wayyin'ōl*) is striking; the same form occurs at Judg. 3.23.

[g]Perhaps the form *'ªmīnōn* instead of *'amnōn* is meant as an ironical diminutive.

[h]The 'and' before the next word can indicate that a second word (two words also in LXX Luc.) has fallen out. *mārā* has been put in as a suggestion; the word is also used in Ruth 1.20 for the desolate widow. It could easily have been overlooked after the same consonants at the end of *tāmār*, especially if it was defectively written.

desolate in her brother Absalom's house. [21]When King David heard of all these things, he was very angry; but he did nothing to harm his son Amnon,[a] for he loved him, because he was his firstborn.[b] [22]But Absalom spoke to Amnon neither good nor bad; for Absalom hated Amnon, because he had forced his sister Tamar.

This exceptionally tense narrative is connected with the rest of the work in two ways. First, the reader sees that the son is dominated by the same sensuality as his father, a sensuality which takes no notice of men's lives, and will notice divine retribution in the fact that David has to experience this in his own flesh and blood. Secondly, however, after the birth of Solomon, Yahweh's favourite, the future king and bearer of the promises of ch. 7, the question of the position of the older sons arises. They are higher in the line of succession than he, and chief among them is the crown prince Amnon. The fate which befalls Amnon through his own sin is not unconnected with the divine plans, even though this is not stated explicitly.

[1] In fact, the matter is told quite simply as an episode and is also introduced as such. The *dramatis personae* are David's eldest son Amnon, the son of Ahinoam, his half-brother Absalom and Absalom's sister Tamar, children of the princess Maacah, and the king himself. All four are introduced in the very first verse. Tamar is the tragic figure of the drama, but in the general context she is merely a subsidiary figure whose fate is only important for the light it sheds on the struggle between the two oldest[c] princes and its further consequences for the history of the kingdom of David. The consummate skill of the narrative lies in the way in which these two elements are woven together: the recognition of the historical significance of a purely private matter and the tragic fate of the young princess which is related with deep sympathy.

[2] Amnon's love for Tamar is described from the beginning as a strong sensual emotion; he desires the maiden so much that he becomes quite ill. Neither at the beginning of the narrative nor during its development is it thought at all strange that the object of his affection should be his half-sister; the position of Abraham and Sarah in Gen. 20.12 is precisely the same. Such marriages, well known out-

---

[a]Literally, 'he did not trouble himself . . .'

[b]The addition is made following LXX. Perhaps it was overlooked because the sentence began in the same way as the one following (*weˡō*).

[c]Chileab, whose birth occurred between these two, is mentioned only in the list at 3.2ff.

side Israel (notably in Egypt), were afterwards emphatically prohibited by the law (Lev. 18.9, 11; 20.17; Deut. 27.22), but that is not (yet) the case here. A further element in Amnon's position is the fact that he sees no possibility of gaining access to Tamar, as the virgins were evidently kept under a particularly close guard; Amnon could not therefore act as did his father with Bathsheba. [3–7] It is Jonadab, the son of David's brother Shimeah (Shammah, I. 16.9; 17.13), who sets things in motion. His cunning advice, the consequences of which he has apparently not made clear (see below), is immediately taken up and put into effect by Amnon, who is obviously ready for anything. The basis of it is evidently the custom of preparing a special meal for the sick (*biryā*); the root *bārā* is also used for 'bread of consolation'. In addition, the dish in question is—only in this case?—described as *lebībā*, for the making of which the related verb stem *lābab* (piel) is a customary term. This has been thought to be connected with *lēbāb*, heart, and hence heart-shaped cakes have been envisaged. But such a view is highly improbable. The more likely meaning is 'what the heart desires' (the heart being the 'seat of feelings, emotions and manifold internal agitations', GB); in other words, what the invalid has an appetite for, his favourite dish. Despite a detailed description of the way in which the food was prepared, it is impossible to tell whether it was 'baked' or 'boiled'. In any case, the invalid can count on such a degree of consideration during his nursing as will even temporarily set aside the fixed custom of keeping a young woman under close surveillance. Jonadab's plan is based on this. Moreover, he counts on the king visiting the invalid, a valid assumption in view of Amnon's position as crown prince, and David's love for him. Only the bare essentials are narrated here; such a call in the East would, in fact, be extremely protracted (with continual inquiries about the patient's state of health!).

[8–14] The king agrees, and Tamar comes. The food is prepared in a vestibule or side room, so that Amnon, lying on a bed 'in the chamber' can see everything that goes on, and in the presence of at least one servant (and probably several, cf. 9b). The servant is then evidently meant to take the food to the invalid. Amnon's refusal to eat is regarded as a whim of the crown prince, who is so used to giving orders, and perhaps also respected as a symptom of his illness. He succeeds in this way in getting the men out and Tamar, who alone remains, has to bring the food to his bed. So he reaches the desired goal, and even the touching request of the girl, which is as wise as it is warmly put, cannot prevent him from forcing her. Neither a consideration of the consequences for her and for himself (and here there is a clear reflection of what happens later) nor the possibility of asking for the girl in marriage has any effect. He does the 'wanton folly', folly which is not simply 'stupidity' but a culpable misdemeanour.

[15–17] The sudden change from passionate love to passionate hate is certainly not a characteristic of the 'spoilt sensualist, indeed even libertine' (Budde) nor a consequence of the girl's furious struggles (Ehrlich). It is a sexual, psychological factor ('sexual hatred') which provides a parallel to the almost morbid passion at the beginning. Moreover the disenchantment which now sets in could make room for the pangs of conscience which Tamar had wanted to awake. As thoughtless now as before, he orders Tamar to be put outside, and despite her urgent representations—the 'ōdōt at the beginning seems, as in v. 13, to contain the request that he will still look at her situation—this is immediately done by the servant who has been summoned for the purpose.

[18–20] Tamar knows well enough what is in store for her; it will now become clear what has happened to her and that means that she must now lead a solitary life, as there will be no one who will desire her. Her wearing of the long-sleeved robe, a specially cut garment and the sign of the virgin princess, must seem to her a mockery when she is thrown out into the street like an irksome prostitute; this may be the reason why the remark about her dress is inserted at this point. She runs home as though in deep mourning; the ashes, the torn garments, the hand laid on her head, are all well-known expressions of such a situation. What her brother Absalom says to her is little enough. But what else is he to say? It is no comfort to her that the matter is 'kept in the family'. Her fate is sealed, as we are told in blunt words; here the word šōmēmā is particularly impressive; it properly means 'desolate', 'laid waste'. She remains in her brother's house, i.e. in the same place as before (against Budde), a widow who has never been a wife. We hear nothing of any other consequences of Amnon's action.

[21–22] The reaction of David and Absalom is more important to the narrator. Anger breaks out, but nothing is done; David's love for his children (cf. later in ch. 19) has something unmanly about it. In Absalom there is a hate which he does not express, but which eats into him and is thus all the more dangerous. What David does not do

possibilities. Either Ephraim is the present *eṭ-ṭaiyibe*, about twelve
miles north-east of Jerusalem as the crow flies; in that case the name
Baal-hazor would be that of the mount *el-'aṣur*, north of *eṭ-ṭaiyibe*. Or
the LXX reading Gophraim (*'ephrōn*?) is right (Josh. 15.9) and the
neighbourhood is therefore that of *khirbet ḥazzur* (between *en-nebi
samwil* and the main road). This is much nearer to Jerusalem, about
four miles away as the crow flies.[a] We will return to this question
later.

[24–27] Absalom at first invites the king's sons; this is perhaps a
stereotyped expression for the other princes apart from the successor
to the throne (quite clearly so in v. 27). Then he goes to the king,
perhaps already assuming that he himself will not come, but in the
hope that he will send the crown prince. The king courteously de-
clines and by his blessing (the present Arabic *ma'salame*, 'go in peace')
declares that the audience is ended. While, as it were, on his way out,
Absalom extracts the king's consent, which is evidently necessary for
Amnon to go. The royal permission was presumably not absolutely
necessary for the participation of the others.

[28–29, 34a] So the plan can be carried out. Late in the day and
at a given signal Amnon is killed by Absalom's daring servants.
A turbulent scene follows. Everyone mounts and rides off (on mules,
an evident sign of nobility). Even Absalom, apparently quickly
sobered, takes flight. We hear nothing of what happens to the murderers. The responsibility, as Absalom has said earlier, lies completely
with the man who gave the orders.

[30–33] The report goes ahead of the princes; how this is possible
is not said. The event has already been considerably exaggerated; all
the princes are said to have been killed. The effect on the king and on
the court is as might be expected. Here Jonadab once again intervenes. He once again proves 'his wisdom; but it is prompted by a
guilty conscience' (Budde). The voice of reason speaks rightly and
persuades the king. But even the truth would be small comfort! [34b–
35] Jonadab is, in fact, right: the watchman announces the approach
of a group of men. The question of the locality of the murder is not
made any clearer here. The place name used to describe the road
occurs only once in the MT and is clearly corrupt (*'aḥᵃrāw* means
'behind him'); it occurs twice in the LXX, but even here the picture
given by the manuscripts is completely confused. 'Horonaim' is
usually accepted as the reading. The road of this name runs north-

[a]Cf. *PJB* 24, 1928, pp. 13–15 and 25, 1929, pp. 11f.

west from Jerusalem to the two Beth-horons, but it cannot be seen from the south-east hill of the city of Jerusalem, whereas the messenger expressly states that he has seen the people approaching by the road in question. As a result, there is much to be said for the conjecture Eissfeldt and Alt that we should read 'Bahurim' for the uncertain place name.[a] In that case, the princes would be coming under the slope of the mount of Olives, on the same road along which David is later to flee, and by crossing the Kidron valley would quickly have reached Jerusalem. This route could have been seen from the city. All in all, then, if we think back to the two possible locations for the sheep-shearing, the first mentioned (Ephraim = et-ṭaiyibe) must be preferred.

[36–37] The sorrowful reunion is reported very briefly; it is followed by a long period of mourning kept by the king. Amnon, as we learnt from the previous section, occupied a special place in his heart. Moreover, he has now lost two sons. For Absalom, now gone into exile—to his grandfather (3.3), the king of Geshur (a tribe in present-day Syria; cf. my commentary on Josh. 13.11, 13)—was in David's own opinion to be regarded as lost and could hardly count as a successor. Thus these events conclude with deep distress, which has been caused by equally deep guilt.

7. ABSALOM RETURNS TO FAVOUR: 13.38–14.33

13 [38]So Absalom fled, and went to Geshur, and was there three years. [39]And David gradually began to lose his abhorrence of Absalom;[b] for he was comforted about Amnon, seeing he was dead. 14 [1]Now Joab the son of Zeruiah perceived that the king's heart went out to Absalom. [2]And Joab sent to Tekoa, and fetched from there a wise woman, and said to her, 'Pretend to be a mourner, and put on mourning garments; do not anoint yourself with oil, but behave like a woman who has been mourning many days for the dead; [3]and go to the king and speak thus to him.' So Joab put the words in her mouth.

[4] When the woman of Tekoa went in[c] to the king, she fell on her face to the ground, and did obeisance, and said, 'Help, O king.' [5]And the king said to her, 'What is your trouble?' She answered, 'Alas, I am

---

[a]Cf. *PJB* 22, 1926, pp. 30–32.

[b]A passage which only makes sense with conjectures. It is quite wrong to suppose that David ceases to 'go out' against Absalom, although MT seems to have thought this. Here, the first verb has been pointed as a qal (*wattēkal*, cf. *ekopasen* LXX), the final *l* before 'David' written once again, and *happallāṣūt* read for *hammelek lāṣēt* (cf. Caspari). The confusion may have arisen by the beginning of this word becoming illegible and being taken for the present 'the king'. On the other hand, it is now striking, as elsewhere 'the king' stands before, not after 'David'.

[c]See BH.

a widow; my husband is dead. [6]And your handmaid had two sons, and they quarrelled with one another in the field; there was no one to part them, and one struck the other and killed him.[a] [7]And now the whole family has risen against your handmaid, and they say, "Give up the man who struck his brother, that we may kill him for the life of his brother whom he slew"; and so they would destroy the heir also. Thus they would quench my coal that is left, and leave to my husband neither name nor remnant upon the face of the earth.'

8 Then the king said to the woman, 'Go to your house, and I will give orders concerning you.' [9]And the woman of Tekoa said to the king, 'On me be the guilt, my lord the king, and on my father's house; let the king and his throne be guiltless.' [10]The king said, 'If anyone says anything to you, bring him to me, and he shall never touch you again.' [11]Then she said, 'Pray let the king invoke the LORD your God, that the avenger of blood slay no more, and my son be not destroyed.' He said, 'As the LORD lives, not one hair of your son shall fall to the ground.'

12 Then the woman said, 'Pray let your handmaid speak a word to my lord the king.' He said, 'Speak.' [13]And the woman said, 'Why then have you planned such a thing against the people of God? For in giving this decision the king convicts himself, inasmuch as the king does not bring his banished one home again. [14]We must all die, we are like water spilt on the ground, which cannot be gathered up again; but God will not take away a life, and he devises means not to keep his banished one an outcast. [15]Now I have come to say this to my lord the king because the people have made me afraid; and your handmaid thought, "I will speak to the king; it may be that the king will perform the request of his servant. [16]For the king will hear, and deliver his servant from the hand of the man who would destroy me and my son together from the heritage of God." [17]And your handmaid thought, "The word of my lord the king will set me at rest"; for my lord the king is like the angel of God to discern good and evil. The LORD your God be with you.'

18 Then the king answered the woman, 'Do not hide from me anything I ask you.' And the woman said, 'Let my lord the king speak.' [19]The king said, 'Is the hand of Joab with you in all this?' The woman answered and said, 'As surely as you live, my lord the king, one cannot turn to the right hand or to the left from anything that my lord the king has said. It was your servant Joab who bade me; it was he who put all these words in the mouth of your handmaid. [20]In order to change the course of affairs your servant Joab did this. But my lord has wisdom like the wisdom of the angel of God to know all things that are on the earth.'

21 Then the king said to Joab, 'Behold now, I grant[b] this; go, bring back the young man Absalom.' [22]And Joab fell on his face to the ground

[a]Free translation. Text perhaps corrupt, see BH.
[b]Perfect, meaning 'I have decided to . . .'

and did obeisance, and blessed the king; and Joab said, 'Today your servant knows that I have found favour in your sight, my lord the king, in that the king has granted the request of his servant.'[a] 23So Joab arose and went to Geshur, and brought Absalom to Jerusalem. 24And the king said, 'Let him dwell apart in his own house; he is not to come into my presence.' So Absalom dwelt apart in his own house, and did not come into the king's presence.

25 Now in all Israel there was no one so much to be praised for his beauty as Absalom; from the sole of his foot to the crown of his head there was no blemish in him. 26And when he cut the hair of his head (for he used to cut it from time to time; when it was heavy on him, he cut it), he weighed the hair of his head, two hundred shekels by the king's weight. 27There were born to Absalom three sons, and one daughter whose name was Tamar; she was a beautiful woman.

28 So Absalom dwelt two full years in Jerusalem, without coming into the king's presence. 29Then Absalom sent for Joab, to send him to the king; but Joab would not come to him. And he sent a second time, but Joab would not come. 30Then he said to his servants, 'See, Joab's field is next to mine, and he has barley there; go and set it on fire.' So Absalom's servants set the field on fire. 31Then Joab arose and went to Absalom at his house, and said to him, 'Why have your servants set my field on fire?' 32Absalom answered Joab, 'Behold, I sent word to you, "Come here, that I may send you to the king, to ask, 'Why have I come from Geshur? It would be better for me to be there still.' Now therefore let me go into the presence of the king; and if there is guilt in me, let him kill me." ' 33Then Joab went to the king, and told him; and he summoned Absalom. So he came to the king, and bowed himself on his face to the ground before the king; and the king kissed Absalom.

The circumstances surrounding the succession to the throne of David make such a chain of unfortunate events that we can only wonder continually at the unsparing frankness of the biblical chronicler. The account of Absalom occupies the greatest amount of room and this, too, is characterized by considerable misery and guilt. It is thus all the more astonishing that the narrator at this point introduces a chapter which notwithstanding the seriousness of the matters to be described has about it an atmosphere of relaxation, a chapter which lingers comfortably over events and is even suffused by a humorous light. This is true principally of the conversation between David and the woman, but later also of Absalom's dealings with Joab.

[13.38–39] If the third mention of Absalom's flight does, in fact, form part of the original text,[b] it must be regarded as the introduction

---

aAs in v. 20, 'do the thing' stands both times for 'grant the request'.

bThis is the most probable thing. Why should a later writer wish to report the same happening for a second or even a third time?

to ch. 14. This is also supported by the indication of time given. The three years are long enough to heal the wounds caused by Amnon's death, even in David. A reconciliation with Absalom is thus possible. [14.1–4] The reason for Joab's intervention is not given. Is it sympathy for Absalom? It is he who later brings about Absalom's death against David's express orders. Joab is probably concerned about David's successor, and the energetic young man, resembling him in so many ways, seems to him the best possibility. He does not use direct conversation to further his purpose, but a method similar to that employed by Nathan in ch. 12. This is itself surprising, as he acts differently in 3.24 and 19.6ff. Perhaps Joab had made unsuccessful attempts earlier. David's remark in v. 19 might be confirmation of this.

[14.5–11] The 'wise woman' is to be imagined as a person distinguished by her gifts and her authority (cf. 20.16), somewhat like the present Arabian *sheha*. She comes from Tekoa, the village of Amos, which lies two hours' journey south of Bethlehem. The woman is absolutely right for her supposed role. The story of the two sons could happen even today among the Bedouins living round Tekoa. Blood vengeance on a brother's murderer is to be exacted by the family of the dead man. Such customs prevail even today in Palestine; conflicts between them and the laws of the Government were particularly noticeable during the time of the foreign mandate. Behind the account lies the intention of the family to lay aside the 'heir' and thus take over his possessions.[a] David here appears strong enough to assert himself against such ideas. The special element of this story, which is also well constructed from a psychological point of view, is that the woman wishes to involve the king completely in his decision. She is therefore not content with interesting the king in her case, or appealing to his mercy, as in the image of quenching her coal. Nor, therefore, is she content merely to receive his assurance that he will put the matter right. Not that she means to express any doubt about his will or his memory. But she is afraid—if she refers to the king's words—that she herself and her family (see the case of Samson's wife, Judg. 15.6) will be called to account, instead of the king, who is responsible for the decision. She therefore requires the king to support his decision by calling upon the name of Yahweh. In this way she makes sure that the king and not herself now appears

---

[a]The same problem, but with completely different antecedents, occurs in the Book of Ruth.

as the 'opposite number' to the vengeful family. And above all, in her fictitious case, the king has formally, by a sacred oath, affirmed that he will not expiate the killing of a brother by new killing, but will allow grace to prevail so that the 'name' may be preserved.

[14.12–14] The woman can now disclose her intentions. She does it carefully, but unmistakably. The people of God takes the place of the family. Absalom is not mentioned by name; he is described as the 'banished one'. The woman dares to call the king 'guilty'—against the people of God—if he does not allow the banished one to return home. Just as the continuation of the family was at stake earlier, so, too, the progress of the cause of the land and of the people is involved, and in the last resort therefore probably the succession to the throne. If Absalom is not pardoned, the woman implies, his fate will be to die in a foreign land. The next sentence is probably meant to remind the king: we must all die some time, even Absalom, whether abroad or at home. Is this said against a possible objection on the part of the king? Perhaps, however, the half verse is meant to recall Amnon (cf. Thenius) and to say: the dead cannot be brought back to life, even by harshness against the living. This is then appropriately followed by the conclusion that God does not will 'to take away a life', but to bring his banished one home again. It seems better to understand the passage in this way than to accept the usual emendation of *weḥāšab* into *weḥōšēb* (Ewald) and so reach the remarkable meaning that God will not take away one who concerns himself to bring back an exile—as though the woman wished to give David a guarantee of a long life in return for his expected act of mercy. If the text remains unemended, as has been suggested, it will mean to the king that God wills the same for Absalom's case as he, the king, confirmed by his oath was his will in the case of the woman's son.

[14.15–17] The conclusion of the woman's speech is particularly fine. In it she returns to her own case, still heard with great patience by the king. For this reason, Budde thought that the verses belonged after v. 7. This is, however, to mistake the position. The three verses are not to be regarded as a gush of feminine loquacity, though this, too, is not wholly lacking; two things in particular are to be noted. First, the woman means to give the impression that her own personal problem is the reason for her appearance and the case of the exiled king's son is mentioned only incidentally, as a related instance. By the construction of her address she means to make what is, of course, her main concern, the case of Absalom, seem to be a subsidiary matter. This way of proceeding will have made the old audiences smile; the men of the East would do the same today. There is, moreover, a kind of *double entendre* in the woman's words, so that she appears to describe her own case when, in fact, she is referring to the king's case. This can already be seen in the remark that she hopes that her request will be fulfilled; indeed she has certain hope (v. 16a) that the king for his part will hearken; we should also notice the hint that the killing of the son would affect both her son and herself; in the case of the king this means that Absalom's removal would considerably affect not only the son but also the father. The mention of the 'heritage of God', which means primarily the land— as God's fief to his people—can equally well allude to the situation of the king and his dynasty. The fact that the king decides what is good and what is evil—here virtually what is right and what is wrong—could mean that the woman wishes the king to do just this in his own case also. Even the prayer of blessing could have pregnant significance to the effect that Yahweh who has always been 'with' David will be with him again in the decisions which are now necessary. The speech is further characterized by the pathos of the suppliant position of the woman who speaks and the exalted position of the person whom she addresses; this can still be seen in the eastern style of today.

[14.18–20] The king immediately sees what is afoot. His immediate mention of Joab shows that he knows the latter's views on the banishment of Absalom. The woman answers charmingly once David has uncovered her connection with Joab. She feels that the only thing to do now is to lay all her cards on the table; by comparing the king to an angel of Yahweh, who knows everything, she pays extravagant compliments to his wisdom—the same word 'wise' which was used earlier to describe the woman herself[a]—and thus delivers herself entirely to his judgment and his mercy. She already knows that the victory is hers, but as a really 'wise woman' she must let the man appear the victor.

[14.21–24] The woman then disappears without further mention and the writer proceeds to his goal. The recall of Absalom is arranged by David as briefly as possible, and there is no expression of his personal share in the matter. David's restraint, which immediately

[a]For the characterization of 'wisdom' of this sort see Cazelles in *SVT* 3, 1955, p. 267.

manifests itself, seems already to be hinted at here. Joab's thanks and joy are real. The remark that he 'blesses' the king evidently refers to one of the prayers for blessing which are still known even today; he presumably makes a gesture of blessing. Here and also between the lines there is much evidence of a court ceremonial which seems already to be developed, despite the short duration of the Davidic kingdom. 'Falling on the face' and 'doing obeisance' (*hištaḥᵃwōt*: it seems that two successive acts are imagined) and also 'in the king's presence' (occurring frequently), even 'going in' and, in the circumstances of the previous remark, the kiss at the conclusion of the interview, are all parts of this ceremonial, which perhaps also includes the 'blessing' (by the king, 13.25; Joab's blessing at 14.22 differs) and perhaps the call for 'help' at the beginning of the interview (v. 4). We might further ask whether Joab's 'arising' at v. 23 marks the end of a sitting posture to which the king will have directed him after the initial *proskynesis*—this would in itself be remarkable, as the subordinate usually stood in the presence of his superior—or whether here it merely means 'depart'. Joab then goes to Geshur and brings back Absalom, who is not yet, however, fully restored to grace, contrary to his own and Joab's expectations. But his position is not some kind of house arrest, though vv. 28ff. might suggest this.

[14.25–27] Some remarks about Absalom's person are inserted at this point, perhaps because the gap of two years seemed appropriate to the compiler for their interpolation. In any case, it is unsatisfactory to put the verses before ch. 15; v. 28 is formed in such a way that it will not join directly to v. 24, but presupposes the intervention of something (cf. Budde 264). Absalom's appearance is depicted in bright colours, just as his sister Tamar is described as being beautiful and desirable in 13.1ff. The anecdote about his hair would have been passed round among the people; the weight of the hair, cut occasionally (yearly?), is put at four and a half pounds (LXX halves the weight).[a] This figure is far too high, but so the story went. The details about his family contradict 18.18; according to that, he has no son. The daughter is mentioned here, not because she bears the name of her unfortunate aunt, but because the sons

[a]For the weight see Galling, *BRL*, p. 187. The 'king's' weight is hardly, as he thinks, a *special* standard; it is rather a *reliable* one. (See also C. H. Gordon, *Ugaritic Handbook* [Analecta Orientalia 25], 1947, p. 36, n. 1. We might compare the British 'Imperial' weights and measures.—Tr.)

will have died young, leaving only her to him. The picture of Absalom, drawn here with evident admiration, shows a refined, attractive prince, who seems well suited to represent his people in the highest office.

[14.28–33] The episode at the end also pictures him as a determined man, who knows well enough what he wants. When he is unsuccessful in summoning Joab to his house for an interview he has his barley field burnt down out of hand; the fact that Joab, like Absalom, possessed fields, and also Absalom's sheep-shearing, shows how the members of the court shared in the agrarian character of the people and the land. In this way, Absalom compels Joab to come to him, to hear his representations and to take them to the king. Absalom now stakes everything on one last chance. His wishes are heard. The king receives him and with his kiss ratifies his acceptance back to favour. Nowhere is it said that the delay in restoration has left its mark on Absalom, but this is to be presumed if we are to understand what happens next. The whole handling of the case of Absalom and Amnon by the king is clumsy. Just as in the section about Uriah and his wife, so here a clear verdict is given about David, not only that—as the previous section told us—he sees his own sins re-enacted in the persons of his sons, but also that here he largely fails. All the time the unseen Ruler stands in the background, seeing and avenging sin, but still generally displaying astonishing mercy, despite the human failure in respect of the promise.

8. ABSALOM'S REBELLION: 15.1–12

15 ¹After this Absalom got himself a chariot and horses, and fifty men to run before him. ²And Absalom used to rise early and stand beside the way of the gate; and when any man had a suit to come before the king for judgment, Absalom would call to him, and say, 'From what city are you?' And when he said, 'Your servant is of such and such a tribe in Israel,' ³Absalom would say to him, 'See, your claims are good and right; but there is no man deputed by the king to hear you.' ⁴Absalom said moreover, 'Oh that I were judge in the land! Then every man with a suit or cause might come to me, and I would give him justice.' ⁵And whenever a man came near to do obeisance to him, he would put out his hand, and take hold of him, and kiss him. ⁶Thus Absalom did to all of Israel who came to the king for judgment; so Absalom stole the hearts of the men of Israel.

7 And at the end of four[a] years Absalom said to the king, 'Pray let

[a]MT and some ancient witnesses read 'forty'. The error may be a result of mishearing; the endings of 'arbāʿīm šānā and 'arbaʿ šānīm were confused.

me go and pay my vow, which I have vowed to the LORD, in Hebron.
[8]For your servant vowed a vow while I dwelt at Geshur in Aram,
saying, "If the LORD will indeed bring me back to Jerusalem, then I
will offer worship to the LORD." ' [9]The king said to him, 'Go in peace.'
So he arose, and went to Hebron. [10]But Absalom sent secret messengers
throughout all the tribes of Israel, saying, 'As soon as you hear the
sound of the trumpet, then say, "Absalom is king in Hebron!" ' [11]With
Absalom went two hundred men from Jerusalem who were invited
guests, and they went in their simplicity and knew nothing. [12]And
while Absalom was offering sacrifices, he sent for[a] Ahithophel the
Gilonite, David's counsellor, from his city Giloh. And the conspiracy
grew strong, and the people with Absalom kept increasing.

[1] With short strokes, but with extreme vividness, Absalom's rise
from being a recently exiled prince to the seat of power is now depicted. Absalom's recognition of the propaganda value of first surrounding himself with a bodyguard fits what we hear of his external
appearance in ch. 14. It was not the custom in Israel to act in this
way. We hear similar things of Joseph in the court of Pharaoh at
Gen. 41.43, and I. 8.11 includes the keeping of chariots and horses
and the appointment of attendants among the things which will lay
the monarchy open to the charge of being a pagan institution. A
similar evaluation is intended in II. 15; Absalom introduces strange
customs—which he perhaps learned from his grandfather, the pagan
king! Adonijah also begins his attempt on the crown in similar
fashion (I Kings 1.5). [2–6] Absalom's dealings with the men who
have a summons to the court have a more serious effect. The 'gate',
at the approach to which Absalom stations himself—presumably on
the appointed days of judgment—is, of course, a door, or the door,
to the palace building and not the gate of the city. Absalom seems
to have been particularly concerned with the members of the tribes
of Israel. Here lay the root of the problem; the northern tribes were
the uncertain part of the people. Evidently the king held regular
days of judgment, perhaps specially for the northern tribes, such as
there had been during the institution of the judges.[b] The king is the
supreme authority. It emerges indirectly from this account that
there was discontent about the way in which David exercised the
office of 'judge of Israel', particularly in 'Israel' (cf. on 8.15–18).
The same is recorded of Moses (Ex. 18.33ff.), who was not equal to

[a]See BH.
[b]Cf. Judg. 4.4 and Hertzberg, 'Die Kleinen Richter', *TLZ* 79, 1954, esp.
col. 289.

the task by himself. Inadequacies and above all, of course, injustices in the administration of the law always aroused criticism among the people of Israel, particularly from the prophets. So this side of David's government was the area in which Absalom could gain ground. His winning personality (cf. 14.25f.) here affords him considerable help. He commends himself as a judge and underlines this by an act which seems to overcome social differences. Such a thing will have run like wildfire through the villages, so that the verdict that he 'stole the hearts of the men of Israel' is in no way exaggerated.

[7–9] Absalom thus acts calmly and with consideration. He does not hurry anything. For four years—after his reconciliation with the king—he waits; in this way the incidents involving Amnon can retreat more and more into the background, and the seed spread over Israel has time to grow. He evidently thinks that he has nothing to fear from the men of Judah. At all events, the blow is to be struck at Hebron, their most important city and a holy place. Hebron is the city where Absalom was born (3.2f.); perhaps moreover, it was hostile to David, because he had transferred his residence thence to Jerusalem. The reason which Absalom gives for his journey to Hebron sounds plausible to the king (though he may have wondered why Absalom should have waited so long to have paid his vow); it is also skilful, as the great sacrificial feast 'before Yahweh in Hebron' provided him with the opportunity of gathering a large body of men around him without exciting suspicion. [10–11] Moreover, the two hundred men who, all unsuspecting, are invited with him must now for good or ill become Absalom's partisans. At the same time, the flame of rebellion will be stirred up in Israel by $m^e ragg^e lim$ (scouts, agents with a special commission directed against the régime), and preparations will be made to seize power; the official expression of this is the word $mālak$, he is made king (Isa. 52.7). From all this it once again becomes clear that the Israelites in the narrower sense are the decisive factor for Absalom. He means at least to keep the men of Judah neutral; he already knows the political significance of 'sympathizers', as the example of the two hundred shows.[a] [12a] Among those whom Absalom knows how to win over to his side, Ahithophel is especially mentioned. He is the grandfather of Bathsheba (11.3; 23.34). It is possible that David's treatment of his granddaughter may have put him in opposition to the king; on the other hand, Bathsheba's subsequent position would

[a]On this see also Alt, *Kleine Schriften* II, p. 57.

have been sufficient to settle any conflict. The fact that he does not set out from Jerusalem with Absalom but is summoned from his home at Giloh[a] suggests that this 'counsellor' of the king no longer functioned as such. The name Ahithophel ('my brother is folly') seems purposely to have been distorted, perhaps from the form Ahiphelet. The proper name Eliphelet is evidenced more than once, cf. II Sam. 5.16; 23.34. Only a transposition of consonants (with the alteration of the t into a t) would then be necessary, along with the pointing of $b\bar{o}\check{s}et$, shame (cf. Meribbaal, Ishbaal).

[12b] So without any suspicions on David's part a political crisis brews up behind his back which seriously jeopardizes the existence of his kingdom. Seen in its entirety, Absalom's undertaking is an attempt to turn the further history of the people of God to his own ends. This is alarming not only in respect of the history itself, but still more in respect of the theological situation. For in the background are always two questions: Who is now the successor intended by the supreme guidance? and Who is it that in the last resort shapes history?

9. DAVID'S FLIGHT FROM JERUSALEM:
15.13–16.14

15 [13]And a[b] messenger came to David, saying, 'It is certain;[c] the hearts of the men of Israel have gone after Absalom.' [14]Then David said to all his servants who were with him in Jerusalem, 'Arise, and let us flee; or else there will be no escape for us from Absalom; go in haste, lest he overtake us quickly, and bring down evil on us, and smite the city with the edge of the sword.' [15]And the king's servants said to the king, 'Behold, your servants are ready to do whatever my[d] lord the king decides.' [16]So the king went forth, and all his household after him. And the king left the[e] ten concubines to keep the house. [17]And the king went forth, and all the people after him; and they halted at the last house. [18]And all his servants remained[f] at his side; and all the Cherethites and Pelethites, and Ittai the Gittite[g] and all the six hundred Gittites who had followed him from Gath, passed on before the king.

[a]Josh. 15.51, according to which it lies in the region of Hebron (cf. 54); cf. Abel, *Géographie de la Palestine* II, p. 338. On this possibility see Alt, *PJB* 23, 1927, pp. 28f.
[b]In the text there is 'the' = the one in question, GK § 126q, r.
[c]This must be the meaning of the prefaced $h\bar{a}y\bar{a}$.
[d]The LXX emendation 'our lord' is intentional. 'My' lord is the usual form.
[e]On the mark of the accusative (*'ēt*) with indeterminative nouns see GK § 117d. The 'ten concubines' are thus 'those who are known', although they are only mentioned later.
[f]See BH.
[g]The words *we'ittay haggittī* have been omitted through a scribal error.

19 Then the king said to Ittai the Gittite, 'Why do you also go with us? Go back, and stay with the king; for you are a foreigner, and also an exile from your home. 20You came only yesterday, and shall I today make you wander about with us, seeing that I go I know not where? Go back, and take your brethren with you; and may the LORD show[a] steadfast love and faithfulness to you.' 21But Ittai answered the king, 'As the LORD lives, and as my lord the king lives, no; wherever my lord the king shall be, whether for death or for life, there also will your servant be.' 22And David said to Ittai, 'Go then, pass on.' So Ittai the Gittite passed on, with all his men and all the baggage he had with him. 23And all the country wept aloud as all the people passed by, and the king stood at[a] the brook Kidron, and all the people passed on before him toward the wilderness.[a]

24 And Abiathar[b] came up, and lo, Zadok came also, with all the Levites, bearing the ark of the covenant of God; and they set down the ark of God, and Abiathar offered (sacrifice) and poured out (drink-offerings),[c] until the people had all passed out of the city. 25Then the king said to Zadok, 'Carry the ark of God back into the city. If I find favour in the eyes of the LORD, he will bring me back and let me see both it and his habitation; 26but if he says, "I have no pleasure in you", behold, here I am, let him do to me what seems good to him.' 27The king also said to Zadok the priest, 'Look, you and Abiathar; go[d] back to the city in peace with your two sons, Ahimaaz your son, and Jonathan the son of Abiathar. 28See, I will wait at the fords of the wilderness, until word comes from you to inform me.' 29So Zadok and Abiathar carried the ark of God back to Jerusalem; and they remained there.

30 But David went up the ascent of the Mount of Olives, weeping as he went, barefoot and with his head covered; and all the people who were with him covered their heads, and they went up, weeping as they went. 31And it was told David,[a] 'Ahithophel is among the conspirators with Absalom.' And David said, 'O LORD, I pray thee, turn the counsel of Ahithophel into foolishness.'

32 When David came to the summit, where God was worshipped, behold, Hushai the Archite, David's friend,[a] came to meet him with his coat rent and earth upon his head. 33David said to him, 'If you go on with me, you will be a burden to me. 34But if you return to the city, and say to Absalom, "I will be your servant, my lord king;[a] as I have been your father's servant in time past, so now I will be your servant",[e] then you will defeat for me the counsel of Ahithophel. 35Are not Zadok

[a]See BH.

[b]Preserved in LXX as *apo beithar*, in MT as *berīt*.

[c]MT has *wayyaṣṣīqū* = 'they poured out' instead of the *wayyaṣṣigū* = 'they set down' which might have been expected. Perhaps the former stood after 'of God' or, as *wayyaṣṣēq*, after 'Abiathar'. This course has been taken above.

[d]The text, which now does not mention Abiathar (despite its fluctuation between the second person singular and, at the end, the second person plural), appears to have been altered later; cf. BH.

[e]For the construction, see GK § 134d.

and Abiathar the priests with you there? So whatever you hear from the king's house, tell it to Zadok and Abiathar the priests. ³⁶Behold, their two sons are with them there, Ahimaaz, Zadok's son, and Jonathan, Abiathar's son; and by them you shall send to me everything you hear.' ³⁷So Hushai, David's friend, came into the city, just as Absalom was entering Jerusalem.

16 ¹When David had passed a little beyond the summit, Ziba the servant of Meribbaalᵃ met him, with a couple of asses saddled, bearing two hundred loaves of bread, a hundred bunches of raisins, a hundred of summer fruits, and a skin of wine. ²And the king said to Ziba, 'Why have you brought these?' Ziba answered, 'The asses are for the king's household to ride on, the bread and summer fruit for the young men to eat, and the wine for those who faint in the wilderness to drink.' ³And the king said, 'And where is your master's son?' Ziba said to the king, 'Behold, he remains in Jerusalem; for he said, "Today the house of Israel will give me back the kingdom of my father." ' ⁴Then the king said to Ziba, 'Behold, all that belonged to Meribbaal is now yours.' And Ziba said, 'I do obeisance; let me ever find favour in your sight, my lord the king.'

5 When King David came to Bahurim, there came out a man of the family of the house of Saul, whose name was Shimei, the son of Gera; and as he came he cursed continually. ⁶And he threw stones at David, and at all the servants of King David; and all the people and all the mighty men were on his right hand and on his left. ⁷And Shimei said as he cursed, 'Begone, begone, you man of blood, you worthless fellow! ⁸The LORD has turned back upon you all the blood of the house of Saul, in whose place you have reigned; and the LORD has given the kingdom into the hand of your son Absalom. See, your ruin is on you; for you are a man of blood.'

9 Then Abishai the son of Zeruiah said to the king, 'Why should this dead dog curse my lord the king? Let me go over and take off his head.' ¹⁰But the king said, 'What have I to do with you, you sons of Zeruiah? If he is cursing because the LORD has said to him, "Curse David", who then shall say, "Why have you done so?" ' ¹¹And David said to Abishai and to all his servants, 'Behold my own son seeks my life; how much more now may this Benjaminite! Let him alone, and let him curse; for the LORD has bidden him. ¹²It may be that the LORD will look upon my affliction,ᵇ and that the LORD will turn back to me good for this cursing of me today.' ¹³So David and his men went on the road, while Shimei went along on the hillside opposite him and cursed as he went, and threw stones at him and flung dust. ¹⁴And the king, and all the people who were with him, arrived weary at the water;ᶜ and there he refreshed himself.

ᵃSee BH and on 4.4 and 9.6.
ᵇSee BH.
ᶜʿad-hammayim could easily have been overlooked alongside ʿayēpīm. It is also possible that the striking plural form ʿayēpīm is a miswriting of ʿad-hammayim (on the nomenclature, see 17.21) (so Joüon, Biblica, 1928, p. 312).

The account of David's flight from Jerusalem to the Jordan, though engagingly and vividly told, gives only the essential details, in accordance with the normal biblical style. For example, we are not told that David was in any way grateful for the circumstances and declarations that were in his favour; he does not say a word of thanks either to Ittai or Hushai or Ziba. As the attitude of these men is not something that could be taken for granted—otherwise it would not have been reported at all—this mention will have been left aside as being less important. David shows his true greatness on this his day of misfortune. He humbly bows himself under the bitter blow and leaves the future to the Lord, without, however, neglecting to take what steps he can. The direction of his flight is wisely chosen. Going towards the south, to the tribe of Judah, he would run straight into the hands of Absalom, although—as becomes clear later—he has many friends there. The Israelite territory in the north and the conquered land of the Philistines to the west are too unsafe, so that at first the wilderness, the classic goal of all fugitives, with the land east of Jordan in the background, is the only remaining possibility.

[15.13–15] The decision to leave Jerusalem is taken as soon as the news comes. This, significantly enough, does not say that Absalom has Judah behind him. As is proved later, that is not, in fact, the case; but at the moment, as David knows, he cannot count upon Judah. Now Israel is in any case lost; this is reported to the king as the real piece of bad news and in a form which makes it clear that here is no act of force on the part of Absalom, but a manifest transfer of the allegiance of the people to a new king and their desertion from the old. Absalom has acted very skilfully in choosing Hebron as his starting-point; not only has he won Israel over to his side, but he has also crippled Judah. So the king decides to evacuate the city, not only to save himself and his men, but also so as not to expose Jerusalem to the devastation which would take place were it really besieged and captured.[a] [15.16] David takes his family with him, as he must fear that the usurper will carefully do away with his half-brothers (cf. Judg. 9.5).[b] The concubines, whom he does not imagine to be in any danger, are to 'keep house' in the strict meaning of the phrase during the hours or days of the interregnum. [15.17–18] In addition, the king takes out of Jerusalem all the loyal troops

[a]At the end of 1917 the German and Turkish armies evacuated Jerusalem for the same considerations and abandoned the city to the enemy without a struggle.
[b]The question of Absalom's mother, sister and children is left open.

under his command, the Jerusalem garrison proper, the 'servants of David', the guard in the strict sense of the word. Of course, David will have asked other able-bodied men to go with him from Jerusalem, but the host as a whole, either from Judah or from Israel, was not at his disposal. So the mention of 'all the people' will mean all the troops with the exception of the 'servants of David' (v. 23.) Also involved is the foreign legion of the Cherethites and Pelethites (cf. on 8.15ff.), whose leader Benaiah is not mentioned here; in addition, apparently as a separate contingent, there is the Philistine detachment under Ittai, six hundred men strong. A special group among the warriors, mentioned often, is formed by the '*gibbōrīm*' (v. 6), the 'mighty men', whose leader Abishai (23.18f.) is mentioned by name (v. 9). The king makes the troops march past him, except for the 'servants of David', who remain with him. The parade is held at the 'last house', which will have been at the bottom of the Kidron valley, at the place where the crossing of the stream—usually dried up—was to be made to the Mount of Olives.

[15.19–22] The account then continues by giving a number of separate pictures, first of all the conversation with Ittai. We are not told why he left Gath with a considerable number of able-bodied men; it might, however, be concluded from v. 19 that he was exiled from Gath. Perhaps the friendly attitude of Ittai—and his men— towards David may have been the very reason for his exile; the personality of the great king will have won the hearts of men from other subject peoples, just as in Goethe's boyhood Frederick the Great captivated the youths of Frankfurt despite their hostile attitude towards the Prussians. Ittai's faithfulness towards the person of the king shows clearly enough what he thinks. David loyally makes his return easy, but precisely in so doing shows that he knows how to handle men. The way David calls Absalom king is not meant as irony; it takes into consideration existing conditions and is, moreover, the appropriate way of speaking to the foreign soldier. Ittai's answer is brave and clear; it shows his friendship for David in life or death and is high praise for David. As has been said, there is no word of thanks from the king, but the later appointment of Ittai to be commander of one third of the army (18.2) is the way in which a king expresses his thanks. [15.23] So the parade goes on; the troops leave the outskirts of Jerusalem in an easterly direction, and the 'land' ('all the country'), which here means the people who are left behind, watches with sorrowful concern an event which means a farewell to a much-admired personality and a period of splendour, and the beginning of a path into an uncertain future.

[15.24–29] Before the king's personal entourage sets out, the conversation with the priests takes place. The text is unreliable here, but it can be reconstructed. Of the two priests, Zadok seems to be the one who is specially entrusted with the care of the ark, and so at this point he stands in the foreground. The note about the Levites could be a later addition; on the other hand, Zadok must have had personnel trained in transporting the ark and serving it. It is evidently his intention to accompany the king with the ark. In addition, sacrifices are offered during the parade of the troops— this is the way the text is to be understood[a]—an action which is quite reasonable in the circumstances. Here Abiathar, the real court priest, makes an appearance. The grounds for David's order to the priests to go back with the ark are theological, but there is also a practical thought behind his command. On the one hand, he leaves the decision to the grace of God in a way which would accord with the feelings and expressions of Eastern peoples even today; the king is quite serious in his belief. On the other hand, however, he sees a possibility of gaining information about events in the city with the help of the priests' two sons. The writer does not feel that he is reporting two irreconcilable elements here—David, man under God and man engaged in human activities, and, as king, both of these things to a heightened degree, is as wise as a serpent and as innocent as a dove.

[15.30] The king now climbs the Mount of Olives, fully given over to the bitter needs of the hour, in the attitude of a mourner and a penitent. His conduct primarily stems from the sorrow of the situation, but at the same time, like that of the Ninevites in Jonah 3, it is also directed towards the Lord. Everyone, and particularly David, knows that these events are not a matter of chance or luck; the question is what further action God is planning with his king and his people. It is therefore the right and the duty of king and people not to sit and await the divine decisions, but to do everything possible to show themselves worthy of the Lord. [15.31] David's reply to the news of the desertion of Ahithophel into Absalom's

---

[a]The word wayya'al is to be understood to mean 'offer sacrifices' (for the construction see I. 2.28; II. 24.22), especially as wayyaṣṣēq stands alongside it (see above ad loc.). It cannot mean 'he went up' (gal), as in that case the sentence would be meaningless. For as David himself was at the deepest part of the valley, this could only refer to Abiathar's ascent of the Mount of Olives.

camp is in accord with such a train of thought. 'The only strength of his, David's, position was Absalom's inexperience. Therefore the news is a bitter blow.'[a] Against this David makes the prayer that the Lord may turn Ahithophel's wisdom, which is fully recognized as such, into folly. [15.32–37] But once again there is not just a prayer. David's decision about Hushai is also an integral part of the matter. Hushai is described as 'the king's friend', a title which implies not merely a relationship of trust but also a definite office at court. He comes from an enclave in the border territory between Benjamin and Ephraim (Josh. 16.2), originally Canaanite, but long assimilated. Like Ahithophel, he is already elderly, as is clear from David's remark that he will be a burden if he accompanies him, and also from the wisdom which he has at his disposal. Hushai meets David on the summit of the Mount of Olives; David's route is the Bahurim road mentioned in 13.34, which will be identical with the later Roman road.[b] It is not clear from the language used whether the place of worship, which lay, as often (Tabor, Gerizim, etc.) on the summit of the mount, was still used;[c] the holy character of the land has not, however, been forgotten.[d] Hushai is one of the king's really true friends. This can be seen not only from the way in which he comes in mourning, but also from his immediate readiness to play the dangerous game which David asks of him: in accordance with the words which David himself frames exceedingly wisely, he is to find his way into the innermost circle of Absalom's counsellors, to become Ahithophel's antagonist, and then to make contact with David through the priests. Hushai is thus given a decisive role. He returns to the city just as Absalom is entering—and as David is leaving the heights of the Mount of Olives with the last of his people.

[16.1–4] Before David comes into the wilderness proper, two further incidents take place, the first of which augurs well for him, the second badly. Both are connected with the house of Saul, which again casts its shadow over David's flight into the wilderness, and not without purpose. The first is the encounter with Ziba, mentioned in ch. 9 as the servant and steward of Meribbaal. He offers the king some small help for his wearisome journeying. The description of his gifts reminds us of those which Abigail brings to David in I. 25.18.

[a]Kreyssig, *Gerechtigkeit für David*, p. 115.
[b]Cf. Alt in *PJB* 22, 1926, p. 30.
[c]Caspari's rendering, according to which David 'prays' there, is surely not right.
[d]Cf. Dalman, *Jerusalem und seine Gelände*, 1930, pp. 44f.

The account suggests that Ziba acted on the spur of the moment and took with him what he had. The king receives this action, which is physically and spiritually a refreshment for him, with friendly thanks. We may ask whether Ziba's spontaneous action is not the result of certain calculations. If Absalom emerges victorious, then nothing much can happen to him, but if David proves the victor—and this seems to Ziba more probable—he will immediately be in favour with the king. In any case he becomes an object of suspicion through what he says about Meribbaal. The latter must have been not merely crippled, but completely naïve if he believed that as a member of the house of Saul he could gain anything at all out of a change of rule. Ziba's remark seems to be distorted or invented. David's immediate trust in him, and his gift of the whole of Saul's estates, shows how he is influenced by Ziba's action in his present position and also how mistrust of the house of Saul has not really been banished from his innermost thoughts.

[16.5–14] The meeting with Shimei, who is introduced as a distant relation of Saul, is of quite a different character. Bahurim, already mentioned at 3.16 and probably also at 13.34, lies on the edge of the wilderness.[a] The route taken by David's column goes along a valley running from west to east, about half-way up the hillside. On the other side of the slope, separated by the deep valley, is Shimei. His description of David as a 'man of blood' is certainly connected with the events of II. 21, which, as has been said, preceded David's treatment of Meribbaal in ch. 9. It is also, of course, possible that Shimei further accuses David of the murder of Abner and Ishbaal, if not of the death of Saul himself—to say nothing of Uriah. The view of David's present fate as a punishment for past sins is a natural one, credible even to David. This may be connected with David's refusal that Abishai should cross the valley and kill Shimei. He sees Shimei's curses not as the subjective expression of human anger, but as the performance of a divine commission. It is remarkable that in v. 12 the phrase 'my affliction' ($b^{e^c}ony\bar{\imath}$) is read in the $k^e th\bar{\imath}b$ as $ba^c{}^aw\bar{o}n\bar{\imath}$ 'my iniquity'; according to this, presumably the correct text, David not only took his present fate upon himself with humility but also recognized the justification of the divine retribution. Nevertheless, the outrage of the cursing, which David readily allows to pass over him without taking any counter-measures, is in his eyes more

[a] Perhaps it is *ras eṭ-ṭmim*, Alt, *PJB* 22, 1926, p. 30, and 25, 1929, p. 58. Dalman, *Jerusalem und seine Gelände*, 1930, pp. 38f.

than he has deserved, and he hopes in this way to increase his favour in the sight of God. The extent to which the thought lies in these categories can be seen from the fact that the word *hēšib* (the Lord has 'turned back' your guilt upon you, literally 'made to return') is first used by Shimei (v. 8) and then (v. 12) taken up again by David. David's hope for the future wavers between trust in the righteousness of God and trust in his grace (15.25f., 31b). He can therefore only regard Abishai's well-intentioned desire as a temptation and refuse to take the law into his own hands. Exhausted not only by the long and hot road but also by the long and unwelcome company of the cursing Benjaminite, who constantly throws stones and lumps of sand, the king and his company reach the bank of the Jordan and go right up to the Jordan, to be ready for anything (and, of course, also to procure water). The Lucianic recension of the LXX is certainly right in assuming here such details as are presupposed in 17.21f.

Although all of David's life's work is in jeopardy, the report of his flight marks a kind of climax to his career. In an unexpected way, he is now thrown completely upon God's mercy. It is up to the Lord either to take up the possibilities he offers or not. This emerges several times as the real significance of his position. We must be surprised that David's proud kingdom was brought to such a crisis almost overnight; this did not happen to much worse kings of a later time. The crisis is, however, meant to show that while the history of David is not that of a great man, but of a man with faults, in spite of everything it is still the history of the Lord using his chosen instrument.

10. ABSALOM IN JERUSALEM: 16.15–17.23

16 ¹⁵Now Absalom and all the people—the men of Israelᵃ—came to Jerusalem, and Ahithophel with him. ¹⁶And when Hushai the Archite, David's friend, came to Absalom, Hushai said to Absalom, 'Long live the king! Long live the king!' ¹⁷And Absalom said to Hushai, 'Is this your loyalty to your friend? Why did you not go with your friend?' ¹⁸And Hushai said to Absalom, 'No; for whom the LORD and this people and all the men of Israel have chosen, his I will be,ᵇ and with him I will remain. ¹⁹And again, whom should I serve? Should it not be his son? As I have served your father, so will I serve you.'

20 Then Absalom said to Ahithophel, 'Give your counsel; what

ᵃSee Commentary.
ᵇSee BH.

shall we do?' [21]Ahithophel said to Absalom, 'Go in to your father's concubines, whom he has left to keep the house; and all Israel will hear that you have made yourself odious to your father,[a] and the hands of all who are with you will be strengthened.' [22]So they pitched a[b] tent for Absalom upon the roof; and Absalom went in to his father's concubines in the sight of all Israel. [23]Now in those days the counsel which Ahithophel gave was as if one consulted the oracle of God; so was all the counsel of Ahithophel esteemed, both by David and by Absalom.

17 [1]Moreover Ahithophel said to Absalom, 'Let me choose[c] twelve thousand men, and I will set out and pursue David tonight. [2]I will come upon him while he is weary and discouraged, and throw him into a panic; and all the people who are with him will flee. I will strike down the king only, [3]and I will bring all the people back to you as a bride comes home to her husband. You seek the life of only one man, and all the people will be at peace.'[d] [4]And the advice pleased Absalom and all the elders of Israel.[e]

5 Then Absalom said, 'Call Hushai the Archite also, and let us hear what he has to say.' [6]And when Hushai came to Absalom, Absalom said to him, 'Thus has Ahithophel spoken; shall we do as he advises? If not, you speak.' [7]Then Hushai said to Absalom, 'This time the counsel which Ahithophel has given is not good.' [8]Hushai said moreover, 'You know that your father and his men are mighty men, and that they are enraged, like a bear robbed of her cubs in the field. Besides, your father is expert in war; he will not let the people rest overnight. [9]Behold, even now he has hidden himself in one of the pits,[f] or in some other place. And when he falls on the people at the beginning and some of them get killed,[g] whoever hears it will say, "There has been a slaughter among the people who follow Absalom." [10]Then even the valiant man, whose heart is like the heart of a lion, will utterly melt with fear; for all Israel knows that your father is a mighty man, and that those who are with him are valiant men. [11]But my counsel is that all Israel be immediately[h] gathered to you, from Dan to Beersheba, as the sand by the sea for multitude, and that you go to battle in person.[i] [12]So we shall come upon him in some place where

[a]Apparently a variant set of readings: *nib'aštā be'ābīkā* and *hib'aštā 'et-'ābīkā*.
[b]Hebrew has '*the* tent'; probably a technical term for the bridal tent.
[c]See BH.
[d]Here the vivid reading of LXX is unquestionably better; MT has a corrupt text.
[e]Literally: And the word was right in the eyes of Absalom and in the eyes of all the elders of Israel.
[f]The word is here used in the feminine, unlike 18.17.
[g]The original text probably ran *kinpōl bāʿām wenāpelū bāhem*, see LXX. The copyist could easily have overlooked the words *bāʿām wenāpelū*.
[h]Infinitive absolute.
[i]Usually *beqirbām* (in their midst) is read with LXX, etc., instead of *biqrāb*, but the MT makes good sense.

he is to be found, and we shall light upon him as the dew falls on the ground; and of him and all the men with him not one will be left. ¹³If he withdraws into a city, then all Israel will bring ropes to that city,ᵃ and we shall drag it into the valley, until not even a pebble is to be found there.' ¹⁴And Absalom and all the men of Israel said, 'The counsel of Hushai the Archite is better than the counsel of Ahithophel.' For the LORD had ordained to defeat the good counsel of Ahithophel, so that the LORD might bring evil upon Absalom.

15 Then Hushai said to Zadok and Abiathar, 'Thus and so did Ahithophel counsel Absalom and the elders of Israel; and thus and so have I counselled. ¹⁶Now therefore send quickly and tell David, "Do not lodge tonight at the fords of the wilderness, but by all means pass over; lest the king and all the people who are with him be swallowed up." '

17 Now Jonathan and Ahimaaz were waiting at En-rogel; a maid-servant used to go and tell them, and they would go and tell King David; for they must not be seen entering the city. ¹⁸But a lad saw them, and told Absalom; so both of them went away quickly, and came to the house of a man at Bahurim, who had a well in his courtyard; and they went down into it. ¹⁹And the woman took and spread a covering over the well's mouth,ᵇ and scattered grain upon it; and nothing was known of it. ²⁰When Absalom's servants came to the woman at the house, they said, 'Where are Ahimaaz and Jonathan?' And the woman said to them, 'They have gone from here in the direction of the water.'ᶜ And when they had sought and could not find them, they returned to Jerusalem.

21 After they had gone, the men came up out of the well, and went and told King David. They said to David, 'Arise, and go quickly over the water; for thus and so has Ahithophel counselled against you.' ²²Then David arose, and all the people who were with him, and they crossed the Jordan; by daybreak not one was left who had not crossed the Jordan.

23 When Ahithophel saw that his counsel was not followed, he saddled his ass, and went off home to his own city. And he set his house in order, and hanged himself; and he died, and was buried in the tomb of his father.

Absalom spent only a short time in Jerusalem. It would have been even shorter—and in the end very much longer!—had he followed Ahithophel's advice and struck at once. As it is, there is a delay, even if not a very long one, until the Israelite host has assembled.

ᵃThe hiphil of *nāsā* is unusual, but not meaningless.

ᵇLiterally 'countenance of the well'. An emendation to the more usual *pī* ('mouth of the well') is unnecessary.

ᶜOn the puzzling word *mīkal*, see BH. The MT perhaps imagined a place in or near Bahurim which bore the name Michal (cf. 3.16).

The account essentially contains only the struggle between Ahithophel and Hushai; the former really sees what is in the interest of
Absalom, while Hushai is on David's side, so that the events in
Jerusalem are a preliminary decision in the battle between Absalom
and David, a decision in which the latter clearly remains on top.
It is thus sufficiently clear from the very moment when Absalom is
at the height of his success that it is not this son who is destined to
occupy the throne of David. It was not Amnon, the man of unbridled sensuality, and it is not Absalom, the usurper.

[16.15] Absalom, as is confirmed by this verse, has the bulk of
the 'men of Israel' behind him. Perhaps the words '$i\check{s}\ yisr\bar{a}$'$\bar{e}l$ are only
a gloss, but if so the gloss is correct. Here, as earlier with David,
'all the people' means the troops at Absalom's immediate disposal.
Ahithophel is mentioned by name as being the most important man
in the camp of Absalom and David's most dangerous adversary.

[16.16–19] Hushai's defection to Absalom may only have been
one detail in the rush of events; defections and desertions from one
régime to another occur frequently at such times. For the writer,
however, it is the decisive event. Hushai acts completely in the spirit
—if not in the words—of the commission which David gave him at
15.34. As 'king's friend' he has evidently unhindered access to
authoritative circles and approaches with a cry of homage which is
even uttered twice. He is nevertheless not accepted with open arms
by Absalom, but is reminded with some scorn of the person to whom
he belongs by virtue of his title and his previous attitude. At the
beginning of Hushai's extremely skilful reply there occurs a formula
which contains the deciding factor in the choice of a king, such as
obtained in the case of Saul and of David: the divine designation
and the assent of the people, here above all the 'men of Israel'.[a]
Hushai thus declares Absalom to be the duly elected king, evidently
referring to the appropriate events in Hebron. We hear nothing
more about these, but from Hushai's remarks we can assume them
to have taken place.[b] Hushai says nothing about his own view of
Absalom's actions; he merely gives the fact of the legitimacy of the
new king as the reason for his transference of allegiance, adding his
connection with the father and hence with the son. He is thus
accepted by Absalom, though this is nowhere explicitly stated, and

[a]This 'acclamation of the people' has been worked out in particular by A. Alt,
Kleine Schriften II, p. 23, etc.
[b]Alt views the matter differently, *Kleine Schriften* II, p. 58 n. 2.

now belongs to those who serve 'in the presence' of the king. He can therefore register his first success in the cause of his master David.

[16.20–22] A reverse, however, follows immediately. Ahithophel recommends the young king as a first step to take possession of his predecessor's harem. David is reported to have acted similarly with Saul's harem (12.8), and this may have been the usual custom. Here, however, there is the added point that Absalom's predecessor was also his father. Reuben, who lies with his father's concubine, incurs a curse (Gen. 35.22; 49.3f.) and loses the right of a firstborn. Absalom's act must have been assessed in the same way by those who narrated it and heard of it. What at first sight is a move of infamous skill, in practice and in the long run proves to be the reason for Absalom's failure, in that he sets himself above human and divine law. This verdict stands, even if Absalom only formally proved that he was the master of these women by openly and visibly going into the tent which was specially pitched upon the roof. Absalom may really have had other things to do! But this does not alter the fact that the son has now 'made himself odious' in the eyes of his father. The bond between father and son is thus broken. Absalom's act has this personal effect and is a state act equivalent to a declaration that the previous king is dead (Budde). The cunning Ahithophel knows this; he is clear about the consequences, one of which is that the supporters of Absalom are now strengthened in their position. Now Absalom is associated with them for better or for worse, and he has burnt his boats behind him. We may not exclude the possibility that Ahithophel, the grandfather of Bathsheba, enjoys a belated revenge for what David has done to his family in the same context. The narrator stresses how infallible Ahithophel's counsel is held to be at court. It is not said that by this diabolical counsel which he has given he is leading the king, and, as is apparent later, himself, on the road to disaster, but the thought lies in the background.

[17.1–4] At first, of course, he is sure of success. As he knows that the king is now occupied, he declares himself ready to set out immediately and to destroy David. He knows David from long years of close collaboration. He may also imagine that David, who has taken women and children with him, will be prevented from travelling quickly. He therefore means to use the proven stratagem of a sudden night attack, which will throw everything into confusion and enable David to be killed. Here, too, we are given the impression that he is concerned to satisfy personal feelings of hatred. The plan is once again diabolically good, not least because peace can then immediately be achieved in the land by a general amnesty; the image used here—mutilated in the MT but preserved in the LXX—of the young wife (*kallā* = Arabic *'arus* means newly wed) who after a short quarrel returns to her husband (there is an example of this in the behaviour of the concubine in Judg. 19) describes the political and military situation splendidly. Here both the immediate needs and the future consequences are considered. This is therefore the most dangerous moment of all, especially as Absalom immediately agrees, together with 'all the elders of Israel', who are present as the supreme authority of the northern tribes. Their position can also be seen at David's enthronement (5.3).

[17.5–13] Luckily Absalom expresses the desire to hear Hushai's opinion; the latter is therefore not to be imagined as having been present at the earlier meeting. His speech is a masterpiece of oriental eloquence. His aim is clear, to gain time for David. He, too, speaks in pertinent images: the she-bear robbed of her young as a description of David and his men in a desperate fight; the sand on the sea-shore as a simile for 'all Israel' who are to be called out; the dew of heaven to depict the irresistible and all-embracing scope of the action, and the ropes round the city wall, another image of the same irresistible force of the troops. To begin with, he tries to disenchant the men who are swayed by Ahithophel's advice: do you think that David will wait until you come and kill him? The skill at arms of the old king and his 'mighty men' (*gibbōr* = professional soldier) make an initial defeat possible and this would mean Absalom's losing both men and prestige; so Hushai recommends a levying of the whole host from Dan to Beersheba. He does this without noticing that in so doing he is going far more into the realm of the utopian than Ahithophel himself. His fantasy increases from sentence to sentence; he speaks with an ever-increasing pathos, as is shown chiefly by his remarks about the demolition of the city. 'A glittering garment designed to cover the weak spots'.[a] But that is Eastern eloquence. He knows just how to make up to Absalom. Ahithophel has suggested himself as the leader of the expedition against David; Hushai considers it important to stress that Absalom (literally 'his countenance') must be there in person. As well as displaying a certain mistrust of Ahithophel (the old man?), this remark contains an appeal to the

[a]Rost, *Thronnachfolge*, p. 125.

vanity of the prince. [17.14] The speech does not fail to make its effect: the whole gathering is infected by Hushai's oratory—a phenomenon frequently to be observed in the East—and holds the worse counsel to be the better. A firm decision is not yet apparently taken, as the message sent to David reckons on the possibility that Ahithophel may still prevail. Perhaps the compiler thinks that Hushai departs again once he has made his 'report' and that the decision is made by a small nucleus to which Ahithophel belongs. But the compiler, who knows the sequel, has allowed the reader to have a glimpse behind the scenes. Behind the events on the stage where Ahithophel, Hushai and Absalom find themselves, stands the Lord, who assigns them their places and the parts they are to play and guides the history of David in a way which corresponds to the promise of ch. 7.

[17.15–17] The sequel, too, is dramatic; the hearer is constantly kept in tension. To relay the state of affairs to David and to advise him to cross the Jordan whatever happens, Hushai makes use of the way provided for him by the priests' sons. These have prudently left the city—perhaps so as not to place their fathers under suspicion, for if all were discovered even the priestly garment would have been of little use (cf. I. 22.6ff. and I Kings 2.26f.)—and are at En-rogel, the present *bir ayyub* (Job's fountain, presumably originally Joab's fountain),[a] near where the Valley of Hinnom and the Valley of Kidron meet. It is not surprising that a maid should go to the watering-place. The verse says nothing of the 'repeated comings and goings of the young men' (so Budde, who deletes it), but of the repeated coming of the maid, on whose trustworthiness much depends; the young men, of course, only went to David once, but were constantly in readiness and were continually kept informed. [18–22] Despite all precautions, they are observed, so that all could yet have miscarried. They realize this, however, and quickly go to the farm of an acquaintance in the village of Bahurim, which thus houses partisans of David as well as the family of Shimei. The messengers can do nothing but hide in the well,[b] which the woman covers carefully with a firm covering or mat on which grains of wheat are spread to dry.[c] As soon as the coast is clear, they can

[a]Cf. *PJB* 22, 1926, p. 95.
[b]Presumably this is not a natural well (*be'ēr*), but a cistern (*bōr*). The terminology changes, cf. Dalman, *Arbeit und Sitte* I, pp. 526–8.
[c]Cf. Dalman, *Arbeit und Sitte* III, pp. 271f.

rush off to David, who immediately draws his conclusions, and on the night following the day of his flight from Jerusalem crosses the Jordan with all his people. Hushai's plan has succeeded and David is safe for the time being.

We hear nothing of the return of the priests' sons; they almost certainly remained with David. [**17.23**] We do, however, have a report of the death of Ahithophel. It is supposed that Absalom finally decided against his counsel. Ahithophel does not decide on the step of suicide, rare in the Old Testament (I Kings 16.18, cf. Judg. 9.54; I Sam. 31.4f.; later II Macc. 10.13; 14.41) because of wounded pride, but because he rightly recognizes that Absalom's cause is lost and that he can only expect a cruel death after David's victory. He is wise enough to foresee the consequences; his fate is a prelude to that of Absalom and, like the last days of his life, a counterpart to the fate of the traitor Judas. With it, the melancholy sign of divine ordained failure stands over Absalom's plans to succeed to the throne.

11. ABSALOM'S DEFEAT AND DEATH:
17.24–19.8a (Heb. 19.9a)

17 **24**Then David came to Mahanaim. And Absalom crossed the Jordan with all the men of Israel. **25**Now Absalom had set Amasa over the army instead of Joab. Amasa was the son of a man named Ithra, an Ishmaelite,[a] who had gone in to Abigal the daughter of Nahash, sister of Zeruiah, Joab's mother. **26**And Israel and Absalom encamped in the land of Gilead.

27 When David came to Mahanaim, Shobi the son of Nahash from Rabbah of the Ammonites, and Machir the son of Ammiel from Lo-debar, and Barzillai the Gileadite from Rogelim, **28**brought beds and coverings,[b] basins and earthen vessels, wheat, barley, meal, parched grain, beans and lentils,[c] **29**honey and curds and cheese from cows' milk and sheep's milk,[d] for David and the people with him to eat; for they said, 'The people are hungry and weary and thirsty in the wilderness.'

18 **1**Then David mustered the men who were with him, and set over them commanders of thousands and commanders of hundreds. **2**And David divided the people into three parts,[e] one third under the command of Joab, one third under the command of Abishai the son of Zeruiah, Joab's brother, and one third under the command of Ittai

[a]Cf. I Chron. 2.17. MT has 'Israelite' (see Commentary). The name Ithra is transmitted as Jether in I Kings 2.5; I Chron. 2.17.
[b]Expand as LXX, see BH.
[c]See BH.
[d]$w^e\bar{s}\bar{o}n$ is better placed after $b\bar{a}q\bar{a}r$.

S.–M

the Gittite. And the king said to the men, 'I myself will also go out with you.' [3]But the men said, 'You shall not go out. For if we flee, they will not care about us. If half of us die, they will not care about us. But you are worth ten thousand of us;[a] therefore it is better if you remain in the city, to aid us from the city.'[b] [4]The king said to them, 'Whatever seems best to you I will do.' So the king stood at the side of the gate, while all the army marched out by hundreds and by thousands. [5]And the king ordered Joab and Abishai and Ittai, 'Deal gently for my sake with the young man Absalom.' And all the people heard when the king gave orders to all the commanders about Absalom.

6 So the army went out into the field against Israel; and the battle was fought in the forest of Ephraim. [7]And the men of Israel were defeated there by the servants of David, and the slaughter there was great on that day, twenty thousand men. [8]The battle spread over the face of all the country; and the forest devoured more people that day than the sword.

9 And Absalom chanced to meet the servants of David. Absalom was riding upon his mule, and the mule went under the thick branches of a[c] great terebinth, and his head caught fast in the terebinth, and he was left hanging between heaven and earth, while the mule that was under him went on. [10]And a certain man saw it, and told Joab, 'Behold, I saw Absalom hanging in a terebinth.' [11]Joab said to the man who told him, 'What, you saw him! Why then did you not strike him there to the ground? I would have been glad to give you ten pieces of silver and a girdle.' [12]But the man said to Joab, 'Even if I felt[d] in my hand the weight of a thousand pieces of silver, I would not put forth my hand against the king's son; for in our hearing the king commanded you and Abishai and Ittai, "Whoever you may be,[e] protect the young man Absalom." [13]On the other hand, if I had dealt treacherously against his life (and there is nothing hidden from the king), then you yourself would have stood aloof.' [14]Joab said, 'I will not waste time like this with you.'[f] And he took three darts[g] in his hand, and thrust them into Absalom's body[h] while he was still hanging alive in the middle[i] of the terebinth. [15]And ten young men, Joab's armour-bearers, surrounded Absalom and struck him, and killed him.

[a]SeeB H.

[b]MT is confused. The *mēʿîr* (from a city) points both to *bāʿîr* (in the city), as LXX, and to *mēhāʿîr* (from the city). The last, equally uncertain, word of MT, transmitted twice in LXX, is to be read *laʿzōr* with the *qᵉrē* and put before *lānû* (us).

[c]Hebrew 'the'; it would, of course, be a certain large tree, well known to tradition.

[d]Literally 'were to weigh in my hand'.

[e]The *lî* (= for me, cf. v. 5) usually read instead of *mî* is a simplifying emendation.

[f]The emendation 'Therefore I will begin before you', suggested by MSS and BH is no improvement on MT. The above rendering is well paraphrased by LXX.

[g](?) Literally 'sticks'; see Commentary.

[h]'In the heart' is not to be taken literally; see Commentary.

[i]Hebrew has the same word 'heart' (*lēb*) as previously.

16 Then Joab blew the trumpet, and the troops came back from pursuing Israel; for Joab restrained them. [17]And they took Absalom, and threw him into a great pit in the forest, and raised over him a very great heap of stones; and all Israel fled every one to his own home. [18]Now Absalom in his lifetime had taken[a] and set up for himself the pillar which is in the King's Valley, for he said, 'I have no son to keep my name in remembrance'; he called the pillar after his own name, and it is called 'Absalom's hand' to this day.

19 Then said Ahimaaz the son of Zadok, 'Let me run, and carry tidings to the king that the LORD has delivered him from the power of his enemies.' [20]And Joab said to him, 'You are not to carry tidings today; you may carry tidings another day, but today you shall carry no tidings; the reason is that[b] the king's son is dead.' [21]Then Joab said to the Cushite, 'Go, tell the king what you have seen.' The[b] Cushite bowed before Joab, and ran. [22]Then Ahimaaz the son of Zadok said again to Joab, 'Come what may, let me also run after the Cushite.' And Joab said, 'Why will you run, my son, seeing that you will have no reward for the tidings?' [23]But Ahimaaz said,[c] 'Come what may, I will run.' So he said to him, 'Run.' Then Ahimaaz ran by the way of the plain (of the Jordan), and outran the Cushite.

24 Now David was sitting between the two gates; and the watchman went up to the roof of the gate by the wall, and when he lifted up his eyes and looked, he saw a man running alone. [25]And the watchman called out and told the king. And the king said, 'If he is alone, there are good tidings in his mouth.' And he came apace, and drew near. [26]And the watchman saw another man running; and the watchman called to the gatekeeper[d] and said, 'See, another man running alone!' The king said, 'He also brings good tidings.' [27]And the watchman said, 'I think the running of the foremost is like the running of Ahimaaz the son of Zadok.' And the king said, 'He is a good man, and comes with good tidings.'

28 Then came Ahimaaz[e] and cried to the king, 'All is well.' And he bowed before the king with his face to the earth, and said, 'Blessed be the LORD your God, who has delivered up the men who raised their hand against my lord the king.' [29]And the king said, 'Is it well[f]

---

[a]The word does not mean that the monument comes from elsewhere. Vulg. has rightly left it untranslated. It underlines the way things have been arranged.
[b]See BH.
[c]The *mōṣēt* seems to be a remnant of the missing clause *wayyōmer 'aḥima'aṣ*, of which LXX has still retained the first word.
[d]Why not the king? The emendation 'to the gate' = 'on the gate' is no better. Is this meant to convey that the coming of the second man seems strange to the watchman, so that he does not mention it directly to the king, as before?
[e]MT 'Ahimaaz cried'. This would mean while he was still running (see Schulz *ad loc.*). But the reading *wayyiqrab* (see BH) is preferable. The word *wayyiqrā'* occurs several times in the passage and could easily be supposed here also.
[f]Literally 'Is the young man . . . well?'; the king takes up Ahimaaz' greeting (*šālōm*) in his question.

with the young man Absalom?' Ahimaaz answered, 'When Joab sent the king's servant and your servant,ᵃ I saw a great tumult, but I do not know what it was.' ³⁰And the king said, 'Turn aside, and stand here.' So he turned aside and stood still.

31 And behold, the Cushite came; and the Cushite said, 'Good tidings for my lord the king! For the LORD has delivered you this day from the power of all who rose up against you.' ³²The king said to the Cushite, 'Is it well with the young man Absalom?' And the Cushite answered, 'May the enemies of my lord the king, and all who rise up against you for evil, be like that young man.' ³³(Heb. 19.1) And the king was deeply moved, and went up to the chamber over the gate, and wept; and as he went, he said, 'O my son Absalom, my son, my son Absalom! Would I had died instead of you. O Absalom, my son, my son!' 19 ¹⁽²⁾It was told Joab, 'Behold, the king is weeping and mourning for Absalom.'ᵇ ²⁽³⁾So the victory that day was turned into mourning for all the people; for the people heard that day, 'The king is grieving for his son.' ³⁽⁴⁾And the people stole into the city that day as troopsᶜ steal in who are ashamed when they flee in battle. ⁴⁽⁵⁾The king covered his face, and the king cried with a loud voice, 'O my son Absalom, O Absalom my son, my son!' ⁵⁽⁶⁾Then Joab came into the house to the king, and said, 'You have today covered with shame the faces of all your servants, who have this day saved your life, and the lives of your sons and your daughters, and the lives of your wives and your concubines, ⁶⁽⁷⁾because you love those who hate you and hate those who love you. For you have made it clear today that commanders and servants are nothing to you; for today I perceive that if Absalom were alive and all of us were dead today, then you would be pleased. ⁷⁽⁸⁾Now therefore arise, go out and speak kindly to your servants; for I swear by the LORD, if you do not go, not a man will stay with you this night; and this will be worse for you than all the evil that has come upon you from your youth until now.' ⁸ᴬ⁽⁹ᴬ⁾Then the king arose, and took his seat in the gate. And the people were told, 'Behold the king is sitting in the gate'; and all the people came before the king.

[17.24] Yet another highly dramatic section. At the beginning, David finds himself in Mahanaim, Ishbaal's old capital, and therefore a particularly well-chosen city in the land east of the Jordan, with suitable fortifications (cf. 18.3f., 24). Hushai's counsel has borne

---

ᵃThe text is unclear. The word order 'et-ʿebed hammelek yōʾāb could suggest that Joab, the 'servant of the king' in the explicit sense, is the subject of the infinitive clause; but in that case it would be necessary to delete the first 'et and the wᵉ behind Joab. It is these two particular words which commend the above translation. In that case, however, the word yōʾāb is better placed after lišlōᵃḥ.

ᵇThe participle mitʾabbēl (Targ.) is an understandable, but impermissible, simplification in the light of MT.

ᶜ'People' occurs in the text here, too.

fruit: the time gained has enabled David to develop a strategy. Absalom is thus at a disadvantage from the start, especially as the host of Israel, unwieldy and rarely used in military actions, cannot begin to match the 'servants of David' in fighting worth. **[17.25]** Absalom has appointed a kinsman named Amasa as commander. The details of his ancestry are extremely obscure. His father is known by name (see above), but the tradition is uncertain whether he is to be described as an 'Ishmaelite' or an 'Israelite'. The first is surely right; the second reading can be explained as giving him a particularly suitable qualification to be leader of the host of Israel. The wife, Amasa's mother, would not, however, have followed her husband to 'Israel'. In any case, all becomes more comprehensible if it was an Ishmaelite, a Bedouin (Gen. 16.12; Judg. 8.24), who 'went in' to Abigal; perhaps the word, which is an unusual one to describe a marriage, here means that something unusual in fact happened; was it a so-called *ṣadiqa* marriage,[a] or had the nomad come upon the young woman of Bethlehem and overpowered her? The description of Abigal is also strange. She is not called a sister of David, but sister, i.e. full sister, of Zeruiah; perhaps both David's half-sisters came from a first marriage of their common mother. Nahash would then have been her first husband, though the identity of name with the Ammonite king mentioned in v. 27 suggests a scribal error. In 19.13ff. it looks as though he remained with the host of Judah. Furthermore, Amasa makes no appearance in the battle. In that case, v. 26, at the beginning of which the phrase 'and Absalom' 'is remarkably lame' (Budde), becomes more comprehensible. Perhaps it is meant to imply that Absalom himself commanded the Israelite host stationed in the land east of the Jordan, thus following Hushai's advice (17.11).

[17.26–29] It is evident that David is not without important friends east of the Jordan. The mention first of all of the son of Nahash, the dead king of the Ammonites (10.11), shows that there are other voices at the court of Rabbath Ammon than those of Hanun and his 'commanders'. Machir is a supporter of the house of Saul (cf. on 9.4f.); David's gracious treatment of Meribbaal may have made him a supporter of David. Barzillai, not known from elsewhere, is described as being old in years (19.32ff.).[b] These men,

---

[a] See my commentary on Judg. 15.1–3.
[b] The place Rogelim is identified by Abel with *tell barsina* (*Géographie* II, p. 437). Glueck (*Explorations in Eastern Palestine* IV, pp. 176f.) rightly objects to this on archaeological grounds. He suggests *zaharet sokʿah*, five miles south-west of Irbid.

all portrayed as well-to-do, act as David's line of communications. No mention is made of troop reinforcements; perhaps it was more important for David that he should use only the well-tried 'servants of David'. The provisioning, on the other hand, was a real help, as it saved him from the unpleasantness of having to make requisitions. Absalom will also have been in a more difficult position in this respect in the 'land of Gilead'.—The substance of the provisions seems to have been chosen practically, and with loving care. Quickly perishable materials (particularly meat) are completely lacking, as are delicacies, surely in view of the number of men to be provided for. The mention of the parched grain,[a] however, shows that here we have no pedantic schematism. Honey and milk products[b] probably do not stand side by side by chance.

[18.1–5] David, the experienced strategist, knows that the striking power of his troops depends on the speed with which they may be organized and put in position. He is therefore concerned to organize them throughout. There is a special reason for the appearance of Ittai rather than Benaiah among the three commanders (see on 15.18–22); perhaps it is a sequel to this that in David's last days we find Benaiah not in Joab's camp but among his opponents. David's intention is to go into battle, but he is made to stay behind at the request of the people. Possibly his wish conceals the intention of saving Absalom's life, that of the troops, Joab's concern to prevent this. The reason given for this desire of the troops is an anxiety for David's person (cf. 21.17), but they also recognize how important it is that David should at any event cover their rear. He therefore has a reserve with him ready to cope with any unfavourable trends. The troops march out into the field past David, urged on by the words and looks of the supreme commander. David's clearly given command 'Deal gently . . . with the young man Absalom' shows his confidence of victory and at the same time his readiness to forgive and his weakness as a father, which was already observed in ch. 13.

[18.6–8] The battle is fought in the forest of Ephraim, an area east of the Jordan settled by this west-Jordanian tribe. It is a territory in which Absalom, who relies on the tribes of Israel, perhaps hopes to find some support. Even today the landscape contains all kinds of trees; although, as becomes clear later, there is no lack of high trees, we are to imagine it as a mixture of deep undergrowth and rock

[a]Cf. my commentary on Judges 2.14.
[b]For 'curds' see Dalman, *Arbeit und Sitte* VI, pp. 307–11.

rather than as forest land proper. The vast amount of cover quickly puts the host at a disadvantage and causes a great many casualties. [18.9–13] Even Absalom himself falls a victim to it; while he is riding at speed his mule takes him into the branches of a terebinth in such a way that he is left suspended in it. It is not said that his vast head of hair is a contributory factor in his entanglement, but it is clear that he cannot get free without assistance. A man who has seen him tells Joab, and there is an informative conversation. The soldier obeys David's instructions, but to the far-sighted commander the demands of the state are more important than the sentiments of the ruler. For Joab knows better than David himself, who is here governed solely by his paternal sensibilities, that a further pardon of Absalom will only lead to a further jeopardizing of the kingdom. His attitude is explained not by antipathy towards Absalom, for whose return he had canvassed vigorously at an earlier time, but by these very considerations. At the same time, however, the attitude of the ordinary man is well summed up by his fluent logic. His ideas are determined not only by a simple observance of the king's command but also by reflection on the consequences which the killing of the prince would have for him, as he would be left quite alone by Joab in the decisive hearing before the king. He also provides charming testimony for the widespread (cf. 14.20) view that nothing could remain hidden from the king. [18.14–15] Joab abruptly breaks off the conversation, which is conducted on an astonishingly comradely basis, takes up three 'darts' ($\check{s}^eb\bar{a}\underline{t}\bar{\imath}m$) and thrusts them 'into the heart' of Absalom. As Absalom is only killed by the ten armour-bearers, Joab's action appears rather to be a symbolic action which opens the way for the killing of the king's son. Perhaps that is why 'darts' are mentioned instead of spears. The expression 'in the heart' here does not mean a part of the body; it occurs once again in the same verse, in connection with the oak, and must therefore both times be understood to mean 'in the middle'. We are not told where Joab wounded Absalom, but this is unimportant; the flow of blood may have marked him as doomed to death. Nor is it now clear why Joab takes 'three' darts; perhaps this stresses the complete and definitive character of the act. The *coup de grâce* is then administered by a group of warriors. In this way the execution is manifestly performed by the troops as a whole. The same happens to Achan (Josh. 7.25 and my commentary *ad loc.*). [18.16–18] Here, as there, a great heap of stones is raised over the body. It will have been pointed out for a long time afterwards. Remarkably, there is also a memorial of Absalom in the neighbourhood of Jerusalem. According to this passage, Absalom himself erected it, as he had no son (but cf. on 14.27); perhaps that is why the obscure word *yād* is used (properly 'hand'; Isa. 57.8 = male member. It is also used to mean a 'monument' in I. 15.12). An emendation of the text to make David rather than Absalom the constructor of the memorial (Budde) can hardly be commended, especially as it requires considerable inroads on the text. The views of his leading citizens would hardly have allowed David to do this. On the other hand, we must ask when Absalom had an opportunity to make such provisions. Hardly in the few days of his 'reign' in Jerusalem. The most obvious time would seem to be while he was still a prince; perhaps he did it out of sorrow (at the death of his sons?) during the time he was waiting. The present tomb of Absalom in the Kidron valley (Hebrew *yad 'abšālōm*) has been connected with Absalom only since the sixteenth century; it is, however, possible that some earlier tradition underlies it. In the general context, the verse, like I. 15.12, could be meant to stress 'that the rejected one himself thought of his reputation' (Schulz II, p. 219).

Thus the battle ends. Joab, who gives the signal for the suspension of hostilities, is of the same view as Ahithophel, but on the opposing side (17.2f.): this war is concerned not with the people but with a man. **[18.19–23]** The host is therefore free to return. There remains the difficult task of sending the news to David. Ahimaaz, the athletic son of the priest, offers himself as a messenger. Apparently he does not know what every soldier knew, and, as a man with unripe judgment, can only think that he is to be a *mᵉbassēr*, a messenger with good news (*euangelion*) for David. Joab, who well knows that kings are accustomed to answer bad news with bad decisions (4.10), seeks, however, to restrain him and instead sends a negro, who is apparently among his followers, *cui etiamsi quid triste accidisset, leve damnum existimabat Joab* (Grotius). Another reason for his choice may be that 'the' Cushite is in a special sense 'the servant of the king' (v. 29) and thus has little to fear. Ahimaaz is, however, all the more unrestrainable; he takes the longer but better road, while the Cushite apparently runs along side paths, so Ahimaaz takes the lead.

[18.24–32] David is 'between the two gates', hardly, as is usually assumed, sitting in the gatehouse itself—this would need a different expression—but in a space between the outer and the inner gate.

From there he can keep in touch with the watchman who is posted at the place where the gate is joined to the battlements. The soldier reports the coming of a solitary man, who is interpreted by David as a messenger of good news; many men running would have had to be regarded as a rout. Soon the second appears, and the first man is shortly afterwards recognized as Ahimaaz. He is thus the first to bring the news of the victory. As the king in reply only inquires after Absalom, Ahimaaz, quickly understanding the significance of Joab's earlier allusions, gives an evasive reply. The Cushite, however, with less presence of mind, although well conversant with the style of language at court, gives an answer to the king's renewed questioning, from which the dreaded truth bursts upon him.

[18.33–19.8a] Filled with deep grief, the king begins his lament even as he departs, and returns to the upper room in the main gate, from where his weeping, with the constant repetition of his son's name, re-echoes quite audibly. The narrator gives the account in such a way that we can see that he understands the king, even if he does not approve of his conduct. By and large this will have been the view of those involved at the time. Joab makes himself the spokesman of the *vox populi*. He sees, moreover, the consequences for the state of the realm and of the dynasty, for he knows that the common man, despite his reverence for the king's person and his consideration for a father's grief, will not in the long run allow a complete disregard of the deeds at arms done on behalf of the king. Indeed, the people's reaction can be perceived immediately. Here the only help is energetic action to repair the situation and to prevent a disintegration of the army. Joab's one-sided but clearly persuasive words are crowned with success. He succeeds in raising the king from his now completely inopportune sorrow and has him watch the march past of the warriors, thereby assuring them of his royal recognition of their deeds. And in this way the danger is overcome.

The whole account is given in an extremely vivid manner. The reader follows the individual scenes in a state of extreme tension. The narrator knows that Absalom is in the wrong, but he is not without sympathy for him. That King David gains the victory and Absalom meets his death is to him a sign of the divine righteousness (esp. 18.28–32), and despite Joab's hardness he regards his action as correct. But we still gain the impression that the king's lament for Absalom is also his own: what tragedy for the cultivated, attractive prince, born to be a ruler! He has been justly dealt with, for the crown of David may not be won by selfish anticipation; but at the end the lament is greater than the satisfaction. And as for the question of the succession, which dominates this whole section, the answer given by the events just past is still only negative.

12. DAVID'S RETURN: 19.8b–43 (Heb. 19.9b–44)

19 [8B(9B)]Now Israel had fled every man to his own home. [9(10)]And all the people were at strife throughout all the tribes of Israel, saying, 'The king delivered us from the hand of our enemies, and saved us from the hand of the Philistines; and now he has fled out of the land from Absalom. [10(11)]But Absalom, whom we anointed over us, is dead in battle. Now therefore why do you say nothing about bringing the king back?'[a]

[11(12)] Now this saying by all Israel (also) reached the king. And King David sent this message to Zadok and Abiathar the priests, 'Say to the elders of Judah, "Why should you be the last to bring the king[a] back to his house? [12(13)]You are my kinsmen, you are my bone and my flesh; why then should you be the last to bring back the king?" [13(14)]And say to Amasa, "Are you not my bone and my flesh? God do so to me, and more also, if you are not commander of my army henceforth in place of Joab." ' [14(15)]And he swayed the heart of all the men of Judah as one man; so that they sent word to the king, 'Return, both you and all your servants.'

[15(16)] So the king came back to the Jordan; and Judah came to Gilgal to meet the king and to bring him[b] over the Jordan. [16(17)]And Shimei the son of Gera, the Benjaminite, from Bahurim, made haste to come down with the men of Judah to meet King David; [17(18)]and with him were a thousand men from Benjamin. And Ziba the servant of the house of Saul, with his fifteen sons and his twenty servants, rushed down to the Jordan before the king, [18(19)]and they had crossed[c] the ford to bring over the king's household, and to do his pleasure. And Shimei the son of Gera fell down before the king, as he was on the point of crossing the Jordan, [19(20)]and said to the king, 'Let not my lord hold me guilty or remember how your servant did wrong on the day my lord the king left Jerusalem; let not the king bear it in mind. [20(21)]For your servant knows that I have sinned; therefore, behold, I have come this day, the first of all the house of Joseph to come down to meet my lord the king. [21(22)]Abishai the son of Zeruiah answered, 'Shall not Shimei be put to death for this, because he cursed the LORD's anointed?' [22(23)]But David said, 'What have I to do with you, you sons of Zeruiah, that you should this day be as an adversary to me? Shall anyone be put to death in Israel this day?

[a]For the arrangement of the text in vv. 11f., see BH.

[b]MT has 'the king' here, too. Perhaps the two infinitive clauses are variant readings.

[c]Read $we^{\varsigma}āb^er\bar{u}$; MT seems to imagine a sort of ferry.

For do I not know that I am this day king over Israel?' 23(24)And the king said to Shimei, 'You shall not die.' And the king gave him his oath.

24(25) And Meribbaal[a] the son of Saul came down to meet the king; he had neither dressed his feet, nor his hands, nor trimmed his beard,[a] nor washed his clothes, from the day the king departed until the day he came back in safety to Jerusalem.[b] 25(26)And when he came to meet the king, the king said to him, 'Why did not you go with me, Meribbaal?' 26(27)He answered, 'My lord, O king, my servant deceived me; for your servant said to him, "I will have my ass saddled,[c] that I may ride upon it and go with the king." For your servant is lame. 27(28)He has slandered your servant to my lord the king. But my lord the king is like the angel of God; do therefore what seems good to you. 28(29)For all my father's house were but men doomed to death before my lord the king; but you set your servant among those who eat at your table. What further right have I, then, to cry to the king?' 29(30)And the king said to him, 'Why speak any more of your affairs? I have decided: you and Ziba shall divide the land.' 30(31)And Meribbaal said to the king, 'Oh, let him take it all, since my lord the king has come safely home.'

31(32) Now Barzillai the Gileadite had come down from Rogelim; and he escorted[a] the king over[d] the Jordan, to bid him farewell at the Jordan. 32(33)Barzillai was a very aged man, eighty years old; and he had provided the king with food while he stayed[a] at Mahanaim; for he was a very wealthy man. 33(34)And the king said to Barzillai, 'Come over with me, and I will provide for you with me in Jerusalem.' 34(35)But Barzillai said to the king, 'How many years have I still to live, that I should go up with the king to Jerusalem? 35(36)I am this day eighty years old; can I discern what is pleasant and what is not? Can your servant taste what he eats or what he drinks? Can I still listen to the voice of singing men and singing women? Why then should your servant be an added burden to my lord the king? 36(37)Your servant will go a little way over[a] the Jordan with the king. Why should the king recompense me with such a reward? 37(38)Pray let your servant return, that I may die in my own city, near the grave of my father and my mother. But here is your servant Chimham; let him go over with my lord the king; and do for him whatever seems good to you.' 38(39)And the king answered, 'Chimham shall go over with me, and I will do for him whatever seems good to you; and all that you desire of me[e] I will do for you.' 39(40)Then all the people went over

[a]See BH.

[b]Misplaced after v. 25.

[c]Read 'aḫbīšā. The defectively written hiphil form—there is no other instance of the hiphil of ḥābaš—was taken as qal. Usually the easier variant, 'saddle me an ass' (see BH) is taken.

[d]The 'et which stands later is better here. The closing phrase 'et-bayyardēn now looks like a conflation of 'et-hayyardēn and bayyardēn.

[e]Lit. 'to my account' as in modern Arabic.

the Jordan, and the king too went over;[a] and the king kissed Barzillai and blessed him, and he returned to his own home. [40(41)]The king went on to Gilgal, and Chimhan[b] went on with him; and all the people of Judah, and also half the people of Israel, brought the king on his way.

41(42) Then all the men of Israel came to the king, and said to the king, 'Why have our brethren the men of Judah stolen you away, and brought the king and his household over the Jordan, and all David's men with him?' [42(43)]And all the men of Judah answered the men of Israel, 'Because the king is near of kin to us. Why then are you angry over this matter? Have we eaten at all at the king's expense? Or did we kidnap him?' [43(44)] And the men of Israel answered the men of Judah, 'We have ten shares in the king, and we are firstborn in respect of you.[c] Why then did you despise us? Were we not the first to speak of bringing back our king?' But the words of the men of Judah were fiercer than the words of the men of Israel.

The king's return to Jerusalem, like his departure, is illustrated by episodes which to some extent reintroduce the personalities of the earlier description. In this way, the change of circumstances is well illustrated, and at the same time the report is connected with the rising of Absalom. It is not clear whether the sequence of scenes corresponds to their historical occurrence. The prime motive of the compiler is to show that at first sight the crisis seems to be over for David. The end of the chapter, however, shows that it only *seems* to be over, and this already prepares for the next section.

At the beginning we learn of a political move behind the scenes in which David plays the principal role, thus showing that he is again in control of himself. On the other hand, the end of the chapter shows that the very way in which David seeks to utilize the opposition between the tribes to his own advantage conjures up a new and dangerous crisis. In the last resort David does not carry all before him.

[8b-10] Such thoughts and words as are now expressed by the tribes of the Northern kingdom are usual after a defeat has been suffered. Since before and during Absalom's rebellion they saw the disadvantages of David's rule, now the advantages seem all the more preferable. Reason and gratitude assert themselves, but not regret. The whole argument is completely pragmatic. The new king is dead, long live the old. In this the men of Israel are not simply wishing the king good luck; they are also concerned to gain influence

[a]Perfect as in v. 41, etc. The reading 'still stood there', badly supported but mostly preferred, as it is easier, recalls 15.23.

[b]Perhaps this was how the (strange) name was pronounced in Jerusalem.

[c]See BH.

over him. Anyone who brings the king back 'to his house', i.e. to his residence, is his guard; they protect him, but at the same time he must respect them.

[11–14] David, who hears of these opinions and plans, immediately grasps the position. He sees that as well as the servants of David, with whom he has won the war, he will soon have at his disposal the Israelite host, the 'men of Israel'. In this situation he must also summon the host of Judah, to act as a counter-balance to 'Israel'. He once again uses the two priests in Jerusalem as go-betweens, but this time we are not told how he makes contact with them. He appeals to the elders of Judah on the strength of his descent, but at the same time, knowing that in the political sphere such factors are not decisive, also declares himself ready to confirm Amasa in the office conferred upon him by Absalom. This represents the passing over of Joab, who by his killing of Absalom in disregard of orders and his behaviour towards the sorrowing king—quite apart from earlier events (cf. especially 3.39)—has made himself so unpopular with David that the latter uses the first possible political opportunity of depriving him of the supreme command.

[15–17] The men of Judah immediately go to Gilgal, the sanctuary lying nearest to the ford over the Jordan,[a] to protect the king's crossing of the Jordan. The Benjaminites, however, to whose tribe the sanctuary and ford belong, are already there to undertake their part of the duty. The word translated 'rushed' is meant to show their eagerness: they could not wait until the king reached the Jordan. It transpires that there are two men behind this eagerness, Shimei and Ziba, both of whom have reason to demonstrate their loyalty. Their association here is a consequence of their membership of the family of Saul. Shimei has raised a thousand men—a sign that the descendants of Saul had considerable support in the tribe of Benjamin—and Ziba has brought all his attendants. [18–23] The latter group principally undertakes to escort the women and children over the river. Ziba thus once again secures for himself the goodwill of the king, of which, as transpires later, he is much in need. Shimei appears to have gone over the river with Ziba's people[b] to throw

[a]Cf. my commentary on Josh. 3.

[b]Commentators seem in some doubt about the bank of the Jordan on which these events are to be imagined as taking place. The decisive clause at the end of v. 18 'on his crossing of the Jordan' can in the original Hebrew refer either to the beginning or to the end of David's passage. Psychologically the former (as RSV) seems more probable.

himself at the king's feet as soon as he arrives. The man gives us the impression of having a certain degree of forthrightness, both earlier in his cursing (which was not without risks for him) and now in his petition. He makes no attempt to excuse his earlier conduct. He openly acknowledges his guilt and as expiation simply points out that he is the first Israelite to be there, that he has as it were broken the ice. This shows a peasant cunning which well fits his character. For he will have imagined that David could hardly reject or even hew off the first hand offered to him from Israel—David explicitly confirms this in v. 22b—and will further have assumed that the king would arrange no executions on such a day. Abishai's intervention is thus to Shimei's advantage rather than to his detriment. The sons of Zeruiah are not much in favour with David, and at this moment Abishai's role can only be that of the *sātān* (as Mark 9.33; Matt. 16.23). The taking over of a new dominion makes an amnesty necessary, and so Shimei's life is guaranteed to him by an oath. David kept the oath, but never forgot the insult offered to him, and took care to see to his later retribution (I Kings 2.8f., 36–46).

[24–30] The meeting with Meribbaal is directly attached at this point, although it is not clear whether historically speaking it belongs here. Meribbaal will hardly have crossed the Jordan, like Ziba; the mere fact of his physical disabilities would have made this difficult. Some commentators would therefore suggest that the scene takes place in Jerusalem; this is supported not only by the final words ('the king has come safely home') but also by the conclusion of v. 24. On the other hand, expressions like 'come from' (v. 24) and 'meet', (v. 25), show that Meribbaal, who was certainly in a position to ride, did not just await the king in Jerusalem, but, having been put in a very bad light by Ziba, did everything possible to justify himself. He will have ridden with the men of Judah as far as Gilgal, so that the episode will have taken place immediately after that with Barzillai; it has been moved forward because Ziba was mentioned just before. Verse 24 is to be given a different explanation and in v. 30 'safely home' will refer quite generally to the king's return. Meribbaal, the grandson of Saul—here we have 'son'—can show his unkempt appearance as a sign of his grief at David's departure. Similar neglect of the care of the body, much practised in the East (cf. Ps. 23.5; 45.8f.; 104.15), is a sign of grief (Job 1.20; Lev. 19.27), so that this, too, confirms the fact that Meribbaal has been calumniated by Ziba (cf. 16.1–4). Using the

same expression as the woman of Tekoa (14.17, 20), Meribbaal leaves
a verdict to the king; this is not simply flattery, but an appeal to
the king's responsibility. David gives a 'Solomonic' verdict. On the
one hand there are tokens of friendship given and received, and on
the other there is the recognition of Meribbaal's evident innocence.
He therefore decides that the inheritance of Saul is to be divided.
The attitude of Meribbaal's earlier protector Machir (cf. on 9.4;
18.27), will certainly have contributed towards David's relatively
good treatment of the grandson of Saul. Meribbaal's answer is to
be taken in the same way as when a seller of goods today says to the
purchaser that he can have them '*baleš*', 'for nothing'. Meribbaal,
however, knows and says that as a descendant of Saul he has no claim
to justice or even to life, so that the king's decision still falls on the
side of mercy.

[31–40] We have most probably to imagine the scene of the last
of the encounters described here as being on the east bank. It is not
necessary to assume that the 'escort over the Jordan' included an
actual crossing by the patriarch. It was an act of co-operation (at
least in intention) on the part of his people; even v. 39 need not be
understood to mean that the parting took place *after* the king had
crossed the Jordan. We would expect Barzillai to accompany the
king only as far as the river boundary. Barzillai evidently provided
for the king very generously and freely while he was east of the
Jordan. Understandably enough the king wishes to give him a royal
recompense. The invitation to Barzillai to spend the rest of his life
at the court in Jerusalem naturally includes his family, so that
David's offer is far greater than appears at first sight. But Barzillai,
who, in this respect also a true man of the East, represents his
services to David (he mentions only the escort) as being very small
and David's recompense as very great, refuses on understandable,
well-expressed grounds. The delights of the court no longer mean
anything to him, his homeland and his family grave mean everything.
By giving the king Chimham (Chimhan), almost certainly a younger
son, he acknowledges the thought behind the invitation and once
again underlines (cf. 15.18ff.) the significance of David's renowned
person in the eyes of the young men of the neighbouring territories.
David's answer is particularly charming in the way in which he
assents to Barzillai's proposal with a slight alteration. The latter
had said, 'Take Chimham and do with him whatever seems good
to you'; David replies, 'I will take Chimham and do with him

whatever seems good to *you*.' In addition he provides a *carte blanche* for any other wishes of the old man. The whole event, right down to the farewell kiss and the parting blessing, shows in the best possible way the chivalrous Eastern way of life, and sheds a particularly happy light on the person and conduct of David *post tot discrimina rerum*.

[41–43] The content of the closing section of the chapter belongs, as has already been said, to the next chapter. Its insertion at the end of ch. 19 is a healthy reminder that the previous accounts are in no way to be interpreted as a 'happy ending'. The very beginning of the section shows us that there are still conflicts between North and South as before, and that David is fully aware of them. Remarkably enough, this discord is locally connected with the plain of the Jordan, like that in Judg. 8.1–3 and 12.1–6.ᵃ The dispute is initiated —as in the earlier instances—by the people of the North. The claim is that the men of Judah have encroached on their rights; apparently they claim the right of escort over the river. The vivid picture of kidnapping is answered on the part of Judah with still more drastic assertions. Israel's counterblast stresses the size of the tribal territory, the ancient right of the firstbornᵇ and the priority of the thought of bringing back 'their'(!) king. What the 'men of Judah' say to this is not quoted, but only described. But the last verse of the chapter is quite enough to hint at the new conflict which leads to 'Sheba's revolt'.

13. SHEBA'S REVOLT: 20.1–22

20 ¹Now there happened to be there a worthless fellow, whose name was Sheba, the son of Bichri, a Benjaminite; and he blew the trumpet and said,

> 'We have no portion in David,
>   and we have no inheritance in the son of Jesse;
> every man to his tents, O Israel!'

²So all the men of Israel withdrew (from the plain of Jordan) from David, and followed Sheba the son of Bichri; but the men of Judah followed their king steadfastly from the Jordan to Jerusalem.

3 And David came to his house at Jerusalem; and the king took the ten concubines whom he had left to guard the house, and put them in

---

ᵃCf. my commentary *ad locc.*

ᵇ'Judah is the *homo novus*, who has only recently come into the picture' (Budde *ad loc.*).

a house under guard,[a] and provided for them, but did not go in to them. So they were shut up until the day of their death, living as if in widowhood.

4 Then the king said to Amasa, 'Call the men of Judah together to me within three days, and be here yourself.'[b] [5]So Amasa went to summon Judah; but he delayed beyond the set time which had been appointed him. [6]And David said to Abishai, 'Now Sheba the son of Bichri will do us more harm than Absalom; take your lord's servants and pursue him, lest he has found[c] fortified cities (before we get there) and snatches away our eyes.'[d] [7]And there went out after Abishai the people of Joab[e] and the Cherethites and the Pelethites, and all the mighty men; they went out from Jerusalem to pursue Sheba the son of Bichri. [8]When they were at the great stone which is in Gibeon, Amasa had just arrived. Now Joab was wearing a soldier's garment, and over it was a girdle with a sword in its sheath fastened upon his loins,[f] and as he went forward it fell out. [9]And Joab said to Amasa, 'Is it well with you, my brother?' And Joab took Amasa by the beard with his right hand to kiss him. [10]But Amasa did not observe the sword which was in Joab's (other) hand; so Joab struck him with it in the body, and shed his bowels to the ground, without striking a second blow; and he died.

Then Joab and Abishai his brother pursued Sheba the son of Bichri. [11]And one of Joab's men took his stand by Amasa, and said, 'Whoever favours Joab, and whoever is for David, let him follow Joab.' [12]And Amasa lay wallowing in his blood in the highway. And when the man saw that all the people stopped, he carried Amasa out of the highway into the field, and threw a garment over him, because anyone who came by, seeing him, stopped. [13]When he was taken out of the highway, all the people went on after Joab to pursue Sheba the son of Bichri.

14 And Sheba passed through all the tribes of Israel to Abel of[g] Beth-maacah; and all the Bichrites[h] assembled, and likewise[i] followed him in. [15]And all the men who were with Joab came and besieged him in Abel of Beth-maacah; they cast up a mound against the city, and

[a]The word-play is evidently intended. Seclusion is meant.

[b]'Commander's orders' (Budde).

[c]This is the significance of the perfect. Most commentators read the imperfect.

[d]Or 'rob us of our fountain'. Both would be images of the irreplaceable.

[e]MT reads 'anšē = the men, but the very similar 'abīšai could have been misread (see LXX) or even overlooked in front of 'anšē; cf. the Commentary.

[f]The text is very confused. wᵉyōʾāb lābūš mādū wᵉʿālāw ḥᵃgōr wᵉḥāgūr ḥereb has been conjectured.

[g]See BH.

[h]MT has 'and all Berim' after 'Abel Beth-maacah'. The name Berim is unknown. bikrīm, which is perhaps to be read, would mean Sheba's fellow clansmen; in that case the word is to be put after 'assembled'.

[i](?) The word 'ap is usually deleted; but who would have inserted it?

it[a] stood against the rampart;[b] and they were battering the wall, to throw it down. [16]Then a wise woman called from the city, 'Hear! Hear! Tell Joab, "Come here, that I may speak to you." ' [17]And he came near her; and the woman said, 'Are you Joab?' He answered, 'I am.' Then she said to him, 'Listen to the words of your maidservant.' And he answered, 'I am listening.' [18]Then she said, 'They were wont to say in old time, "Let them but ask counsel at Abel and Dan";[c] then they settled the matter.[d] [19]We are[e] those who are peaceable and faithful in Israel; you seek to kill a city which is a mother in Israel;[f] why will you swallow up the heritage of the LORD?' [20]Joab answered, 'Far be it from me, far be it that I should swallow up or destroy! [21]That is not true. But a man of the hill country of Ephraim, called Sheba the son of Bichri, has lifted up his hand against King David; give up him alone, and I will withdraw from the city.' And the woman said to Joab, 'Behold, his head shall be thrown to you over the wall.' [22]Then the woman went to all the people and spoke[g] in her wisdom. And they cut off the head of Sheba the son of Bichri, and threw it out to Joab. So he blew the trumpet, and they dispersed from the city, every man to his home. And Joab returned to Jerusalem to the king.

The account of Sheba's revolt is introduced as an appendix to the history of Absalom. Not only does a detail like the matter of the concubines occur again, to be carried through to the end, and the name of Absalom recur (v. 6), but the revolt itself develops from the events which are directly connected with Absalom's rebellion, as is shown by the conclusion of ch. 19. The report of Amasa's death, which has been woven into the account, also belongs to it. The text has been transmitted in worse condition than the other parts of the succession history. There is also a further peculiarity. There are stereotyped phrases which occur often in the same form. The leader of the revolt is always introduced as 'Sheba, son of Bichri' (eight times!); why not, at least once, simply as 'Sheba'? The phrases for

[a]'It' is the mound (fem. in Hebrew). The sentence could also be translated 'and she went up to the wall'. In that case the two words would have to be taken into v. 16, and this would necessitate heavy inroads into the text. This possibility is also to be discarded because of the word used here (see the note below).

[b]This part of the fortifications is described by a different word (ḥēl) from that describing the 'wall' immediately afterwards (ḥōmā). The latter is the city wall proper, cf. v. 21 and de Vaux, RB 65, 1958, p. 125.

[c]Read this with LXX instead of 'and so'.

[d]The pointing hᵃtammū is preferable.

[e]MT 'I am'. The alteration may have been made because 'and Dan' was misread as 'and so' (wᵉkēn).

[f]The expression is chosen to suit the picture of the 'mother in Israel'. The usual emendation of ḥāmīt into ḥaṣḥīt is unnecessary.

[g]A word of this kind must almost certainly have fallen out, see LXX.

the men following Sheba (five times) and the action of the pursuers (four times) are similarly stereotyped, though this is disguised in RSV. Such repetition is to some extent in accord with the Hebrew narrative style, but here seems to have the character of a series of catchwords on which the story is virtually built up.[a] We will return to this later.

[1–2a] We learn virtually nothing about the originator of the revolt. He is called 'worthless' because of the evil work which he undertakes. His derivation from the tribe of Benjamin, on the border between North and South, which was elsewhere a disruptive element in the Israelite constitution, seems to be regarded as particularly appropriate. The mention of his father, which recurs constantly (see above), may have some special significance. In Gen. 46.21, I Chron. 7.6, 8, Becher is mentioned as a son of Benjamin, in I Sam. 9.1 Becorath is an ancestor of Saul. Perhaps Sheba is meant to be represented in this way as a member of the family of Saul; it is understandable that these groups should be a disruptive element in David's kingdom. The saying uttered by Sheba, a rhythmic remark (as I Kings 12.16), calls for an abandonment of David, objects to the personal union, and with the cry 'Every man to his tents' declares the end of the present action of the Israelite host. This does not mean the disbanding of the troops. The same thing took place in the time of Saul, who made himself a bodyguard from men of the host (I. 13.2) and continually joined able-bodied men to his entourage (I. 14.52). At any event, it later transpires that the enthusiasm for Sheba does not last long.

[2b–3] There is first an account of David's return to Jerusalem, made under the cover of the men of Judah.[b] In Jerusalem, the brief era of Absalom is finally brought to a close by the isolation of the ten concubines (15.16; 16.21f.); the human tragedy of these 'widows for life'—so the LXX renders the phrase—is only just hinted at, as in the case of Absalom's sister, Tamar. [4–7] The way to a second tragedy is opened by the appointment of Amasa to lead the troops into action. To assign the host of Judah to an expedition against Israel is in itself a delicate task. For the new man in command, the task is doubly difficult, as he is a replacement of Joab,

---

[a]There are other examples of this in Josh. 3.1–5.1 and Ruth 1; see my commentary *ad loc.*

[b]Shimei, a Benjaminite and member of the house of Saul, is not mentioned. He will, however, certainly—as earlier, 19.17—have attached himself to the men of Judah for obvious reasons.

whose name alone commands respect (I Kings 11.21) both in
Judah and in Israel. Amasa is not in a position to carry out in three
days a command given at such short notice. David therefore sends
the 'servants of David' out northwards under Abishai to prevent
Sheba from establishing a firm position anywhere; David adopts a
military approach to the position similar to that counselled earlier
by Ahithophel (17.1–3). The troops who set out under Abishai are
essentially the same as those at David's disposal on his evacuation
of Jerusalem (15.17f.; 16.6). The *gibbōrīm*, the mighty men (23.18f.),
doubtless under the command of Abishai, are expressly mentioned.
Joab is also present, but whether as a commander of a detachment
or as an ordinary soldier we are not told. The former is more
probable although there is no mention of the 'men of Joab' elsewhere—as here the individual sections of Abishai's command are
given; moreover, the later transference of the supreme command to
Joab is more comprehensible if Joab also holds a position of authority.
Perhaps the ten who kill Absalom in 18.15 belonged to 'Joab's men'.

[8–13a] The mention of Joab prepares for the following scene.
At the great stone in Gibeon,[a] the troops meet Amasa, who has
evidently determined to catch up with David's men as soon as
possible. From the wording, it looks as though Amasa took another,
shorter way. As he knew that Abishai was in front of him, he could
press on without having to bother about covering moves. We are
not, however, given the picture of a closed formation, but rather
of a disordered rabble which follows 'behind' the leader. Be this as
it may, Amasa is first there. Joab is thus able to carry out his plan
for the murder, which appears to be preconceived. Like Ehud, on
an earlier occasion (Judg. 3), Joab has hidden a short, dagger-like
sword on his right side, placed—if this is the right interpretation of
the wording—between the girdle and the long flowing robe (which
was, of course, girded up on the march). The girdle consists, as it
does now, of a broad piece of cloth gathered together, thus making
many folds and pockets in which the dagger could easily be hidden.
Joab wears it with the openings downwards; in this way he can
push away the particular fold in the girdle and let the short sword
'fall' into his hand held out below.[b] By seizing Amasa's beard in his
right hand, Joab makes Amasa feel secure, and as Joab draws him
forward for a kiss, Amasa cannot see what he is doing with his left

[a]On the locality see Dalman, *PJB* 21, 1925, pp. 83f.
[b]It is quite erroneous to assume from the text that the sword fell to the ground.

hand. The 'Old Testament kiss of Judas' (Budde) introduces the murder. Joab once again does all the work, as in the case of Abner and of Absalom. As the advance is hindered by people stopping to look at the body lying in the road, it is put into a field; we do not, however, hear anything about a burial. It is more important for the course of events that the man stationed at the scene of the murder categorically demands of the host whether they will decide for Joab and so for David.

[13b–14] From now on it is a foregone conclusion that Joab again becomes the leader; in v. 10 he is mentioned even before Abishai, whose name need no longer be given. Joab pursues Sheba through the whole territory of Israel. Sheba has established himself far to the north, in Abel Beth Maacah (the present *'abil*, near Dan, north of Lake Huleh). The crucial verse has, however, a very doubtful text. The principal reason for this is that the form *wyqlhw* is read as *wayyiqqāhᵃlū*, 'they assembled' (so RSV), by the *qᵉrē*, but as *wayᵉqil-lūhū*, 'they despised him', by the *kᵉthīb*. The *kᵉthīb* thus found Sheba's apparent lack of success in gaining Israelite support confirmed at this point. The *qᵉrē* will, however, be the correct reading. This states that only his own people followed the rebel. The fact that they 'followed him in' to the city makes it quite clear that here we have adherents of Sheba and not pursuers.

[15–21] Things never get to the point of a battle. The mound which the besiegers throw up against the city wall shows the citizens the seriousness of the position. As in ch. 14, so here a 'wise woman' appears on the scene in the difficult situation. Her conversation with Joab is in some ways as delightful a passage as that between the other wise woman and David. It begins with a proverb which is unfortunately no longer recoverable from the text, which refers to the neighbouring cities of Abel and Dan and is perhaps meant to show that these have the reputation (Dan perhaps as a sanctuary?) of always having made a particularly large contribution to the settling of disputes and the relaxing of tensions in Israel. Would Joab destroy such a 'mother in Israel'? This reference to the situation in Israel immediately bears fruit; nothing can be further from Joab's mind than to accumulate new material for disputes with Israel. A union is thus quickly achieved and Sheba has to pay the price of it with his head.

[22] So the struggle ends, and with it the account. All that remains to be mentioned is Joab's return to the king and the

dismissal of the host. The king's views on Amasa's death are not given; it was never, however, forgiven Joab (I Kings 2.5, 31f.), even if he escaped unscathed for the moment, thanks to his excellent solution of his difficult task. Perhaps the king guaranteed his life to him, as to Shimei, with an oath; we could then understand why David returns to the unexpiated guilt of the two men only in his last will (I Kings 2.1–9).

David's kingdom is now firmer than ever, and the 'heritage of the Lord' is not destroyed. It includes, however, much guilt. And the question of the succession to the throne still receives only a negative answer: not Amnon, not Absalom, not a descendant of Saul. The solution only comes later (I Kings 1f.).

14. THE LEADING MEN (SECOND LIST): 20.23–26

20 ²³Now Joab was in command of all the army of Israel; and Benaiah the son of Jehoiada was in command of the Cherethites and the Pelethites; ²⁴and Adoram was in charge of the forced labour; and Jehoshaphat the son of Ahilud was the recorder; ²⁵and Sheva was secretary; and Zadok and Abiathar were priests; ²⁶and Ira the Jairite was also David's priest.

[23] The reason for the further introduction of the list of David's officials here—cf. 8.15–18—can be found in the restitution of Joab to his old position. It is as though the sentence began 'so once again . . .' The problem is thus not why the list occurs here a second time, but what the alterations mean. The omission of any note about David is explained by the reason just given; Joab, whose office is involved, begins the list, and the opportunity is taken of mentioning the other officials. The insertion of the word 'Israel' after the host seems to refer back to the previous account; Joab is now, or rather, again, leader of the whole force.ᵃ [24] The first new name in the list is Adoram, in charge of forced labour; his name is probably Adoniram (I Kings 4.6; 5.28; in I Kings 12.18 MT reads Adoram, LXX Adoniram). The occurrence of his name only in this list can be explained from the fact that he came to office during the latter period of David's reign and continued in power right through the reign of Solomon (until his violent death in I Kings 12). [25] The

---

ᵃPerhaps there was a choice of readings, 'for the whole host'—'for all Israel'. The 'el has, as often, the sense of ʿal.

name of the secretary is only remotely similar to the Seraiah mentioned in 8.17. The *kᵉthīb* and *qᵉrē* waver between Sheya and Sheva, and I Chron. 18.16 has Shavsha; the variants in LXX include also 'Jesus', corresponding to 'Joshua'. Here then the tradition, or rather the original, was uncertain, unlike that about the recorder. The priests are mentioned without their fathers, unlike 8.17. **[26]** Nor is there further mention of the priestly office of David's sons (8.18). Instead, we find the name of an Ira, 'David's priest', who will have had a special duty connected with David's person. Here, too, the development of organization can be seen. Ira, presumably to be identified with the 'Ira the Ithrite' or 'Jethrite' of 23.38, one of David's 'valiant men', may later have taken over the function of David's sons. The second list is thus a second edition of the first. It forms an appropriate conclusion to the section 9–20, just as the other list closes the previous section, and like it, shows that the kingdom of David is now set in order after the tumult surrounding the succession.

NOTE ON FORMATION AND STRUCTURE: VI

We are fortunate to possess in Leonhard Rost's book *Die Uberlieferung von der Thronnachfolge Davids* a basic work on the problems involved in this section, a work of which even the details have been widely accepted. The most important conclusion of this book is that we have here the main part of a work which is concerned with the question: 'Who will occupy the throne of David?' Our commentary on individual points has confirmed the correctness of this observation. As Rost has seen, in Part VI only the account of the Ammonite war (10.1–11.1; 12.26–31) did not belong to the succession work; this has been added because of the episode of Uriah and Bathsheba and particularly because of its relevance to Solomon. It was necessary to describe the background against which David's shady dealings with Uriah might be understood. The passage about David's adultery and its consequences, which is thus given a firm foundation, is particularly important for the succession work. For here, as Rost shows, we have our introduction to the successor to the throne, and in 9.13–20 our introduction to the history of the succession (p. 92). In other words, the majority of the chapters speak of the possibilities of a successor to David which are to be ruled out.

The story of the succession extends both backwards and forwards beyond chs. 9–20. On the one hand, I Kings 1 and 2 belong to it:

these describe Adonijah's attempt to occupy the throne of his father
and the beginnings of Solomon's reign. On the other hand, it has
also left traces in earlier chapters. Rost (p. 105) has pointed to
7.11b, where it is said that the Lord himself will make David a
house, i.e. will found a dynasty. Nathan's promise is, in fact, the
presupposition, indeed the 'text' for the succession history. Rost
likewise (*ibid.*) points to ch. 6 (vv. 16, 20ff.), where Michal's childlessness is mentioned. This, too, is important (see above, p. 277).
Indeed, we might ask whether the material which now occurs in
chs. 3 and 4 must not originally have had its place in the story of the
succession (see above, pp. 295ff.).

Of one thing there is no doubt: David at least seriously considered
the possibility that his successor might come from his blood-relation-
ship with the family of Saul. Would he otherwise have asked for the
return of Saul's daughter? If he regarded her return as a necessary
prerequisite for the agreement with Abner, i.e. for the union of the
'Northern kingdom' with the 'Southern kingdom', then we are
certainly not to suppose that this was merely a sham wedding.
Michal's childlessness is rather to be regarded as a punishment from
the Lord, who intervened because of a certain incident. David had
intended his successor to be the son of this marriage, but Yahweh
had willed otherwise. Here we come across the view which emerges
later again and again: all Saul's descendants must share in the rejection of Saul. David and his contemporaries will already have
recognized that the Lord would not accept as a successor to David
a descendant of David's marriage with Saul's daughter. And quite
apart from this, it is absolutely clear that another offspring of Saul
who did not derive from 'David's body' (7.12) could not be considered as his successor—a not inconsiderable part of the succession
history is occupied with demonstrating this. For this reason, the
episode of Meribbaal's arrival at court (ch. 9) and probably also
the prelude to it (4.4) belong here. We therefore later hear much of
the attempts of members of Saul's family to further themselves,
about the time of Absalom; we may recall Shimei and Sheba. Even
the matter of Ziba and Meribbaal, the way in which David reacts
to Ziba's calumniation, and the calumniation itself, which is meant
to put the king on a scent which holds the prospect of a descendant
of Saul (16.3) succeeding to the throne, show to what extent things
were, in fact, still in the air. Saul's shadow lies over these accounts.
It is a frequently evident concern of the story of the succession to

show that a descendant of Saul can under no circumstances be entertained as a successor.

It must therefore be a son of David. If we include I Kings 1 and 2 in our survey, there are, in order of their births, Amnon, Absalom and Adonijah, who are the first three in line for the throne. We gain the impression that David at one time imagined first Amnon and later Absalom as his successor. Because of the age of the king, this is no longer discernible in the case of Adonijah; even here, however, it looks as though David would not have made any move against Adonijah without the intervention of Solomon's protector. We may, however, leave this out of account. The story of the succession is meant to show why the real candidates had to be eliminated. Neither the man of unbridled sensuality nor the fratricide (and usurper, see below) are acceptable kings. We should take particular note that these characteristics are mentioned immediately after David has incurred gilt on both counts. He, too, then, should have forfeited the throne; it is only by the grace of God that this has not come to pass. Moreover, the material is ordered in such a way that the defections of Amnon and Absalom come immediately after the entry of Solomon into the world: it seems as if those who are not worthy give place to the one who is regarded as the 'beloved of Yahweh' (12.25), and son by the grace of God (p. 317).

Absalom's attempted usurpation occupies the most room. His name occurs as early as the Amnon pericope, in the very first verse (13.1), and appears again in the story of Sheba. We are given the impression that for the author of the succession story Absalom is the real crown prince; Amnon, and later Adonijah, do not approach his standing. Absalom's person and actions are described with warmth. Not only does he look a prince (15.1), he acts like a prince. His whole appearance is completely appropriate to his position (14.25f.). He acts skilfully, he can wait, he is ready to be given advice, he is energetic (14.29ff.) and ready for battle. One can in no way say that Absalom's picture is painted in dark colours. It is very different from that of Amnon, the author's view of whom is quite plain—it is only right for the latter to disappear from the scene. But the events in which Absalom plays a part are described in such a way as to show that the author not only understands but also joins in the king's lament for this his son. What a tragedy to happen to this fine young man! We can almost hear the man who wrote these chapters say this (see p. 361). But as we have said before, the usurper cannot occupy the throne. Hushai may say to Absalom that he is now the legitimate king, chosen by Yahweh and all Israel (16.18), but Hushai knows, and the author and his readers know, that this is not true. Anyone who anticipates the will of the Lord is not his elect. The same is also true later of Adonijah. And here the theological viewpoint of the succession history emerges. Absalom's sin is the root sin, denounced by Isaiah and the other prophets, the sin of Job, even of Adam and the men who built the Tower of Babel: the sin of the man who is his own master or behaves as though he is his own master. That is not the way that a man becomes king of the people of God.

This is closely connected with another feature of the work. The author of the succession story maintains a critical attitude towards the legitimate king, David, throughout. This is true, of course, most of all in the matter of Bathsheba and Uriah. But even David's treatment of Amnon, and later of Absalom, is portrayed in such a way that we can and are meant to see that here David has brought things from bad to worse, partly by excessive weakness, partly by his severity. Even his actions after the death of Absalom, his measures with Judah and Israel and his decisisions about Amasa and Jaob have serious and damaging consequences. There is a remarkable cogency in the course of events. K. Leimbach's title for chapters 11–20, 'David's sin and its consequences' is right in so far as everything is, in fact, under the curse of the evil action which must go on to produce more and more evil actions. On the one hand we see the judicial righteousness which binds together guilt and punishment in a remarkable way. The sentence put in the mouth of Nathan, that the sword will never more depart from David's house, has a terrifying effect. On the other hand, however, it is clear that the continuance of David's kingdom depends not on any ability of the king, but on the grace of the Lord who stands by his promise. Therefore in these chapters David is humanly and in fact at his greatest when his external circumstances are at their worst, in his flight from Jerusalem. For the grace of God most frequently comes at the time of man's humiliation. Such considerations reveal that these narratives, too, are held together by the recognition that the Lord is directing events even in the smallest detail.

We do not know who wrote the succession history. At all events, he must have been someone who was very close to the happenings described. The name of Ahimaaz has often been mentioned in this connection. Hushai, 'the king's friend', is another possibility. We do not know. It is, however, certain that whoever took up his pen not only knew the facts but could also describe them, pertinently, in a skilful and artistic form, with a clear eye for the theological essentials. The final compiler needed to do no more here than to follow his excellent example.

VII

APPENDICES
II. 21–24

1. THE SEVEN SONS OF SAUL: 21.1–14

21 [1]Now there was a famine in the days of David for three years, year after year; and David sought the face of the LORD. And the LORD said, 'There is a[a] blood guilt on Saul and on his house, because he put the Gibeonites to death.' [2]So the king called the Gibeonites and said to them—Now the Gibeonites were not of the people of Israel, but of the remnant of the Amorites; although the people of Israel had sworn to spare them, Saul had sought to slay them in his zeal for the people of Israel and Judah[b]—[3]And David said to the Gibeonites, 'What shall I do for you? And how shall I make expiation, that you may bless the heritage of the LORD?' [4]The Gibeonites said to him, 'It is not a matter of silver and gold between us and Saul or his house; neither is it for us to put any man to death in Israel.' And he said, 'What do you say that I shall do for you?' [5]They said to the king, 'The man who consumed us and planned to destroy us, so that we should have no place[c] in all the territory of Israel, [6]let seven of his sons be given to us, so that we may hang them up before the LORD in Gibeon,[d] on the mountain of the LORD.'[a] And the king said, 'I will give them.'

7 But the king spared Meribbaal,[a] the son of Saul's son Jonathan, because of the oath which was between them, between David and Jonathan the son of Saul. [8]The king took the two sons of Rizpah the daughter of Aiah, whom she bore to Saul, Armoni and Meribbaal; and the five sons of Merab[a] the daughter of Saul, whom she bare to Adriel the son of Barzillai the Meholathite; [9]and he gave them into the hands of the Gibeonites, and they hanged them on the mountain before the LORD, and the seven of them perished together.[e] They were put to death in the first days of harvest, at the beginning of barley harvest.

[a]See BH.
[b]'A parenthesis without parallel' (Thenius, *ad loc.*).
[c]Loose language in the Hebrew. Emendation is unnecessary.
[d]See BH and Commentary.
[e]The text has 'they fell'. Conclusions about the method of execution can hardly be drawn from this.

10 Then Rizpah the daughter of Aiah took sackcloth, and spread it for herself on the rock, from the beginning of harvest until rain fell upon them from the heavens; and she did not allow the birds of the air to come upon them by day, or the beasts of the field by night. ¹¹When David was told what Rizpah the daughter of Aiah, the concubine of Saul, had done, ¹²David went and took the bones of Saul and the bones of his son Jonathan from the men of Jabesh-gilead, who had stolen them from the public square of Beth-shan, where the Philistines had hanged them, on the day the Philistines killed Saul on Gilboa; ¹³and he brought up from there the bones of Saul and the bones of his son Jonathan; and they gathered the bones of those who were hanged . . . ¹⁴And they buried (them) with the bones of Saul and his son Jonathan in the land of Benjamin in Zela, in the tomb of Kish his father; and they did all that the king commanded. And after that God heeded supplications for the land.

The first question to arise is why this story does not stand in its proper context, in the story of the succession, along with the rest of the dispute between David and Saul's descendants. For both the events of ch. 9 (Meribbaal) and the reasons for Shimei's cursing (16.7f.) presuppose the killing of the seven sons of Saul. Moreover, the event fits better at the beginning of David's reign. In that case, the explanation would have to be that a later editor took the story from its original context—before ch. 9—and added it at the end as a supplement (so Budde, p. 304). Then, however, the editor would have done something not only psychologically incomprehensible, but also quite careless, as the narrative is presupposed in its alleged context both earlier and later. The only answer to the question is therefore that the text derives from elsewhere and was known to the author of the succession work. Should we go on to ask why he did not incorporate this material in his work as he did the account of the Ammonite war in chs. 10–12, the answer seems to be that the Gibeonite pericope was transmitted with other texts, particularly with ch. 24, and he did not feel himself at liberty to separate them. The final compiler may have put ch. 21 in its present position, immediately after ch. 20, because, like large parts of the succession history, it deals with David's dispute with Saul's descendants.

Originally, of course, this was not the case. David appears as one who punishes the family of Saul only under compulsion, and, at the end of the chapter, even as one who is gracious to the family. The historical question whether the sons of Saul did not die 'very opportunely' for David, as did earlier Abner and after him Ishbaal (cf. p. 261) is quite another matter. The narrative, however, is not concerned with this. It deals with two other things, the affliction of the famine and the Gibeonite blood-vengeance. Here, as often elsewhere, we must distinguish between the original meaning of the story and that in its present context.

[1–3] The famine must be regarded as the result of a long dry period. There could be other reasons: a plague of locusts or hostile incursions. Both, however, are improbable, especially as later, when the expiation has been made, rain is expressly mentioned. The lack of rain is in its turn associated with blood guilt. David is informed of Saul's blood guilt against the Gibeonites by a visit to the sanctuary; that is the place where one seeks the 'face of the LORD'. We are given no indication of the place where this is done. First thoughts are, of course, of Jerusalem, but we cannot exclude the possibility that David, like Solomon later (I Kings 3.4ff., cf. II Chron. 1) went to the 'great high place of Gibeon'. This would be in keeping with David's attitude. We can then understand particularly well why the king, asking about the cause of the famine, should be told of Saul's unexpiated guilt towards the Gibeonites. According to II Chron. 1, the great high place of Gibeon preserved the tradition of the tent-sanctuary.[a] We would, of course, like to know how such a decision was obtained. Here we do not have an alternative question, as in I. 14.41f., but a real inquiry, which must have been made of a priest or a prophet working there. According to Josh. 9, the Gibeonites remained in service at this sanctuary even in Israelite times.[b] Moreover, in I Chron. 16.39, Zadok is associated with it. Abiathar, too, may be assumed to have had similar connections with the place, as the priestly city of Nob will have been located in the vicinity of Gibeon. It is more than likely that the blood-bath recalled by the Gibeonites and said to have been perpetrated by Saul had something to do with the massacre of priests recorded in I. 22.6–23.[c] Of course,

[a]There are good reasons for the identification of this sanctuary with that of Mizpah (Hertzberg, *ZAW* 47, 1929, pp. 161–96); it is the central Benjaminite sanctuary. This article takes up again the old conjecture that the place should be identified with the dominating height of the *nebi samwil* in the immediate vicinity of *ed-jib*, which is to be taken as Gibeon (cf. ATD 9, on Josh. 9.3). Alt, too, has recently returned to *nebi samwil* as a possibility (*ZDPV* 69, 1953, pp. 1–27) and assigns the sanctuary (but not the border fortress) of Mizpah to the same place. His conjecture for Gibeon, however, differs.

[b]Cf. ATD 9 on Josh. 9.27.

[c]Cf. A. Bruno, *Gibeon*, 1923, pp. 75–87, esp. pp. 82f. There is much fantasy in the individual detail of Bruno's work, but the basic outline is well worth considering; cf. *ZAW* 47, 1929, pp. 177f.

the text gives the impression that Saul sought to 'unify' the Gibeonites by a national policy aimed at removing the privileges of the Canaanite enclaves. On the other hand, the remark that the Gibeonites would (again) 'bless the heritage of the Lord' once the barrier of the blood guilt had been put aside suggests that the reference here is to special ministerial functions which the Gibeonites had no longer exercised after Saul's action. The old relationship of the Gibeonites to the sanctuary in Josh. 9 has been mentioned; here, too, in v. 2, there is a reference to Josh. 9. Historically, it may have happened that Saul's action against the priestly city of Nob encroached upon Gibeon and its sanctuary—the great high place of Gibeon—so that the words of the Gibeonites need by no means be an exaggeration. After Saul's death they will again have assembled in the locality and around the sanctuary. David's policy of friendship towards Gibeon,[a] continued later by Solomon, fits the whole situation excellently.[b]

[4–6a] The Gibeonites require blood, not money, for expiation.[c] The execution of seven sons of Saul is in accordance with the law of tribal membership; the number seven is chosen as being a holy number. The manner of execution demanded cannot be deduced from the vocabulary used; we need not assume that it was particularly cruel; it is in any case not important how the men are killed, but that their bodies should be exposed.[d] Here the other interest of the narrative again comes to the fore—the matter of the famine.

[6b–9] Before this comes to pass there is a short report of David's consent and his orders for the handing over of the men doomed to execution. It is explicitly said that Meribbaal is excluded; the sentence (added later), connects the content of this chapter with ch. 9. The sons concerned are partly sons of Saul by the Rizpah over whom Abner had his dispute with Ishbaal (3.7f.) and partly the sons of Merab,[e] Saul's daughter, who according to I. 18.17–19

---

[a]Cazelles ('David's monarchy and the Gibeonite claim', *Pal. Explor. Quart.* 87, 1953, pp. 1–14) also connects II Sam. 21 with David's policy of assimilating the Canaanites.

[b]It is also possible that the murder of Ishbaal was connected with this; it was done by two men from Beeroth, a town which for long had connections with Gibeon (Josh. 9.17).

[c]There is provision for money payments in requital for killings in Ex. 21.30.

[d]'A humiliating death'; Kapelrud, *Mowinckel-Festschrift*, pp. 114, 119f.

[e]Stoebe (*Eissfeldt Festschrift*, 1958, p. 229) considers the emendation of the word *mīkal* which stands in the MT into *mērab*, on the basis of the LXX, Syr. and Vulg. as 'inadmissible' (it was last supported by Kapelrud in *ZAW* 67, 1955, p. 199). He claims Michal's marriage with Paltiel as a 'late elaboration' (p. 234); Adriel

was promised to David, but later refused and given to Adriel.[a] The
date of the execution is expressly given as the beginning of the barley
harvest, i.e. about the middle of April. This time was hardly chosen
by chance. The feast of Mazzoth is celebrated at the beginning of
the barley harvest (Ex. 23.15f.; Deut. 16.1–9). We are given the
impression that the execution of the men at the time when the firstfruits of the barley harvest would normally be offered represents a
sacrifice which is intended to have a similar effect to that of Hiel in
I Kings 16.34 and of the Moabite king in II Kings 3.27. [10] The
relationship between the events on the holy hill and the famine are
made most clear by the fact that Rizpah keeps up her watch over the
dead until the rain comes. This need not necessarily be the early rain
at the beginning of November, as is usually assumed.[b] There is from
time to time an extra late rain,[c] and this will have come in this
instance. Indeed, the passage seems to imply that the loving act of
the mother helped to ease the restraint of the heavens.

Rizpah's devoted and moving action, reminiscent of Antigone,
is described with warmth, as is particularly clear from the effect
which it has on David. [11–14] Once the rain has fallen and thereby
Yahweh's favour has again been made manifest, he sees to it that the
dead are worthily buried; at the same time Saul and Jonathan are
laid together in the family grave. It is difficult to determine whether
this was in a place Zela, which otherwise would be unknown to us,
or whether the bodies were put in a special chamber (ṣēlāʿ) of the
tomb, which would then be presumably situated in Saul's Gibeah.
The narrative ends in such a way that throughout it no blame falls
upon David, just as in the case of the deaths of Saul, Abner and
Ishbaal. Indeed, it is emphatically said that now the grace of the
Lord again shines over the people and the land.

The effect of the episode is twofold; it is gruesome and yet at the

---

was, in fact, her husband. His argument, however, in which topography plays a
considerable part (note the references to Bahurim), makes the whole complex
of the daughters of Saul so confused that the reading of the versions seems a much
more plausible course. Cf. also the note on I. 18.19.

[a]Her dwelling-place of Abel-Meholah is in the land east of the Jordan; N.
Glueck, *Explorations in Eastern Palestine* IV, pp. 215ff., identifies the town with the
present *tell el-maqlub*. The Barzillai mentioned has certainly nothing to do with
David's host (17.27; 19.32ff.).

[b]Most recently Kapelrud, *ZAW* 67, 1955, p. 204.

[c]I experienced such rain in Jerusalem on 13 June 1925; it was so heavy that
it even brought water to the cisterns.

same time moving. It is remarkably enigmatic, and with its references to blood vengeance, human sacrifice and rain magic[a] points to a world which was banished by the Old Testament itself. What is said about the sons of Saul, and about Saul, Jonathan and Meribbaal, forms a conclusion to the Saul chapter and shows how despite everything these events help to strengthen David's position. The last word is that of the grace of God.

2. THE GIANT-KILLERS: 21.15–22

21 [15]The Philistines had war again with Israel, and David went down together with his servants, and they fought against the Philistines; and David grew weary, [16]so that they camped in Gob.[b] And there was a warrior,[c] one of the descendants of the giants, whose spear weighed three hundred shekels[d] of bronze, and who was girded with a new sword,[d] who thought to kill David. [17]But Abishai the son of Zeruiah came to his aid, and attacked the Philistine and killed him. Then David's men adjured him, 'You shall no more go out with us to battle, lest you quench the lamp of Israel.'

18 After this there was again war with the Philistines at Gob; then Sibbecai the Hushathite slew Saph,[e] who was one of the descendants of the giants. [19]And there was again war with the Philistines at Gob; and Elhanan the son of Jair,[f] the Bethlehemite, slew Goliath the Gittite, the shaft of whose spear was like a weaver's beam.[g] [20]And there was again war at Gath, where there was a man of great stature,[h] who had six fingers on each hand, and six toes on each foot, twenty-four in number; and he also was descended from the giants. [21]And when he taunted Israel, Jonathan the son of Shimei, David's brother, slew him. [22]These four were descended from the giants in Gath; and they fell by the hand of David and by the hand of his servants.

[a]Kapelrud (*Mowinckel-Festschrift*, 1955, pp. 113–22) investigates the connections between 'King and Fertility' with reference to II. 21.1ff. He also refers to examples from Norwegian history (p. 120). In ZAW 67, 1955, pp. 198–205, too, Kapelrud explains the killing of the sons of Saul as a 'royal sacrifice'. 'The question remains whether the land and the king were so little affected by belief in Yahweh as the writer assumes' (Bardtke in TLZ 83, 1958, col. 106).

[b]This is to be read, with Wellhausen, instead of 'Nob'.

[c]The words $we^{\prime}\bar{i}\check{s}$ $gibb\bar{o}r$ fell out after the similar $wayy\bar{e}\check{s}^{e}b\bar{u}$ $b^{e}g\bar{o}b$; they have been preserved in Syr. Other ancient translations see, almost certainly wrongly, the name of the giant preserved in the two opening words of the verse. So RSV.

[d]See BH.

[e]I Chron. 20.4: Sippai.

[f]The name Jair is uncertain. In 23.24 Elhanan's father is called Dodo. Von Pákozdy (ZAW 68, 1956, p. 257) conjectures the similarly written word $yi\check{s}ai$ (Jesse) in place of Jair. For the text see BH.

[g]See the note on I. 17.7.

[h]MT read the incomprehensible $midd\bar{i}n$ as $m\bar{a}d\bar{o}n$ = pugnacious. The right sense is preserved in I Chron. 20.6.

S.–N

This section enumerates four anecdotal episodes, all occurring during the Philistine wars, which are also held together by the fact that on each occasion the opponent is a man of unusual size. The descriptions are all similar; this is particularly true of the beginnings. The whole is consciously stereotyped in form. We thus have a text which already existed in this fixed form and which comes from a kind of archive in which notable deeds were put down in writing; there is a possibility that such accounts made up the 'Book of the Wars of Yahweh' (Num. 21.14). The reason for the insertion of an extract at this point may be that the last war waged by David was reported in ch. 20; the collection of anecdotes of acts of valour thus found an appropriate context at this point. A second possible reason will be given later.

[15–17] We know nothing of Gob, supposedly the scene of two if not three of the four actions described here. Like Gath, however, it probably belongs to the hilly country west of Judah. We learn that in the first of the battles David grew 'weary'. Later tradition explained this as a result of his old age, and this could be a further reason why the texts were not inserted earlier, perhaps after the Philistine battles in ch. 5. In reality, however, the events belong to an earlier period of David's history. David's weariness is given as the occasion for a strong enemy warrior to plan to kill him. The Philistine is one of the sons of the giants (of Rapha), usually called Rephaim (thus in the parallel account I Chron. 20.4, see also Gen. 14.5; 15.20; Josh. 12.4; 13.12). The Hebrew is meant to describe the unusual size of this and the other men. The name of the warrior seems to be given in the MT, but the text is probably corrupt at that point (see above). The description of his weapons is reminiscent of the Goliath story (I. 17.7), though there the long spear is twice as heavy (six hundred shekels). The announcement of his intention to kill David also suggests Goliath. The Philistine is not, however, killed by David but by Abishai, and instead of opening David's career as a warrior, as the Goliath episode does, this closes it. For in the form of a solemn obligation, the men, solicitous for David's life, adjure him no longer to wield the sword himself. This at least shows that we are in a fairly late period of his life; he must already be king, as otherwise there would be no mention of the 'lamp of Israel'. On the same subject, see also 18.3. Now the beginning looks like a continuation (especially with the word 'ōd, again). Was the report perhaps preceded by a short account of David's victory over

Goliath, which was then omitted in view of I. 17? In that case, the list—we might almost say the official document—began with the two episodes in which David himself played a part. **[22]** If this is so, the closing sentence which mentions both David and his servants is much more comprehensible.

[18–19] Sibbecai the Hushathite[a] is one of David's 'thirty', according to 23.27; we learn nothing about his opponent except his name, which is itself uncertain. Whether Elhanan, the son of Jair, the third of the victors, may be identified with Elhanan, the son of Dodo, who is mentioned early on in the list of the thirty, is questionable.[b] The name and description of his opponent pose a far greater riddle. The Goliath of I. 17 has been readily recognized. There is a widespread view that the fame of the victory over this apparently deadly warrior was in the course of time transferred from the unknown Elhanan to the much better-known David. On the other hand, as has been said at I. 17, the deed there ascribed to David was known to the rest of the tradition; even this anecdotal list presumably knows it, so that it is hardly possible to detach Goliath from the early history of David. The Chronicler (I Chron. 20.5) adopts the expedient of altering the word 'Bethlehemite' of the Samuel text (*bēt hallaḥmī*) to 'Lahmi, brother of Goliath', an attempt which shows his predicament quite clearly. There is therefore nothing for it but to recognize that the tradition testified to here simply stood alongside the other. The compiler of Samuel did not feel inconvenienced at its presence and certainly did not include the note to correct the David story! Perhaps even at this early stage the name 'Goliath' had come to designate a type. The description *dawidum*, commander, in the Mari texts seemed to open up a new approach. Because of it, scholars, von Pákozdy[c] in particular, attempted to demonstrate that Elhanan was the original name of David, which at an early stage was forgotten in view of his title as leader, and was preserved only here. This thesis is not, however, tenable.[d] In any case, it is difficult for such a hypothesis that the name 'David' should occur even here in five out of eight verses, which seem to have been brought together at an early period.

[a]According to I Chron. 4.4 belonging in the neighbourhood of Bethlehem; cf. K. Elliger, *PJB* 31, 1935, p. 44.
[b]But cf. Elliger, *op. cit.*, p. 33.
[c]*ZAW* 68, 1956, pp. 257–9.
[d]Cf. p. 139 note.

[20–21] The last-named giant, whose name is unknown, is described as an abnormal and therefore uncanny man who is also apparently particularly large. His conqueror is a nephew of David's, unknown elsewhere (cf. 13.3, 32). It is hardly possible to identify him with Jonathan the son of Shammah[a] from the list of the thirty in 23.33, as the latter is not a Bethlehemite. It is remarkable that all those named here should come from Bethlehem (or its neighbourhood), so that the whole passage seems to be a page from the honours list of Bethlehem, which is added here to give higher praise to David of Bethlehem.[b]

3. THE KING'S SONG OF THANKSGIVING: 22.1–51

22 ¹Then David spoke to the LORD the words of this song on the day when the LORD delivered him from the hand of all his enemies, and from the hand of Saul. ²He said,

> 'I will love thee, O LORD, my strength,[c]
>   O LORD my rock, my fortress and my deliverer,
> ³my[d] God, my rock, in whom I take refuge,
>   my shield and the horn of my salvation,
> my stronghold and my refuge,
>   my saviour; thou savest me from violence.[e]
> ⁴I call upon the LORD, who is worthy to be praised,
>   and I am saved from my enemies.
>
> ⁵For the waves of death encompassed me,
>   the torrents of perdition assailed me;
> ⁶the cords of Sheol entangled me,
>   and the snares of death confronted me.
>
> ⁷In my distress I called upon the LORD;
>   to my God I cried.[f]
> From his temple he heard my voice,
>   and my cry came to his ears.

[a]David's brother Shimei (q⁽e⁾rē: Shimea) is also called Shammah in I Sam. 16.9.

[b]Gutbrod's hypothesis (II, p. 247) that the four warriors here in the service of the Philistines appear 'as it were as the last of the strange and uncanny race of giants' is attractive; it would in that case have been seen as 'a sign of the stature and achievement of David that under his leadership it was possible to overcome the last of the race of giants which reached right back into the days of pre-history'. This makes the preparation of this list of David's victories comprehensible.

[c]So Ps. 18.1.

[d]See Ps. 18.2.

[e]The words from 'my refuge' to the end of v. 3 do not occur in Ps. 18.

[f]See BH.

⁸Then the earth reeled and rocked;
　　the foundations of the heavens trembled
　and quaked, because he was angry.
⁹Smoke went up from his nostrils,
　　and devouring fire from his mouth;
　glowing coals flamed forth from him.
¹⁰He bowed the heavens, and came down;
　　thick darkness was under his feet.
¹¹He rode on a cherub and did fly;
　　he was seen upon the wings of the wind.

¹²He made darkness around him his canopy,
　　dark water ᵃ(and) thick clouds;
¹³Out of the brightness before him,
　　hail andᵃ coals of fire flamed forth.ᵃ
¹⁴Thenᵃ the LORD thundered from heaven,
　　and the Most High uttered his voice.
¹⁵And he sent out arrows and scattered them;
　　and lightningᵇ in wild confusion.ᶜ
¹⁶Then the channels of the sea were seen,
　　the foundations of the world were laid bare,ᵃ
　at thy rebuke, O LORD,
　　at the blast of the breath of thy nostrils.ᵈ

¹⁷He reached from on high, he took me,
　　he drew me out of great waters,
¹⁸He delivered me from my strong enemy,
　　from those who hated me and were mightier than I.
²⁹Let them come upon me in the day of my calamity;
　　the LORD was my stay.
²⁰He brought me forth into a broad place;
　　he delivered me, because he delighted in me.

²¹The LORD rewarded me according to my righteousness;
　　according to the cleanness of my hands he recompensed me.
²²For I have kept the ways of the LORD,
　　and have not wickedly departed from my God.
²³For all his ordinances were before me,
　　and from his statutes I did not turn aside.
²⁴So I was blameless before him,
　　and I kept myselfᵉ from guilt.

ᵃSee BH.
ᵇ*ūbᵉrāqīm*, Ps. 18.14.
ᶜLiterally, 'and he confused it', viz. the lightning.
ᵈMT here speaks in the third person. But the suffixes in the second person as in Ps. 18 are surely original.
ᵉThe form *wā'eštammᵉrā* represents a conflate reading of *wā'eštammēr* (so Ps. 18.23) and *wᵉ'eštammerā*.

²⁵Therefore the LORD has recompensed me according to my
    righteousness,
    according to my cleanness in his sight.

²⁶With the loyal thou dost show thyself loyal;
    with the blameless man thou dost show thyself blameless,
²⁷With the pure thou dost show thyself pure;[a]
    but with the crooked thou dost show thyself strange.[b]
²⁸Thou dost deliver a humble people,
    but thou dost bring down the eyes of the haughty.[c]
²⁹Yea, thou art my lamp, O LORD,
    and my God[d] lightens my darkness.
³⁰Yea, by thee I can crush a troop,
    and by my God I can leap over a wall.
³¹This God—his way is perfect;
    the word of the LORD is true;[e]
he is a shield for all those who take refuge in him.

³²For who is God but the LORD?
    And who is a rock, except our God?
³³This is a God who girds me with power[f]
    and has made my way free and safe.[g]
³⁴He made[d] my feet like hinds' feet,
    and set me secure on the heights.[d]
³⁵He trains my hands for war,
    so that my arms can bend a bow of iron.
³⁶Thou hast given me the shield of thy salvation,
    and thy help[h] made me great.
³⁷Thou didst give a wide place for my steps under me
    and my feet did not slip;
³⁸I pursued mine enemies and overtook[i] them,
    and did not turn back until they were consumed.
³⁹[j]I smote them to the ground; they did not rise;
    they fell under my feet.

[a]So Ps. 18.26.

[b]This must be the meaning of the MT *tittappāl*; cf. Köhler, *Lexicon*, p. 1037.
The sense would be, 'so that he thinks that God is playing a bad joke on him'.
Ps. 18.26 simplifies, 'thou dost show thyself perverse'.

[c]See BH. MT 'Thine eyes are against pride; thou makest (it) lowly.'

[d]See BH.

[e]It is doubtful whether this line originally belonged to the verse. It fits here
neither in form nor in content, and looks far more like a reference to Ps. 19 (vv.
8ff.), which indeed follows the present psalm in the Psalter.

[f]So Ps. 18.32. MT 'my strong refuge'.

[g]Ps. 18.32 has 'He makes my way blameless'—an inappropriate simplification.

[h]So MT. In Ps. 18 there is 'thy gentleness', which makes no sense.

[i]Read *wā'assigēm*, with Ps. 18. MT 'I destroyed them'.

[j]With reference to Ps. 18.38, another 'I destroyed them' has been wrongly
inserted in MT. It takes up the last word of v. 38.

⁴⁰For thou didst gird me with strength for the battle;
    thou didst make my assailants sink under me.
⁴¹Thou didst make my enemies turn their backs to me,
    and I destroyed those who hated me.ᵃ
⁴²They cried,ᵇ but there was none to save;
    they cried to the LORD, but he did not answer them.
⁴³I beat them fine as the dust of the earth,
    I stamped them like the mire of the streets.ᵇ

⁴⁴Thou didst deliver me from strife with the peoples,ᵇ
    thou didst exalt me above my adversaries.ᶜ
Thou didst set meᵇ as the head of the nations;
    people whom I had not known served me.
⁴⁵Foreigners came cringing to me;
    as soon as they heard of me, they obeyed me.
⁴⁶Foreigners lost heart,
    and cameᵈ out of their fastnesses.
⁴⁷The LORD lives; and blessed be my rock,
    and exalted be my God, my salvation,ᵇ
⁴⁸the God who gave me vengeance
    and brought down peoples under me,
⁴⁹who brought me out from my enemiesᵉ—
    thou didst deliver me from men of violence.

⁵⁰For this I will extol thee, O LORD,
    among the nations,
    and sing praises to thy name.
⁵¹Great salvation he gives to his king,
    and shows steadfast love to his anointed,
to David, and his descendants for ever.'

This chapter provides us with the example, always very welcome, of a text transmitted in two ways, as in all its fifty-one verses it corresponds to Psalm 18. The sense is almost completely the same; the wording differs in some ways, but these very differences are useful in determining the original form of the work. The reader is referred to *The Psalms*, in this series,ᶠ for the exegesis of the chapter as a psalm. It is, however, necessary, as also in the case of I. 2, to

---

ᵃThe two words of the half verse are better transposed; *wā'aṣmītēm* is correct (against BH).

ᵇSee BH.

ᶜThe transposition of this verse, superfluous in v. 49, seems justified by both sense and metre.

ᵈInstead of the impossible *yaḥgerū* 'they girded' in MT, with a little transposition *yaḥreᵍū*, 'they came out', may be read.

ᵉSee on v. 44.

ᶠA. Weiser, *The Psalms*, ET 1962, pp. 182–96.

discuss briefly at this point the independent significance of the psalm. It is an 'individual thanksgiving', indeed a royal one, a type which is extremely ancient in origin, as can be seen from other examples from the Ancient East.[a] The thanksgiving begins with a lengthy 'introduction' which describes the past distress (*op. cit.*, p. 267); here, as often, it is the danger of death. The singer goes on to tell how he called upon the Lord and received help. He leads up to God's help with a description of a theophany, painted in broad sweeps (8-16). Only then does he describe his deliverance (17-19), which is in its turn justified—as in the psalms of the innocent—by the righteousness of the suppliant (20-25). A reference to God's righteousness occupies a special place here (26-28); thereafter the song takes the form of a confession (29-31). From now until the end, the hymn form predominates, though not to such an extent that we have to divide the psalm into two parts, especially as the situation presupposed is the same as at the beginning. It is rather that the structure of the psalm produces an effective contrast at its conclusion to the distress evident at the beginning. At the end, the speaker becomes victor and master of the world, but knows and recognizes full well that it is really only the Lord who is to be praised for his triumph.

The '*Sitz im Leben*' of a psalm like this is not primarily to be sought in a definite, historical situation, and therefore will hardly have its setting in a victory feast, though, of course, such a psalm will always have had its place on such occasions—like our hymn 'Now thank we all our God'. Its primary context is that of cultic action. It is the way from humiliation to exaltation, not only set forth in the cult but effected in the cult, which is realized with praise and thanksgiving. Thus it is all-important that the king himself is the speaker. In his distress and deliverance, he is the focal point of the cultic act which must be imagined here, just as he is the focal point of the people. The king, especially in early Israel, is a sacral figure and therefore one who occupies a central position in the cult. David's participation in the bringing up of the ark in II.6 is no private affair, any more than is Saul's display at the sacrifice in I. 13.15 or Solomon's functioning on the high place of Gibeon and in the consecration of the temple at I Kings 3ff. The king really is the 'lamp of Israel' (21.17). The fact that it is the king who speaks here is more important than the answer to the question which king it is. In view of the parallels from the Babylonian and Egyptian environments

[a] Gunkel-Begrich, *Einleitung in die Psalmen*, 1933, pp. 281, 284ff.

there is nothing against the assumption that the custom of using such a psalm belonged to the earliest period of the monarchy, i.e. to the time of David himself.[a] It is beyond dispute that David was a poet. It is hard to deny that he wrote psalms; had he not done so, the attribution of so many psalms to him would be incomprehensible. This particular psalm belongs to the narrower circle of those which might possibly be of Davidic authorship. It does not, however, make any difference to the character and worth of this psalm if its composer wrote it for or about David. It deals with the typical destiny of the king, the man of God's grace.

This is the reason for the present position of the psalm. We might ask why it was the only one of the psalms 'of David' to find its way into the Books of Samuel. There are further psalms which are associated expressly with situations in David's life (3, 7, 34, 51, 52, 54, 56, 57, 59, 60, 63, 142). Psalm 18 was not, of course, repeated here, because it seemed to be more 'Davidic' than the others. But there was a wish to describe and explain all the king's military action by the psalm. It stands here for that reason. In 21.15-22 we hear for the last time of David's activity as a warrior, and it is expressly said that his men solemnly prohibited him from any further active participation. Moreover, this conclusion of his personal career was fraught with considerable danger. For that reason, too, the psalm fits its position well. Other psalms might have illustrated individual episodes from David's life; [1] Ps. 18 had a comprehensive significance. Indeed, it is a theological commentary on the history of David. The history of David is to be read and heard in the light of this psalm. That is the intention of the final compiler.

[2-4] It will not be possible to stress every individual detail here, but only to point out a series of conspicuous features. The very beginning, as indeed the whole of the psalm, makes it clear and is meant to make it clear that David was a man who had a manifest relationship of personal piety with the Lord. The omission of the beautiful opening phrase, 'I will love thee, O Lord, my strength' from the text in Samuel—it is in the text of the psalm (with the exception of Syr.)—can only be chance. It is explicitly 'Davidic' in character. Otherwise, the introduction is longer than in Ps. 18; here we have the only considerable difference. It seems that the

---

[a]Gunkel's reasons for a 'relatively late origin', i.e. the 'breadth of expression', 'repetitions', etc. (*Die Psalmen*, p. 67), are not conclusive. Here Gunkel has simply not drawn the conclusions from his own conceptions.

speaker cannot stress too much his complete dependence upon the Lord and upon his aid. The words chosen point principally to God as the protector of the person calling upon him. The root *yaša'* 'save, help', occurs four times in the introduction alone and five times more in the rest of the psalm; its derivatives *yeša'* and *yešū'a* are to be translated 'salvation' (cf. vv. 47, 51). God has wrought David's victories, and his saving purpose has shone out in the deliverance which he has accomplished. This is said right at the beginning, and again at the end. Here, too, we hear of 'enemies' for the first time, apart from the superscription.

[5–7] This last feature is important because the description of distress which now begins has no mention of these enemies. We simply find a scene in which the speaker is shown to be at the brink of death; he seems already to be in Sheol (hell = the kingdom of the dead). By itself this could mean either sickness[a] or condemnation; only the prior and subsequent contexts show that he is in peril of war. In the context of the Books of Samuel the particular reference is to the perils of war, David's perils of war. The fact that this is in the framework of the cultic state of humiliation lies unemphasized in the background. Attention may be drawn to a feature which is not generally noticed,[b] the use of the tenses. The distress is described in the perfect tense, often equivalent to our pluperfect. The Hebrews can make a transition from this directly to the imperfect, i.e. expressing the past as present. We, too, can change to the present in describing something particularly vividly. There is also, of course, the element of re-presentation which is part of the cultic event.[c] Now it is significant that in v. 7b—and a further seven times in the course of the psalm—the historic tense of the consecutive imperfect is used instead of the imperfect[d] of Ps. 18. We are given the distinct impression that the typical instance is here made historical.[e] It is

[a]Even today the Arab patient, when asked how he spent the night, can be heard to reply, 'I died three times last night.'

[b]But see Weiser, *The Psalms*, p. 188.

[c]Weiser, *loc. cit.*

[d]Twice with *waw* consecutive, five times without a copula, and once without equivalent. Verses other than v. 7 are 12, 38, 39 (three times), 41, 44. The opposite (imperf. in II Sam., imperf. consec. in the psalm) occurs twice, v. 14 and v. 16; in this case the *waw* seems to have been omitted both times through a scribal error. There is also corruption in v. 48.

[e]The question which of the two is more original is quite another matter. We are principally concerned here in establishing how the final compiler of II Sam. regarded the matter. The approach offered here has most recently been supported by Gutbrod (pp. 258f.).

appropriate here, particularly for David, that his voice was heard by the Lord in time of need.

[8–16] God's reaction is depicted in a theophany full of striking images and anthropomorphisms. This chapter shares with many other descriptions of theophanies a special wealth of catastrophic storm-pictures.[a] When God himself comes on the scene—for this is what is happening—the whole creation is pressed into his service. For this reason heaven and earth are mentioned to begin with (as in Isa. 1.2). As in I Kings 19, earthquake, fire and tempest signal the coming of God.[b] The passionate anger with which he is seized is made visible by the hot breath of his 'nostrils'—in Hebrew 'nostrils' and 'anger' are the same words, cf. v. 16b—and the fire which comes out from his mouth. In the description of his coming he is said to bow the heavens down to the earth and to come on dark clouds; the cherub is identified with the heavenly cloud-chariots (Isa. 19.1; Ps. 104.3) on which the Lord descends from heaven to earth. It is everywhere noticeable that the storm imagery has lent its colour to this colossal picture.[c] It merely serves here to lay due stress on the majesty of the Lord who by the voice of his displeasure lays open the sea to its bed and the earth to its utmost depths. It is not only the God of Sinai who is vividly present (Weiser), it is *God* whose greatness cannot be better described than with a setting of this kind. We should further observe how his righteousness is at the same time included in his power. The Old Testament does not consider God's wrath to be like that of a bull when confronted by a red rag; it is *significant*. This will be discussed later. Suffice it to say how strongly the consecutive imperfects predominate at this point, as in Ps. 18. The colouring of the theophany is not just embellishment which could as well be dispensed with, but is meant to imply that the Lord is consciously and effectively at work to relieve the distress of his anointed. In the view of the final compiler, this is what David experienced, and it was, in fact, granted to him to experience God in the fullness of his power.

[a]Ex. 19; I Kings 19; Habakkuk 3, etc.

[b]Gunkel (as well as others) points out the origin of such symbols in volcanic phenomena (on Ps. 18.13). He is certainly right that the alleged reference to a storm, much stressed, is by no means sufficient. The theological significance is, moreover, more important than whatever roots there may be in the comparative study of religion.

[c]There is also mention of a hailstorm at Josh. 10.11 and a thunderstorm at I Sam. 7.10 (using similar words to those in vv. 14f.) to show openly the divine intervention.

[17–19] This God now brings about deliverance. David's history is here understood as a history of God's dealings with David, the history of a powerful and delivering God. David is a man, subject to sin (ch. 11) and weariness (most recently 21.15). God, whose character has been made plain by the theophany immediately preceding, can save him even from the uttermost depths of his distress (5–7). Here the history of David is seen vertically and is thus incorporated into the larger biblical history. David's history could have been narrated as that of a great and powerful king. *This chapter, however, is concerned that it should be understood as the action of a great and powerful God*, who deals with David as he once did with Moses, in 'drawing him out of the great waters'.[a]

[20–25] We can now see quite clearly the position briefly mentioned earlier. The mighty one is at the same time the righteous one. As has been said, in the course of a psalm such as this, as practised in the cult, we have now come to the point at which the speaker acknowledges his innocence; i.e. he surrenders to God (as Job in ch. 31) and may feel that he is deserving of God. Whoever speaks here can conclude from the deliverance vouchsafed to him that he was 'blameless before him'. The word *tāmīm* (in Job 1.1 applied to Job, as *tām*) means that all is in order between God and man. Man is not, of course, by this token said to be sinless; here, too, things are seen from a theological and not an anthropological standpoint. God 'delighted' in him and recognized the faithfulness and 'righteousness' which he had shown. It would be a misunderstanding of the text to think that man in effect holds his fate in his own hands as a result of his righteous actions. In the end, the operation of God's righteousness is determined by his power and his grace. He need not consider the actions of men, but he does so; this therefore is praised. If this is true in general it is particularly true of David, to whom it is meant to refer here. Any other understanding is impossible, because David's guilt in ch. 11 is in the end also a part of the king's life. The action of the final compiler in putting vv. 20–25 in David's mouth, in other words in regarding it as a testimony to his life, cannot simply be explained by saying that he passes over the king's sin, as does the Chronicler. It is there, but it is forgiven. Righteousness and grace have both been in operation, as can be seen from chs. 11 and 12. And as far as this chapter is concerned, the compiler knows that the working of the divine righteousness towards David is determined by

[a]The expression *māšā*, which we find in Ex. 2.10, occurs here.

the divine saving will. For once again it should not be forgotten that in a significant manner the past and present tenses stand side by side (vv. 20 and 24). What is said here was once true and is still true.

[26–31] In vv. 26–31 matters become still clearer. First of all the righteousness of God is virtually defined in well-chosen words. He is by no means indifferent to the conduct of a man, even that of a king. God is righteous, to each and every one. It is a part of his nature and the actions which stem from it that the lowly are delivered and the 'high eyes' (RSV 'haughty')—a favourite expression for overweening conduct—are brought low. The man who speaks here, i.e. King David, does not therefore place himself among the 'haughty', but among the humble who are directed towards God's grace and salvation. Thus we have the principle, well known and important to the Old Testament, that God's righteousness is manifested as grace, indeed *is* grace.[a] The man who knows this, knows well that he does not accomplish anything by his own action; it is the gracious intervention of God which is effective. God lightens 'my' darkness. Thus the section can end with a confession incorporating a fine testimony to a sure faith, reminiscent of Luther's words, 'If I had the faith demanded of me by the Scriptures, I could fight the Turks single-handed.' Attention is not kept on the believing man, but is fixed on the gracious and righteous God.

[32–43] The second main part of the psalm must be understood from this position. It takes on the characteristics of a hymn and derives the whole life and work of man, and therefore of the king, from the grace and help of God. The first concern is with war and victory. The individual expressions, even 33b, 34b, 36b, all point in the same direction. Endowed with power from on high, he finds an unobstructed way which he traverses with swift feet and skilled hands. These capabilities are not, however, his own; the participles in vv. 34f. and the second person address in vv. 36f. continually point to God as the giver and the helper, and finally he appears as the sole victor. He, the king, receives consolation and direction; the others, like the priests of Baal before Elijah, look in vain for an answer. Thus the king's victory becomes a demonstration of the glory of God, who gives his enemies into his hands. [44–46] At the close the king appears as the ruler of the peoples: God, the Lord of the world, has laid the nations under his feet. No fortress, however

[a] I have attempted to demonstrate this transition from righteousness to grace with the term *mišpat* in ⟨*AW* 41, 1923, pp. 51–61.

strong, has been able to resist his victorious path. If we remember once again that in the description of so favoured a progress the consecutive imperfect occurs six times in vv. 38 to 44 alone in contrast to Ps. 18, we can take it that these verses refer to David's success, his victories and his kingdom.

[47–51] But the palms of victory are due to God, who has in this way shown 'that he lives'. So the psalm can conclude with the praises of the Lord. The express mention of the 'anointed' (*māšîªḥ*) and the explicit naming of David and his descendants—as in Ikhnaton's hymn to the sun and in Merneptah's song of victory, the king's name occurs right at the end[a]—once again makes it clear whose actions and life have met with this fullness of salvation (*yešûʿōt*). It should further be recognized that three times (vv. 31, 33, 48) a verse begins with *hāʾēl* 'this God' (the article here has demonstrative significance); David's whole career is thus regarded as pointing like a finger to this God of salvation.

4. THE LAST WORDS OF DAVID: 23.1–7

23 [1]Now these are the last[b] words of David:

> The oracle of David, the son of Jesse,
>   the oracle of the man who was raised on high,
> the anointed of the God of Jacob,
>   the favourite of the songs of Israel.

> [2]The spirit of the LORD speaks by me,
>   and his word is upon my tongue.
> [3]The God of Jacob[c] has spoken,
>   the rock of Israel has said to me:
> When one rules justly over men
>   ruling in the fear of God,
> [4]he is like the dawn when the sun rises[d]
>   on a cloudless morning,
> and like[e] young grass from the earth as food,[f]
>   sparkling in the rain.

[a]Gressmann, *AOT*, pp. 18 and 25; Pritchard, *ANET*, pp. 369–71 and 376–8.

[b]The translation 'last' is not to be disputed; the rendering *suivantes* (de Boer *SVT* IV, 1956, p. 49) would be a trite truism.

[c]See BH.

[d]The line is unusually long. Budde's proposal to take the word 'sun' to the following line ('he gleams like the dawn, and (like) the sun on a cloudless morning') is worth considering.

[e]*ûkemō*, with LXX. Only the *m* remains in MT.

[f]The words *kî-lōʾ* are completely corrupted from the similar *leʾōkēl*. The mention of food is as in Isa. 55.10.

[5]So lives my house with God,
    for he has made me an everlasting covenant.
Yea, he has made me an everlasting covenant,[a]
    ordered in all things and secure.
For all my salvation is in him,[b]
    and he causes to prosper all my desire.[c]
[6]But godless men are not like this;
    they are all like wind-tossed thorns;
for they cannot be taken with the hand,
[7] and no one touches them.
Man fills himself with iron
    and with the shaft of a spear,
he burns them in the fire,
    he burns them in the flames.[d,e]

The last words of David follow the royal psalm just as the blessing of Moses follows the song of Moses, and the texts have evidently been put together thus on purpose. The presentation of 23.1–7, like the blessing of Moses, as 'last words', is meant to underline their significance, for the 'last wish' or 'last will' of a dying man has always been respected, as it is even in modern law, and has special weight (see also I Kings 1). Of course, these are not express words of blessing, as with Isaac (Gen. 27), Jacob (Gen. 49), and Moses (Deut. 33). Nevertheless, the basic structure of David's life and house is made clear; to this extent the theological programme for the future of the dynasty is to be found here. The context of the poem must therefore be regarded as well chosen, [1a] just as the description 'last words' is engaging and understandable.

Part of the text has suffered in transmission—presumably as a result of the terse and original language—though not to a hopeless

[a]A line seems to have fallen out here (cf. Mowinckel, *ZAW* 45, 1927, pp. 40f.). It seems easiest to assume that the last line was originally repeated.

[b]The word *'immō* could easily have fallen out here.

[c]Read *ḥepṣī*. The words *kī lō'*, as *lō' kēn* (*bᵉnē?*), belong at the beginning of the next verse, see Mowinckel, p. 40.

[d]The presumably original *baššalhebet* (cf. Procksch in the *Kittel-Festschrift*, p. 113, note 7) was miswritten as *baššebet*, as this word occurs in the next line.

[e]de Boer attempts to make sense of this text keeping to MT throughout (*SVT* IV, 1956, pp. 47ff.). In principle, this has much to commend it. But in this case it is necessary to put up with a large number of grammatical peculiarities (cf. especially the four *ki* sentences in v. 5, which are partly translated as conditional, partly as interrogative clauses). It is always important to see how such a translation fits the general context; de Boer's rendering does not present a convincing picture.

extent. Only a very few[a] adjustments are necessary to bring out not only the meaning of the text but also its skilful construction. The poem runs into six strophes, each of four lines; the individual lines are in three-stress metre (see the note on v. 4a); only the last strophe contains four short verses each of two stresses, which makes an effective conclusion. We therefore have here outstanding poetry in every respect. The high quality of the poetry should never have been attacked with the claim that the language has close affinity with the *māsāl* (parable, saying); even the prophets (Isaiah, Jeremiah) sometimes use wisdom sayings as vehicles for their message. The phrase 'everyman's wisdom' (Mowinckel, p. 45) is by no means an apt description of the poem. Today an increasing body of opinion, in accordance with tradition, regards David as the author of the poem from at least v. 3b onwards; there are hardly any decisive arguments to be brought against this position.

[1b] Two strophes go to make up the introduction, which has a striking similarity to the beginning of the third and fourth sayings of Balaam (Num. 24) and the words of Agur (Prov. 30.1ff.), from its construction right down to its wording (the twofold *ne'ūm* at the beginning and the words 'the man' in the second line). This is not a case of literary borrowing, but of a stylistic form. Here at the beginning there is a sort of presentation, of self-characterization. David gives himself his full names, as does Balaam. The word 'king' is given a poetic paraphrase, but the theological vindication of his position is stressed explicitly (cf. 19.22). David can be termed the 'favourite of the songs of Israel' (RSV margin), as he is certainly often sung about (cf. I. 18.7; 29.5), but he may also be 'pleasing in respect of songs', in other words, the sweet singer; the latter is the more probable.[b] [2–3a] The inspiration testified to in the second strophe is not unconnected with what has been said earlier. As the anointed, and as a man equipped with skill at making poetry, David is qualified to be the bearer of the divine spirit and the mediator of the divine word. The king is, as was said on ch. 22, a sacral figure; *this* king, to whom the Lord has given the 'songs of a sweet mouth', can particularly be said to be 'filled with God'; this does not, of

[a]Fewer than has been supposed earlier. Cf. esp. O. Procksch, 'Die letzten Worte Davids', *Kittel-Festschrift*, 1913, pp. 112ff.; S. Mowinckel, 'Die letzten Worte Davids', II Sam. 23.1–7', *ZAW* 45, 1927, pp. 30ff.

[b]The root *nā'am* occurs in this sense twice in David's lament at II. 1; this is sufficient to refute any association with the Arabic *naghama*, sing.

course, refer to ecstasy, but, as each of the four lines explicitly stresses, to the Word, as in the case of the prophets.

[3b–5] The message of the poem makes use of two similes, those of the rising sun and the effect of the rain. The two images may not, however, be amalgamated.[a] The first simile (strophe 3), which presents the saying of God proper, is said of the righteous ruler: righteousness towards men and the fear of God go to make up his person. The comparison with the rays of the rising sun is magnificently done. The association of the sun with righteousness is well known in the East, cf. the Babylonian hymn to the sun-god,[b] who is called the 'incorruptible judge'; Hammurabi similarly compares himself to the sun in his capacity as law-giver.[c] Mal. 3.20 speaks of the 'sun of righteousness', while there are only distant allusions to the association in Ps. 19.7b. The second simile, too, is still current in the East. After the long summer drought, the rain makes the young grass 'sparkle',[d] a bold piece of imagery, which is not to be questioned. Here it is not a question of the relationship of the ruler to man and to God, but of God's dealings with him; the results of the covenant made between God and the house of David are life-giving, fructifying, producing blessings, like the beginning of the rains (Isa. 55.10). We may be reminded of ch. 7, but also in addition that in Samuel it is often stressed that the Lord is 'with' David. The fifth strophe emphatically points out that this is the key to the understanding of the guidance in David's life. As from the fourth strophe onwards it is no longer the Lord, but the singer who speaks, these statements have the character of a confession: the Lord has stood by his covenant and has made the king share in salvation—here again, as in ch. 22, we have the important expression yeša', 'deliverance'. The original, poetic, lofty words should be noted carefully.

In contrast to those who receive the blessing are the godless men, of whom the two final strophes speak. [6–7] Here, too, we once again have surprising imagery, which has often been misunderstood because of its boldness. The children of the devil are compared with 'thorns that are blown away'; these are hard desert plants which,

---

[a]Against Budde, Kittel, Rehm,[2] etc.

[b]Printed in Gressmann, *AOT*, pp. 242ff.; Pritchard, *ANET*, pp. 387ff. The word *deše* occurs in the creation story, which is also recalled sometimes; this is not surprising, as the Old Testament is fully aware of the *creatio continua*.

[c]*AOT*, p. 381; *ANET*, p. 164.

[d]See Johnson, *Sacral Kingship in Ancient Israel*, 1955, p. 17. The connection with Ps. 132 is striking.

pulled up from the ground, are tossed by the wind over the land; a man can hardly touch them with the hand without getting hurt. It is necessary to have a steady implement to put them to their only useful purpose, to be burnt. The expression 'fill himself with iron' is again strange, but not impossible; in Ex. 28.17; 39.10 the word 'fill' is associated with precious stones in the sense of 'setting' them. This is also the meaning here: a man must be as it were completely set in iron, or have a long spear shaft, to be able to get at the thorns. These are strong expressions to be used of the enemies of the king; at the end of his life he was, in fact, in the position that all the thorns which goaded him had been withered and burnt.

The whole poem is a prophetic interpretation of what David was and did; here, too, in a different and more concise fashion, we are shown the essential elements of his character and of his life. Chapter 22 does it by way of a psalm; 23.1–7 is prophetic. Both point to God, who is 'with' David and his house.

5. DAVID'S 'MIGHTY MEN': 23.8–39

23 [8]These are the names of the mighty men whom David had: Ishbaal from Beth Kerem was chief of the three; he wielded his spear[a] against eight hundred whom he slew at one time. [9]And next to him among the three mighty men was Eleazar the son of Dodo from Ahoah.[b] He was with David in Pas-dammim and[c] when the Philistines gathered for battle there, the men of Israel withdrew. [10]But he stood and smote the Philistines until his hand was weary, and his hand clove to the sword; and the LORD wrought a great victory that day; and the men returned after him only to strip the slain. [11]And next to him was Shammah, the son of Agee from Harar.[d] The Philistines gathered together at Lehi,[e] where there was a plot of ground full of lentils; and the men fled from the Philistines. [12]But he took his stand in the midst of the plot, and defended it, and slew the Philistines; and the LORD wrought a great victory.

13 And three[f] of the thirty went down at the beginning of the

[a]The alterations—up to *bēt-hakkarmī* (cf. Budde *ad loc.*); on *bēt-kerem*, a place in Judah, cf. Jer. 6.1 and Neh. 3.14, are according to I Chron. 11.11.

[b]See BH. For Ahoah as a possible place name in southern Judah see Elliger, *PJB* 31, 1935, pp. 44–46.

[c]See BH. The place is almost certainly the same as Ephes-dammim in I. 17.1, in the hill country of western Judah.

[d]On the place, see Elliger, pp. 54–56.

[e]See BH. On the place-name Lehi see ATD 9 on Judg. 15.9–19.

[f]See BH.

harvest[a] and came to David at the hold[b] of Adullam, when a band of Philistines was encamped[c] in the plain of Rephaim. [14]David was then in the stronghold; and the garrison of the Philistines was then at Bethlehem. [15]And David said longingly, 'O that someone would give me water to drink from the cistern[d] of Bethlehem which is by the gate!' [16]Then the three mighty men broke through the camp of the Philistines and drew water out of the cistern of Bethlehem which was by the gate, and took it and brought it to David. But he would not drink it; he poured it out before the LORD, [17]and said, 'Far be it from me before[e] the LORD that I should do this. Shall I drink the blood of the men who went at the risk of their lives?' Therefore he would not drink it. These things did the three mighty men.

18 Now Abishai, the brother of Joab, the son of Zeruiah, was chief of the thirty.[e] And he wielded his spear against three hundred men and won a name among the thirty.[e] [19]He was the most renowned of the thirty[e] and became their commander; but he did not attain to the three. [20]And Benaiah the son of Jehoiada was a valiant man[f] and mighty in deeds; he came from Kabzeel. He smote two lions from Moab;[g] he also went down and slew a lion in a pit on a day when snow had fallen. [21]And he slew the Egyptian, a terrifying man.[h] The Egyptian had a spear in his hand; but Benaiah went down to him with a staff, and snatched the spear out of the Egyptian's hand, and slew him with his own spear. [22]These things did Benaiah the son of Jehoiada, and won a name among the thirty[e] mighty men. [23]He was renowned among the thirty, but he did not attain to the three. And David set him over his bodyguard. [24]Asahel, the brother of Joab, was one of the thirty . . .

Elhanan the son of Dodo of Bethlehem, [25]Shammah of Harod, Elika of Harod, [26]Helez from (Beth)pelet, Ira the son of Ikkesh of Tekoa, [27]Abiezer of Anathoth, Sibbethai[e] the Hushathite, [28]Zalmon from Ahoah, Maharai from Netophah, [29]Heleb the son of Baanah of Netophah, Ittai the son of Ribai of Gibeah of the Benjaminites, [30]Benaiah of Pirathon, Hiddai of the brooks of Gaash, [31]Abibaal[e] of (Beth)-arba, Azmaveth of Bahurim,[i] [32]Eliahba of Shaalbon, Jashen of Gimso,[i] Jonathan the son of [33]Shammah from Araru,[j] Ahiam the

[a]The word *qāṣir* is to be added to the otherwise incomprehensible *rōš*. An *'el* is then to be deleted.

[b]See BH. Cf. also on I. 22.1.

[c]*hayyat* = *hawwat*.

[d]I Chron. 11.17 reads 'cistern' (*bōr*), whereas here the *kethīb* means a well (*be'ēr*). But it is hardly to be assumed that Bethlehem had such a thing at that time. The 'wells of David' pointed out later are cisterns.

[e]See BH.

[f]The words *ben* and *'īš* are variant readings.

[g]Instead of *'arī'ēl mō'āb*, perhaps *'ariyyīm lemō'āb* is to be read.

[h]Read *'īš mōrā*.

[i]On the deduction of this name see Elliger, pp. 53f. The word *benē* is, as *ben*, to be put at the end of the verse.

[j]Perhaps cf. Elliger, pp. 54–56.

son of Sharar from Araru, [34]Eliphelet the son of Ahasbai of Maacah,[a] Eliam the son of Ahithophel of Gilo, [35]Hezro of Carmel, Paarai from Arab, [36]Igal the son of Nathan of Zobah, Bani the Gadite, [37]Zelek the Ammonite, Naharai of Beeroth, (both) armour-bearers of Joab the son of Zeruiah,[b] [38]Ira from Jatthir, Gareb from Jatthir,[c] [39]Uriah the Hittite: thirty-seven in all.

The phrase 'mighty men', which is usually adopted as a title for this section and as a translation, properly means 'mercenary', 'the professional soldier'.[d] These are a special group of men which David gathered round him (I. 22.2), following the precedent of Saul (I. 14.52). As Elliger in his much-quoted article has decisively shown, this group was fixed at the number thirty, most probably after an Egyptian pattern. His hypothesis that the group was inaugurated when David was made king at Ziklag (I. 27.1ff.) is also to be accepted. The list of the thirty has its own special history. The remarks about the 'three', which are partly of anecdotal character, were prefixed to the list from another tradition. Unfortunately the text is in a bad state; at no time is there a distinction drawn between the three and the thirty. It is, however, largely possible to restore much of the text. As is obvious, the document is of considerable age and is of special value for the history of David.

[8–12] The whole consists of four parts and a postscript. First we are told of the 'three'. Nothing is said outright about their relationship to the thirty; we are probably to assume that they belonged to it, but were distinguished from it as a special group, 'the three'. The names of the men are not mentioned elsewhere, which is quite astonishing, when we reflect that they are placed even before Abishai and Benaiah. This may be connected with the question of their distinguishing features. This is least clear in the case of the first mentioned, even the name of whom is uncertain. He is mentioned first because of the magnitude of the deed which he did. It is obviously meant here, as in the case of the other two—and also in the case of the giant-killers—that he distinguished himself in the war against the Philistines; this is expressly said of Eleazar and

---

[a]Cf. I Chron. 2.48; in ATD 12 *ad loc.* the word Maacah is omitted in error. The word *ben* (son) could indicate membership of this family, which belongs to the south (cf. Elliger, pp. 56f.).

[b]The tradition fluctuates between 'the armour-*bearers*' and 'the armour-*bearer*'. As ten armour-bearers are mentioned in 18.15, the former is more probable.

[c]See BH.

[d]Elliger, p. 66.

Shammah. Here we also learn that both times the men of Israel had withdrawn and that the 'mighty men' saved the situation. We have, then, something similar to what is narrated of David in I.17. It is particularly important that we are twice told that the Lord worked 'great salvation' ($t^e\check{s}u^c\bar{a}$; again an allusion to the significance of the root $y\bar{a}\check{s}a^c$, 'deliver') through these deeds. These men, like the giant-killers, participate in the divinely ordained salvation. In both cases these are not simply brave men, 'heroes' in the usual sense of the word, but warriors in the Holy War, whose deeds are particularly valued. Here, too, we can imagine that such instances were written down in the 'Book of the Wars of Yahweh'.

[13–17] The adjacent anecdote is given no such 'saving' significance, but is an attractive indication of the relationship between David and his men. The event takes place at the time indicated in 5.17–21; the Philistines have advanced on the plain of Rephaim, in the neighbourhood of Jerusalem, to sever David's connections in the direction of Israel, and have set up a 'post'a in Bethlehem. David is in the stronghold of Adullam (cf. on I. 22.1ff. and II. 5.17ff.). The event now described precedes by a short interval David's attack on the Philistines reported in 5.17–21. David's 'longing' is not to be interpreted as a special need for water; it is just an idle remark about which he will have thought very little. Perhaps the cistern at the gate had particularly cool and good water. The bold move is successful, but like Alexander at a later date in the famous story told by Arrian, David pours the water away, though, of course, for another reason: he will not refresh himself with something for which his men have risked their lives. His conduct makes it easy to understand why his men went through fire for him, and throws a clear light on the personality of the king, who could gather knights about himself, like King Arthur and Charlemagne. The incident with the Gittite Ittai (15.19–22) shows that even at a later date there were still men who would go through thick and thin with David. It is not said who the three men concerned here were. The final compiler certainly supposed that they were the 'three' mentioned earlier. The final clause 'these things did the three mighty men', which Wellhausen wished to attach to v. 12, is in any case meant to connect in one unit the episode of the well and the remarks about the three. But the three were hardly meant

aThe word 'camp' in v. 16, Hebrew mah^ane, does not mean the same as in v. 13, where we have $hayy\bar{a}$.

originally; the introduction expressly stresses the anonymity of the men concerned, and were we to think of looking for their names, the sons of Zeruiah, who were familiar with Bethlehem, would seem the most obvious persons to whom such a venture would suggest itself in the first place.

[18–19] They are, in fact, explicitly mentioned in the third section. It has often been remarked that Abishai and Asahel are mentioned as brothers of Joab, while Joab himself is not mentioned as one of the thirty. He did, of course, belong to it; we will return to the point later. Evidently he formed an exception; it was not felt necessary to mention him specially by name. An action of Abishai's is recorded which is reminiscent of that of 'Ishbaal', the leader of the three, though it does not reach quite the same magnitude. He is also mentioned here by name as the leader of the thirty; we know that he was at David's disposal for some special tasks and was always among those nearest to David, who remained true to him in times of difficulty. Although David was not always in agreement with this overhasty man (I. 26.8f.; II. 3.39; 16.9f.; 19.21f.), he was nevertheless always ready to trust him implicitly. In 21.17 he even appears as one who saved David's life. Nevertheless, he was still not numbered among the three! [20–23] The same is true of Benaiah from Kabzeel in southern Judah (Josh. 15.21). He is a rugged veteran, used later by Solomon for 'liquidating' political undesirables, a man who can be trusted to deal with the Egyptian, whom he attacks with a staff, robbing him of his spear, just as he can to come out on top in the episode of the lion. It is not clear whether the 'ariels', 'lions of God', describe men or real lions. The latter is more probable, as there is a further instance immediately afterwards, where Benaiah goes down into a cistern and there kills the beast that has fallen into it; the snow is mentioned because it may have betrayed the track of the lion and because the event was more than usually impressed upon the memory because of the rareness of such snowy days. Even this adventurous man, whom David later put in charge of his body-guard—he thus became what David once was to Saul (I. 22.24)—did not attain to the three. The reason for this being mentioned twice is presumably that given above, that the deeds of the three belonged to the Holy War. What is reported of Benaiah has nothing to do with that, and the matter is at least left open in the case of Abishai; these are daring deeds, but not 'saving' deeds. [24a] Asahel is next mentioned in third place; his death is reported in ch. 2. He seems to belong in the list of the thirty, which now follows. It is, however, hardly by chance that the list contains exactly thirty names without that of Asahel. Moreover, the mere way in which he is mentioned ('Joab's brother': almost always elsewhere 'son of . . .'; and 'belonged to the thirty': not said of any of the others) shows that here we have something exceptional, presumably the beginning of a longer note which may have run: 'Asahel, Joab's brother, also was one of the thirty. He was as swift of foot as a wild gazelle (2.18) and he had a name among the thirty. He was honoured above the (others of) the thirty, but he did not attain to the three.' Why the continuation of this note was omitted remains obscure.

[24b–38] The list of the thirty proper owes its recognition above all to the work of Elliger mentioned earlier. By investigating the derivation of the men mentioned, he has made it very probable that the list follows a definite sequence. The first ten—except the man from Anathoth, the birthplace of Jeremiah—all belong to the territory of the tribe of Judah; this corresponds with the early period when David was an outlaw. The list is then expanded by people from the North; these are the men from Ittai of Gibeah to Jashen from Gimso. The fact that the names mentioned between v. 33 and v. 35 point to origins in the South fits the increasing activity of David in that area. To that point, i.e. to Paarai from Arab (a place in the vicinity of Hebron?) there are twenty-three names. If we add the 'three', together with Abishai, Benaiah and Asahel, that makes twenty-nine. The missing thirtieth is then, of course, Joab, who while not named directly, is still sufficiently clearly taken for granted. We will therefore be correct in assuming that to this point we have the oldest list of the thirty, in the form which it had during the time that David was resident at Ziklag. The list did not, however, remain fixed in this form, as the institution of the thirty was something alive, which could be extended, and which needed to be extended. Asahel, for example, was killed at the beginning of David's stay in Hebron. Benaiah, as we are told, was given another assignment; the cases of Abishai and, of course, of Joab will have been similar. The 'three', being a special group, may not at a later date have formed part of the 'thirty' in the proper sense. This goes to explain the addition of the seven men whose names now stand at the end of the list. Coming, as some do, from the regions east of the Jordan, they show the extension of David's position and, with it, of his reputation. The form in which they are mentioned, somewhat different from the earlier names, appears to support this conclusion. The list is complete up to the time when Uriah was accepted in the number of the thirty. The fact that Chronicles adds a further sixteen names seems to suggest that there was still a recollection that the list was brought up to date, e.g. after Uriah's death and other vacancies in the ranks, to maintain the number thirty (I Chron. 11.41b–47). It is further striking that the additions made by the Chronicler all come from the territory east of the Jordan. Was the reason for this that 'the lack of heroes from east of the Jordan was felt',[a] when there were three representatives of this territory even in the old list (vv. 36f.)? True, it must always remain questionable whether the additions made by the Chronicler really represent the extension of the old list. But the fact that the thirty remained a living and an ever-replenished nucleus can be underlined by a glance at what is said in the books of Chronicles.

[39] Two further points must be made about the end of the list. The mention of the number thirty-seven is a later addition. It includes the thirty names of the list proper, the three, Abishai, Benaiah and Asahel, and, of course, as the thirty-seventh or the first, Joab. For this reason, its insertion is not unimportant. A second point is, of course, more important. The mention of Uriah in the last place may be pure chance; we have the list up to the time when Uriah, as it were the novice, was accepted into the order. But the final compiler and the audience will hardly have regarded it in this light. The name Uriah at the end of the list leads us to recall what is associated with his name. The list of the men who were David's 'bodyguard' ends with the name of one who did not betray the king, but was betrayed by him. The end of the list is meant to tell us, 'Do not forget the name of the last of David's mighty men'! We are thus prohibited from making heroes of David (and his men). Even here, history was not made by men, but by the grace of God, whose help and forgiveness were needed even by David and his time.

6. THE CENSUS AND THE TEMPLE SITE: 24.1–25

24 [1]Again the anger of the LORD was kindled against Israel, and he incited David against them, saying, 'Go, number Israel and Judah.' [2]So the king said to Joab and the commanders of the army, who were with him, 'Go through[a] all the tribes of Israel, from Dan to Beersheba, and number the people, that I may know the number of the people.'

[a]Galling, ATD 12, p. 44; similarly Elliger, p. 36. Rudolph, *Chronik*, 1955, p. 101, differs.

[3]But Joab said to the king, 'May the LORD your God add to the people a hundred times as many as they are, while the eyes of my lord the king still see it; but why does my lord the king delight in this thing?' [4]But the king's word prevailed against[a] Joab and the commanders of the army. So Joab and the commanders of the army went out from the presence of the king to number the people of Israel.[b] [5]They crossed the Jordan, and began in Aroer, and from[a] the city that is in the middle of the valley, towards Gad and on to Jazer. [6]Then they came to Gilead, and to Kadesh[a] in the land of the Hittites; and they came to Dan, and from Dan they went[c] around to Sidon, [7]and came to the fortress of Tyre and to all the cities of the Hivites and Canaanites; and they went out to the Negeb of Judah at Beersheba. [8]So when they had gone through all the land, they came to Jerusalem at the end of nine months and twenty days. [9]And Joab gave the sum of the numbering of the people to the king: in Israel there were eight hundred thousand men who drew the sword, and the men of Judah were five hundred thousand.

10 But David's heart smote him because[a] he had numbered the people. And David said to the LORD, 'I have sinned greatly in what I have done. But now, O LORD, I pray thee, take away the iniquity of thy servant; for I have done very foolishly.' [11]And when David arose in the morning, the word of the LORD came to the prophet Gad, David's seer, saying, [12]'Go and say to David, "Thus says the LORD, Three things I offer you; choose one of them that I may do it to you." ' [13]So Gad came to David and told him, and said to him, 'Shall three[a] years of famine come to you in your land? Or will you flee three months before your foes while they pursue you? Or shall there be three days' pestilence in your land? Now consider, and decide what answer I shall return to him who sent me.' [14]Then David said to Gad, 'I am in great distress; let us fall into the hand of the LORD, for his mercy is great; but let me not fall into the hand of man.'

15 So the LORD sent a pestilence upon Israel[d] from the morning until the appointed time; and there died of the people from Dan to Beersheba seventy-seven thousand men. Those were the days of the wheat harvest.[e] [16]And when the angel stretched forth his hand toward Jerusalem to destroy it, the LORD repented of the evil, and said to the angel who was working destruction among the people, 'It is enough; now stay your hand.' And the angel of the LORD was by the threshing-floor of Araunah[f] the Jebusite. [17]Then David spoke to the LORD when he saw the angel who was smiting the people, and said, 'Lo, I have

[a]See BH.

[b]The text offers a choice between 'people' (warriors) and 'Israel'.

[c]So Wellhausen, up to now the best attempt at making the difficult text comprehensible.

[d]LXX has here another form of the text: 'So David chose the pestilence.' But MT is preferable; in no event are the two sentences to be put side by side.

[e]This clause stands at the beginning of the verse in LXX.

[f]See Commentary.

sinned, and I have done wickedly; but these sheep, what have they done? Let thy hand, I pray thee, be against me and against my father's house.'

18 And Gad came that day to David, and said to him, 'Go up, rear an altar to the LORD on the threshing-floor of Araunah[a] the Jebusite.'[19] So David went up at Gad's word, as the LORD commanded. [20]And when Araunah looked down, he saw the king and his servants coming on toward him, and Araunah was threshing wheat.[b] And he came out and did obeisance to the king with his face to the ground. [21]And Araunah said, 'Why has my lord the king come to his servant?' David said, 'To buy the threshing-floor of you, in order to build an altar to the LORD, that the plague may be averted from the people.' [22]Then Araunah said to David, 'Let my lord the king take and offer up what seems good to him; here are the oxen for the burnt-offering, and the threshing-sledges and the yokes of the oxen for the wood. [23]All this Araunah gives to the king.'[c] And the king said to Araunah, 'You shall not make a gift to the king.' Then Araunah said to the king, 'The LORD your God accept you.' [24]But the king said to Araunah, 'No, I will buy it of you for a price; I will not offer burnt-offerings to the LORD my God which cost me nothing.' So David bought the threshing-floor and the oxen for fifty shekels of silver. [25]And David built there an altar to the LORD, and offered burnt-offerings and peace offerings. So the LORD heeded supplications for the land, and the plague was averted from Israel.

The final chapter is connected with ch. 21 in a strange way. In both cases we have expressions of the Lord's anger, which makes expiation necessary. Both times, too, there is a catastrophe (famine and pestilence), which in its turn has something to do with a definite transgression, committed by each of the two first kings. Moreover, a holy place is concerned in each of the chapters, though not the same one. The disastrous situation each time leads to a blessing of a special nature, which can be regarded as the final goal of the text. Whereas in ch. 21 attention is focused on the dispute between David and Saul, ch. 24 looks into the future, to what was regarded as the most important event in the reign of Solomon, the building of the temple. For this reason, Budde has described the *pericope* as 'one of the most important in the Old Testament' (p. 326): it contains the

[a]'Aranyah' in text, see Commentary.
[b]Expanded after I Chron. 21.20.
[c]The text also contains the strange address 'O king'. Wellhausen conjectures *'ebed 'ᵃdōnī*, 'the servant of the king' for *'ᵃrawnā*. But the original text is very different from this new conjecture and the content is not improved. Better to assume a clause to have fallen out—see the textual lacuna: *wayyōmer hammelek la'ᵃrawnā lō' tittēn lammelek*. This has been done above. The clause could easily have been overlooked.

hieros logos of the sanctuary at Jerusalem. This will be the reason
why it was separated from ch. 21 and put at the end of the book.[a]
For here David leaves to his successor not only the kingdom, but
also the holy place for the manifestation of the presence of God.

[1] The reason for the wrath of God 'again' being kindled over
Israel is not clear from a reference to ch. 21; it is 'anger for an unknown reason' (Caspari, p. 662). We may nevertheless ask why the
plan for the census was not simply described as an idea of the king's.
We must assume that even here the importance of the consequences
of this decision, which include not only the pestilence but also the
establishment of the holy place, was the occasion and indeed the
final cause of seeing in the whole proceedings a divine instigation
which, while beginning in anger, ends in blessing. As is well known,
the Chronicler gave 'Satan' (without an article) as the instigator of
the census. This is without doubt a theological vindication of God,
but it is not a theological simplification by any means. The idea,
occasionally expressed in the past, that the Chronicler's view is the
original one, has now rightly been almost universally abandoned. The
description in Samuel is of naïve consecutiveness, precisely because
it at first sight appears arbitrary and incomprehensible. The course
of events is reminiscent of the flood-narrative, in which the new
blessing comes as a consequence of punishment and destruction.

[2] In the way that the decision to hold the census is introduced,
the matter seems to have been enjoined by a divine command
(oracle). The narrator does not feel himself obliged to give any
reason why the census should have been regarded as so reprehensible
a course of action, as he says nothing about it. The criticism of the
census is quite comprehensible to him. Nor is the census associated
only with divine anger; even Joab, who elsewhere is not represented
as a thoughtful man, raises objections to David's measures, following
up the pricking of David's own conscience, and regards the ensuing
punishment as not unjustified. If we seek the reason for this apparently harsh judgment, the general answer would be that God's blessing
may not be investigated in detail; it should be received thankfully
and reverently and not made the object of speculation. On closer
examination, it seems that David intended to alter or disband the

[a]It is not certain whether or not the puzzling passage I Chron. 21.20 is meant
to refer to Solomon. If the 'four sons' really means David's sons, Solomon could
be thought of as the fourth son in respect of I Chron. 14.4 (cf. Galling in ATD 12,
p. 62) and therefore imagined as present at the purchasing of the site of the temple.

levy.[a] Now this represents a direct inroad into the sacral sphere, the replacement of a charismatic institution by the measures of human organization. It is a challenge to God himself.

[3–9] Joab, the old commander of the host, sees this clearly, but cannot make his view prevail. The census of the 'people', again an enrolment of the host, therefore takes place. The military character of the undertaking is clear from the fact that the men appointed to number the tribes pass before the king on their departure (as in 15.18, 22, and 18.14). The work begins in the southern part of the land east of the Jordan, in the Arnon valley, in the neighbourhood of Aroer (*khirbe ʿarāʿir*; Josh. 12.2; 13.9, 16), which is held to be in the territory of Reuben, as Jazer (cf. Josh. 13.25) is given as a district of Gad.[b] The description of the territory compassed is a summary one; we are given as it were only the boundaries within which the lists were made. Kadesh in the land of the Hittites could be a reference to the well-known sanctuary on the Orontes (*tell en-nebi mend*), which would fit David's kingdom. On the other hand, the place Kedesh in Naphtali, which is mentioned in Judg. 4 as one of the two points of departure for the battle against the Canaanites, is more in accord with the mention of Dan (*tell el-qadi*) and Sidon, especially as the recruiting of the host would preclude ranging so far to the north; in that case the king would have designated the area to be covered as that 'from Dan to Beersheba'—both places are expressly mentioned in the list. 'In the land of the Hittites' would then merely indicate the general direction taken by Joab and his men; 'kings of the Hittites' are also mentioned in I Kings 10.29; they, like the 'Aramaean kings' mentioned in the same passage, are to be located in present-day Syria. The length of time needed confirms the fact that considerable work was involved in the action. The numbers involved are astonishingly large, and in Chronicles, of course, are still larger, though these can be explained from the original form in Samuel.[c] In this way not only is stress laid on the magnitude of the manpower standing behind David, but we are shown at the same time how right Joab was in objecting and how wrong David was in his undertaking.

[10–15] It is therefore quite understandable that immediately

---

[a]Cf. G. v. Rad, *Der Heilige Krieg im alten Israel*, pp. 37f.

[b]On the location of Jazer (*yaʿzēr*) see Schultze, *PJB* 28, 1932, pp. 68–80: *tell yadude*. Abel, *Géographie*, pp. 356f., differs and suggests *khirbet jazzir*.

[c]On the details see Rudolph, *Chronikbücher*, 1955, pp. 144f.

afterwards there occurs the remark that David becomes conscious of his guilt. He recognizes it—though without saying in what it consists!—and asks for forgiveness. Meanwhile the divine command has already gone out to Gad, 'the seer of David', briefly mentioned as early as I. 22.5. He is to put before David three possible punishments, in which the shortening of the duration (three years, three months, three days) corresponds with an intensification of their content. It is impossible to regard one punishment as lighter or harsher than any others. David merely decides against the second punishment and leaves it to the Lord to decide between the first or the third. His reasons are excellent. David at all events prefers to fall into the hands of God, whose heart he is sure is ready for pardon. The form of MT is here more to the point than that of the LXX, according to which David himself 'chooses the pestilence'. The express note that so many people were smitten 'from Dan to Beersheba' is meant to point to the area which was the scene of the king's sinful action. The remark about the time of the barley harvest, preserved in the LXX, prepares for the happening at the threshing-floor of Araunah.

[16–17] In the text as it now stands, it is the Lord who determines the duration of the punishment, just as it was he who appointed its character. It sounds as though he stayed the anger of the angel of the pestilence before the due time had come. David was thus right in abandoning himself to the mercy of the judge. It would be no improvement if we were to put v. 17 between v. 16a and v. 16b and to feel that God's 'repentance' was brought about by David's noble appeal to punish him instead of the 'sheep'. Through the present arrangement of the text, however, it becomes more clear that the whole matter is arranged by Yahweh, and this is important as being the aim of the narrative. The pestilence is ended not by David's prayer, but by the Lord's mercy, and it is therefore the Lord's mercy which saves Jerusalem and at the same time appoints the place of the future sanctuary. The question of the relationship in time between David's prayer and the divine decision may be left open; the prior element is, in fact, the latter and not the former.

The name of the owner of the threshing-floor is by no means certain. Chronicles says quite plainly Ornan, the LXX Orna, and this is at least presupposed in the $k^e th\bar{\imath}b$ of MT at v. 16 ($q^e r\bar{e}$ is Awarna—remarkably enough the article is added). [18–25] In v. 18 the man is called Aranyah, the remaining seven (or nine) times Araunah. Chronicles evidently preserved the final customary form of the name. Nevertheless, the MT in Samuel so overwhelmingly attests the name Araunah that we will have to recognize it as the oldest expression.[a] The man is one of the original inhabitants of Jerusalem, and had his threshing-floor on the hill immediately to the north of the oldest of the city's hills.[b] It is emphatically affirmed that the site of the threshing-floor is not already a sanctuary; it only *becomes* a sanctuary on the appearance of the angel. David is explicitly instructed to erect the altar on the threshing-floor, and the theophany is expressly given as the reason for this, more clearly still in Chronicles than in Samuel. In Samuel it is for David's eyes alone; we can hardly assume that this was altered by Chronicles.[c] Araunah the Jebusite is one of the 'quite ordinary people'—as in Volkmann-Leander's beautiful fairy-tale of the invisible kingdom—; he sees only his threshing-floor, on which he threshes. In accordance with the prophetic instructions, David and his entourage—according to I Chron. 21.20 there are, as has been said, four of his sons (including Solomon) present—go to Araunah. The latter 'comes out', i.e. he leaves the threshing-floor, pays homage to the king and learns his purpose. In saying that he wishes to erect an altar, to stay the plague, David makes it clear that he knows as little about the scene between the Lord and the angel as Job does of the council of God in heaven. In both cases, however, it is this scene in heaven which is vital for the understanding of the consequences. The dealings between the king and Araunah have a distant similarity to Gen. 23, the conversation between Abraham and the sons of Heth. Courtesy requires that not only the place sought after but also the necessary objects for the sacrifice be provided by the present owner. Here we have the same expression 'give' as in Gen. 23.11; in the same way one can hear 'I give you everything' even today in the East. But David, like Abraham in the earlier instance, here refuses the gift. The site of the sanctuary, like the cave of Machpelah, cannot be

---

[a]One plausible possibility is that suggested by H. B. Rosen (*VT* 5, 1955, pp. 318–20), who tries to derive the name from the Hittite *a-raw-wan-ni* or *a-ra-u-wan-ni*, '*libre, aristocrate*'. This would explain the article in v. 16.

[b]The 'holy rock', particularly in its present form, does not correspond with the 'threshing-floor'. 'We can, however, assume that it belonged to the ground which was used as a threshing-floor and would represent its highest point' (Hertzberg in *JPOS* 12, 1932, p. 33).

[c]It is much more likely that in v. 20 *hammal'āk* (the angel) should be emended to *hammelek* (the king). Cf. also Galling *ad loc.*; Rudolph differs.

owed to pagan generosity, but is formally purchased.[a] In this way the altar is built, and, as we hear rather inconsistently, the plague is stayed; in this way the connection between the text of ch. 24 and that of ch. 21 is once again made quite clear. Chronicles has the sacrifice further authenticated by fire from heaven, thus making it certain that from now on the legitimate place of worship is here— and not in Gibeon. This underlines what was said above about the reason for the present position of the narrative of the census: the site of the temple is ready, and the man who is to build it may now appear on the scene.

NOTE ON FORMATION AND STRUCTURE: VII

The content alone shows that this closing section of the books of Samuel is a supplement; we have a story which is set in the time of the disputes with the house of Saul (21.1–15), a further narrative which in its ultimate concern is connected with David's plans for the temple (24.1–25), accounts of acts of valour from the time of the Philistine wars (21.14–22; 23.8–17), and following that, the list of 'mighty men' proper (23.18–39). Finally, we have the royal psalm, which also occurs in the Psalter as Psalm 18, and which is given a theological interpretation bearing on David's activities in war (22.1–51), and the poem 23.1–7, which is rightly called 'the last words of David'. There is, then, no doubt that these form 'Appendices'. The problem lies in the sequence in which the material is presented. If we number them consecutively, as has been done in this commentary, then the two narratives 1 and 6, the two lists 2 and 5, and the two poetic sections 3 and 4 each belong together. As far as the first pair are concerned, the connection with the beginning of the second story is quite clear. Moreover, the content, as was said in discussing ch. 24, affords clear parallels (the divine wrath, the sanctuary, the ending of the plague). In the lists, the chief similarity is between 21.15–22 and 23.8–12. Their poetic form puts the two poems into a special group, although they have no other connection with each other, but it is precisely these alone of the three pairs of *pericopes* which stand together.

Now this order is to be attributed to the final compiler; the texts follow one another like Deut. 32 and 33. We are not to assume any earlier affinity here. This may, however, be so in the case of the

[a]The purchase price of fifty silver shekels is multiplied by twelve in I Chron. and the more valuable gold takes the place of silver.

other texts. The narratives 1 and 6 were certainly connected at an
earlier stage of literary tradition. This must have been felt so strongly
(and may indeed also have been known) that the compiler did not
feel himself free to add the sections either to the succession narrative
or to the history of the ark. The reason why despite this they were
not left immediately side by side is obvious. It was necessary to put
the first narrative, which dealt with the disputes with the house of
Saul, as near as possible to the rest of this material. The second
narrative, on the other hand, needed to be put as near as possible
to the accounts of the building of the temple and the person who built
it. We can therefore well understand why the connections with
material which both preceded and came after this section made it
necessary to put the narratives at diametrically opposed ends of the
section. It is harder to discover why the lists 21.15–22 and 23.8–12
were not left side by side. They give a strong impression of coming
from the same source (the 'Book of the Wars of Yahweh'?). There
are two possible reasons for their present position, as mentioned above.
First, 21.17 suggests that at this point a line is being drawn under
David's warlike activities. For that reason, one section belongs
as near as possible to the last account of these. The psalm may then
have been added, because, as we have said, it illuminates and interprets them. We can hardly be surprised that the second poetic
section is immediately attached to the psalm. Now it was possible
to 'go on', and for the lists about the three and the thirty, which
must in every respect be regarded as interconnected, to follow. Chapter 24 then formed the conclusion, for the reasons mentioned above.

In this way the 'Appendices' effectively round off the whole picture. We might, of course, ask whether it would not have been more
skilful to end the Second Book of Samuel with the account of the
end of David's life, as, in fact, I Kings 1 and 2 demonstrably belong
to the original succession story. On the other hand, these events are
so closely connected with Solomon that we can quite understand
their having been put in the part to which they are relevant. Moreover, it is precisely the chapters in the 'Appendices', which could
hardly have been introduced after David's death, which divided
II Sam. 20 and I Kings 1 and 2. So the conclusion of the Books of
Samuel does not show the picture of the aged king, not in full control
of his mental and physical capacities, but shows him still, indeed
again, at the prime of life, conscious of what he has to do, devoted
and blessed, the man 'with whom' the Lord is.